Crisis *of* Conscience

Also by Tom Mueller

Extra Virginity: The Sublime and Scandalous World of Olive Oil

Crisis *of* Conscience

WHISTLEBLOWING
IN AN AGE OF FRAUD

TOM MUELLER

RIVERHEAD BOOKS *New York* 2019

RIVERHEAD BOOKS

An imprint of Penguin Random House LLC
penguinrandomhouse.com

Library of Congress Cataloging-in-Publication Data

Names: Mueller, Tom, 1963– author.
Title: Crisis of conscience : whistleblowing in an age of fraud / Tom Mueller.
Description: New York : Riverhead Books, 2019. |
Includes bibliographical references and index.
Identifiers: LCCN 2019016249 (print) | LCCN 2019980032 (ebook) |
ISBN 9781594634437 (hardcover) | ISBN 9780698405103 (ebook)
Subjects: LCSH: Fraud—United States. | Whistle blowing—United States. |
Corporations—Corrupt practices—United States. |
Administrative agencies—Corrupt practices—United States. |
Political corruption—United States. | Corruption investigation—United States.
Classification: LCC HV6695 .M84 2019 (print) | LCC HV6695 (ebook) |
DDC 364.16/30973—dc23
LC record available at https://lccn.loc.gov/2019016249
LC ebook record available at https://lccn.loc.gov/2019980032

Printed in the United States of America
1   3   5   7   9   10   8   6   4   2

Book design by Cassandra Garruzzo

Contents

"A time comes when silence is betrayal."

Martin Luther King Jr., "Beyond Vietnam,"
a speech delivered at Riverside Church, New York City, April 4, 1967

Crisis *of* Conscience

CHAPTER 1

Becoming a Whistleblower

Resolved, that it is the duty of all persons in the service of the United States . . .
to give the earliest information to Congress or other proper authority of any
misconduct, frauds or misdemeanors committed by any officers or persons in
the service of these states, which may come to their knowledge.

Legislation of July 30, 1778,
reprinted in *Journals of the Continental Congress, 1774–1789*

Some of the worst crimes, and the most wrenching tests of character, happen by slow degrees, steady as sunrise. This is the story of how Allen Jones, an investigator at the state Office of the Inspector General in Harrisburg, Pennsylvania, moved in gradual, irrevocable steps to a crossroads in his life, and one day made a fateful choice.

On July 23, 2002, Jones learned that a check for $2,000 had recently been deposited into an unnamed bank account used by Steven J. Fiorello, the state's chief pharmacist. Hardly a remarkable sum, yet Jones's instincts, honed by years of investigating multimillion-dollar fraud schemes, were aroused. Fiorello and his superiors had failed to register the account's existence with the state comptroller, which was a felony offense in Pennsylvania. Worse, the check was from Janssen Pharmaceuticals, a subsidiary of Johnson & Johnson. Since Fiorello's job was to choose which drugs were available for purchase by state hospitals, foster homes, prisons and elder care facilities throughout Pennsylvania, this money looked suspiciously like a bribe.

"It was the first of a series of 'Oh my God!' moments I had over the next months and years," Jones remembers. "That check was like a loose pebble that started an avalanche."

Today Jones is a slope-shouldered, rough-handed man of sixty who resembles a heavyset Chuck Norris. His close-cropped, grizzled beard is stained with nicotine around his mouth, and his face is reddened by weather. Beneath gray bangs and seams of concern across his forehead, his clear green eyes seem wary, though as he gets to know you they occasionally glint with humor. Jones likes to build things in wood and stone—houses, barns, drywall terracing—and spends much of his time alone in the forested foothills of the Appalachian region of central Pennsylvania, where he grew up. This is Pennsylvania Dutch country, where the Amish drive horse-drawn buggies with two gas lanterns for headlights, and the barns and clapboard houses stand square across the roof beam but often need a coat of paint. Jones grew up working with the Amish, and has some of their calm reserve. He chooses his words judiciously, like a good mason laying bricks, like a man accustomed to living at hazard before the law. He even swears judiciously: "The only way to accurately describe my state of mind at that moment," he says of his realization that his own office was covering up massive pharmaceutical fraud, "was 'fucking devastated.'" Jones has many friends who drop by his cabin at odd hours, to drink a beer and swap deer-hunting stories, but occasionally he'll leave their company, walk out on his back porch and look over the frozen pond into the bare woods beyond, drawing hard on a cigarette.

Jones continued exploring Fiorello's finances and found more checks written by Janssen, as well as by two other pharmaceutical companies, Pfizer and Novartis. "As an investigator I was taught to look for the big picture," Jones says. "Not just what happened, but why it happened. So I started looking into what these drug companies were doing in Pennsylvania in the first place." The funds were being used to support and expand the Pennsylvania Medication Algorithm Project (Penn-MAP), a protocol to diagnose and treat bipolar disorder, schizophrenia, ADHD and major depression. This protocol required doctors in all state facilities to treat these conditions with a new generation of drugs, called atypical antipsychotics, in preference to older, generic antipsychotic medications that had previously been prescribed. Jones discovered that the protocol was a carbon copy of one being used in Texas, TMAP, which Johnson & Johnson and other pharmaceutical companies had launched in the late 1990s, with generous funding to mental health officials, who in return had often helped market the drugs. Jones also found evidence that Johnson & Johnson, together with acquiescent state officials, was rolling out similar programs in at least ten other states.

The more Jones learned about these protocols, the more disturbing they seemed. They made Risperdal and other atypical antipsychotics the treatment of choice for a wide range of mental disorders. Since atypicals were far more expensive than first-generation antipsychotics—Risperdal cost about 45 times more than previous medications—Texas Medicaid payments for atypicals had skyrocketed from $28 million in 1997 to $177 million in 2004. The same was happening in Pennsylvania: between 2000 and 2003 alone, Medicaid spending for atypical antipsychotics rose by 55 percent.

Yet despite their cost, Jones discovered that much of the supposedly impartial medical research used by pharmaceutical marketers to convince state officials that Risperdal and other atypicals worked better than older medications had been ghostwritten by the pharmaceutical companies. Unbiased clinical trials not only suggested no increase in effectiveness but revealed serious side effects caused by atypicals, which the pharma-sponsored studies had downplayed. Risperdal could cause muscle spasms, medically serious weight gain, and an increased risk of diabetes, stroke, pituitary tumors and death. Patients on Risperdal might develop disfiguring and irreversible twitching of the face, torso and limbs. Some male patients grew lactating breasts, and required mastectomies. Though Johnson & Johnson apparently concealed major research from the Food and Drug Administration (FDA), the FDA knew enough about Risperdal to forbid the company from claiming that the drug was superior to earlier antipsychotics; to require warnings of the neurological side effects, weight gain and diabetes it could cause; and to impose, in one demographic, the agency's strongest, or "black box," warning, reserved for drugs with life-threatening side effects. The FDA approved extensive use of the drug only for adult schizophrenics. Johnson & Johnson, Jones found, had ignored many of these prohibitions, and downplayed or denied them in its marketing campaigns; in Texas, the company had aggressively marketed Risperdal for children, adolescents and elders, to treat anxiety, insomnia, mood disorders, agitation and mild emotional discomfort. In fact, the Texas protocol mandated Risperdal for these conditions in state prisons, hospitals, reform schools and nursing homes, whose captive patient populations had little or no say in their medical care. Now the company and Pennsylvania officials were starting to impose the same regime in Jones's home state.

Thinking he might be misunderstanding the evidence, Jones traveled to Janssen headquarters in New Brunswick, New Jersey, to question marketing executives and company lawyers. Apparently dismissing him as a harmless paper-shuffler, they blandly confirmed his worst suspicions. "I'd never seen anything so blatant," he remembers. "They had co-opted state healthcare, and were using it to sell billions of dollars of dangerous drugs in illegal ways." Among the documents that Jones reviewed was a "drug usage evaluation" that Steven Fiorello, at the request of Janssen Pharmaceuticals, had performed on 756 diagnosed schizophrenics in eight Pennsylvania mental hospitals, who were given Risperdal or one of four other atypicals. Janssen then paid for Fiorello to fly to New Orleans and present this research to pharmacists from across the country. Behind the chill, clinical language, Jones saw evidence of terrible suffering. One patient on Risperdal had lost 59 pounds during the study, while another had gained 85 pounds. A patient on Zyprexa, an atypical produced by Eli Lilly, had gained 240 pounds. "Someone in a white coat sat by and watched those poor people, and jotted everything down," Jones says. Certain patients exhibited extreme swings in serum glucose and cholesterol levels, putting them at high risk of diabetes, heart disease and other conditions. Stefan Kruszewski, a psychiatrist working as a reviewer at one of the hospitals, told Jones that he believed the deaths of several children in mental health facilities had been linked to the use of atypical antipsychotics.

Healthcare fraud, like other thefts of taxpayer dollars, creates countless victims, yet few of us see them. They are hidden behind a scrim of marketing and earnings reports and objective-looking research, presented by executives and researchers in suits and white lab coats who are clever and ambitious, perhaps a bit like us. This is the subtle treachery of corporate crime.

Jones knew firsthand what it meant to be invisible, powerless. He'd grown up at the end of a mile-long dirt road, in a solitary house in the middle of an apple orchard, with an outdoor privy and no hot water. When Jones was three, his father was hit by a car while helping another motorist; he was an invalid, in and out of hospital, for several years, and was left with permanent damage to his left arm and leg. His mother worked in a shoe factory and a chicken processing plant, and the rest of the time cared for his father. They ate souse, scrapple, occasionally chops or ham, and game shot by Jones and his relatives. His paternal grandmother, a stout, hard, profane woman straight out of Faulkner, stole the family Christmas tree from a tree farm one foggy December morning, and made squirrel stews that sometimes had fur and claws lurking at the bottom of the pot.

A hard life took its toll on Jones's parents, and on their relationship with him. He was drawn to work with addicts and the mentally ill, he says, to "prevent others from living through the kind of things I had." Once, after staying with a neighboring family of farmers for a couple of nights to help with chores, he called his mother to ask if he could stay a night or two longer. She brought a box of his clothes and told him, "Stay as long as you want." Jones explains: "I learned to distance myself from them. I cared for them, but spent very little time with them."

Instead, Jones worked. He tanned deer hides for five dollars a skin, planted and tended half-mile rows of tomatoes, and was a chaser at a local chicken ranch. In ultraviolet light the birds are blind to, he'd herd them to one end of a long barn and snatch them up, scratching and pecking, by a leg. "It was like a vision from hell," he remembers. Later he began building houses up from the bare studs, and renovating dilapidated buildings with minimal cash down and lots of sweat equity. He'd built a house of his own by the time he was twenty-five.

Perhaps because of his solitary childhood, Jones sought out tight-knit communities. He often worked as a hired hand with local Amish farmers, and was the only "Englishman," or non–Pennsylvania Dutch speaker, invited to several barn raisings. He was also drawn to outsiders and underdogs. The 1972 massacre of Israeli athletes at the Munich Olympics stunned and horrified him, and awakened an affinity for Israel. He moved to a military base in the central Galilee, and served two tours of duty as a civilian volunteer in the Israel Defense Forces, helping soldiers with nonmilitary jobs like painting and building repair. Although he was an atheist, he spent Shabbat weekends with Israeli families on nearby moshavim, and accompanied them to services.

Early in his stay, Chaim, the patriarch of his host family, pointed inland to the horizon. "See that line? That's the Mediterranean." He turned 180 degrees. "And that line? That's the West Bank. This is the narrow waist of Israel. The people in those hills want to put us in that sea." At the top of the hill on which the settlement was built stood a playground, a concrete defense tower at its center. At first, Jones wondered how Israel had survived, even prospered, in such adverse conditions. Gradually, he says, he understood. People lived with an intensity he'd never before experienced: "You have good food, you eat it," an old Israeli man told him. "Cigarettes? You smoke them. Today, you live!" His host family led a communal existence utterly unlike his own solitary upbringing. "When they broke the bread together, I saw all the love and respect they showed to each other, and to Chaim. All the men at the table were soldiers; all the women were, too. And I said to myself, 'Okay, so this is how Israel has survived.'"

Back in the States, Jones continued to be drawn to underdogs. After a few years at the newly founded Pennsylvania Office of the Inspector General (OIG), he took a job as a state probation and parole officer, where he specialized in working with addicts, foster children and the mentally ill. To this day, when he visits poor inner cities, he often buys two fast-food dinners and offers one to a homeless person, then coaxes out his new acquaintance's story as they eat together. "I try to give them the respect and attention they deserve. I take them seriously. I guess I've always tried to stand up for the little guy, the person with no voice," he says. "These are my people."

Now, on his second tour of duty at the OIG, Jones knew that Pennsylvania, following Texas's lead, had begun to medicate countless voiceless wards of the state with strong, unproven and potentially harmful chemicals, at huge cost to taxpayers and enormous profit to the pharma companies. He also knew this was the kind of wrongdoing the OIG had been created to fight.

Soon after his trip to New Jersey, the atmosphere at his office changed. His superiors instructed him to treat the case strictly as a personnel matter concerning Fiorello, and to stop investigating the pharmaceutical companies that were paying him. When Jones objected, his boss, Dan Sattele, told him, "Morally and ethically, you're right, but politically this is dead." Sattele suggested that the drug firms had purchased impunity by contributing money to state politicians in both parties. "These companies are very aggressive marketers. They write checks to both sides of the aisle."

Nevertheless, Jones continued to gather evidence about the pharma protocol in Pennsylvania and Texas. He requested clearance to conduct interviews with officials in Corrections, the Department of Public Welfare, and other state agencies that also appeared to be receiving pharma money and taking part in the Pennsylvania protocol. Sattele refused. "These are not the good old days," he told Jones. Then, visibly dejected, he added: "If you want to find waste, fraud and abuse, you don't have to look outside the OIG. It's all here." (Sattele, in a later deposition, remembered their conversation differently, saying that Jones expressed frustrations— many of which Sattele shared—about changes that had occurred in the OIG since his first stint there. "Allen, accept the team concept," Sattele says he told Jones. "Accept the attorneys are here to stay.") Soon an order came down from the office of Tom Ridge, the Republican governor of Pennsylvania, to close the investigation and to shred Allen Jones's fat dossier of corruption.

When Jones persisted in his pharma investigation, Henry Hart, the deputy inspector general, stopped at his cubicle and announced in a voice audible throughout the office that they needed to talk. He led Jones past the desks of the other investigators to the law library, where they sat in full view of the office. There he announced a "problem": the office receptionist had accused Jones of sexual harassment, for which he could be disciplined or fired. Jones concluded that the charge had been fabricated as a way of shutting down his probe.

Later that day, in what Jones calls "a classic good cop–bad cop routine," Dan Sattele took Jones aside in the lunchroom and asked him what had happened. Jones repeated what Hart had said, and told Sattele he was worried he would be fired. "Am I a marked man? Is there a conspiracy against me? What do I have to do?"

Sattele said there was no conspiracy against him among front-line investigators, though his eye contact and body language told Jones there was probably one higher up. "Quit being a salmon," Sattele told him. "Quit swimming against the current with the pharmaceutical case. Go with the flow."

It had taken Allen Jones nearly six months of "Oh my God" moments to reach this point. Now he made a rapid mental inventory. He had settled his parents in a comfortable home that he had built. His daughters had finished college and were financially independent. If he lost this job, he could still work construction for a living. He was free to act.

"But the odd thing was, even while I was running through these facts, I never actually felt there was a choice," Jones remembers. "I'd just been ordered to go against the principle and mandate of my office, and to participate in the cover-up of corruption. I felt like a soldier who has received illegal orders. At the same time, I now knew that defenseless, mentally ill people were suffering and dying, and taxpayers were being ripped off by the pharma companies. Once I knew all this, I couldn't let it go, or I'd have become complicit, and part of the moral responsibility for these crimes would have been mine. I realized I'd become a whistleblower."

Jones pretended to submit to his superiors, while continuing his investigations of the drug companies as an undercover operative in his own office. "I was thinking, 'You're the enemy,'" he recalls. "'And I'm going to prove what you're doing, when you're doing it, and why it's wrong.'" Jones surreptitiously gathered more evidence about the protocols in Texas and Pennsylvania, and traced their deep political root structure. He sent letters detailing the fraud to the Department of Justice and the Department of Health and Human Services (HHS) in Washington, DC, as well as to the attorneys general of Texas, Arkansas, Louisiana, Virginia, South Carolina and other states where Johnson & Johnson and its competitors were operating some version of the scheme. The DOJ and HHS took no action. Some states declined to investigate the case. Most simply did not answer.

Eventually, his bosses at the OIG discovered that Jones hadn't stopped digging, and they relieved him of all investigative duties. But Jones was ready. He had made copies of the most incriminating documents in his case file. He published a lengthy "whistleblower document" on the Web, detailing his investigative findings about patient harm, pharmaceutical wrongdoing and corruption by state officials in Pennsylvania and Texas. He contacted patients' rights advocates, who put him in contact with reporters at the *New York Times*, the *British Medical Journal* and other publications, where he gave interviews. In response, the leaders of the OIG assigned Jones to menial jobs and subjected him to a steady stream of intimidation and public humiliation. His officemates, even former friends, avoided him. "Everyone at work looked at me like I was a cobra," he remembers. "I couldn't have been more alone if they'd put me in the toilet." His desk was searched, and members of his office formed what he termed the "Jones Strikeforce" to monitor his movements and communications. When he called in sick or took a day off, a squad car from the OIG appeared near his house; when he returned to work, a manager would question him: Who was he talking to outside the OIG? Was he under a subpoena? If so, was he testifying? "They kept trying to do things that would make me behave like them, so they could control me," Jones says. "There was this huge disconnect—they just couldn't conceive of a whistleblower identifying with the greater mission of the office, instead of blind loyalty to his bosses."

Finally, on April 28, 2004, his superiors summoned Jones to a second-floor conference room. They placed him on administrative leave, took his badge and identity card, and told him to stay off OIG property. A security guard handed him a box containing a few belongings from his desk and escorted him out of the building. He still remembers the sharp, terminal click of the security door shutting behind him. Two months later, the OIG fired him for acts of insubordination: sharing confidential information with persons outside the OIG and speaking with the press.

Allen Jones knew he was a whistleblower. But how, he wondered, could he use his newfound status to fight against the OIG and a pharma multinational? Jones began a ten-year education in public and private whistleblowing, and in the complex and rapidly changing array of laws that both encouraged and protected it. In the process, he would walk the two very different legal paths that modern whistleblowing has taken in America.

With the help of lawyers at the Government Accountability Project (GAP), a nongovernmental organization based in Washington, DC, that has represented whistleblowers since 1976, Jones brought suit against Sattele, Henry Hart and other

members of the Pennsylvania Office of the Inspector General. They had violated his
First Amendment rights, he argued, by preventing him from speaking freely on two
matters of urgent public concern: the wrongdoing by pharmaceutical companies
that he had uncovered, and the OIG's attempts to conceal that wrongdoing. Later,
after being terminated by the OIG, he filed a second whistleblower retaliation suit
for wrongful discharge.

"When Allen Jones came to us, he was in a very bad spot," remembers Jason
Zuckerman, one of the attorneys who defended Jones on behalf of GAP. "He was
living in a cabin in the woods without indoor plumbing, and he didn't have any
money. He just barely got by. Once he was fired by the IG, he was both unemployed
and unemployable." (Recognizing the importance of the case, GAP represented
Jones pro bono.)

Zuckerman was impressed by Jones's commitment. "Whenever I meet with prospective clients, I try to go in with skeptical eyes, and ask a lot of hard questions. I
didn't really feel the need to take that approach with Allen. It was obvious, from the
moment I met with him, that he was absolutely credible, and that he had put a lot
on the line in order to do the right thing. This wasn't about Allen. He was extremely
concerned about all the kids and adults in the state mental hospitals who were
being put on atypical antipsychotics, and as a result would be harmed for life, by
diabetes or other complications. And it was clear that he was never going to back
down, until the people who were doing it were held accountable."

Zuckerman and his colleagues at GAP, on Jones's behalf, filed a First Amendment suit, one of the oldest whistleblower defenses in the United States, whose
guiding ethos predates the nation. On March 25, 1777, Marine captain John Grannis came before the Continental Congress to denounce crimes committed by Esek
Hopkins, commander in chief of the Continental navy. Grannis spoke for himself
and for nine other sailors and Marines who served aboard the USS *Warren*, a frigate
in the Continental navy. He stated that Hopkins had treated British prisoners "in
the most inhuman and barbarous manner"; negligently failed to intercept British
shipping; and publicly ridiculed the members of the Congress as a "parcell of lawyers clerks" and "a pack of damned fools." The Congress swiftly relieved Hopkins

of his command, and when he jailed several of the whistleblowers for criminal libel and conspiracy, it unanimously issued the following act on July 30, 1778:

> Resolved, that it is the duty of all persons in the service of the United States, as well as all other inhabitants thereof, to give the earliest information to Congress or other proper authority of any misconduct, frauds or misdemeanors committed by any officers or persons in the service of these states, which may come to their knowledge.

The Continental Congress, showing a clear understanding of the risks run by subordinates when they denounce powerful superiors, also ordered that Grannis and his shipmates receive any government documents they needed to defend themselves in court, pledged to pay their legal fees, and hired a distinguished attorney to represent them. The ten men eventually won their case and were reinstated, while the embittered Hopkins retired to private life.

This early law shows how central the basic tenets of whistleblowing were to the intellectual climate of Revolutionary America. In writing this law, and the First Amendment eleven years later, the Founders drew on two millennia of ancient thought about individual conscience, egalitarianism, free speech, and the citizen's duty to denounce public wrongdoing. They knew the English Bill of Rights of 1689, with its stress on the "freedom of speech and debates" in Parliament, and John Milton's defense of a free press in the *Areopagitica* forty-five years earlier. They likewise employed conceptions established during the Enlightenment and the Scientific Revolution, like Locke's ideas on personal conscience and the social contract, and Galileo's courageous stand for the objective truth of the heliocentric universe against the obscurantist, authoritarian pronouncements of the Inquisition. The Founders were also familiar with classical precedents for whistleblower-like behavior, particularly the free, bold speech against unjust power that the ancient Athenians called *parrhesia*, which Socrates famously defended to the death during his trial for impiety in Athens.

The Founders themselves were practicing these same principles in their wrenching break with Mother England and their Divine Monarch—a rejection of authority whose radicalism we can hardly imagine today. On the day they passed the law, British troops occupied New York, and George Washington and his fledgling Continental Army were fighting for survival in New Jersey. They knew well the danger that the USS *Warren* whistleblowers were running, for they, too, risked life and limb if their uprising failed. Repeatedly in their laws and writings, the Founders underscored the moral duty of virtuous dissent, and of following individual conscience against blind obedience to unjust, brutal rulers. "If the freedom of speech is taken away," wrote George Washington, "then dumb and silent we may be led, like sheep to the slaughter." Benjamin Franklin was more succinct: "Rebellion to tyrants is obedience to God." The Founders had expressed similar sentiments a year earlier, in the Declaration of Independence, whose preamble stresses the "right" and the "duty" of citizens to overthrow unjust rulers, and the fundamental equality of all men. They set these precepts in still more binding form in the First Amendment, which made free speech and a free press the birthright of all American citizens.

This foundation for whistleblowing laid down by the Founders became actionable through a series of new laws and court rulings that began with the Civil Rights Act of 1871, progressed through the new civil rights era of the 1960s and 1970s, and has continued to evolve to the present day. By 1968, public servants who discovered wrongdoing at their jobs and were silenced by superiors could rely on a powerful First Amendment defense. This was the legal basis of Allen Jones's claim against the Pennsylvania OIG. Now he had to win his case in court.

To help his lawyers, Jones wrote a series of memoranda describing corruption at his former employer, which reveal a taste for legal combat he'd developed as an investigator. Jones described the essential changes that had taken place at the OIG. The office had been created in 1987 by Governor Robert Casey, as an independent body required to "deter, detect, prevent, and eradicate waste, fraud, misconduct, and abuse" in all agencies under the governor's jurisdiction, in a sense an institutional whistleblower force built into the state government. Shortly after taking over as governor in 1994, however, Tom Ridge stripped the OIG of its independence: before investigating a state agency, the office now had to obtain permission from that agency and approval from the governor's office. The staff of special investigators was cut by two-thirds. Ridge instituted a new policy of shredding old case files, which might destroy valuable evidence. Lawyers who reported to the governor's office began to keep careful watch on the OIG's activities.

The result, Jones noted in a memorandum, was an office that had lost its original fraud-fighting mission and become a façade. Paraphrasing Leon Uris, he described the prevailing atmosphere in the Ridge-era OIG: "It is I against my brother—my brother and I against our father—our family against the tribe—the tribe against the nation—our nation against the world." Most employees, he said, had forgotten the public interest they had sworn to protect; some, whom Jones called "the walking wounded," had resigned themselves to playing the new game. His colleagues had made an example of him, Jones believed, in order to discourage other honest employees from coming forward with evidence of political corruption. For his part, Jones was determined to make an example of *them*, and to show other OIG employees how they, too, could expose and defeat such corruption. He wrote:

> The only "fame" I desire is among government administrators who may be tempted to set aside their duty in service to corrupt politics. I would like them to "see" my face in their mind's eye before they act—to have to consider that the person they are about to crush just might turn the tables on them. It would please me if middle managers everywhere invoked my name as a Boogeyman to frighten their children (and their bosses) into good behavior.

Despite expert help from GAP, as the litigation ground through the courts, one by one the defendants were granted immunity and Jones's charges were pared back. Eventually, lawyers for the remaining defendants in his wrongful discharge case offered to settle it for $37,500. By now, Jones had been forced to sell the house he'd built for himself, and was living in a hunting cabin with plywood floors that he owned with a friend. "I felt that I was losing everything I'd built, everything in my life I cared about." He accepted the settlement. After paying off creditors, replacing the tires on his pickup and filling his propane tanks for the winter, he was left with $1,200.

"Allen Jones had been a distinguished law enforcement officer for many years, but once he blew the whistle, it was all over—he was almost homeless," says Jason Zuckerman. "I think his claim is a good response to what I hear out of the Chamber of Commerce and the Wall Street firms, that whistleblower laws create the wrong incentives, and provide a way for disloyal employees to get very wealthy overnight. That's utter bullshit. The reality is that all of the whistleblowers I've worked with would probably have been 'smarter,' and served their economic interests better, just to look the other way. If you calculate what they would have earned if they'd kept below the radar and continued their professional careers, it would be a hell of a lot more money than they earned blowing the whistle."

Worse, Jones was haunted by the knowledge of myriad helpless patients still being abused by pharmaceutical companies. Building walls to pay for food, Jones continued to investigate the various drug protocol schemes around the country. Eventually he learned of another whistleblower law that might allow him to bring suit against Johnson & Johnson in the name of the United States of America. It had been passed at the height of the Civil War, and at its heart was a Latin phrase that sounded like a sorcerer's incantation: *Qui tam pro domino rege quam pro se ipso in hac parte sequitur.*

The phrase, which means, "He who sues on behalf of our Lord the King and on his own behalf," originated in early medieval England, where the king, having no regular police unit, often relied on private individuals to help enforce his laws. The "qui tam" mechanism allowed common citizens to become private prosecutors and to bring suit on behalf of His Majesty, even when the Crown took no part in the proceedings. It also paid these citizens a bounty if they won the suit. The earliest known qui tam provision appears in a 695 declaration of King Wihtred of Kent: "If a freeman works during the forbidden time [i.e., the Sabbath], he shall forfeit his *healsfang* [i.e., pay a fine in lieu of imprisonment], and the man who informs against him shall have half the fine, and [the profits arising from] the labor." Other qui tam provisions that accumulated over the centuries helped control the sale of wine at universities and the brewing of beer; the manufacture of clogs and other wooden shoes; the importation of silk and grain; the practice of games like kailes, half-bowls, hand in and hand out, and queckboard; together with what one legal commentator has called "a tawdry bag of poaching, bastardy and theft." William Shakespeare's father was sued, and perhaps ruined, by qui tam informers who accused him of usury and the illicit sale of wool. From the fourteenth century, an increasing number of qui tam laws enabled private persons to sue public officers, including mayors, sheriffs, bailiffs and customs officers, for negligence and for engaging in private business related to their public duties.

The thirteen British colonies in America adopted numerous English laws that contained a qui tam provision; at the First Congress in 1789, shortly after signing the Constitution, the Framers passed several qui tam laws of their own. But the most momentous private prosecutor law in America was enacted a century later, in 1863, when the Union army suffered from sweeping fraud by defense contractors. Two years earlier, at the beginning of the Civil War, the Union's fledgling Department of Defense had rushed to equip a fighting force, at a moment when the North–South split was causing severe shortages in basic supplies like wool, horses and gunpowder. The result was, as one congressman put it, "a mania for stealing that ran from the general to the drummer boy." When Brooks Brothers ran out of wool, the company began pressing rags together with glue to make "shoddy" uniforms, which, as the *Sacramento Daily Union* reported in 1861, "resolved themselves into their original elements within a week after being put on by the soldier." Horse traders sold blind mules and lame horses to Army quartermasters at $110 a head; armorers supplied defective rifles that blew off soldiers' thumbs at the first shot, then collected the weapons, repaired the defects, and sold them back to the Army at a markup. Artillery crews in the heat of battle pried open gunpowder barrels only to find them brimful of sawdust. Jim Fisk, a circus performer turned stockbroker who became one of the most notorious robber barons of the Gilded Age, made millions selling shoddy blankets and cardboard boots to the US military. "You can sell anything to the government," he once bragged, "at almost any price you've got the guts to ask."

Abraham Lincoln detested such war profiteers, and agreed with New York congressman Charles H. Van Wyck, an abolitionist and vehement opponent of contract fraud, who wrote: "Worse than traitors in arms are the men who pretend loyalty to the flag, feast and fatten on the misfortunes of the nation, while patriotic blood is crimsoning the plains of the south and their countrymen are moldering in the dust." At the beginning of the war, Van Wyck chaired a House Select Committee on Government Contracts, which questioned hundreds of witnesses and produced a long and lurid chronicle of defense chicanery. "Nearly every man who deals with the Government seems to feel or desire that it would not long survive," Van Wyck observed, "and each had a common right to plunder it while it lived."

To rein in such abuse, which threatened the Union war effort, in 1863 Senator Jacob M. Howard and a group of reform-minded congressmen sponsored the False Claims Act, a vigorous and inventive new fraud-fighting measure. The law fined offending contractors $2,000 for each misrepresentation, or "false claim," that they made in their request for payment from the government. In addition, defendants were liable for double damages—they had to return to the Treasury twice what they had stolen. But the law's most incisive feature was its qui tam provision, which allowed individuals to prosecute fraud with or without the government's participation. Allowing private citizens to sue on behalf of their government was essential to the effectiveness of the False Claims Act, not only because no central law enforcement agency or Department of Justice yet existed, but also because high-ranking officials in the government, including Secretary of Defense Simon Cameron and Secretary of the Navy Gideon Welles, were implicated in the fraud. In return for insider information, the whistleblower, which the new law termed a "relator," received 50 percent of the money recovered by that suit. Senator Howard explained that he favored the qui tam provision because "'setting a rogue to catch a rogue' . . . is the safest and most expeditious way I have ever discovered of bringing rogues to justice."

Lincoln championed the law, urging Congress to send an army of "citizen soldiers" against corrupt military contractors and their creatures within the government. After Congress passed the False Claims Act by a generous majority, it became known as the "Lincoln Law."

Predictably, defense companies disliked the new act and eventually found a way to defang it, with help from the executive branch. In 1943, with the United States deep in World War II, leading contractors urged Congress to repeal the law, claiming that it impeded their ability to deliver vital war matériel. Attorney General Francis Biddle agreed. Biddle had learned that a few enterprising lawyers had begun hanging around courthouses, copying criminal complaints as soon as they were filed by the Department of Justice and refiling them as civil False Claims Act lawsuits. Although these new lawsuits often resulted in further recoveries for the Treasury, Biddle viewed them as dishonest. "Informers' suits have become mere parasitical actions, occasionally brought only after law-enforcement offices have investigated and prosecuted persons guilty of a violation of law and solely because of the hope of a large reward." He petitioned Congress to eliminate the qui tam provision, arguing not only that it enabled parasitic behavior but that such meddling by private attorneys general could harm the war effort. Biddle asserted that the DOJ should be in complete control of all litigation that concerned the federal government.

Senator William Langer of North Dakota, a lawyer like Biddle, objected. "What harm can there be if 10,000 lawyers in America are assisting the Attorney General of the United States in digging up war frauds?" In fact, he pointed out, the DOJ had not diligently pursued fraudulent defense contractors, though their crimes often endangered soldiers' lives. But the law's opponents won the day: although Congress didn't repeal the FCA entirely, it curtailed the role of the relator, cut the potential bounty and added a "government knowledge" clause that required the dismissal of all cases in which the wrongdoing had previously been known to a public official—which was almost always true. The defense contractors and the DOJ had succeeded in neutralizing the FCA.

Yet while imaginative lawyers, by angering Attorney General Biddle, had led to the weakening of the act, forty years later, during a further season of defense scandals, another such lawyer found a way to revitalize the law and turn it into the US government's most powerful fraud-fighting tool.

John Phillips first heard of the False Claims Act in 1983, as he sat in a breezy, light-filled office in Century City, the headquarters of the Center for Law in the Public Interest (CLIPI). The office bore little resemblance to a law firm, though it was a step up from CLIPI's original location in a strip mall, where the Formica furniture and orange shag carpet had exuded a lingering fug of fried food from the burger joint next door. Phillips had cofounded the Center in 1971, having left the august law firm of O'Melveny & Myers after revealing, in a case he'd taken pro bono without telling the firm's partners, that their biggest client, Union Oil, had broken the law by secretly funding a referendum against public transportation. Three other O'Melveny associates also left the firm with Phillips to cofound CLIPI.

The firm's shabby-chic office was one of many iconoclastic moves. "At first we had virtually no money, except a small grant from the Ford Foundation," Phillips remembers. "We hardly had jobs at all, because public interest law was in its infancy. So we took the cheapest offices we could find. But the contrast with the oak-paneled gravitas of big law firms really worked. It signaled to everyone that we weren't just doing your average lawyering, but were up to something different."

Just so: Phillips isn't your average lawyer. He's lean and tanned and voluble, and seems restless until he hears an idea that really interests him. Then his jaw and his posture firm, and his eyes get the distant, inward-looking commitment of a marathoner at the starting line, as he latches on to the idea, teasing out ways make it better. Some of his ideas come from deep left field. "One time John decided that pregnant women being forced to carry babies for nine whole months was cruel and unusual, a kind of slavery," his wife, Linda Douglass, a former distinguished television journalist and director of communications for the White House Office of Health Reform under Barack Obama, told me. "He talked with a bunch of biotech experts, and generated some interesting theories. Including bringing babies to term in the uteruses of cows." She cocked her head pertly and watched my reaction, while Phillips held his chin with a hint of contrition.

"That idea never got much traction!" Douglass cackled. You could see from Phillips's expression, tinged with wistfulness and tenacity, that he hadn't completely given up on it. "Tricky to put all the pieces of the puzzle together, sure," he said quietly, almost to himself. "But something like this still could work."

Phillips has a flair for calculated rebellion. As a boy barely able to see over the dashboard, he borrowed cars from his father's Ford dealership and drove them around woodlots in Leechburg, the coal and steel town in western Pennsylvania where he grew up. Around ten o'clock in the evening he'd often drive down to the Elks Club to collect his father, who'd been drinking there for hours and was usually in no condition to drive himself home. Upon graduating from high school in 1960, he enlisted in the army, rather than risk being drafted after college. He reported for duty to Fort Knox, Kentucky, but learned when he arrived that there weren't enough empty bunks in the barracks; he and his fellow recruits had to stand in formation in the courtyard all night. "I've never been so cold," he remembers, obviously still irritated. "Can you imagine? Your first day in the service of your country, and you spend it standing in the cold like an idiot?" The next year, starting a new tour of duty at Fort Benning, Georgia, he discovered that his name was missing from the roll call roster. For the first three months, while his comrades in arms went through basic training, he read philosophy in the local library, returning to the barracks for dinner and sleep. Later, the recruits' belongings were being pilfered while they trained, so he set a trap with ink-stained money and caught the culprit, a cook's assistant; when the commanding officer refused to discipline the thief, Phillips wrote one of his congressmen and had the officer reprimanded. After the army, he earned a degree in government and international studies at Notre Dame, then attended law school at the University of California at Berkeley, at that time a nexus of protests against the Vietnam War.

When Dupont Circle was still druggy and dangerous, he bought the Blaine Mansion, the enormous 1881 residence on the Circle that is now his Washington residence and the headquarters of his law firm, Phillips & Cohen. He fell in love with Borgo Finocchieto, an abandoned hilltop village in the Tuscan countryside, bought it all, and, with eight years of effort and expense, restored it into an oasis in the sky. His eye for future value is occasionally off. He was an early investor in Theranos, the biotech company that seemed poised to revolutionize laboratory blood testing and reap a fortune before the company's leaders were charged with massive civil and criminal fraud. But far more often than not, his risks pay off. The False Claims Act certainly did, and handsomely.

Phillips's rebelliousness, tenacity, entrepreneurialism and strategic brilliance all helped CLIPI win a series of landmark cases in civil rights and First Amendment rights, environmental quality, consumer protection and affordable housing. When the City of Los Angeles ran the Century Freeway through some of its poorest neighborhoods, evicting thousands of residents, Phillips and his partners sued the city for civil rights and environmental violations, forced the construction of high-quality replacement housing, and eventually caused the freeway to be redesigned. They blocked the construction of nuclear power plants, saved public art master-pieces from demolition and championed the rights of blacks and women in the Los Angeles Police Department and in private sector jobs. After the Watergate investi-gators revealed that the defense giant Northrop had given $50,000 to the Nixon administration, some of which had gone to the Watergate burglars as hush money, CLIPI sued Northrop for illegal use of corporate funds, and eventually got Tom Jones, the Northrop president and CEO, to admit under oath that his company routinely paid bribes to foreign governments to secure contracts, in order to keep pace with competitors like Lockheed, who were doing the same. The revelation made nationwide news, triggered Senate hearings on defense contracting fraud, and led to the passage of the Foreign Corrupt Practices Act, a potent statute against corporate bribery abroad. Phillips also pioneered a new California law that could force defendants to pay the plaintiff's attorney fees if the suit served the public good. "CLIPI was a fantastic job," Phillips says. "I'd found a way to do good, and to do well doing it."

In 1981, however, soon after an assailant shot John Lennon at point-blank range with five hollow-point bullets from a .38 Special, the ever-restless Phillips went on a leave of absence from his firm, cashed out his pension fund and took up arms against the National Rifle Association. He drafted Proposition 15, a California initiative to freeze new handgun sales, which received statewide support and was endorsed by Tom Bradley, the popular mayor of Los Angeles who was running on the same ballot to become the state's first black governor. Four months before the election, pollsters predicted that Prop 15 would pass by a 2-to-1 margin, and gave Bradley an insurmountable 7-point lead.

Then the NRA arrived. Pro-gun activists launched a $7 million fear campaign among white rural inhabitants of California's Central Valley, many of whom owned guns. They ran television ads in which armed, black-swathed burglars broke in on defenseless white grannies. They set up voter registration centers in gun stores throughout the state, and signed up three hundred thousand new voters. Prop 15 was voted down overwhelmingly, and Tom Bradley lost by a narrow margin.

In 1983, sitting in Century City after the NRA debacle, Phillips tried to rein- vent himself once more. He asked an aide at CLIPI to assemble a list of little-known statutes that might be enhanced to create leverage against corporate power. Half- way down the list he found a nearly defunct nineteenth-century statute with a curi- ous Latin phrase. Though in much-watered-down form, the False Claims Act still existed in the US legal code in 1983. And one case was currently working its way through the courts, brought by a three-hundred-pound machinist and Vietnam combat veteran, Jack Gravitt, against General Electric, then the nation's largest corporation and a leading defense contractor, which Gravitt accused of defrauding the federal government to the tune of $40 million. Phillips called Gravitt's lawyer, a young Cincinnati employment attorney named Jim Helmer, who explained that the DOJ was attempting to end the case with a patently inadequate $264,000 settlement with General Electric, and was threatening both Helmer and Gravitt with legal action if they didn't go along.

Phillips was riveted. At that moment, the defense industry was embroiled in public scandals as virulent as those of 1863, when Abraham Lincoln had signed the original False Claims Act. Forty-five of the top hundred defense contractors were under investigation for multiple offenses, and four of the largest—General Electric, Rockwell, GTE and Gould—had been convicted of criminal fraud. The Depart- ment of Defense, under Caspar Weinberger, was being ridiculed for paying $640 for toilet seats on military planes. Lincoln had signed the original law to stop army and navy contractors from stealing taxpayer dollars, but also to push complacent or complicit government agencies to act. Phillips wondered: Could the Lincoln Law be revived and fortified to fight modern defense fraud? Could its all-important qui tam provision force the DOJ to discipline politically powerful fraudsters? Could Ronald Reagan be made to understand that private whistleblowers teaming up with prosecutors to recover taxpayer dollars was an ideal example of his vaunted public-private partnership?

Qui tam pro domino rege quam pro se ipso in hac parte sequitur. As John Phillips murmured the Latin phrase, his eyes got that familiar faraway look.

———

Eighteen months later, Phillips had achieved the impossible. He had persuaded a coalition of left-leaning Democrats and hard-right Republicans to join forces and amend the False Claims Act, reversing the damage done to the law during World War II and adding sharp new penalties, anti-retaliation protection for whistleblowers, and a stronger qui tam provision that made relators a formal party to their cases, allowing them to object to inadequate settlements and to prosecute cases alone when the government declined to intervene. The revitalized law guaranteed whistleblowers between 15 and 30 percent of funds recovered in successful cases; wrongdoers in these cases were also required to pay the whistleblowers' legal bills.

The coalition was led by Chuck Grassley, the conservative Republican senator from Iowa, and Howard Berman, a liberal Democratic congressman from California. Polar opposites on most social issues, together they were a political odd couple of formidable energy and reach. When I asked Grassley, who receives millions of dollars in contributions from large corporations, why he backed a law that, according to many of his fellow Republicans, stacks the deck against American industry and enriches a lot of clever lawyers, he smiled his tart, preacherly smile. "I'm no enemy of corporations, and I'm certainly no great friend of lawyers," he said. "But this law just works. It breaks the fraud cycle."

A closer look at Grassley's record reveals telltale anomalies that have made him whistleblowing's most effective champion in Congress for the last four decades. He's known for his attentiveness to ordinary citizens and regularly meets with Iowa farmers, housewives and small business owners visiting Washington even when he has ostensibly more significant work on his DC calendar. He is a tireless watchdog against abuse of authority by the executive branch. "Senator Grassley firmly believes that individuals have a right of conscience, and that they need to be protected from bureaucratic uniformity and repression," says Ralph Nader, who over the years has fought many battles both with and against Grassley. "He loves civil servants who have conscience and speak out."

Above all, Chuck Grassley hates fraud, waste and abuse. Though pharma and healthcare companies help bankroll his elections, he has pursued Medicare corruption more relentlessly than anyone else in Washington. Grassley sees whistleblowing as a way of fighting fraud and protecting the individual simultaneously: of allowing individual citizens to make themselves heard by Big Government and Big Business alike. Since he first came to Washington as an Iowa representative in 1975, he has helped pass more than thirty whistleblower laws and provisions against both corporate and government misconduct, ranging from air safety to healthcare, shareholder rights to national security.

"Whistleblowing is a great act of courage and patriotism, yet all too often, whistleblowers are treated like a skunk at a picnic," Grassley says. "The Founding Fathers recognized whistleblowing as one of the central rights, and duties, of the citizen to his society. This is about individuals healing the disease of bureaucracy and public thievery."

On September 17, 1985, at the height of public outrage over defense contract fraud, Grassley chaired hearings before a subcommittee of the Senate Judiciary Committee that paved the way for the False Claims Act amendments—the opening salvo in a bitter war over whistleblowing that continues to this day. An odd assortment of witnesses had gathered for the event. Jack Gravitt, the Purple Heart recipient and whistleblower against General Electric, sat at the front of the room, beside attorney Jim Helmer and not far from John Phillips. Nearby were two senior Department of Justice officials, Jay Stephens and Stuart Schiffer, who soon made clear that the DOJ, as the prosecutorial arm of the executive branch, opposed the new law even more vehemently than GE did.

"Contractor fraud may well be the world's second oldest profession," Grassley said in his opening statement. "Certainly after 122 years of experience with contract fraud in this country, the U.S. government should have come to grips with how to solve this age-old problem." In an obvious swipe at the DOJ, Grassley continued, "If we wish to deal effectively with rampant fraud, we must ask ourselves if the current system is institutionally capable of doing that. The evidence suggests it is not."

Jay Stephens countered that Justice was actually doing an excellent job at fighting defense fraud, and that a stronger False Claims Act would hamper its work. The law, he said, was an anachronism from a time when the United States had no central investigative force; now that the DOJ and the FBI existed, most qui tam whistleblowers were parasitic "bounty hunters" who interfered with legitimate law enforcers and ultimately provided little useful evidence of wrongdoing. Finally, Stephens suggested that the act was unconstitutional. (This followed an earlier legal opinion, written by Assistant Attorney General William Barr, according to whom the False Claims Act, with its crucial qui tam clause, represented "a devastating threat to the Executive's constitutional authority and to the doctrine of separation of powers.") Stephens and his colleague Stuart Schiffer concluded that they were "quite proud" of the DOJ's record of prosecuting defense contractors without the False Claims Act.

"It seems like every Department of Justice witness paints a rosy picture [of their prosecutions]," Chuck Grassley observed drily, "even though the evidence contradicts what they say." Then he introduced John Gravitt, whose experiences as a plaintiff against General Electric demonstrated why the False Claims Act needed fixing—not least because the DOJ had been winking at fraud. Gravitt testified that GE was overbilling the Department of Defense with counterfeited time stamps at its Evendale, Ohio, aircraft engine plant, where he worked. Yet his numerous, detailed reports of this fraud, which amounted to $40 million over five years, had been ignored by his bosses and later by the Defense Department. The only concrete outcome of Gravitt's actions was to get himself fired.

As a last resort, Gravitt had brought a false claims suit against GE, but the DOJ's response had been to arrange a tiny settlement with the company, for a fraction of what it had stolen. When Gravitt and Helmer announced that Gravitt intended to pursue the case alone, as a false claims relator, the DOJ promptly opened a civil case against GE, which under the terms of the 1943 amendments to the False Claims Act blocked Gravitt from proceeding against the company. Then the DOJ closed the investigation. A senior DOJ lawyer threatened to prosecute the two men criminally if they didn't drop their suit.

Gravitt, who had been badly injured in battle near Da Nang, told the committee that he had brought his suit mainly for patriotic reasons—"to force General Electric to stop overcharging the taxpayers and the US government"—and expressed bafflement at the DOJ's obstructionism. "It appears they don't want somebody doing their job for them," he said, "but it is quite evident from what we have seen thus far with the situation at General Electric that somebody hasn't done their job for a long, long time." He urged Congress to pass the amendments, including a strengthened qui tam provision.

Helmer agreed, stressing that the amendments were needed to protect whistleblowers from retaliation, curtail widespread fraud, and prevent the DOJ from striking sweetheart deals with powerful contractors. "So long as Mr. Gravitt is not involved, nothing prevents the United States Government and General Electric Company from 'settling' his case for a nominal amount to avoid adverse publicity concerning defense procurement efforts," Helmer said. If, on the other hand, relators like Gravitt were allowed to take an active part in their litigation, they "could act as watchdogs over taxpayers' funds and ensure that fraudulent contractors pay an appropriate amount of damages."

Six weeks later, on a groundswell of popular resentment against defense fraud, Congress amended the venerable False Claims Act as Phillips, Gravitt and Helmer had urged. However, the new law still needed the president's signature; Congress had adjourned, and if Reagan didn't sign the bill within ten days, it would automatically die by pocket veto. As days went by and Reagan didn't sign, the law's proponents began to wonder whether the defense lobby, which had long enjoyed Reagan's favor, had convinced him to veto it. "That was an extremely stressful time," John Phillips remembers. "We pulled out all the stops. I notified the press, and they asked Reagan whether he was being pressured by contractors. Chuck Grassley and his staff called everyone they knew." Finally, on October 27, a day before the veto took effect, Ronald Reagan signed the revised act into law aboard Air Force One.

The amendments reversed the changes made in 1943 and added important new provisions. They prescribed substantial penalties, which have since been increased: a company or person found guilty must repay three times the amount that they stole, plus a minimum of $11,463 for each of their false claims, which typically are contracts to provide the government with goods or services that, in reality, were never provided. Depending on factors including the quality and quantity of the evidence that the relator supplied, he or she is eligible to collect between 15 and 30 percent of the total funds recovered for the state or national Treasury. The lawyers of a successful relator also receive their expenses from the defendant—the fraudster—as well as a portion of the relator's share.

Despite its passage into law, and its obvious merits as a fraud-fighting tool, large sections of the federal government, particularly the DOJ, remained hostile to the new FCA. Two years later, DOJ lawyers argued before the Supreme Court that qui tam was unconstitutional and unnecessary, and that the FCA should be repealed. The court rejected their arguments, noting among other things that numerous laws containing qui tam provisions had been passed by the same men who had written the Constitution—how then could qui tam be unconstitutional?

Since then, the FCA has weathered many more juridical storms, and it remains at the heart of a fierce debate within American society, between two different visions of justice.

The premise of the 1986 False Claims Act—that insiders could reveal fraud and collect a reward for the consequent career and legal risks they ran—was later embodied, often at Chuck Grassley's prompting, in a series of state laws designed to encourage and protect qui tam whistleblowers. One of these, a Texas law to fight healthcare fraud, ultimately provided the legal tools that Allen Jones used against Johnson & Johnson. If the company had lied about Risperdal's effectiveness and real costs when it sold the drug to state healthcare authorities or to Medicaid and Medicare, then it had made wrongful representations, or "false claims"; like the shoddy contractors during the Civil War, Johnson & Johnson had defrauded taxpayers and could be brought to justice. Even if the federal government or a state attorney general chose not to intervene—and Jones had already uncovered enough collusion by state employees to understand why this might occur—the Texas Medicaid Fraud Prevention Act had the crucial qui tam provision that would allow him to prosecute the case himself as a private attorney general. But Jones had limited legal experience and no money: he needed lawyers at the state or federal level who understood the legal labyrinth of qui tam whistleblowing to run—and to fund—his case.

After the DOJ, federal healthcare officials and several state attorneys general declined to take the case, Jones finally found someone who listened. Charles Siegel, a lawyer at the Dallas firm of Waters & Kraus, which had some false claims experience, was impressed by Jones's account. Siegel introduced Jones to Tom Melsheimer, a former federal prosecutor and standout trial lawyer at Fish & Richardson, a large litigation firm that had the deep pockets required to pursue a whistleblower case on a contingency basis, and the connections with the Texas state government necessary to enlist the support of the attorney general. Melsheimer and Jones met Cynthia O'Keeffe, a senior lawyer in the state's Civil Medicaid Fraud Division. "My first impression of Allen was that he looked a lot like Chuck Norris in *Walker, Texas Ranger*, a popular TV show," says O'Keeffe in her clear East Texas soprano. "I was sitting there thinking, 'This is so ironic! This guy looks like Walker, Texas Ranger, but he's from Pennsylvania, and here he is telling us about what's going on down here in Texas.' I saw right away that he was very credible and very earnest, but the scheme he was describing was so huge and complex that I couldn't help wondering, 'Can this all be true?' At the time I didn't think it could be. It seemed too fantastic."

Nevertheless, O'Keeffe felt that the seriousness of Jones's allegations required a thorough investigation by her office. Like Jones, she had a personal stake in the case. Before joining the AG's office, she'd worked for twenty years as a family lawyer, where she'd devoted herself to protecting vulnerable children. "I was absolutely horrified to think that foster children in Texas might have been targeted, that they were part of the marketing plan for this project," she remembers. "I could not have slept at night if we didn't bring this to light." O'Keeffe formed a team of lawyers and investigators from various departments in the Texas AG's office. Together they began interviewing state employees and perusing an ever-growing stream of documents. They traveled to DOJ headquarters in Washington to pore over twenty more boxes of documents subpoenaed from Johnson & Johnson in a related case. Soon O'Keeffe sent the company a civil investigative demand, which yielded another three hundred boxes. "Our team was there with those documents every day, every week, every month, for a whole year. And that's what convinced us that Allen Jones was right. We went in thinking he wasn't, but after we'd investigated for a while, we realized that the vast majority of what Allen brought to us was actually documented in the evidence, and we could prove it to a jury. That he could figure it all out with only two banker's boxes of documents is a testament to what a fantastic investigator he is."

In the end, on O'Keeffe's recommendation, state attorney general Greg Abbott joined the case on behalf of the State of Texas, and sued Johnson & Johnson under the Texas Medicaid Fraud Prevention Act. In doing so, the state and Allen Jones formed an alliance that is vital to private whistleblowing, and explains much of its success. Texas supplied investigative clout, legal acumen and public credibility, while Jones, as relator, provided insider knowledge, expert document analysis and a willingness to testify in court. Jones also brought veteran lawyers at law firms with the staff and money required to litigate the case, and the trial experience to succeed before a jury. "Cynthia told me that she wanted and expected us to do a lot of heavy lifting on the case," says Tom Melsheimer, whose firm eventually spent about $20 million in staff time and direct expenses. "They did an enormous amount of work on their own, but in such a huge case, it was essential for all of us to work side by side, as a team." Fish & Richardson hired several expert witnesses, which would have been difficult for the Texas AG's office to do, given its limited funds and time-consuming bureaucracy. Melsheimer brought in famed Austin trial attorney Tommy Jacks, who together with Patrick Sweeten, a senior lawyer in the AG's Civil Division, led most of the 140 depositions across the country. "We were building a wall, a brick at a time," Sweeten says.

Finally, Melsheimer introduced Jones to a young associate in his firm, Natalie Arbaugh, slender, blond, petite, with a husky contralto and a clear green gaze. Jones met Arbaugh high in a glass-sided Dallas skyscraper one chilly winter day in 2004; as his day-to-day counsel and confidante, she soon became one of the most important people in his life. Arbaugh explained to Jones the basics of being a whistleblower, including the bounty provision, which seemed to surprise him. "One of the things that immediately struck me about Allen was that he had clearly gone into this process with no idea he could make money out of it," Arbaugh says. "He was just trying to do the right thing. I believe he would have proceeded even without the money. But the fact is, the chance of substantial monetary rewards allows whistleblowers who don't have Allen's rock-solid convictions, or who have more economic risk, to take a chance on behaving ethically." The prospect of a large bounty also enables a law firm like Fish & Richardson to invest millions of the firm's dollars on the expectation that they will eventually prevail—and profit.

Another surprise for Jones was the secrecy that enveloped his case as soon as it was filed. False claims complaints are filed under seal, meaning that the defendant is not notified of the charges, and the whistleblower is forbidden to discuss the case, or even mention its existence, with anyone save his lawyers. The seal is designed to allow the government to investigate a case thoroughly without alerting the defendant and, where appropriate, to run a parallel criminal investigation. It's also intended to protect the whistleblower from retaliation. At the same time, however, the seal places relators in a psychological pressure cooker, expressly forbidding them from speaking about something that is usually the dominant concern in their lives. For Jones, who until that moment had been doing everything he could to call attention to big pharma's wrongdoing, the transition was a shock. "My neighbors used to say I was living up here in my cabin like a hermit, that I'd gotten into big trouble, and it had something to do with drugs." His smile fades, and he adds somberly, "It was hard not to be able to explain to people what I was up to. That I wasn't just some washed-up fifty-something guy who'd been fired from his job."

He had to keep his secret for eight years, a period in his life he calls the "dark times," during which he and his lawyers painstakingly built cases in Texas and elsewhere, while the rest of his life collapsed. He went through a bitterly contested divorce from his wife. When he wasn't poring over documents from his court cases or combing the internet for "pharma whores"—doctors and researchers who took pharmaceutical money in return for marketing drugs—whom he tabulated in enormous Excel spreadsheets, Jones continued to work construction jobs for cash, laying stone in the bitter Pennsylvania winters and blazing summers until his hands bled. As his debts mounted, he borrowed money from friends, skipped meals to economize, shot a deer when he could. "I was always glad for that protein," he re-members.

The economic and psychological vulnerability of whistleblowers, the strictures of the seal, and the duration of many false claims cases, some of which last over a decade, lead whistleblowers to seek support in a range of places. Jones found strength in a late-blooming religious faith of which he'd had the first inklings during his stay in Israel. "I saw the sincere worship of Christians, Muslims and Jews in some of their holiest places. And I realized there wasn't that much difference between a Jew davening in prayer chambers in the Wailing Wall and a Muslim a few hundred feet away, prostrating in the Dome of the Rock. All were expressing their love and fealty to God. I was still an atheist then. But God had found me before I found Him."

He came to believe that God had given him a mission to reveal wrongdoing in the pharmaceutical industry. "I felt that He opened up a door, and asked me to step through. And that He enabled me to do it—gave me the necessary blend of talents, skills and determination. God gifts everybody differently. He gave me the ability to look at disparate facts and see a larger order, how things are interrelated. Which is what I brought to the document analysis, the discovery requests, the FOIA requests and the other work I did in my cases."

Many whistleblowers also form strong, symbiotic relationships with their lawyers, as Jones did with Natalie Arbaugh. "She was the one who kept me sane through the dark times," Jones says. "She was always the one to call when there was bad news." Tom Melsheimer agrees. "A lawyer for a whistleblower is not just a lawyer: they're often a psychologist, a therapist, a marriage counselor, a dietician, and any number of other things that Natalie got called upon to assist Allen with." When destitute relators lose their homes, their attorneys have been known to take them in for months on end, like kinfolk fallen on hard times. "Once we had a relator and her son living with us, along with an Ethiopian kid we'd adopted," remembers Mary Louise Cohen, cofounder of Phillips & Cohen and a pioneering false claims attorney. "So many people were in and out of our house that we called it 'Camp Cohen' or 'Casa Chaos.' Bruce, my husband, just rolled with the punches."

Gradually Jones's work brought results. In Pennsylvania, Steven Fiorello was convicted on felony conflict-of-interest charges, and the state's mental health director, Steven Karp, resigned. Most important, the Pennsylvania protocol itself was dismantled. Jones began working as a consultant on a series of false claims cases, personal injury suits and multidistrict litigation lawsuits that were being brought against pharma companies by other whistleblowers. He supplied vital insights on how the companies had subverted state healthcare systems and defrauded government programs.

Jones embraced the role of whistleblower. "Having worked with addicts as a probation officer helped me a lot," he says. "Addicts have to fight the beast of their addiction, and keep beating it back when it raises its ugly head. For me, my condition as a whistleblower and the fraud I had uncovered were like fighting the beast. I kept swinging, which sustained me. Despite the financial and emotional hardship, I was never just a victim." He made several trips to Washington to discuss healthcare fraud with aides of Chuck Grassley, who, as the chair of the Senate Finance Committee, had launched a major investigation of illicit funding of scientists and medical schools by pharmaceutical companies. Jones met people who had lost relatives to mass murders and suicides apparently sparked by antidepressant use, which several clinical trials had linked to violent acts and suicidal ideation. "I met widows trying to make sense of the suicide of their husbands. I met parents shattered by the loss of a child, including the parents of a kid shot eleven times at Columbine. If you could comprehend all their grief in an instant, it would crush you utterly, annihilate you."

As legal discovery continued, internal documents from Johnson & Johnson and other pharmaceutical companies poured in. Jones, Fish & Richardson and several expert witnesses analyzed ten million pages of data, and explained in lay terms what it meant. Gradually the contours of the fraud emerged, more massive and malignant than anyone had imagined.

Johnson & Johnson had systematically created the medical and scientific environment necessary to turn Risperdal, a medication with stringent FDA-imposed limits on the diseases and age groups it could be used to treat, into what the company called a "$2 billion brand." To overcome the uncomfortable medical realities of the drug—negligible therapeutic improvements over earlier antipsychotics and dangerous new side effects—Johnson & Johnson had paid illustrious MDs to serve as "key opinion leaders," helping to create a false scientific consensus on Risperdal's superiority among doctors, patients, advocacy groups and third-party payers (such as Medicaid).

Next, the company devised a treatment protocol to push their future blockbuster. According to internal company documents, as early as May 1995, Johnson & Johnson began discussing the creation of treatment guidelines for schizophrenia with three key opinion leaders in psychiatry: Dr. Allen Frances, who chaired both the Department of Psychiatry at the Duke University School of Medicine and the influential American Psychiatric Association's *Diagnostic and Statistical Manual of Mental Disorders (DSM)*; Dr. David Kahn of the Columbia University Medical School; and Dr. John Docherty of the Cornell Medical College. The three doctors founded their own company, Expert Knowledge Systems (EKS), which in tight collaboration with Johnson & Johnson surveyed eighty-seven opinion leaders in psychiatry, all selected by them and by Johnson & Johnson, whose responses they used to formulate treatment guidelines. These guidelines, which Johnson & Johnson self-published in the fall of 1996 as a supplement to the *Journal of Clinical Psychiatry*, made Risperdal the first- or second-choice treatment for all schizophrenia patients.

Johnson & Johnson paid the three doctors over $600,000 to conduct the survey, compose the guidelines, and publicize them. EKS sent sixty thousand copies of the guidelines to various influential "decision makers," including high prescribers of antipsychotics, psychiatric residents in training, and officials at Medicaid and other third-party payers. The commitment of Drs. Frances, Kahn and Docherty to the commercial goals of their sponsor was striking. "Janssen and EKS share a vision of effective healthcare . . . ," they wrote. "We are also committed to helping Janssen succeed in its effort to increase its market share and visibility in the payor, provider, and consumer communities. . . . EKS is now ready to move forward in a strategic partnership with Janssen: We are now ready to maximize the impact of the guideline on clinical practice with a range of educational and implementation programs designed to facilitate your strategic marketing plan." They traveled the country to promote the guidelines that they and their corporate sponsor had created. In all, the company paid the doctors almost $1 million for their services.

In 2002, Johnson & Johnson opened another front in its consensus-building efforts concerning Risperdal. In partnership with Harvard Medical School professor Joseph Biederman, then perhaps the world's most influential child psychiatrist, the company founded a research center for child and adolescent psychiatry at Massachusetts General Hospital, with Biederman as its director. One of the center's three stated research aims, according to its 2002 annual report, was to "move forward the commercial goals of J. & J." In 2002 alone, according to court documents, the company paid Biederman at least $700,000. An investigation by Chuck Grassley's staff revealed that, between 2000 and 2007, Biederman had received an additional $1.6 million in "consulting" and "speaking" fees from Johnson & Johnson and other drug companies, which he hadn't disclosed, in violation of federal law and university regulations. Between 1994 and 2003, in part thanks to the work of such prominent researchers, the diagnosis of pediatric bipolar disorder increased by 4,000 percent, which in turn drove the sales of expensive, powerful drugs with serious side effects for use on children. Johnson & Johnson was employing a familiar— and highly profitable—strategy used by many other pharmaceutical companies: not just to invent new drugs to cure existing diseases, but to create new diseases for their existing drugs.

Texas turned out to be the ideal state in which to roll out treatment guidelines driven more by marketing than by science. The company had cultivated strong ties with leaders in the University of Texas medical community, as well as with Medicare and Medicaid officials, and together with other pharmaceutical companies had donated generously to numerous prominent politicians. Such connections were particularly valuable in a notoriously political state, where the regents and administrators of state universities, hospitals and prisons are routinely nominated by the governor. What's more, Texas had enormous prison, juvenile detention and state mental hospital populations, all ripe targets for Risperdal.

Through the efforts of key opinion leaders and their own employees, Johnson & Johnson persuaded Drs. Steven Shon, A. John Rush and other Texas state healthcare leaders to adopt in full, as TMAP, the antipsychotic guidelines that the company and its consultants had created, and to represent TMAP as the product of unbiased science endorsed by independent medical authorities. State officials and pharma executives soon produced a parallel protocol that pushed Risperdal use in children (though the FDA had never approved the drug for pediatric use). Next, Johnson & Johnson and other pharma companies paid for extensive travel by Steven Shon and other Texas officials, to meet with healthcare leaders in other states and launch antipsychotic protocols of their own. One of the states they visited was Pennsylvania, where they met with Steven Fiorello and his boss, Steven Karp. Here Allen Jones picked up their trail, when he ran across the suspicious payment from Janssen Pharmaceuticals to Fiorello.

Johnson & Johnson's marketing strategy was highly successful. Risperdal and related Johnson & Johnson drugs using the same active ingredient became the world's best-selling antipsychotic, with sales of over $4 billion in 2006 alone. More broadly, efforts by Johnson & Johnson and other pharmaceutical companies to modify the perceptions and prescribing habits of psychiatrists throughout the United States produced a global second-generation antipsychotics market with sales of $13 billion per year.

Sifting through the documents, Allen Jones and his team of lawyers and expert witnesses also uncovered the powerful political alliances that enabled Risperdal's growth. He learned that Governor Tom Ridge, who in October 2001, a month after 9/11, had been called to Washington by President George W. Bush to head the newly formed Department of Homeland Security, had appointed senior members of the Pennsylvania mental health system to lead the state's new antipsychotic program. One of these leaders was Gerald Radke, former marketing director of Eli Lilly, producer of a top-selling atypical antipsychotic, Zyprexa. Ridge had also appointed Radke's predecessor, Charles Curie, who had no medical training but strongly advocated pharmaceutical sales and psychiatric testing. George W. Bush himself, Jones learned, had approved TMAP when he was governor of Texas; he had even mentioned it in a presidential debate with Al Gore. Bush had made Charles Curie the director of his New Freedom Commission on Mental Health, an organization that planned to screen preschoolers and schoolchildren nationwide for mental illness, and aggressively to medicate with atypical antipsychotics those judged to have mental disorders.

Jones and his team delved into the details of Johnson & Johnson's skewed science—how the company had designed misleading clinical trials to exaggerate Risperdal's effectiveness, concealed unfavorable evidence, and misrepresented dangerous side effects and other health risks. When doctors began to report that Risperdal was causing neurological disorders in their patients, Johnson & Johnson mounted a misinformation campaign to "neutralize" the doctors' concerns. Jones also saw the lies face-to-face, when he attended a number of depositions of Johnson & Johnson employees, some of whom he himself had interviewed while working at the OIG. "They had been coached by Johnson & Johnson lawyers to deny, deny, deny," he remembers. "They could have pulled out a dead rat and taken a bite, and then denied adamantly that they'd done any such thing. '*What rat?*'" Hopes that former Johnson & Johnson employees would reveal irregular practices were dampened by the company's practice of paying them "consulting fees" to support the company in litigation, essentially buying their testimony.

Back in his cabin, Jones continued scouring the internet, tracing a vast web of pharma conspiracy. Now and then his eyes strayed from the screen to the rough pine walls of the cabin, where he'd posted inspirational sayings by Schopenhauer, Theodore Roosevelt and Winston Churchill:

All truth passes through three stages. First, it is ridiculed. Second, it is violently opposed. Third, it is accepted as being self-evident.

It is not the critic who counts; not the man who points out how the strong man stumbles, or where the doer of deeds could have done them better. The credit belongs to the man who is actually in the arena . . . who knows the great enthusiasm, the great devotion, who spends himself in a worthy cause, who at the best knows in the end the triumph of high achievement and who at the worst, if he fails, at least he fails while daring greatly. So that his place shall never be with those cold and timid souls who know neither victory nor defeat.

Never, never, in nothing great or small, large or petty, never give in except to convictions of honour and good sense. Never yield to force; never yield to the apparently overwhelming might of the enemy.

Late in the night, he stared out the window at the bare tree trunks and pondered the movements of the human heart.

Natalie Arbaugh, for her part, learned things about healthcare that permanently changed her behavior. When shopping for her young daughter, she says, "I started going to great lengths to avoid buying the products of Johnson & Johnson or any of its divisions. That wasn't easy. They were everywhere."

Together, Arbaugh and Jones prepared for trial. They decided that Jones would take the stand. Arbaugh knew the jury would be impressed by his remarkable grasp of the evidence and his unmistakable sincerity. Yet preparing him to testify was stressful. "He desperately wanted to say what he knew. He couldn't wait for that day. But testifying meant opening him to cross-examination. Which can be a bloodbath."

The trial of *State of Texas ex rel. Allen Jones v. Janssen et al.* began on January 9, 2012, in the gray granite megalith of Austin's Travis County Courthouse. Here, after years of silence, the seal of the case would at last be broken. Allen Jones could tell his story, and hear others speak the crimes he had long fought in secret.

Certain voices and gestures are seared in Jones's memory: The diminutive yet unquestionably Right Honorable John K. Dietz, cautioning jurors on the first day of proceedings, in his Texas twang, not to feed the lawyers, and when they stared back at him nonplussed, adding, "That was a joke. Y'all're supposed to laugh." Cynthia O'Keeffe, her gentle voice taut with outrage, explaining how Johnson & Johnson had stolen $579 million from Texas Medicaid by targeting the state's poorest and most vulnerable citizens, many of whom were children and pregnant women. Tom Melsheimer, describing how the company had repeatedly assured state healthcare officials that Risperdal was better, safer, and more cost-effective than other drugs, when they knew very well, from their own clinical research, that it was none of these things; and how, at the very moment when the FDA notified the company of its concern about Risperdal causing diabetes, the firm had accelerated its marketing to children. "Often in this country we can feel powerless to combat the actions of large companies," Melsheimer told the jury. "Our jury system empowers you like no other system in the world to send a message to companies like Janssen, a message to tell the truth, don't conceal it, a message to put patients first, not profits, and a message to refuse to let corporate greed feast on taxpayer dollars." Jones remembers, too, the smooth tenor of Dr. Steven Shon, as he acknowledged taking generous honoraria from Johnson & Johnson to spread the gospel of Risperdal in Texas and other states. How he'd briefed the main architect of the Risperdal marketing plan, Janssen vice president Alex Gorsky, on the progress of TMAP.

Then came a series of Johnson & Johnson voices, some defensive, some forthright, describing the marketing scheme they'd used to make Risperdal a $2 billion brand, in open disregard of the law and patient safety. Most seemed to Jones the voices of decent people doing indecent things—people who should have sensed something was wrong, and who could at any time have stepped forward to report it. For the long years of the protocol schemes in Texas, Pennsylvania and elsewhere, none of them did. Here, incarnate, was the banality of evil.

Finally Jones heard the voice of his friend and counselor, Natalie Arbaugh: "Your Honor, we call Allen Jones."

Arbaugh led Jones's testimony. She had him talk about building houses in the woods of central Pennsylvania, and his work with addicts, foster children and the mentally ill. About finding that first check to Steven Fiorello, and the ominous drumbeat of discoveries that followed.

She closed with the same straightforward yet slippery question that Jones had been asking himself for years.

MS. ARBAUGH: *Tell the jury, Mr. Jones: Why did you blow the whistle?*

MR. JONES: *The first people affected by TMAP, known in Pennsylvania as PennMAP, were the residents of mental health hospitals, the people in the back wards who were helpless and defenseless to take care of themselves. They needed to trust the people taking care of them. The people responsible for them were betraying them. I couldn't be a part of that. I wouldn't be a part of that. So I blew the whistle.*

MS. ARBAUGH: *Pass the witness.*

Soon after Jones spoke, Johnson & Johnson's lawyers informed his attorneys that their client wanted to end the trial through a negotiated settlement. The two teams of attorneys conferred and rapidly agreed on a number: $158 million. This figure was only a quarter of the $579 million that the State of Texas said it had lost. It made no attempt to quantify the harm done to patients by a decade's worth of Risperdal—the diabetes, heart disease, neurological damage, lactating male breasts, suicide. Nevertheless, it was the largest healthcare settlement in Texas history. In view of Allen Jones's exceptional contribution to making the case—there would, in fact, have been no case at all without him—prosecutors recommended that he receive a 24 percent relator's share of the settlement.

"I felt huge disappointment when they stopped the trial after a week," Jones says. "We could have filled a yearlong trial with evidence against Johnson & Johnson, and damned them every day. I wanted all that evidence to come out, every last expert witness, every last damning email. Though I confess"—here he makes one of his rare grins, like he's trying to smile through novocaine—"part of me breathed a sigh of relief."

Following common practice in legal settlements, Johnson & Johnson admitted no wrongdoing, accepted no liability. "The company expressly denies the government's civil allegations," the firm announced in a press release. No executives were prosecuted or penalized. Then it struck back at Allen Jones. Shortly after reaching the settlement, lawyers from the company made a presentation to high-level members of the Texas attorney general's office. They argued that Jones's relator's share should be sharply reduced, and threatened to lobby the state legislature to cripple the Texas Medicaid Fraud Prevention Act if it wasn't. In the end, the attorney general's office reduced Jones's share to 17 percent. Jones still received a substantial sum of money—a little under $8 million after legal fees and taxes. But he was disturbed by this last lash of the dragon's tail: despite all the grotesque wrongdoing revealed during the trial, the company was still able to pressure state officials into penalizing the whistleblower who had revealed it. "They are trying to produce a chilling effect on the ability of whistleblowers to come forward," Jones told a reporter after the settlement. "It was brazen, and it was disgusting," Margaret Moore, a former attorney at the AG's office, remembers today. "But political power is political power, and they knew how to use it."

After Allen Jones's trial in Texas, more Risperdal suits rolled in, all initiated by whistleblowers, many drawing on information revealed during Jones's litigation. A jury in Louisiana ordered Johnson & Johnson to pay $258 million for the harm the company had done with Risperdal. In South Carolina, the jury put the bill at $327 million. An Arkansas jury said $1.2 billion. Civil suits were brought against the company by patients who had suffered severe harm from Risperdal. Finally, prodded by these state-level successes, the federal government got into the act; in November 2013, the DOJ settled further Risperdal charges with Johnson & Johnson for $2.2 billion.

Again, with a few trivial exceptions, Johnson & Johnson admitted no wrongdoing in these cases, accepted no liability. None of its employees was prosecuted. The jury verdicts in Louisiana and Arkansas were voided on technicalities by the supreme courts in those states; the penalty in South Carolina was halved on appeal. And though Risperdal suits have cost the company nearly $3 billion, it sold $34 billion of the drug between 1993 and 2011 alone, sometimes at profit margins approaching 97 percent. Viewed like this, $3 billion in fines seems a smart investment. That's evidently how the company felt. In April 2012, two months after the Texas trial, the board of Johnson & Johnson made Alex Gorsky, the mastermind of Risperdal marketing, the firm's new chief executive. Wall Street cheered: the company's share price held firm throughout the trial and, aside from brief blips, has climbed steadily ever since. (Johnson & Johnson stock now sells for more than twice what it was worth during the trial.)

The Department of Justice showed little more respect for whistleblowers. Its press release on the $2.2 billion umbrella settlement praised the hard work of DOJ lawyers and celebrated the government's victory over fraud. The release did not name Jones or any of the other whistleblowers, without whose knowledge and courage the case against Johnson & Johnson would never have been brought in the first place. Allen Jones had testified about the state betraying vulnerable people, people who needed to trust that state to take care of them. But reading the DOJ press release, he, too, felt betrayed, by government entities that had long ignored his contribution and at times seemed to have conspired against him.

Today, seven years after the trial and seventeen years since his odyssey began, Allen Jones still spends much of his time in the cabin in the Pennsylvania woods where he lived through the lean years. He has a new Silverado pickup, and the stew bubbling on his stove isn't freshly killed venison as in former times, but caribou, from a recent hunting trip he made to Newfoundland. But his Rumford fireplace is still the only source of heat in the cabin, which has a flush toilet now but no hot water. Jones wears the same loose-fitting gray jeans and olive T-shirts he was wearing in photos from before the settlement, and still sleeps in the loft where he once slept with a gun under his pillow. "Now Mr. Smith and Mr. Wesson are on the bedside table," he says, with another of his novocaine grins.

When he became a whistleblower, Allen Jones began a new life, of secrecy and intense legal scrutiny, of loss and paranoia and, now and then, a powerful sense of freedom. This life has brought him wealth, yet with that wealth has come disillusionment, a bitter taste of justice denied. Legal success as a whistleblower rarely brings closure or satisfaction. Cheryl Eckard, in financial terms the most successful false claims whistleblower in history, has wept openly every time she has discussed with me her case against GlaxoSmithKline, remembering the documents she saw that suggested widespread patient harm, but which were sealed away by the settlement agreement she signed, and which she can no longer discuss. Jones, whose lawsuits have been far more successful than those of most whistleblowers, is likewise left with a lingering sensation that the world, having turned on him so violently for stating the truth, is itself broken, corrupt. "It is hard to fully trust anyone or anything again," he says.

Seventeen years on, he is still trying to make sense of what happened. He wonders how the central figures of his drama could have lived with their acts, and whether they've had a change of heart. (He has written to Steven Fiorello, Charles Curie and others involved in TMAP, and seems puzzled, even saddened, that they haven't responded.) He asks himself what justice was done, when nearly everyone at the pharmaceutical companies and public health institutions who orchestrated the alleged fraud, and who covered it up at the Pennsylvania OIG, went unpunished, and many have prospered. He doubts that the wanton harm he identified has stopped. "In this particular case, I believe I was successful in halting the mayhem and death, the robbing of the public treasury," he says. "TMAP is dead, its ashes are scattered. But I'm sure there are other programs, other schemes out there, happening right now. I'm sure it's happening in the military—soldiers are going into combat with a thirty-day supply of Seroquel [an atypical antipsychotic produced by AstraZeneca]. Until a drug company executive goes to jail, this won't stop. They simply say, 'We're going to kill X many people, injure Y. Of those, only A percent will know, and of those, only B percent will be able to do something about it.' Factor all this into the price of doing business, including payoffs to the families of the ones they kill, and they're still making huge profits. Whether someone is actually so diabolical as to put it into those words, or whether it's just the way things work out, I don't know. The result is the same."

Above all, Jones strives to explain to others and to himself precisely why he did what he did, retelling his story as if it still amazes him. Given the level of corruption and human harm he encountered, Jones insists that he had no real choice: he was compelled to blow the whistle, because inaction would have made him an accessory to the crime. In this telling, there is an inevitability to what happened, as if he were the protagonist in a Greek tragedy, walking the path that the Fates had foretold. Few who hear his story would question his moral calculus. Yet few could survive the fear, solitude and punishment he faced.

Allen Jones's story presents us with an unsettling challenge. In his place, would we do what he did, risk what he risked? Few know that we would. For most of us, setting ourselves against a government agency and a multinational corporation is an almost unimaginable step, because we sense that when provoked, they will pursue us like the Furies to the ends of the earth. Throughout our lives, we've all had moments, great and small, when we could have played the whistleblower, and we know that we haven't always measured up. Allen Jones's story is partly our own, but we are less likely to be the tragic hero than a member of the chorus, looking on fascinated, appalled, yet silent, one of countless mute witnesses too fearful or stunned to react. Or perhaps we've played the Furies.

This is the age of the whistleblower. Over the past two decades, continuing legal and social trends that originated in the late 1960s, a vital new figure has emerged: the insider who reveals malignant behavior by his organization, earning a measure of protection from the law and of acceptance, even acclaim, from society. In lawsuits that grow more numerous every year, private antifraud whistleblowers have disclosed crimes by Fortune 500 healthcare companies, banks, automakers and weapons manufacturers. Government whistleblowers have unmasked wrongdoing throughout federal, state and local government: dishonest meat grading at the USDA, theft of revenues from oil contracts in the Bureau of Indian Affairs, hazards at nuclear facilities like Los Alamos and Hanford, violations of mine safety standards that killed hundreds of miners, malfeasance by US Marines procurement officials that killed hundreds of frontline soldiers in Iraq and Afghanistan. Civil servants at the Environmental Protection Agency, Homeland Security, the Department of the Interior and the White House have revealed what they see as systemic betrayals of the legal mission of their offices.

In the past five years alone, whistleblowers determined to safeguard public well-being have disclosed Cambridge Analytica's use of Facebook data to help skew elections; toxic levels of lead in Flint, Michigan, drinking water; deadly abuses and delays in Veterans Administration hospitals; the billion-dollar looting of Malaysian public funds by government insiders and Goldman Sachs; conspiracies to hide emissions by VW and other carmakers; the Theranos blood testing scandal— endless revelations we'd likely know nothing without having an insider speak up. In fact, whistleblowing as an essential fraud-fighting paradigm is one of the few things that liberal and conservative lawmakers can agree on. Each year Congress passes new whistleblower laws, which frequently improve job protection and offer larger money incentives to encourage employees in an ever wider sphere of the public and private workforce to step forward. Shortly after the Enron and WorldCom financial scandals of 2001 and 2002, lawmakers wrote whistleblower legislation to fight corporate crime; after bank fraud and regulatory corruption triggered the 2008 financial collapse, they created whistleblower offices in the Securities and

Exchange Commission (SEC) and the Commodity Futures Trading Commission. In 2015, after deadly ignition switch failures at General Motors and gas pedal malfunctions at Toyota, Congress passed the new Motor Vehicle Safety Whistleblower Act to encourage (and pay) automotive workers to reveal future car hazards. Recent university admissions scandals and Boeing jet crashes, even a Trump tweet criticizing leakers, have prompted public calls for whistleblowers to step forward.

Whistleblowing is spreading because it works. In 2018 alone, the SEC whistleblower office received 5,282 whistleblower reports from people in all fifty states and seventy-two foreign countries, and has since its founding in 2010 caused wrongdoers to pay $1.7 billion in sanctions. Since 1986, the False Claims Act has been used to recover some sixty billion stolen tax dollars, and has deterred an estimated $1 trillion more in fraud. Every dollar spent on building a false claims case brings back to the Treasury about twenty stolen tax dollars; the return on other government fraud investigations is a fifth the size.

Beyond fighting crime, whistleblowers are raising some of the fundamental questions of our democracy. They are forcing debate on the pervasive influence of corporations, and the proper balance between free speech and secrecy, between citizen rights and state power. Whistleblower suits are being heard in the highest courts in the land. The Supreme Court itself has reviewed almost a score of them in the past two decades alone, deliberating on the evolving rights, duties and definitions of public and private whistleblowing: what constitutes a material disclosure, when does the statute of limitations run out, who actually qualifies for whistleblower status in the first place, and how free is their speech. US whistleblower laws are increasingly being used to fight corruption abroad, by companies that do business in the United States. Since 1998, fifty foreign nations have enacted whistleblower statutes of their own (nine since April 2018), often modeled on US law and the lessons of American whistleblowing. Rarely have the voice and conscience of private citizens had more resonance. Whistleblowers join a long line of social critics and questioners, known at various times in history as prophets, philosophers, rebels, freethinkers, poets, muckrakers, and civil rights activists, who risked their freedom and their lives for their ideas.

This book explores the rise of whistleblowing, the character and role of the whistleblower, and the nature of the whistleblowing act, familiar and yet mysterious to most of us (and to many whistleblowers themselves). It examines the root causes of the whistleblowing act, which often arises from malevolent authority in organizational cultures turned toxic. Ultimately, too, this book considers what the growth of whistleblowing suggests about our society. Superficially, the advent of whistleblowing is a David-and-Goliath tale, a rare instance in these times of the individual empowered to confront and even correct institutional wrongdoing, public and private. But ultimately, as we'll see, the power of whistleblowers is often illusory: their rise is a symptom of a society in deep distress.

We are in the midst of a battle over whistleblowing, part of a larger struggle between personal conscience and group solidarity, between the rights of individuals to know what their corporations and their government are doing, and the ever greater power of organizations to keep their secrets. How these conflicts are ultimately resolved will say much about the future strength of our democracy.

CHAPTER 2

Question Authority

In most social systems obedience is the supreme virtue, disobedience the supreme sin. In fact, in our culture when most people feel "guilty," they are actually feeling afraid because they have been disobedient. They are not really troubled by a moral issue, as they think they are, but by the fact of having disobeyed a command.

Erich Fromm, *On Disobedience and Other Essays*, 1981

Obsta principiis [halt the beginnings], nip the shoots of arbitrary power in the bud, is the only maxim which can ever preserve the liberties of any people. When the people give way, their deceivers, betrayers, and destroyers press upon them so fast, that there is no resisting afterwards. . . . The people grow less steady, spirited, and virtuous, the seekers more numerous and more corrupt, and every day increases the circles of their dependents and expectants, until virtue, integrity, public spirit, simplicity, and frugality, become the objects of ridicule and scorn, and vanity, luxury, foppery, selfishness, meanness, and downright venality swallow up the whole society.

John Adams, *Novanglus* essays, February 6, 1775

On August 31, 2006, Franz Gayl was standing with General Richard Zilmer in the headquarters building at Camp Fallujah in Anbar Province, scene of some of the fiercest fighting in Iraq. Zilmer, once Gayl's supervisor at the Pentagon, now commanded the I Marine Expeditionary Force (Forward) in Iraq. "We need innovative capabilities against an adaptive enemy, and we need to provide our Marines with more effective protection," Zilmer told him. "I have requested equipment from the support establishment, but requests have gone unfulfilled. I want you to make it your mission to do something about it." In plain English, Zilmer meant,

"My Marines are dying because they aren't getting the right gear from headquarters. Go get it for them, *now*."

Gayl (whose German surname is pronounced like "guile") had served in the Marine Corps for twenty-two years before retiring as a major in 2002. He had been working as a civilian science and technology adviser to the Corps when Zilmer asked him to come to Iraq. Gayl promptly volunteered. "I wanted to pay my dues, not just sit out the war in some cubicle in the Pentagon," he told me years later.

At Camp Fallujah, he gave blood regularly, because the field hospital needed a lot of it, and service members on the base were the only source. In the base's junkyard, he saw the perforated, burned-out hulls of vehicles destroyed by mines and improvised explosive devices (IEDs). Many of the wrecks were Humvees, the light truck widely used by American forces for moving troops and cargo.

Since January 2005, six hundred Marines had been killed and another two thousand wounded by mines and IEDs, placed by Iraqi insurgents. At that time, 90 percent of coalition soldiers killed and 60 percent of those wounded in Iraq were victims of IEDs, which were often far from "improvised": blocks of Iranian-made C-4 explosive ignited by industrial timers or motion sensors, which drove a milled copper-alloy slug through many kinds of armor. Humvees were widely known to be vulnerable to IED attacks, especially when the explosion occurred beneath their flat, low-slung undercarriage; already in 1994, Marine Corps analysts reporting on Operation Restore Hope in Somalia had stated that underbody blasts turned them into "death traps." The military began to add blast-resistant plating to the Humvees' undercarriage, but they remained a soft target.

Instead of Humvees, General Zilmer wanted MRAPs, or "mine-resistant ambush-protected" vehicles, hulking polygons on four or six wheels that had been developed by the South African army to fight insurgents in Rhodesia and Angola, whose high, V-shaped hulls, produced from a single piece of specially forged carbon steel, provided far better protection from IEDs. However, despite repeated requests by Zilmer and his predecessor in Anbar Province, General Dennis Hejlik, to Marine Corps high command in Quantico, Virginia, no MRAPs had arrived, and soldiers continued dying in Humvees, often two and four at a time. Zilmer had also asked for several other devices for surveillance and nonlethal deterrence, which already existed and which he believed would save lives. None made it to Iraq.

Zilmer is widely credited for his achievements in Iraq, particularly the ticklish job of convincing Sunni warriors in Anbar to join US troops in fighting al-Qaeda, and Gayl revered him. So when Zilmer told him to push the MRAP and the other missing equipment through the maze of military bureaucracy, he set to work with his full energy.

From certain angles, Gayl's deep-set hazel eyes have a bruised look. His face is mobile and expressive, and he smiles readily, especially when remembering his time on active service. He speaks with the accent of his native Minnesota, and blends a soldier's fluent stream of acronyms with chunks of vintage Americana, like "Jeez Louise" and "holy cow." He has put on weight since the photos he shows me of his Iraq deployment, but still has the short-cropped hair, muscular arms and commanding presence of an active Marine. He's a rare breed: a voluble talker who also listens carefully, watching your face with slightly raised brows as if in suspense about what you might say next.

From an early age, Gayl loved to invent and to destroy. His father, an architect and ecologist who had served as a paratrooper in the German air force during World War II, let him help build the scale models for his commissions, as well as constructing elaborate toy houses out of sticks, which young Franz then set alight. Gayl devised complex thought experiments involving lasers, and projects with explosive chemicals. After dropping out of high school, he enlisted in the Marines the day he turned seventeen. As an infantry antitank assaultman, he gave free rein to his creative and destructive tendencies. He designed and built a two-wheeled cart for transporting grenade launchers and machine guns in night combat, a new safety mechanism for the M16 rifle, and an innovative boat trap to launch and recover amphibious vehicles and landing craft.

Later, as a civilian sci-tech officer, he invented a device called the Gayl Blaster, which used pulsed laser light and high-frequency sound to immobilize rioters without injuring them. While earning a master's degree in space systems operation at the Naval Postgraduate School, he made predictions about the electromagnetic emissions produced by free-electron lasers, which his supervising professor dismissed as improbable. "He said that I didn't understand the science, and that I should stop speculating," Gayl remembers. "In fact, he said I was full of shit." Yet when the laser system he'd written about was tested, his predictions proved correct. Gayl says that although he hadn't analyzed the emissions with mathematical rigor, he had visualized the physics of the problem.

Richard Zilmer thought Gayl's unusual abilities—a gift for finding unorthodox solutions to old problems, a deep commitment to the uniformed Marine Corps, and a certain fearlessness (his critics might say recklessness) in fighting bureaucracy— might enable him to get the much-needed matériel to Iraq. "Franz knew how to get money, he knew how the Hill operated, how the Pentagon operated," Zilmer said in a 2012 interview.

The bottleneck for the equipment, and the target of Gayl's future efforts, was the Marine Corps Combat Development Command (MCCDC), the Quantico-based department responsible for supplying weapons and other hardware to soldiers in the field, which had been headed by General James Mattis for most of Zilmer's time in Iraq, and was now overseen by General James Amos. At Camp Fallujah, together with his supervisor and fellow sci-tech expert, Colonel Martin LaPierre, Gayl worked eighteen-hour days to identify the technological tools the Corps needed to reduce casualties and fight more effectively. They filed more than thirty requests for laser dazzlers, surveillance systems, unmanned aerial vehicles and mine-detection devices. Most urgently, they repeated the requests for MRAPs. Still the equipment failed to arrive.

Gayl's superiors at the Pentagon warned him to tone down his vocal and email communications with Quantico procurement officials. Agents of the Naval Criminal Investigative Service (NCIS) visited Camp Fallujah to question him about his contact with a Chinese diplomat whom he had interviewed in the United States the previous year while completing a postgraduate degree at the National Defense University. The interview had been authorized by security officials at the time, but now became the subject of a formal investigation, the first of three the NCIS would open against him. Gayl was eventually cleared, but he believes this investigation, like the others, was a response to his activism.

After nearly six months in Iraq, Gayl returned to the Pentagon in February 2007, to continue his mission on behalf of General Zilmer and the Marines. Zilmer wrote him a glowing performance evaluation: "Mr. Gayl is one of our brightest minds, and as a service, we are fortunate to have him among our ranks." He also braced Gayl for his coming struggles with the Quantico and Pentagon bureaucracies. "You're going back into the lion's den," Zilmer told him. "I can't protect you anymore."

"The general officer's culture," Gayl says, is "never criticize a fellow general officer. Their loyalty to each other, and their political reliability, seems to be more important to them than protecting society." Yet he points out numerous exceptions to this rule, including Zilmer and his deputy in Anbar, General Robert Neller. "They did a great deal for me in the months and years that followed," Gayl remembers.

Back at his cube in the Pentagon, Gayl began to see why the MRAP and other systems had gotten hung up at Quantico. Each of the delayed technologies, he discovered, was competing for funding and visibility with alternative weapon programs. The MRAP itself was pitted against several other vehicles, each of which had strong supporters within the military procurement hierarchy. "People get invested in pushing one program over another, sometimes regardless of their merits," Gayl observes. "You are selling your wares at conferences, in meetings. The success or failure of that program becomes attached to you: your opportunities for promotion, your career, and even your post-career employment."

Gayl began digging into the history of requests for MRAPs from Iraq. A February 2005 "Urgent Universal Need Statement" (UUNS) drafted by Marine major Roy McGriff and signed by General Hejlik, at a point in the war when IED casualties had begun to spike, explained how the MRAP would save countless lives and requested specific models of the vehicle, already being manufactured by a company in South Carolina. Hejlik pointed out the absurdity of the Marines' suffering grave casualties because of a problem to which an off-the-shelf solution already existed. "Without MRAP, personnel loss rates are likely to continue at their current rate," he concluded. "Continued casualty accumulation exhibits potential to jeopardize mission success." In other words, Hejlik felt the missing MRAPs were losing the war.

Gayl called McGriff, who explained that, back in 2005, he had briefed Mattis himself about the MRAPs, and Mattis had agreed that the vehicles should ship as soon as possible. But Gayl discovered that in the spring of 2005, when top procurement officials from MCCDC and other departments met to discuss the request, their primary concern had not been how MRAPs would help frontline soldiers, but how supplying large numbers of these expensive vehicles would divert funds from competing projects, including the up-armored Humvee, the Light Armored Vehicle, and the Expeditionary Fighting Vehicle (EFV), a costly prototype built by General Dynamics and championed by some top brass, including Mattis himself. (In 2011, after spending a total of about $3 billion to develop it, the Marine Corps canceled the EFV due to its poor reliability and ballooning costs.) A later audit by the Department of Defense inspector general confirmed that MCCDC officials had not considered the causes of IED casualties, much less accelerated MRAP deployment to prevent them.

"They had killed the [UUNS] request, and then 'disappeared' it to hide it from leadership," Gayl says. "When I saw that, I was pissed!" Partisanship over weapon systems and strategic priorities has likely been a part of military procurement since the birth of standing armies. Yet after serving as an adviser at Camp Fallujah, he knew firsthand the human cost of these bureaucratic turf wars. "The disappearance of that single document below the radar led to the unnecessary deaths of many, many Marines. I believed the Marine Corps needed to make this ugly story part of our lessons learned, to help us avoid similar tragedies in the future."

When Gayl told his civilian and military supervisors of the frustration Generals Zilmer, Neller and other frontline commanders were feeling about the failure to supply MRAPs and other technologies, they took no action. So Gayl attempted to alert the higher echelons of the Department of Defense. Together with Martin LaPierre, he prepared a PowerPoint presentation for the Department of Defense Research and Engineering office. Beneath the dry, technical language of the slides was a powerful indictment of how bureaucratic gridlock was compromising the war effort. "Process worship cripples operating forces," one slide read. "Unnecessary delays cause US friendly and innocent Iraqi deaths and injuries," said another.

In the rarefied bureaucratic realm of Pentagon weapons procurement, such straight talk is rare. After reviewing the presentation, Gayl's supervisors canceled the meeting and ordered Gayl to delete all copies of the slides. They informed him that high-ranking officers in the procurement establishment, including General James Mattis, the former head of MCCDC, had objected to the presentation, and that he was henceforth "persona non grata at their commands." When an article in *Defense Technology International*, citing an anonymous military source, claimed that delays in the delivery of the laser dazzler had resulted in 50 dead and 140 wounded Iraqi civilians in Anbar, Mattis fired a Marine colonel close to Gayl who had agreed with the assessment. (The anonymous source had been Gayl; the colonel was reinstated soon after, and joined Zilmer's staff.)

Despite increasing hostility from his supervisors, Gayl persisted. He began writing an even more scathing report, "Five Recent Examples of Marine Corps Gross Mismanagement," which asserted that the Marine Corps procurement establishment, in failing to supply MRAPs, dazzlers and other requested devices, had been blatantly, even criminally, negligent.

Finally, in May 2007, Gayl saw an article in *Inside the Pentagon*, an influential Web newsletter on military policy, in which General James Conway, commandant of the Marine Corps, told the Joint Chiefs of Staff that field commanders hadn't asked for MRAPs until 2006—when, as Gayl knew, they'd actually been formally requested in February 2005. "My first reaction when I saw the article was, 'The Commandant of the Marine Corps just told a serious lie!'" Gayl remembers. "Then I thought, 'No, the Commandant wouldn't lie. But the people who briefed him might.'"

Gayl notified *Inside the Pentagon* of the error, and when the publication failed to correct it, he sent a copy of the MRAP request from 2005, an unclassified document, to another defense industry blog, Wired.com's *Danger Room*. On May 22, Wired.com published a harsh criticism of the MRAP delays, titled "Military Dragged Feet on Bomb-Proof Vehicles." The article drew immediate attention. Two prominent senators, Joe Biden from Delaware and Kit Bond from Missouri, demanded an explanation for the delays in fielding MRAPs. Biden's staff contacted

Gayl, whose role in the disclosure had not yet become public knowledge but whose name had come up in their research. They asked if he'd be willing to brief Biden on the MRAP, and to speak with the press.

Gayl had reached the Rubicon. His repeated attempts to fix the MRAP emergency and other instances of supply mismanagement within the Marine Corps establishment had failed. A number of peers and mentors had cautioned him to back down. "You have done enough," one supportive general told him. "Any more would be willful suicide." But Gayl could not let go. He sensed that in order to achieve his mission, he would have to go public.

He told his mother what he was planning to do. "Oh, Franzie, you're going to be a whistleblower?" she replied in disbelief.

"I was so insulted," he told me. "To me 'whistleblower' was a fuckin' narc. Worse than a narc: an opportunistic narc. I told her, 'No I'm not going to be a whistleblower—that's ridiculous!' But later, when I cooled down, I began to think, 'Aw, Jeez Louise, is this what it is?'" Gradually the term took on a more positive connotation in his mind. "After all, the only reason I'm still surviving is because I had that status. But the first time I heard that word from my mom, I was mortified."

Gayl was torn between two powerful emotions. "On the one hand, it seemed to me unthinkable to speak outside of this tight, self-sufficient family called the US Marine Corps. On the other hand, Marines on active duty were dying, because of a corrupt culture of money and career advancement completely divorced from their operational realities. And those Marines, the men and women in harm's way, were my real family. The Marines had taken me in at seventeen, a high school dropout with problems—selfish indiscipline, alcohol, delinquency. From the very first day, standing on those yellow footprints on the pavement at basic training, they gave me an identity, a purpose in life."

His loyalty to that "real family," he says, left him no other option. "I had exhausted all internal channels. I felt nothing would change unless I went outside command. I found myself standing at an intersection of personally observed events and unique personal knowledge. It would have been criminal for me not to act."

The military code of justice he'd learned in basic training states that soldiers must not obey orders that they know are wrong or illegal. "In fact, you have a responsibility to reject bad instructions and to correct wrongs, and that responsibility overrides everything else," Gayl told me. And the "request mast," a time-honored military convention, gives every uniformed Marine, even a lowly private, the right to bring any concern, personal or professional, directly to the first general or flag officer in his chain of command, in complete secrecy. "The request mast is a sacred right, and we cherish it. It's legendary in boot camp. You hear stories of young guys using it to get all the way to the commandant of the Marine Corps, even to the president." Though the request mast is technically only available to people in uniform, Gayl said that it, too, influenced his thinking when he decided to blow the whistle.

Then he flashed his toothy grin. "I'm making my decision to speak out sound complicated. But in another way, it was simple. *Das macht man nicht* [One doesn't do that]. What was happening was just wrong, and I couldn't let it happen." His smile faded. "Look, I was far from an exemplary Marine. Otherwise I would have advanced further. I've fallen short in many things in my life. But on this very important thing, I felt, 'No! I've gotta look myself in the mirror.'"

Before he acted, he also consulted his wife, Conchita, a Filipino national, whom he calls "my backbone, my beautiful, beloved Rottweiler." He remembered telling her, "'Honey, they stopped me, but I have to go forward. But it's going to change things in our lives.' Her only response was, 'We'll make it somehow. Kids are getting killed. Do what you need to do for the Marines.' She supported me one hundred percent, trusted me one hundred percent, even though I couldn't tell her what I was going to reveal. Without that support, most whistleblowers do poorly. Their lives fall apart."

Conchita told me that she also gave her husband a word of caution. "I told Franz what my grandmother in the Philippines always said: 'When you point a finger at someone, you're pointing three other fingers back at yourself.' I wanted Franz to be sure he was doing it for the right motives. To save lives, and not just to get back at people who had stood in his way."

Jane Pejsa, Gayl's mother, gave a different kind of advice. "You need a lawyer *right now*," she remembers telling him. "You need protection." She searched the internet, and quickly found three organizations that served whistleblowers as advisers and legal advocates: the Office of Special Counsel (OSC), which investigates cases of whistleblowing in federal agencies and defends the legal rights of whistle-blowers against those agencies; the Project on Government Oversight (POGO), a nonprofit government watchdog; and GAP, whose lawyers represent whistle-blowers in courts and before administrative boards. She gave Gayl the telephone number and email of GAP's legal director, Tom Devine.

Gayl tried to reassure her that he'd be all right on his own—he had faith in the people he was dealing with, he said, and ultimately, there were legal protections for whistleblowers. But she was adamant. "Nope. Call these people, Franz. I have a feeling."

"Boy, was she right," Gayl said. "If I had waited, I would have been dead."

On May 23, Gayl blew the whistle—characteristically, at full volume. He explained the details of the MRAP affair to the staffs of Senators Biden and Bond, and gave them his report on "gross mismanagement" at the Marine Corps. He also briefed the staffs of Senators Jay Rockefeller, chair of the Senate Select Committee on Intelligence, and Carl Levin, chair of the Senate Committee on Armed Services. Days later, Biden and Bond grilled General Conway about the MRAP affair. Gayl also gave on-the-record interviews to a series of newspapers and radio and television programs, including *USA Today*, NPR's *On the Media* and *PBS NewsHour*, declining to seek permission from Marine Corps Public Affairs as he'd been ordered. "I already knew they would shut me down."

His whistleblowing brought results. Secretary of Defense Robert Gates swiftly made fielding MRAPs a top priority, and by July 2008, the Defense Department had approved the construction of 15,838 of the vehicles, of which 2,225 were allocated to the Marines. By November 2008, 12,073 MRAPs had been shipped to Iraq. Casualty rates from IED attacks dropped from 60 percent with Humvees to 5 percent with MRAPs. Fatalities fell by 85 percent.

Independent authorities repeatedly verified Gayl's criticisms of the MRAP affair. A September 2007 report by the Naval Audit Service identified serious flaws in the UUNS process. An audit by the inspector general of the Department of Defense condemned MCCDC's handling of the MRAP affair, observing that the Marines had recognized the dangers of IED attacks in Iraq well before the invasion and had known the Humvee's vulnerability to IEDs since the early 1990s, yet had failed to act on repeated warnings and requests. The Government Accountability Office confirmed Gayl's claims about wrongful delays in fielding other urgent technology.

The military had accepted Gayl's message about the MRAPs. Yet it swiftly attacked the messenger, for having committed the two cardinal sins of the defense establishment: speaking to Congress and speaking to the press. The Pentagon's bitter and elaborate persecution of Gayl would last for eight years.

Both in uniform and as a civilian, Gayl had always earned high performance ratings. At his retirement from active duty in 2002, General James Amos, later to become commandant of the Marine Corps, wrote, "You have been a super-star for the Marine Corps for your entire career." In 2007, General Zilmer recommended him for the Senior Executive Service, the civilian equivalent of a general officer's rank, writing in his performance review, "Mr. Gayl's dedication and passion for design, development and delivery of technology solutions to our warfighting needs is matched by no one I know."

Yet only months after speaking out, Gayl received a performance rating in the bottom 30 percent of his rank. By 2008, it had dipped to the bottom 3 percent. He was no longer given the pay raises and awards that had once been routine. He was ordered to take a psychological examination to determine his fitness for duty. He received a series of written reprimands and recommendations for unpaid suspension. His military boss subjected him to frequent, public humiliation, calling his whistleblowing acts "cowardly, unethical and immoral." Gayl's superiors rewrote his job description to eliminate the scientific and technological skills for which he'd been hired and then worked to demote him to fit this new, diminished position. He was repeatedly denied permission to take part in continuing education, essential for a science and technology officer.

Gayl's work assignments became booby traps. His supervising colonel repeatedly criticized a report on procurement reform he'd been tasked with, and demanded numerous additions but, once Gayl delivered it to Congress, reported him for unauthorized release of classified information contained in two footnotes— even though the information came from unclassified documents, and Gayl's report itself had already been cleared as unclassified. NCIS investigators opened a second probe for this purported breach, which they said made Gayl a potential insider threat. They soon dropped this investigation, but then began a third, for possible psychological instability, after Gayl was accused of using an unauthorized USB flash drive in the Sensitive Compartmented Information Facility (SCIF), the restricted area where he worked that was designated for the handling of highly classified material. Gayl does not recall using a flash drive in the facility, and no evidence has ever been produced that links him with the drive. In fact, the drive's manufacturer stated that it had never produced a drive with the serial number cited by investigators, which suggests that the accusation was fabricated. Nevertheless, the Pentagon inspector general supported the charges against Gayl, as well as the decision to suspend him.

On October 4, 2010, in an elaborately choreographed ritual of public humiliation, Gayl was "read out" of his security clearances. Without them, Gayl could not do his job, or even enter the SCIF. He was put on paid administrative leave and escorted off the Pentagon premises. Most observers believed that he was gone for good.

When I visited Gayl at his home in Burke, Virginia, a Washington, DC, suburb, in April 2015, he suggested a walk in a nearby park with his two Rhodesian ridgebacks, Phoenix and Goldie. As we walked, I observed that a number of Marine Corps officers involved in the MRAP affair had left the military soon after, to work for defense contractors that were manufacturing armored vehicles that competed with the MRAP. As commandant of the Marine Corps, James Conway had initially voiced strong opposition to the MRAP; in April 2011, less than six months after retiring from the military, he joined the board of directors of Textron, a defense firm that was building a rival vehicle. General Mattis had vigorously championed the EFV built by General Dynamics and became a director of that firm five months after he resigned from the Marines in May 2013.

"As Marines, right from basic training, we are taught that officers must be 'above reproach' at all times," Gayl said. "I have fallen far short of standards of all kinds, on many occasions. When I look in the mirror, I try to correct myself. But some people develop such a sense of comfort, even a cult of the personality, that they do questionable things repeatedly, right in plain sight. And when they get called on it, they go on the counterattack. 'Don't question my character—*how dare you question my character!?* I am *incorruptible.*' Their actions may survive legal scrutiny, because of a Marine legal opinion that there's no conflict of interest, but in taking certain jobs, standards of propriety are violated."

Gayl believes that such people have departed from the teachings every recruit learns in basic training: to refuse to participate in wrongdoing, and to alert others when it happens. "These are the basic moral foundations that are instilled in every one of us. That's unique to the military—I don't think you'll hear that when you go into an industry, when you're being indoctrinated into a new company. And it relates directly to the highest-stakes situation there is: to combat. What the drill instructor strove for us to embody was the sense of personal accountability for every action that we took, or failed to take. If your superiors directed you to knowingly harm innocents, or overlook lethal threats to your own comrades, you would be expected to refuse such orders, whatever the consequences. And you would be expected to report it."

It may be no coincidence that the first US whistleblower law concerned sailors and Marines on active duty. The life-and-death nature of combat demands absolute honesty. But as officers work their way up the ranks, Gayl observed, they sometimes become susceptible to what Germans call *Ehrgeiz*, the fierce ambition for power or advancement that can be indistinguishable from egocentric pride. "Men and women are weak," he said in a low, resigned voice, as if suddenly weary. "We are all corruptible. Even general officers. The lure of money is a powerful force."

When we returned home, Gayl showed me his basement library, an eclectic collection of physics texts, Mandarin Chinese phrase books, Hegel and Kant in the original German, and classics of Marxist political theory. Like any good soldier, he had a copy of Sun Tzu's *Art of War*, and, like several whistleblowers I know, he had William Golding's classic on groupthink and tribal horror, *Lord of the Flies*, as well as plenty of Kafka. ("I know what it's like to wake up one day transformed into a cockroach!" he said.) His collection of religious texts included the Bible, the

Pentateuch and Haftarah, introductions to Buddhism and Taoism, three editions of the Qur'an, the *Fiqh-us-Sunnah* on Sharia law, and *The Sealed Nectar*, a recent biography of Muhammad. "I've read the Qur'an five times. I used to read it in the courtyard of the Pentagon." He plans to get the Talmud, which runs to over six thousand pages. "I'm gonna buy that thing when I have cash to spare, though I'm not sure where I'll put it."

During his readings, which Gayl started after joining the Marine Corps, he was struck by the correspondences among the three great monotheistic religions. "It is all the same story, and it is all the same message," he said, pointing to parallels between the dietary laws of Islam and Judaism, which require that animals be killed without cruelty and forbid the eating of predators, because they don't kill humanely, and we inherit their cruelty if we eat them. Such laws, Gayl told me in a delighted rush of words, "connect us to bigger things we all have in common, but have forgotten because we no longer speak the same language. All of the prophets were talking about the same things, but at different times and in different languages. It's the Tower of Babel problem, the arrogance and defiance of humankind. The Talmud says that whenever a brick would fall from the tower, the people would burst into tears, but when a man fell they never shed a tear." He shook his head. "The world suffers from a lack of reading. If everyone knew what I know about this stuff, there would not be fighting."

Gayl pulled out a slender book with a cream linen cover, *Soldaten fallen vom Himmel* (Soldiers Fall from Heaven). On the frontispiece is a dedication to Gayl's father, "for distinguished achievements in service," dated Christmas 1941. The book, Gayl explained, was a present from the much-decorated German general Hermann-Bernhard Ramcke to his father, Franz Josef Gayl, who fought in the Luftwaffe. Franz Senior had wanted to join the SS, Hitler's elite shock troops, but because one of his grandmothers would have been considered a Jew under the laws of the Third Reich, he entered the crack Fallschirmjäger (paratrooper corps) instead, where racial background checks were less stringent. He had served in Rommel's Afrika Korps and had been taken prisoner by British troops, interned in an American prison camp and repatriated after the war. He had returned to the United States as one of the first German foreign exchange students in the postwar period, to study architecture at the University of Chicago, with the intention of going back home to help rebuild Berlin. But instead he had met an American woman, Jane Pejsa, and decided to stay.

Gayl says his father, like many Germans of his generation, was demoralized by the loss of the war and struggled to find a new worldview. Beginning in the 1950s, he took up the cause of Native Americans and African Americans, and in the 1960s he embraced the architectural style and the counterculture ideals of the early ecological movement. Over time he became disillusioned with the materialism and environmental destructiveness he saw in the United States, which seemed to him a cancer on the natural world. He eventually built a home for the family on a tiny island in Lake Minnetonka, Minnesota. Gayl remembers it as a wonderful place to grow up, though isolated. But the idyllic setting didn't appear to help his father.

"He was a visionary, the strongest and yet the most humane person I have ever known," Gayl says. "But his anti-Semitism ran deep all his life, surely due to Third Reich indoctrination as a child, and in spite of the fact that he was part Jewish himself. Being the embodiment of such extreme contradictions was pretty explosive stuff to live with. And as a former German paratrooper in the bourgeois circles of his American wife, he always felt under suspicion." Gayl says his father suffered from debilitating depression, particularly in later years. "He was bipolar, decades before there was anything effective to treat it, and he may have been when he was younger as well. He just had to suck it up." Gayl adds that he himself has taken Prozac since 1992.

At such moments, I felt for Gayl's superiors. After all, what is the average military official to make of a federal civil servant with high security clearances reading the Qur'an in the courtyard of the Pentagon and discussing his daily dose of Prozac? Gayl also told his colleagues that he thought society was in rapid decline, and that he had started buying guns in preparation for darker times. "I'm not a psychologist," one of Gayl's former supervisors, Colonel James Wilkinson, said in a 2012 interview, "and I don't know what to look for in guys who may be ready to go over the edge." ("After he did everything possible to push Franz over," Gayl's lawyer would add, when I repeated the comment to him.)

But consider: What kind of person can resist the United States Marine Corps' almost overwhelming pressure to submit to superiors, and knowingly risk job loss, financial ruin, humiliation, divorce and jail, to do the right thing? Many people who blow the whistle are able to do so precisely because they are *not* like most of us, or how we're told to be. They're not "team players," not "go along to get along" personalities. They can be prickly and doctrinaire. They can seem obsessive, even unstable. Franz Gayl may be all of these things. Yet those very traits may have enabled him to save thousands of lives in Iraq.

Tom Devine is the legal director at GAP whom Gayl's mother found for him on the internet. He is a small, tousled, soft-walking, soft-looking man of sixty-six. He owns one pair of black shoes, which he wears to court, to restaurants and on long walks in the country. He has two suits, blue and gray, which he wears only when testifying before Congress, together with one of his several dozen Jerry Garcia signature ties. A sign on his office door reads RESIDENT ANARCHIST, and he salts his conversation with hippiespeak ("good trip," "cool city") and random rhymes at the end of his sentences ("later, gator," "no big deal, Neal"). His voice is gentle, almost feminine, so the dry, steady crush of his handshake is startling. "Tom really has the Howdy Doody routine down," says Rick Parks, one of his whistleblower clients who later worked at GAP as an investigator, "to the point where his opponents think they can reach out and tickle him beneath the chin. And soon they may find they're tickling the belly of a dragon." Devine says he loves his work because it lets him speak truth to power and get away with it. "I'd be a whistleblower, but I don't have a martyr's complex," he says, with a mirthless chuckle. "This is the perfect job, because I get to keep it." He doesn't mention that the job nearly killed him.

Devine received his law degree from Antioch, a hotbed of public interest law founded in 1972 in answer to Ralph Nader's call for a new breed of lawyers willing to defend the general public. Antioch held its first lectures in a condemned stone mansion, and its commencements in a Unitarian church. On the wall of its largest classroom was a bright red QUESTION AUTHORITY bumper sticker. To earn their degree, students were required to spend a third of their time defending the poor, the physically and mentally handicapped, and foster children. As a first-year law student, Devine attended a conference on government transparency hosted by the Institute for Policy Studies, a left-wing think tank that had helped Daniel Ellsberg pass the Pentagon Papers to the *New York Times*. Among the featured speakers was J. Anthony Morris, an FDA vaccine specialist who had revealed that the swine flu vaccine of 1976 was a Big Pharma boondoggle. "That speech and that entire situation were completely inspiring," Devine remembers. "My eyes were a river. I knew immediately this was my calling." Helping victims was all well and good, he felt, but by defending whistleblowers, he'd be striking at the heart of society's problems. While completing his law degree, he worked at the Institute for Policy Studies' new whistleblower program, called the Project on Official Illegality, which he soon developed into the GAP legal clinic. He broke his first major case in 1980, when a private detective and group of whistleblower welders revealed to him that the William H. Zimmer nuclear power plant, then being completed near Cincinnati, was so riddled with defective materials, faulty welds and safety violations that it represented a threat of catastrophic failure. Thanks to a nearly four-year battle by Devine, Cincinnati antinuclear activist Tom Carpenter, and fifty whistleblowers, the facility was halted at 97 percent completion and converted to coal power.

Since then, Devine has represented about a thousand whistleblowers and helped some six thousand more, who have revealed wrongdoing ranging from institutional recklessness at the Three Mile Island nuclear plant to the FDA's irresponsible authorization of the deadly drug Vioxx, wrongdoing being winked at by the USDA and the Department of Homeland Security, and fraud in the Star Wars missile defense system. He and his colleagues at GAP, today a world leader in strategy and defense for government and corporate whistleblowers, have worked with Congress to help pass or defend thirty-two national statutes, including every federal law concerning whistleblowing enacted over the last twenty years. GAP attorneys have also shaped better whistleblower legislation in seventeen countries, often serving as representatives of the State Department. They helped to draft whistleblower policies for the UN, the World Bank and the African Development Bank, and then to pass laws ensuring that the United States would not fund these and other NGOs unless they had valid whistleblower policies in place.

By the early 1990s, he'd had too much of a good thing. "Working with such high-impact cases and such remarkable people, it's inspiring. I found it irresistible. But it became all-consuming. I was working eighty- to hundred-hour weeks." Devine had been an all-American debater in college, captain of a team that still holds the national record for tournament championships. "This was my gift: analytical warfare. I knew that I could win any argument that I had with myself. So rather than fool around with the bullshit of thinking every single thing through, I started just following my gut. Which made a lot of sense at times, but isn't a good way to live your life. It means you're driven by your inner child: you're reacting to everything, you're not taking control of your life. And gut reactions are pretty primitive sometimes—you need facts to flesh them out. But that was the way I lived my life until I was forty. Then everything started falling apart."

His wife left him. He developed a chronic cough and headaches, and strange, wandering pains that no doctor could explain. "I thought I was dying," he says with a bemused look, as if remembering the antics of a spoiled child. Doctors eventually located and removed an egg-size cyst behind his left eardrum, which had it burst would have ended his life. With the help of meditation and yoga, Devine learned to detach himself from his clients, while continuing to empathize with their struggles and respect their values. Today he teaches his clients to do the same. "Many whistle-blowers come in here with a strong 'They're not going to get away with this!' attitude. They want to shout the wrongs they've seen from the rooftops. Sometimes they're pretty vindictive. I'm not afraid of conflict, but unless there's a public health threat that needs to stop right now, I've learned to view conflict as a last resort. If you want whistleblowers to survive and to continue in their professions, you have to make their speaking out a healing process, not a vindictive confrontation. Whistle-blowers should be perceived as problem solvers, exercising their freedom to warn on behalf of the long-term well-being of their organization, not critics who say 'Gotcha!'"

Devine takes my notepad and draws his model of whistleblower dynamics. "Here is the whistleblower," he says, making a dot in the middle of the page. He draws a circle around it. "This circle is the whistleblower's organization. A lot of our work is about out-Machiavelli-ing the Machiavellis, about fleshing out the plan for staying under the radar. Because the longer you prevent the institution from perceiving the whistleblower as a threat, the longer the information keeps flowing, which makes the whistleblower's case stronger. But as soon as they're seen as a threat"—here he draws a series of arrows converging from the circle to trap the dot—"then they are walled off and can no longer access the information. They're isolated, and isolation is fatal. If you're isolated, it's really dangerous to know too much. Solidarity is crucial to survival. So what we do next is this." Devine traces a larger circle that encompasses the first, then draws more arrows radiating from the dot through the first circle to reach the second. "We get the information out past the organization, to the places where people can access and use it. When this happens, instead of an organization surrounding the individual, it's society surrounding the organization."

Doing this effectively often requires the timing and finesse of an orchestra conductor. "I play the information matchmaker, and call in as many fact finders as possible who can't be bought off or intimidated. Law enforcers, prosecutors, media, local community leaders, public interest groups. I try to involve politicians of opposing parties and trigger government investigations at different levels, so that people will be competing against each other, and no one institution will be able to cover up what they find. I may try to draw in competing factions within organizations or, if it's a business, to alert their competitors."

In 2007, when he went to work for Franz Gayl on the MRAP issue, the situation looked bleak. "A lawyer for the Marines told me, 'We can settle, and won't criminally prosecute him, if he drops the case and doesn't speak further,'" Devine says. "I asked, 'What are the charges, sir?' He answered: 'Everything he told Congress he stole from the Marine Corps—it's the intellectual property of the USMC.'" Devine hoots with laughter. "That wasn't much of a basis for dialogue!"

Step by step, Devine parried the Marine Corps' attacks, while coordinating Gayl's whistleblowing about the MRAP with the press and Capitol Hill. When the Marines threatened Gayl or gave him bad performance reviews, Devine and Danielle Brian, director of POGO, wrote letters of protest to Congress, prompting Senators Biden and Bond to warn the Marine commandant not to punish someone who was helping to save lives. Devine established Gayl's status as a whistleblower under federal law; after the Marines changed Gayl's paid leave to unpaid leave—essentially firing him—he persuaded the Office of Special Counsel (OSC) to file a stay request with the Merit Systems Protection Board (MSPB), claiming that the Marines' action had violated the federal Whistleblower Protection Act of 1989. The MSPB granted a forty-five-day stay, blocking the Corps' action until the OSC had investigated and agreed that Gayl was indeed a whistleblower who was suffering retaliation. Devine and Brian also delivered petitions to Defense Secretary Leon Panetta that demanded an end to this retaliation.

Gradually Devine's strategic moves began to pay off. The Marine Corps reversed Gayl's suspension, making him eligible for a security clearance, albeit at a lower level of responsibility. Gayl resumed limited work duties. Devine and the Marine Corps lawyers, with extensive help from the OSC and other offices, began to negotiate a settlement agreement. Finally, on September 23, 2014, the Marines and GAP reached an agreement that allowed Gayl to keep his job, receive an undisclosed payment for damages and a citation for his whistleblowing, and be entrusted with formulating whistleblower guidelines for the Marine Corps.

I sat with Devine in his office at GAP that day, as he answered a stream of calls from lawyers and reporters. He spoke with them in a firm, low-key, matter-of-fact voice, without a trace of jubilation. "I'd just love to gloat about this," he told me after yet another dour phone conversation, "but Franz has just been freed after seven years in hell. My gloating would be self-indulgent."

Tom Devine's successes with Franz Gayl were built not only on the general public's recognition of whistleblowing as a legitimate and beneficial act, but also on a series of federal laws to protect whistleblowers that began to take shape a half century earlier. Between 1968 and 1972, a time of crisis in the United States, four pioneer whistleblowers fought back against illegitimate authority in ways that galvanized the nation. They revealed corporate crime and systemic government abuse on an unprecedented scale, and proved whistleblowing to be both an effective and a necessary tool against institutional wrongdoing. They became voices of the country's conscience and helped catalyze the legislation, create the government bodies, and generate the public support for whistleblowing that attorneys like Tom Devine and John Phillips would use to empower and protect their clients.

On November 13, 1968, a short, dark, slightly plump man with graying brillian-tined hair and thick glasses slipped into Room 1202 of the New Senate Office Building during a hearing of the Subcommittee on Economy in Government and took a seat in the audience. Soon the committee chairman, Senator William Prox-mire, recognized the man, called him to the witness table and asked for his state-ment. In a rich Alabama drawl, the man explained that he had not prepared a statement but would speak extemporaneously. He then delivered a mind-numbingly detailed disquisition on cost control in major weapons systems, including the Min-uteman missile, the F-111 fighter and the C-5A Galaxy, the massive new transport plane that Lockheed, its manufacturer, promised would revolutionize warfare.

Proxmire, known for his bluntness as well as his parsimony with the public purse, heard the man out. Then he said that in a letter of October 18 he had asked the man to prepare a written statement in advance.

"You have told us this morning you did not prepare a statement for the record. Why not?"

"Mr. Chairman, I was directed not to prepare a statement," the man answered. He explained that his superiors in the Pentagon had done the directing.

"Well, this is very troublesome to this committee, very disturbing!" Proxmire erupted. He asked a Pentagon representative seated at the witness table, Commander Edward Dauchess, "Did [Air Force Deputy] Secretary Clifford provide instructions to muzzle this witness?" Dauchess said he didn't think so.

Proxmire returned to the man from Alabama. "Have you done work in connec-tion with the procurement of the C-5A?"

Not procurement per se, the man replied, though he had analyzed the likely costs of the plane.

Then Proxmire asked the question that the man had been dreading, one that his Pentagon superiors had specifically warned him not to answer. "Is it true that the costs of that contract will be approximately two billion dollars more than was orig-inally estimated and agreed on?"

The man hemmed and hawed, producing documents and explaining the difficulty of making such estimates, due to "repricing clauses which would be applied to the follow-on production if the option for the follow-on production is exercised."

Proxmire glared at him silently, waiting for an answer.

The man paused, as if listening to a distant voice. Then, as he later put it, he "committed truth." If the current cost trends for the plane and its engines remained unchanged, he told Proxmire, and if a series of other reasonable assumptions proved valid, then "your figure could be approximately right." He felt that he'd answered the question circumspectly, as a "maybe" rather than a "yes." And after all, he was merely commenting on a figure that Proxmire himself had produced.

When the hearing ended, however, he was mobbed by reporters demanding to know why the Air Force's new wonder plane was going to cost $2 billion more than Lockheed had pledged. "I knew then that I was in the soup," he wrote later. When he returned to his office in the Pentagon, his phone was ringing nonstop. "Have they fired you yet?" his worried secretary asked.

This man was A. Ernest Fitzgerald, a Pentagon cost control engineer, whom his many friends and secret admirers at work knew as "Ernie," the Air Force considered its most hated man, and President Richard Nixon called "that son of a bitch." For the next forty years, with a potent combination of mulishness, strategic brilliance and southern irony, Fitzgerald helped create the figure of the modern whistleblower in the public imagination, and to craft the laws that, to this day, determine how whistleblowing works.

Fitzgerald committed truth at a tumultuous moment in US history, when public questioning of authority carried extreme risks but could sometimes produce remarkable results. The country was at war in Asia, and with itself. The twin military disasters of the Tet Offensive and the siege of Khe Sanh had shattered the myth of US invincibility, and though many political and military leaders, including Secretary of Defense Robert McNamara, had begun to admit privately that the United States could not win in Vietnam, almost half a million US troops were there, more than a thousand of whom died every month. The motives and moral purity of the nation were widely questioned as reports began to surface of civilian massacres by American soldiers. In 1965, Norman Morrison, a thirty-one-year-old Quaker from

Baltimore, doused himself with kerosene and burned to death below McNamara's office in the Pentagon, to protest the endless killing of the Vietnam War. By the time Fitzgerald spoke out, students had held over 220 antiwar protests at universities across America. The previous year, two hundred thousand protesters had gathered in Central Park and burned the American flag, prompting Congress to criminalize flag burning. A growing number of conscientious objectors destroyed their draft cards and refused to fight; one objector was Cassius Clay, world heavyweight boxing champion, who changed his name to Muhammad Ali and declined to enlist in the Army because, as he said, "I don't have no personal quarrel with them Vietcongs."

The upheaval of war and dissent joined deeper swells of violence, hope and transformation in American society. For over a decade, Martin Luther King Jr. and other civil rights leaders had led protests throughout the South. In Ernie Fitzgerald's hometown of Birmingham, Alabama, widely considered the most racially segregated city in the United States, white nationalists bombed churches, police crushed rallies, and King wrote his historic "Letter from Birmingham Jail," affirming the moral duty to break unjust laws. In 1964, Lyndon Johnson pushed the Civil Rights Act through Congress, improving the prospects for racial equality in the United States yet simultaneously turning historically Democratic southern states into Republican strongholds and sparking a savage backlash. Civil rights activists were shot, beaten and burned throughout the South. On April 4, 1968, King was murdered in Memphis by white supremacist James Earl Ray, igniting race riots in a hundred American cities. On June 5, Robert Kennedy was killed in Los Angeles by a Palestinian-born Jordanian, Sirhan Bishara Sirhan. Three months later, Chicago police and National Guardsmen armed with billy clubs, mace and attack dogs brutally suppressed an antiwar rally during the Democratic National Convention, leading Senator Abraham Ribicoff to denounce the use of "Gestapo tactics in the streets of Chicago." On November 5, Republican Richard M. Nixon, promising "peace with honor" and an end to war in Vietnam, was elected president. Eight days later, Ernie Fitzgerald spoke.

Fitzgerald was neither a civil rights activist nor a war protester. What fueled his outrage was a love of precision, efficiency and thrift, and what he saw as the betrayal of these principles by the Pentagon. He had studied industrial engineering at the University of Alabama, and worked summers in the family iron foundry in Birmingham, where his father taught him pattern making, the meticulous art of preparing exact wooden replicas of objects to be cast in metal, which are then used to create molds to receive the molten metal. The foundry's watchwords were quality products, minimal waste, fair prices, and on-time delivery. "I liked foundry work," Fitzgerald said in a 1999 interview. "My grandfather was a foundryman, his father was a pattern maker, and my father was a pattern maker. It's in the DNA, I suppose." After college, Fitzgerald worked in industrial engineering and quality control for several Alabama companies, one of which built aircraft, before joining the accountancy and management consulting firm Arthur Young & Company. He came to see the method and rigor of industrial management—the subdivision, measurement and organization of human labor—as the cornerstone of American economic strength, and the reason why American products outcompeted foreign goods even though American wages were higher. Eventually he started his own consultancy, where he performed searching and often harshly critical financial analyses of major military contracts like the F-111 fighter-bomber and the Minuteman II missile. Air Force managers came to respect his sharp eye for cost management and efficiency. In September 1965, the Air Force offered him the influential job of deputy of management systems in the Pentagon—a decision that many in the Air Force and the Pentagon would soon come to regret.

In *The High Priests of Waste*, his sardonic, data-dense and eerily prescient 1972 memoir of his early Pentagon career, Fitzgerald explained that he had accepted the Department of Defense position, though it meant a 30 percent pay cut from his consulting job, because he saw a unique chance to help end the monstrous growth of military spending, a disease that he felt had afflicted the United States since his childhood. Fitzgerald had served in the Navy as a teenager during World War II, and he grew to adulthood during the Korean War and the beginning of the Cold War. He felt the waves of fear of Soviet military superiority roll through the nation, the successive alarms about Sputnik, the "bomber gap," and the "missile gap," which supposedly proved Russia's military superiority. He saw the US defense establishment undergo a fundamental transformation. Until the 1950s, large industrial firms like Ford and Boeing made cars and passenger planes in peacetime, then retooled to make jeeps and bombers in war. Armies and navies stood down after each major conflict, as they did after World War I and World War II. But the Korean War, the threat of Communist China, and especially the specter of nuclear war with the Soviet Union spurred the creation of a permanent, massive military, run by a caste of professional warriors that had less and less in common with a citizen army or with civilian life. Manufacturers of sophisticated new weapons like intercontinental ballistic missiles, nuclear submarines, supersonic fighters and bombers became increasingly specialized in, and dependent on, contracts with the Pentagon.

Fitzgerald knew the Founders' warnings about the dangers of military power to the American Republic; he quoted the Declaration of Independence on how the tyrant King George III had made "the Military independent of and superior to the civil power," James Madison on how a large standing army could be "fatal to the liberties of a nation," and Thomas Jefferson on how "endless war" would destroy democracy. Fitzgerald had grown up during a period of unprecedented US militarization, and had himself heard another legendary American denounce war. In 1953, when the US and the USSR had both developed thermonuclear devices, Eisenhower gave his moving "Chance for Peace" speech:

> Every gun that is made, every warship launched, every rocket fired signifies, in the final sense, a theft from those who hunger and are not fed, those who are cold and are not clothed. This world in arms is not spending money alone. It is spending the sweat of its laborers, the genius of its scientists, the hopes of its children. The cost of one modern heavy bomber is this: a modern brick school in more than 30 cities. It is two electric power plants, each serving a town of 60,000 population. It is two fine, fully equipped hospitals. It is some fifty miles of concrete pavement. . . . This is not a way of life at all, in any true sense. Under the cloud of threatening war, it is humanity hanging from a cross of iron.

Eight years later, Fitzgerald had heard the old soldier, in his farewell address to the nation, use the phrase "military-industrial complex," for what Eisenhower by now saw not as a potential threat but as a terrible, all-encompassing reality:

In the councils of government, we must guard against the acquisition of unwarranted influence, whether sought or unsought, by the military-industrial
complex. The potential for the disastrous rise of misplaced power exists and will
persist. We must never let the weight of this combination endanger our liberties
or democratic processes.

Working in the defense industry in the early 1960s, Fitzgerald began to believe
that waste, not war, was the greatest threat to America. The pattern maker and cost
cutter in him recoiled at the massive overstaffing, grotesquely high levels of pay and
abysmal industrial efficiency among large military contractors, who offered plush
postretirement jobs to the same military officers who'd managed their contracts
while in uniform. After Fitzgerald objected to the inflated overhead budgets at one
contractor, a general charged with reining in such costs replied, "Look, Fitzgerald,
I'm going to retire in a year or two and I'll become part of some contractor's overhead. If I cut overhead allowances, I'll be cutting my own throat."

Some Pentagon contractors spent twenty times as many labor hours as a properly run factory required to do the same amount of work. Fitzgerald discovered an
entirely new category of worker, the "expediter" or "parts chaser," who hunted
down critical parts that had gone missing somewhere in the manufacturing
process—as they often did. An executive at a major missile contractor said he lost
no sleep over solving a thorny engineering puzzle: "I just assign a thousand or so
guys to the problem." Another manager told him outright that he was strongly
against competition, which could "ruin the whole business climate." Downright
dishonesty, Fitzgerald saw, was becoming the industry norm: companies routinely
underbid to secure the contract to produce a piece of military hardware and then
steadily ratcheted up the cost, a practice known as "contract nourishment." "Cost-
plus" contracts guaranteed contractors a profit over and above all expenses they ran
up, which often meant that they intentionally spent more in order to earn more.

Such behavior not only pilfered tax dollars and destroyed competition, but also
yielded inferior products: the industrial, managerial and intellectual sloppiness en-
gendered by unlimited funds yielded weaponry that was plagued by design defects,
high failure rates and frequent project terminations. "Bad management has shot

down more airplanes, sunk more ships and immobilized more soldiers than all our enemies in history put together," Fitzgerald told one congressional committee. In short, Fitzgerald said, the American people were getting "a lot less bang for a lot more bucks."

Finally, on a macroeconomic level, Fitzgerald saw how systemic waste in arms manufacturing, with its parasitic relationship to Washington as its sole client, was infecting the efficiency, work ethic and quality standards in civilian industry, undermining American industry at its base. The cozy, symbiotic relationships between contractors and the military effectively eliminated free-market competition, and with it the drive to make the best weapons at the lowest prices. Most insiders Fitzgerald met seemed to find this state of affairs beneficial. "Inefficiency is national policy," General John "Zeke" Zoeckler told him. "We are not here to save money. We want to use these projects to employ people who really don't have jobs." Some economists actually claimed that overspending and waste in military procurement strengthened the economy by creating jobs and stimulating research; one defended US bombing in Southeast Asia on such grounds. "To such economists," Fitzgerald wrote, "the economic products of the bombing program were jobs and corporate profits. . . . Like primitive witch doctors, they had their idols and their mysterious, esoteric rituals which required long training to perform, but they neither questioned nor thought much about fundamental causes and effects. They were our high priests of waste." Fitzgerald watched this dogma spread to other industries that fed on government money. "On the Pentagon pattern, private-sector managers prospered if they were skillful at justifying higher costs as a way to get higher prices," he lamented. "This was particularly true in the medical and health care industry and contributed to the skyrocketing costs of medical treatment."

The homespun pragmatism he'd been raised with helped Fitzgerald see through this pseudo-religion and its countless apostles. He explained the high priests' theories to his father, who had retired from the foundry business and started a cattle ranch. "I never saw a cow get fat sucking herself," his father replied. He was describing orosthenic syndrome, or "self-sucking," a disorder that causes dairy cattle to suck their own teats to satisfy their hunger. If left untreated, the animals stop eating grass altogether, suffer a general decline in health, and eventually die. To Fitzgerald, "self-sucking" seemed an apt metaphor for the United States under the influence of the arms drug.

> Our military establishment may not have won a war in forty-three years, but it has managed to pull down the world's greatest industrial colossus. This could not have happened without the concomitant disintegration of institutional checks and balances in business, government, and society. When the tribunes and the senate neglect their vigilance, the Praetorian Guard takes over the treasury for itself. The collapse of management controls and moral standards radiated outward from the Pentagon's acquisition community, the ripened fruit of the noxious military-industrial complex weed that President Eisenhower warned us about. The problem is that the fruit, though deadly to liberty and lasting prosperity, is addictive. Almost all who partake are hooked, and the addiction has spread far beyond the military and its suppliers. The weed now chokes formerly productive industrial fields not directly involved in supplying the military. Greed, institutionalized dishonesty, and legalized stealing have corrupted not only the military but also segments of Congress, prestigious universities, and even whole civilian communities that have become dependent on military money.

Fitzgerald accepted the job at the Pentagon in 1965 because he saw a historic opportunity to use his own skills and knowledge to help cure what senior defense officials at the time seemed to agree was a national scourge. The ballooning costs of America's military had recently drawn public outcry. An influential 1962 study concluded that the average weapons system ended up costing more than three times its original budget. John F. Kennedy's new secretary of defense, Robert Strange McNamara, was an economist, accountant and executive who had taught at Harvard Business School and had a brilliant career at Ford Motor Corporation. Here, Fitzgerald believed, was just the man to reform the defense behemoth.

With his hair slicked marble-smooth off a razor-sharp part, his gleaming spectacles and his intimidating facility with numbers, McNamara was the embodiment of the Best and the Brightest. Barry Goldwater, an admirer, called him "an IBM machine with legs," while critic Richard Barnet referred to him as "the leading specimen of *homo mathematicus*." McNamara's obsession with data often seemed to crowd out his humanity. During World War II, working with Air Force general Curtis E. LeMay, he analyzed statistical data from bomber missions, adjusting plane altitudes, bomb hit-rates, and civilian deaths to maximize the impact of nearly a thousand B-29 firebombing missions on Japanese cities. "In that single night we burned to death 100,000 Japanese civilians in Tokyo: men, women, and children," he remembered in a 2003 interview. "LeMay said, 'If we'd lost the war, we'd all have been prosecuted as war criminals.' And I think he's right. He, and I'd say I, were behaving as war criminals." In 1965, however, McNamara showed no such qualms, and began applying his rigorous analytical methods to the war in Vietnam.

Fitzgerald liked the new secretary of defense, at least initially, because he planned to run the military like a business, according to the principles of free enterprise, and to end the cronyism and pork-barrel spending between the military and arms contractors. "The Defense Department cannot and should not assume responsibility for creating a level of demand adequate to keep the economy healthy and growing," McNamara stated. "Nor should it, in developing its programs, depart from the strictest standards of military need and operating efficiency in order to aid an economically distressed company or community." Competition, not protectionism, was to be the new Pentagon watchword. McNamara brought a team of fellow Ivy League economists and technocrats into the Defense Department, whom the press soon dubbed the "Whiz Kids," in a nod to McNamara's brain trust at Ford, to run his revolution. Charles Hitch and Alain Enthoven, economists at the Air Force–funded think tank RAND, became his budget director and head of systems analysis, a decision-making methodology developed at RAND to break down complex, uncertain environments—like nuclear war planning—into component elements in order to weigh their expected costs, benefits, and risks. Harold Brown, a nuclear physicist whom admirers called "the smartest man in the world," headed the Air Force. Brown replaced the disastrous "cost-plus" contract with a businesslike new agreement, which required a bidder to include all costs—initial design, manufacture, testing, and spare parts—into a binding final bid, and to pay for all subsequent overruns.

Brown himself had noticed the cost-cutting expertise on Fitzgerald's résumé, and had urged his hiring.

Fitzgerald moved into a spacious office on the fifth floor of the Pentagon, where he hung a framed copy of the civil service code of ethics, ten principles that each federal employee swore to follow when they joined the government, which Fitzgerald called the "Ten Commandments." The first commandment was to "put loyalty to highest moral principles and to country above loyalty to persons, party, or government department." Further down the list was the directive to "find and employ more efficient and more economical ways of getting tasks accomplished." Commandment nine was the pithiest of all: "Expose corruption wherever discovered." These were rules that Ernie Fitzgerald had lived by as an engineer, accountant and cost manager. He proceeded to apply them to the world of military procurement, unbendingly and against increasingly sharp resistance, for the next forty years.

Though Fitzgerald's Alabama drawl and public college education made him feel something of an outsider among the Whiz Kids—he referred to himself as a "sharecropper industrial engineer" surrounded by "bright, beautifully educated Harvards"— he won respect, and several awards, for his accounting and business instincts. He began trying to trim the fat off a series of major weapon systems by replacing the prevailing method for setting prices, the so-called historical price method, according to which the current price of a fighter jet or a submarine was determined by what such items had previously cost. Nonsense, Ernie Fitzgerald argued, because historical prices factored in previous contract inflation, waste and fraud; what was needed wasn't "did cost," he said, but "should cost," based on a hard look at existing numbers. Hot on the trail of "should cost," Fitzgerald rooted out overspending in missiles and fighter jets, serious waste and fraud by General Electric, Northrop and other major Air Force contractors. Along the way he discovered a number of technical flaws in the weapons, which had been caused by inefficient management.

His most controversial assignment, which launched his whistleblowing career, was the C-5A Galaxy transport plane, known in the Air Force as the "tin balloon," then being built by Lockheed under what was then the largest contract ever signed by the Air Force. The C-5A ultimately became one of the most troubled and disastrous aircraft in US history, and from his first glance at Lockheed cost sheets and his first visit to the Marietta, Georgia, plant where the plane was being built, Fitzgerald saw why. Already two years prior to Fitzgerald's testimony, Air Force auditors had found that the C-5A project was some $2 billion over budget, though this news was kept to a select few within the company and the Air Force. In November 1967, McNamara learned that Air Force officials were lying to him about C-5A costs. Nevertheless, despite the defense secretary's tough talk, Fitzgerald realized that many long-term Pentagon employees, particularly military officers, instinctively fought any action that reduced the flow of money to their pet contractors.

As the sole supplier of the Poseidon and Polaris missiles, bulwarks of the US Cold War arsenal, Lockheed was held in particular regard by the Pentagon. Yet its financial health was fragile. Unlike Boeing and Douglas, its two main competitors, Lockheed had never designed a successful commercial airliner, and over 90 percent of its revenue came from the military. In the early 1960s, the Air Force found it needed a larger cargo aircraft than the company's bread-and-butter C-130 Hercules transport plane and the C-141 Starlifter. To help Lockheed, the Pentagon had already purchased several of its facilities, including the Marietta plant where the C-5A was being built, effectively nationalizing parts of the company. Lockheed executives warned that if the company failed to secure the C-5A contract, for which it was competing against Boeing and Douglas, it would have to make severe job cuts, and perhaps even file for bankruptcy.

Trouble for Lockheed, the company's leaders pointed out, would also mean economic hardship for Americans in every factory where the plane was being produced. This got the ear of powerful politicians and Lockheed backers, including senior Georgia senator Richard Russell, chair of the Senate Armed Services Committee, and South Carolina congressman L. Mendel Rivers, who chaired the House Armed Services Committee. In fact, Ernie Fitzgerald discovered that such "financial engineering" was a standard practice by military contractors, leading to a widely used extension of Eisenhower's famous phrase, "the military-industrial-congressional complex." Lockheed had bulletproofed the C-5A by spreading its manufacturing facilities across two thousand subcontractors in forty-one states, ensuring that most politicians who voted against the aircraft would be voting against jobs in their home states. The company launched a massive PR campaign, jointly managed with the Air Force, to portray the plane as not only vital to national defense but essential to local economies, a marvel of technological achievement, and reasonably priced as well. All who criticized the plane faced the military-industrial-congressional complex in full panoply.

Ernie Fitzgerald continued to push for accountability in the C-5A project, but to his alarm, support from his Pentagon managers melted away. He wrote a caustic but uncontroversial study on military contract inefficiencies, which the secretary of defense's office suppressed as a security risk, forbidding its distribution even within the DOD and the Air Force. His demands for financial information from Lockheed, which he suspected to be falsifying official records to increase the flow of government money, were rebuffed. Air Force officers grew openly hostile to his cost-cutting measures, and civilian former allies and proponents of financial common sense lost their economizing zeal. Fitzgerald watched with disgust as tough clauses were deleted from the C-5A contract, and new language added that enabled the company to make more money on future production runs of the C-5A by wasting money on the first batch. Defense Secretary Harold Brown, once critical of the aircraft's overruns, began expressing more concern for the financial welfare of the company, and the power of its political backers, than for honest accounting. It was at this tense moment that Senator Proxmire called Fitzgerald, who the senator's staff had learned was critical of the program, to testify.

Twelve days after he committed the truth in Congress, Pentagon payback began. Fitzgerald was informed that his civil service tenure, which had been confirmed a few months earlier, was being revoked—it had been issued, his superiors explained, by a computer error. (Fitzgerald protested, to no avail, that the letter announcing his tenure had been handwritten, and signed by the head of Pentagon personnel—hardly a computer glitch.) He was excluded from important meetings, and most office mates avoided him. He was relieved of cost management duties in all important weapons systems and was instead assigned to make-work projects like cost-cutting for Air Force mess halls and for a twelve-lane bowling alley in Thailand. (When he found that the alley's budget required significant cuts, he lost that project, too.) The new secretary of the Air Force, Robert Seamans, accused him before

Congress of leaking classified documents—a lie Seamans eventually retracted, though it permanently damaged Fitzgerald's reputation in Pentagon circles.

Fitzgerald soon discovered that his mail was being opened and that a former Air Force officer, now working for a major defense contractor on the West Coast, had questioned his friends about possible extramarital or homosexual affairs and abuse of alcohol or drugs. He later learned that this questioning was part of Investigation HQD 24-12052, headed by General Joseph Cappucci, director of the Air Force Office of Special Investigations, and by the infamous FBI agent and Hoover hatchet man William "Crazy Billy" Sullivan, who had been instructed to root out anything untoward in Fitzgerald's past that might merit his firing. The juiciest information that the investigators turned up on Fitzgerald was that he saw things as either "black or white," "right or wrong"; that he worked long hours, sometimes late at night; and that he was a "pinchpenny" who drove a beat-up old AMC Rambler. Cappucci began collecting allegations by secret informers, designated as T1, T2, T3 and T4, in a "dirt file," which he circulated to damage Fitzgerald's reputation. (Cappucci later admitted that he'd kept only derogatory allegations against Fitzgerald in the file, and deleted any evidence that contradicted them.) The file was classified, and Fitzgerald was never allowed to view it, or to know the identity of his four secret accusers, though he soon worked out who they were.

Finally, on November 4, 1969, in a move purportedly aimed at reducing costs, the Pentagon carried out a "reduction in force" that actually eliminated only one staff position—Ernest Fitzgerald's. (The irony of a cost cutter's being fired to save costs was not lost on him.) Fitzgerald packed up the contents of his desk, posed for a photo by his office blackboard where someone had written "Time wounds all heels," climbed into his battered Rambler, and left the Pentagon for what appeared to be the last time.

But Ernie Fitzgerald wasn't through. "I won't give up on this," he told reporters. "I plan to give them hell." Though no one in the arms industry would hire him, he had some money saved up from his previous consulting work, and the strong backing of his wife, Nell, who had urged him to tell the truth at the 1968 Senate hearings: "I told him that I didn't really think I could live with a man I didn't respect," she told a reporter in 1985, "and if he went over there and lied, I'd have no respect

for him." Fitzgerald's sense of humor also helped keep him sane. He called the
C-5A scandal "the Great Plane Robbery," and the Pentagon's use of cost-plus contracts "the Golden Fleece." Fitzgerald soon discovered he had both a gift and a taste
for DC infighting, knowing instinctively when to play the slow-talking good old
boy, and when to fire off a volley of dart-like data. Fitzgerald had documents, contacts, insider knowledge and a prodigious memory. His combined mastery of accounting, weaponry and the bureaucratic mind made him a redoubtable foe to the
military-industrial complex. He also had a knack for cultivating powerful supporters across the political spectrum.

Fitzgerald embarked on a thirty-year campaign of lawsuits against a wide range
of persecutors. First he sued the Pentagon for illegal termination. ("I was the only
bureaucrat in the world suing for more work," he told one House subcommittee.)
After four years of hearings and legal wrangling, he finally won, and the Pentagon
had to take him back, but they assigned him a position with drastically inferior
duties and no input on arms procurement. So he brought more lawsuits, challenging this arbitrary demotion and calling out those who had originally conspired to
fire him. In his conspiracy suit Fitzgerald aimed high, naming as defendants two
secretaries of the Air Force, three generals, several high White House officials, and
additional "person or persons unknown," one of whom eventually proved to be
President Richard Nixon.

As a result of his activism, Fitzgerald was in the news for decades. He gave lectures to local business groups and political organizations in Washington about the
fundamentally anticapitalistic practices of the defense welfare establishment, and
how the military was swindling the citizens it was meant to defend. He testified
more than fifty times before Congress. A year after his first testimony, Senator
Proxmire held a follow-up hearing, "The Dismissal of A. Ernest Fitzgerald by the
Department of Defense," during which the senator grilled a series of Air Force officials and deplored their "shooting the messenger" instead of addressing the enormous waste in military procurement that he had revealed.

Instead of attacking the problem, the man who had the guts to point out the
problem was sacked. Instead of giving him a medal, the Air Force has fired him.

In the meantime the defense of this country has been weakened, the hard earned income of millions of American taxpayers has been squandered, and funds for the myriad of military and civilian priorities facing this Nation have been wasted. This makes us weaker, not stronger, and if the Air Force can get by with such deliberate acts it will also weaken the moral fabric of this Government and this country by putting every honest civil servant on notice if he tells the truth and tries to save money, even under circumstances which are properly authorized, his job is at stake.

A group of influential DC supporters, including senators of both parties, journalists, lawyers and even members of the White House staff, began to fight Fitzgerald's corner. He advised several key lawmakers on how to curb defense contractor fraud and, subsequently, to write better whistleblower laws. Fitzgerald's wholehearted espousal of the whistleblower's role, and his righteous anger, tenacity and David-and-Goliath vulnerability, inspired more insiders to speak out. During one speech to a group of government employees, he insisted that true integrity meant understanding that "government money" was a meaningless concept—it remained the *taxpayers'* money. He urged his audience to cut out waste, accept lower budgets and help achieve lower costs. The *Federal Times*, a newspaper for government employees, described the audience's reaction.

Hands were shooting up. Stories about waste, mismanagement, corruption, and cover-ups began pouring out from all sides. Complaints went uninvestigated, complainants were punished, documents destroyed. . . . It seemed an endless orgy of accusations in southern lilts, midwestern drawls, and Bronx accents. . . . There were many Fitzgeralds now, countless numbers, and all of them felt that the big shots who commit crimes go scot free, while the little guys, honoring their Code of Ethics, get slammed for revealing wrongdoing.

Within the Pentagon, Fitzgerald's efforts drew a wave of support from insiders who kept him supplied with revelations about the C-5A and other military boondoggles, a growing army of grassroots resistance fighters whom he called "closet patriots" and "secret admirers." Others were as outspoken as Fitzgerald himself, though they employed very different tactics. John Boyd, a brilliant fighter pilot and self-taught genius in aeronautics and military strategy, led a team of mavericks inside the Pentagon, which included decorated fellow pilot and contrarian Chuck Myers; subtle French-born statistician and aeronautics engineer Pierre Sprey; senior defense adviser and brilliant bureaucratic strategist Tom Christie; and clear-thinking, plainspoken former Air Force captain Chuck Spinney. "I wasn't a whistleblower—I was just doing the job I'd been hired for," Spinney says. "I was on a premeditated attack. I knew what I was in for, and I was never reactive like whistleblowers. Calling people 'whistleblowers' is a bureaucratic tactic that allows the powers that be to focus attention on the whistleblowers and distract attention away from the problem they're trying to fix." Fitzgerald agreed. "I have never, incidentally, liked the newspaper term 'whistle blower,'" he wrote, "because it tends to set apart and isolate taxpayers' employees who do what they're paid to do—tell the truth."

While they may have disapproved of the term "whistleblower," however, the strategies that Fitzgerald, Spinney and Pentagon colleagues used to win their battles and avoid destruction, many of which they drew from classic treatises on warfare by Sun Tzu and Clausewitz, eventually became part of Tom Devine's whistleblower defense toolkit. One of the central lessons was Sun Tzu's maxim, frequently paraphrased by John Boyd, "Cultivate fear, mistrust and betrayal within your enemy." Which is what successful whistleblowers often do.

Another key member of the so-called Pentagon Underground was Dina Rasor, a young journalist from California who worked closely with Boyd and Pierre Sprey, and became Fitzgerald's disciple and confidante. "Boyd and Fitzgerald had completely different approaches. Boyd was a warrior; he'd listen to 'Ride of the Valkyries' while working on his computer, he'd grab people by their lapels and spit in their face if they were doing wrong. Ernie was subtle, gracious, and had so much southern charm that it took his targets some time to realize they'd been skewered." She remembers how Fitzgerald made allies of surprising people, like Pat Robertson, the conservative television evangelist, whom Fitzgerald called "Brother Pat." During one of his several appearances on Robertson's show, he got Robertson to lead an "industrial-strength prayer" for military reform, which he called "jail a general for Jesus." Rasor believes that Fitzgerald and Boyd, successful insiders and critics working in the open, were the exceptions that proved the rule. A safer and more effective way for someone to get information out of a bureaucracy, she says, was and remains to blow the whistle anonymously. "I knew eight to ten insiders, and each of them knew ten to twenty more whose names I never learned, and so on down the line, creating this huge pyramid of what Ernie called his 'fellow travelers in military reform.' They developed procedures to prevent the documents they passed to him or to me from being traced back to the source. I had tremendous success with people who are still working in the Pentagon, even twenty years later."

Fitzgerald's crusade was facilitated by endless revelations of mismanagement and fraud by defense contractors. His worst predictions about the C-5A proved correct. One of the first planes to be finished burned on the runway in May 1970, and later planes that did become airborne developed stress fractures in their wings due to their excessive weight, forcing Lockheed to cut the plane's payload from the original 110 tons it had guaranteed the Air Force to 50 tons. The plane's supposedly advanced (and fabulously expensive) radar and flight control systems proved defective and had to be ripped out and replaced with simpler technology. Parts of the landing gear of one C-5A tore off on touchdown and rocketed down the runway; another plane caught fire and exploded during maintenance, killing one mechanic and injuring another. A 1971 engineering report warned that the C-5A's rear cargo door was "a monster system that was unreliable and unsafe"; Lockheed failed to fix the door, with predictable results: during Operation Babylift, a 1975 airlift of Vietnamese war orphans, a rear door on one aircraft blew open at 23,000 feet, causing a crash that killed 138 people, including most of the orphans. Despite a series of "golden handshake" adjustments that the Pentagon offered Lockheed, which increased profits and forgave extra costs, the company again threatened to declare bankruptcy. So the Department of Defense invoked Public Law 85-804, which allowed it to designate Lockheed "essential to the national defense," whether or not the company actually produced anything, and gave it $1 billion in loan guarantees. The US government had declared Lockheed too big—or at least too powerful—to fail.

As bad as the C-5A was, it was only one of a series of military procurement scandals that made the news in the late 1970s and early 1980s, a host of defective and overpriced missiles, tanks, aircraft and ships that Ernie Fitzgerald helped explain to increasingly irate politicians and the American public. ("I don't see why everyone has picked on the C-5A," former comptroller of the Defense Department Robert Anthony said. "There are many examples of defense contracting that are much worse.") Because of the inherent complexity of high-tech weapons systems and the byzantine manner in which they were funded, Fitzgerald and his allies sought ways to make the magnitude of the waste comprehensible. One of the most effective techniques, which he devised with Dina Rasor, was to reveal the price tags of spare parts, banal items often gussied up with sophisticated names and sold to the Pentagon at stunning markups. While it was difficult for the average person to know whether an ICBM or a nuclear submarine was fairly priced, the spare parts for that weapon were easy to visualize—and the parts gave a vivid snapshot of the monumental wastefulness of the whole. "Think of a fighter jet as a bunch of spare parts flying in close formation," Fitzgerald said.

Among the outrages that Fitzgerald and Rasor uncovered, and delightedly dangled before legislators and the media, were a $4 hammer that one contractor rebranded as a "handheld impact device" and charged the government $435 for; an "antenna hexagon wrench" that was an ordinary Allen wrench with a fancy handle that cost the government $9,609; $91 screws, $660 ashtrays, $2,043 nuts and a $100 box of tools that ended up costing a tidy $10,820.56. Even in this gallery of the absurd, the C-5A distinguished itself, with a seat armrest that ran $670, and a $7,622 coffeemaker. But the most infamous overpriced spare parts were toilet seats, ranging from the C-5A's rather modest $286.75 model to the $640 version in another Lockheed aircraft, the P-3C Orion antisubmarine plane, which, as Senator William Cohen observed, gave new meaning to the word "throne." The $640 toilet seat frequently appeared in vignettes by noted cartoonist Herblock, hanging around the neck of Caspar Weinberger, Reagan's defense secretary.

One evening in early 1983, Fitzgerald gained his staunchest and most influential supporter of all. He received a telephone call at home from someone with a strong midwestern accent.

"Are you the Fitzgerald who wrote *The High Priests of Waste?*" the man wanted to know. Fitzgerald said he was.

"Is all the stuff you wrote in that book true?"

It was, Fitzgerald assured him.

"Are the same kinds of things going on in the Pentagon now?"

Fitzgerald said that things were worse than ever.

"Well, I'd like for you to come in and talk to me about this."

The curious midwesterner turned out to be Chuck Grassley, the Iowa senator known both for his thrift and for his outspoken criticism of government waste. From then on, Grassley and his staff drew on Fitzgerald's boundless knowledge of government wrongdoing and bureaucratic dysfunction to cut costs and increase transparency in the military, as well as to improve whistleblower legislation. He repeatedly called Fitzgerald to testify before the Senate; once, when Fitzgerald's superiors resisted, Grassley drove to the Pentagon in his battered orange Chevette— like Fitzgerald, he considered thrift a badge of honor—waded through the flustered crowd of Pentagon officials outside Fitzgerald's office, and hand-delivered a subpoena to the delighted cost cutter. "Ernie Fitzgerald was the first whistleblower I'd ever met," Grassley says today. "He taught me just how courageous, and precious, they can be." Fitzgerald was one of the first people to encourage Grassley to reform the False Claims Act, which the senator soon did with John Phillips's help. "How would you like to put Abe Lincoln's law back to work?" Fitzgerald asked him.

For the next twenty-three years, until Fitzgerald's retirement in 2006, the two men were allies in the fight against fraud in the defense industry, and for the rights of whistleblowers. To this day, Grassley remains the most steadfast ally of whistleblowing in Congress.

On March 29, 1969, four months after Ernie Fitzgerald gave Congress the bad news about the C-5A, another minor member of the military-industrial complex risked his career and his life to follow his conscience and his sense of higher duty. Sitting in a low apartment building on a long, heat-shimmery boulevard in Phoenix, he typed a three-page letter that helped end the Vietnam War.

In it, he described an engagement a year earlier, by members of his former out-
fit, the C (or "Charlie") Company of the 11th Brigade, 23rd (Americal) Infantry
Division. Initial reports had described the battle as a stunning success, a pincer
movement that had annihilated an entire Vietcong battalion in Quang Ngai Province, in a village that local people called Xom Lang. The supreme commander of
US forces in Vietnam, General William Westmoreland, congratulated Charlie
Company on its performance. But one by one, in bars or during the endless waiting
between battles, members of the unit had told Ronald Ridenhour a different story.

Ridenhour was a hardened combat veteran. After serving as a door gunner in
an aeroscout helicopter, flying low and fast over the countryside to draw enemy
fire, he'd transferred to a LRRP (long-range reconnaissance patrol, pronounced
"lurp") unit, a heavily armed Special Forces team that carried out reconnaissance
and search-and-destroy missions behind enemy lines. He had seen, and done,
much killing. Yet he was deeply disturbed by what the soldiers of Charlie Company, part of the same Americal Division as his unit, told him about events in
Xom Lang, which the soldiers called "Pinkville" and military maps identified as
My Lai 4.

In his letter, Ridenhour laid out the evidence neatly, like a prosecutor. He gave
the map coordinates of the village, named the eyewitnesses he had questioned, and
summarized what each had said. "Exactly what did, in fact, occur in the village of
'Pinkville' in March 1968 I do not know for certain," Ridenhour concluded, "but I
am convinced that it was something very black indeed. I remain irrevocably persuaded that if you and I do truly believe in the principles, of justice and the equality
of every man, however humble, before the law, that form the very backbone that
this country is founded on, then we must press forward a widespread and public
investigation of this matter with all our combined efforts. I think that it was Winston Churchill who once said, 'A country without a conscience is a country without
a soul, and a country without a soul is a country that cannot survive.'" Ridenhour
added that he had considered contacting the press, but preferred to have the government investigate, because "as a conscientious citizen I have no desire to further
besmirch the image of the American serviceman in the eyes of the world."

Ridenhour made thirty photocopies of the letter. He mailed the original to

President Richard Nixon, and the copies to senior officials at the State Department and the Pentagon, and to twenty-four congressmen. The letter triggered a series of military investigations and congressional hearings into the My Lai massacre, and court-martial trials that were followed by 92 percent of Americans.

Here is the story Ridenhour told. At 7:30 a.m. on March 16, 1968, waves of helicopters began landing near a group of hamlets, greenery swirling in the rotor backwash. The men of Charlie Company leaped out and made for My Lai, across a landscape of emerald rice paddies, irrigation ditches, dikes and dirt roads. They were equipped for heavy combat: the night before, senior officers had told them that the elite Vietcong 48th Battalion was in the village, and that all civilians would be away at a market—anyone still in My Lai would be Vietcong or a VC sympathizer. One soldier asked, "Are we supposed to kill women and children?" Captain Ernest Medina, commander of Charlie Company, reportedly replied: "Kill everything that moves."

There were in fact no Vietcong in the area, and the people Charlie Company found in the village were almost exclusively women, children, infants and elderly men. Only one firearm was discharged against the unit that day, when Private Herbert Carter shot himself in the foot to escape the horrors his comrades were perpetrating. For four and a half hours, soldiers shot women and children in the head. They raped women and girls as young as ten years old, then cut open their vaginas with knives and killed them. They bayoneted pregnant women, cut off ears and scalps from victims as war trophies. They burned thatched huts, killed livestock, blew up food. They lined up 150 villagers at the edge of an irrigation ditch just south of town and machine-gunned them. In all, the soldiers killed somewhere between 350 and 500 civilians. The body count is uncertain because of the unchecked butchery, and the subsequent cover-up by senior Army officers.

The first My Lai participant whom Ridenhour interviewed, over drinks in a bar in Vietnam a few months after the massacre, was Private Charles "Butch" Gruver. "Men, women and kids, everybody, we killed them all," he told Ridenhour. "We didn't leave anybody alive—at least we didn't intend to."

As he listened, Ridenhour had an epiphany. "It was an instantaneous recognition and collateral determination that this was something too horrible, almost, to comprehend and that I wasn't gonna be a part of it," he wrote years later. "Just simply having the knowledge, I felt, made me complicit, unless I acted on it."

He began to investigate, tracking down other soldiers who had been at My Lai that morning. This was relatively easy, because within days of the massacre, five of them had transferred out of Charlie Company and into his LRRP unit. Between missions in the jungle, Ridenhour asked them what had happened at Pinkville. "And it would be like lancing a boil," he remembered later. "I mean, if you asked them, they were compelled to talk. They couldn't stop talking."

Sergeant Larry La Croix told Ridenhour how soldiers had pulled three separate groups of villagers out of their huts, twenty to forty people each, and shot them with a heavy M60 machine gun—"like so many sheep," he told Ridenhour. Lieutenant William "Rusty" Calley, head of Charlie Company, had killed many people himself, repeatedly ordered his men to shoot unarmed villagers, and even pointed his sidearm at one of his own soldiers who was reluctant to take part. But most of Charlie Company apparently took part without much coercion, caught up in thirst for vengeance, blood lust, fear or mindless obedience.

Private Michael Terry had also been at My Lai. He and Ridenhour had done basic training together and were close friends. Terry was an ardent Mormon; Ridenhour called him "one of the finest people I ever met." The two men often discussed questions of religion and morality. "He didn't cuss, discuss women, lie, cheat, steal or speak badly of anyone," Ridenhour wrote later.

Terry told him about the 150 villagers machine-gunned beside the irrigation ditch. He described the scene as a bad dream, "a Nazi kind of thing." Terry said he had refused to take part—at least at first. But at around 11:00 a.m., he and a mutual friend, William "Billy" Daugherty, had sat down for lunch beside the ditch. "Billy and I started to get out our chow," Terry told Ridenhour, "but close to us was a bunch of Vietnamese in a heap, and some of them were moaning. [Calley] had been through before us and all of them had been shot, but many weren't dead. It was obvious that they weren't going to get any medical attention so Billy and I got up and went over to where they were. I guess we sort of finished them off." Terry and Daugherty then returned to their packs and ate the rest of their rations.

After Terry finished his story, he and Ridenhour lay silent in the darkness for several minutes, staring up at the stars. Then Ridenhour said, "Mike, my God, Mike . . . don't you know that was wrong?" Terry's expression suddenly changed, Ridenhour remembered, "as if I saw a wall roll down behind his eyes."

"I don't know, man, I don't know," Terry replied. "It was just one of them things." He rolled over and fell asleep.

Ridenhour's last witness was Private Michael Bernhardt, one of the few soldiers of Charlie Company who had refused to kill civilians in My Lai—a refusal that made his superiors suspicious. The evening after the operation, Bernhardt said, Captain Medina had warned him not to talk about what had happened in the village. After My Lai, he was repeatedly denied medical treatment, and often ordered to walk point at the head of patrols, where he would be the first to be killed by a booby trap or an ambush.

Ridenhour's discussion of these testimonies was so sincere, relentless and authoritative that it proved impossible to ignore. High-level officials in the Army, the Pentagon and Congress opened separate investigations. Another My Lai whistle-blower came to light, a helicopter pilot named Hugh Thompson, who had witnessed the murders of My Lai from the air, and had even landed and rescued a few of the civilians from the killers; Thompson had filed a detailed report on the massacre, but the Army ignored it and instead retaliated against him for speaking out. After Ridenhour's letter, investigators finally listened as he described several murders in detail and had him identify Lieutenant Calley in a lineup. Army prosecutors brought charges of war crimes and crimes against humanity, murder, rape and assault against Calley, Medina and eleven other members of Charlie Company. Higher-level officers, including Major General Samuel Koster, head of the Americal Division, were accused of covering up a war crime. During the trials, numerous soldiers stated that the order to kill civilians had come from above. Eventually Calley was convicted of murdering twenty-two "Oriental human beings" and was sentenced to life in prison.

The public outcry at this outcome was overwhelming. Conservatives saw Calley as a simple soldier carrying out his duty as an Army officer—just following orders—while liberals who opposed the war felt Calley was a scapegoat for senior officers and the political leaders who had sent soldiers to Vietnam in the first place. FREE

CALLEY bumper stickers and billboards appeared across the nation. A country western single, "The Battle Hymn of Lt. Calley," sung to the tune of "The Battle Hymn of the Republic," played on radio stations throughout the South, and nearly two million copies of the record were sold. In it, Calley tells God: "Sir, I followed all my orders and I did the best I could." The White House received countless thousands of letters and telegrams, reportedly 100 to 1 in Calley's favor. Nixon eventually pardoned him. Charges against all other defendants were dismissed—the foot soldiers because, *pace* Nuremberg, they were just following orders, and their superiors because they were too senior to have known what their foot soldiers had been up to.

Many observers felt that the real villains of the story were the whistleblowers. Hugh Thompson was attacked as a traitor by war-hawk congressmen while testifying. He received death threats, and dead animals were left by night at his door. Nationwide polls revealed that many Americans didn't believe Ridenhour, while many others felt that atrocities like My Lai were inevitable in wartime. Even some experts who saw Calley and his fellow soldiers as murderers, like General William Peers, leader of the Army's investigation into the massacre, viewed My Lai as an aberration.

In time, Ron Ridenhour came to a very different perception of My Lai and its aftermath. He recognized the immense power of authority to make people do virtually anything they are ordered to do, even against their conscience. He also understood that organizations that demanded and enforced such authority had self-defense mechanisms that led them to conceal or to defend their crimes. He was certain that My Lai hadn't been the work of a few corrupt soldiers; rather, he felt, the military culture itself corrupted many soldiers. On his first combat mission he'd seen an Army corporal execute a civilian prisoner in cold blood. Soon after, he'd heard one sergeant tell another how his company had killed women and children in a night raid on a hamlet, saying he had just closed his eyes and followed orders. While investigating My Lai, Ridenhour learned that a similar massacre had occurred the same morning at a hamlet less than two miles away. Civilian massacres weren't an aberration, but part of a master plan.

Ridenhour was right, and the Pentagon knew it. In August 1967, seven months before My Lai, a 208-page DOD report produced for Defense Secretary McNamara had revealed that the majority of Army and Marine officers questioned would willingly torture or kill prisoners. In April 1971, Vietnam veteran John Kerry reported to the Senate Committee on Foreign Relations that widespread rape, torture, random shooting of civilians and other atrocities by US forces "were not isolated incidents but crimes committed on a day-to-day basis with the full awareness of officers at all levels of command." Beginning in the early 1970s, a secret Pentagon task force, the Vietnam War Crimes Working Group, compiled 9,000 pages of investigative records detailing hundreds of atrocities against civilians; many of these records were rediscovered in the National Archives in 2002, by investigative journalist Nick Turse.

"What was happening all around us in Vietnam was not a strategy that went awry, or one that had some unforeseen and regrettable consequences for civilians, but one in which the deliberate military aim was to lay waste the countryside," Ridenhour wrote. "Yes, yes, kill them all. Let God sort 'em out. The brass knew what they were doing. They knew what we were doing. It took me a long time to really understand that."

Ridenhour saw that Robert McNamara, the homo mathematicus, had reduced war to technology, people to data. McNamara had proclaimed that American supremacy in money and technology would overwhelm this stubborn third-world nation: Agent Orange, developed by researchers at the University of Chicago, the University of Hawaiʻi, Monsanto and Dow Chemical, would burn away Vietcong ground cover, just as napalm, invented in a secret laboratory by scientists from Harvard, Standard Oil and DuPont, would burn the Vietcong themselves. IBM computers predicted when and where the enemy would attack, and portable radar units and sweat and urine "sniffers" tracked him in the jungle. Unprecedented use of bombs and artillery were expected to win the war. (The US dropped on Vietnam more than three times the bomb tonnage it had dropped in all of World War II.) This focus on firepower made mass civilian killings inevitable.

Employing the managerial methods he'd learned at Harvard Business School and honed in the Air Force and at Ford, McNamara quantified the progress of the Vietnam War in bomb tonnage, people flows, infiltration rates, targets hit, weapons seized and, above all, body counts. Enemy body counts were set against the tally of American dead to create "kill ratios," by which the Pentagon measured success in battle, units distinguished themselves, and officers won promotions. Philip Caputo, a Marine Corps lieutenant in Vietnam, wrote: "Our mission was not to win terrain or seize positions, but simply to kill: to kill Communists and kill as many of them as possible. Stack 'em up like cordwood. Victory was a high body count, defeat a low kill ratio, war a matter of arithmetic. The pressure on unit commanders to produce enemy corpses was intense." Dead civilians were routinely reclassified as Vietcong to boost body counts.

"Gooks," "slopes," "dopes," "dinks," "slants," "slant-eyes"—Ridenhour recognized that the slurs routinely used by US troops allowed them to see Vietnamese as subhuman, even verminous, much as Nazis had degraded Jews. This, he saw, made killing easier. In the abstract, the dehumanization process could be rationalized as a cultural difference between East and West. "The Oriental doesn't put the same high price on life as does the Westerner," General Westmoreland famously said. "Life is plentiful, life is cheap in the Orient." On the front lines, the process was more direct. According to an Army psychiatrist who examined William Calley before the trial, "Lt. Calley states that he did not feel as if he were killing humans but rather that they were animals with whom one could not speak or reason." (The jury at Calley's trial was not allowed to hear this report.)

Ridenhour exposed My Lai in part because of his anger at its perpetrators. "I wanted to get those people," he remembered later. "I wanted to reveal what they did." He also spoke out because of his horror at the acts themselves. But perhaps the main cause of his whistleblowing was his anger and disgust at himself—for allowing himself to become part of the Plan. "I knew the first time I heard the story that My Lai was not some grunt's idea," he wrote in 1994. "These dirty motherfuckers, I thought. Look at what they've gotten me into."

After returning home, as he agonized over whether to blow the whistle, even his most trusted family members, friends and mentors urged him to "go along to get along," just as the Army had. "They all, almost to the person, said, 'Shut up. Shut up. This is none of your business—leave it alone.'" After he spoke out, most people asked him not why the soldiers of C Company had done what they'd done but why *he* had blown the whistle on them. They did not seem to recognize the disturbing similarities that Ridenhour saw between Nazi atrocities and the US murder of civilians in Vietnam, or to understand that both were often the direct result of geopolitical policy. In a 1994 article, "Jesus Was a Gook," he pointed out that the United States was running Vietnam-style counterinsurgency campaigns, some camouflaged as drug wars, throughout Central and South America, as well as in various parts of Asia and Africa. "In every case, amazingly enough, the enemy happen to be citizens, usually large numbers of them, who oppose the government we support. Gooks, I guess you'd say."

> The U.S. is nevertheless still orchestrating the slaughter of gooks throughout the world. Massacres, assassinations, disappeared ones, forced relocation of the rural poor, government "secure" zones, death squads, the torture of prisoners, the labeling of any and all opposition as "terrorists"—all have a familiar ring. Call it Nixon's revenge. It is Vietnamization that seems to work. We provide the money, the guns, the strategies, and plenty of on-the-scene advisors to our friends, the good gooks. They in turn steal most of the money, do the dirty work on the bad gooks, and if someone gets caught, take all the blame. A whole continent with gooks on one side and potential Lt. Calleys on the other. Gooks and Lt. Gooks. What could be more perfect in a world of perpetual war?

Ron Ridenhour had recognized a fundamental aspect of human behavior that lies at the heart of organized criminality. In theory, we say that people are responsible for their acts, and that orders from above are no excuse for evildoing. In practice, most of us act as if such orders absolved us of responsibility. Why do whistleblowers behave differently? In Ridenhour's case, the power to speak out derived from a larger view of humanity he had developed; he identified with the "gooks" of the world much as Allen Jones saw himself in the homeless and mentally ill. From the time he first spoke out until his death from a heart attack on a handball court at the age of fifty-two, Ridenhour spoke from his own conscience about the conscience of the country, drawing a moral from My Lai in hopes of creating a better America.

———

Around the time that Ernie Fitzgerald was settling into his new job at the Pentagon and Ronald Ridenhour was about to start jump school in Hawaii with the future murderers of My Lai, a fresh Harvard Law graduate began a battle with the world's largest auto maker.

Ralph Nader had been thinking about car safety since his teens, after several high school and college friends were killed or maimed in car accidents. He witnessed more wrecks during hitchhiking trips he took around the country. "Once in a while the truckers who picked me up would reach the scene of a crash before the ambulance or the police," he says today. "I began seeing how these vehicles crumbled, how people were thrown out of the car, or burned to a crisp after a fuel tank rupture. It made a deep impression on me." One accident in particular stuck in his mind, a simple 15-mph collision during which a sharp-edged glove compartment door had snapped open on impact and decapitated a child passenger. In 1955, in a law school term paper, he proposed to reassess liability in such cases. Against the car makers' contention that accidents were caused by driver error or poor highway conditions, Nader argued that companies that manufactured faulty or dangerous vehicles should themselves be held responsible for damages.

In 1963, after brief stints in the Army and working as an attorney in Hartford, Connecticut, Nader hitchhiked to Washington, settled in a boardinghouse, and joined the staff of Daniel Patrick Moynihan, assistant secretary of labor and future US senator. Moynihan, a strong advocate of highway safety, set Nader to study the issue further. Nader crystallized this work in *Unsafe at Any Speed: The Designed-In Dangers of the American Automobile*, published in November 1965, which expressed his vision of the industrial and governmental problems that plagued the automotive industry—the basis of his future consumer rights revolution.

Although automobile accidents took a $16 billion toll on American society— over 2 percent of the national GDP—that cost was not borne by the manufacturers, who were far more intent on making cars faster and flashier than safer to drive. In the book's opening chapter, Nader took aim at General Motors and its popular new compact car, the Corvair, which had been introduced in 1960 to compete with

Robert McNamara's Ford Falcon and the VW Beetle. Known as the "poor man's Porsche" for its power and sporty handling, the Corvair crashed a great deal, because its swing-axle design and rear-mounted engine made it susceptible to oversteering, spins and rollovers. It was so notoriously unstable that a GM suspension engineer had attempted to add an anti-roll bar to its design, but senior management had nixed the change because it would have made the car more expensive. By the time Nader began looking into the Corvair, more than a hundred lawsuits had been filed against GM for deaths and serious injuries caused by its many crashes. The car, he wrote, represented the triumph of "stylistic pornography over engineering integrity" and a massive ethical failure of government and society.

Nader denounced the President's Committee for Traffic Safety and the National Safety Council, two quasi-governmental bodies, as industry-funded front groups that papered over problems and perpetuated driver injuries and fatalities. Nader said that insurance executives, automotive repairmen and police, far from fighting traffic accidents, earned their living from them, and had become "a service industry" to injury and death. Government regulators, automotive engineers, doctors and lawyers, by ignoring the predictable carnage, were violating the basic ethical codes of their professions. To reverse this moral decline, Nader called for a renaissance in professional and civic responsibility: "The roots of the unsafe vehicle problem are so entrenched that the situation can be improved only by the forging of new instruments of citizen action," he wrote in *Unsafe at Any Speed*. "A great problem of contemporary life is how to control the power of economic interests which ignore the harmful effects of their applied science and technology." Much of Nader's future work would be devoted to forging and using these new instruments of civic action, with fervor and ingenuity.

One such new instrument was whistleblowing. In fact, in his denunciation of the automobile industry Nader himself had become an external whistleblower like Allen Jones, an interested outsider who learns from internal sources about wrongdoing, and makes it known to a wider audience. Nader had received crucial information about the dangerous design features of the Corvair and other cars from two dozen internal whistleblowers, most of them automotive engineers at major car companies. "Some would send me information in plain envelopes, and I never found out who they were," Nader remembers. "Others I'd meet with surreptitiously, in airports. It was ridiculous when you think of it now." Soon Nader went a step further, and became what might be called a "meta-whistleblower"—a megaphone, consultant and advocate for whistleblowers everywhere.

Unsafe at Any Speed was widely reviewed. The automobile industry issued formal rebuttals of Nader's critiques. Partly in response to the debate set off by the book, Senator Abraham Ribicoff, who had held hearings on traffic safety the previous year, organized further hearings in February 1966, and called Nader to testify. Later that year, largely because of the hearings and Nader's continuing activism, Congress would create a new, cabinet-level Department of Transportation, pass two epoch-making auto safety laws, and form a new agency to set and enforce auto safety standards, eventually called the National Highway Traffic Safety Administration. Familiar features such as seat belts, shatter-resistant windshields, safe door mechanisms and headrests, as well as crash testing and manufacturer recalls of defective cars, would stem from these developments.

Since his facts were hard to refute, General Motors hired a private detective agency headed by Vincent Gillen, a former FBI special agent, to dig up compromising information on Nader—"his politics, his marital status, his friends, his women, boys, etc., drinking, dope, jobs, in fact all facets of his life," as Gillen instructed his investigators. (When GM denied that they had requested such prying into Nader's private life, Gillen revealed that he had taped his conversations with the company.) Claiming that they were vetting Nader for an important job, private detectives questioned over fifty of his relatives, friends, former teachers and colleagues at work. Nader and his family received late-night phone threats. He began to suspect that his phone had been tapped, that he was being followed, and that the attractive young women who had suddenly begun to throw themselves at him in public were sex lures.

Newspapers got wind of the story and published scathing articles about GM's attempts to discredit Nader. An outraged Ribicoff and other members of Congress called for a DOJ investigation, and held further hearings. GM's clumsy stalking made Nader front-page news and turned *Unsafe at Any Speed*, whose initial sales had been modest, into a bestseller. Nader eventually sued the company for invasion of privacy and won a settlement of $425,000, at that time the largest in the history of privacy law.

He used the money to fund other consumer protection initiatives and investigations. Supporters and fellow activists, many of them law students, flocked to Washington, becoming what the *Washington Post* was first to call Nader's Raiders. Teams of Raiders began to infiltrate government agencies and their related industries, sometimes as employees and summer interns; helped by internal whistleblowers, they produced seventeen detailed reports/exposés, which revealed that the FTC, the FDA, the USDA and other agencies suffered widespread corruption, excessive secrecy, toxic partisan politics, and regulatory capture by the industries they were tasked with policing. Time and again Nader demonstrated his central thesis: that large corporations, with their vast wealth and political power, were single-mindedly growing their profits at the expense of the well-being of American citizens.

Nader's denunciations struck a nerve. Since the end of World War II, many Americans were increasingly concerned about corporate power; beginning in 1950, a series of influential books explored how large corporations were curbing individual conscience and personal freedom. David Riesman's *The Lonely Crowd* described how "tradition-directed" and "inner-directed" individuals who followed ancient societal norms or the teachings of their elders were giving way to "other-directed" people who molded their beliefs to match their peer groups and the media, and whose yearning for approval enabled them to thrive at big firms. William Whyte's *The Organization Man* argued that corporations demanded complete loyalty from employees at the expense of individuality, and created an atmosphere in which the group rather than the individual was considered the source of creativity. C. Wright Mills's *The Power Elite* and Vance Packard's *The Hidden Persuaders*, as well as Sloan Wilson's novel *The Man in the Gray Flannel Suit*, examined other insidious aspects of corporate and governmental control. Critics also condemned the conscience-numbing effects of large organizations. Summing up several decades of his work on obedience and dissent, Erich Fromm, the German-born social psychologist, wrote that "the organization man has lost the capacity to disobey, he is not even aware of the fact that he obeys. At this point in history the capacity to doubt, to criticize and to disobey may be all that stands between a future for mankind and the end of civilization."

In his 1965 sermon "The Transformed Nonconformist," Martin Luther King Jr. observed that "'Do not conform' is difficult advice in a generation when crowd pressures have unconsciously conditioned our minds and feet to move to the rhythmic drumbeat of the status quo. . . . Success, recognition, and conformity are the by-words of the modern world where everyone seems to crave the anesthetizing security of being identified with the majority."

Ralph Nader saw how bureaucratic practices at the major car manufacturers could dull individual morality, particularly after Robert McNamara, together with the other nine Air Force Whiz Kids, was hired to remake an ailing Ford Motor Company. McNamara and his team were pioneers of managerialism, a movement rooted in the Industrial Revolution that had taken on new rigor at Harvard Business School in the 1930s. Managerialism arose from the twin convictions that organizations should be run according to scientific, quantitative principles, and that professional managers skilled in these principles were the best leaders for any large organization, whether a corporation, a hospital, a university, an NGO or an army. "Management is, in the end, the most creative of all arts—for its medium is human talent itself," McNamara said in a 1967 college convocation address. "Management is the gate through which social, political, economical, technological change— indeed change in every dimension—is rationally and effectively spread through society. Some critics, today, keep worrying that our democratic, free societies are being overmanaged. The real truth is precisely the opposite. As paradoxical as it may sound, the real threat to democracy comes from undermanagement."

Firm in their faith in the new corporate gospel, McNamara and his colleagues centralized procurement at Ford, computerized accounting and inventory management, and quantified each step of the production process. By building hierarchies of loyal deputies throughout the organization, they ensured a steady flow of data from the production areas to the firm's leaders. They gave particular power to the finance and marketing departments, from which the future leaders of the firm were often recruited, including a star salesman from Pennsylvania named Lee Iacocca. The key tools of the new scientific management included clear numeric goals to incentivize workers, data gathering to measure their performance, and the wide-spread use of cost-benefit analysis to make strategic decisions.

McNamara's myopic focus on numbers and abstractions caused much needless bloodletting on American roadways, as it later did in Vietnam. The Pinto fiasco, a consequence of the goal-driven, cost-benefit culture McNamara instilled at Ford, shows why. The Pinto was a small, cheap compact car designed by his successor, the hard-charging, cigar-chomping Lee Iacocca, to compete with inexpensive foreign imports. Iacocca decreed that the Pinto would weigh two thousand pounds and cost $2,000—not one pound or one dollar more. The Pinto, first produced in 1971, was rushed from initial design to production in twenty-five months, just over half the normal time. In the process, the gas tank was inadvertently placed too close to the rear bumper, creating a serious fire hazard in rear-end collisions. In fact, eighteen months before the first Pinto left the assembly line, Ford engineers had spotted the flaw and proposed several simple modifications, which would have cost between $0.22 and $6.00 per car. Yet since these fixes would have increased the Pinto's list price and delayed its launch, proposing them to the fiery Iacocca was widely viewed as career suicide.

Instead, Ford engineers performed a cost-benefit analysis titled "Fatalities Associated with Crash-Induced Fuel Leaks and Fires," which considered two courses of action: redesign the Pinto to fix the flawed fuel system, or make the car with the current design and deal with the resulting traffic deaths as they came. In tidy rows of figures, the authors showed that design changes would cost $137 million, while the cost of burn deaths and serious injuries—primarily legal fees estimated at $200,000 per fatality and $67,000 per serious injury—would be $49.5 million. Ford chose the deaths. And Ford's approach was no anomaly. That same year, General Motors drew up a similar cost-benefit study to assess fire risks in the fuel systems of several of its cars, and similarly concluded that driver deaths were the preferable option. The study's only uncertainty was how many victims had actually died by fire and how many had been killed by the initial impact. "The condition of the bodies almost precludes making this determination," one author wrote.

A cost-benefit analysis calculates the price of various courses of action in net present dollars and mandates the selection of the lowest-cost option. It is a useful tool in management. Like body count, however, it requires assigning a specific value, usually modest, to human life. At his cabin in the Pennsylvania woods, Allen

Jones, describing the cold logic of pharmaceutical executives as they weighed the potential profits from illegal sales of dangerous drugs against the costs of dealing in court with the victims of those drugs, added that he wasn't sure whether anyone was so diabolical as to write down their reckoning. The Ford and GM cost-benefit analyses are his answer. And while these documents came to light only many years after they were written, Ralph Nader had already spoken of the "Medea-like [sic]" capacity of a corporation "to paralyze conscience, initiative, and proper concern for people outside the organization."

On January 30, 1971, in the midst of the Calley trial and Ernie Fitzgerald's fight for reinstatement, Nader held a "Conference on Professional Responsibility" in Washington, DC. Ernest Fitzgerald and other pioneering whistleblowers spoke at the gathering, along with scholars, lawyers and lawmakers like Senator William Proxmire, Fitzgerald's congressional ally, all of whom recognized the vital role of the whistleblower in fighting fraud and fostering social justice. Ronald Ridenhour's story and several other whistleblower narratives were told, to serve as role models for ethical action. The proceedings of the conference were published the following year in a book, *Whistle Blowing*. Both conference and book helped redefine the whistleblower as a model citizen.

Since Elizabethan times, "to whistle" and "to blow" had meant to reveal secret information, but the words were ambiguous: the whistleblower could be either a friend or an ill-intentioned informer. By the early twentieth century, "to blow the whistle" and the compound noun "whistle blower" referred either to blowers of literal whistles—police and umpires—or to people who attempted to stop illegal or immoral activity by making a public fuss about it. Sportswriter Jack Miley wrote in 1936 of a disillusioned pro wrestling promoter, Jacob Pfefer, who had turned on his sport: "Jake is a whistle-blower, which is unforgivable. Not only that, but he twee-tles his cop-caller with thick Yiddish overtones." In 1938, the *Washington Post* used the term to describe a former Tammany Hall leader who revealed the political machine's illicit operations to the Manhattan district attorney, "despite the scorn with which the testimony of a 'whistle blower' usually is received."

Through the 1960s, the "whistle blower" could also be a somewhat seedy witness who aimed to stop real wrongdoing. In a 1958 article in a local Ohio newspaper, a woman described as a "witch" and an attempted blackmailer was also called a "whistleblower" because she had revealed a prostitution ring. In 1960, a union rival called Teamster boss Jimmy Hoffa a "whistle blower" as well as a "notorious wink" and an "opportunist." But gradually the positive connotations of the term grew more pronounced. Arthur Schlesinger Jr., writing in 1965, lamented his failure, as a member of President Kennedy's cabinet, to "blow the whistle" on the "nonsense" of the disastrous Bay of Pigs invasion of Cuba. In 1970, the *New York Times* used "whistle-blower" approvingly, to celebrate a principled councilman from the Bronx who had courageously denounced the secret machinations of the New York City Council and was subsequently ousted. A series of widely publicized whistleblowers of the late 1960s and early 1970s, including Frank Serpico at the NYPD, the anonymous "Deep Throat" who helped reveal the Watergate scandal (later revealed to be senior FBI official W. Mark Felt), and Karen Silkwood at the Kerr-McGee nuclear facility, each the subject of high-profile books and films, spread both the meme of whistleblowing and an awareness of its positive potential.

In the opening address to his landmark 1971 conference, Nader linked whistle-blowing to the courageous rejection of British tyranny and oppression by the Founders, and to the triumph of individual conscience over arbitrary government action. This same resolve was now needed, he said, to free America from new forms of tyranny and oppression by large organizations. Nader argued that the best way to fight organizational wrongdoing was from within. "Corporate employees are among the first to know about industrial dumping of mercury or fluoride sludge into waterways, defectively designed automobiles, undisclosed adverse effects of prescription drugs or pesticides. They are the first to grasp the technical capabilities to prevent existing product or pollution hazards. But they are very often the last to speak out." He blamed this problem on groupthink, hierarchy and obedience to authority within organizations, which made ordinary dissent into an act of "uncommon courage." Nader concluded with a call for a new "ethic of whistle blowing," which, "if carefully defined and protected by law, can become another of those adaptive, self-implementing mechanisms which mark the relative difference between a free society that relies on free institutions and a closed society that depends on authoritarian institutions."

The remainder of the conference raised a number of critical questions about whistleblowing, and sketched ways to turn isolated acts of individual conscience into a widespread movement for social justice. William Proxmire proposed "a peaceful professional revolution against the massive buildup of political and economic power in the executive branch of government, and specifically in the Department of Defense." Robert Townsend, a retired president of the Avis car rental company and fierce critic of corporate bureaucracy, secrecy and dishonesty, denounced the leaders of large corporations as having been so "distracted and corrupted by luxuries and the trappings of corporate success, [that] they have no time to consider fundamental values like honesty, truth and justice." Arthur S. Miller, a professor of constitutional law, noted the existence of ancient qui tam statutes and stressed the importance of passing new laws to ensure that whistleblowers could speak without endangering their careers. The conference ended by introducing a score of lesser-known whistleblowers as instances of individual conscience clashing with organizational malfeasance in numerous industries.

Robert Vaughn, a professor of constitutional law and former Nader's Raider who attended the conference, says it marked a new stage in the evolution of whistleblowing. "Ralph Nader helped to undermine the old loyalties to boss and organization, and to give public servants and corporate workers alike a new idea of duty and responsibility, a higher loyalty to society." Further successful books and films on whistleblowing soon followed, increasing the intellectual weight and charisma of the nascent movement.

Corporate America was alarmed by Nader's initiatives. Soon after the Conference on Professional Responsibility, James Roche, the CEO of General Motors, denounced both Nader and his whistleblowers as anti-American subversives. "Some of the enemies of business now encourage an employee to be disloyal to the enterprise," he told a meeting of executives in Detroit. "They want to create suspicion and disharmony and pry into the proprietary interests of business. However this is labeled—industrial espionage, whistle blowing or professional responsibility—it is another tactic for spreading disunity and creating conflict." A more far-reaching reaction came six months later, from Lewis Powell, a corporate lawyer from Richmond, Virginia, who had made a fortune defending tobacco companies and sat on eleven corporate boards. At the request of the US Chamber of Commerce, Powell wrote a memorandum that began with a call to battle: "No thoughtful person can question that the American economic system is under broad attack." Powell singled out Nader as the most serious threat: "The passion that rules in him—and he is a passionate man—is aimed at smashing utterly the target of his hatred, which is corporate power." But attacks on the corporation and on capitalism itself were coming from other opponents as well: reporters, politicians, scientists, artists, religious leaders and judges.

To combat this pernicious assault, Powell proposed that corporations build their political power and burnish their public image with a series of carefully planned and well-funded initiatives, to be coordinated by the Chamber of Commerce. In academia, the Chamber should form a "faculty of scholars" with sympathetic views. The Chamber should likewise assemble a staff of "eminent scholars, writers and speakers" to argue the corporation's case in the media and before the general public, as well as carry on "surveillance" of the media and demand equal time for their positions. Powell urged the extensive use of political lobbying in Washington, because business must recognize that "political power is necessary; that such power must be assidously [sic] cultivated; and that when necessary, it must be used aggressively and with determination." If progressive lawyers like Ralph Nader had formed centers for law in the public interest, then corporate lawyers should, Powell argued, create legal centers funded by the business community to press the interests of business. Finally, he urged American corporations to cultivate judges: "Under our constitutional system, especially with an activist-minded Supreme Court, the judiciary may be the most important instrument for social, economic and political change."

Two months after he wrote this memo, Powell himself was nominated to the Supreme Court by Richard Nixon, who told him that joining the court was his patriotic duty. Powell went on to pen a series of legal arguments that, in line with his memorandum, strengthened the legal status of the corporation. Most notable of these, the 1978 decision in *First National Bank of Boston v. Bellotti*, gave corporations a right to free speech under the First Amendment, and supplied crucial arguments for several of the court's later pro-corporate rulings, including *Citizens United v. Federal Election Commission*.

As Nader, Fitzgerald and the other participants at the Conference on Professional Responsibility were discussing the theory of whistleblowing in Washington, a senior military analyst on the other coast, in Santa Monica, California, was putting it into practice, in one of history's highest-stakes whistleblowing acts. Daniel Ellsberg had already made multiple copies of a massive, top-secret study of the Vietnam War, which came to be known as the Pentagon Papers. In November 1969, he began to release it, first to five members of Congress, and then, when the congressmen balked at revealing the explosive data, to the press.

Even some friends called Ellsberg "dangerous." Unlike Fitzgerald and Ridenhour, who were at the periphery of the military-industrial complex, Ellsberg worked in the control room. Since 1958 he had been a security analyst at the RAND Corporation, a think tank based in Santa Monica and funded by the Air Force. There he developed the ideas of his Harvard economics PhD on decision making in uncertainty, analyzing the fraught choice of whether—and how—to wage nuclear war. RAND was a hotbed of thinking about radical questions like this, never before faced by humanity. Some of the brightest minds in physics, mathematics and economics, including twenty Nobel laureates, worked there in the 1950s and 1960s. When Eisenhower, in his farewell military-industrial-complex speech, warned of public policy becoming "the captive of a scientific-technological elite," he likely had RAND in mind. (Certainly Stanley Kubrick did in his film *Dr. Strangelove*, in which the mad ex-Nazi scientist working for the BLAND Corporation and willing to destroy the world in a nuclear war was modeled on several Cold War strategists at RAND.)

One of RAND's approaches to the problem of nuclear brinksmanship was game theory, a method of determining ideal outcomes in uncertain contests invented by brilliant Hungarian polymath John von Neumann. Best known in one of its thought problems, the prisoner's dilemma, game theory generally implied a model of mankind as totally rational, selfish, suspicious, cynical, ambitious and greedy— beings who always seek to extract the greatest personal advantage from any competitive situation. Though many theorists recognized this was a simplified model of the human mind, they found it a useful representation of the minds of Americans and Soviets in a nuclear showdown. Game theory and the related field of decision theory influenced the evolution of the two main doctrines of nuclear conflict in the US, deterrence by mutually assured destruction and nuclear utilization target selection, better known by their apt acronyms, MAD and NUTS. Thanks to John von Neumann's *Theory of Games and Economic Behavior*, the game theory approach to human psychology also became influential in economics.

Ellsberg, the brilliant, data-driven, aggressive, ambitious economist, seemed a perfect fit both with RAND game and decision theorists and with McNamara's data-driven team of systems analysts in Washington. At Harvard and at RAND, he had absorbed McNamara's heady blend of economic analysis and real-world engagement. He was a self-defined "cold warrior" whose fervent anti-Communist beliefs were forged in the Berlin blockade of 1948 and the Soviet coup in Czechoslovakia that same year, and tempered during the Korean War, which prompted him to enlist in the Marine Corps. Holding multiple security clearances beyond top secret, Ellsberg ranged at will in the nation's most highly guarded data, advising the Department of Defense, the Department of State and the White House on nuclear war plans and crisis decision making. During the Cuban Missile Crisis in October 1962, he was urgently summoned to Washington to serve on high-level work groups that advised the National Security Council. Two years later, he joined the Defense Department, to analyze what was then a low-level US engagement in Vietnam.

On August 4, 1964, Ellsberg's first day at work in the Pentagon, the Gulf of Tonkin incident occurred—or rather, didn't: North Vietnamese gunboats appeared to launch torpedoes at a US Navy cruiser, but within hours the Navy commander reported that the torpedoes had actually been sonar glitches. The real story, however, was concealed from Congress and the American public; that same day, in a speech replete with lies, Lyndon Johnson accused the North Vietnamese of carrying out an unprovoked attack, and soon used the incident as a pretext for open warfare in Vietnam. Early the next year, when McNamara wanted to justify a heavy new bombing campaign, Ellsberg stayed up all night searching for evidence of Vietcong atrocities against Americans. Finally, at about 4:00 a.m., he learned of the deaths of two American advisers—possibly the only such fatalities to have occurred in Vietnam until that time—which McNamara then used to convince Johnson to escalate the war. Even as Johnson assured the nation that "we seek no wider war," Ellsberg was helping to prepare secret plans for a massive escalation of US military force.

Ellsberg had no illusions about the war in Vietnam. He had visited the country in 1961, as part of a high-level Pentagon task force, and had frank, discouraging conversations with veteran commanders and read stacks of field reports that had, as he later wrote, "the smell of rot, of failure." Later, as a State Department adviser, he walked point on combat patrols through forests and rice paddies, and took fast, dangerous drives with legendary Vietnam specialist John Paul Vann, a grenade in his lap and an M16 pointed out the window. By the time of the Gulf of Tonkin incident, Ellsberg knew that Vietnam was a war of futile brutality that the US would eventually lose. Nevertheless he did his job, and ferreted out atrocities to justify an escalation that he totally opposed. Ellsberg calls this work "the most shameful act of my life."

Ellsberg returned to RAND in the summer of 1967, where he joined a team of military officers, historians and security analysts charged with writing the *true* history of the Vietnam War. Despite his confident public façade, Robert McNamara was dismayed at the seemingly endless series of errors that had led the United States into the quagmire in Southeast Asia. He created a task force to document these errors in a top-secret study titled "United States–Vietnam Relations, 1945–1967," later known as the Pentagon Papers. Using vast quantities of CIA reports, State Department cables and other original documents, it examined the decisions that had led to the impasse in Vietnam, and the lessons to be learned from them. McNamara concealed the project from President Lyndon Johnson, Secretary of State Dean Rusk and National Security Advisor Walt Rostow. The report remained so secret that it was omitted from the list of classified documents at RAND, and when an inventory of documents was being prepared in April 1969, Ellsberg removed it from the safe in his office and rolled it around the halls of RAND in a grocery cart.

By late 1968, the project was completed, in forty-seven volumes. Ellsberg, one of only three people to have access to all seven thousand pages of the study, had read them by the middle of 1969. He later called the Pentagon Papers "a continuous record of governmental deception and fatally unwise decision-making, cloaked by secrecy, under four presidents."

Ellsberg was still a Pentagon insider actively prosecuting the war. Yet as US involvement in Vietnam escalated, he had developed a parallel personality that tended to pacifism. (Unlike absolute pacifists, Ellsberg believed, as he believes today, that military self-defense was appropriate in exceptional circumstances, such as World War II.) His insider's knowledge of the realities of the defense establishment broke his faith in the honesty of the highest civilian and military leadership. He saw irrefutable evidence that the "bomber gap" and the "missile gap" that had driven the feverish US Cold War arms buildup had been fabrications by Air Force and SAC intelligence officials to increase fear among Americans and amp up the arms trade. Likewise, since his insider role in the Gulf of Tonkin incident and his time in Vietnam, he had known that the Vietnam War was causing pointless death and suffering. By mid-1969, the Pentagon Papers confirmed his worst suspicions, and suggested that the secrecy, lies and death were likely to continue. By then Mc-Namara had resigned, Johnson had refused to run for reelection, and Nixon had defeated Johnson's incumbent vice president Hubert Humphrey on a campaign promise of "peace with honor" to end the war in Vietnam. Yet Ellsberg learned from his sources in the White House that Nixon was actually planning a further escalation, and even considering the use of tactical nuclear weapons. "The history in the Pentagon Papers offered no promise of changing this pattern from within the bureaucracy," Ellsberg wrote later. "Only a better-informed Congress and public might act to avert indefinite prolongation and further escalation of the war."

Ellsberg's metamorphosis from Pentagon war hawk to near-pacifist truth teller is one of the most striking transformations in whistleblowing history. A few people gave him clear reasons to renounce his old life entirely, to consider the pacifist position, and eventually to fight wholeheartedly against the war. Janaki Tschannerl, a peace activist from Madras, explained Mahatma Gandhi's view that since nearly all evil required the obedience or acquiescence of countless people, the only appropriate response to it was firm, open, nonviolent resistance, even at the risk of one's life. "Janaki inspired me to think of truth-telling (we didn't use the word 'whistleblowing' back then) as a form of nonviolent civil disobedience, of Gandhian *satyagrahi*," Ellsberg remembers.

Over several days of intense conversation, Tschannerl provided the intellectual and historical pedigree for the antiwar movement that the rigorous rationalist Ellsberg seemed to need before he could be persuaded to espouse open dissent. Like a thesis adviser, Tschannerl set him texts to read. Ellsberg pored over the essay "On the Duty of Civil Disobedience" by Henry David Thoreau, who had protested against the Mexican War by refusing to pay a poll tax that was funding it, and had gone to prison. Thoreau argued that a civilian's obedience to leaders in an unjust cause was the equivalent to a soldier's service in an unjust war, and must be refused. Ellsberg studied Gandhi's acts and writings, and other pacifist classics like Barbara Deming's *Revolution and Equilibrium.* He also considered what further inactivity on his part would mean. He read how Albert Speer, the prominent Nazi architect, admitted his guilt for Nazi atrocities because he had failed to take personal responsibility for his regime's acts, and willfully suppressed his conscience: "Being in a position to know and nevertheless shunning knowledge creates direct responsibility for the consequences," Speer wrote. Tschannerl also helped Ellsberg to see the Gandhian influence on the civil rights movement, and encouraged him to read *Stride Toward Freedom* and other writings by Martin Luther King. Tschannerl even proposed to introduce him to King, whose comprehension of and early resistance to the Vietnam War stunned Ellsberg, but King was assassinated before they could meet.

The last, dramatic act in Ellsberg's transformation took place at a peace conference at Quaker-founded Haverford College in Pennsylvania, where several young men about to be jailed for draft evasion publicly explained their repudiation of the war in Vietnam as an act of civil disobedience. These face-to-face encounters shattered Ellsberg's long-held stereotypes of draft evaders as cowards and traitors. He was struck by their thoughtfulness, patriotism and willingness to sacrifice, their loyalty not just to an abstract goal of national security but to higher principles of peace and human welfare. The last speaker was Randy Kehler, who spoke with quiet enthusiasm about their many friends who had already been imprisoned and how eager and proud he was to be joining them, in full confidence that the others present would carry on the struggle when he was gone.

Kehler's words overwhelmed Ellsberg. In tears he staggered to his feet and made his way to a men's room outside the auditorium, where he cried convulsively for over an hour. "When Randy said, 'I'm going to jail,' it felt as if an ax had split my head and my heart in two," Ellsberg says today. "Clearly my life had split—before and after were very different. But it was also a physical sensation, as if I'd been stunned by an ax-blow. I cried hysterically at the feeling of what my country had come to: that the best thing which Randy Kehler, or my son, or any other young man could do for America was to go to prison."

Kehler had shown him the way forward. Ellsberg was ready to leave his old life behind. He was ready to go to prison, perhaps for the rest of his life. He was finally free to act. He vowed never again to take part in killing simply because he was ordered to kill—such orders had lost their authority for him. Nor would he continue to lie about the killing, as he'd done for many years. "I'm not going to be part of this lying machine, this cover-up, this murder, anymore," he wrote afterward.

Critically, Ellsberg already knew the power of whistleblowing. In early 1968, he had shown to Senator Robert Kennedy a top-secret, "eyes only" report by the chairman of the Joint Chiefs of Staff for President Johnson, requesting that 206,000 more American troops be sent to Vietnam—an escalation that Johnson had publicly promised would never happen. When the *New York Times* published a detailed account of the proposed troop buildup, which the paper had received from another whistleblower, the outcry in Congress caused by that disclosure startled him, and made him see his civic responsibilities in a new light. Johnson's ability to escalate the war, Ellsberg suddenly realized, was predicated on insiders' not breaking the code of secrecy and revealing his lies. In such circumstances, truth telling could alert the president that he had lost the power to compel silence and keep certain secrets from the American public. Ellsberg saw that leaking was not necessarily treacherous, as he had previously believed, but could be an act of patriotism.

In mid-March 1968, Ellsberg made his first leak, when he passed secret and top-secret reports and cables to Neil Sheehan at the *New York Times*. The resulting news stories caused a sensation with their revelations that US forces had been unprepared for the Tet Offensive, had distorted enemy troop numbers, and aimed for further advances, with additional troops, into Cambodia, Laos and North Vietnam. Johnson promptly relieved General Westmoreland of his command in Vietnam, and days later announced not only an end to bombing in parts of North Vietnam but also his desire to open negotiations with Hanoi. That November, Nixon won the presidential election in part by promising peace. The war seemed to be coming to an end.

Most Americans wanted the war to end. The majority of South Vietnamese did too—no matter who won. Yet the killing continued. Searching for answers to the origins of this war, which seemed increasingly indefensible, Ellsberg reread the early volumes of the Pentagon Papers, covering the years from 1945 to 1960. He saw how the US had urged and funded the French colonial power in its repression of a Vietnamese national independence movement backed by overwhelming popular support. How the US had repeated all the blunders, lies and follies of the French, and betrayed Ho Chi Minh, a genuine patriot and freedom fighter backed by the majority of North and South Vietnamese. History showed Ellsberg that America was not protecting South Vietnam from foreign aggression by the North—*we* were that foreign aggressor, committing mass murder in Southeast Asia.

In the summer of 1969, Ellsberg learned that Nixon, despite his public promises, had no intention of leaving Vietnam, and in fact was considering further escalation—mining harbors, carpet bombing, even the use of nuclear weapons. Immersed in the lessons of the Pentagon Papers, Ellsberg recognized that the historical pattern followed by four presidents since 1945—all believing they could eventually cow the North Vietnamese with threats and violence, none wanting the war to end on their watch—was continuing in a fifth. Ellsberg felt more than ever an urgent moral imperative to take action to end the war, by whatever means necessary.

At the prompting of Tony Russo, a close friend and former RAND analyst who had been fired for writing damning reports on the widespread torture of enemy prisoners, Ellsberg decided to release the Pentagon Papers, the compendium of official lies on which the war had been built. But unlike his first leak to the *New York Times* the previous year, he would make this disclosure in his own name.

In October 1969, Ellsberg smuggled the first volumes past the RAND security guards. With Russo's help he photocopied them night after night. After failing to persuade prominent senators, including William Fulbright and George McGovern, to release the papers, he gave them to the *New York Times*, which began publishing excerpts and analysis in June 1971. When Nixon's attorney general, John Mitchell, forced the *Times* to halt publication with an injunction claiming that they caused "irreparable injury to the defense interests of the United States," Ellsberg and his wife, Patricia, in hiding to elude a massive FBI manhunt, passed a copy of the papers to the *Washington Post*, and successively to seventeen other newspapers as new injunctions arrived. Finally, on June 28, 1971, Ellsberg surrendered himself at the federal courthouse in Boston. His statement to reporters captured his new mentality, and is a crux of modern whistleblowing: "I felt that as an American citizen, as a responsible citizen, I could no longer cooperate in concealing this information from the American public. I did this clearly at my own jeopardy and I am prepared to answer to all the consequences of this decision."

Ellsberg and Russo were indicted by a grand jury in Los Angeles on multiple counts of theft, conspiracy and novel non-espionage offenses under the Espionage Act of 1917, a harsh, anachronistic law originally passed during World War I to prosecute German spies. Ellsberg faced 115 years in prison.

In Daniel Ellsberg, the world saw its first high-level whistleblower, a researcher at Harvard, RAND and MIT, an adviser to cabinet secretaries, the Joint Chiefs of Staff and the president, whose eloquence and mastery of the facts made him as impressive to the general public as he was difficult for the administration to dismiss. Unlike more recent defendants in Espionage Act cases, Ellsberg was granted bail and remained at liberty before and during his trial. He appeared frequently on television and in the press, providing Americans with a vivid image of a person of conscience who had thrown away a glittering career to tell the world the truth about the war.

Ellsberg's revelation triggered a rapid-fire series of investigations, legal decisions, low crime and high theater. The White House continued to claim that the publication of the Pentagon Papers had caused irreparable harm to US interests; Nixon accused the *Times* of giving "aid and comfort to the enemy" by publishing them.

Nevertheless, on June 30, 1971, the Supreme Court upheld the *Times'* First Amendment rights to do so. "In the First Amendment the Founding Fathers gave the free press the protection it must have to fulfill its essential role in our democracy," wrote Justice Hugo Black for the majority. "The press was to serve the governed, not the governors. And paramount among the responsibilities of a free press is the duty to prevent any part of the government from deceiving the people and sending them off to distant lands to die of foreign fevers and foreign shot and shell."

The trial of Ellsberg and Tony Russo began in February 1972, in Los Angeles Federal Courthouse. From the beginning, during jury selection, it raised thorny questions of dissent and obedience, conscience and conformity that are central to the whistleblowing act. Psychiatrist Ralph "Romey" Greenson, who served as a consultant to Ellsberg's lawyers, advised disqualifying middle-aged professional men from the jury during voir dire: "These are people who in the course of their lives might possibly have sacrificed principle for the sake of career, for the sake of family, and they lived with that compromise, and they will have a lot of disdain, even contempt for two men who did it for the sake of principle and took the risk." To avoid other anti-whistleblower bias, Ellsberg's legal team supplied Judge William Byrne with a list of 268 questions to ask the jurors. They included: "Do you believe that overpermissiveness on the part of parents and schools contributes to the breakdown of order in the country?" "Do you believe the government of the United States should have the right to censor the news?" "Do you believe it was correct for many Americans to help free black slaves prior to the Civil War even though it was against the law at that time?" "Do you believe that Jesus Christ was justified in throwing the money changers out of the temple by force?" (Judge Byrne did not allow the questions.)

The prosecution, in turn, aimed to exclude prospective jurors who had antimilitary or counterculture leanings, as well as ACLU members and readers of publications that had published Ellsberg's articles or extracts of the Pentagon Papers.

After a suspension, the trial resumed in January 1973, and lasted four months. Few observers felt they could guess how it would end. On the one hand, by releasing the Pentagon Papers, Ellsberg had revealed the war as a systematic lie perpetrated by the US government, which seemed highly relevant to the public's ability to decide whether to support or condemn the war. On the other hand, Ellsberg and Russo admitted having released top-secret documents and violated numerous confidentiality agreements they had signed with RAND and with the US government.

Prosecutors had also insisted, and Justice Byrne had agreed, that the jury be instructed not to consider the larger questions raised by the defendant's acts: the morality of the Vietnam War, the public's right to know, the freedom of the press, or the Supreme Court's recent First Amendment decision in favor of the *Times*. Ellsberg still remembers his shock when the prosecution prevented him from explaining his motives for releasing the papers. When his lawyer asked him straightforwardly why he'd done it, a prosecutor objected that the question was "immaterial," and Judge Byrne sustained. "My lawyer was stunned," Ellsberg remembers. "He told Judge Byrne that he'd never heard of a case where a defendant wasn't allowed to tell the jury why he'd done what he did. 'Well, you're hearing one now,' Byrne said." This restrictive interpretation of the Espionage Act presaged subsequent espionage prosecutions after 9/11, which forbade Chelsea Manning, Tom Drake and other national security whistleblowers from explaining why they blew the whistle.

The trial ended abruptly, in a series of dramatic revelations. On April 27, a grim-faced Justice Byrne revealed to Ellsberg's attorneys that White House operatives Gordon Liddy and Howard Hunt, later imprisoned for their role in the Watergate burglary, had on orders from the White House broken into the office of Lewis Fielding, a California psychiatrist who had treated Ellsberg, in an attempt to discredit or to blackmail him. A few days later, Byrne informed the court that, while Ellsberg's trial had been in session, he had met twice with top Nixon aide John Ehrlichman and once with Nixon himself, and had tentatively been offered the directorship of the FBI, reportedly his life's ambition. (Nixon implied that he hoped Byrne would end the Ellsberg-Russo trial soon.) Finally, on May 10, Byrne told the court that the FBI had illegally recorded conversations between Ellsberg and Morton Halperin—the first public acknowledgment that the Nixon administration had used wiretaps against its political enemies.

The next day, after learning that the FBI could not find the records and logs of those wiretaps, Judge Byrne dismissed all charges against Ellsberg and Russo. "The totality of the circumstances of this case which I have only briefly sketched offend

'a sense of justice,'" he told the courtroom. "The bizarre events have incurably infected the prosecution of this case." Byrne dismissed the charges with prejudice,
meaning that the defendants could never be tried again on them, because he felt
they might not receive a fair trial under the current administration.

With this abrupt conclusion, the Ellsberg trial left unresolved several critical
questions concerning his whistleblowing. How far was the US government entitled
to commit crimes, carry on illicit domestic surveillance, even wage wars, in secret?
Did an individual have the right, or even a duty, to violate that secrecy, in order to
inform the public of illegal acts by their own leaders? In later years, Ellsberg was
increasingly recognized as a hero and a prototypical whistleblower: someone willing
to risk his job, his family's well-being and his freedom to end an unjust war. Atten-
tive readers of the Pentagon Papers saw that they had been no threat whatsoever to
national security: their chronicle of the war ended a year before Nixon was elected.
Erwin Griswold, who as solicitor general had told the Supreme Court that the Pentagon Papers caused "grave and immediate danger to the security of the United
States," later admitted that he had "never seen any trace of a threat to the national
security" from their publication. "It quickly becomes apparent to any person who
has considerable experience with classified material that there is massive overclassification and that the principal concern of the classifiers is not with national security,
but rather with governmental embarrassment of one sort or another."

Immediately after the charges against him were dismissed, Ellsberg stated his
belief that, had his trial proceeded to a verdict, the jury would have exonerated him.
But for reasons we'll consider in later chapters, Ellsberg does not think he would
receive a fair trial today—and he believes that his truth telling would ultimately
have ended, if not for a series of fortuitous circumstances involving Watergate, in a
lengthy prison term.

Daniel Ellsberg's release of the Pentagon Papers did not initially appear to hasten
the end the war. Just over a year after they first began to appear in newsstands,
Nixon won a landslide 1972 reelection, and privately pursued the idea of intensify-
ing the war to defeat the North Vietnamese. The US Navy mined Haiphong, the

main North Vietnamese port, and during the so-called Christmas Bombing campaign dropped over ten thousand tons of bombs a week on Hanoi and Haiphong, killing some 1,600 civilians. Yet Ellsberg's act of conscience had triggered extreme responses in the White House that soon brought Nixon's downfall and hastened the US withdrawal from Vietnam.

Already in 1969, furious that Operation Menu, their secret bombing campaign in Cambodia and Laos, had been leaked to the press, Nixon and National Security Advisor Henry Kissinger had directed the FBI to tap, without warrants, the phones of prominent reporters and senior Nixon officials including Morton Halperin. In 1970, White House attorney Tom Charles Huston drew up what came to be called the "Huston Plan," which proposed to give broad new powers to the CIA, the NSA, the FBI and other intelligence agencies to perform wiretaps, break-ins, surveillance on college campuses, and other illegal tactics aimed at controlling, discrediting and defeating war protesters and civil rights activists. Ellsberg's release of the Pentagon Papers fueled Nixon's paranoid fear of a left-wing conspiracy to bring down his presidency, led by shadowy forces he and his inner circle variously identified as Communist subversives, radical antiwar activists, Black Power leaders, and the Democrats. Though the Pentagon Papers did not implicate Nixon, he suspected that Ellsberg had other sensitive documents on Nixon's national security policy that he might publish, including analysis of the option of using tactical nuclear weapons in Vietnam. (Nixon's fears were correct, as Ellsberg revealed in his 2017 book *The Doomsday Machine: Confessions of a Nuclear War Planner*.) Henry Kissinger, who had known and confided in Ellsberg, scrambled to distance himself from his former protégé, telling Nixon and other top White House aides that Ellsberg was "the most dangerous man in America, who must be stopped at all costs."

Alarmed, Nixon warned his loyal inner circle that Ellsberg's disclosures put the US government at risk, and ordered them to discredit or destroy him by any means necessary. "We've got a countergovernment here and we've got to fight it. I don't give a damn how it's done. Do whatever has to be done to stop those leaks." Senior Nixon aides formed the Plumbers, a team to locate and plug the leaks. Its first job was to discover information that could be used to discredit Daniel Ellsberg. It was on this mission that they broke into his psychiatrist's office and discussed a physical attack on Ellsberg. They considered burglarizing or fire-bombing the Brookings Institution, where they believed another copy of the papers and other compromising documents were being held. The growing paranoia and lawlessness sparked by Ellsberg's revelations eventually led to the idea of bugging the Democratic Party headquarters at the Watergate, and in turn to the arrests of the burglars and to Nixon's fall. Former White House counsel John Dean has remarked, "The seeds of all of Watergate occur in the Pentagon Papers."

Fortunately, an insider was watching this dark drama unfold, and he spoke out. W. Mark Felt, then acting associate director and second-in-command at the FBI, was angered by the White House's obstruction of his ongoing investigation into the Watergate burglary, and by Nixon's attempts to control the bureau. (Felt had also recently been passed over for promotion to the directorship, after the death of historic bureau head J. Edgar Hoover in May 1972, which may have contributed to his decision to reveal Nixon's wrongs.) Acting as an anonymous whistleblower (he only revealed his identity in 2005, shortly before his death), Felt guided Bob Woodward, a young *Washington Post* reporter whom he had met by chance some years earlier, in his inquiries into the scandal, passing on clues during 2:00 a.m. meetings in an underground parking garage in Rosslyn, Virginia, a DC suburb. Felt helped Woodward and his colleague Carl Bernstein to see the vast iceberg of conspiracy, slush funds, spying and criminality of which the bungled burglary at the Watergate was merely the tip.

Watergate also helped Ernie Fitzgerald. In fact, many of his legal battles, however determined and inventive, would likely have failed without evidence that emerged during the Watergate hearings, which demonstrated that high-level White House leaders, including Nixon himself, had retaliated against him for his whistleblowing. A January 1970 memorandum came to light that concerned Fitzgerald's 1968 congressional testimony and subsequent firing, written by one of Fitzgerald's chief tormentors, Alexander Butterfield, an Air Force colonel who later served as a Nixon aide. "Fitzgerald is no doubt a top-notch cost expert," Butterfield wrote, "but he must be given very low marks in loyalty; and after all, loyalty is the name of the game." Butterfield called Fitzgerald a "basic nogoodnik," and recommended punishing him by stalling for a time before offering him another job: "We should let him bleed, for a while at least. Any rush to pick him up and put him back on the Federal payroll would be tantamount to an admission of earlier wrong-doing on our part."

The Watergate tapes provided even juicier details. During a meeting in January 1973, Nixon and several top aides discussed how they had handled Fitzgerald, whom John Ehrlichman identified as "the guy that, uh, ratted on the C-5A overruns."

"This guy that was fired," Nixon remembered in another conversation, and admitted that he himself had approved the termination of Fitzgerald, which Air Force Secretary Seamans had promptly carried out. "That's how it happened. I said, 'Get rid of that son of a bitch!'"

"He was a . . . he was a thorn in everybody's side," Ehrlichman said.

Nixon interrupted. "Yeah, well, the point was not that he was complaining about the overruns, but that he was doing it in public."

"That's the point. And cutting up his superiors," Ehrlichman said.

"That's right."

"Yeah," echoed Ehrlichman.

"And frankly, not taking orders," Nixon concluded.

These statements had caught the Watergate investigators' attention both because the Fitzgerald firing was a well-known case, and because the question of blind loyalty by staffers to the hierarchy and the president, rather than to the Constitution or the nation, had become the signature corruption of the Nixon White House. Fitzgerald observed that the Nixon administration's "code of silence about military waste was enforced as effectively as the Mafia's code of omertà."

Yet Fitzgerald believed that Nixon's attitudes toward the military-industrial complex, loyalty and the appropriate treatment of whistleblowers were characteristic of the executive branch. "Four other presidents—one earlier (Lyndon Johnson) and three to come—were equally determined to silence me or get rid of me," Fitzgerald wrote. "Because of Nixon's uniquely candid record of unsavory conversations in the Oval Office, we tend to think of him as something of an anomaly, a singularly amoral politician who somehow was able to con his way into the Oval Office while we weren't looking. I can't agree. His attitudes and actions in regard to the problems that have always concerned me were quite consistent with the actions of his predecessors and successors. All five presidents, under the guise of national security, systematically exploited the American people. And all five were equally fierce in concealing what was going on. Richard Nixon was part of a continuum."

In Watergate, Fitzgerald also saw unmistakable signs of the military asserting its primacy over civilian authority, which he had opposed throughout his whistle-blower career in the Pentagon. He drew attention to a widely overlooked statement made by General Alexander Haig, White House chief of staff, when Attorney General Elliot Richardson refused to carry out Nixon's command to fire special prosecutor Archibald Cox in October 1973. Haig reportedly passed Nixon's directive to Deputy Attorney General William Ruckelshaus, saying, "Your commander in chief has given you an order."

"This was more than the usual Al Haig bluster," Fitzgerald said.

It was a general's symptomatic misconstruction of the Constitution. The president is commander in chief of the armed forces, not of the entire nation. With respect to the rest of us, our elected leader's primary function is "to take care that the laws be faithfully executed." But the military mind was formed with the Macedonian phalanx of hoplites, where unquestioning obedience was the key to victory. When a commander gives an order, legality is irrelevant. The Pentagon, from my worm's eye view, had the ethic of the phalanx, though it had no Alexander. The military men knew by heart every bureaucratic detail, every arcane regulation for what many considered the only legitimate function of government: the common defense, or at least expenditure for defense. They were the only ones with the right vision for the nation. They knew what would make the United States both secure and prosperous: military discipline and military spending.

With proof of Nixon's involvement in his illegal firing, Fitzgerald pursued the president of the United States all the way to the Supreme Court. There, in 1982, a 5–4 majority led by Chief Justice William Rehnquist granted Nixon immunity from all acts, even crimes, that he had committed while he was president. Fitzgerald

was appalled, but not speechless: "Rehnquist, who as Richard Nixon's assistant attorney general had denounced whistle blowers, did not recuse himself this time," he
wrote. Justice Byron White, in a scathing dissent, wrote, "Attaching absolute immunity to the Office of the President, rather than to particular activities that the
President might perform, places the President above the law. It is a reversion to the
old notion that the King can do no wrong." In a sense, though, Fitzgerald still had
the last laugh. Before the Supreme Court judgment, he had already secured a
$142,000 civil settlement from Nixon, by promising not to take him to trial.

The Watergate investigations also shed new light on My Lai. Among the mass of
documents that Watergate investigators pored over was a page from a yellow legal
pad with notes in bright blue ink, dated December 1, 1969. The right-sloping cur-
sive hand was H. R. Haldeman's.

Task force—My Lai—Kl, Buch, K, Nof, A
dirty tricks—not too high a level—
discredit one witness
get out facts on Hué
admin. line
may have to use a Senator or two

Haldeman's notes are from a meeting he had with Nixon, to create a task force
to downplay the recent news of the My Lai massacre. In his recent biography of
Hugh Thompson, journalist Trent Angers fleshes out the memo line by line, showing how Nixon and his staff worked behind the scenes both to undercut the whistleblowers and to derail the prosecution of the killers.

Nixon had known about My Lai since he received Ronald Ridenhour's letter in
April 1969, but the United States only learned of the massacre in November, when
an exhaustively reported story by Seymour Hersh appeared in thirty papers nationwide. Nixon worried about potential damage to public support for the ongoing war
in Vietnam.

The members of the proposed task force, whose names were abbreviated in Haldeman's notes, were senior members of Nixon's staff: Herb Klein, the president's

director of communications; Pat Buchanan, his consultant for media analysis and speechwriting; Henry Kissinger, his national security advisor; and Franklyn "Lyn" Nofziger, deputy assistant for congressional relations. ("A" may have been special assistant Martin Anderson or Alexander Haig.) "Get out facts on Hué" suggests using the massacres of civilians by the Vietcong when they took the city of Hué in 1968 to make My Lai seem less exceptional.

But the most explosive part of the memo is Nixon's order to "discredit one witness," with the help of "a senator or two." Angers points out that Lyn Nofziger met soon after with Nixon ally Mendel Rivers, chair of the House Armed Services Committee, and that Rivers and his fellow committee member and war hawk Edward Hébert promptly opened hearings on My Lai, to which they called important prosecution witnesses, then sealed their testimony and refused to provide it to the military courts that were then hearing the My Lai prosecutions—a clear attempt to stonewall the proceedings. In some instances, the tactic worked: one military judge refused to let the prosecution call witnesses who had already testified before Rivers's committee. Rivers and Hébert also subjected Hugh Thompson, the whistleblower and eyewitness to the massacre, to many hours of repetitive and belligerent questioning, which one observer called "more of an inquisition than an investigation." Again and again they pushed him to admit that he had ordered his crew to point their weapons at soldiers from Charlie Company, a court-martial offense. The actions of Rivers and Hébert fit the script laid out in Haldeman's memo, to use compliant congressmen to discredit a key My Lai witness. One army prosecutor later stated that the two congressmen had "tried, calculatingly and technically," to sabotage the trials.

Watergate even had a gift for Ralph Nader. In May 1973, Congress authorized the attorney general to appoint a special Watergate prosecutor, with wide-ranging powers to investigate the Watergate break-in, the 1972 presidential election, and activities of the president and his staff. That summer, when Watergate special prosecutor Archibald Cox learned of the secret taping system that Nixon had installed in the White House, he subpoenaed Nixon to get the tapes. During the so-called Saturday Night Massacre, after Attorney General Richardson and Deputy Attorney General Ruckelshaus refused to fire Cox and resigned in protest, Nixon ordered

Robert Bork, who had begun the day as solicitor general and was now, thanks to the resignations of his two superiors, the acting attorney general of the United States of America, to do so. Though Bork disliked the idea, he complied, and subsequently attempted to abolish the office of the Watergate special prosecutor entirely.

Days after these events, Ralph Nader and three members of Congress sued Bork for illegally firing Cox. In the statute that instituted the special prosecutor, it was clearly stated that the prosecutor could not be dismissed unless he committed "extraordinary improprieties." Since no one had accused Cox of improprieties, Nader argued, his dismissal had been illegal. Later that year, a federal judge agreed with Nader, further eroding Nixon's popularity and paving the way for his resignation the following year.

The carnage of Vietnam, the Pentagon Papers' revelations about the lies behind the war, and the crimes and conspiracies of Watergate all substantiated Ralph Nader's most vehement antiestablishment claims. During the Watergate hearings, and subsequent congressional and criminal investigations held after Nixon's resignation, Americans began to understand the extent to which Nixon and his staff had subverted the federal government to serve their narrow political ends, attempting to concentrate White House power to create an "imperial presidency," employing political espionage and government secrecy on the pretext of national security, and nepotistically assigning government grants and contracts to administration allies. Watergate also underscored the essential role to be played by upstanding insiders in resisting the illegal behavior of powerful, secretive organizations, further highlighting the emerging figure of the whistleblower. "Watergate taught many Americans that secrecy, bureaucratic power and unquestioning obedience to authority could become acute threats to democracy," Robert Vaughn says. "Whistleblowing, which had recently gained public attention as a way principled individuals could fight such abuses and assert ethical resistance from within, addressed these concerns."

Some political leaders specifically proposed whistleblowers as an antidote for the institutional malevolence of Watergate, and urged new laws to protect them. In 1978, Senator Patrick Leahy authored *The Whistleblowers: A Report on Federal Employees Who Disclose Acts of Governmental Waste, Abuse and Corruption*, which described the battles of Ernie Fitzgerald and other pioneer whistleblowers, and the conflict they faced between the civil service code of ethics they swore to uphold and their superiors' demands for loyalty, teamwork and silence. Among the abuses of power spotlighted in Leahy's report was the so-called Malek Manual, an eighty-page guide written by Nixon officials Fred Malek and Alan May on how to exploit loopholes in civil service rules in order to punish and remove any employee with insufficient political and personal devotion to the president, and to ensure that "loyal members of the team" controlled their agencies. Among the methods recommended in the manual are the "Frontal Assault Technique" ("Simply call an individual in and tell him he is no longer wanted. . . . There should be no witnesses in the room at the time"); the "Transfer Technique" ("By carefully researching the background of the proposed employee-victim, one can always establish that geographical part of the country and/or organizational unit to which the employee would rather resign than obey and accept transfer orders"); and the "Shifting Responsibilities and Isolation Technique" ("The setting up of a parallel organization to one already in existence, and giving that new organization most of the real authorities previously vested in the old organization it parallels . . . [thus] isolating those bureaucrats who have not quit in disgust into meaningless technical positions out of the mainstream of the Department's operation"). The Malek Manual revealed to Congress and the public the utter ruthlessness of some civil service leaders, and the vulnerability of ethical bureaucrats who resisted unjust authority.

After Watergate, Congress passed a series of new laws to restrict the power of the executive branch, improve government transparency and increase the personal accountability of public employees. For the first time, a number of influential politicians considered whistleblowers to be important figures in achieving these goals. Jimmy Carter, who ran for president in 1976, specifically made empowering whistleblowers part of his platform. At a campaign speech in Arlington, Virginia, he mentioned Ernie Fitzgerald by name. "I intend to seek strong legislation to protect our federal employees from harassment and dismissal if they find out and report waste and dishonesty by their superiors or others," Carter told the crowd. "The Fitzgerald case, where a dedicated civil servant was fired from the Defense Department for reporting cost overruns, must never be repeated." Carter was the first president to publicly use the word "whistleblower."

After his election, Carter's initiatives to reduce waste, fraud, abuse and political patronage in government included laws to protect and empower whistleblowers. The 1978 Civil Service Reform Act (CSRA), a centerpiece of his declared war on bureaucratic dysfunction, explicitly forbade whistleblower retaliation. The CSRA also established offices to investigate, prosecute and adjudge whistleblower retaliation and other prohibited practices, which included the Merit Systems Protection Board and the Office of Special Counsel. Still more fundamentally, the CSRA affirmed the First Amendment right of public servants to speak out about official malfeasance, and underscored their duty to refuse to carry out unconstitutional or illegal orders. That year, two other important laws were passed that fostered whistleblowing. The Ethics in Government Act introduced more protections for whistleblowers, especially to guard against politicization of federal offices, and the Inspector General Act, which created a new, nominally independent office within twelve government agencies (since expanded to seventy-three government bodies) to investigate fraud, waste and abuse within their parent organization, and to shield whistleblowers who further these aims.

The new laws formalized the shift in attitudes toward unauthorized disclosures that had taken place during the Watergate era. Whistleblowers were now widely seen as vital agents against government wrongdoing; in a few years, with the 1986 amendments to the False Claims Act, they became corporate fraud fighters as well. Yet the Italian proverb *"Fatta la legge, trovato l'inganno"* (The loophole is made with the law) held true. While the new, positive position of the whistleblower, both public and private, had been impressed on the American consciousness and consolidated in new laws, many methods remained for leaders determined to enforce loyalty to twist the law to their own ends.

How did the president of the United States and his most senior aides lose sight of basic ethics and their sworn duty to defend the Constitution, in a downward spiral of criminality? How did a group of highly trained yet otherwise ordinary Americans lose their grip on morality at My Lai? How could automotive engineers coolly tally up the number of future burn victims their cars would produce? Why did top military and civilian leaders systematically lie to the nation about the horror and futility of the Vietnam War? And why, in all of these cases, did so many insiders and onlookers remain silent? These questions of early 1970s America echoed those that the world had asked itself insistently since World War II. The savage genocides by the Imperial Japanese Army in China and the Pacific; the purges, pogroms and forced relocations ordered by Stalin and Mao; and the Allied slaughter of German and Japanese civilians with incendiary and nuclear bombs—all brought into focus how easily individuals could lose their humanity and sense of justice under the intense pressures of loyalty and hierarchy. Above all, the horrors of the Holocaust showed age-old virtues in a grim new light: Nazis in the dock at Nuremberg justified their various atrocities as obedience to their commanders and the rule of law, devotion to their supreme leader and patriotic allegiance to their fatherland. The tribunal rejected their arguments, later termed the "Nuremberg" or "superior orders" defense, by affirming the abiding responsibility of every individual to live by his or her own personal morality, even in the face of coercion by peers, authorities or the state. "Crimes against international law are committed by men, not by abstract entities, and only by punishing individuals who commit such crimes can the provisions of international law be enforced," the justices proclaimed. Another legal doctrine to be refined by World War II, "command responsibility," also asserted that military leaders who knowingly ordered or failed to halt atrocities were guilty of committing them.

Yet as we've seen, responsibility within a group is evanescent, often adhering to no one individual. Despite the landmark pronouncements at Nuremberg and other post–World War II tribunals, less than twenty-two years later the soldiers who wiped out the village of My Lai successfully defended themselves by arguing that they had merely been following orders, while their commanders pleaded innocence for having been too far up the chain of command to be responsible for the killings. Here is the paradox of group criminality, and of its polar opposite, whistleblowing. When we think as individuals, in the abstract, about the crimes that organizations commit, most of us assume that we would resist and denounce them. Disobedience and public denunciation seem the only moral choice. Yet time and again, in actual instances of group wrongdoing, dissenters are rare or absent: most group members suppress their personal values and participate in the crime more or less willingly. Society routinely accepts, sometimes even commends, those who comply with such acts—seeing them as the "good soldiers" who stick with their comrades and make the best of a dirty job—while condemning as traitors those few who publicly condemn the wrongdoing. "I've never met an organizational leader who is against whistleblowing in theory," Tom Devine observes, "and in practice, I've never met a leader who believed there actually *were* any whistleblowers in their own organization. They seem to be thinking, 'Those people [in my organization] aren't whistleblowers. They're assholes.'"

The field of social psychology arose after World War II in an attempt to explain this massive gulf between individual conscience and group behavior, as a number of brilliant researchers, many of whom were European Jews haunted by the annihilation of their world, strove to comprehend how so many outwardly humane Germans, Austrians and other Europeans could have committed such monstrosities. Each also added a piece to the puzzle of explaining those rare dissenters, including whistleblowers, who, even at enormous cost, maintain their values in a society gone mad. Solomon Asch explored people's unreasoning conformity to group pressure and propaganda, demonstrating the sometimes extreme malleability of people's ideas under social duress. Henri Tajfel revealed the inexorable gravitational pull of in-groups, demonstrating that even when strangers were divided into groups randomly, by coin toss, people formed strong bonds with their fellow coalition members, and corresponding dislike and distrust of out-group members. Irving Janis explored what, in a nod to George Orwell, he called "groupthink"—how people's loyalty to their teams can lead to severe conformity of thought, instinctive censorship of dissenting views, and illusions of group invulnerability. Theodor Adorno published *The Authoritarian Personality*, which linked the signature traits of the Fascist mind—anti-intellectualism, submissiveness to authority, aggression, and striving for power—to extreme discipline in childhood.

Perhaps the most influential researcher of those fertile decades was Stanley

Milgram, a junior professor in social psychology at Yale who devised the famous "shock" experiments. Milgram, a former doctoral student of Solomon Asch, devoted himself to understanding how obedience to authority can negate individual conscience—and how exceptional individuals, including whistleblowers, succeed in resisting authority. Milgram, whose Jewish family had been ravaged by World War II, was obsessed by the Holocaust. He watched raptly the 1961 trial, the first ever televised, of Adolf Eichmann, the logistics expert in the Central Office for Jewish Emigration, who had faithfully ensured that trains to the liquidation camps ran full and on time. Balding, middle-aged, with a scrawny neck and thick glasses, Eichmann showed the world another face of the Holocaust: not the fearsome warriors in the dock at Nuremberg, but the bland functionaries who made the Nazi killing machine run smoothly. Israeli attorney general Gideon Hausner, in his opening statement for the prosecution, called Eichmann "a fastidious person, a 'white-collar' worker," for whom "the decree of extermination was just another written order to be executed." Political theorist Hannah Arendt, who attended the trial in Jerusalem, observed, "The trouble with Eichmann was precisely that so many were like him, and that the many were neither perverted nor sadistic, that they were, and still are, terribly and terrifyingly normal." Arendt famously wrote that Eichmann embodied the "banality of evil."

Listening to Eichmann's bland account of his work in the logistics of genocide, and his repeated insistence that he'd had no independent responsibility for his acts, Milgram asked himself, "Could it be that Eichmann and his million accomplices in the Holocaust were just following orders? Could we call them all accomplices?" He devised an experiment to test these hypotheses, which placed participants in the role of unwilling torturers.

In July 1961, three months after the Eichmann trial began, a series of volunteers from a wide range of occupations and backgrounds joined Milgram in the basement of the Yale psychology department, to participate in a one-hour memory experiment. They were divided into "Teachers" and "Learners," while a man in a lab coat with a stern, professional demeanor served as the "Experimenter," and directed the proceedings. The Experimenter explained that the purpose of their work was to test the effects of punishment on learning, adding that it was essential to complete the procedure, or the entire experiment would be compromised. He and the Teacher seated the Learner in a chair, bound his arms firmly to the armrests with leather straps, and attached an electrode to his wrist. Then the Experimenter led the Teacher into another room, where they could speak to the Learner but not see him. The Teacher sat at a desk with a large, impressive-looking electrical device labeled "shock generator," with a voltage scale marked in 15-volt increments, ranging from "slight shock" to "intense" to "danger: severe shock" at 375 volts to a final, menacing "XXX" for the last three gradations at the top of the scale. Under the direction of the Experimenter standing beside him, the Teacher gave the Learner a simple memory test. When the Learner made an error, the Teacher used the generator to administer a shock, increasing the voltage with each error.

The experiment was actually an elaborate sham. The "generator" produced no electric current, and the Learner was Milgram's accomplice, a plump, middle-aged Irish American named James McDonough, who had been trained to play the part of a slow and suffering Learner. But as far as the Teachers knew, they were inflicting increasingly severe pain on an innocent person. Starting at 75 volts, the Learner began to grunt in discomfort; as the voltage increased he complained loudly, then groaned in apparent pain. At 150 volts, he urgently demanded to be released from the experiment, and continued shouting until 285 volts, when he screamed in simulated agony. At 300 he pounded on the wall. Above 315 volts the pounding stopped, and the Learner fell ominously silent.

Nevertheless, every participant continued to at least 300 volts, the level of shock marked "danger," and well past the point at which the Learner had begun crying out. A total of 65 percent of participants reached 450 volts, the maximum shock, which they delivered three times to the long-silent Learner. No one seemed to enjoy inflicting pain; Milgram noted that some trembled, groaned, shouted and sweated profusely as they administered the shocks. Yet they continued the experiment.

Milgram concluded that humans have a powerful instinct to obey orders, Eichmann-like, which often overcomes their personal morality. "A substantial proportion of people do what they are told to do, irrespective of the content of the act and without limitations of conscience," he wrote, "so long as they perceive that the command comes from a legitimate authority." He noticed that many participants began to treat the experiment itself as an almost organic entity of great significance; for them, respecting the rules of the experiment became more important than respecting the humanity of the victim. Milgram's experiments, a landmark in the understanding of human obedience to authority, soon became the subject of popular and scholarly articles, radio broadcasts, documentary films and novels. They were frequently invoked to explain My Lai, Watergate and other crimes of obedience. They were also cited in court briefs and hundreds of law review articles. One such article, published in 1977 by Nader's Raider and legal scholar Robert Vaughn, used Milgram's work to stress the dangers of blind obedience in government bodies, and called for guarantees to the legal right of employees to disobey illegal or unconstitutional orders. "Milgram's experiments changed the way the nation, and some members of Congress, thought about authority," Vaughn says today. "They helped create the atmosphere that, in 1978, produced landmark laws to protect federal employees who became whistleblowers."

Milgram's work highlighted four psychological mechanisms which the Teachers in his experiments used to reduce the strain of harming a helpless victim: authorization, agentic state, routinization and dehumanization. These mechanisms, since refined by other scholars, are also vital for understanding how a few participants in his experiment managed to remain independent of harmful authority—and how whistleblowers and other truth tellers can break free from the powerful psychological pull of group wrongdoing, while so many of their colleagues in corporations, government bureaucracies and the military fail to do so.

Authorization, according to Milgram, is the process by which an individual accepts the legitimacy, power and expertise of an authority, and agrees to perform tasks at the authority's command. The authority almost always justifies these tasks by linking them to a higher ideological mission, such as the furtherance of science or national security, and uses rewards and punishments to compel compliance by its subordinates. Once individuals accept this relationship, Milgram explained, they transfer judgments of right and wrong to the authority figure, and their sense of personal responsibility for their actions fades.

Milgram's second psychological mechanism—the "agentic state," which some later psychologists have termed "doubling"—is an outgrowth of authorization.

According to Milgram, many individuals under the influence of strict authority leave their normal "autonomous state," in which independent moral individuals take responsibility for their own actions, and become the agents, or tools, of the authority. This creation of a distinct, subservient self allows people to set aside the dictates of their conscience and focus instead on obeying orders: morality itself becomes a function of how well they carry out their orders, not of what they actually do. This dual state resembles Orwell's "doublethink," a condition in which people could tell deliberate lies while simultaneously believing them, and also the institutional hypocrisy that a business executive interviewed in *Moral Mazes*, the classic study of corporate psychology, had in mind when he observed: "What is right in the corporation is not what is right in a man's home or in his church. What is right in the corporation is what the guy above you wants from you. That's what morality is in the corporation."

A third psychological process revealed by Milgram's experiment is routinization, by which members of organizations break down large activities into a series of discrete steps, which they perform almost automatically. Routinization employs euphemisms to shield people from the moral implication of their acts, reframing their choices as professional rather than personal or moral—"just business." As a result, the individual's attention shifts from an ethical assessment of the work to how efficiently they perform it; terms like "loyalty," "duty" and "discipline" are defined with reference to the organization rather than to society, humanity or the environment. Milgram's contemporary and fellow student of group deviance, Herbert Kelman, described how a bureaucracy can routinize harmful behavior: "By proceeding in routine fashion—processing papers, exchanging memos, diligently carrying out their assigned tasks—the different units mutually reinforce each other in the view that what is going on must be perfectly normal, correct, and legitimate." Milgram concluded that the atomization of social relations in the modern world often grayed out wrongdoing. "Beyond a certain point, the breaking up of society into people carrying out narrow and very special jobs takes away from the human quality of work and life," he wrote. "A person does not get to see the whole situation but only a small part of it, and is thus unable to act without some kind of over-all direction. He yields to authority but in doing so is alienated from his own actions."

The fourth mechanism that Milgram observed, both in his experiments and in several widely known crimes of obedience, is the dehumanization or derogation of the victim. As his shock experiment progressed into the higher voltages, Teachers often berated the Learner as so stupid and stubborn that he deserved to be shocked. Milgram inferred that Teachers were attempting to neutralize their stress and guilt by portraying the victim "as an unworthy individual, whose punishment was made inevitable by his own deficiencies of intellect and character"—a process similar to the psychic balancing act of cognitive dissonance that had been identified a decade earlier by Leon Festinger. Also, because of our strong innate resistance to harming fellow humans, viewing the victim as in some sense subhuman makes inflicting pain on him less disturbing. "Those who participate in any bureaucratic apparatus increasingly come to see their victims as bodies to be counted and entered into reports, as faceless figures that will determine their productivity rates and promotions," Kelman wrote. In a related phenomenon, the greater the physical distance separating aggressors from their victims, the easier crimes of obedience are to carry out, just as the proximity of the authority figure tends to increase the level of compliance.

Elements of Milgram's four mechanisms are present in a number of major crimes of obedience committed in the 1960s and 1970s. At My Lai as in Watergate, the men involved felt they had been authorized by their superiors to carry out what they would normally have recognized as criminal, even inhuman, acts; and they demonstrated an agentic shift by assessing their behavior according to how strictly they followed their superiors' orders, rather than how those orders brought them to break laws or kill innocent civilians. Routinization took place at many levels, from the Pentagon's emphasis on body counts to the use of high-tech, long-distance weapons to prosecute the war. Dehumanization was evident in the pervasive use of slurs like "gook" and "slant"; various enemies of the Nixon administration were likewise mentally recategorized as foreign, deviant and dangerous—threats to national security to be eliminated by whatever means required. In similar ways, the Watergate conspiracy occurred in part because of the powerful influence that Nixon exerted over his collaborators; they became his "agents," extensions of his presidential authority rather than independent moral beings.

These four mechanisms of obedience to emerge from Milgram's work also help make sense of the organizational wrongdoing in the whistleblower stories we've heard so far. The systematic work of Johnson & Johnson employees and healthcare workers in Texas, Pennsylvania and other states to break federal laws and endanger vulnerable populations; the bureaucratic machinery in Quantico that helped kill thousands of active-duty Marines; and the cost-benefit analyses at Ford and GM that priced out human deaths and found them preferable to lost profits; all illustrate how the interrelated processes of authorization, doubling, routinization and dehumanization can drive members of an organization to dissociate their jobs from real human outcomes, and to think with their group minds rather than with their own hearts.

Though the overwhelming majority of participants in Milgram's experiment gave in to authority and obeyed harmful orders, a few Teachers followed their conscience instead. How they managed to do so helps to explain why whistleblowers and other principled dissidents reject the status quo. Milgram carried out nineteen variations on his original experiment, modifying certain conditions in order to clarify the psychological processes involved. When he moved the experiment from Yale University's psychology department to a shabby office building off campus, or when the Experimenter wore civilian clothes instead of a lab coat, the percentage of Teachers who reached maximum voltage dropped. Obedience declined even more when the Teacher sat in the same room as the Learner and could see his (simulated) pain face-to-face, or when he was required to push the Learner's hand down onto a metal plate when administering the shocks. Perhaps most strikingly, obedience fell to a meager 10 percent when participants performed the experiment in cooperation with another Teacher, another Milgram confederate, who loudly refused to obey the Experimenter's commands. On the other hand, when Teachers questioned the Learner but delegated the administration of the shock to someone else, 93 percent proceeded to the highest voltage; most later explained that they felt the responsibility for harming the Learner belonged to the person who actually triggered the shock.

In other words, changes that reduced the authority figure's aura of prestige, increased the Teacher's empathy for the Learner, provided a dissenting role model, or accentuated the Teacher's sense of direct responsibility for inflicting harm, all reduced the hypnotic power of the experiment, and helped participants follow their own better instincts. Additionally, a few Teachers appeared to possess a higher level of empathy, or stubbornness, whether because of their innate character or their life experiences. A forty-seven-year-old factory inspector, after administering a 120-volt shock and hearing the victim demand to be released, refused to continue the shocks until he could see the victim for himself. When the Experimenter declined, the Teacher said, "I don't think I'd like to take that myself, what he's taking right now." He soon halted the experiment. Another Teacher, a thirty-nine-year-old salesman, began to resist after the Learner flatly refused to continue answering questions. When the Experimenter pressed him to continue, saying he had no other choice, the Teacher protested, "I have *no* other choice? Hmm. Hmm. I think I have," and would not go on, perhaps in part from annoyance at the Experimenter's domineering manner, and a sense that the fairness of the experiment had been violated.

Herbert Kelman, who coined the term "crimes of obedience," draws broader conclusions about why certain people are able to escape the twin pulls of obedience and groupthink. Like Milgram, Kelman notes several situational factors, which he calls "binding forces," that enhance or erode obedience: the level of surveillance by the authority, the presence of widely recognized symbols of authority, and the level of obedience that subjects observe among their peers, as well as the existence of a clear organizational hierarchy and the extent to which embarrassment or other sanctions are used to punish disobedience. On the other hand, people are more likely to resist performing such harmful acts when they are able to recognize the people they are harming as victims and as fellow human beings; or when they realize that the authority figures themselves are human, which dims their aura of infallibility. In both instances, actors realize they have choices, and are not simply being swept along by fate. Other people, trapped in their own prestige and identity bestowed by the organization, must distance themselves from the organization in order to see through its mystique. Disobedience also requires that the individual recognize the authority under whose orders they are acting as either illegitimate or subservient to another, higher authority, like human morality or god.

Many of the whistleblowers we have encountered have, through circumstance or genetic disposition, disabled the mechanisms that their organizations relied on to enforce obedience. Allen Jones, Franz Gayl and Ron Ridenhour, thanks to their pronounced empathy and personal experiences in the front lines of their professions, perceived with painful intensity the ongoing human harm to which their colleagues seemed oblivious. They came to see the victims as fellow humans who shared a universal right to respect, kindness and justice; almost as kin. In very different ways, Ernie Fitzgerald and Daniel Ellsberg gained a clear, compelling sense of an alternative, higher authority that deserved their allegiance—the commonweal, the Constitution, the human and divine prohibitions against killing—that enabled them to pierce the conscience-numbing power of the Pentagon. The ability of all these men to act was enhanced by a certain independence of character, a lack of awe of authority often accompanied by a sarcastic sense of humor, a sense of options in their lives beyond their specific career, a relatively modest need for approval from their peers, and a confidence that they could act independently and effect real change with their acts. Many of the whistleblowers we've met so far were outsiders, both culturally and professionally, who felt fewer bonds with their coworkers and bosses, and were unlikely to fall under the spell of a rarefied team. Many had also grown up in small communities with old-fashioned values, where the sense of common good and duty to others was strong, and where they saw that their actions had consequences for specific people. In the process of blowing the whistle, too, many enjoyed the support of like-minded colleagues or fellow whistleblowers at their workplaces, as well as of family members who urged them to speak out, and supported them during the war of bureaucratic and psychological attrition that followed.

These days when Franz Gayl takes his dogs for a walk, he feels a change in the air. "Ah, Jeez Louise, life is good," he says. "Things are friggin' good. My world has been transformed." After a life-threatening bout of diverticulitis, he is healthy again. And he is finally doing real work at the Pentagon once more.

In 2011 Gayl passed a mandatory psychiatric examination that found him fit for duty, had most of his clearances restored, and returned to the Pentagon. After years of busywork at a borrowed desk, he has resumed his science and technology duties, and is now working on a major project to augment strategic decision making with artificial intelligence. Some of his worst enemies at the Pentagon and at Quantico have retired or moved out of his chain of command; others are, if not friendly, at least collegial. "I'm now working with some of those guys," he says. "And I can extend the olive branch. Some of them, people who may have been very angry with me in the past, have extended the olive branch, too, all credit to them. I do what they tell me to do. I've returned to the good order and discipline of the Marine Corps. In the end, I recognize I could have done a lot of things different—better. And in the process of giving back and forth, I believe some other people learned that, too."

Franz Gayl talks the way very few whistleblowers ever can. Yet he can hardly be happy with the ultimate outcome of his acts. He successfully revealed mismanagement in the MRAP program, but the root causes of that mismanagement—the conflicts of interest, the revolving door and the disproportionate economic and political power of the major defense contractors—remain. Even when their efforts fix specific problems, most whistleblowers are forced to acknowledge that the underlying abuses still occur. Allen Jones halted the horrors of TMAP, but widespread abuses by pharmaceutical giants continue. Ernie Fitzgerald, Chuck Spinney and Dina Rasor revealed gross waste and fraud in military contracting, which resulted not only in inferior weapons but also in direct risk to soldiers, yet the same kind of wrongdoing persists. Daniel Ellsberg and Mark Felt unmasked the malevolent power of the presidential office and big bureaucracies alike, but that power remains, as malevolent as ever.

In the military-industrial complex, things are worse than Fitzgerald or Eisenhower could ever have foreseen. The United States currently spends more on weapons than the next ten leading weapons-producing nations combined. The defense budget has almost doubled in real dollars since 1998, and each year over the last decade has been higher than at any other time since World War II—more than during the Cold War, the Vietnam War, the Korean War. Despite this enormous outlay, the US military has not won a significant war since 1945 (the First Iraq War had to be refought, and the protracted conflict in Kosovo ended only when the Russians stopped supporting Milošević); the current conflicts in Iraq and

Afghanistan have degenerated into grinding, slow-motion defeats that show the mismatch between American military strategy and real combat. "These low-intensity, piss-ant wars now cost so much that they have stretched the supposedly mighty US military to the snapping point," says Chuck Spinney. "Today the cost of the so-called War on Terror in inflation-adjusted dollars exceeds any war in US history except for World War II. I hate to think what would happen in a real war." Waste and fraud are rampant. Already in 2011, the bipartisan Commission on Wartime Contracting estimated that somewhere between $31 billion and $60 billion had been misspent or stolen by defense contractors and the military itself in Afghanistan and Iraq, largely because, the commissioners stated, the US government "had no effective way of overseeing contractor spending" in these countries. (The Costs of War project at Brown University has put the price tag of conflicts in Afghanistan, Iraq and Syria at $5.9 trillion, with an additional $8 trillion in interest costs over the next forty years.) The fraud, bad enough in itself, also causes failure: according to a September 2016 report by the Special Inspector General for Afghanistan Reconstruction, the endless billions of US dollars poured into the country fueled unprecedented corruption in the Afghan ruling class, degraded military performance, discredited American forces, and even helped to fund anti-US insurgents. But the biggest scams are back home, in the heart of the Pentagon. In the latest in a series of accounting scandals that have run for decades, in August 2016 the DOD's inspector general revealed that Army accountants had intentionally misstated their 2015 accounts by $6.5 *trillion*, inventing tens of thousands of false line items in order to close their year-end books, a practice so common that the Army has a name for it: "the grand plug." "They don't know where all that money goes," says Chuck Spinney, "and if they don't know, the Congress and the American people sure as hell don't. The accounting scandal is a direct assault on the basic requirements of a representative republic enshrined in the Accountability and Appropriations clauses of the Constitution—yet every member of the military has taken a sacred oath to protect and defend the Constitution."

After a series of consolidations in the 1990s urged and facilitated by Bill Clinton, defense giants like Lockheed Martin and Northrop Grumman now exert more power than ever over the government. Lockheed, Ernie Fitzgerald's old nemesis, is the world's leading arms maker, with revenue of $39 billion from government contracts in 2018 alone—70 percent of the firm's sales. (The top five contractors consumed about 110 billion tax dollars in 2018.) Defense conglomerates have a sleek new media image: their planes, helicopters and submarines star in Hollywood films and in television ads during Super Bowls, and they sponsor college football championships. But many of the dodges that Ernie Fitzgerald described fifty years ago remain unchanged. Cost overruns and cost-plus contracts (which Fitzgerald called "blank check contracts") are widespread. Once, a $640 toilet seat constituted a scandal; today the toilet seat of the Boeing C-17 costs $10,000, and no cartoonist has hung it around the defense secretary's neck. Congressional engineering, or the distribution of contract work across numerous districts to insulate a weapons program from cancellation, has grown so effective that programs like the C-17 and the M1 Abrams tank march ahead, zombielike, for many years after the DOD itself says it no longer wants them. In return, contractors spend uncounted millions a year on Congress, in campaign contributions and lobbying. Some payments seem open bribes. In 2013, for example, the members of the Senate Committee on Foreign Relations who voted in favor of air strikes on Syria received 83 percent more campaign donations from defense contractors, per person, than did those who voted against the strikes.

The looting of the public purse continues. Lockheed's F-35 Joint Strike Fighter, the most expensive arms program in US history, has cost $1.4 trillion to date, and is already more than 200 percent over budget. Although seven years behind schedule, the plane still cannot fly, navigate or shoot reliably; it has major problems with its software system, ejector seat, fuel tanks and other elements, and has experienced unexpected engine fires and sudden, unexplained drops in altitude. Yet Air Force cheerleaders continue to tout it as a triumph of technology, and to decommission working planes that compete with it. These include the most effective US air-to-ground aircraft in existence, the A-10 Thunderbolt, on which frontline commanders in Iraq, Afghanistan and Syria rely for ground support. Despite protestations from the field, dozens of A-10s are removed from service or destroyed each year. The Air Force is so set against the A-10, and behind Lockheed, that Major General James Post, another leading F-35 supporter, announced that servicemen who communicated the A-10's impressive capabilities to Congress were "committing treason." Backers of another monstrous project, the Air Force's new B-21 stealth bomber being built by Northrop Grumman, avoid awkward questions about funding simply by refusing to reveal the price tag. In May 2016, the Senate Armed Services Committee voted in a closed-door session to keep the development costs of the bomber secret, because, the Air Force claimed, this information would tell enemies too much about the plane—a transparent lie, since the Air Force had already revealed the plane's unit cost and a list of major components. It's the same old story as in Ernie Fitzgerald's day: while soldiers die and taxpayers lose, Lockheed and its military minders keep their money machine humming.

The high priests of military waste continue to corrupt civilian industry; in the 2018 and 2019 crashes of 737 MAX aircraft and reportedly slipshod manufacturing practices at a plant that produces its 787 Dreamliner, Boeing shows all the symptoms of the bloated, Lockheed-style, too-big-to-fail behemoth that Ernie Fitzgerald knew well; these kinds of systemic failures, in fact, seem to coincide with the rise of military contracting executives to leadership roles at Boeing. The F-35 and B-21 likewise prove Fitzgerald's contention that bang is frequently inversely proportional to buck. Contractors push high-tech weapons because they are hugely profitable, but such malfunction-prone systems violate one of the central principles of modern combat: KISS, or "Keep It Simple, Stupid." "Today's military is addicted to gold-plated weapons," says Chuck Spinney. "Costly items like the F-35 and the B-21 siphon away money that the military badly needs to maintain its existing equipment and train its troops, further degrading its readiness for real fighting." Such long-distance bombers and air-to-air fighters are relics of the Cold War, largely useless in the low-level counterinsurgency against guerrilla forces that the United States is likely to be fighting in the future. "Spending more on bad ideas actually makes things worse," says Spinney. "Pumping more money into the French military in 1933 and its obsession with the Maginot Line would not have given you a better outcome in 1939."

Money, though, is more and more openly accepted as the supreme goal. The last two decades have seen a major shift in ethics and expectations among senior military officers. After retirement, General George Marshall, the World War II leader and mastermind of postwar European recovery, refused to join a defense corporation or to collect royalties from his biography; he even declined to ask FDR for a specific command during the war, stating that he was "here to serve and not to satisfy personal ambition." While not all of Marshall's contemporaries met his high standards—Eisenhower worried privately about certain revolving-door generals— he embodied an accepted ideal. "Many general officers considered joining a defense contractor after they left the service a questionable action at best," says Bill Astore, a retired Air Force lieutenant colonel who has taught history at the Air Force Academy and the Pennsylvania College of Technology. "It was considered a stain on their public service. Military service, in those days, was about sacrifice and selflessness. It wasn't about private gain." As late as 1998, according to an incisive study in the *Boston Globe*, fewer than half of senior generals and admirals went to work in the defense industry after they retired. A decade later, 80 percent of them did, and the number remains at comparably high levels today. (In 2007, a stunning thirty-four of thirty-nine retiring senior generals and admirals immediately joined defense companies.) "What was once a stain has now become a badge of success," Astore says.

Dina Rasor agrees. "The generals are a scourge, a priestly caste, the biggest barriers to ever making the Pentagon work," she says. "They claim to act in the interests of the nation, but actually follow their own. Their refrain is, 'We need the best for our boys, or we're all gonna die!' When people suggest trimming some fat out of the Pentagon budget, they shout, 'You don't want the best for the boys!' Meantime, they're already thinking about their future careers." Rasor says the revolving-door mentality, which she prefers to call "self-dealing," starts long before they leave the military. "If you're a general running a major weapons program worth ten or twenty billion a year, when you get out, you aren't satisfied just playing golf with your friends. You don't want to lose that power. So you start mentally self-dealing the minute you get into a position of authority." This has serious implications for potential whistleblowers. "To self-deal successfully, you have to make sure there are no bombs in your projects, no hidden risks. If you ever let a whistleblower get the better of you, people don't trust you. If you have a whistleblower scalp on your belt, you're more impressive."

Chuck Spinney captures the shift from public service to self-dealing by comparing portrait photographs of Eisenhower and General David Petraeus. Eisenhower,
the hero of Normandy and North Africa, stands at an angle to the camera against
a drab gray background, his lips compressed in a firm line, one slender strip of
decorations above his left breast pocket. The portrait exudes modesty and restraint.
David Petraeus, a leader in two disastrously failed wars, stands with three American flags behind him, shoulders squared to the camera and face alight with a horse-
toothed smile, his entire torso covered with medals, ribbons and badges. After his
military career, Eisenhower became president of Columbia University, commander
of NATO, then president of the nation for two terms, before retiring to private life.
After his military career, Petraeus became CIA director, but resigned after only a
year when the FBI caught him sharing highly classified material—identities of covert officers, code names for secret intelligence operations—with his biographer,
Paula Broadwell, with whom he was having an extramarital affair, and then lying
about this to bureau investigators. (The FBI recommended felony charges against
Petraeus, but he eventually pleaded guilty to a misdemeanor charge of mishandling
classified material.) Unchastened, Petraeus continues to serve as a senior fellow at
Harvard's Kennedy School, where he launched a new initiative on strategic leadership while he was still on probation. He remains a partner at KKR, the investment
giant, and holds prominent positions at multiple think tanks and NGOs, where he
speaks at length about halting terrorism and winning wars in the Middle East—
things he himself failed to do. The Petraeus brand is booming.

So, too, is the military brand. Despite all the waste and the fraud, despite the
endless, illegitimate, losing wars that have bled the nation's economy dry, Americans remain obedient to military authority. Ten years of Gallup polls show that,
while the percentage of respondents expressing strong confidence in the presidency
has often been in the 30s, and faith in Congress in the teens and single digits, US
trust in its military has remained in the mid- to high 70s. War as a government
policy is not questioned as it was during Vietnam or even in the run-up to World
War II, largely no doubt because in a nation without the draft, civilians leave the
country's wars to a professional class of "war fighters," whom they thank unend-
ingly for their "service." Bill Astore observes that our economic, social and moral

malaise, though in part caused by our hypertrophic military, ironically has helped to create an obsession with weaponry, large and small—assault rifles for the home, new stealth fighters and aircraft carriers for the homeland's military. "Our personal insecurities, due to debt, lack of affordable healthcare, low-paying jobs, weather catastrophes, and fears of various sorts—like 'invading' hordes of 'bad hombres'— have driven a cult of security in which guns and related military technologies have been offered as a palliative or even a panacea. Feel secure—buy a gun. Feel secure— build a new stealth bomber."

The supreme public servants have become the supreme self-servers—Eisenhower has mutated into Petraeus—and somehow we've failed to notice. "There is an asymmetric burden of risk," Chuck Spinney says of the military leadership. "Whether in the Pentagon or in industry, these people spend other people's money and spill other people's blood, but they pay no price for their decisions." Behind the close-cropped grizzled hair and lithe, upright bearing, beneath the uniforms with the chest candy that have become as sacred in many minds as the American flag, the generals have become a corporation, which like most other corporations unswervingly pursues its own interests, even at the expense of the common good.

CHAPTER 3

The Money Dance

The corruption of the best things gives rise to the worst.

David Hume, *The Natural History of Religion*, 1757

O n August 25, 2011, Arvin Lewis, vice president of Patient Business and Financial Services at Halifax Hospital in Daytona Beach, Florida, called the office together for a biweekly management meeting on the broad floor of the hospital's administration building. As his colleagues watched in silence, Lewis, a short, rotund, balding man with a close-cropped gray beard, announced that the "Million Dollar Hour" had arrived. "Here comes the Money Man!" he crooned. He switched on a boom box, and Petey Pablo's rap tune "Show Me the Money" blasted across the floor. Swaying to the music, Lewis lip-synched the lyrics:

Come on, let a momma work for me
Make a playa wanna spend some moneeeeeeeeey. . . .

As the music played, three women, all senior hospital officials, approached Lewis holding ritualistic objects, like priestesses at some bizarre initiation. Wanda Gerson, the chief nursing officer, pinned a green towel decorated with gold dollar signs around his shoulders like a cape. Joni Rahn, director of Patient Financial Services, set a black hat with large white dollar signs on his head. And Shelly Shiflet, the associate legal counsel, hung a thick gold chain around his neck with a gold dollar sign as big and bling as a Mercedes hood ornament.

Elin Baklid-Kunz, director of Physician Services, stole a glance around the room. "I was watching all this," she remembers, "and I was wondering whether anyone else saw what I was seeing, or thought it was unusual. Is this really okay behavior at a nonprofit hospital? Shouldn't we be talking about patient care? Beth Hollis, the nurse manager who was about to retire, looked at me and rolled her eyes. The rest just laughed, or clapped their hands to the music. Everybody was just going with the flow, like the Milgram experiments. It was horrible. I literally thought I was losing my mind."

Not that Lewis had made a mystery of his priorities as a manager at Halifax. On the hospital intranet, he had a personal page dedicated to what he called "Arvinisms," seventeen aphorisms that outlined his philosophy of work and personal success. These included:

- The only thing better than cash is lots of it.
- The system is a beast and it is always hungry (for cash).
- We do not have any problems that cash can't fix.
- Regardless of what the bank commercial says, I did want to grow up to be a money man.
- Success is getting what you want, happiness is wanting what you get and I just want some cash.

A video on the Halifax website showed Lewis dressed up as a monkey, which employees were told represented the monkey on their backs to make more money. Another showed Lewis and Halifax CFO Eric Peburn dancing to celebrate a big collection day. A hospital employee composed a song, "The Twelve Days of Collections," set to the tune of "The Twelve Days of Christmas." At one office meeting, Lewis distributed green umbrellas printed with white dollar signs to Halifax employees. "Our management meetings never opened with a discussion of patient care," Baklid-Kunz remembers. "The meetings were always about cutting costs."

There was another reason why Baklid-Kunz saw Lewis's money dance in a different light. The hospital knew she had filed a whistleblower suit that alleged that

Halifax had, in essence, paid too much attention to money, by overbilling Medicare, paying kickbacks to doctors, and committing other forms of profitable wrongdoing. Perhaps, she thought, the money dance "was some kind of signal to people who knew about the lawsuit, that everything was fine. In fact, things remained business as usual at the hospital, just like before the subpoenas." Before learning that Baklid-Kunz was the whistleblower, one manager told her that the hospital leadership wasn't particularly concerned about the subpoenas, but that he felt almost sorry for the person who'd alerted the authorities. Whoever they were, he said, Halifax would make them regret it.

Baklid-Kunz grew up in the 1960s and early 1970s, first in Jostedal, a village of four hundred inhabitants in western Norway, and then in the slightly larger town of Hokksund, where the local accent sounds folksy to the ear of city dwellers in Oslo an hour to the east. After thirty years in the States, she speaks perfect colloquial American, but now and then hesitates over a word choice, or stretches a vowel, turning "do" into "düü," "moon" into "myyyyn." The Norway she was raised in hadn't yet grown wealthy on oil reserves, and people in Hokksund lived by thrift and hard work. Baklid-Kunz's father dropped out of high school after World War II and worked on a whaling ship in the Antarctic for a year at a time; later he worked in a local paper mill, where his own father had taken only two sick days in fifty-five years, a feat that earned him a medal from the king. "We didn't have much, but everybody had the same, and we all felt we had everything we needed," she remembers. "We spent a lot of time outdoors, didn't watch television. Many people didn't own a television."

Her mother was a seamstress who worked at home, and her grandfather—the famous worker—lived next door. Two doors down were two pairs of uncles and aunts, and eight cousins. Hokksund itself was a tight-knit community. When the general store got a new bolt of cloth, all the children wore matching clothes for that season. People lived according to the Jantelov, or "Law of Jante," an informal Scandinavian social code that encourages group harmony and discourages overachievers. "A lot of people hate the Jantelov because they say it doesn't teach people to progress and reach for higher heights," Baklid-Kunz says. "But we're kinda taught as kids never to think you're better than anyone else. Just because someone is in a high position, like the CEO of a company, doesn't mean you should follow them blindly. For me this was important later on at Halifax."

Baklid-Kunz excelled in school, which, like other children in Norway at the time, she started at seven years of age, but there were no programs for "gifted" students: she and other faster learners were encouraged to help slower learners. "We had no grades until middle school, just general evaluations. So no one gets labeled as having 'bad grades in math.' You all work as a group, and move forward together. And if someone gets hurt—it's kinda the sandbox rule—you don't look the other way. If you're the stronger person, you're always looking out for those who are not." Baklid-Kunz, following the family tradition, was a hard worker. During high school she worked in a cafeteria, and she juggled three jobs over the summer. (She spent the money she earned on books and other school expenses, as well as brief trips in Europe.) She's proud that in her twenty years of work in Florida—even during her whistleblowing ordeal at Halifax—besting her grandfather, she never took a sick day.

At nineteen, she moved to Miami as an au pair. After her childhood, Florida was like exotic fruit: hot, lush, fragrant. "The palm trees, the Latino culture, the warm wind off the Gulf—I would love to live here!" she remembers thinking. After her au pair stint ended, she enrolled in a business program at a local community college, then transferred to Florida International University in Miami, where she initially studied business but, daunted by the mandatory speech class, transferred to hospitality management. "I could never get up in front of a room full of people—I was petrified," she says. "I only overcame this much later, when I started speaking about coding regulations and explaining to my colleagues at the hospital that we were breaking all those laws."

With an immigrant's endurance, she paid her way through school, sometimes holding three jobs at a time as she had in Norway. She met her husband, Russel, a power company operator and licensed welder and plumber, while in college, and moved with him to Orlando, where she took a job at a restaurant after she'd completed her hospitality degree. Their first child, Michelle, was born six years later. Baklid-Kunz received her MBA from Stetson University on Mother's Day, when

Michelle was two years old, a memory that seems to trigger un-Jantelovian emotions: "That was probably the hardest thing I've ever done: study, work full-time, breastfeed and have a toddler. After that, I remember thinking, 'I can do anything!'" The couple's second child, Eric, arrived six years after that.

In February 1994, Baklid-Kunz took a job as food service manager at Halifax, a hospital in nearby Daytona Beach that now has 764 beds and over five hundred physicians in forty-six medical specialties. From a starting salary of $9.50 an hour, she worked her way up over the next fifteen years, through successive promotions in the finance department, compliance, and business and financial services, where in 2008 she became director of Physician Services. "Halifax was like a family for me. All of my friends were there, and I really looked up to some of my bosses. I was incredibly proud of that hospital, and the work we did in the community."

However, after transferring to the compliance department in 2005 and undergoing intensive training to earn certification as a compliance officer and professional coder, Baklid-Kunz began to see problems. When she was asked to standardize the hospital's employment contracts with its various specialists, she found that oncologists, neurosurgeons and other specialists were being paid bonuses based on the hospital's operating margin, which she believed to be illegal. "I thought that doctors should not have profit-sharing from the hospital. But my boss, Arvin Lewis, said that Halifax wanted them to have 'skin in the game,'" as he put it. She reported this observation to her former boss, George Rousis, head of compliance. Rousis was a widely recognized expert in compliance, at the hospital and across the state of Florida, so Baklid-Kunz felt she could rely on his judgment. Rousis told her not to blow the issue out of proportion. "But when I went to a compliance seminar in Philadelphia in October 2008, a lawyer who was speaking there, Bob Wade, explained that contracts that involved profit-sharing from the hospital violated the Stark Law. That it was illegal. And I thought, 'But wait, that is exactly what we're doing!'"

Elin Baklid-Kunz speaks like this: she states names, legal statutes and exact dollar amounts, often the date and day of the week when something important occurred. Occasionally she'll stop in the middle of a sentence and her eyes will drift slightly to the side as she considers; after a second or two, she'll retrieve the word or figure she's just scanned her mental RAM for, often spelling out longer names one letter at a time. She says she's always had a retentive memory—"I still remember the birthdays of each of my elementary school classmates. It's always been a curse." It was a blessing, of course, for her lawyers and the prosecutors in her case. She remembers exact phrases she heard years before; some apparently stuck in her memory because they were new to her, and she had to look them up. She remembers an ER director saying that some doctors' practices were "rife" with overpayment, which she googled. When she asked Rousis how he could sleep at night, knowing that the hospital was breaking the law, he replied that he supposed he'd become "jaded."

She was right about the contracts. The Stark Law prohibits doctors from referring Medicare patients to hospitals where they have a financial relationship, because such arrangements create a conflict of interest and can induce doctors to recommend testing, surgery and other medical procedures that earn them money but aren't in the best interests of their patients, potentially harming those patients and shortchanging Medicare. Baklid-Kunz explains the conflict with a reference to her own family, whom she often mentions: "When my mom had cancer, if a doctor could have earned more for himself by prescribing cheaper drugs, even a drug that didn't help her as much, that's illegal." Stark also prohibits paying doctors above fair market rates for their services, which is how some hospitals have concealed paying doctors for referrals. Baklid-Kunz suspected she was seeing something of that sort in Halifax's employment contracts with oncologists, neurosurgeons and psychiatrists.

When she returned from the conference, she gingerly suggested to hospital managers that they might want to review the terms of these contracts. "I knew how they talked about other people who tried to bring up valid concerns: they were always called a troublemaker, no matter what had been brought up. Then they soon would be gone." Rousis was clearly concerned. "He said that if we ever had the government look at these contracts, it would be a 'firestorm.' That word stuck in my mind, because I had to google it." An attorney in the legal department, Audrey Pike, wrote a memo that detailed how Halifax was violating the Stark Law and said the hospital should consider self-reporting this violation to the government. Ulti-mately, however, the consensus among senior managers was that the contracts were acceptable: they had already received qualified approval from McDermott Will & Emery, the corporate law firm that handled much of the hospital's legal business. Pike told Baklid-Kunz, her friend, that this interpretation wasn't likely to hold up in court, but that if they lost, they could sue McDermott for malpractice. In the end, Halifax did not self-report, nor did it rewrite the contracts to comply with the law.

During her eight years in the hospital's finance department, Baklid-Kunz says, "we were only looking at the money side of things, and never really thought about the patients. They were just numbers in a spreadsheet for us." A popular maxim in the department was "Just do, don't think." Baklid-Kunz's move to compliance changed her perspective. She began to review medical records, Medicare claim forms and other documents, where she saw vast differences between the clinical care that the hospital said it was providing—and for which it was claiming reim-bursement from the government—and the treatment it was actually giving some patients. One of the first sets of medical documents Baklid-Kunz looked at was from a patient who had been hospitalized for brain cancer and eventually died. The Medicare claim form showed that the neurosurgeon had billed for critical care every day of that patient's hospital stay. Yet the patient's medical record showed that the doctor had provided no critical care at all. "We had billed the insurance com-pany, Medicare, and the patient's family for co-pay, and we didn't even perform the service, because the office manager had automatically entered charges for every day the patient was in the hospital, without looking at the physician's documentation. Once you start reading the medical records, you're not in the spreadsheet anymore. This is an actual person that is being billed for stuff that didn't happen. The family has lost their relative, and now they're stuck with this bill?"

Reading the declarations on every claim form that Halifax submitted to Medi-care and Medicaid for reimbursements, Baklid-Kunz also got a stern sense of her own responsibility. "Each form stated that submitting false claims could re-sult in fines and penalties, including imprisonment. My compliance certification, my higher training, meant to me that I would be held to a higher standard. It's harder to say you don't know. I saw that I could be legally liable for not reporting violations."

She began to see further ways in which the hospital was noncompliant, and how these failures could put patients at risk. Hospitals earn far more money by admitting patients than by treating them on an outpatient basis or by holding them for observation and then releasing them. To avoid excessive admissions, the Centers for Medicare and Medicaid Services (CMS), the government entity that runs Medicare and Medicaid, passed stringent rules on patient admission. Halifax compliance had in fact produced its own protocols that laid out the appropriate decision-making tree for caregivers to follow. Yet hospital records from 2000 to 2006 indicated a steady rise in one-day admissions, and a nearly 50 percent decline in patients placed in outpatient observation. An internal audit of sixty-four short-stay admissions in March 2009 concluded that twenty-nine had been improper. A Halifax document estimated, based on this error rate, that the hospital was overcharging Medicare on one-day stays alone over $2.2 million per year.

Unnecessary admissions can do more than inflate government healthcare costs. When patients are admitted to any hospital, they are exposed to a range of health risks variously known in the medical profession as "iatrogenic illness," "medical misadventure" or "adverse events": hepatitis C infections, transfusion reactions, postoperative hemorrhage, and a great deal more harm than most people imagine. A 2010 report by the Inspector General of Health and Human Services found that 134,000 Medicare patients suffered accidental harm in US hospitals every month, and 15,000 of them died. A study published two years earlier in the *Annals of Internal Medicine* concluded that some 320,000 people die annually of serious yet preventable medical errors; a 2013 report in the *Journal of Patient Safety* put the number even higher, at about 440,000 patients a year, which would make adverse events in hospitals the third leading cause of death in America, behind coronary heart disease and cancer. This same 2013 report estimated the number of cases of serious but nonfatal patient harm at between four million and eight million per year.

While reviewing the internal audits, Baklid-Kunz encountered other problems, concerning the admission of patients complaining of chest pains. Nationwide, many chest-pain admissions are medically unnecessary, since chest pains can be caused by gastric reflux and other relatively benign conditions. Yet such symptoms are widely abused to justify increased patient admissions. In October 2007, Halifax had opened a specialized chest pain center with a clear case-management protocol, designed to receive chest pain patients from the ER and treat them on an outpatient basis, but an internal review the following year revealed that 61 percent of chest pain admissions had violated the protocol, an error rate that continued to climb. Apparently under pressure from hospital administration to increase revenues that many of them would share in, doctors were ignoring the established policies.

Halifax's revenue-above-all philosophy was widely espoused by managers and doctors alike. During a January 2008 meeting to discuss the audit results on the problem of improper one-day admissions, Baklid-Kunz was told by the director of cardiology, "The hospital will not make any money if these patients are treated as outpatient cases." Arvin Lewis relayed an estimate by CFO Eric Peburn that the hospital had lost $3 million already that year, as a result of assigning too many patients to observation; Lewis suggested not being "too aggressive" in that practice going forward, lest it "hurt our revenue cycle by millions." Some physicians said that the payment they received for admitting patients for observation or other lower levels of care was not worth their time coming to the hospital. During more than one staff meeting, Baklid-Kunz heard physicians say that if they couldn't routinely admit a patient as an inpatient, they would "leave the patient in the emergency room."

As part of an internal billing review and outside insurance reviews, the compliance department also discovered that one of the hospital's three neurosurgeons, Dr. Rohit Khanna, had systematically billed at the highest level of service for over ten years, producing a 100 percent error rate on one audit report. In a memo she wrote about this overbilling, Baklid-Kunz drew a man pushing a wheelbarrow full of cash, with the caption RETURN TO THE GOVERNMENT. The review also determined that Khanna and his neurosurgeon colleague Dr. Federico Vinas had used their physician's assistant or registered nurse to do their rounding, yet billed the government as if they had performed the procedures themselves. An internal review and external audit also revealed that Vinas's annualized RVUs (relative value units, a measure of the value of physician services to be reimbursed by Medicare) were 450 percent above the national average, yet Vinas had not been present for approximately 90 percent of the hospital rounding visits he billed for. Again, the overbilled amounts were paid directly to the doctors.

Most disturbing of all to Baklid-Kunz, the compliance department had received allegations of unnecessary spinal fusions, a high-reimbursement procedure, by Dr. Vinas, who was performing as many fusions as both of his fellow neurosurgeons, Rohit Khanna and William Kuhn, combined. Some of the complaints about Vinas came from other doctors at Halifax. Kuhn himself said that he had refused to assist in surgeries with Vinas, at least in part because, as he stated in a May 2, 2012, deposition, "I had felt somewhat uncomfortable regarding the procedure that was being performed." Another hospital employee was less diplomatic, telling compliance officers that referring patients there felt like "sending lambs to slaughter," because they were almost invariably operated on.

By May 2008, concern about Vinas's record had reached the point that hospital administrators decided to carry out an external peer review of his work by board-certified neurosurgeons; in December 2009, Baklid-Kunz was finally authorized to assist in obtaining the review. Medical staff director Cheryl Owen suggested that she retain Allmed Healthcare Management, a medical consulting firm in Portland, Oregon, which was widely recognized for its peer review work and had been used by Halifax in the past. Allmed's medical director, Skip Freedman, MD, instructed Baklid-Kunz on how to choose relevant cases for his company to examine; his criteria included operations on patients below the age of fifty-five, those that had led to readmissions, or those that had involved more than one level of fusion. The hospital's medical records department sent case files meeting these criteria to Allmed, where they were reviewed by four board-qualified neurosurgeons. The results of the Allmed report, which was sent to Halifax in March 2010, were worrying: the Allmed specialists concluded that, among the cases they had reviewed, one out of the five surgeries Khanna had performed, two of the five by Kuhn and a startling nine out of the ten by Vinas had been medically unnecessary. The report also observed that some of the procedures had been incorrectly performed or improperly documented in the medical records, and might have harmed the patients. Baklid-

Kunz read the Allmed report at the request of her supervisor, and was so upset at the opinion of an Allmed reviewer on one surgical error—that the patient would likely never be able to walk again—that she went to the bathroom and vomited. (The hospital disputed the validity of the Allmed report, and commissioned a second review of Vinas's surgeries, by Kentucky neurosurgeon Timothy Schoettle; a hospital spokesman said this new report had found all ten of Vinas's surgeries to be necessary, though he declined to supply a copy of this report, or to explain how Halifax had selected Schoettle to perform it.)

Baklid-Kunz alerted a number of high-level hospital managers to the problems she was seeing. She continued to burnish her credentials, taking further education courses in coding and billing practices and in compliance, sometimes at her own expense. She published articles on compliance, coding and reimbursement regulations in professional journals, and she began teaching physician billing methodology at a nearby public college. She attended conferences on healthcare compliance, and was soon invited to speak at them. "I did all this education hoping that the higher executives at Halifax would respect me more. If people knew I was speaking at national conferences, maybe they would take my opinions more seriously. I was constantly asking myself, 'If I do this, this, this, will they listen?'"

In June 2008, she was promoted to director of Physician Services, a position that put her back in the finance department, where she thought she might have the authority to fix some of the problems she now recognized at the hospital. Before accepting the position, she consulted with the hospital's general counsel, Dave Davidson. "I was concerned about the responsibilities in taking on this job. I felt that our issues were huge—upcoding, wrongful admissions, all the rest. So I asked him, 'What do I do if somebody shows up at my door at nine o'clock at night, and they're the FBI?' He told me not to worry, that we were a public hospital and couldn't be hurt by the False Claims Act. He said that he had friends high up at the DOJ and would know if there was any investigation going on." (Davidson left the hospital shortly after Baklid-Kunz's case ended, and is working as a lawyer in private practice.)

She continued to bring the numerous irregularities she was encountering to the attention of executives in the legal, business and compliance departments. During one particularly heated exchange, George Rousis told her that her loyalty was to

Halifax Hospital, not to the government, and that if she ever thought about becoming a whistleblower she should leave right away. "I never wanted to become a whistleblower," Baklid-Kunz says. "I gave the information to so many people, in compliance, in legal, because I thought they'd have to do something with it once they knew. I never imagined that people in their positions could just walk away." Yet this seemed to be exactly what they were doing. The lack of response began to take its toll. Baklid-Kunz suffered from continuous stomach pain and nausea. She began stress eating and eventually gained fifty pounds.

Matters came to a head later that summer when the hospital underwent an inspection by the HHS Inspector General's Office as part of a nationwide investigation of unnecessary admissions for a spinal surgery called kyphoplasty. Although the inspectors concentrated solely on this one procedure and did not seem to notice the other infractions Baklid-Kunz had been encountering, the inspection made her feel even more exposed. "I saw that I could be legally liable for not reporting violations. I felt that I could go to jail for this."

In March 2009, Baklid-Kunz learned that the hospital's oncologists had just received their annual incentive payments. She had assumed that these had been discontinued after she had pointed out the clear violation of the Stark Law, but now she understood that the money dance had continued. Driving home from work on March 25, 2009, the day before her nineteenth wedding anniversary, she pulled over to the shoulder, slumped forward on the wheel, covered her face with her hands and began to cry. She thought about her upcoming anniversary, and the toll her troubles at work had taken over the last two years on her husband, their marriage, their children. "I was in a shambles over all these things that were wrong. I was devastated that they hadn't self-disclosed, that nothing had changed. I would have given anything to get them to listen, but it was like we were speaking different languages. It must be like having a child that's a drug addict. You do everything you can to fix the problem, and then one day you realize that it doesn't matter what you do. It's beyond your scope."

Her first thought was to resign and move on. "I spent a great deal of time thinking if I could walk away from this and not do anything. I wanted to do that so bad, to just get another job and forget that this had happened." Ultimately, however, she decided she couldn't allow the harm to patients to continue. "When defenseless people are getting hurt, you can't turn your back. That's how I was raised."

She understood that she had already made what she now calls a "choiceless choice." Still sitting in her car by the side of the road, she made two calls. The first was to her husband. She told him that she had to do something to stop the wrongdoing at Halifax. "I'm probably going to lose my job," she told him. "We may lose our house. But I cannot do this anymore. I just know it's the right thing to do. We'll figure out the rest." Her husband, long troubled by her emotional turmoil, said he would support whatever she needed to do. "But no more speaking at conferences, no more extra work," he told her. "You're killing yourself, and it won't change a thing."

Her second call was to Marlan Wilbanks, an attorney in Atlanta, Georgia, who works exclusively with whistleblowers. She had found his name on the website of Taxpayers Against Fraud, a nonprofit legal advocacy group, and had noticed that he'd successfully handled a number of false claims cases, including a small Stark Law suit in Georgia. She had ruled out speaking with Florida lawyers, for fear that they might have connections with Halifax and would betray her to her employer. She worried about Wilbanks, too, given her general counsel's claim to have high-level contacts at the DOJ, but she dialed his number anyway. It was after business hours, so she planned to leave a message on his voicemail.

Instead, Marlan Wilbanks himself answered the phone.

In April 2015, I joined Marlan Wilbanks, his mother and his stepfather for a breakfast of flapjacks, grits and hash browns at a diner in Habersham County in northeast Georgia. Wilbanks grew up in this area, where, he points out more with pride than discomfort, much of the movie *Deliverance* was filmed. His speech is studded with southern pearls: he calls a fellow trial lawyer "smarter'n a tree full of owls" and indicates he's got one corporate fraudster dead to rights by saying, "I've got photos of him and the goat." Wilbanks did his undergraduate degree in political science at the University of Georgia, though he says he spent more time with his fraternity than at his books, earning money teaching tennis lessons and spending it on spring breaks in Florida. "He always was a risk taker, and did whatever he needed to do to win," says his mother, looking at Wilbanks with affection but also a hint of bafflement, as if amazed he turned out so well.

Wilbanks is still an opportunist, with an exuberant, often raunchy sense of humor. At the two country clubs he belongs to, where his name is on all the golf trophies, people "Hey Marlan!" him with obvious respect, and swap convivial abuse. Yet just below the easygoing surface is another man, edgy and unconventional, a long way from down home. He shares glimpses of a dark childhood, describing his father as "a cold, hard, non-gun-loving car salesman who worked all the time, and taught me how not to live my life." Wilbanks is chairman of Voice Today, an organization that fights child abuse. "Child abuse is the attempted murder of the soul, and it's happening all around us," he says quietly, faint red patches rising in his cheeks. His mother is also a supporter of Voice Today; Wilbanks explains that, as a child, she was sexually abused by her father. "One out of every four children is abused at some point in their life. But less than ten percent of cases are ever disclosed. For most people, it's easier to pretend child abuse is not happening." In 2016, he founded the Childhood Endangerment and Sexual Exploitation Clinic at the University of Georgia School of Law, the first organization of its kind in the nation, which helps provide legal help and social justice for victims of child sexual abuse.

The appeal of my syrupy pancakes wanes. "The key to addressing this problem is breaking the silence," he continues, "speaking up for people who don't have a voice. And outing the opposition—the people who'd rather keep their heads in the sand, when it's a big-money beach." He says that lobbyists for insurance companies and the Catholic and Baptist Churches were pressuring Georgia legislators to pass a statute of limitations on sex acts against children, in order to limit their own liability. In various "green door" committees where the matter was being debated more or less in secret, several prominent state lawmakers were going along. He and his mother confronted them during a public hearing at the statehouse. In the end, the Georgia legislature passed new laws that provide better protection for at-risk children and harsher penalties for abusers.

His work with abused children gives an edge to his description of how he came to practice whistleblower law. "Right out of law school I went to work in a small firm as a commercial litigator, in a general law practice that did some family law. One time my partner and I represented a woman on a child custody case. We did a terrific job for our client. The mother got full custody. But she was an alcoholic, and was keeping the kids to get more child support. I knew this all along. We won all right, but I didn't feel like celebrating. I didn't go to law school to feel like that." He says that he sleeps better as a whistleblower attorney. "You never have to doubt yourself or be in a moral dilemma, like a defense lawyer who deep down knows there was fraud, and tries to prevent the right evidence from coming out." Even the mechanics of whistleblower law work better for him. "I only get paid when I do a good job for my client. And when I do, the defendants—the fraudsters—write my checks. I know I'm from a turnip farm in North Georgia, but this is too good to be true."

A day later, touring his large house in Buckhead, a densely wooded suburb of Atlanta, with its hunting trophies and its views through the green twilight of the trees, he paused in the doorway of a small bedroom and pointed to the bed. "This is where I found Madie." I knew that his eighteen-year-old daughter had died suddenly three months earlier, from complications of juvenile diabetes, but I hadn't known how to broach the subject with him—whether to offer condolences or to remain respectfully silent. Now I mumbled something about how hard it must be to get over such a loss. Wilbanks gave me a blank look, weary and slightly bewildered. "We're not thinking about getting over it," he said. Not a reproach, just a statement of fact. "I will see her again. I am sure of that."

There is something naked, fierce, even a little frightening about Marlan Wilbanks's candor. He seems to be living one moment to the next, and has gone through enough hardship that he has no more time for lies. Perhaps this is what creates his bond with whistleblowers, and makes him such a good listener and ally.

He says that when Elin Baklid-Kunz first called him from that palm-lined road in Daytona Beach, "Everything came out in a rush. It had been so long since anyone had listened to her, believed her story, that she was a little desperate—as if she'd been talking a different language to her coworkers, and no one understood her. But what really struck me were the facts. Names, dates, documents—her recall was amazing."

Baklid-Kunz drove to Tampa a month later to meet with Wilbanks at the offices of James Hoyer, the Florida law firm Wilbanks contacted to assist with the case. Soon after, he accompanied her to Orlando to meet with members of the DOJ's Civil Division, who would be partners in prosecuting their False Claims Act case. Then Baklid-Kunz and Wilbanks rapidly drafted a complaint detailing the ways in which Halifax Hospital had presented false claims to state and federal healthcare offices. "The abuse was so long-term and so flagrant that we were sure other people at the hospital would be filing suits," Wilbanks remembers. "We wanted to be first." (False Claims Act legislation gives the first relator to file their case what often amounts to an exclusive right to a reward.) They filed the complaint in June 2009, at the US District Court for the Middle District of Florida, in Orlando. Then the waiting started.

Wilbanks told Baklid-Kunz that as long as she continued to work at Halifax, she must do her job just as she'd done it before filing the suit. While access to further compromising documents might be valuable in proving her accusations, such materials would need to come to her in the normal course of her work: more and more companies are suing whistleblowers for using internal documents that don't meet this criterion, accusing them of stealing company property and violating corporate confidentiality. Wilbanks also advised Baklid-Kunz to resign and find another job before her case was unsealed, because her chances of being hired in healthcare would be nil after her identity as a whistleblower became public. "She wouldn't believe me. She was so wonderfully naive. She thought the best of people, and assumed that if she was right, people would respect her for speaking up. She found out different. Whistleblowers always do. They are almost always disappointed when they assume that compliance matters to a company as much as revenue."

Wilbanks shakes his head, as if disappointed not just by Halifax employees, but by humanity. "Wherever government healthcare dollars are up for grabs, the business model usually ends up sounding like a country western song—'Lyin', Stealin' and Cheatin'." His poor opinion of the US healthcare industry is born of long experience representing whistleblowers at hospitals and clinics. His first false claims case, back in 1997, involved a major hospital chain, Columbia/HCA, which his client and more than thirty other whistleblowers accused of sweeping and systemic fraud; the suit ended in one of the biggest healthcare fraud settlements in history, with combined civil and criminal fines of $1.7 billion. Since then Wilbanks has represented whistleblowers in scores of false claims, kickback, Stark Law and other suits against healthcare organizations, recovering more than $3 billion for US taxpayers and his clients. When we met, he and his clients were in litigation concerning hundreds of millions of dollars of alleged Medicare and Medicaid fraud by DaVita, a dialysis company (this ended later that year in a settlement of $450 million); Adventist HealthCare, a nonprofit hospital company (which settled in 2016 for $115 million); and two of the nation's largest for-profit hospital chains, Tenet Healthcare Corporation and Health Management Associates (in 2016 Tenet agreed to pay a $368 million settlement and $145 million in criminal restitution). He was also suing Wells Fargo, JPMorgan, Bank of America and several other banks for mortgage fraud against veterans and the government (seven of the banks have since settled, for a total of $270 million), and other major corporations he couldn't name because those lawsuits were still under seal.

Wilbanks has an unusual business model, which some attorneys believe represents the future of corporate whistleblower law. For each case, he assembles a team of local and national lawyers whose skills and contacts match the specific client and case. When working on large lawsuits outside of Georgia, Wilbanks regularly joins forces with other litigation firms, including Phillips & Cohen. But his A team is in Atlanta. His law partner, Susan Gouinlock, rounds off Wilbanks's high-energy rainmaking with calm, organization, and an almost scholarly love of documents. "I'm a big believer in looking at every page," she says, describing how she immersed herself in a twenty-thousand-page cache of documents subpoenaed from Tenet. "You see the signatures of people signing off on documents, you see dates, people who were present at meetings, all of which tells you who knew what, when. Looking at documents is like working a big jigsaw puzzle. It's strangely meditative: part of the mind has to be able to see the bigger associations." Gouinlock also helps translate some of Marlan Wilbanks's sports metaphors and southern aphorisms for clients. "He'd keep saying, 'We've got to move the ball down the field,' or 'It's fourth and one,'" Elin Baklid-Kunz remembers. She'd ask Gouinlock, "Is that good?"

Another long-standing collaborator is Scott Withrow, a partner at the Atlanta firm of Withrow, McQuade & Olsen, LLP. An experienced healthcare lawyer with expertise in Stark and kickback regulations, Withrow also advises hospitals and other healthcare companies on how to stay out of trouble, which helps him assess the merits of a case from the defendant's perspective. Wilbanks also calls in his "pit bulls," a handful of experienced, pugnacious Atlanta trial lawyers. Jim Butler, who is working on his banking case, has won more jury verdicts over $1 million than any other lawyer in the United States. A further hired gun is Lucian Lincoln "Lin" Wood Jr., a handsome, tanned, statuesque fellow whose silvery hair sweeps back from his high forehead and touches his collar behind. Wood drives a canary-yellow Lamborghini, competes in horse jumping, and made his name in high-profile libel suits in the 1990s. He represented Elin Baklid-Kunz against Halifax.

"We're a great team," Wood says. "I can take hard positions with the defense that Marlan might not want to take. I can rant and rave, and walk out. We've got the good cop–bad cop thing going for us when we need it." The presence of experienced litigators like Wood and Butler signals Wilbanks's readiness, even eagerness, to take cases to trial, while historically most whistleblower suits have been settled out of court. Several whistleblower attorneys see this as an important trend. "More whistleblower cases are going to trial, which I think is a good thing," says false claims pioneer Eric Havian, a former prosecutor and now a leader of the whistleblower practice at Constantine Cannon, a major litigation firm. "I get to depose witnesses, write briefs, do cross examinations—to do real lawyer work."

Essential to Wilbanks's litigation strategy is close collaboration with federal prosecutors, particularly those in the Middle District of Georgia. He's more reserved about his relations with certain attorneys at DOJ headquarters in Washington. In whistleblower suits, the DOJ officially represents the government agency from which tax dollars were stolen—not the taxpayers, the whistleblower-plaintiff or the people actually harmed by the scheme. In most healthcare fraud cases, for example, the DOJ represents the CMS, HHS or the FDA, while in nuclear energy cases its client is the Department of Energy (DOE). Like many experienced qui tam attorneys, Wilbanks says these agencies often hesitate to call out fraud that happened on their watch, whose existence suggests that they themselves were negligent, or worse.

Wilbanks's case against Wells Fargo, JPMorgan and other major banks illustrates this dysfunctional dynamic. Two of his whistleblower clients, who worked as mortgage brokers with veterans, informed him that the banks were charging inflated or illegal fees to refinance home loans, under a program guaranteed by the VA and specifically designed to protect veterans from predatory lenders. "The banks were ripping off the vets, tricking the government to guarantee the loan, then flipping the paper and getting extra value for the government guarantee of the loan. The scheme was rampant, with a substantial number of major lenders involved. But when my clients Victor Bibby and Brian Donnelly revealed the scheme, we got one lie after another not only from the banks, but from the VA as well. The VA told us not to believe our lyin' eyes. They claimed that veterans had incurred no damages, even though our review of the mortgages showed that thousands of loans were clearly tainted by unallowable fees—so they were illegal loans from the get-go. Tens of thousands of loans went into default, leaving the taxpayer on the hook. Some veterans lost their homes in foreclosure. Through all this, the ugly truth is that the VA was in bed with the banks, and is still in bed with the banks. They didn't care about the veterans, or the taxpayers. The VA made money at the closing table on every loan."

When its official client drags its heels, the DOJ has a hard time aggressively prosecuting a whistleblower suit. In this case, the DOJ obtained seventeen extensions of the seal, causing a delay of nearly eight years, while waiting for the VA to announce whether they believed there had ever been fraud in the banks' mortgage-writing practices. In the meantime, the banks and the VA continued writing mortgages to veterans using those same practices (which in fact turned out to be fraudulent). Finally, in 2011, the federal judge hearing the case lost patience with the DOJ and removed the seal, allowing Wilbanks, Jim Butler and their client to pursue the case on their own. Within months they had recovered $162 million from JPMorgan, Bank of America/Countrywide Mortgage, CitiMortgage (a subsidiary of Citigroup) and other banks involved in the scheme. (They later extracted an additional $108 million settlement from Wells Fargo, and expect to recover still more from Mortgage Investors Corporation when that case ends.)

But recalcitrant client agencies aside, many experienced qui tam lawyers say that the DOJ itself is often deficient in its handling of whistleblower complaints and sometimes antagonistic to the whistleblowers. Main Justice can be slow to intervene, which benefits the defendant; as the whistleblower attorney Tom Melsheimer has observed, prosecutors often prefer to settle rather than go to trial. Moreover, their settlements are frequently far lower than qui tam attorneys believe the government could get if it really pushed the plaintiff, and routinely less than what the government lost to the scheme in question—too low to represent an effective deterrent. "There's little incentive to be honest," Wilbanks says. "Companies that realize they're breaking the law and self-report can end up paying stiffer fines than if they'd stayed quiet and fought it in court when they got caught. This is screaming to the industry: 'Don't self-disclose! Roll the fraud dice, and you'll probably get away with it.'"

Ultimately, Wilbanks believes, the government's stance puts the interests of major corporations ahead of the welfare of ordinary citizens. "They know that taxpayers are being ripped off, yet they're also worried that innocent stockholders or employees will be hurt if they hit a company hard. Or in healthcare, that patients will suffer. But hold up a minute! Should a company's massive illegal profits be a defense of their acts of fraud? The mantra 'too big and fraudulent to fail' doesn't make sense to me."

The DOJ's softness on corporate criminals is often matched by its harshness toward whistleblowers. "I always warn my clients, 'Sooner or later, your government will turn against you,'" says Jim Helmer, whose 1986 qui tam case helped John Phillips and Chuck Grassley amend the False Claims Act. "They're glad to take all the information the whistleblower has, but when it comes to giving, to treating them like a partner in the case, few prosecutors do. I think it's the instinctive reaction of people in a big hierarchy, against people who, at some point in their career, have broken the chain of command." This adversarial attitude toward whistleblowers often becomes overt when the time comes to determine a whistleblower's award. The DOJ routinely ignores the 15 to 30 percent guideline for the relator's share established in the law and proposes significantly lower rewards. While no DOJ lawyer would comment officially on this practice, off the record some underscore that they are legally obligated to maximize the return of stolen tax dollars to the Treasury. When a prosecutor and former law school classmate of Tom Devine mentioned this rationale, Devine replied, "Sure, but if you abuse your own key witnesses like this, other whistleblowers won't come forward, [and] you'll soon be returning 100 percent of nothing to the Treasury."

Some DOJ lawyers have a low opinion of whistleblowers and the attorneys who represent them. While working on a settlement agreement for a major false claims case against Singer, the sewing machine manufacturer, Joyce Branda—who until recently led the DOJ's Civil Division—blew up at John Phillips and his colleague Robert Montgomery, who were representing the whistleblower in the case. "This is so wrong—this is outrageous!" she shouted at Montgomery. "We do all the work, and you get all this money!" A former senior prosecutor who worked closely with Branda on whistleblower suits but now defends companies against whistleblowers told me that the evidence whistleblowers provide is often of minimal use to prosecutors, and claimed that they interfere with the investigative priorities of the DOJ. "And it's outrageous how wealthy some qui tam lawyers have become," he said, before suggesting that defending whistleblowers was a dishonorable occupation. Several qui tam lawyers have told me that Branda's successor as head of the Civil Division, Michael Granston, shares her dim view of whistleblowers. In fact, in a leaked memorandum dated January 10, 2018, Granston urged prosecutors to dismiss more false claims cases, including not only those that lacked merit or threatened national security but also those that interfered with a government agency's policies or programs. In previous writings and interviews, Attorney General William Barr has called the qui tam provision of the False Claims Act "an abomination" and "a devastating threat to the Executive's constitutional authority." The Supreme Court was recently asked to review a case that questioned the constitutionality of the FCA. Though the case was withdrawn, other challenges may come under this hostile DOJ and lead to the court's declaring the FCA to be unconstitutional.

Wilbanks says he's pursuing a new paradigm in his false claims cases. Most qui tam attorneys eagerly court government intervention, because the DOJ brings to the table powerful tools like subpoena powers and the threat of criminal prosecution, and because the government's presence lends a case gravitas. Wilbanks sees things differently. "We used to want to get all the government support we could.

But the more cases I did, the more I realized that the government agency in play is sometimes a bigger problem than the defendant. We're supposed to be partners, but they're not always on our side. You start out wanting government support, but can end up wanting them to stay as far away as possible." Working with his own team and his network of legal allies, Wilbanks has achieved record-breaking recoveries without DOJ intervention—though he notes that the government has gladly helped itself to its portion of the spoils.

In the Halifax case, however, a team of DOJ prosecutors, led by Adam Schwartz, Patricia Fitzgerald and Ralph Hopkins, worked closely with Baklid-Kunz and her lawyers, proceeded expeditiously with their preliminary investigation, and intervened in the portion of the suit involving Stark violations. (They also stressed that their declining to intervene on the unnecessary surgeries and unnecessary admissions in no way diminished the merits of these allegations.) The suit was unsealed in June 2010, a year after it was filed, and Elin Baklid-Kunz's name appeared on the public docket. Yet no one at Halifax appeared to know.

"Every time someone would come into my office, I was sure they had found out that I was a whistleblower," Baklid-Kunz remembers. Finally, on September 21, DOJ prosecutors summoned hospital managers to a meeting in Orlando, at which they revealed Baklid-Kunz's identity. "It was a huge relief in one way," remembers Baklid-Kunz. "At least I didn't have to keep pretending." Many of the reactions were predictable. At team meetings, people would avoid sitting next to her. "Now and then a new employee would see the empty chairs next to me and sit down." She laughs. "But someone would tell them who I was, and by the next meeting, they were standing at the wall with the rest. It was like I had the plague." Her performance evaluations, which had been uniformly stellar, suddenly plunged; she received zeros in leadership. One longtime colleague stopped her at the entrance to the hospital and said loudly, in front of patients, "How dare you come back here? You should be ashamed of yourself!" (When she reported the incident to the hospital's legal department, the associate legal counsel dismissed it with a shrug: "What else can you expect, after what you've done?") She was moved to a small, unpainted office at the end of a long hallway.

Preparations for the trial proceeded. At the request of Halifax lawyers, Judge Gregory Presnell split the case into two prongs, one concerning the Stark violations, the other the unnecessary admissions and surgeries. Defense and prosecution began to take depositions, which brought further disappointments for Baklid-Kunz. One by one, Baklid-Kunz's friends and colleagues turned against her. George Rousis stated under oath that she had commissioned the medical peer review of the neurosurgeons to further her case, though it had actually been requested by other hospital officials long before she had any notion of filing suit. Lisa Tyler, with whom she'd met weekly to discuss oncology and neurosurgery incentives, said she could only remember talking about their kids during those meetings. Attorney Audrey Pike, who'd written the memorandum stating that Halifax was violating the Stark Law, testified that Baklid-Kunz had been plotting her whistleblowing for years.

In their discovery log, McDermott lawyers called Pike's memorandum "the document that shows the Stark violation." Yet they and Halifax did their best to prevent it and other compromising documents from coming to light. They omitted it in responding to Wilbanks's and Wood's discovery requests, claiming that it was protected by attorney-client privilege. What they didn't know was that Pike had emailed a copy of the memo to Baklid-Kunz. When Baklid-Kunz produced the document, lead McDermott lawyer Tony Upshaw accused her of stealing it, though she was able to prove that she had received it from Pike in the ordinary course of her work. This smoking-gun document made proving that Halifax had violated the Stark Law "as easy as killing baby seals in the bathtub," Wilbanks says.

The day before trial, Halifax agreed to pay $85 million to settle this portion of the suit, plus millions in legal fees to Wilbanks and his team. In the settlement agreement, the hospital explicitly admitted having violated the Stark Law and accepted a stringent corporate integrity agreement designed to help prevent future violations. But this was only part of Baklid-Kunz's lawsuit against Halifax. Some of the charges that mattered most to her concerned the alleged wrongful admissions and unnecessary surgeries, which she believed had injured and killed some patients.

———

When he was a boy, Mark Twain learned an important lesson about money from a young slave named Jerry. "You tell me whar a man gits his corn pone," Jerry told him, "en' I'll tell you what his 'pinions is." In later life, Twain saw the truth of this assertion: the average person, he wrote, "is not independent, and cannot afford views which might interfere with his bread and butter"; even while remaining convinced that he's acting honorably, he will instinctively behave in ways that earn himself money, all too often "dump[ing] his life-long principles into the street, and his conscience along with them."

This is an ancient theme. Socrates observed, "When wealth and the wealthy are valued or honored in a city, virtue and good people are valued less." The Old and New Testaments abound with warnings about money corroding faith and hardening hearts—the difficulty the rich have gaining entrance to heaven, and the love of money as the root of all evil. In legends and folktales, gold is Satan's favorite lure to steal away a person's soul or firstborn child, for corrupting friendships and families.

Over the past fifteen years, neuroscientists have found strong scientific grounding for this ancestral mistrust of money. Magnetic resonance images of the brain show that earning money activates the same neural circuitry that is lit up by food, sex and psychotropic drugs, and triggers the release of dopamine as a rewarding stimulus. Losing money, by contrast, stimulates the same parts of the nervous system that respond to pain and fear. "Money excites and motivates people by activating deep, subcortical circuits," says Stanford neuroscientist Brian Knutson, who performed groundbreaking brain imagery experiments. "On our fMRI scans, the possibility of making or losing money aroused the brain more consistently than seeing attractive naked bodies, or food that looked delicious." The existence of an addiction to money, gambling and financial risk-taking is by now widely accepted. Economist Andrew Lo testified before a congressional committee investigating the causes of the 2008 financial crisis that "prolonged periods of economic growth and prosperity can induce a collective sense of euphoria and complacency among investors that is not unlike the drug-induced stupor of a cocaine addict."

Money can also change our behavior toward others. "There is mounting evidence that increasing someone's wealth or power increases their indifference and dehumanization toward distant others, perhaps also their contempt," observes Daniel Fessler, an anthropologist at UCLA. "The increased rule-breaking, exploitation, and cheating by wealthier individuals is consistent with a reduced concern for others." In recent experiments by behavioral economists, people primed to think about money were twice as likely to lie, deceive and otherwise behave unethically in order to earn money; they socialized less with other participants and preferred to work alone rather than in groups. Economics majors tended to make more selfish choices than students in other departments, and, in turn, were more inclined to assume that their competitors would behave selfishly. When people focus their energies on money, they tend to lose sight of the ethical dimensions of an activity and its potential impact on others, a phenomenon known by behavioral scientists as "framing."

Other scholars see money as both a symptom and a cause of broad shifts in worldview. Classical historian Richard Seaford asserts that, with the appearance of a money economy in fifth-century BCE Athens, people began conceptualizing coins, whose value was guaranteed by the city's official seal, as a new kind of ideal essence that was more significant than the gold or silver from which they were made—much as the forms or ideas posited by Plato around the same time also in some sense upstaged concrete reality. Psychiatrist and philosopher Iain McGilchrist points out how money, like language, creates metaphoric virtual realities of often hypnotic power.

Money, then, is a highly psychoactive substance. Using it as an organizational principle for society seems a risky strategy. Yet over the past four decades of market triumphalism, the accepted wisdom among conservatives and market-friendly liberals alike has increasingly been that markets are the path to social well-being, that private wealth is identical with public good, and that freedom from government regulation and social obligation are the only authentic freedoms. At the same time, long-standing ethical prohibitions against commodification have lost their normative edge. The result is that money has unparalleled significance in today's society, not only as the fuel of markets, but as the measure of human success and fulfillment. "We've never had this kind of influence of money in society before," observes business psychology scholar Max Bazerman. "It's a profound influence, in countless and sometimes quite terrible ways."

Economic historian Karl Polanyi painted the broad canvas of the ascent of money in his 1944 masterpiece, *The Great Transformation*, which traces the rise of the "market society," where economic exchanges are considered the most natural, and in some sense the ideal, human interaction. But perhaps the most detailed, disturbingly pointillist picture of the triumph of cash in the West is *What Money Can't Buy: The Moral Limits of Markets*, by Harvard legal scholar Michael Sandel. More than at any time since the Gilded Age, Sandel argues, people can purchase social privileges with money: they can buy their way to the front of a line at airports, amusement parks or the Supreme Court; acquire a green card to live in the United States; or obtain a permit to shoot critically endangered animals. Corporations, likewise, can purchase the right to pollute; to "brand" public parks, squares and stadiums; to market their products and ideologies in schools; and to take out life insurance on their unknowing, unconsenting employees (and to collect premiums when those employees die). Many economists and politicians regard financial incentives as the best way to mold human behavior: to encourage kids to read, to prod teachers to teach better and smokers to quit, to convince women to sterilize themselves with a hysterectomy. Some devotees of the free market go further: Richard Posner, an influential federal judge and legal scholar at the University of Chicago, has suggested that kidneys in organ banks, and babies available for adoption, should be auctioned off to the highest bidder.

Sandel argues that the intrusion of money into realms where a deeper human morality is actually paramount—sexuality and reproduction, child rearing, education, medicine, criminal justice and the environment, for example—is not progress, but corruption. Yet it is a corruption we often seem powerless to define, and therefore to prevent, as formerly widespread conceptions of virtue and human dignity on the one hand, and of the intrinsic tawdriness of cash on the other, lose force. Thanks to a half century of intellectual groundwork laid by economists and lawyers, the proposition that human behavior is, at some level, best understood as a cost-benefit analysis holds sway with legislators, judges, public policy experts and financiers, who have helped to create a world in which money is considered unambiguously good. Earning money for shareholders is put forward as the supreme obligation and statutory responsibility of all public corporations. Laws and legal penalties are widely viewed as mere economic strictures, with no inherent moral force. The Supreme Court asserts that cash is equivalent to free speech, and the medium through which corporations exercise their First Amendment rights.

Most of us sense that we shouldn't buy and sell babies or vital organs, just as we believe, in general, that the primary obligation of doctors is to heal the sick, of engineers to build safe bridges and nuclear power plants at a fair price, of bankers to husband their clients' wealth, and politicians to serve the common good. We instinctively know that when corporations pay politicians, in most cases they are buying influence, and that a historic stadium renamed for an energy company or a bank has lost its soul. Yet in the workplaces where many of us get our corn pone, money dances are in vogue, leading many to ignore or even relish the psychotropic and moral-anesthetic powers of cash.

Elin Baklid-Kunz saw how money eroded Halifax Hospital's stated mission to heal the sick and the injured. She dates the most serious problems at the organization to the arrival of the current CEO, CFO, and chief revenue officer, none of whom had formal medical training. "I think in a hospital you need to keep clinical people in some of those positions, but in our case, they were all finance people," she says. "I know from when I was involved in budget that when you have a good year, the money doesn't go to increasing nursing staffing ratios for better patient care. It goes to their salary increases, their executive pension plan." The gulf between the hospital's high-minded, publicly stated goals and its real, day-to-day behavior also became clear to her when she trained new employees in the hospital's ethical standards, one of her responsibilities in compliance. Her presentation, "Our Values in Action," had been carefully scripted by top hospital executives. It included a letter from the CEO, Jeff Feasel, which stressed the hospital's "tradition of strong moral, ethical and legal standards of conduct," and a set of core values, which included respect, honesty, integrity, compassion and trust. She identified several "risk areas" where the new hires would need to be vigilant, like conflicts of interest, kickbacks for patients and referrals, wrongful billing, and false claims. But she also reassured them that they didn't have to be experts: when in doubt, she told them, "let your values be your guide."

In light of the accusations in Elin Baklid-Kunz's whistleblower lawsuit, her compliance presentation at Halifax reads like a catalog of the very practices and attitudes that the hospital failed to enforce. As Baklid-Kunz realized this, teaching compliance became almost unbearable. "I remember standing in front of that group and telling them how proud Halifax was that we'd had a compliance program since 1998, and we do this so that we don't become the Enron of Daytona Beach—that was my script," she says. "And once I learned what was going on, I felt that I was two personalities. I felt like I was getting up there lying to these people, because we weren't doing any of the things our policy said we would. That's why when I learned all this I told my boss, 'I can't do this anymore. I can't sleep at night.' And that's when he told me that my loyalty was to Halifax, not to the government— our goal was to protect Halifax."

As Baklid-Kunz explained in her presentation, the compliance industry was born in 1986, after the series of defense procurement scandals that gave John Phillips and Chuck Grassley the necessary leverage to amend the False Claims Act. That year, Ronald Reagan formed a commission to study the scandals, headed by former deputy secretary of defense David Packard, one of Ernie Fitzgerald's perennial foes and CEO of Hewlett-Packard, a major defense contractor that had itself been implicated in contracting fraud. Reagan was an advocate of outsourcing government activity, including the enforcement of laws and regulations, to the private sector; perhaps unsurprisingly, Packard's commission concluded that self-policing was the best way for defense companies to stop fraud in their ranks. Lockheed, Northrop and twenty-two other contractors, many of whom were undergoing fraud investigations, formed the Defense Industry Initiative, whose stated aims were to improve the business practices, regulatory compliance and (perhaps most important) public image of the defense industry. Their methods for creating an ethical business culture—drawing up written codes of ethics, training employees in appropriate behavior, and instituting anonymous hotlines to report wrongdoing— became cornerstones of a new compliance movement that rapidly spread to other industries. The judicial branch officially endorsed this self-regulatory approach, stipulating that only organizations that formed compliance programs would be eligible for reduced sentences if convicted of wrongdoing. In 2002, after a spate of massive financial scandals including Enron and WorldCom, Congress passed the Sarbanes-Oxley Act, which introduced new compliance requirements for all US public companies. Chuck Grassley further boosted the compliance industry with a provision in the Deficit Reduction Act of 2005, which required most healthcare organizations receiving $5 million or more a year in Medicaid reimbursements to educate their employees in the False Claims Act and other whistleblower laws.

In principle, the compliance department is an institutionalized whistleblowing body within an organization, like the inspector general's offices instituted in many government agencies a few years earlier. In practice, compliance programs often become an elaborate game that a company plays with itself, while proceeding toward its real goal of making as much money as possible. This shouldn't surprise us. In sports, after all, players are told to follow the rules and to exhibit good sportsmanship, but umpires remain on the field to blow the whistle on every foul. In business, by contrast, most of the referees have been sent home. Compliance is now a multibillion-dollar industry whose members run research institutes, organize worldwide conferences, publish best practice guidelines and design specialized software. Despite these efforts, corporate crime has continued unabated; by many measures, it has grown. "A company has an informal, hidden culture whose norms, signals and pressures often influence employee behavior far more than its formal compliance and ethics programs ever will," Max Bazerman observes. "This hidden culture isn't announced in official declarations, but is passed along informally among employees, teaching what the company really expects of them." Generally, what the company really expects is profits: bonuses and promotions usually depend on revenue, not on honesty or integrity.

Some firms use ethics-speak as PR to reassure regulators and investors, even though studies have shown that the more often words like "ethics" and "corporate responsibility" appear in a firm's annual report, the more likely it is to have a poor corporate governance record and a history of class action lawsuits. Incessant messaging about how ethical and law-abiding an organization is also appears to reassure its employees that all of its activities are aboveboard, blinkering them to wrongdoing. Often, as at Halifax, the compliance department reports to the legal department, allowing management to classify employee complaints, internal audits and other potentially compromising documents as legal communications, protected from legal discovery by attorney-client privilege. Compliance is often overseen by the very people who are relentlessly focusing the organization on money, like Arvin Lewis, a member of the Compliance Committee at Halifax. In a criminogenic organization, compliance often becomes an exercise not in avoiding bad behavior but in covering it up. Elin Baklid-Kunz describes how her superiors instructed her not to put potential violations of healthcare law in writing, and to replace charged words like "fraud" with more neutral terms like "potential overpayment." She also found that internal reporting mechanisms at the hospital could become traps for critics of the organization, including whistleblowers: a colleague in the food service department lodged a complaint about her boss with the human resources department, only to be met at the elevator, as she returned to her floor, by the boss, who had already been alerted by HR.

Ultimately, compliance departments and ethics training, like their guiding philosophy of self-policing, are based on the false assumption that people are fully aware of ethical dilemmas whenever they encounter them, and consciously decide whether to behave ethically or unethically. This idea contradicts the work of Stanley Milgram, Solomon Asch and other groundbreaking social psychologists, who proved that bad behavior is caused less by bad morals than by the pressures of authority, group conformity and self-interest. More recently, behavioral economists and behavioral ethicists have shown how subconscious mechanisms can cause honest, well-intentioned people to cross ethical lines without seeing them. In a classic experiment, Uri Gneezy and Aldo Rustichini persuaded ten day-care centers in Haifa, Israel, to introduce a fine for parents who arrived late to pick up their children—which, surprisingly, caused late pickups to double. Gneezy and Rustichini concluded that, before the fines were instituted, parents viewed the teachers who looked after their children after the school closed as kind, generous people of whom they should not take advantage. After fines were introduced, the scholars suggested, parents felt differently: "The teacher is taking care of the child in much the same way as she did earlier in the day. In fact this activity has a price (which is called a 'fine'). Therefore, I can buy this service as much as needed." Similarly, compliance programs often reframe an ethical choice between right and wrong as a commercial decision, an analysis of the costs and the benefits of obeying the law.

In short, compliance can serve as a façade that conceals an organization's wrong-doing from outsiders and insiders alike. At the same time, like the gleaming marble credo in the Johnson & Johnson global headquarters or the Halifax "core values," compliance intensifies institutional hypocrisy, forcing employees to "double"—to live secret lives that are disturbingly at odds with what they and their colleagues profess to the rest of the world. For some people, this split personality becomes intolerable. A few, like Elin Baklid-Kunz, cry out.

After Halifax lost the first prong of the lawsuit with Baklid-Kunz, the hospital went on the offensive. It hired a major public relations firm, and as the second trial approached, began a barrage of press appearances and community outreach in the Daytona Beach area. During town hall meetings, hospital leaders insisted that Halifax had done nothing wrong, and was a victim of what CEO Jeff Feasel called arcane and "draconian" healthcare legislation. They depicted Baklid-Kunz's lawsuit as an attack on a vital safety net of the community, and on the selfless doctors who worked there. "We take care of everyone in our community," Feasel said at one meeting. "These physicians that were raked over the coals and made to feel like they criminally did something wrong are the very physicians who get up in the middle of the night on Christmas Eve, on the weekend and take care of people who can't pay for their health care."

Hospital officials stressed, in direct contradiction of court records, that no inappropriate care had ever been provided, nor had bills been submitted to Medicare for services not rendered. They emphasized the big payoff that Baklid-Kunz stood to receive from her whistleblowing and characterized her lawsuit as motivated purely by greed. Retired accounts payable clerk Pat Franklin called Baklid-Kunz's acts "beyond morally obscene."

Marlan Wilbanks counterattacked, rebutting the hospital's claims in a series of interviews. He pointed out that the law Halifax had broken—and had admitted to breaking—was crystal clear, and was anything but a technicality: the Stark statute existed, he explained, in order to prevent doctors from putting personal gain before their patients' health. "It wasn't a single line in a contract," Wilbanks told Skyler Swisher, a local reporter for the *Daytona Beach News-Journal*. "It was about creating a bonus pool for physicians that the more procedures they did, the more money that the hospital made. It's asking people to disregard the facts, disregard the law and pretend that the mistake wasn't so monumental that it cost them $85 million. That's a fantasy." He said that Halifax's attempt to portray Baklid-Kunz's lawsuit as an attack on the community turned the truth on its head. "If you admit patients to your hospital who don't need to be admitted, if you operate on the wrong limbs, then *you* are an attack on this community," he told me in August 2014, as the case approached trial. "When you steal funds with illegitimate expenditures, then there will be no money to pay for legitimate services. This is a culture of fraud, a culture of putting profit over patient safety. It's a cancer that is metastasizing all over the American healthcare system."

Wilbanks noted that the same executives who had led Halifax into wrongdoing were still in charge, so the hospital's ethics were unlikely to improve. Indeed, despite a document retention order issued by Thomas B. Smith, another judge involved in the case, Halifax destroyed all records for short inpatient stays between 2002 and 2004, when many of the alleged irregularities had taken place. Smith called the hospital's conduct "reprehensible" and recommended further sanctions against it. As the date of the new trial approached, teams of lawyers from both sides entered settlement negotiations.

Then, on July 1, 2014, just before the trial, Judge Presnell ruled that damages suffered by the government in unnecessary admissions were not, as Wilbanks and Lin Wood had argued, the $82.2 million in payments that Halifax had received, but only the difference between that figure and the cost of the outpatient services the hospital ought to have supplied—a figure that Baklid-Kunz's expert witness had not calculated. According to a lawyer who was familiar with the settlement negotiations, Halifax had been ready to pay a major fee, in the tens of millions of dollars, to conclude this part of the case. Now, however, they reduced their offer to $1 million, plus $4.5 million in attorney fees. With no time and few clear options, Baklid-Kunz and her attorneys accepted. Halifax admitted no wrongdoing and accepted no liability.

Wilbanks thought the court's pronouncement on damages sent precisely the wrong message to the healthcare industry. "If this ruling is right, and all a hospital has to do is pay the difference between the treatment they should have given a patient and the fraudulently inflated treatment they actually gave him, it's an open invitation to take their best shot. Ninety-plus percent of the time, they won't get caught. No wonder American healthcare is going broke. It's sad when committing fraud makes business sense."

Baklid-Kunz's whistleblowing was widely considered a success. She was named the 2014 "Whistleblower of the Year" by Taxpayers Against Fraud, which also made Marlan Wilbanks its "Lawyer of the Year." In financial terms, her whistleblowing was unusually lucrative. The DOJ, in recognition of her vital contribution to the case, approved a relator's share of 24.5 percent of the total settlement, which amounted to $20.8 million before taxes and attorney fees. Yet she would probably have made more money in the long run by simply keeping her head down and executing, or even embracing, the hospital's practices, which would have won her perhaps two more decades of an executive's salary, bonuses, benefits and pension.

"A lot of people look at whistleblowers like bounty hunters," Baklid-Kunz says. "They look at the reward as blood money. But people don't understand that most whistleblowers are motivated to act by something more than money, because there's really no guarantee of any reward at all. So many things can go wrong, and you can end up with nothing: no relator's share, no job, no future. I feel really bad for people who go through what I've done, and lose everything."

Meantime she feels like a pariah in her own community, where she's widely blamed for harming the hospital by causing it to spend more than $120 million in attorney expenses and settlements. To make up this shortfall, the hospital took on debt, announced a round of layoffs, and defunded the employee pension plan, converting it to a cash-balance account similar to a 401(k). "People think they lost their pensions because of me," Baklid-Kunz says. The executive pension plan remained intact, however, and most senior executives during her tenure have continued to prosper at the hospital. Arvin Lewis is now senior vice president and chief revenue officer, and Shelly Shiflet, associate counsel during Baklid-Kunz's tenure, was promoted to vice president and chief compliance officer in 2015. Even the registered nurse who did the alleged illicit rounding on behalf of Dr. Federico Vinas was promoted, and nominated for employee of the month. Drs. Khanna, Kuhn and Vinas, who have since left Halifax, were never accused of any wrongdoing, and all remain practicing neurosurgeons in good standing with the medical profession. Eric Peburn, who as CFO had ultimate responsibility for certifying that its cost reports were truthful, correct, complete, and did not violate any laws, was recognized by a major healthcare trade publication as a standout financial manager, as was Jeff Feasel, who remains president and CEO. Both Feasel and former Florida governor Rick Scott, healthcare entrepreneur and erstwhile CEO of the fraud empire that was Columbia/HCA, were recently honored by Daytona Beach's Bethune-Cookman University for their services to the community. As governor, Scott appointed all members of Halifax's seven-member board.

Over the past three years, Baklid-Kunz has applied for dozens of jobs in healthcare and related fields, but despite her impressive résumé, she hasn't yet been hired. In a recent experience that she views as symptomatic, she was recruited by the local office of a nationwide healthcare firm. A senior vice president at the local office invited her for an interview and promptly made her a job offer. Baklid-Kunz replied that she preferred to wait to respond until the offer was cleared at headquarters, although the vice president assured her that board approval would be a formality. A week later, the vice president sent her an apologetic email, saying that the board, and particularly the firm's general counsel, had objected to hiring a whistleblower. "I did all I could to make the argument for why it makes sense to hire you," she wrote. "The concern is how our larger clients will handle knowing that we're employing a whistle blower and that they could drop us as a client." (The disillusioned vice president resigned soon after.)

Some compliance professionals have also given Baklid-Kunz the cold shoulder.

When Marlan Wilbanks discussed her case at a major compliance conference in April 2015, organizers declined to include her in the panel that discussed the case, apparently, Wilbanks heard, because they didn't want to appear to favor whistle-blowers. "But whistleblowing is one of the core practices that compliance officers are supposed to defend!" Baklid-Kunz blurts. After paying $1,500 out of her own pocket to attend, she noticed that people seemed to be avoiding her. A friend who also attended told her why: "A lot of people here are thinking, 'What are you doing here? You got your money. Just move on.'"

"In a sense, I don't have anything to complain about," Baklid-Kunz says. "It's more that I don't know how to deal with the emotional side, of me doing the right thing and being punished for it, while the people who did the wrongdoing are fine. And the people who were really hurt, the patients, got nothing, and probably never will. I don't feel that I was successful as a whistleblower. Yes, I got the relator's share, but the good that I was looking for, that I thought should have come out of this, didn't come. I have to figure out how to move forward with that."

Baklid-Kunz told me this in the fall of 2017. By the following summer, a way forward seemed to have appeared. She abruptly realized that she actually didn't want a normal job with a boss, the kind she'd held all her working life. Almost im-mediately, she began to receive requests to serve as an expert witness and auditor in healthcare lawsuits, and as a speaker and teacher of compliance. "It feels good to reinvent myself, and find ways to continue fighting fraud and abuse," she says today. "It is not in my nature to be entrepreneurial, so maybe the grieving process of the last few years helped me to grow."

In October 1978, Dr. Roy Poses, an intern at the University Hospital in Boston's South End, the teaching hospital of Boston University, had just completed the first twenty-five hours of another brutal, sleepless shift. "People were horrendously over-worked," Poses remembers. "You walked in at seven a.m. and worked to seven p.m. the next day, with about two hours of sleep—no night floats, no day floats, no hours restrictions." Waiting for an elevator, eyes glazed and head bowed with fa-tigue, he wondered how he'd get through the day. When the elevator finally arrived, he stepped on, and found himself surrounded by men and women whose perfumes and colognes contrasted with the alcohol and disinfectant of the ward he'd just left, much as their tailored business suits contrasted with his body fluid–flecked, sweat-soaked scrubs. Conversation ceased. The well-groomed visitors were all watching him.

"It took me a while to figure out who they were," Poses remembers. "They certainly weren't doctors or patients. They were too well-dressed to be vendors. I thought they might be bankers." Eventually he understood: these were the hospital's financial executives, just arriving for their day's work in the management suite on the top floor. "I felt like rubbing up against them and saying, 'Go ahead, folks, take a whiff! I'm the guy you're paying minimum wage to keep this friggin' place running.'"

So began Poses's transformation into, if not a whistleblower in the strict sense, then a meta-whistleblower like Ralph Nader—a figure that has been essential to the rise of whistleblowing. Such figures interpret and provide context for the information that whistleblowers reveal, helping the public to understand its significance. And they lend whistleblowers themselves the moral support of being heard, which helps them to persist. Poses has used his experiences during a forty-one-year career in medicine to create *Health Care Renewal*, an erudite, sharp-tongued blog that is a sweeping indictment of healthcare in America. Poses's blog helps explain how the money dance came to Halifax Health, and why Elin Baklid-Kunz and so many other healthcare professionals end up blowing the whistle on their organizations.

After his encounter with the financial managers, still deranged by overwork and understaffing, Poses confronted Norman Levinsky, the hospital's chairman of medicine and physician in chief. "How is it that we get destroyed physically, working such long hours and drawing blood and doing IVs, so that when the patient crashes, we're a wreck?" he asked Levinsky. Most young interns wouldn't dream of speaking so bluntly with their chairman of medicine, who has a large say in their future job prospects. "I was so tired that my filter was off. Right after I spoke, I thought, 'My career is over.'"

Instead, Levinsky agreed. In fact, he explained, he'd been trying for some time to get money from the administration to pay for routine technical support, such as round-the-clock IV nurses. But hospital management had refused to pay for it. "At a much higher level, he was seeing what I saw," Poses says. "He was puzzled, and frustrated, by a sense that the hospital was being run by people who didn't understand medicine, or seem to care particularly either about patients or doctors."

This was Poses's first encounter with managerialism, which has seen financial managers take control of major hospital chains and other healthcare providers. He initially believed that the problem was limited to Boston University. "I just assumed that the chief of medicine and the chief of surgery ran most hospitals, and that the business people worked for them, to keep the finances straight." In fact, at that point CEOs, CFOs and COOs were a rarity at hospitals. "There might have been an 'executive director' or a 'hospital superintendent,'" Poses remembers, "but he was a retired doctor, and his office wasn't too grand. There were 'hospital administrators,' but you'd only contact them if the lights went out or there were no linens on the beds." However, as he moved to other posts at university medical centers in Pennsylvania, New Jersey and Virginia, before ending up at Brown University medical school in 1994, he found the same widening gulf between the values of medicine and the methods of hospital leaders, most of whom were skilled in capital rather than health.

Roy Poses's career spans a dramatic transition in US healthcare over the last half century, during which control over most aspects of the medical profession, from routine checkups to the education of doctors at medical schools to the development and marketing of new drugs, passed from doctors to financial managers, unmooring medicine from its original ethical and humanitarian basis. The triumph of managerialism in medicine is part of the broader rise of a professional management class that began in the early 1900s, with Frederick Taylor's groundbreaking studies in productivity, and accelerated after World War II as economists and accountants like Robert McNamara, possessing new quantitative skills rather than expertise in any particular field, began to move freely among leadership positions in government, industry, business schools and international financial institutions. The result was a new breed of generic executives who, as business historian H. Thomas Johnson writes, "believed they could make decisions without knowing the company's products, technologies, or customers. They had only to understand the intricacies of financial reporting."

One of McNamara's disciples applied the Whiz Kids' data tools to healthcare. Alain Enthoven, an MIT- and Oxford-educated economist, had led McNamara's systems analysis unit at the Pentagon before working at the defense and electronics firm Litton Industries, and then going on to teach economics, business management and healthcare policy at Stanford. In 1977, he wrote a white paper for President Jimmy Carter on US healthcare policy, replete with the cost-benefit analyses, planning-programming-budgeting systems and five-year plans of his Pentagon days. Subsequently he helped design Bill Clinton's plan for universal healthcare. Enthoven's central scheme, which he called "managed competition," was predicated on breaking up the close-knit "guild" of doctors that ran healthcare, an arrangement long guarded by the American Medical Association (AMA), which strove to ensure that doctors controlled their relationships with patients, hospitals, insurance firms and pharmaceutical companies, and protected them from having to think like businessmen. "The practice of medicine should not be commercialized, nor treated as a commodity in trade," declared the AMA's 1934 ethics guidelines. After a 1975 Supreme Court ruling that professional societies like the AMA were unlawfully limiting the professional freedom of their members with such norms, however, the AMA struck such financial prohibitions from its guidelines. Having abandoned the ethical high ground, the AMA rapidly moved from a grudging acknowledgment to an eager embrace of corporate money in medicine; today the organization lobbies for major healthcare firms and frequently criticizes whistleblower laws designed to combat wrongdoing by those firms.

In 1980, the Bayh-Dole Act allowed universities to patent inventions discovered in federally funded research, which had previously belonged to the government, and the Supreme Court ruled in *Diamond v. Chakrabarty* that genetically modified bacteria, and by extension any living organism, could be patented. Fields like pharmaceuticals and biotechnology were deregulated and became enormously profitable; they demanded new research—and were willing to pay academics handsomely to perform it. These developments vastly increased the flow of corporate dollars to medical schools and university science programs; at the same time, public funding to higher education entered a decline that grew steeper after the mid-1990s, and became a plunge after the 2008 Great Recession. To compensate for this lost income, universities began to accept more corporate money, to enter into joint-venture agreements with industry, to open intellectual property offices, and to encourage their faculties to launch for-profit enterprises. Whereas researchers had previously tried to keep their distance from industry, fearing that such cooperation would shift their attention from basic research to the more short-term—and marketable— problems of applied research and would also inhibit the free flow of scientific information in academia, now industry funding, collaboration and confidentiality became the norm. What a previous generation of researchers had considered selling out came to seem necessary, sensible, even shrewd. Researchers became entrepreneurs, as biochemists and geneticists launched biotech ventures or joined the boards of pharmaceutical corporations, just as economists opened their own investment vehicles and academics in other fields spun off consultancies and startups. Research in the public interest morphed into a search for private (and personal) gain. "It was once considered unseemly for a medical or science researcher to be thinking about some kind of commercial enterprise while at the same time doing basic research," says bioethicist Sheldon Krimsky. "The two didn't seem to mix. But as the leading figures began intensively finding commercial outlets and get-rich-quick schemes, they helped to change the ethos of the field. Now it is the multivested scientists who have the prestige."

As universities, medical schools and academic health centers felt these pressures to engage with industry, the managerial revolution arrived in academia. A growing class of professional university administrators, with MBAs rather than PhDs or MDs, assumed leadership roles in many parts of the academic world, much as they were doing in hospitals. They encouraged university researchers to welcome rather than to mistrust collaboration with industry, and declared that potential conflicts of interest could be managed as they were in business: with self-regulation. In these same years, hospitals were undergoing their own managerial revolution. Lyndon Johnson instituted Medicare and Medicaid in 1965, which together with new government subsidies of hospitals' physical plants and medical research, and the rapid spread of employer-based health insurance plans, brought billions of new tax dollars into medicine. Government healthcare spending soared in the 1960s. By 1969, President Nixon warned that the US healthcare system was on the verge of collapse. "The management of medical care has become too important to leave to doctors," *Fortune* magazine proclaimed.

Wall Street sensed a superb investment opportunity in this flow of funds, guaranteed by the government, into medicine, and helped finance a series of for-profit, publicly traded hospital chains—Hospital Corporation of America (HCA), Humana, Tenet Healthcare, Columbia Healthcare—which rapidly bought up nonprofit, community-owned hospitals across the nation and imposed on them a business model explicitly borrowed from the fast-food industry. (Jack Massey, founding partner of HCA, was the marketing virtuoso who had built Kentucky Fried Chicken into a nationwide franchise.) "A business that had begun as a charity had turned into an irresistible investment opportunity," writes Maggie Mahar in *Money-Driven Medicine*, her magisterial analysis of American healthcare corruption. The share prices of for-profit hospital corporations shot up, which allowed them to buy up more hospitals with their own skyrocketing stock. Salaries of top hospital management, which had been modest when doctors were in charge, rose like the pay packages of senior executives at publicly traded enterprises in other industries.

This, then, was the tide of perfumed and cologned managers whom Roy Poses first encountered in Boston in 1978. Their peers soon occupied the C-suites of hospitals around the nation, and increasingly decided how medicine would be practiced.

Shortly after his arrival at Brown, Poses met his first whistleblower. On November 22, 1994, Dr. David Kern, Poses's division chief in internal medicine at Brown's school of medicine, and a longtime director of the Brown University program on occupational medicine at Memorial Hospital of Rhode Island, examined a thirty-six-year-old textile worker with a peculiar lung condition, whose symptoms included patches of opacity in CT scans of his lungs and crackling sounds during chest auscultation, apparently caused by interstitial fluid in the lungs. The patient had been referred to Kern by a local pulmonologist, who had diagnosed the condition as hypersensitivity pneumonitis, an inflammatory condition caused by allergies to organic dust, which the pulmonologist believed he had inhaled at his workplace. Kern was skeptical—tests had revealed findings never before associated with hypersensitivity pneumonitis. Nevertheless, he contacted the worker's employer, Microfibres, in nearby Pawtucket, which manufactured textiles covered with finely cut nylon flocking for upholstery, clothing and automobiles.

Kern asked to visit the worksite, both to investigate possible causes of the worker's condition and to create a relationship between Microfibres and Brown University that might help resolve future industrial health problems. The company agreed, and on December 2, Kern, a Brown industrial hygienist and several students visited the plant, signed a generic, two-page confidentiality agreement, and collected air samples to test for the existence of mold spores that might cause allergic reactions. Kern concluded that the worker was extremely unlikely to have hypersensitivity pneumonitis and recommended he undergo a lung biopsy to explore his condition further. The biopsy was not performed, but after taking time off work and receiving treatment with corticosteroids, the worker recovered.

Over a year later, however, Kern saw another young textile worker, who had been referred to him for the same condition. This time a biopsy was performed, revealing interstitial lung disease (ILD), a scarring of lung tissue often caused by long-term exposure to hazardous material, which reduces the amount of oxygen that reaches the bloodstream. When he learned that this worker was also employed at Microfibres, he became concerned. ILD is a rare condition, with an expected annual incidence rate of one case in three thousand people. Yet Kern had just seen two cases in a workforce of fewer than two hundred people. He contacted the National Institute for Occupational Safety and Health (NIOSH) and notified Microfibres of his concern. Further research revealed that five other cases of ILD had been reported in a Microfibres facility in Kingston, Ontario, where one worker had almost died of acute respiratory failure and two others had suffered extensive, irreversible lung damage. During a meeting with the Microfibres CEO and senior management on February 26, 1996, Kern learned of a third cluster of ILD that had been detected at the Canadian plant. He proposed to carry out a comprehensive investigation of the Rhode Island facility; company officials agreed, formally requesting a consulting arrangement with the Brown occupational medicine program and a health hazard evaluation by NIOSH.

The researchers eventually discovered a total of nine Rhode Island workers, active and retired, with this condition, which they concluded was the same as that suffered by the workers in Canada—a serious new respiratory disease that they called flock worker's lung, which was evidently caused by the inhalation of tiny fragments of nylon and other synthetic materials produced in the manufacture of flocking. They believed it could kill workers or leave them permanent invalids, and knew the manufacturing method that apparently caused it was widespread—the international trade organization of companies that made similar products counted at least fifty members. Kern believed that many workers might be at risk.

Over time, his relationship with the company deteriorated. Microfibres executives were increasingly critical of Kern's contact with the workers' union, which was essential to his gathering information about the nature and causes of the disease. One worker he had evaluated called him to report that his condition had improved, and that he would be returning to work; however, he wished to use a respirator. When Kern wrote to the Microfibres personnel director to recommend that the employee be given a simple, half-face respirator, he received an angry call from James Fulks, an executive vice president at the company, who accused him of coddling his employees, legitimizing their claims of work-related illness, and opening the door to workers' compensation claims. Fulks ended the conversation by stating that he would not authorize a respirator for the employee in question. (After returning to work, that employee suffered repeated incidents of nausea, and after six days was hospitalized for chest pains.) Kern and his team also noticed delays and lack of cooperation by NIOSH, and heard a rumor that NIOSH's refusal to give him sampling data on patients at the Canadian plant was due to pressure from company management.

Matters came to a head on October 29, 1996, when Kern, convinced he had uncovered a potentially serious threat to public health, announced his intention to present his findings at the following year's meeting of the American Thoracic Society, both to alert the medical community to be on the lookout for the disease and to elicit advice from doctors elsewhere on how to analyze and treat it. Two days later, Microfibres threatened legal action against both Kern and Memorial Hospital if he did so. Kern wrote a watered-down version of the abstract, which omitted references to the nylon flocking industry and the Canadian cases, but the company rejected this, too.

When Kern turned to senior officials at Brown University and Memorial Hospital for support, they instead sided with Microfibres. Frank Dietz, president of the hospital, denied the existence of a public health risk and expressed his concern that Kern might destroy the company. H. Denman Scott, the physician in chief at the hospital and associate dean of medicine for primary care at Brown, criticized Kern for losing the confidence of the company's management by his handling of the incident and denied that his academic freedom was being infringed. Peter Shank, associate dean of medicine and biological sciences, stated that he believed the confidentiality agreement Kern had signed fifteen months before—long before he suspected the existence of flock worker's lung—prohibited him from releasing this sensitive information about Microfibres without the company's permission, and instructed him not to publish it. Hospital and university administrators also forbade Kern to continue providing medical care to those of his patients who worked at the company.

In reality, the confidentiality agreement Kern had signed merely prohibited disclosure of Microfibres' trade secrets, such as its machinery, materials and production processes. The operating principles of Kern's occupational health group, which he had given to the company when they began their consulting work, clearly stated that the group would communicate results to the scientific and public health communities as it deemed appropriate. Kern concluded that the demands of academic freedom and public health, and the central professional responsibility of doctors to patients, all required him to publish the abstract. He did so on September 26, 1997, in *Morbidity and Mortality Weekly Report*, a publication of the US government's Centers for Disease Control and Prevention. Since then, flock worker's lung has become widely recognized as a serious, chronic and potentially lethal condition.

In response to Kern's publication, Memorial Hospital promptly shut down his occupational and environmental health program and terminated his research funding. Months later, Brown University informed him that it would not be renewing his employment contract. But Kern would not be silenced. During his contacts with officials at the hospital and the university, Kern had learned of their personal and financial ties with the company, which, in his mind, raised serious questions of conflicts of interest. In an article he published in 1998 in the *International Journal of Occupational and Environmental Health*, Kern described these ties as follows:

> Perhaps worthy of note is that Microfibres is one of eight benefactors responsible for construction of the hospital's histology laboratory. Three members of the company owner's family serve as members of the Memorial Hospital Corporation. More troubling, however, is that the company was asked to contribute to the hospital's Primary Care Center Capital Campaign at approximately the same time as Frank Dietz and Dr. [H. Denman] Scott were attempting to allay the company owner's anger about our having submitted a scientific abstract on the disease outbreak. Moreover, the solicitation was made jointly by Rick Dietz [assistant vice president at Memorial Hospital] and the Chairman of the Capital Campaign. The Chairman of the Capital Campaign also serves both as Vice Chairman of the hospital's Board of Trustees and as hospital attorney. In the latter role, he has provided guidance to Frank Dietz on how to deal with the confidentiality agreement, the submitted scientific abstract, and me.

At a talk on the controversy Kern gave at MIT in March 1999, he said that his situation reminded him of Henrik Ibsen's play *An Enemy of the People*. In it, Dr. Stockmann, a Norwegian physician, learns that his town's medicinal baths have been contaminated. He makes this discovery just in time to avert disaster: his brother, the town's mayor, has been advertising the baths as a powerful cure for various diseases, and numerous visitors are expected to begin taking the waters soon—a boon to the local economy. Stockmann writes an article describing the dangers of the spa, but his brother demands that he retract it: repairs to the spring would be too expensive, and the bad publicity would threaten the town's economic well-being. "Soon the doctor is branded 'an enemy of the people,'" Kern told the audience. (To be clear, Kern does not consider himself a whistleblower or an advocate of unrestricted free speech; rather, following legal scholar Owen Fiss in his book *The Irony of Free Speech*, Kern believes that since truly free speech can be stifled by powerful private actors, government intervention may be required to ensure a robust and balanced debate on important social issues.)

Three months later, Brown allowed Kern's contract to expire, and he left the university.

Today, remembering the flock worker's lung controversy, Poses says, "No one in leadership at the hospital or the university seemed to want to contest it at all, even though they could easily have done so just by getting a competent lawyer. Instead, they just wanted to be nice to the company—that's the way it appeared." Poses, who sports thick glasses, a dense, woolly mustache, and an expression that tends toward pleased surprise—a hint of Groucho Marx without the cigar—is a careful person. His father was a noted New York lawyer whom he calls "Edwardian, and tough as nails." As an undergraduate at Brown, Poses earned a double major in electrical engineering and English. All three influences—linguistic precision, style, and a certain juristic punctilio—emerge in his speech and his writing. He is circumspect about what he says, and clearly wishes to avoid being sued for libel. Yet he manages to speak his mind; in fact, the calm restraint of his delivery makes his denunciations all the more devastating.

Poses says he was bewildered at how something so egregious could happen without any official remedy being available. "I thought there had to be someplace David Kern could go. I assumed that when this kind of thing happened, there was somebody—the university, a state-level department of health, a national medical society, a licensing board—somebody who would sort this out. Then I realized that there is no such organization. If something like this happens, as a researcher you have no one to appeal to. Certainly, nobody that David appealed to was interested in sorting it out, and apart from some press reports, no serious investigation was done of the flock worker's lung affair, by the university or any other body. We still don't know what really happened." This persistent, stubborn silence in the face of potential ethical failures and serious abuses is a recurrent theme in Poses's writing.

Understanding that no official or body was going to set the record straight in the David Kern case, Poses attempted, together with sympathetic fellow faculty members, to mount some kind of defense for Kern. He wrote two letters of protest to the president and other senior administrators of Brown University. He admits that his efforts were somewhat halfhearted. "I didn't speak up much. I didn't go marching around with a picket sign. I wasn't an activist." In fact, in a list of "courageous supporters" on the Brown faculty whom Kern acknowledges in an article he published about the affair in 2000, Poses doesn't appear. Poses says that Kern's most vocal supporters left Brown, or were pushed out by the university. Yet eventually, even his own comparatively mild objections began to make him feel isolated. "I started to realize that if I make protests, now I'm the nail that is sticking out, where a hammer may find me." Poses believes that his support for David Kern led to his losing his associate professorship in internal medicine at the university and being barred for a time from teaching at the hospital. "Without really wanting to, I had become a dissident, which made me very unpopular. And then I realized that there were more and more things to be dissident about."

Around the time of David Kern's troubles, Poses became aware of another kind of whistleblower story. Between 1994 and 1998, Martin Keller, the head of psychiatry at Brown, served as the principal investigator of Study 329, a placebo-controlled, randomized clinical trial of paroxetine, a new antidepressant produced by Smith-Kline Beecham (the company that merged in 2000 with Glaxo Wellcome to become GlaxoSmithKline, or GSK) and widely sold under the trade name Paxil. The trial, substantially funded by SmithKline Beecham, involved 275 adolescents suffering from major depression, who were recruited, treated and studied by Keller and his coauthors at twelve psychiatric centers in North American research hospitals. In 2001, Keller published its results in the prominent *Journal of the American Academy of Child and Adolescent Psychiatry* (*JAACAP*). In the article, Keller and coauthors stated that Paxil was safe, "generally well tolerated and effective for major depression in adolescents."

GSK promptly made this study the centerpiece of an enthusiastic marketing campaign. A 2001 memorandum that the company distributed to drug salespeople stated that "Paxil demonstrates REMARKABLE Efficacy and Safety in the treatment of adolescent depression." In 2002 alone, over two million prescriptions were written for American children and adolescents, according to a fraud lawsuit brought against GSK by New York attorney general Eliot Spitzer in 2004. However, as with Johnson & Johnson's Risperdal, each of these prescriptions was off-label—the FDA had not approved Paxil for children. What's more, in 2002 an FDA scientist had pronounced Study 329 a "failed trial, in that neither active treatment group showed superiority over placebo by a statistically significant margin." Two other Paxil clinical trials, 377 and 701, likewise indicated no improvement over placebo and increased risk of suicide; these were "suppressed and concealed" by the company, according to Spitzer's lawsuit.

Alison Bass, a reporter for the *Boston Globe*, wrote a series of articles describing irregularities in Keller's management of clinical trials and industry funding, based in part on revelations by Donna Howard, an administrator in Brown's department of psychiatry. Howard, whose daughter suffered from depression and had taken a number of popular antidepressant medications, handed Bass a box of documents, some of which suggested that Keller had suppressed instances of suicidal acts by patients taking part in Study 329, in order to make Paxil appear safer. At the same time that the New York state lawsuit against GSK began to reveal that the company had concealed negative studies and data, internal documents from Brown and GSK suggested wrongdoing had occurred in the clinical trial and publication of Study 329. The article, it emerged, had been ghostwritten for Keller and his coauthors by Sally Laden at Scientific Therapeutics Information, Inc., a "medical communications" company hired by SmithKline Beecham, GSK's predecessor; though Laden was paid to research, write and edit the article from materials supplied by the company, and her firm even sent Martin Keller an electronic copy of the text to print on his letterhead, she was identified in the published text only as an editorial assistant. This article mischaracterized the actual results of Study 329: far from being "well tolerated and effective," trial data showed that the drug was no better than a placebo, and that eleven patients had experienced serious adverse effects including suicidal behavior, worsening depression, mania and aggressiveness—11 percent of patients had suffered a possibly suicidal event, compared with 1 percent of patients on a placebo. (The article underreported suicidal thoughts and acts by classifying most of them as "emotional lability.") In 2012, a series of whistleblower lawsuits brought against GSK for off-label marketing and other misdeeds involving Paxil and other drugs were settled for a combined total of $3 billion, which to date remains the highest legal settlement ever paid by a drug company. In its plea agreement, GSK admitted that its labeling of Paxil, founded in large part on Study 329, was false and misleading.

As part of a 2004 settlement of Spitzer's New York lawsuit, GSK was required to release the raw data behind the study. A team of psychiatric researchers, including Mickey Nardo, who attended Allen Jones's trial in Austin, Texas, reanalyzed the data. In September 2015, they confirmed, in a definitive report published in the *British Medical Journal*, that Paxil was no more effective than a placebo at treating depression. They also demonstrated that Study 329 and other contemporary clinical trials had not only shown that Paxil produced "clinically significant increases in harms" to patients, "including suicidal ideation and behaviour and other serious adverse events," but that the studies had actively concealed such facts, evidently to favor GSK.

Despite the misdirection by GSK and other pharma companies, word about the risks of this class of antidepressants was getting out. By 2004, the FDA had added a black box warning to Paxil and eight other antidepressants. Not long after, Chuck Grassley began an extensive investigation into financial conflicts of interest in psychiatry; his staff eventually identified prominent professors at ten universities, including Harvard's Joseph Biederman, Stanford's Alan Schatzberg, Emory's Charles Nemeroff, and two researchers in the University of Texas system, A. John Rush and Karen Wagner (both leading figures in TMAP), all of whom had accepted but not revealed significant consulting fees from pharma companies—some received several million dollars—while carrying on research funded by the NIH, in violation of NIH and university conflict-of-interest policies. Another researcher named in Grassley's probe was Martin Keller at Brown, who had received substantial fees and research funding from GSK, Pfizer and other pharma firms.

Despite ample evidence of Study 329's flawed science and potential to cause human harm, none of the study's twenty-two authors, most of whom were university researchers and members of noted professional societies, made corrections. To this day, the *JAACAP* has refused numerous requests to retract it, or even to publish errata. (In October 2014, the editor in chief of *JAACAP*, Andrés S. Martin, a psychiatrist at Yale University, stated that after extensive consultations with the authors, other clinical experts, and "a whole range of attorneys," no action was necessary on the part of the journal.) The American Academy of Child and Adolescent Psychiatry (AACAP), the professional society to which several authors of the study belong, has not commented on the paper. On the contrary, the AACAP recently elected Karen Wagner, a coauthor of Study 329 and an outspoken advocate for Paxil and TMAP alike, as its next president.

Most disturbing of all for Roy Poses, Brown University did not reprimand or discipline Martin Keller, who, though stepping down as chair of the psychiatry department, remained a full professor in good standing until his retirement in 2012. To this day, his Brown webpage lauds Keller's leadership of the department, his numerous grants from research foundations and pharmaceutical companies, and his honors, including selection as one of "The World's Most Influential Scientific Minds" in 2015 for the many widely cited papers he had published. Poses remembers his dismay at Brown's radically different handling of Kern and Keller. "I was caught in this yin and yang of whistleblowing. One scientist tried to do the right thing, and was punished. Another did the wrong thing, and prospered. And my university and my hospital were right in the middle of it."

With the Study 329 scandal, as with the flock worker's lung affair, Brown University officials mounted no public investigation, nor did they comment substantively on what had actually happened. "They handled both cases the same way," Poses says. "At the time, they said, 'We've looked into it, there's no problem, there's nothing more to say, there's nothing to be done. Just keep moving, folks—nothing to see here.' Nowadays, when they're asked about Study 329, the new administration says, 'This happened a long time ago, we don't know anything about it.' But these aren't minor issues, trivial disputes that you can just shrug off. These are big-deal issues, disputes over science, with very important implications for patients and public health. . . . We should say, we will look into it, and either we're fine or we're not fine. Instead, Brown handled things, and continues to handle things, as if this were a legal settlement. Officials simply refuse to confirm or deny anything, and no individual gets into trouble."

As a member of a newly formed Medical Faculty Executive Committee, Poses attempted to understand how the flock worker's lung and the Study 329 whistle-blowing scandals had happened, and why nothing was being done to investigate them properly. He also reviewed the university's conflict-of-interest policy, which he was surprised to discover actually appeared to approve of commercial entanglements between Brown faculty and industry as a boon to the university, the community and science. The policy stated that conflicts of interest

are not unusual; they do not imply wrong-doing or inappropriate activities. Rather, research universities encourage interactions and the establishment of relationships between faculty and business and industry. The experience and knowledge gained through outside consulting and service on advisory committees is valued for its synergistic return to both research and student training. Commercialization of faculty inventions and discoveries through technology transfer brings the benefits of university research to the public good. Faculty often play an important role in successful commercialization efforts as scientific consultants and in continuing research development projects.

"When I read that, I thought, 'Holy cannoli, look at this!' Written right there in the conflict-of-interest policy, it said that conflicts were unavoidable, and in fact very positive—something you just had to manage or disclose to someone, and you were fine. This was the mentality of a corporation, not of the university as I'd known it." Poses soon found other examples of what seemed to him questionable ways of managing conflicts of interest by the university. "Regulations said that you had to disclose, but only to the administration, not publicly. Administrators looked at faculty disclosures, but the administrators didn't have to disclose their own conflicts. The Brown University president at the time, Ruth Simmons, was on the board of Pfizer, so I was disclosing my conflicts to someone with serious conflicts of her own . . . What did that mean? It was all a complete sham."

———

At conferences and other professional gatherings, Poses heard colleagues from around the country tell similar stories of financial conflicts and the erosion of evidence-based medicine at their institutions. In 2002, he began a series of informal interviews on these topics, in person or by telephone. Some colleagues were reluctant to speak, or had been forbidden to do so by lawyers at their universities or hospitals; others, however, were eager, even desperate, to share their concerns. "I didn't pick people with the biggest problems. I just picked people I thought would come to dinner, or who'd be willing to talk to me for half an hour. There was a general sense that things were going terribly wrong, which many of my colleagues and I were feeling, but didn't really understand. I set out just to get a handle on the scope of the problem, and get a first draft of what might be behind it. It was remarkable to have a group and discover how many common concerns we shared. We'd often be talking about the same issues, their local version of the issue: 'Oh, you have that, too? Well, here's my version.' We started to realize: this is everywhere."

From these conversations, Poses wrote a first sketch of healthcare dysfunction in America, which he published in 2003 in the *European Journal of Internal Medicine*. What Poses and many of his colleagues were experiencing, he wrote, was a progressive abandonment of medicine's basic values, caused by widespread conflicts of interest, the impersonal bureaucracies of large organizations, and a generalized breakdown of scientific integrity. Behind these processes stood the people Poses had seen and smelled in the elevator that morning back in 1978: financial managers, who had once helped doctors keep the hospital accounts in order, and somewhere along the line had begun to run, and sometimes to own, those hospitals.

Poses was still doing his best to be collegial, not confrontational. Yet his determination to do something about the distortions and abuses in US healthcare grew in 2000, when he received a diagnosis of colon cancer. "Sitting there with the chemo running in, you think differently. You think: 'What if this is like really . . . *real*? What's going to be written on the tombstone? I ought to be dealing with the big stuff here, rather than just getting the next grant, publication or promotion. I only have so much time.'" As part of his treatment, Poses took part in a clinical trial, which he believed, as a medical researcher, he should see from the inside. He underwent surgery. His cancer went into remission. But the urgency to denounce the corruption of US healthcare remained.

In late 2004, Poses and a group of medical professionals whom he'd first contacted during his 2002 interviews began to publish the *Health Care Renewal* blog, to continue their conversation about grave and growing problems in American medicine. In his posts, Poses searches for larger themes among the sordid minutiae and scandals in the daily news on healthcare, and for ways to impress their significance on laypeople. Witnessing the flock worker's lung and Study 329 incidents taught Poses how success or failure in whistleblowing—and in his form of meta-whistleblowing—often depends on the ability to generate outrage in the wider public, through the press, lawyers and advocates. His central premise is that healthcare corruption has become endemic in the United States and many other nations, yet is a taboo topic in the press, both because wrongdoers accumulate so much wealth and influence that they can keep their crimes out of the public eye and because Americans believe that healthcare corruption happens only in less developed countries. The result is what Poses calls the "anechoic effect"—the failure by media and other observers to denounce wrongdoing by powerful healthcare interests in a clear and consistent manner, which has allowed that wrongdoing to become chronic.

Poses's strategy for overcoming the anechoic effect is to repeat, tirelessly and with a wealth of particulars, the stories of corruption that typically appear once in local media and then vanish from public view. His posts are replete with mantric catchphrases—"As we have said until blue in the face," "Once more with feeling," "It's déjà vu all over again"—to introduce the latest outrage, each a replica of previous outrages he has already dissected in the blog. Repetition is, in fact, Poses's point. He's creating an echo chamber, a sound box to amplify stories about healthcare crimes that would otherwise be lost in the background noise. He strives to make each new iniquity unforgettable.

GSK, Pfizer, Merck, AstraZeneca, Novartis, Medtronic and scores of other healthcare multinationals appear again and again on the blog. Johnson & Johnson has been tagged sixty-one times, as Poses has covered the company's repeated frauds and abuses, including several posts on its Risperdal court cases, the company's subversion of state healthcare systems, Allen Jones's victory at trial in Austin, and the company's $2.2 billion federal settlement. Time and again Poses decries the legal settlements with which big healthcare firms buy their way out of the frauds and crimes they've perpetrated, settlements that routinely deny wrongdoing and guarantee impunity for the executives who designed and conducted the fraud. "How many legal settlements does it take to lead to real change in Johnson and Johnson leadership?" one of his posts asked in September 2012, when, despite the federal Risperdal settlement, CEO Alex Gorsky remained in charge.

Poses explores the perversion of healthcare science by pharmaceutical and medical device companies, and has compiled an endless litany of wrongdoing by hospitals, chronicling how many of them, lured by the promise of technology, have hired IT contractors to build fabulously complex and expensive computer systems that, instead of increasing efficiency, routinely cause operational failure and patient harm. He decries the depredations of executives who collect multimillion-dollar pay packages even as they preside over extensive salary cuts and layoffs among nurses, doctors and other medical staff, and quotes finance professor Henry Mintzberg of McGill University: "All this compensation madness is not about markets or talents or incentives, but rather about insiders hijacking established institutions for their personal benefit." And he shows how financial conflicts degrade healthcare by shifting the attention of executives, politicians, research scientists and medical school administrators from patients to profits. "Not only are there revolving doors connecting the national government and large commercial health firms, but also connecting state government and regional hospital systems, and non-profit health care insurers/managed care organizations and device companies. This is just some more evidence that people in the leadership of large health care organizations have more in common with each other, even if their organizations are supposed to be competing or negotiating at arm's length, than they have with patients, clients, customers and the public at large."

After the 2008 economic crisis, Poses realized that the dysfunctions that were rampant in healthcare also pervaded many other industries, government sectors and areas of American society. "I began to see that the takeover by mission-hostile financial managers and the false assumptions of neoliberal economics, especially free-market fundamentalism, had created the same kinds of corruption and immoral behavior in finance, academia, government and many other places." He came to understand these concerns as new manifestations of moral and ethical dilemmas that have plagued people forever. "It's actually an age-old problem. The first books of the Old Testament, the Jewish Torah, were written to establish rules and laws that would prevent wealth from corrupting the way we treat others." Age-old, perhaps, but Poses's blog chronicles how Donald Trump's 2016 presidential victory has ushered in a Golden Age of fraud. By calling out healthcare corruption and challenging doctors, healthcare workers and common citizens to do the same, Poses seems determined to make this a Golden Age of truth telling and principled dissent as well.

Running through Roy Poses's blog are some of the central causes of whistle-blowing's rise over the last five decades. Some are circumstantial: the increasing number of laws to protect and pay whistleblowers and news stories to spread their paradigm; new computer and internet tools that facilitate the capture and release of confidential data; and the decline of watchdog functions like investigative journalism and government regulation, which leaves whistleblowers as a last line of defense against much organizational deviance. But on a deeper level, whistleblowing has thrived because of three important trends in American society, which are prominent in the whistleblower stories we've examined so far and are regular refrains in *Health Care Renewal*: the rise and normalization of fraud, the growing interpenetration of corporations and the government, and the spread of secrecy.

Frequent news stories capture an apparent epidemic of fraud and corruption committed by corporations, government agencies and individuals: from cybercrime to credit card scams to identity theft, from criminal college admissions conspiracies to systemic wrongdoing by automobile companies to wholesale money laundering and looting of national treasuries by banks: fraud seems rampant, in the US and elsewhere. Bike racers, baseball players and Olympic athletes routinely use banned drugs, in collusion with coaches and teammates; FIFA, the world soccer authority, has been a fraud mafia for decades. University professors also cheat; a 2012 study of over two thousand science research articles revealed a nearly tenfold increase over the past twenty years in the rate of retractions due to fraud. Corporations and wealthy individuals have squirreled away somewhere between $7 and $36 trillion in secret offshore accounts, leaving only Leona Helmsley's "little people" to pay taxes. Even noble causes are plagued by grift and graft: Wounded Warrior Project executives skim funds meant for injured veterans, Little League managers embezzle from the team accounts of their young players, and the American Red Cross misspends hundreds of millions of dollars donated for disaster relief after Superstorm Sandy and the 2010 earthquake in Haiti.

Yearly surveys by accounting firms and auditors reveal an across-the-board rise in illegal behavior in many industries; in the 2017/2018 *Global Fraud and Risk Report* prepared by Kroll, the business intelligence and investigations firm, 84 percent of 540 senior executives polled at major corporations had witnessed fraud, and 86 percent had seen cybercrime—an all-time high in both categories since Kroll began the annual survey ten years ago. In the United States alone, fraud siphons away perhaps $1 trillion a year from the legitimate economy, 5 percent of GDP. (The World Bank puts the global figure lost to fraud at nearly $4 trillion.) Each year in the United States, tax evaders steal over $450 billion, and healthcare offenders make off with between $200 and $400 billion more. Contractors at government bodies like the Department of Energy, Homeland Security, the Environmental Protection Agency and the Department of the Interior are notorious for inflating prices, rigging bids and fudging standards for the products they sell to their government minders. The Department of Defense and its big-name contractors constitute an entire fraud fiefdom. The GAO High Risk List for 2019, which identifies government programs and operations most prone to fraud, waste, abuse and mismanagement, singles out no fewer than nine Pentagon and national security areas, two of which, DOD weapons systems acquisition and DOD contract management, manage nearly $2 trillion in taxpayer funds, and have been on the GAO's High Risk List for over twenty-five years.

Of course, part of this perception of epidemic may be due to our improved ability to detect fraud in the first place, with sharper oversight and better transparency laws. Yet many scholars and laypeople alike feel that the country is undergoing a crisis of ethics—that, as jurist and political activist Lawrence Lessig has written, "we have allowed core institutions of America's economic, social, and political life to become corrupted." Many see the growth of systematic wrongdoing as the result of a breakdown of long-standing moral norms, together with new standards and expectations that tend to institutionalize greed. In *Cultivating Conscience*, Cornell law professor Lynn Stout shows how fifty years of bad laws and regulations, based on misguided models of human behavior, have helped to foster our inner cheater. Harry Lewis, longtime Harvard computer science professor and author of *Excellence Without a Soul*, an indictment of the ethos of higher education in America, worries that universities, and US society more broadly, are "losing sight of the idea that people are more than the sum of their skills and expertise, their intelligence and effectiveness—of foundational principles like character, virtue and values, which are what hold us together in times of stress and crisis."

Morality in large corporations can be particularly murky. Scholars of business ethics like Marianne Jennings, Max Bazerman, Ann Tenbrunsel, Dan Ariely and Linda Treviño have pointed out the myriad ways in which corporations reframe wrongdoing as acceptable business practice, helping to transform them, in economist William Lazonick's phrase, "from producers to predators." Entire industries have created an alternative moral universe where behavior that would be immoral or illegal for an individual is considered savvy—and obligatory—for organizations: "creative" accounting, "aggressive" marketing, legal "hardball." During the last decade, nineteen of the twenty largest pharmaceutical companies in the United States have been prosecuted for serious criminal and civil violations, and most of the top thirty US banks by total assets have been convicted of or have settled a range of charges including mortgage fraud, insider trading, market rigging and facilitating Ponzi schemes. "Crime by corporations inflicts far more damage to society, in deaths, injuries and dollars lost, than all street crime combined," says Russell Mokhiber, editor of the *Corporate Crime Reporter*, a weekly publication he founded in 1987. "It's impossible to say for sure if corporate crime is increasing, because the Justice Department doesn't produce reports on it, only on street crime—an omission which is a political favor to corporations. But by all indications, corporate crime is getting worse, while the resources to fight it are being cut. Recent administrations have been very soft on corporate crime."

Impunity is pervasive. The Pentagon cooks its books to the tune of $6.5 trillion, but no heads roll. Director of National Intelligence James Clapper lies under oath to Congress about bulk domestic surveillance, yet keeps his job. Corporations under prosecution cut deals with the DOJ—money settlements, deferred prosecution agreements, nonprosecution agreements—and escape meaningful punishment. In fact, corrupt behavior has been increasingly normalized in business, government and the courts. Virginia governor Bob McDonnell takes cash and Ferraris from an entrepreneur keen to have McDonnell push his interests. A federal jury in Virginia convicts McDonnell of corruption, yet the Supreme Court overturns the conviction, pronouncing that nothing short of outright bribery—the simultaneous exchange of money for specific political favors—qualifies as corruption. Activities that were once illegal—stock buybacks, unlimited corporate contributions to politicians, gambling in casinos and sports betting—are now ubiquitous.

The second major cause of whistleblowing's rise—and of the fraud that whistleblowing fights—is the growing share of public work being performed by private corporations, which creates sweeping conflicts of interest and undercuts the basic conception of public service. Bipartisan rejection of Big Government and celebration of the private sector have encouraged a sweeping transfer of government activities to for-profit businesses that took off under Reagan and has continued under every successive administration, Republican or Democrat. Corporations and NGOs that benefit from this trend trumpet the gospel of small government and free markets, though these are the last things many of them want: they thrive on parasitic relationships with a gargantuan, absentminded US government, which is by far the largest consumer, customer and funder in the world. (In 2018, federal, state and local government distributed about $7 trillion, in healthcare, defense, education and other industries, about a third of the nation's GDP.) This money is ripe for misuse because it's being managed by revolving-door public servants who will soon return to the private sector, and it comes from anonymous taxpayers—it's "other people's money," as Justice Louis Brandeis called the savings accounts of unwitting depositors that bankers like J. P. Morgan used to make risk-free profits for themselves. Or as Benjamin Franklin said: "There is no kind of dishonesty into which otherwise good people more easily and frequently fall, than that of defrauding Government of its revenues."

Industries routinely capture their regulators by pressuring politicians via lobbying and campaign finance to fund or defund the regulator's budget, or by paying a substantial part of this budget themselves. Each year since 1992, for example, pharmaceutical companies have supplied half to three-quarters of the operating budget of the FDA. Similar financial conflicts of interest exist in banking, energy, telecommunications and other industries. "Perhaps the greatest threat to freedom and democracy in the world today comes from the formation of unholy alliances between government and business," George Soros has said. "The outward appearances of the democratic process are observed, but the powers of the state are diverted to the benefit of private interests."

The extreme interpenetration of public institutions and private enterprise means that major crimes by private firms often have a public component. Johnson & Johnson and other pharmaceutical companies co-opted the departments of health in a dozen states, nearly shut down an investigation by the Pennsylvania Inspector General's Office into this activity, and successfully pressured the Texas attorney general to reduce Allen Jones's whistleblower award. Franz Gayl witnessed behavior in the Marines supply chain that, de facto, valued the lives of frontline soldiers less than lucrative contracts with defense manufacturers, where many senior officers were taking jobs after retirement. Elin Baklid-Kunz watched federal healthcare dollars flow steadily into Halifax Hospital, as they do into countless other medical facilities across the nation, and believed that many were diverted by fraud.

Civil servants positioned at the cusp of the government-corporate interface often experience a glaring disjunction between their stated and real jobs. Many turn a blind eye. Others become co-conspirators. A few, insiders with the conscience of ordinary citizens, become whistleblowers.

A third reason for the rise of whistleblowing is the spread of secrecy, whistleblowing's nemesis. When crimes occur within an organization that is hermetically sealed by confidentiality, its members are trapped on the inside with burning information they know is invisible to regulators, prosecutors, politicians and the press.

A few of these insiders feel an overwhelming need to reveal it. And despite universal recognition that transparency breeds accountability, and that secrecy fosters misconduct and a sense of impunity, secrecy has become an increasingly accepted standard for running corporations, government agencies, NGOs, universities, and many other organizations, spreading Roy Poses's "anechoic effect" throughout society. Corporations routinely hide their activities behind walls of confidentiality, invoking attorney-client privilege or expansive protections of proprietary and competitive information, just as they conceal their financial dealings within labyrinths of anonymous shell corporations and offshore tax vehicles. (The Tax Justice Network's Financial Secrecy Index identifies the United States as the world's second most secretive jurisdiction, just behind Switzerland, and well ahead of tax havens like the Cayman Islands, Dubai, Guernsey and Panama.) Organizations often force their employees to sign nondisclosure agreements to prevent them from blowing the whistle on wrongdoing, and compel them to conduct all labor disputes in secret arbitration tribunals rather than in public courts of law.

Questions to NGO and university employees are routinely referred to the legal and PR offices of those organizations. Government agencies have developed an obsession with controlling access to their own ostensibly public information, denying its release by invoking threats to data privacy, trade secrets or national security. "There was tremendous retrenchment in government information policy in the years immediately following 9/11," says Steven Aftergood, director of the Federation of American Scientists' Project on Government Secrecy and an authority in classification policy. "Documents were withdrawn from public archives, government websites were censored or taken offline, public and press access to government officials was curtailed." Before then, Aftergood remembers calling senior DOE and DOD officials directly—not their public affairs liaisons—with questions, and getting answers. "Sometimes I would even meet them for lunch or for a beer after work to continue the discussion. That largely ended after 9/11. There is greater emphasis within agencies on message control. So unsupervised and uncoordinated comments by individual officials are discouraged and may even be punished."

In 2009, shortly after his election to the presidency, Barack Obama promised to introduce an "unprecedented level" of government transparency, acknowledging that most information was being withheld from the public "for self-serving reasons or simply to avoid embarrassment." Yet the increase in the classification of federal documents during his administration led one authority on government secrecy to call overclassification "an epidemic," and two other experts to decry its use by "officials who are involved in misconduct . . . to hide the evidence." Most of the $700 billion annual budget of the Department of Defense is secret, and Pentagon officials routinely refuse to explain line items even to Congress. The IRS says it's being shortchanged over $450 billion in taxes each year, yet will not reveal who the evaders are or why they're not being stopped. The DOJ concludes multibillion-dollar settlements with corporate fraudsters, yet routinely keeps the details of the fraud schemes secret, and allows the perpetrators to seal compromising court documents. Steven Aftergood deplores the practice of sealing court records. "Instead of becoming collectively smarter and better as a society, we are denied the lessons of experience. It's a bad model." Louis Brandeis famously observed that "sunlight is said to be the best of disinfectants," but the default nowadays is darkness; the public no longer expects, much less demands, access to vital information that might change their perceptions and their lives. As secretary of state, Hillary Clinton illegally moved her official email servers to her home, for convenience but also to avoid scrutiny; during the 2016 presidential election, Donald Trump refused to release his tax returns, as candidates had done for over thirty years. Political campaigns are awash in unprecedented amounts of dark money, an existential threat to any democracy. Journalistic freedom in the United States, once a beacon of free expression, has declined: Reporters Without Borders ranks the United States in forty-fifth place, behind Surinam, Burkina Faso and Romania. In 2014, Professor David Cuillier, director of the Society of Professional Journalists, told the Senate Judiciary Committee that the nation is "approaching a crisis when it comes to access to information."

Taken together, secrecy, public-private interpenetration and pervasive fraud corrode public trust. They create a strong though opaque sense of an economic and political "rigged game" engineered by corporations and financial elites, of stark inequities built into our society, and the suspicion that the basic tenets of American society—equal opportunity and equal justice, truly free markets, and the social contract itself—are being subverted. This, in turn, creates a devastating sense of impotence, a fear that individuals are losing their voice—that We the People are being shut out of our own commonwealth.

The rise of whistleblowing signals that many citizens demand a realignment of legality and morality, a new conception of personal and organizational ethics. Yet whistleblowers routinely face retaliation that jeopardizes their livelihood, their health and sometimes their lives. The mismatch in power between whistleblowers and the organizations they challenge, which command vastly more resources— time, legions of defense lawyers, influence with politicians and judges—remains immense. Pro-whistleblower laws are multiplying, but troubling gaps in legislation allow continued victimization. And despite the newfound popular support for whistleblowers, much of society still mistrusts their motives and their methods.

Whistleblowers highlight some of America's greatest strengths and most danger- ous weaknesses. They are a characteristically American phenomenon, an expression of cherished national values: egalitarianism, free speech, individualism, fair play, a hatred of tyranny, and the courage to rebel against it. In their words and their ac- tions, the Founders often behaved like whistleblowers. Yet the violent retaliation many whistleblowers suffer—and the fact that we as a society tolerate it—also sug- gests that many of us sense something deeply foreign in them. If whistleblowing fits with our much-heralded love of justice and freedom, it also clashes with other marked American traits like loyalty, respect for authority, and a reflexive patrio- tism. Sociologist Claude Fischer has pointed out that, despite our fond images of a national character of self-reliance and uncompromising righteousness, long- running studies of national beliefs like the World Value Survey and the Interna- tional Social Survey Programme suggest that Americans are substantially more obedient to the demands of the state, and less respectful of the individual morality, than the citizens of many other countries. When asked, "Would you say that people should obey the law without exception, or are there exceptional occasions on which people should follow their consciences even if it means breaking the law?" fewer than half of American respondents said that people should sometimes follow their conscience—far fewer than the Swedes (70 percent) or the French (78 percent). Americans were the most likely of all nationalities surveyed to agree with the proposition that "people should support their country even if the country is in the wrong," and the least likely to agree that "right or wrong should be a matter of personal conscience." "Americans insist on the reality and value of individual free choice, including, critically, free choice to join or leave groups, be they companies or countries," Fischer concludes. "However, Americans also believe that, once individuals are members of the group, they must be loyal."

Whistleblowers excite violent and contradictory emotions because they pose demanding questions about our national character, and at the same time set us face-to-face with a fierce, almost frightening ideal that most of us wonder whether we could live up to—or whether we even want to.

CHAPTER 4

Blood Ivory Towers

We few, we happy few, we band of brothers;
For he to-day that sheds his blood with me
Shall be my brother. . . .

William Shakespeare, *Henry V* ("St. Crispin's Day Speech")

Few men have the honor to withstand the highest bidder.

George Washington, letter to Major General Robert Howe, August 17, 1779

Lynn Stout, a professor of corporate governance and securities regulation at the UCLA law school, had thought a fair bit about conscience, but her ruminations took on a new intensity in July 2010, when a wave of nausea began to hit her every morning as she arrived at work. A new plaque had been hung prominently on the law school's "Wall of Honor," where memorials commemorated generous donations by famous alums. The plaque read, LOWELL MILKEN, VISIONARY, and celebrated a $10 million gift from Milken, a California-based billionaire and philanthropist, to fund the creation of the Lowell Milken Institute for Business Law and Policy.

Lowell Milken is the brother and former close associate of Michael Milken, the so-called junk bond king of Drexel Burnham Lambert, the now-defunct investment bank. Reckless speculation and shady dealings had bankrupted Drexel in 1990 and earned both men multi-count indictments for racketeering, securities fraud and other crimes. Michael eventually pleaded guilty to six felonies, and was sentenced to ten years in prison. The DOJ dropped all charges against Lowell as part of its plea deal with his brother. Both men were banned for life from dealing with securities, and from becoming officers or directors of companies listed on the New York Stock Exchange.

"'Visionary'?" says Stout of the plaque. "If they'd said 'visionary criminal,' I'd have been fine with it. Here is a man who was up to his elbows in the most blatant and incredibly costly white-collar fraud of the 1980s. There are probably still retirees eating cat food in Texas thanks to Michael Milken. And my institution was holding the Milkens up as a model for students. I literally couldn't go to work and look at that sign without feeling sick to my stomach. It provoked physical nausea."

A friend and colleague, anthropologist Daniel Fessler, told Stout that her queasiness was an exaptation: a behavior or trait that evolved for one purpose and is coopted to serve another, more recent need. (For example, the brain circuitry of sex and euphoria that engages when we deal with money is an exaptation of far older drives, which urge us to continue to eat and to reproduce.) In this case, Fessler explained, disgust, an ancient sensation designed primarily to protect us from harmful substances, either by discouraging us from eating them or by making us vomit them up, had been redirected as moral disgust, which helps us to steer clear of grifters and rule breakers. "The behavioral features associated with disgust—avoidance, rejection—are an efficient means of creating social distance between the self and someone who violates an important norm," he told her.

To Stout's surprise, few others in the business or law schools seemed to feel at all queasy about the proposed donation. A statement issued by the law school called Milken "a leading philanthropist and pioneer in education reform." Rachel Moran, dean of the law school, celebrated Milken's "transformative gift," which she said showed "that our students, alumni and friends share the vision and values that define us as a great public law school." No mention was made of Milken's career at Drexel.

"It was shocking," Stout remembers. "The law school issued a series of press releases designed to whitewash his past and misrepresent him, not only to the student body but to the public. What I found most disturbing was the way UCLA actually seemed to be participating in rewriting history, and presenting Lowell Milken as some kind of a hero to our law students. There was a level of deception and hypocrisy that I found inexcusable. In fact, the damage from this kind of hypocrisy is potentially even greater than the damage from the fraud, because it fertilizes the ground for people to act like that, and perpetuate even more fraud. The message is, if you rip off someone, that makes you a leader, makes you a businessman, someone who can win the deal. And if you make—if you steal—enough money, you can buy history, you can buy the truth. As a professor, someone who spends her professional life in the quest for understanding reality and the truth, that just struck me as completely unconscionable."

Stout sent a letter to UCLA chancellor Gene Block and to the president of the University of California system, Mark G. Yudof, stating that a business law and policy center named in Milken's honor not only posed "serious ethical problems and reputational risks for UCLA," but would "damage my personal and professional reputation, as I have devoted my career to arguing for investor protection and honest and ethical behavior in business." She said the same in interviews with major newspapers. "I don't think someone who has been banned from the security industry and barred from the New York Stock Exchange is an appropriate model for UCLA alumni and students," she told the *Los Angeles Times*. Several UCLA professors and administrators disagreed with her, publicly and vehemently. Gene Block said the university was "deeply grateful for the vision and philanthropic leadership of Lowell Milken" and had carefully weighed all potential ethics concerns before accepting the gift. "The UCLA School of Law represents and teaches the rule of law, justice and fairness," he concluded, "and consistent with those principles we are proud to count Lowell Milken among our alumni and to have him associated with this Institute." "Everybody else here is thrilled with this gift," law professor Kenneth Klee told the *Los Angeles Times*, asserting that Lowell Milken was an entirely appropriate role model—"I think we would want more of our alumni to become leading philanthropists." Dean Moran said she was "mystified" by Stout's criticism. In a private meeting with Stout, she pointed out that Lowell Milken had never been convicted of any crime. "Well, neither was O. J. Simpson," Stout remembers telling her, "but you wouldn't create the 'O. J. Simpson Center for Domestic Violence Law and Policy,' would you?" (At the time, Simpson had not yet been criminally convicted of robbery.) Stout describes Moran's reaction: "She was not amused."

Having blown the whistle on her organization, Stout received a whistleblower's welcome. She was accused of being the only member of the business law faculty who objected to the gift, which was true, although a number of scholars in other departments had objected. Critics pointed out that she had used Lowell Milken's money before without protest, which again was true but misleading: yes, she'd used $50,000 of it to help organize a conference long before Milken had proposed to fund an institute, but she'd never objected to taking Milken's money. "In fact, I'd much rather we take it than he keep it!" she says. "My objection was to holding him up as a role model for our students, by naming a center after him." Like many whistleblowers, she also received a series of supportive emails, letters and phone calls. A retired math professor who'd taught at Stanford during the McCarthy era sent her "good wishes and praise," and recalled how few of his colleagues had stood up to McCarthy's witch hunts. A financial professional wrote that he'd just been interviewed under oath by the Securities and Exchange Commission after telling the commission that Michael Milken was still advising a securities management firm, Guggenheim Partners, despite his lifetime ban on such work. A managing director at Kroll, the business investigations firm, offered his aid, and noted that he'd written "extensively about the Milken junk bond world and the damage that was done by those two brothers." A professor at Harvard Business School stated that the Milkens "operated hand in glove throughout the hay [sic] days of Drexel Burnham. Michael has spent years and hundreds of millions trying to rewrite his history. Now Lowell is trying to do the same thing!" A woman who'd worked at Drexel Burnham set up an anonymous meeting with Stout. "She said she was at the Drexel office the weekend they destroyed all the documents," Stout remembers. "That they did what people know about, but a lot more as well. She said she was terrified of those people."

In fairness, Lowell Milken's gift to UCLA, and the Milken brothers' philanthropy elsewhere, may be entirely disinterested and well-intentioned. Since their Drexel days, both Lowell and his brother Michael have contributed to various worthwhile causes, and some students and professors at UCLA have no doubt benefited from Lowell's gift. Harry Lewis, the Harvard professor and former dean, says that a university can accept certain donations of dubious origin and still turn them to the common good. "Universities are the kidneys of the nation," he says with a smile. "The price of accepting money is the moral burden we have to do good for the world, to graduate people of whom we can be proud, to produce knowledge for the public good, not just the silly 'learning for its own sake' version of what we do." (Lewis himself, as dean of the engineering school, helped secure a $400 million donation from John Paulson, the hedge fund manager involved in the infamous ABACUS 2007-AC1 transaction—a deal whose implications we will consider in Chapter 6.) But Lewis also stresses that the recipient should scrutinize each donation with care. "Anything that smacks of quid pro quo or the donor's hands, dead or alive, binding the future in any but the broadest terms is off-limits for me."

It was the donor's hands, very much alive, that concerned Lynn Stout about the UCLA institute. Lynn Stout believed that Lowell's generosity to UCLA, like certain other acts of philanthropy by the Milkens, had ulterior motives—and it's easy to see why. Intertwining one's name with a distinguished institution gives that name gravitas, and the sanction of civil society. Shady characters routinely launder their reputations in this way. Marianne Jennings, in her classic book on corporate crime, *The Seven Signs of Ethical Collapse*, identifies philanthropy as a frequent symptom of wrongdoing; Jennings documents how crooked executives at Enron, WorldCom, Tyco and other firms made lavish donations to universities, charities and communities in order to generate positive press, attract more business and reduce the pressure of cognitive dissonance by balancing their private wrongdoing with public good. "Their philanthropic and social goodness became the salve for a conscience grappling with cooked books, fraud, insider trading—all the usual activities of ethical collapse," Jennings writes.

A foundation can also create a platform from which to propagate certain beliefs, defend certain behaviors, and, in so doing, cast one's career in a new light. UCLA chancellor Gene Block insists that Lowell Milken's gift wasn't about "putting his name on the door," and that the university "would have received his gift had the institute remained nameless." This seems improbable. Lowell Milken's name appears a great deal at his institute: he has met with faculty and sits on the advisory board, and his name is relentlessly branded into events, prizes and sponsored activities, as well as cross-sold on the institute's website with the Milken Family Foundation, which Lowell also runs. Insiders at UCLA report that Milken has met with members of the UCLA business law faculty, and has a significant say in the topics that his institute chooses to address. There seem to be parallels here with a third organization, the Milken Institute, a Santa Monica–based think tank run by Michael and Lowell. This organization has held conferences to promote peace in the Middle East and improve relations between Wall Street and Main Street, but also to defend junk bonds, decry "frivolous" lawsuits against securities fraud (for which Michael went to prison), and place the Milkens onstage among Nobel laureates and other luminaries. Journalist Edward Cohn writes that the Milken Institute "has not quite been able to resist taking on issues that seem intended less to expand knowledge than to help transform a felonious businessman into a respected public intellectual."

In the end, Stout resigned, walking away from nearly $1 million in pension benefits, and took a job at Cornell. She recognizes that her whistleblowing path was smoother than many. Still, she says, "From my own experience, no one in their right mind would ever aspire to be a whistleblower. Whistleblowing is definitely not free. But I felt I had no choice: I felt I couldn't live with myself, or continue to go to work at UCLA, without publicly taking the position that this was wrong."

In her public denunciations, Stout was blowing the whistle not only on her university, but also on her colleagues who went along with the deal. "It was remarkable how frightened, how terrified they were of raising any questions. And I'm not even talking about publicly raising questions, but of rocking the boat in any way. Which, given that they all had tenure, I found shocking. . . . They really seemed to believe that if it was good for UCLA and the law school in the short run, then it was morally acceptable, and there was no need to think about the social consequences or the nature of what the Milkens had done."

She believes their stance reflects a broad decline in academic ethics over the last several decades, for which she proposes several possible causes. "Academics are taught to be as 'objective' as possible, and this easily translates into moral relativism. Also, academia is not an industry that attracts people with enormous amounts of intellectual courage!" She laughs. "There's shockingly little of it, given how safe a tenured professorship is. What person is better prepared to take an ethical stand? But I think tenure tends to attract people who are on the timid side, who aren't risk-takers, and who care a lot about job security. Also, after spending five or seven years or so of really avoiding risk in order to get tenure, that habit gets even more deeply ingrained." Harry Lewis agrees that many tenured academics have little absolute commitment to independence of thought, or sense of responsibility to step outside their job description to address larger ethical issues. "When you hire people for either faculty positions or administrative and executive positions, there's a feeling that you're really not supposed to be taking character into account—that you shouldn't trust your instincts as to whether someone is a good person or not. You're hiring the résumé, not the person. Then that person arrives, and they say, 'Okay, my job is to do the job I was hired to do. And if I see something to my left or to my right that doesn't seem right, well, there's probably a person to my left or to my right whose job it is to sort that out.'"

Perhaps Milken's most determined champion is Daniel Fischel, a legal scholar and former dean of the University of Chicago law school. In his book *Payback: The Conspiracy to Destroy Michael Milken and His Financial Revolution*, Fischel claims that, despite Milken's conviction, nothing he did was actually illegal—or if a few of his acts were indeed just over the legal line, that line had been sloppily drawn, because Milken's actions had caused negligible financial harm, and immense good. Ultimately, Fischel's thesis springs from a philosophical position held by some conservative economists and legal scholars that most corporate crime isn't actually crime at all. People who make (or lose) money in the free market, this argument runs, know what they're doing and deserve, good and bad, what they get; practices like Michael Milken's are not only permissible but "visionary," because they unleash far more economic energy than they destroy; most laws and regulations are wrongheaded attempts to limit the freedom of markets and the individuals, rational self-maximizers one and all, who participate in them; and, ultimately, morality has no place in law or public life. These are some of the fundamental assumptions of law and economics, a vastly influential movement born a half century ago at the University of Chicago that has since spread to many law schools, business schools and think tanks, and from there to the actual practice of law and creation of social policy.

Law and economics, like the Chicago School of economics ideology it channels, is founded on the idea that something more rigorous and quantifiable than morality is required to shape laws and public affairs. Already in the 1650s, during the English Civil War, Thomas Hobbes, arguably the first political scientist, formulated a theory of governance based on the notion that human nature, being basically selfish and greedy, required control by a stern tyrant lest it end in *bellum omnia contra omnes* ("a war of all against all"). In the next century, Jeremy Bentham, founder of utilitarianism, thought that morality was poppycock, and that human welfare, concretely measured, was what counted: "It is the greatest happiness of the greatest number that is the measure of right and wrong." Oliver Wendell Holmes proposed shaping law to fit the mind of the "bad man," who cares nothing for ethics or "the vaguer sanctions of conscience," and is concerned only with avoiding punishment. But the vision of the cynical, self-serving, conscienceless man was elevated to a science during the Cold War at RAND, where game theory and a new logic of zero-sum competition influenced attempts to comprehend and win the high-stakes nuclear arms race with the Soviet Union. In his foundational book, *Theory of Games and Economic Behavior*, John von Neumann first applied the mathematics of game theory to economics. A fellow RAND mathematician, the clinically schizophrenic John Nash, won the Nobel Prize in economics for his game theory work that expressed life as a dark, lonely struggle, in competitive scenarios with names like "So Long, Sucker" (Nash originally called this experiment "Fuck Your Buddy"), which required a player to betray any partner at the first hint that the partner might cooperate. By the late 1950s, when Harvard economist and decision theorist Daniel Ellsberg joined RAND, there were more economists at the think tank than mathematicians or physicists, and the conception of relentless competition among calculating, amoral participants engaged in maximizing their own self-interest, already present in a strain of economic thought for over a century, grew still more influential.

At the University of Chicago, a group of gifted right-wing and libertarian economists and legal scholars, which included Milton Friedman, Ronald Coase, Eugene Fama, Gary Becker and Richard Posner, embraced this view of human nature, often termed "homo economicus," and built an ambitious new approach to economics and the law around it. The radical simplification of the homo economicus model, with its focus on rational self-interest, allowed economists, and later other social scientists, to appear to reduce human behavior to a series of logically consistent axioms, falsifiable hypotheses and satisfyingly crisp mathematical equations. Just as important, the simplifying assumption that humans are best understood as rational actors reinforced and meshed with theories of free-market economics that had been popular since Adam Smith and John Stuart Mill, and lent new analytic rigor to the fervent ideology of Friedrich von Hayek, the Austrian economist who had taught at the University of Chicago during and after World War II. Hayek argued that central economic planning led inevitably to totalitarianism, and that markets were a self-ordering mechanism which could spontaneously organize society itself—thus the ideal antidote to totalitarianism. At Chicago, a version of neoliberal economics emerged that cast markets as the supreme mode of human interaction, and the royal road to optimizing collective well-being. The view of human nature was often deeply pessimistic, which contributed to homo economicus. As University of Chicago economist and Nobel laureate James Buchanan wrote in his 1975 book *The Limits of Liberty*, "Any person's ideal situation is one that allows him full freedom of action and inhibits the behavior of others so as to force adherence to his own desires. That is to say, each person seeks mastery over a world of slaves." This became a central part of the US Cold War ideology: the free market as a vital precondition of human freedom, set against the grim, state-dominated slavery of Soviet socialism. This strong ideological polarity helps to explain the near-religious fervor with which key exponents of the Chicago School proselytized their views, a fervor often, as in religion, inversely proportional to the amount of concrete evidence available to support their contentions.

Chicago School economists applied their analysis to a dizzying range of human behavior. Gary Becker, one of the school's pioneers, identified "hedonic" trade-offs that he claimed were present in drug addiction, slavery, sex, love, friendship, race and gender discrimination, divorce, fads, lotteries and the market for vital organs. Becker insisted that his concept of self-interest meant more than crass materialism. "Behavior is driven by a much richer set of values and preferences" than just goods or money, he said in his 1992 Nobel lecture. "Individuals maximize welfare as they conceive it, whether they be selfish, altruistic, loyal, spiteful, or masochistic." In practice, however, this collapsing of all human emotion into a single "rational" metric, in addition to being a striking case of circular reasoning—defining every-thing that humans do as "rational self-interest" simply because humans do it—ultimately reduced human motivation to pleasure, and to pleasure's most easily quantifiable metric, money. Homo economicus is a living cost-benefit analysis, whose behavior is sharply divorced from hazy questions of right and wrong.

The law and economics movement revolutionized jurisprudence, advancing the notion that incentives and punishments were the best tools to modify the behavior of homo economicus, and that morality, so messy and hard to model, was irrelevant to the law. As Richard Posner writes with characteristic trenchancy, "In legal as well as private life we can get along without doing or even thinking about moral theory," which he suggests is "a mystification rooted in a desire to feel good about ourselves—to feel that we are more than just monkeys with big brains." Indeed, he dismisses the views of scholars like Ronald Dworkin and Judith Jarvis Thomson, who believe that law should follow the dictates of morality, as "prissy, hermetic, censorious, naive, sanctimonious, self-congratulatory." Human behavior should instead be conceptualized as a matter of profit and loss to society.

To see how this works, consider Posner's analysis of crime. "The major function of criminal law in a capitalist society is to prevent people from bypassing the system of voluntary, compensated exchange—the 'market,' explicit or implicit—in situations where, because transaction costs are low, the market is a more efficient method of allocating resources than forced exchange," he writes in a 1985 article. "Market bypassing in such situations is inefficient—in the sense in which economists equate efficiency with wealth maximization—no matter how much utility it may confer on the offender." The only reason murder is wrong, Posner asserts, is that it creates vastly more disutility for the victim than it does utility for the murderer. Posner discusses rape in similar terms.

> Suppose a rapist derives extra pleasure from the coercive character of his act. Then there would be (it might seem) no market substitute for rape, suggesting that rape is not a pure coercive transfer and should not, on economic grounds, anyway, be punished criminally. . . . Given the economist's definition of "value," even if the rapist cannot find a consensual substitute (and one such substitute,

prostitution, is itself illegal), it does not follow that he values the rape more than the victim disvalues it. There is a difference between a coerced transaction that has no consensual substitute and one necessary to overcome the costs of consensual transactions; only the second can create wealth, and therefore be efficient. Indeed, what the argument boils down to is that some rape is motivated in part or whole by the negative interdependence of the parties' utilities, and this, as I have argued in connection with crimes of passion, is no reason for considering the act efficient.

There is a flat-affect, inhuman, even monstrous quality to these arguments, which resemble the dead-eyed tallying of burn victims and company profits by automobile engineers, or the quantifying of levels of acceptable loss in nuclear war devised by RAND technocrats. There is also, in Posner's analysis, something of the thrill of mastery, as if over life itself, through pure brainpower. The hubris of this view is suggested by Harvard economist Gregory Mankiw, in the preface to the first edition of his influential textbook *Principles of Economics*. Mankiw calls the discipline a true social science that nevertheless enjoys "the dispassion of a science." "Economics is a subject in which a little knowledge goes a long way. (The same cannot be said, for instance, of the study of physics or the Japanese language.) Economists have a unique way of viewing the world, much of which can be taught in one or two semesters."

But the once-radical ideas of law and economics are now mainstream. In *The Rise of the Conservative Legal Movement*, Steven Teles, a political scientist at Johns Hopkins University, calls law and economics "the most successful intellectual movement in the law of the past thirty years." Its founders and proponents include numerous Nobel-laureate economists (twelve alone at the University of Chicago), whose influence on their field and its application to jurisprudence and public policy has been powerful. Milton Friedman was a key adviser to Ronald Reagan and Margaret Thatcher, who adopted Friedman's ideas about privatization, free markets and human nature. Frank Easterbrook, Guido Calabresi and Richard Posner applied its precepts from the bench, during long tenures as federal judges. The movement has colonized many influential law schools: Harvard, Yale, Chicago and Stanford each

boast a well-funded law and economics research center with at least a dozen influential professor-practitioners. Harvard is home to Mankiw, who as chair of the
Council of Economic Advisers under George W. Bush advanced a strong deregulatory agenda that helped pave the way for the 2008 economic collapse, and to Andrei
Shleifer, the celebrated economist who played a leading role in the disastrous privatization of the Russian economy after the dissolution of the USSR.

Law and economics proponents have aggressively evangelized their messages,
not only in tens of thousands of articles, books, lectures and courses, but through
law boot camps for economists and educational programs for legal professionals
that have been attended by nearly a thousand state attorneys general and their senior staff, and by over five thousand federal and state court judges, including three
members of the current Supreme Court. In 1988, the United States Sentencing
Commission employed a law and economics analysis of crime to develop federal
sentencing guidelines for judges. Law and economics proponents have also turned
the movement into a lucrative industry, founding consultancies like Charles River
Associates, the Berkeley Research Group and Compass Lexecon, whose employees
can earn $1,350 an hour as expert witnesses, typically in defense of corporations or
individuals accused of white-collar crime. Daniel Fischel, who cofounded Lexecon
with Richard Posner, made a fortune testifying on behalf of noted corporate criminals like Charles Keating, Ken Lay, and Jeffrey Skilling, as well as Michael Milken
himself, in whose defense he wrote the book *Payback*. (The title of his book assumed new meaning three years after it was published, when Milken bought
Fischel's company for $60 million.)

By explicitly excluding matters of morality from their analyses, proponents of
the rational self-maximizer model often appear to condone, even to celebrate, behavior that most non-economists would call unethical. Nobel laureate economist
Oliver Williamson asserts that "economic agents" (such as individuals and corporations) are entitled to employ "calculated efforts to mislead, disguise, obfuscate, and
confuse" in their dealings with other agents. Andrei Shleifer argues that corruption
is a natural by-product of competition. Judge Frank Easterbrook and Daniel
Fischel, in a 1982 article, assert that the choice of whether to obey the law is a
straightforward cost-benefit analysis, devoid of moral weight: "Managers do not

have an ethical duty to obey economic regulatory laws just because the laws exist. They must determine the importance of these laws. The penalties Congress names for disobedience are a measure of how much it wants firms to sacrifice in order to adhere to the rules; the idea of optimal sanctions is based on the supposition that managers not only may but also should violate the rules when it is profitable to do so." University of Chicago's Henry Manne argued that insider trading should be legal, both because it leads to more accurate share valuation and because it more effectively pays entrepreneurs at large corporations for their innovations.

Gregory Mankiw, commenting on the systematic looting of savings and loan institutions by their chief executives during the S&L crisis of the 1980s, stated that, given the lax regulatory environment then in force, CEOs would have been acting irrationally, and therefore wrongly, had they *failed* to loot their institutions. Bill Black, an economist who served as a senior bank regulator during the S&L crisis, still remembers his surprise when Mankiw made this statement during a public discussion—and his even greater amazement when none of the other economists in the audience challenged it. "Many practitioners of neoclassical economics flatly deny the existence of fraud," Black writes, "because it clashes with one of their central dogmas, the total transparency of markets. They prefer to assume that would-be fraudsters are soon discovered by other market participants, and excluded from the market. In reality, of course, hidden fraud and criminal behavior exist and cause massive human harm, but because these phenomena don't square with the neoclassical worldview, many economists studiously ignore them, and consider the harm they do as an externality." Black points to influential neoclassical economists like Mankiw, Fischel and the "Maestro" himself, Alan Greenspan, whose stalwart refusal to recognize the existence of fraud during his long tenure as chair of the Federal Reserve caused immense economic and social harm during the increasingly violent economic booms and busts of the 1990s and 2000s. (To his credit, though far too late, Greenspan eventually admitted his error, testifying before Congress shortly after the 2008 crash that "those of us who have looked to the self-interest of lending institutions to protect shareholders' equity [myself especially] are in a state of shocked disbelief," and conceding that the crash demonstrated a "flaw" in his economic worldview.)

Because of the inherently competitive, zero-sum nature of markets, those who "win" in the marketplace, by making the most money, are its success stories, and their ends are assumed to justify pretty much any means. Thus do corporate law-breakers become visionaries. In 1986, in his heyday, Michael Milken told investors, "The force in this country buying high-yield securities has overpowered all regulation." Evidence that emerged at his trial suggests that, like Easterbrook and Fischel, he viewed the decision of whether to obey the law as a cost-benefit choice. Since his release from prison, despite his guilty pleas, Milken has repeatedly denied he did anything wrong, and still seems willing to push the envelope on securities laws. In 1998, Milken paid the SEC a $47 million settlement, while admitting no wrongdoing, for allegedly offering financial advice to Rupert Murdoch, Ronald O. Perelman and others, in violation of his lifetime ban from the securities industry. In 2015, Bloomberg reporter Matt Levine wrote that a $20 million fine levied by the SEC against Guggenheim Partners suggested that Milken had again offered covert investment advice—as one of Lynn Stout's supporters had informed her in an email four years earlier.

Since corporations are economic agents in their own right, composed of a number of homines economici, Chicago School economists and law and economics proponents hold that they too should behave without regard to morality. Daniel Fischel wrote that since companies were simply assemblages of private contracts, they were "incapable of having social or moral obligations much in the same way that inanimate objects are incapable of having these obligations." Milton Friedman famously stated that the corporation's sole responsibility was to make money for its shareholders, and that any attempt on the part of its directors to promote "desirable social ends" was not only wrong but "highly subversive to the capitalist system." Taking Friedman's theory of shareholder value to another level, economists Michael Jensen and William Meckling, both former graduate students at Chicago, identified the maximization of shareholder value as the supreme obligation of every corporation, and paying executives in stock as the best way to ensure that they acted in their firm's best interests, by aligning their financial incentives with those of shareholders.

This, then, was Lynn Stout's economic worldview, until shortly before her run-in with UCLA and Lowell Milken. Law and economics was so pervasive in her field, in fact, that she says she'd studied few other perspectives on the law. "It has something for everyone," she points out. For Americans, it plays into "a national narrative of independence and lack of obligation to others." It removes stigma "for those who want to ruthlessly pursue their own self-interest at the expense of others, which is why it's raised as the banner of Wall Street." And for academics, Stout says, "law and economics offers a very simple, even reductionist approach to understanding the relation between law and human behavior. By excluding culture and history and evolutionary psychology and developmental psychology, you have a lot less reading to do!"

Stout first began to question some of her assumptions in 1999, when she joined the board of Eaton Vance, an asset management company, and met several executives who didn't fit the homo economicus mold at all. "It was shocking to me how decent they all were! Many showed great respect for others, willingness to cooperate, determination to stick to the truth." Having once coauthored a textbook on law and economics, Stout started a book with a different worldview altogether. In it she explored how laws shape human values, drawing on areas of research that were new to her, including social psychology, behavioral ethics and the growing field of prosocial behavior, which seeks to understand the psychological and evolutionary drivers of voluntary acts that benefit other people or society as a whole. "I started to think about the basic assumption of law and economics, and of the Chicago School, that human beings only care about material incentives. What that really means is that humans have no conscience. They are totally amoral, and will cheerfully lie, cheat, steal, break agreements, manipulate and deceive their fellow humans, even murder, if it serves their material interests. And I realized that this model, the homo economicus model, didn't match the way I saw people, or the world."

Her clash with UCLA opened an extended period of soul-searching about her profession, her future and her values, as many whistleblowers experience. She remembers that writing her new book, which she eventually called *Cultivating Conscience: How Good Laws Make Good People*, "was really good preparation, because I was prepared to think about ethics carefully." Conversely, she credits her whistleblowing with clarifying her thinking and hardening her resolve to delve even deeper into matters of conscience. "I was not expert in ethics until this whole Milken business," she says. "I didn't get interested in bad behavior until it hit me over the head." She continued her research and writing on altruistic and prosocial behavior, and why such instincts are often suppressed. "A lot of recent behavioral research shows that the subconscious lessons associated with the homo economicus approach to human nature have a degrading effect on conscience," Stout says. "We're teaching people that they don't owe anybody anything, and we're teaching them that the ruthless pursuit of their own self-interest makes society a better place, and we're talking about other people as if they were selfish, untrustworthy social actors. And those are the Big 3 social cues for triggering the purely selfish parts of our personalities. It's a self-reinforcing downward spiral, because the more people behave like this, the more people think it's normal, the more we think that other people have no sense of obligation to us, and we are entitled to manipulate or abuse them any way we like. Homo economicus is literally a psychopath—he fits the *DSM-5* designation. So when you tell people and businesses that that's how they're supposed to behave, you shouldn't be surprised to get psychopathic behavior."

Stout also began to trace the specific ways in which decades of ardent advocacy by prominent law and economics practitioners have baked this noxious paradigm into many areas of public and private life. One of the great victims of the law and economics revolution, Stout found, was the American corporation. "Some of the best, most basic and time-honored assumptions of American business are antithetical to the homo economicus model," she says. "Managers have long believed that corporations which develop customer and employee loyalty through cooperation and prosocial behavior, that work for the long-term goals, will thrive. But as homo economicus assumptions started to get hardwired into federal law, these assumptions began to fade—or were actually driven out. In the business sector, we've had a whole bunch of rules based on the homo economicus approach, none of which attracted much attention, which have collectively changed the entire structure of incentives in the business world. They're responsible in large part for many of the corporate scandals of the last thirty years."

Beginning in the 1970s and accelerating in the 1990s, changes in federal regulations, securities rules and the tax code drove companies to target short-term shareholder value, with major growth in mutual funds, pension funds and hedge funds, all focused on stock earnings over a brief timescale. As financial deregulation became Washington's and Wall Street's byword, Milken's novel junk bonds funded a series of highly leveraged takeovers that dismembered established companies and sold them off in pieces, often loading the spun-off business with ruinous burdens of debt. In 1992, the SEC changed its proxy rules, making it easier for activist share-holders and hedge funds to mount proxy battles; the following year, the IRS passed the carried interest deduction, giving hedge funds and private equity even more power. All this helped to create a new financialized ethos in business, according to which, as management scholar Paul Hirsch has observed, "the corporation itself is increasingly defined as a salable bundle of liquid assets, rather than as a producer of goods and services." The time-honored bond between employer and employee weakened, to the detriment of ethics. "People used to stick with the same industry and the same employer for decades," Stout says. "That's a world where character matters, because you're dealing with people repeatedly. In a world where people are constantly changing jobs, in the gig economy, you don't feel as much attachment to an institution or connected to its people—and the institution cares less about you."

In the early 1990s, incentives spread throughout securities law and the tax code, both rewarding and requiring homo economicus–style behavior. "Pay for perfor-mance" became the mantra, following the assertion of economists Jensen and Meckling that harnessing the self-serving greed of managers would improve a firm's economic efficiency. Starting in 1992, the SEC passed several new rules that made share price and dividends the essential indices of corporate performance. In 1993 the IRS added Section 162(m) of the corporate tax code, which allowed companies to deduct executive pay only if they linked it to objective performance measures, causing a boom in executive bonuses paid in stock options. "Basically, the federal government was mandating the homo economicus view of corporate America," Stout says. "Pay for performance signals to employer and employee alike that their relationship is strictly arm's length, one where selfishness and opportunism are not only expected but encouraged, and other concerns like loyalty, trust, generosity, ethical norms, or laws, are all crowded out."

Stout also saw how the dogmas of incentives and shareholder value, when ap-plied to executive pay in order to align the interests of managers with those of their organization, paradoxically had the opposite effect. How this works is elegantly explained by Roger Martin in his book *Fixing the Game*. Comparing corporate

America to the National Football League, Martin points out that NFL leadership strenuously prohibits its players, coaches and referees from betting on the sport, because they know the specter of point-shaving and tanking by shady players with money riding on their own games would dramatically undercut the integrity of the league and the loyalty of fans. By prohibiting betting, the NFL forced its employees to concentrate exclusively on what Martin calls the "reality market"—winning football games—and to ignore the "expectations market"—the bookmakers' predictions about those games. Corporate America, Martin shows, has done the opposite. Senior managers are paid in shares whose value they themselves can manipulate, through cost cutting, stock buybacks and other financial techniques, thus riveting their attention squarely on the "expectations market" (the stock exchange, where pundits bet on how a company will perform in the future) rather than the "reality market" (the products and services the company actually provides).

Stout has shown that the single-minded focus on "shareholder value" has actually hurt many shareholders. If, like most investors, you're a long-term owner of diversified stock (as opposed to a hedge fund trader working on minuscule time horizons), over the last thirty years you have suffered a sharp reduction in companies to invest in, especially those willing to reinvest in their businesses with a view to long-term growth. In fact, according to the S&P 500 return calculator, the returns small investors receive on public equities are lower than they were thirty years ago. At the same time, executive compensation has soared, with the average ratio of CEO-to-worker pay increasing from 20:1 in 1965 to 30:1 in 1978, to 361:1 in 2017. (Since 1978, CEO pay has grown almost 1,000 percent, while worker pay has grown 10.2 percent.) This pay inequality has itself fueled corporate wrongdoing, Stout says. "When the game is exclusively about money, that message moves throughout the organization. The principle here is, if you want people to be good, don't tempt them too much to be bad, but the rules in place now really do. All of the scientific evidence suggests that people will follow the rules except when temptation gets too big." You might not sacrifice your integrity for a vacation home, she notes, "but if sacrificing your integrity allows you to make a billion dollars, suddenly you're going to think about it more at night."

"Conscience" and "character" are recurring terms in Stout's work. So is "integrity," which she uses in the Aristotelian sense, from the root word "integer," or "whole number." "If you have integrity, you're a whole person," Stout says, "which means that your thoughts, words and actions sit neatly with each other and are not in conflict. You don't say one thing and do another. You don't think one thing and say something different. It doesn't mean you're necessarily nice—you can be an asshole with integrity. Even so, everybody knows exactly who they're dealing with." Integrity, character, and conscience, a certain old-fashionedness, and an inclination for honesty over irony: these are some of the whistleblower's key characteristics and habits of mind. Stout has tried to understand these traits more clearly in her scholarship, and to apply them in her life. Growing up with an alcoholic father gave her early intimacy with human hardship. A 2016 diagnosis of lung cancer brought a solemn new clarity to her worldview. "An event like this makes you really think back on your life very deeply. I'm not going to be here forever, and the world's going to go on without me. From that perspective, I'm so glad that I stood up in the UCLA situation. At the end of the day—and I hope this isn't the end of the day!— when you look back at your life, feeling that you've acted with integrity and done the right thing is so much more important than any short-term benefit you could have gotten from going along with something that's against all your principles, and makes your gut churn. I'm proud of my legacy. It may not be the biggest or most significant, but there's nothing that I look back on that I'm ashamed of." And she continues to do what she can to further a collective rediscovery of conscience. "A world where everyone ruthlessly pursues their own self-interest is a horrible world to live in," she says. "For our own collective sake, we need to hold ourselves to a higher standard." (Stout died in 2018, during the writing of this book, having devoted the rest of her life to causes in the public interest.)

Ultimately, the psychological mechanisms that trigger whistleblowing—which Lynn Stout calls character and integrity, and others would refer to as morality or justice—arise from human evolution, and the ways in which our struggle to survive has molded our biology and neurology, our instincts and our minds. For nearly all of our evolutionary history, humans lived as nomadic bands of hunter-gatherers, drifting across the savannah; our experience with agriculture and writing, by comparison, falls on the last page in the encyclopedia of our genetic code. Essential to our survival was the ability to act as a tight-knit group, which provided enormous advantages in finding food and shelter; rearing our large-brained, slow-maturing young; hunting big game; and defending ourselves against animal and human aggressors. Today, often unwittingly, we employ the instincts and cognitive processes of the hunter-gatherer in our family lives, sports, work, worship and politics; as evolutionary psychologists Leda Cosmides and John Tooby like to observe, "Our modern skulls house a stone age mind." We see this ancient mind in exaptations like Lynn Stout's nausea at corporate crime: instincts and drives honed during an earlier evolutionary stage frequently emerge in our modern lives, in ways that can be badly mismatched with the present.

Some of these drives increase group cohesion. Social animals like wolves, lions, zebras and vampire bats exhibit behaviors toward fellow members of their group—affection, trust, reciprocity, a sense of social contract—that help them thrive as a larger unit. Primate and hominid ancestors shared in such traits, and in *Homo sapiens sapiens*, one of earth's most intensely social species, they gave rise to instincts like justice, empathy and morality. They are the basis for some of our most powerful urges, joys, fears and revulsions—our horror at injuring or killing other humans; our outrage at immorality or cheating; our uncanny skill at recognizing faces and reading the emotional states of others—which have been optimized by millions of years of evolution into high-throughput neural circuits. We practice subtle social morality long before we can talk: in a series of elegant experiments with infants, developmental and evolutionary psychologist Kiley Hamlin at the University of British Columbia has shown that at as early as six months of age, humans display strong moral impulses to help others and not to hinder them, and prefer people who help to those who hinder. "Many of our powerful social motivations include the injunction 'do not harm other humans'—at least in a vacuum," says Hamlin. Such research suggests that the homo economicus model of rational self-maximization contradicts central features of human nature. We evolved to cooperate, not to go it alone. Prosocial behavior is adaptive.

Yet against our deep social instincts for justice, fairness and morality, evolution has also honed other, often opposing drives. Cognitive neuroscientist Joshua Greene points out that, in general, our moral instincts evolved to enhance cooperation only within groups, not between them. Each band of ancient hunter-gatherers contended with other, similar bands for food, water and shelter, honing impulses to distinguish between in-group allies and out-group enemies, between Us and Them. The taboos against harming humans lose force when we deal with members of out-groups, whom we are programmed to see as scheming, threatening, even subhuman. Kiley Hamlin discovered that nine-month-olds prefer certain people based on their physical characteristics and familiar group status, and like to see dissimilar or unfamiliar people punished. Anthropologist and behavioral economist Francisco Gil-White has shown that the parts of our brain that light up when we think about out-groups are the same as those that engage when we think about prey.

These drives elevate loyalty, as opposed to justice. When finishing off a wounded mammoth or joining battle with an opposing band, knowing someone "has your back" is often more crucial than knowing that they are virtuous. Within the group, too, peaceful cooperation is balanced against energetic striving for higher rank in the social hierarchy, which ensures better access to food, shelter and mates. Andrew Baron at the University of British Columbia and Marco Schmidt at the University of Munich have demonstrated that babies of six to nine months already manifest strong sensitivity to social hierarchy, including deference to authority figures.

These ancient drives are often triggered in modern contexts, helping to explain our visceral, disproportionate, often violent reactions in relatively mundane situations—road rage, office feuds, soccer riots. Cognitive scientist Denise Cummins has shown that the human neuroendocrine response to competitive sports is essentially identical to that triggered by dominance battles, making it "difficult for competitors and fans to remember that these contests are, after all, just games. Physiologically, they feel like the real thing: a competitive contest between rivals that will determine where we stand in the hierarchy and hence what our chances of long-term survival are likely to be." Andy Thomson, a practicing psychiatrist and an expert in evolutionary psychology at the University of Virginia, points out parallels in the workplace. "The psychology of co-workers in a pharmaceutical company, for example, is the same psychology we developed in small, kin-based hunter-gatherer groups. We feel powerful instincts to sign off on group decisions or actions, even if they're dubious, and deep anxiety about being marginalized if we don't." The mesmeric power of some corporate cultures, Thomson says, derives from their ability to harness ancient mechanisms that promote unity.

The deep evolutionary roots of human justice and morality on the one hand, and of loyalty and obedience on the other, help explain the explosive emotions that often arise in whistleblowing cases. Whistleblowers embody a struggle between two opposing ways of being human, which they and their peers alike often seem to experience as powerfully as if they were still fighting for their lives on an African savannah. In our daily lives, we all mediate the struggle between our individual sense of right and wrong and our group-centric devotion to others—to family, team, firm, nation, God. We usually do so in silence, often unconsciously. The whistleblower, by speaking out, brings the tensions between individual and larger social units into the open. "I had to choose between my team—the OIG—and my 'family'—the citizens whom the OIG was supposed to protect," Allen Jones says. "There was loyalty, and betrayal, in either choice. I believe this is true for many whistleblowers. Our choice is which entity to betray and still preserve a sense of self." Whistleblowers feel moral outrage at violations of their instincts to fairness, horror at human harm, disgust at the violation of the morality that makes us human. At the same time, fellow members of their team feel a no less powerful outrage at what they perceive to be the whistleblower's betrayal of social bonds, their attempt to freeload on the group's resources without shouldering its responsibilities, and their refusal to obey authority figures, all of which could cost the group dearly. The pain whistleblowers feel at being ostracized from their group, and the fury and exaggerated, unrelenting retaliation of their peers, have the intensity of life-and-death conflicts.

However vital the whistleblower's message, we are instinctively wary of the messenger. Even if we admire, in the abstract, his devotion to justice, we may still mistrust him for betraying coworkers, superiors and the organization—even when those coworkers are crooks, or that organization is the Mob. When confronted with the whistleblower's act, however objectively noble, many of us feel a quick, hot pulse of disapproval, followed by a cascade of negative associations: *informer, bounty hunter, mole, snitch, rat, turncoat, traitor, Judas.* For our status- and consensus-hungry species, even the very magnitude of the whistleblower's sacrifice may inspire doubt: What kind of person, we wonder, could knowingly commit such an extreme and irrevocable act, trading the status of privileged insider for that of pariah, re-nouncing career and former life with the finality of religious conversion? We won-der whether the whistleblowers' apparent selflessness might actually be megalomania or narcissism, whether their uprightness and determination are actually symptoms of the stickler, the poor "team player," the disgruntled employee getting even. We instinctively adopt the language of retaliation. Part of human nature prefers collu-sion to truth.

In the end, why certain people turn toward justice while their companions move toward loyalty remains one of the central mysteries of whistleblowing, and of human nature. Andy Thomson speculates that some whistleblowers act because their instinct to avoid hurting fellow humans has somehow been activated: "We all have an innate subcortical aversion to harming another person, but it isn't always triggered in everyone. Possibly the people who step forward to report serious crimes are those whose emotional areas of the brain have been engaged. They realize, 'I'm part of a personal force that is harming other individuals!' This stirs the moral out-rage, gives them the emotional energy to resist." Ultimately, whether someone will choose justice or loyalty may be determined by where they draw the line between in-group and out-group, between fellow humans deserving of equal respect and foreign enemies beyond the pale of morality. Which way we lean probably has a lot to do with our life experiences and social training: the beliefs and worldview we receive from families, teachers and leaders.

If our dominant narrative of society and the world is one of mistrust and conflict—if we live in a perceived state of siege, like Lynn Stout's homo economicus "psychopaths"—then we may instinctively derogate outsiders. Behavioral econo-mist Karen Stenner has identified what she calls the "authoritarian dynamic," a predisposition among certain individuals toward obedience to authority, moral abso-lutism, ethnic and racial prejudice, and often punitive intolerance of outsiders and dissidents, which grow in proportion to those individuals' belief that their physical and psychic well-being is under threat. If, instead, we hold human dignity to be a more or less universal and unquestioned norm, our in-group may expand to embrace the world. Some students of Holocaust rescuers and bystanders have noted, among those who risked their lives to save Jews during the Nazi regime, a tendency to view all people first and foremost as members of the human species, and therefore entitled to just and moral treatment. "We do not know what a Jew is," said André Trocmé, Protestant pastor in a small French village that saved some thirty-five hundred Jews during World War II, when asked by collaborationist Vichy authorities to identify the Jews in his town. "We know only men."

Today in America, as in many parts of the world, the widespread sense of uncertainty and fear caused by political polarization, economic chaos, protracted wars abroad and threats (both real and imagined) of terrorism at home all accentuate the emotive urgency of the choice between justice and loyalty, between dynamic morality and unquestioning obedience. Most of us, at some level, are being forced to decide whether to speak truth, at our own hazard, or to repeat the lie and join the liars. Whistleblowers press each of us with the question: Which side are you on?

On January 5, 2004, Justice Antonin Scalia flew with Vice President Dick Cheney on a government jet to southern Louisiana to spend a week duck hunting in St. Mary Parish, ninety miles southwest of New Orleans. A few weeks earlier, the Supreme Court had agreed to hear the appeal of a lawsuit that the Sierra Club had brought against Cheney, seeking to compel him to reveal the identities of energy executives who'd taken part in secret meetings of his National Energy Policy Development Group, shortly before the United States invaded Iraq.

When news of this hunting trip got out, Scalia was widely called upon to recuse himself. The case for his recusal seemed clear. Federal law requires disqualification whenever a judge's impartiality might reasonably be questioned, which appeared to be the case not only for the hunting trip, but also for the fact that Scalia and Cheney were close friends. Other circumstances that normally lead to recusal are the acceptance of anything of value (like an all-expenses-paid hunting trip) and the opportunity for ex parte communications with a litigant.

Instead, in 2004 Scalia wrote a twenty-one-page memo dripping with scorn and offended pride. "Since I do not believe my impartiality can reasonably be questioned," he began, "I do not think it would be proper for me to recuse." Citing instances of previous Supreme Court justices who had socialized with or befriended senior politicians, and subsequently ruled on legal matters involving those politicians, Scalia argued that conflicts of interest were an integral part of his job and his world. Any prohibition against justices hearing cases involving their friends, he wrote, "would be utterly disabling" to the court. Most important, Scalia said, his stature and professional ethics as a member of the highest court in the land immunized him from the effects of friendship and money. "If it is reasonable to think that a Supreme Court Justice can be bought so cheap," he concluded, "the Nation is in deeper trouble than I had imagined."

Scalia was right: the nation *is* in deep trouble when a Supreme Court justice can demonstrate such profound ignorance of the law and of the human psyche. Conflicts of interest are widely recognized to cause two separate kinds of harm: material harm to the commonweal, when a conflicted party pursues his own private gain instead of the public good; and damage to society's confidence in public office itself, when a conflict of interest is manifest (even when it hasn't actually produced corruption). Canon 1 of the American Bar Association's Model Code of Judicial Conduct directs all judges to "avoid impropriety and the appearance of impropriety," in order to maintain the independence, integrity and impartiality of the judiciary. Scalia knew the importance of senior officials' eschewing even the appearance of impropriety: he stressed this precept in a memo he wrote in 1974, as assistant attorney general, to an adviser of President Lyndon Johnson. He simply chose to ignore it in his own case, evidently because it threatened to curtail his extensive social life. (Between 2004 and 2014, Scalia took more than 250 privately funded trips. He died in 2016 during the last of them, at Cibolo Creek Ranch in Texas, a lavish resort where he was staying free of charge courtesy of its owner, industrialist John Poindexter, one of whose firms had benefited the previous year when the Supreme Court declined to hear an appeal against it.)

But more disturbingly, Scalia's memo reveals his ignorance of (or willful blindness to) seventy years of research on human psychology. In his memo, Scalia describes moral behavior as based on conscious choices by rational persons who easily recognize conflicts of interest and decide how to deal with them. Probity, intellect, strength of character and lustrous reputation, he feels, inoculate persons like him from the nefarious pull of conflicts. Only corrupt people abuse the public trust, and they do so premeditatedly.

Yet research in diverse fields including anthropology, social psychology, cognitive economics and behavioral ethics, particularly in the last twenty years, comprehensively refutes such a conception of human behavior. Much of our decision making takes place well below the waterline of the conscious, and our desires have been revealed to shape our interpretation of the facts far more than previously believed. "Moral reasoning is not like that of an idealized scientist or judge seeking the truth, which is often useful," observes Jonathan Haidt, a behavioral psychologist at New York University. "Rather, moral reasoning is like that of a lawyer or politician seeking whatever is useful, whether or not it is true." Psychologist Daniel Kahneman and colleagues identify a number of cognitive heuristics, or shortcuts, that our brains employ to short-circuit reason and to take certain actions without our even being aware we are doing so. One of these many cognitive traps is the "anchoring effect," demonstrated by experienced German judges whose proposed sentences for putative shoplifters were strongly influenced by, or anchored to, the results of dice rolls they made before their judgment; and Israeli parole judges whose approval rates for parole petitions declined sharply as their levels of hunger and fatigue increased. Kahneman described other heuristics, including the "confirmation bias," which leads us to search for, remember and favor data that confirm our pre-existing beliefs, while irrationally discounting alternative hypotheses that may be more valid; and "in-group favoritism," which likewise leads us to prefer the members, beliefs and behaviors of our own group over those of people we perceive to be outsiders.

Kahneman calls such swift instinctual reactions "System 1" thought, in contrast to more deliberative, logical "System 2" thinking. Jonathan Haidt expresses this dual nature of human cognition with the metaphor of a frail human driver perched on the back of a strong and clever elephant. The driver represents conscious, controlled thought, which humans have been doing for perhaps half a million years. It uses words, is effortful and slow, and represents "cool" cognition, meaning that it's not directly connected to the behavioral centers of the brain that initiate action. The elephant, on the other hand, denotes automatic cognition, which operates by pattern recognition, and which we and our ancestors have been doing for hundreds of millions of years. The elephant's work is unconscious, swift, effortless and "hot"—integrally linked to neural circuitry that prompts physical action. Ultimately the rational driver, for all of his clever talk, is only along for the ride. "The rider can try to steer the elephant," Haidt says, "and if the elephant has no particular desire to go one way or the other, it may listen to the rider. But if it has its own desires, it's going to do what it wants to do."

Nevertheless, the rational rider still believes he's in the driver's seat, and passes his time creating ex post facto rationalizations for the path that the elephant has taken. Haidt illustrates how this works with several thought experiments, which concern intrinsically harmless acts that nevertheless clash violently with our moral intuitions: a one-off act of consensual incest between sister and brother, cleaning a toilet with the national flag, eating the family dog that has been killed by a car or a chicken carcass that has just been used for masturbation. Haidt shows that our unconscious moral intuitions, which are formed by deep-seated biological drives as well as by cultural training, cause us to reach almost instantaneous judgments about the moral rightness or wrongness of certain activities, whereupon our conscious mind, convinced it is in control, begins to marshal evidence to support these intuitive initial judgments.

These widely accepted findings have profound implications for dealing effectively with conflicts of interest. Many of the most hazardous and widespread conflicts do not, as Justice Scalia claimed, involve rational choices, but more subtle relationships of affinity, reciprocity and dependence that are unconscious and therefore largely beyond our control. In fact, some methods commonly used to inoculate people against conflicts actually make them more susceptible. The public disclosure of potential conflicts, for example, has been shown to accentuate many abuses.

Unconscious forces warp our behavior in often invisible but highly predictable ways. Most of us cling to a view of ourselves as ethical, intelligent and deserving people, so we instinctively reframe evidence to the contrary. If we are basically good, after all, how could we ever indulge in gross self-dealing? Anthropologists have long recognized that gift giving and reciprocity, the heart of many conflict-of-interest situations, often create binding social bonds: "The gift not yet repaid debases the man who accepts it," writes anthropologist Marcel Mauss of the powerful sense of indebtedness and obligation felt by the recipient of a gift. Much of our reciprocity is hardwired: fMRI scans of the brain during experiments involving gift giving reveal increased activity in areas of the brain associated with pleasure and social bonding—activity that increased the participants' receptiveness to the ideas of people who'd given them gifts, though they professed to be entirely unaware of this new inclination. Lawrence Lessig has described the dependency cycle between giver and recipient that gift giving creates. Dolly Chugh, a behavioral ethicist at the New York University business school, explains that such "invisible" conflicts of interest, though far more widespread and pernicious than blatant bribery, are often regarded as opportunities, and even obligations, to demonstrate loyalty and generosity for one's company, team, ethnic group or nation.

Conflict of interest isn't personal, therefore, but structural: it's not about a few bad apples spoiling the barrel, but about bad barrels, which can spoil even the best apples. Yet in countless fields where conflicts of interest are rampant, the research is ignored and the misguided, outmoded "Scalia" model is allowed to stand. The business world is rife with examples of mismanaged conflicts. In nearly every major accounting scandal of the last thirty years, "independent" auditors with strong business ties to their clients either missed or suppressed a brewing financial storm until it broke in economic disaster. In perhaps the most celebrated example, Arthur Andersen had increasingly lucrative contracts with Enron for fifteen years, from the company's founding until 2001, when it collapsed in a $63 billion fraudulent bankruptcy. The accountants' blind spot is easily explained. Major accounting firms know that if they refuse to approve a client's books, that client will probably fire them and hire a more compliant accountant. Accounting firms often sell profitable consulting services to the same firms they audit, and accountants routinely resign to take jobs at client firms. "This is absolutely insane!" says Max Bazerman, who for years has denounced conflicts inherent in the accounting industry. "The entire industry was created to provide independent audits, yet because of their multiple, serious conflicts, the one thing Final Four accounting firms cannot provide is independent audits. I view these companies as very corrupt. Their conflicts of interest have cost investors many billions of dollars."

Similar conflicts exist throughout the financial world. Management consultants are hired and fired by a company's board, and often parrot what the board wants to hear. Credit rating agencies are paid by the same investment banks whose securities they are charged with rating, which nudges them to issue positive ratings. Stock analysts work for investment banks that also compete to supply lucrative banking services to the companies whose stocks they rate, which often leads to glowing reviews rather than dispassionate analyses. Conflicts are particularly pernicious— and ignored—in scientific research. Clinical trials of pharmaceuticals, even those not ghostwritten like Study 329, frequently exhibit a "funding bias" in favor of the firm or industry that paid for the trial. Study after study has revealed what the *British Medical Journal* announced in 2003: "Strong and consistent evidence shows that industry sponsored research tends to draw conclusions favourable to industry and industry sponsored studies were much more likely to reach conclusions that were favourable to the sponsor than were non-industry studies." Results are similarly skewed in consumer health research and safety tests performed by independent versus industry-funded researchers.

A few academics, like some on the payroll of the tobacco, fast-food or hedge fund industries, may be consciously corrupt, and may intentionally shape their results to please their paymasters. More often, however, basically honest researchers are unknowingly corrupted by the conditions under which they work, and respond in highly predictable, human but ultimately distorting ways to the invisible pull of their sponsors' money. In fact, for all its aura of objectivity, science, like finance, involves countless subjective choices where invisible biases can germinate. Social psychologist Elliot Aronson, an authority on cognitive dissonance, explains: "If you are an impartial scientist working on your own dime, and your clinical trial shows an ambiguous but potentially harmful result for the new drug you're testing, you might say, 'I'm worried about this result. Is this apparent increase in adverse effects caused by the drug, or by patients who were particularly sick? We need to know more.' But if your research is being paid for by the company who makes that drug, you'll unconsciously tend to downplay your concerns and resolve the ambiguity in the company's favor, and ultimately conclude that there's no need to look further. You'll say, 'Let's assume the drug is safe until proven otherwise.'" Unwittingly, even experienced researchers tend toward the interests of their sponsors, Aronson says, "like a plant turning toward the sun." Recent science confirms what immemorial experience with human behavior has long suggested: most major conflicts of interest cannot be managed. The only sure way to avoid the corruption they engender is to eliminate them.

And yet they are allowed to thrive. In a January 2017 interview, Peter Thiel, the billionaire venture capitalist who advised a newly elected president Donald Trump on tech matters, applauded conflicts as the way of the world. "I think in many cases, when there's a conflict of interest, it's an indication that someone understands something way better than if there's no conflict of interest. If there's no conflict of interest, it's often because you're just not interested." Justice Scalia said essentially the same about a 2009 Supreme Court opinion, *Caperton v. A. T. Massey Coal*, a case so extreme that it inspired John Grisham's legal thriller *The Appeal*. It's worth summarizing the case, to show the facility with which certain lawyerly minds essentially argue conflict of interest out of existence—and the moral decay that ensues.

In 2002, Massey's CEO, Don Blankenship, lost a lawsuit before a West Virginia court to Hugh Caperton, the head of a smaller mining competitor who claimed that Massey had driven his company out of business by fraudulently canceling a contract. The jury set damages at $50 million. Blankenship, a coal baron whose naked predatory instincts seem straight out of Dickens (he was later jailed for conspiring to violate mine safety and health standards at a Massey mine in West Virginia, where an explosion had killed twenty-nine miners), appealed the verdict. While waiting for his appeal, Blankenship spent $3 million to support the election to the West Virginia Supreme Court of Brent Benjamin, a little-known conservative lawyer, to replace incumbent Warren McGraw, a liberal justice who had found against Blankenship in the trial. Blankenship also financed "And for the Sake of the Kids," a political organization that ran a series of vicious, unfounded attack ads against McGraw. Sure enough, McGraw lost his seat to Benjamin in the 2004 election. Benjamin refused repeated demands to recuse himself from the Massey appeal, insisting on his own impartiality even though Blankenship had essentially bought his judgeship. Benjamin cast the deciding vote in a 3–2 decision that voided the previous guilty verdict and damages against Massey.

When the US Supreme Court reviewed the case in 2009, a majority of the justices held that Benjamin should have recused himself, because the Fourteenth Amendment's Due Process clause requires a judge to do so not only when actual bias has been demonstrated or when he has an economic interest in the case, but also when "extreme facts" create a "probability of actual bias." The majority decision added that the defendant had a "significant and disproportionate influence in placing the judge on the case." Scalia, however, disagreed. In a sarcastic dissent reminiscent of his duck hunt memorandum, Scalia argued that, far from preserving the public's confidence in the judicial process, the majority's opinion would reinforce the cynical popular view that litigation was a game invariably won by the highest bidder.

It is hard to imagine a more counterintuitive interpretation. But one thing we can say for sure about Scalia: the man was consistent. A year later, Scalia joined the majority in *Citizens United v. Federal Election Commission*, which declared that free speech is equivalent to money, that individuals and corporations have the constitutional right to give unlimited sums of money to politicians, and that such contributions are not corrupting in fact or in appearance.

At five a.m. on June 30, 1982, four members of the Polish security militia burst into a three-room apartment near Saski Park in downtown Warsaw where Janine Wedel, then a PhD candidate in social anthropology at the University of California, Berkeley, was living with two Polish women, Antonina Dachów and her daughter Ela. Wedel had come to Poland to study the tight-knit social networks that people living behind the Iron Curtain formed in order to elude the rapacious bureaucracy of state socialism. "My professors initially wanted to set me up investigating community life in some sleepy Polish farming village," she remembers. "But I was young, and already knew farmers—I'd grown up in a small Mennonite community in Kansas with relatives who were farmers. I didn't want to spend five years studying people with shit on their shoes. I wanted to be where the action was, in an urban context."

In Antonina Dachów, whom she came to call "Mama," Wedel had certainly found the action. Dachów was a master of day-to-day life under totalitarianism. Her training had started as a teenager, in 1941, when the Soviets deported her and her well-to-do family to a Siberian labor camp as part of the forced resettlement of some 1.5 million Poles from Soviet-occupied Polish territories. In the camp, she distinguished herself as bright, resourceful and skilled at manipulation, able to earn an administrative job and help the family get favors and food. Upon repatriation to Poland in 1946, foreseeing the long-term Soviet domination of her country, she joined the Communist Party apparatus, and eventually became head of the party-sponsored Women's League in the Polish city of Szczecin.

During the dawn raid in Warsaw, Wedel saw her housemother's full repertoire of antitotalitarian misdirection. While the agents searched the apartment for subversive leaflets and other evidence of involvement with the underground, Dachów dogged their steps, barraging them with quips and questions to keep them off balance, and now and then concealing compromising evidence when their backs were turned. She informed the commander of the squad that she belonged to the same state-sponsored Polish–Soviet Friendship Society that he did. When an agent began to search Wedel's room, the fetching Ela, dressed in a bathrobe that showed her long legs to advantage, put her arm around him and laughingly told Wedel that she was in luck: "The best-looking one of all is going to search your room." By the time the agents finished their search, they had become Dachów's allies; they warned the women to watch what they said and whom they met, because their phone would be tapped and their apartment under surveillance.

"It was a bizarre scene," Wedel says. "Here was Antonina, who had spent her career as a party operative, manipulating and misleading Communist officials. It was a classic case of the two-faced life people often lived under totalitarian regimes."

Wedel observed firsthand the institutionalized hypocrisy of the totalitarian state, which the Czech poet and dissident Václav Havel called "living within a lie." "Life in the system is . . . thoroughly permeated with hypocrisy and lies," Havel wrote in 1978, while living in hiding. "Government by bureaucracy is called popular government; the working class is enslaved in the name of the working class; the complete degradation of the individual is presented as his ultimate liberation." This state of extreme institutional hypocrisy and Orwellian doublespeak seemed calculated to trigger whistleblowing, yet there was no authority to whom one could blow the whistle—the state itself had created these contradictions and abuses, and hunted down anyone who, like Havel, objected.

With the thoroughness and tenacity of a field anthropologist, Wedel recorded how Mama navigated her contradictory world, much as she'd manipulated the security militiamen in her apartment. Wedel watched her secure the best cuts of meat and much-coveted rolls of toilet paper by flattering and secretly tipping stall keepers; acquire black market gasoline and alcohol and elusive permits by currying favor with government bureaucrats. Dachów taught her the full weight of the Polish verb *załatwic*, which means "to arrange" or "finagle" a transaction in a shady or illegal way. Wedel came to call Dachów's technique of winning over key elements of the socialist state "personalizing bureaucracy."

Beneath the surface of the Polish day-to-day, apparently so bleak and monolithic, Wedel began to recognize a teeming, ebullient clandestine world organized into almost tribal units of clique, network, clan and family. The most essential commodity in a repressive society was secret information, and the creation of a tight-knit group of trusted allies—relatives, friends, neighbors and coworkers— was essential to obtain and exploit it. Survival meant engaging in sometimes illegal activity that was nevertheless widely embraced throughout the population, with powerful loyalties among group members that Polish sociologist Adam Podgórecki called *brudne wspólnoty* ("dirty togetherness").

"Poles had survived revolution, invasion and occupation, and learned to play their cards close to their chest," Wedel says. "Not surprisingly, they didn't trust the official state, which tried to creep into every corner of their lives with its monopolistic control over politics, culture, and the economy. Individuals could not form organizations—only the Communist Party could—and central economic planning meant that there were shortages of many commodities and services—meat, cheese, shoes, petrol. So people created parallel, unofficial systems to gain access to them. Mama, her survival skills honed in Siberia, possessed a huge, instinctive Rolodex of people who could do or get things. Sometimes she made me uncomfortable by peppering friends who came to visit with questions about themselves and their families—as she was coaxing them with home-baked goodies, of course."

What started as a way of surviving under Communist regimes soon became a competitive advantage of a different kind. Wedel had come to Poland just in time to witness the country's disintegration. Two months before her arrival in February 1982, General Wojciech Jaruzelski, the Polish dictator, declared martial law, closed airports and national borders, severed major roads as well as phone lines, shut schools and universities, and outlawed free labor unions, notably the enormously popular Solidarity, the only non-state-sponsored union in the Communist East Bloc. The totalitarian regime, here and throughout the Iron Curtain, was melting away, and a new world was coming into being, a wide-open, often lawless landscape where vast amounts of state-owned property and businesses, the assets of entire societies, were suddenly available to individuals. "The same strategies that Antonina and Ela used to outwit an authoritarian system gave them and other well-placed people a head start when that system collapsed," Wedel says.

Another valuable commodity in the post-Communist East was foreign aid, which the West supplied in large quantities to smooth the transition from a socialist planned economy to free-market capitalism. Wedel recognized that this aid was vital to Polish leaders not only economically, but as a symbol of support and legitimation by the West. She began to study the distribution of Western aid in Eastern Europe using classic methods of anthropology and ethnography, including participant observation, in-depth interviews and analysis of social networks. Instead of studying people with shit-covered shoes, Wedel found herself doing fieldwork among people in loafers and brogues, members of the carpetbagger army of consultants, facilitators and self-proclaimed "transition" experts who converged on the former East, whom she called the "Marriott Brigade." "For a few months the Marriott was the only place that had a business center where photocopying wasn't a problem. It was wonderful for me—I had everyone in one place. And the staff didn't yet know they weren't supposed to give out information. I'd call and ask, 'When is So-and-so coming to town?' and they'd tell me!"

As an American who was experienced in socialist Poland and knew many influential Poles—a photo on her wall at George Mason University shows her planting a kiss on the cheek of a young and obviously delighted Lech Wałęsa—Wedel was frequently contacted by Western government officials, foundations and companies seeking access to the East. She attended meetings, fascinating for an anthropologist, where members of vastly different and mutually opaque cultures came into contact after decades of enmity and misinformation. Westerners typically behaved with a blend of capitalist triumphalism over their fallen Cold War adversary, zealous free-market ideology and boundless ignorance about the history, culture, society and governance of the Eastern Bloc. On the other side, Wedel repeatedly witnessed what she termed "the ritual of listening to foreigners," during which Poles greeted aid-bearing Westerners warmly while secretly ridiculing their naiveté and devising ways to extract as much money as possible from them.

Wedel is a petite woman with large brown eyes, who dresses conservatively and speaks in a calm, melodious midwestern voice. In Poland in the late 1980s and early 1990s, notepad in hand, she looked to be precisely what she said she was: a scholar doing research. Perhaps, in the guise of a mere observer—someone without any skin in the great game of privatization—she came across as harmless or naive. ("I ask naive questions because I sometimes *am* naive," she says.) Wedel also developed the knack, crucial for field anthropologists and investigators alike, of instilling trust in her subjects, and choosing the right moment in the conversation to spring the tough questions. Numerous insiders granted her revealing interviews, passed her restricted agency documents and internal memoranda. Investigators shared personal insights and confidential reports. "I was a crazy woman, running around and collecting all this absolutely riveting stuff. These were the countries the West at the time saw as most likely to succeed and worthy of aid. I built up a real archive. I felt a bit like a little spy."

In all, Wedel filled a hundred notebooks with interviews and gathered documents that now fill a score of banker boxes in a storage facility in Washington, DC.

These materials became the basis not only of her anthropological research but of her investigative journalism on how the Western aid effort was going awry. She began to denounce the lucrative, often hypocritical, and sometimes deeply harmful industry of US foreign aid in Central and Eastern Europe, and to condemn by name a number of Western insiders, many of them fellow academics, who were engaged in it.

She noticed evolved versions of the subterranean cliques and clans she had first seen in Poland: an amphibious elite of government officials, NGO activists and scholars who glided between state and private roles, forming tight-knit, under-the-radar networks to take full advantage of Western aid. Some insiders were foreigners. The US government had deputized major accounting firms as agents of reform. The historians and political scientists who'd long been central to policy making with the Eastern Bloc were now less in demand, while economists, auditors and bankers were in vogue.

She eventually called this class of domestic and foreign operators "flexians," to suggest the fluidity with which they changed roles and public personae. Wedel's flexians had four key characteristics. First, they captured confidential, often governmental information, and used it to co-opt public goods for their own private ends. Second, they circumvented official channels by "personalizing" bureaucracy, either by creating special relationships with trusted bureaucrats or by supplanting existing bureaucracies with their own quasi-private, quasi-governmental organizations. Third, they played a series of overlapping roles that fused state and private power, usually in ways that were invisible to people outside their networks. "If you're the head of Agency X," says Wedel to illustrate such a flex net, "then I'm the managing director, and your wife or your closest buddy from school is the CFO. And if he's the CEO for Commission Y, then I'm the managing director and you're the president." Fourth, as operators in a world where trust in public entities and the concept of public service had been decimated by decades of communism, flexians showed little or no loyalty to official institutions, and a fervent allegiance to fellow members of their flex net, whose ideology, friendships and financial interests they shared.

As the aid frontier moved eastward from Central Europe, Wedel followed. In Hungary and Czechoslovakia she saw the same flexian behavior. "The watchwords were always 'deregulation,' 'privatization,' 'free markets' and 'democracy,'" she says.

"They were repeated with ideological zeal, almost obsessively, by reformers from the East and the West. But behind the rhetoric, on the ground in each country, something very different was happening. Insiders with massive, hidden conflicts of interest were making sure that a great deal of property and information stayed in private hands—their hands—through means that were anything but free-market or democratic."

By 1994 she'd reached Moscow, where she began to study the rituals of Western aid in the capital of the old Soviet Empire. Here, too, flexians were at work. A familiar cast of economists and consultants were pushing the radical privatization of the Russian economy, according to abstract free-market doctrines, which, in Russia even more than elsewhere in the East, ignored the country's past. After nearly a century of planned economies, most Russians had never seen a retail store or owned private property apart from their household belongings. The rule of law had been totally delegitimized by generations of totalitarian police-state repression, and powerful clans dominated entire sectors of the economy. In short, the prerequisites for a rapid transition to free-market capitalism and democracy were lacking. Nevertheless, the official US prescription for Russian economic reform remained "shock therapy" through high-speed privatization. "A USAID [United States Agency for International Development] representative told me, 'Privatization is our first, second and third priority,'" Wedel remembers. "That was of course without a legal infrastructure in place, without a tradition of private property ownership or civil society, because the 'transition experts' didn't consider those things to be preconditions for a market economy. The law and economics movement had minimized the role of regulations, essentially saying you don't need them." As elsewhere in the East, Wedel saw how Western financial aid and high-speed privatization created vast wealth and influence for a small number of Russians who managed to gain control of the process.

Just how great the wealth and influence, and how small the number of beneficiaries, Wedel began to see at a meeting she attended in February 1994. A group of seasoned, middle-aged consultants and Russian ministry officials sat around an oblong table, with two inexperienced men in their late twenties in their midst who were clearly directing the proceedings. One, Dmitry Vasiliev, was a member of a group of dynamic young St. Petersburg economists led by Anatoly Chubais, former vice mayor of the city, whom Boris Yeltsin, president of the new Russia, had brought to Moscow to spearhead economic reform. Allies often called this group the "Young Reformers," while critics referred to them as the "Chubais clan" or the "St. Petersburg mafia." The other leader of the meeting was a tousled American named Jonathan Hay, a recent graduate of Harvard Law School. "I saw these seasoned, very high-status people, openly deferring to little old Jonathan Hay, who had scant, if any, real work experience," Wedel says. "And I thought to myself, 'What the hell is going on here?'"

To find out, Wedel visited the various offices that were ostensibly leading the Russian privatization process, which had impressive and official-sounding names like the State Property Committee, the Russian Privatization Center, and the Federal Securities Commission. Her interviewees handed her glossy brochures that described the aims and goals of each organization. Eventually she would put away her notepad and start asking her real questions: Who actually showed up and ran this operation? What were its true agendas? The same seven or eight people cropped up as the formal or informal heads of each organization. Some were members of the Chubais clan, including Dmitry Vasiliev, Maxim Boycko and Anatoly Chubais himself. Others worked for the Harvard Institute for International Development, as part of a program, widely known as the "Harvard Project," that aimed to help Russia transition from state socialism to a free-market capitalism by privatizing Russian companies, reforming laws, building a capital market, and facilitating other structural changes. Jonathan Hay, it turned out, was the Moscow-based general director/field coordinator and second-in-command of the Harvard Project. Hay reported to project director and principal investigator Andrei Shleifer, the Russian-born wunderkind economist who earned tenure at Harvard at age thirty.

Shleifer's plan for full-speed Russian privatization matched his avid, Milton Friedman–style neoliberalism and jibed with the theories of his Harvard teacher and patron, Lawrence Summers. The Harvard Project, far from being an ivory tower experiment, was operating almost as an arm of the US government. USAID, a federal entity that administered civilian aid in foreign countries, had basically delegated its economic reform operations in Russia to the project, funding it directly with over 40 million tax dollars and making it the gatekeeper to hundreds of millions more. Members of the Chubais clan received further millions in Western aid and subsidized loans. No wonder those veteran consultants were so deferential to young Jonathan Hay.

Wedel gradually saw that the impressive agency names and their bright brochures were Potemkin façades, behind which the same handful of Harvard and Chubais people ran the show. At the State Property Committee, for example, Wedel found that Chubais was the chair and Vasiliev was deputy chair, Hay was senior legal adviser, Shleifer was an adviser, and Maxim Boycko was the chief economic adviser. At the Russian Privatization Center, Chubais was again the chairman of the board and Vasiliev was deputy chair, Hay and Shleifer were also board members, and Boycko was the CEO. At the Federal Securities Commission, Chubais was chair, Vasiliev was deputy chair and executive director, Shleifer was an adviser paid by USAID, while Hay had an office in the commission and led the Institute for Law-Based Economy, a US-supported body that, in turn, funded the commission. Such interlocking engagements often involved friends and family as well. Vasiliev put Hay's girlfriend (and future wife) Elizabeth Hebert, a budding mutual fund manager, on a working group of a major US-Russian economic commission. Andrei Shleifer's wife, Nancy Zimmerman, a brilliant hedge fund manager and fixed income securities expert who was intimately involved with Shleifer's Russian investments, had worked at Goldman Sachs under Robert Rubin, and routinely counseled Lawrence Summers and other Treasury leaders. (Summers reportedly called the elite nexus of public and private players in Russia, which included Shleifer, Zimmerman and a few others, "our little world.") Later, Veniamin Sokolov, head of a Russian investigative unit, gave Wedel documents showing that the Harvard-Chubais axis had managed to ensure that Maxim Boycko and Jonathan Hay headed a tiny committee that approved privatization decisions.

"Neither of these guys had a formal position in the Russian government at the time, and Jonathan was an American citizen," Wedel says. "It was stunning! All the agencies had different formal purposes, but were being run by the same shadow elite of seven or eight people, which most people except those deep inside the process never had a clue about, including foreign aid officials." She eventually spoke with members of the Moscow office of USAID as well, including some who had denounced wrongdoing internally. "All this was like a metastasis of the cliques and clans I'd seen earlier in socialist Poland, a tumor grown huge on the foreign aid money, economic ideology and cultural ignorance of the West. Flex networks simply appropriated large portions of the state. This was 'dirty togetherness' on a whole new level."

Wedel also traced threads of influence leading to Harvard and to Washington, which had made this Harvard Project possible in the first place. Jeffrey Sachs, a peripatetic economist who advised several Central and Eastern European countries on economic reform after Communism, had brought together key members of the project; both Hay and Shleifer had obtained funding from the Finnish government via his consultancy, Jeffrey D. Sachs and Associates, and Sachs had introduced Shleifer to Chubais in 1991. (Sachs and Shleifer later had a falling-out and stopped working together.) A still more vital node in the flex network was Lawrence Summers. While teaching economics at Harvard, Summers had been close to Shleifer; he was also close to Chubais. After becoming deputy Treasury secretary in 1995 (he became secretary four years later), Summers pushed the agenda of the Harvard Project and the Chubais clan, which he called a "dream team" for Russian privatization. Another Harvard Project booster was David Lipton, a Harvard PhD economist and former vice president of Jeffrey D. Sachs and Associates, who later worked for Summers at Treasury and helped set the US foreign aid agenda in Russia and elsewhere. Another influential ally was Robert Rubin, former Goldman Sachs co-chair turned Treasury secretary, who had been Summers's longtime political mentor at Treasury, and made him deputy secretary in 1995. Together with Alan Greenspan, Rubin and Summers had spread the triumphant doctrine of deregulation, privatization and free-market economics throughout the US economy, Eastern Europe, Asia and beyond. (In 1999, they appeared together on the cover of *Time*, which called them "The Three Marketeers" and "The Committee to Save the World.") So when the Gore-Chernomyrdin Commission, led by the vice presidents of the United States and Russia, was formed to facilitate joint projects, including petrochemical deals, between the two countries, Rubin was named a chair of the commission's capital markets forum, together with Chubais and Vasiliev on the

Russian side. Later, as president of Harvard, Summers brought Rubin onto the Harvard Corporation, the university's secretive governing body.

In 1996, in the diminutive scholarly journal *Demokratizatsiya*, Wedel blew the whistle on the Harvard-Chubais network, describing how its members had contributed to the rape of Russia. Drawing on a wide range of official documents and conversations with insiders to Russian privatization, she detailed the Harvard Project's vast economic resources and influence, and suggested that their exclusive support for Chubais and his circle, despite the existence of other valid reformers and Chubais's growing unpopularity among the Russian people themselves, was partisan politics masquerading as arm's-length development aid. She showed how Chubais's unique access to Western money, facilitated by loyal supporters at the Harvard Project and in Washington, allowed him to form a faction of unparalleled political power in Russia. She explained how he and his Harvard Project partners pushed through their agenda by willfully bypassing Russia's rulers and even its legislature, a practice that, for all their rhetoric about freedom and self-determination for the Russian people, was profoundly antidemocratic. She also demonstrated that the Harvard Project, with help from Lawrence Summers and other influential supporters, had circumvented normal competitive bidding rules in Washington, by claiming that its work was vital to US national security.

Such dealings, Wedel wrote, created serious conflicts of interest among the leaders of the Harvard Project, who were "in the unique position of recommending US aid policies in support of market reforms while being a chief recipient of the aid, as well as overseeing some other aid contractors, some of whom are its competitors." At times, the Harvard-Chubais axis had clearly put its own interests ahead of those of the Russian people: Wedel showed how, after their USAID-funded program to reform laws on mortgages and title registration failed to receive additional USAID money as they had expected, "they promptly blocked legal reform activities . . . launched by agencies of the Russian government."

Worse still, the antidemocratic cronyism of the Harvard-Chubais axis had produced a series of disastrous failures in the Russian privatization process. Their attempt to create open capital markets, from which they had preemptively excluded many of the logical participants, was a flop. The "vouchers for shares" program, lavishly funded by USAID, was meant to privatize thousands of state-run companies by transferring their ownership to ordinary Russians, but had in the end concentrated property in the hands of a few tycoons—the nascent oligarchs—with disappointing returns for the Russian government; economist James Millar has called the vouchers for shares program "de facto fraud." The even more catastrophic "loans for shares" scheme handed many of Russia's most valuable industrial assets, including several large metals and oil companies, to seven oligarch-controlled banks, at fire-sale prices in rigged auctions. As corruption mounted, the originally enthusiastic Russian public began calling the program *Pri-hvatizatsiya*, a play on the Russian words for "privatization" and "grabbing"—"The Big Grab." Polls showed that a large and growing number of Russians believed the program was part of a US plot to destroy their country.

By 1996, when Wedel wrote her article in *Demokratizatsiya*, the vaunted miracle of US-led economic reform had contributed substantially to the collapse of Russia's economy and its fragile incipient democracy. Output dried up, and inflation hit peaks of 2,500 percent, wiping out the savings of ordinary Russians. Death rates spiked and life expectancy plummeted, to levels far worse than in Soviet times. As the economists of the Harvard Project carried out their grand, cerebral experiment, Russians marched in the street with signs that read, NO MORE EXPERIMENTS! Far from creating real property rights or true competition, as promised, Harvard-Chubais programs led to wholesale looting, asset stripping and illicit financial flows. Wayne Merry, senior political adviser at the US Embassy in Moscow from 1991 to 1994, later observed, "The United States . . . created a virtual open shop for thievery at a national level and for capital flight in terms of hundreds of billions of dollars, and the raping of natural resources and industries on a scale which I doubt has ever taken place in human history." Economists, Merry suggested, had insisted that an injection of greed would free individual initiative and inevitably create a free-market economy. Instead, he said, "what was really needed in the post-Soviet Russia was a new culture of law, a new culture of civic society."

Wedel's previous experience with flexians showed that, in addition to circumventing official bureaucracy and guarding valuable information for themselves, flexians often served their own interests, to the direct detriment of the state. So it proved in Russia. Wedel's 1996 accusations, together with a series of news articles in the *Boston Globe* and the *Wall Street Journal*, prompted officials to take a closer look at the activities of the Chubais clan and its Harvard allies. Anatoly Chubais was eventually accused of accepting bribes and helping to launder billions of dollars from Russian "privatizations" through the Bank of New York and other Western banks. In 1996, the GAO began an investigation of the Harvard Project; the following year, the inspector general of USAID opened its own inquiry. In May 1997, amid accusations of mismanagement and self-dealing, the Russian government and USAID both suspended the project; USAID canceled an additional $17 million in funding it had earmarked for the project. The Harvard Institute for International Development, now directed by Jeffrey Sachs, fired Hay for violating conflict-of-interest policies, and removed Shleifer from his leading role in the project, though Shleifer remained—and remains—a full professor in the economics department.

The FBI and a federal grand jury in Boston opened investigations of their own. The Forum Financial Group, LLC, a mutual fund manager, sued Harvard, Shleifer and Hay for cutting them out of the Russian mutual fund market. USAID accused Farallon Fixed Income Associates, LP, founded by Nancy Zimmerman, of misuse of resources and self-dealing. In 1997, Boston assistant US attorney Sara Miron Bloom, an experienced False Claims Act practitioner, also began probing; in September 2000, her office brought a civil suit against Harvard, Shleifer, Hay, Hebert and Zimmerman, on eleven charges including False Claims Act violations, common-law fraud, breach of contract, unjust enrichment, and civil conspiracy. District Judge Douglas P. Woodlock dismissed all charges against Hebert and Zimmerman, and many charges against the other defendants. But on June 28, 2004, in a hundred-page summary judgment memorandum, Woodlock ruled that Shleifer and Hay had conspired to defraud the US government under the False Claims Act; that Hay had also presented false claims and made or used false records or statements under the FCA; and that Harvard had breached its contract with USAID. A civil jury later found that Shleifer, who claimed to be merely a consultant and therefore not bound by associated conflict-of-interest rules, was in fact the director and therefore bound by and in violation of those rules. Hence he and Hay were both liable for treble damages under the FCA.

In the view of the prosecutors and of Judge Woodlock himself, what had happened was a classic case of conflicting public and private interests, in a historical context where massive and enduring social harm could result. In contracts with USAID, Harvard had pledged to serve as "a completely neutral third party, void of any vested interest in the contracting process," in order to "ensure competition, transparency and fair play" and to "develop the complete confidence and trust of the host government and also the array of donor agencies." Instead, according to Judge Woodlock's memorandum and other court documents, Hay, Shleifer, their romantic partners and other associates had engaged in shady dealings that violated the letter and the spirit of these contracts. Among a considerable range of wrongdoing, prosecutors accused Shleifer and Zimmerman of investing $200,000 in major Russian companies that were being privatized under plans that Shleifer, as a key adviser, had helped or was helping to craft; Shleifer, Zimmerman and Hay of purchasing oil stocks under the name of Zimmerman's father, Howard Zimmerman, evidently to conceal their involvement in the transaction (Judge Woodlock referred to this tactic as an "attempt to 'launder'" the share ownership); and Hay and Hebert, using funds loaned by Zimmerman and Shleifer, of launching the first mutual fund management company and the first specialized depository in Russia, and bringing to bear their considerable insider influence, both financial and managerial, over the Federal Securities Commission to ensure that both organizations obtained the first operating licenses, ahead of far more experienced competitors like Credit Suisse First Boston and Pioneer Group. Court documents also indicate that Hay and Hebert had run their private business from an office largely paid for by USAID, and that Shleifer and Hay had attempted to intimidate, marginalize or fire certain employees who had objected to their questionable activities within the organization.

Soon the settlement dance began. In 2002, Harvard quietly resolved the suit with Forum Financial Group for an undisclosed sum, and managed to have many court papers sealed. In 2004, Farallon Fixed Income settled with USAID for $1.5 million. And in 2005, the defendants settled the charges brought by the DOJ. Harvard paid $26.5 million, the largest legal settlement in its history. Shleifer paid $2 million. Hay settled for between $1 and $2 million, depending on his future earnings.

The typical settlement terms applied: no defendant admitted wrongdoing, or accepted any liability. "I strongly believe I would have prevailed in the end," Shleifer commented after the settlement was announced, "but my lawyers told me my legal fees would exceed the amount that I will be paying the government." In a press release, US attorney Michael Sullivan put a slightly different face on the outcome. "The defendants were entrusted with the important task of assisting in the creation of a post-communist Russian open market economy and instead took the opportunity to enrich themselves. Such conflict of interest activities only serve to undermine important development programs."

As usual, much uncertainty remained in the post-settlement gray area. For one thing, how much had the Harvard Management Corporation (HMC), the university's investment arm, and the Yale Investments Office, the equivalent body at Yale, profited from investments in Russia, perhaps at times through insider information? Statements made by Andrei Shleifer in his deposition indicated that regular contacts had taken place between the Harvard Project and HMC. Finance writer Anne Williamson, who was reporting from Russia during much of the affair and in 1999 testified on US aid in Russia before the House Committee on Banking and Financial Services, has suggested ways in which HMC profited from some of the most lucrative deals in the loans for shares program, despite the Russian government's prohibition of foreign participation in the program, and from trading in Russia's high-yield domestic bond market. (Some senior managers at HMC have declined to comment about Russian investments by their organization, while others have denied that they made any.) In the early 2000s, documents released by a Yale union indicated that Nancy Zimmerman had also been investing Yale's endowment funds in Russia. Janine Wedel thinks the foreign investments were extensive. "Does it make sense that the Harvard Project people would only be investing on behalf of Harvard and Yale?" she says. "I was hearing stories of them bragging about such activity at cocktail parties, so was it just these few players, or was a wider network involved?" The fact remains that Harvard's endowment grew from $5 billion in 1992 to $11 billion in 1997, during the rape of Russia, with impressive 30.5 percent returns on its emerging-markets investments in 1997.

Wayne Merry, the former adviser at the US Embassy in Moscow, says that still more serious uncertainties underlie the Harvard Project story and its tidy set of settlements. "Thanks are due to Dr. Wedel for her efforts to document this failed policy process," Merry wrote in 2000, in response to an article on the Harvard-Chubais case that Wedel had just published in the *National Interest*, "but, sadly, she has so far seen only the tip of the iceberg—what remains 'classified' is much worse."

As her denunciations began to gain attention, Wedel was contacted by numerous people who had sensed misconduct by the Harvard Project in Russia, but hadn't known what to do about it. "People were really coming out of the woodwork," she remembers. "I'm not the only one who smelled a rat, but most people only saw the rat's head or body or tail and had access only to a tiny bit of what was really going on. I think my story helped them put some pieces together, and make sense of what they had been seeing. Some doors open up, and people that you didn't think would ever want to talk to you now really want to talk, to share information, add to the story, even give you an audience."

A few of these unexpected doors opened on Wall Street, while others emerged in the intelligence community, which in Wedel's experience had a more accurate understanding of what was happening on the ground in Russia than most of their ideology-driven Treasury and State Department colleagues. She met Colonel Ronald Childress, a lawyer with an advanced degree in political science focusing on Russian studies who had worked with one of the consulting firms in Russia, and who was now at the National Intelligence Council, as well as Fritz Ermarth and Anne Jablonski, two experienced Russian experts at the CIA. "I'm a Mennonite girl from Kansas. These are not people that I usually hang out with. But they were people that I found common ground with, because they understood what was going on. They didn't think that the Russian story was about a group of reformers: they understood that we were choosing these people and we were alienating others, that there was a lot of money going out of the country, and that this wasn't about true reform." Ermarth told Wedel, only half jokingly, that people in the CIA carried her first article in *Demokratizatsiya* around in a paper bag, because it revealed the hypocrisy and wrongdoing behind the US government party line.

Like most whistleblowers, Wedel also received considerable ad hominem retaliation as well. "They knew I had all those internal documents, and they were never able to point to facts that were inaccurate," she says of her detractors. "So they tried to discredit me personally, in a thousand ways." Jeffrey Sachs contacted her repeatedly by letter and phone, she says, in a tone that was initially cajoling but grew intimidating. In a reply to Wedel's 2000 article in the *National Interest*, Sachs wrote, "Wedel's twisting of facts and outright misrepresentations go on and on." Anders Åslund, a Swedish financier who had extensive Eastern European involvements with Sachs, George Soros and others, whose flexian activities Wedel had criticized, called Wedel's piece a "mixture of lies, half-lies, sly allusions and sheer misunderstandings." (In the same venue, Wedel responded point by point to what she termed "unsupported counter-assertions" by Sachs and Åslund, while other commentators, including Wayne Merry, political scientist Peter Reddaway, and economists Michael Hudson and Steven Rosefielde, praised her article.)

Wedel points out that she would never have been able to blow the whistle on the Harvard Project and the malfeasance of economists in Russia if she'd been a conventional, tenure-track academic, much less an economist. "I was able to get away with this because I was in this somewhat marginalized field, anthropology, that doesn't look up to economists or economics. Though I have a ton of sources in the economics profession who told me what was going on here, of course most of them could never have spoken openly about this, or their careers would have been thwarted or even finished." Subsisting mostly on grants rather than trying to protect a tenure-track position, Wedel was able to say what she saw.

Like Lynn Stout, Wedel believes that the tenure system tends to reward people who avoid taking strong intellectual or ethical positions. "Tenure is a bean-counting exercise that looks at how many journal articles you've published, the ranking of those journals, the citation indices. Well, if you're doing something that's truly groundbreaking, you're just not going to be cited. Many people in the field may not even understand what you're saying, and you sure as hell won't be published in the 'leading journals.' I think the tenure system is bereft of true standards, and rewards people who play it safe, not people who do something original or courageous. And I think tenure has something to do with the lack of whistleblowers in academia."

After sounding the alarm in *Demokratizatsiya*, Wedel continued over the next decade to tell the Harvard-Chubais story in ever richer detail, in a series of scholarly articles and news stories, and a book, *Collision and Collusion*. Her analysis grew into a broader kind of whistleblowing, in which she denounced not only a handful of dubious actors in Russia but numerous other scholars who spread neoliberal economic theory and generous dollops of Western aid money throughout Central and Eastern Europe, frequently doing great harm. Like Lynn Stout, she came to see neoliberal economics as a massive intellectual shortcut, which oversimplifies and often misjudges the social, historical and psychological realities of individual nations. Yet the ascendancy of economic theory over real-world experience has continued, she says. "Analysis by numbers is taking over analysis by words. This process is the result of digitization and several generations of economists and social scientists who believe that all you need to do is perform a lot of sophisticated statistics and regression analysis on data from a lot of different countries, without any sense of where this data came from, what it really means, or what's actually happening on the ground in those countries. You don't actually have to know anything." Data enjoys what mathematician Cathy O'Neil, an expert in algorithms, has called "the authority of the inscrutable."

Above all, Wedel blew the whistle on flexians, that new breed of operator on the national and international stage whose actions elude conventional lines drawn by the law and professional ethics, yet whose activities, if seen in toto and with clarity, look patently corrupt to most outsiders. She showed that economic aid in Eastern Europe was sometimes an exercise in institutional hypocrisy, as transition gurus preached free markets, open competition, transparency and democracy for local populations, while they themselves engaged in secret deals, cronyism, conflicts of interest and self-enrichment. In the last few decades, she has examined these self-serving buccaneers through the lens of social anthropology, showing how they evade conventional prohibitions against conflicts of interest and present their appropriation of public power as efficient, entrepreneurial and antibureaucratic. Wedel's research helps to identify the harm flexians do, not only to the economy but to society as a whole.

Wedel's work also challenges the narrow conventional definitions of corruption, in part shaped by economists who are flexians themselves, and who conveniently exclude the "new corruption" they engage in. In a 1993 paper, Andrei Shleifer, an authority on the economics of corruption, defines government corruption as "the sale by government officials of government property for personal gain"—essentially bribery—and follows Gary Becker and other neoliberal economists in affirming that the principal-agent model is the key to understanding corruption. Shleifer explains: "This model focuses on the relationship between the principal, i.e., the top level of government, and the agent, i.e., an official, who takes the bribes from the private individuals interested in some government-produced good." Principal-agent analysis, founded on some of the same basic assumptions about human nature as game theory, cost-benefit analysis and homo economicus, holds that the agent will inevitably betray the principal (and the public trust) when he can derive more benefits by working in his own interest than in working for the good of the principal (and of society). "Corruption with theft spreads because observance of law does not survive in a competitive environment," Shleifer states, as if repeating an ineluctable law of physics. According to this viewpoint, the best way to keep the agent honest is to use incentives—essentially counterbribes—to keep his self-interest aligned with the interests of the principal.

Wedel's flexian analysis shows why the principal-agent model is wholly inadequate to model corruption: it assumes a clear distinction between principal and agent, public and private—the same borders that flexians, by their very nature, break down. "With shadow elites and shadow lobbyists, as roles and affiliations spread, overlap, and interact, there is no clear principal or clear agent," Wedel says. "One party does not employ another party to do a job for him. Is someone a principal or an agent, when he sits on the boards of companies that make a product, the government task force that decides whether to buy it, and is also a professor engaged in research on the product?" She demonstrates that self-dealing involved in structural corruption usually goes far beyond simple bribes and the appropriation of public property, and involves the accumulation of decision-making authority, status and prestige as well.

Unlike the definitions of corruption proposed by many corruption "experts"— who, as in foreign aid, have fostered the growth of a substantial industry—flexian behavior is often celebrated as innovative, effective and entrepreneurial. Wedel calls instead for corruption to be reconceived to include the flexians' subterranean, undemocratic and fundamentally noxious activities. "There are too many things that are allowed, or at least not prohibited, by laws, regulations, or official policies, which are nevertheless gross self-dealing, cause immense public harm, and simply don't pass the smell test," she says. Like Lynn Stout, Wedel demands a renewed attention to ethics, not homo economicus amorality, in the law governing public and private behavior. "We need to realign official accountability with ethics. This isn't some radical new idea, just a return to standards of behavior as old as the Bible and the Koran."

Wedel left Eastern Europe with her eyes opened to the existence of flexians, and promptly began to see this same form of corruption back in the United States, where stateside flexians added new elements to her model. Her latest books, *Shadow Elite* and *Unaccountable*, capture their escapades and modus operandi. Lawrence Summers and Robert Rubin, whom she had encountered in Russia, taught her the bewildering range of interconnectedness possible among American elites: the "small-town incestuousness," as she terms it, with which they devised and advocated public rules that later made them privately rich. In the late 1980s and early 1990s, as a star economist at Harvard and at the World Bank, Summers energetically urged privatization and financial deregulation, while Rubin served as the cochairman of Goldman Sachs. Starting in 1993, from senior roles at Treasury, Summers and Rubin helped to pass a series of "modernization acts" that gutted regulation on financial institutions. In 1999, they facilitated the repeal of Glass-Steagall, triggering massive consolidation in financial services and conferring legitimacy on the illegal 1998 merger of banking, insurance and securities firms that had created the financial giant Citigroup. (Months later, after seeing the repeal through, Rubin left government to take a senior board position at Citigroup, where he reputedly earned $126 million in the next decade.)

In 2001, Summers moved back to Harvard University, where despite his key role in the twin debacle of the Harvard Project and his Treasury-led economic aid program in Russia, he was elected president, with energetic lobbying from Robert Rubin and Andrei Shleifer. (Summers returned the favor, flexian style, by orchestrating Rubin's election to the board of the Harvard Corporation, and helping to shield Shleifer from negative consequences of his lawsuits.) While president of

Harvard, Summers also worked as a consultant for Rubin's Citigroup, the hedge fund D. E. Shaw & Co., the asset management firm Alliance Partners, the operator of the Nasdaq stock exchange, and other organizations. In 2006, Summers resigned the Harvard presidency after a vote of no confidence by the faculty, which for some professors had been prompted by his suggestion that women might have less aptitude for math and science than men, but for others was due to his role in the Harvard Project debacle. "For my own part, the Russia scandal was much more important," says Harry Lewis, who took part in the no-confidence vote, "because it was about institutional corruption, and Summers lied about it to the Faculty." Summers promptly joined his erstwhile advisee D. E. Shaw as a part-time managing director, making $5.2 million in twelve months, and an additional $2.8 million over the same period speaking at Citigroup, Goldman Sachs, JPMorgan Chase and other major banks. By then the economy had melted down, thanks in large part to the deregulations that he and Rubin had championed. Nonetheless, Barack Obama consulted extensively with Rubin, and chose Summers to lead the National Economic Council in 2009, in effect engaging two of the Three Marketeers on the Committee to Save the World to clean up the mess they had made. Under Summers's watch at this critical time, hedge funds like D. E. Shaw, the source of much of his wealth, effectively escaped new regulation.

Using her new paradigm like a nightscope in the jungle, Wedel pinpointed flexians throughout American life. She watched former Environmental Protection Agency administrator and New Jersey governor Christine Todd Whitman run her own eponymous lobbying firm while joining multiple think tanks, corporate boards, and an industry-funded faux grassroots group promoting nuclear power; after the disastrous 2010 oil spill at the BP drilling rig Deepwater Horizon, Whitman wrote a Bloomberg op-ed arguing against a ban on offshore drilling, without revealing that she sat on the BP board, and in the media she advocated the use of nuclear power without consistently disclosing her ties to that industry. Wedel saw Peter Orszag transition from director of the powerful Office of Management and Budget under Obama to a senior role at Citigroup, the bank that was the greatest single beneficiary of the government stimulus and bailouts he'd just helped to craft, a move that, according to veteran DC journalist James Fallows, illustrates "the structural rather than personal corruption that . . . is taken for granted in American public life." Wedel tracked former Senate majority leader Tom Daschle's work as key adviser in writing the Affordable Care Act while he served as a healthcare consultant, and his profitable stints at private equity firms, lobby shops and think tanks involved with healthcare.

In the fields of intelligence and defense, Wedel saw how Richard Perle, Douglas Feith and a handful of other neoconservatives created a flex net that worked outside of official diplomatic, intelligence and military channels, and successfully pushed the invasion of Iraq over objections from senior State Department, Pentagon and intelligence officials. Elsewhere Wedel pointed out how flexians weave threads of government and private sector power into a seamless, invisible web, and remain accountable only to themselves. She watched Navy admiral Mike McConnell and Air Force general James Clapper slide back and forth between leading government intelligence posts and the giant intelligence contractor Booz Allen, melding public office and private business into one vast entity with its own aims, momentum and allegiances. She traced General David Petraeus's constellation of roles in academia, think tanks, and a strategic advisory position at KKR, along with lucrative speaking engagements and media appearances. She explored former assistant attorney general and Homeland Security secretary Michael Chertoff's parallel careers as a member of the powerful DC law firm Covington & Burling, director of defense giant BAE Systems, frequent media "expert," and head of his own defense consulting and private equity firm, the Chertoff Group. Wedel even found prominent flexians just down the hall from her at George Mason University, including General Michael Hayden, whose former and current leadership roles in the Air Force, the NSA, the CIA, the Chertoff Group, and various manufacturers of arms and drones reinforce and enrich one another.

Wedel notes how American flexians tend to turn conflict of interest on its head, and present their many overlapping roles as beneficial rather than harmful. In his 2002 deposition for the Harvard Project lawsuit, for example, Lawrence Summers stated that, speaking from extensive personal experience with foreign policy making, "there was no aura of wrongness of any kind that would be associated with providing advice on a financial issue in which one had an interest," and that, based on his knowledge of Russian mores, he believed that leading Russians would actually value advisers more highly if they were engaged in self-dealing. Another Harvard professor whose career Wedel has studied, Steven Kelman, rebranded similar conflicts "the evolving door," and embodied them frequently in his own career. Kelman, who taught public management at Harvard's Kennedy School until he was chosen by President Bill Clinton in 1993 to head the Office of Federal Procurement Policy, led a sweeping "reform" of the contracting process under Al Gore's "Reinventing Government" program, stripping away many rules intended to promote transparency and prevent collusion between contractors and their government minders, and rendering much previously public information and many such processes secret and proprietary. Starting in 1997, Kelman encouraged similar developments at the Department of Defense, as a member of a task force created to improve the health and competitiveness of the US defense industry. While on this task force, he joined the board of GTSI Corp. (now UNICOM Government, Inc.), a firm with a multibillion-dollar business in government contracts in intelligence and defense, and lobbied for Accenture and FreeMarkets Inc., two companies with a major presence in government outsourcing. Shortly after the inspector general of the Small Business Administration recommended that GTSI be disqualified for government contracts for circumventing rules to protect smaller contractors, Kelman wrote a scathing op-ed in the *Washington Post* titled "The IG Ideology," in which he criticized inspectors general for demoralizing public servants and undermining public management—without revealing that he served on the GTSI board. Kelman also writes blog posts and a regular column for *Federal Computer Week*, a publication for government IT workers and contractors who influence how the United States spends over $112 billon in technology; here he has endorsed contractor-friendly policies, while identifying himself as a Harvard professor and former procurement official and seldom revealing his industry connections.

Here is another common trait of Wedel's flexians: despite their claims that their own conflicting roles are beneficial, they typically conceal these conflicts by identifying themselves only with their most impartial-appearing, balanced-sounding jobs, omitting others that might raise eyebrows among people not properly versed in the flexian credo. For example, when quoted by the *Washington Post* as being strongly in favor of "share-in-savings" contracting, a controversial plan supported by the George W. Bush administration to allow contractors to earn more money if their goods or services contributed to achieving an agency's mission, Kelman was identified as a Harvard professor and former Clinton procurement policy chief, without noting that he was also a registered lobbyist for a government contractor that would be one of the largest beneficiaries of share-in-savings contracting. Likewise, when Lawrence Summers penned op-eds in the *New York Times* in favor of financial deregulation, he styled himself as Harvard president and former Treasury secretary, not a highly paid adviser to hedge funds and banks; and when Michael Hayden wrote a vehement *New York Times* op-ed, "To Keep America Safe, Embrace Drone Warfare," he appeared as retired general and CIA director, and not as a member of two corporations involved in the manufacture of drones. In Michael Chertoff's many media appearances after the 2009 underwear bomber incident, he urged full-body scanners in airports, identifying himself as a former Homeland Security chief but omitting the fact that his consulting firm, the Chertoff Group, represented Rapiscan Systems, then the only company qualified to make such scanners for the government.

Flexians and their networks use university affiliations to lend an aura of objectivity to their advancement of partisan ideas and lucrative schemes. Fueled by Koch Brother money, George Mason has become a hotbed of libertarian activism that hosts the first center devoted to law and economics to have been founded at an American university, and the Mercatus Center, a conservative think tank and free-market policy mill that is a major nexus of flexian behavior in academia. (The university's law school, renamed for Antonin Scalia after a $30 million gift from the Kochs and an anonymous donor, plays a similar function in jurisprudence.) "I'm conflicted about how to operate in my own university," Wedel says of her work at George Mason. "I have a policy to maintain a professional relationship, a collegiality, with all of my colleagues. Yet of course I have strong feelings about what a few of them have done. It's uncomfortable, because we want to think that the people we're writing about are just these horrible people—and of course some of them have done pretty bad things. But it's also good for me, in a way, because when I encounter them in the halls, I'm reminded that they are human. Makes me have that sort of conversation with myself, 'Okay, what kind of a person was Hitler?'" She perks up and adds, "It's also good to see who they show up with, who they go to lunch with. Anthropologists talk about going in the field, but I'm always in the field!" In 2012 the Mercatus Center hosted a familiar face, Andrei Shleifer, who was speaking about aspects of his research. When Wedel asked a student who had attended the talk with her whether he was troubled by the fact that Shleifer had received a lot of money from, and then had been accused of conspiring to defraud, the US government, he seemed baffled.

Perhaps the most striking common denominator among Wedel's flexians is what she calls "failing up": their ability to ride out wrongdoing, if it's discovered at all, with impunity, and to move swiftly on to new and greater heights. Shleifer's legal troubles seem not to have hurt his career. As his lawsuits were grinding through the courts and the disastrous reality of Russian "reforms" was becoming public, he continued to write articles in major journals defending the US approach to economic reform in Russia—often without revealing his own central role in designing and implementing those reforms. During this same period, Shleifer also wrote articles that helped define international corruption, testified about corruption before a congressional committee, and published, with University of Chicago economist Robert Vishny, *The Grabbing Hand*, a collection of essays on topics including corruption, privatization, and the role of central governments in managing their economies. In 1999 he received the John Bates Clark Medal, the highest annual award to American economists under forty; in 2001, with the strong backing of then president Lawrence Summers, he received an endowed chair in economics at Harvard. In 2003, Shleifer was also named to edit the influential *Journal of Economic Perspectives*, one of several prestigious editorships he has held. For his part, in the bio on his Harvard website, Shleifer perhaps understandably makes no mention of his work in Russia. He does observe, however, that he is "the most cited economist in the world." His parallel career as a financier, which he has pursued while working as a university professor, has likewise bloomed. With his frequent coauthor Robert Vishny, he cofounded LSV Asset Management, which now oversees $116 billion in investments. His wife, Nancy Zimmerman, meanwhile, has $27 billion in assets at her hedge fund, Bracebridge Capital. A 2018 issue of *Forbes* featured her as one of the sixty richest self-made women in America.

Shleifer has never publicly acknowledged any wrongdoing, and his fellow economists and university administrators seem to agree. When he won the John Bates Clark Medal, the president of the association that gives the award, Dale Jorgenson (also a professor in the Harvard economics department), stated that Shleifer's alleged misdeeds in Russia were "not even mentioned" in their decision making. In 2006, shortly after Harvard and Shleifer had finally lost their high-profile legal battle with the DOJ, a Harvard economist, David Laibson, said of Shleifer: "By any measure, he is on a Nobel Prize winning trajectory. We are very lucky to have Shleifer as a colleague. And that view is shared by everyone in our department."

"None of his colleagues seems to think he did anything wrong," says Harry Lewis, the Harvard computer science professor. "Even ten years later, it amazes me. We are still living with the consequences of the failure of US-led economic reforms in Russia." Lewis points to a rift between the Harvard economics department and Harvard itself, with diverging allegiances and agendas. "Economists here really have their own university. . . . They teach what they're going to teach, but with a few illustrious exceptions, they're not public-spirited in the sense of contributing to the broader missions of the university. They're not going to speak up about unethical behavior. They feel more important than Harvard. And if you're not invested in the welfare of the institution as your primary motivator, it's not good."

While Shleifer, Summers, and Rubin fell upward, the rest of us were left to deal with the problems that US meddling in Russia helped to create. The rise to power of Vladimir Putin, now the unchallenged head of a sprawling kleptocracy that is aggressively hostile to Western democracies, was facilitated by the Chubais clan, with whom Putin had been deeply intertwined since the early 1990s. The oligarchs who arose in those same years from the rigged privatizations of Soviet assets began to secrete their stolen billions abroad, in jurisdictions where they would be shielded by the rule of law, and couldn't be summarily seized, together with their families and their persons, at Putin's whim. The United States, being the world's leading tax haven and anonymous shell company jurisdiction, became a favored destination. This tsunami of dirty liquidity accelerated the corruption of entire classes of handlers and enablers: the American lawyers, bankers, real estate brokers and incorporation agents whose services were required to park that money in anonymous shell companies and exclusive properties, as well as the corporate intelligence firms, lobbyists, public relations experts and noted academics whom the oligarchs employed to make their presence palatable, even desirable. The opprobrium of dealing with such unsavory, sometimes murderous robber barons was rapidly washed away by their money. "What would once have been a career-ending scandal became a normal business relationship, without stigma or shame," Janine Wedel observes. "It's remarkable what a distinguished professional can do nowadays for a Russian billionaire, and still be considered 'reputable.'"

In fact, many of the activities performed by these enablers were legal, if morally questionable. "Someone like Paul Manafort illustrates one of the biggest changes from Soviet times," says Ilya Zaslavskiy, an expert in Russian oligarchs and their corrosive effect on Western society. "Now kleptocratic regimes like Russia not only have uncontrolled, amazing wealth, but can employ it openly, legally. They only have to use spying, bribing, and killing as a last resort. Instead, they employ absolutely legal avenues like reputation laundering and corporate intelligence, buying media outlets and making generous donations to academic and cultural institutions." The oligarchs who establish themselves in Western countries become highly placed operatives, able to further Putin's agendas with considerable resources of money and soft power. Zaslavskiy says the term "oligarchs" is outdated; he prefers to call such people "underminers," whom he defines as "undercover, noxious-to-democracy emissaries and magnates, who often export their corrosive practices to Western democracies through business practices that are considered partly or completely legal in the West."

Noxious, perhaps, but the oligarchs had amassed their wealth according to the same neoliberal playbook—rapid privatization and deregulation, unlimited corporate payments to politicians, the fiduciary responsibility to evade taxes, the virtue of conflicting interests, and the pure self-justificatory power of money—that US officials themselves had applied in Russia in the 1990s. Their swagger, legal impunity and conspicuous consumption, and even their louche, piratical air, contributed to a new model of billionaire behavior. In the East and in the West, oligarchs and billionaires alike rose on an upsurge of free-market fundamentalism, and took advantage of the wholesale privatization of natural resources, public assets and government work. In both places, this process produced widespread economic distress—the collapse of the Russian economy in the mid-1990s and of the US economy a decade later, soaring unemployment, drug and alcohol abuse, and suicide and sharp drops in life expectancy. Flexians looted Russia and America alike, wielding the same economic arguments and weapons, creating their own parallel reality where only experts were admitted, and only expert rules applied; a realm of immense institutional hypocrisy and doublespeak where grotesque insider dealing could be committed in the name of free markets, and secretive cliques could control information and power in the name of democracy. Philanthropy became a means to purchase legitimacy. Leonard Blavatnik, a Ukraine-born American citizen, helped Shleifer and Zimmerman make their first Russian investment in 1994, in the petroleum and aluminum industries in whose often violent privatization Blavatnik made billions. Since then, Blavatnik has given over $700 million to various universities and art museums, including a $200 million grant to the Harvard Medical School, and £75 million to Oxford to found the Blavatnik School of Government.

Several of the clearest-sighted critics of elite wrongdoing in America, including Matt Taibbi, Gillian Tett and Anne Williamson, were working in Russia in the 1990s, where they witnessed flexian behavior firsthand. Like Wedel, they returned to the United States with expatriate eyes, and saw what many other Americans missed. Wedel observes that being an outsider likewise enabled a few critics to warn of the flexian-driven crisis of the 2008 economic crash before it broke. Two of her favorite truth tellers from that time are a former chair of the Commodity Futures Trading Commission, Brooksley Born, and a former head of the Federal Deposit Insurance Corporation, Sheila Bair. Born and Bair, unlike most of their male, Ivy League colleagues in DC, were women born and raised in the West and the Midwest, respectively. Perhaps their atypical backgrounds allowed them to challenge the assumptions of their intellectual tribe, and to speak up even at the risk of losing their place in that tribe. They could recognize the victims of elite power games, because they grew up with people who had sometimes been those victims.

In her book *A Fighting Chance*, about her time in Washington in the aftermath of the 2008 collapse, Elizabeth Warren, another woman from the geographic periphery, describes a rough-and-tumble Chinese dinner she shared with Lawrence Summers.

> Late in the evening, Larry leaned back in his chair and offered me some advice. By now, I'd lost count of Larry's Diet Cokes, and our table was strewn with bits of food and spilled sauces. Larry's tone was in the friendly-advice category. He teed it up this way: I had a choice. I could be an insider or I could be an outsider. Outsiders can say whatever they want. But people on the inside don't listen to them. Insiders, however, get lots of access and a chance to push their ideas. People—powerful people—listen to what they have to say. But insiders also understand one unbreakable rule: *They don't criticize other insiders.* I had been warned.

The fact is, the games played by insiders can produce real victims, which the insiders find ways not to see: the patients behind the spreadsheets at Halifax Health, the reform school kids and asylum-dwellers being medicated according to the Gospel of Risperdal, the Marines incinerated in their lightly armored Humvees. Perhaps only those who remain outsiders at heart retain the empathy and independence of mind to see the faces of those victims. Outsiders alone retain the freedom of spirit to recognize, and sometimes to renounce, corruption concealed beneath the mantle of authority, status, wealth.

CHAPTER 5

Reaping the Nuclear Harvest

There is not a crime, there is not a dodge, there is not a trick, there is not a swindle, there is not a vice which does not live by secrecy.

Joseph Pulitzer, remark to Alleyne Ireland, 1911

Most of the classification, in my judgment, is not to keep our enemies from finding out information. It is to keep the American people and the Congress from finding out what in God's world various agencies are doing and how they are throwing away money, wasting it. They preach economy and they throw money away like dirt, and lie and cheat and hide to keep Congress from finding out, and, for God's sake, they don't want the American people to find out.

Congressman Jack Brooks, congressional testimony, October 15, 1987

The Columbia—Nchi'i-Wána in the Sahaptin language—sweeps fast and wide out of Canada, still cold from the glaciers and snowpack of the Rockies as it crosses a stretch of hot tan grassland near the Washington–Oregon line, its broad waters mirroring hot blue sky. Upstream in the high desert of Eastern Washington, and downstream clear to the evergreen forests of the Cascade Mountains, the riverbanks are crowded with orchards, vineyards and farms. But here it traverses some of the most pristine desert steppe in the Americas, preserved as if by magic. From the stern of our boat, a twenty-foot Lund Pro Angler with a 150-horsepower Mercury outboard, Tom Carpenter points out the tumbleweed and greasewood, hopsage and Sandberg bluegrass. Mergansers and pelicans feed in the shallows on stonefly larva and freshwater clams. A great blue heron stalks the waterline, pauses, spears a glistening fish with its javelin beak. A mule deer, grazing among the mulberry trees and cottonwoods by the riverbank, raises its head to watch us slip by.

Carpenter says he often sees coyotes and jackrabbits, too, as well as muskrats and beaver in the water. On a slender island ahead, a flag flaps over the frame of a wigwam, bearing a tribal symbol of the Wanapum people, whose ancestral lands these are. They still catch Chinook salmon, which they hold sacred, during the plentiful fall run.

As we round a broad river bend, a smokestack pans into view, rising beside a battleship-gray building with sharp right angles that looks to have been constructed from cinder blocks. So isolated and austere is the structure on this broad brown grassland that it might be a megalith from some lost civilization.

"B Reactor," says the skipper, John Swain. These are the first words he's said since we hit the water; his voice is gravelly and low. As we soft-throttle around the bend, slipping with the current, more chimneys and blockish gray buildings appear on the plain, and Swain names them: the K Reactors, the N Reactor, the D Reactors. Just above the high-water mark on the riverbank berm, we pass a faded yellow warning sign: HAZARDOUS AREA, DO NOT ENTER.

The high-desert purity of this place is an illusion. This is the Hanford Nuclear Reservation, one of the most polluted and dangerous places on earth. B Reactor was the world's first full-scale nuclear reactor, built by Enrico Fermi and other Manhattan Project physicists together with a team of DuPont engineers. B Reactor made the plutonium for Fat Man, the bomb that flattened Nagasaki at the end of World War II. During the subsequent forty years of the Cold War arms race, the military and engineering corporations built eight more reactors along the Columbia in rapid succession, using its glacier-fed water to cool them and water-generated electricity to run them. If Los Alamos was the brains of the Manhattan Project, Hanford was the brawn, an enormous factory to make the active ingredient of America's nuclear arsenal: plutonium. At its height in 1944, about fifty thousand people worked at the Hanford site, which comprises 2,800 buildings, 386 miles of roads and 158 miles of railway tracks, on a 586-square-mile site large enough to hold the city of Los Angeles, with room to spare. Five eight-hundred-foot-long underground processing canyons are nicknamed "Queen Marys," because they are as long as ocean liners.

During World War II and for much of the Cold War, Hanford produced plutonium for America's nuclear arsenal at a feverish pace. Uranium-238 mined in the Belgian Congo, and later Colorado and Canada, was shaped into slugs like rolls of quarters and fed into the reactors, where they were irradiated with neutrons until tiny amounts of uranium decayed into plutonium-239. The intensely radioactive slugs, with their traces of plutonium, were pushed out the back of the reactors into basins of water, where their most lethal short-term radioactivity dissipated, after which they traveled in remote-controlled railcars to separation canyons located back from the river on the Central Plateau. Here they were dissolved, and the plutonium was extracted. The canyons, like many other buildings at Hanford, are now far too radioactive for anyone to enter except in full-body suits, for only minutes at a time. They will remain so for tens of thousands of years.

A lot of Hanford is like this; though recently declared part of the Manhattan Project National Historical Park, many areas of the park will be off-limits to two thousand generations of visitors. Every gram of plutonium extracted at Hanford entailed the production of tons of high-level nuclear waste and toxic chemicals. For Hanford's first forty years, during World War II and the subsequent arms race, the site's overwhelming priority was to turn out as much weapons-grade plutonium as possible, in order to avert the threat of Soviet invasion. "This is the best weapon we have—it is our one real hope of deterring Stalin," Henry "Scoop" Jackson, a Democratic congressman from Washington state, told the House of Representatives in October 1951. "How can we conceivably not want to make every possible atomic weapon we can?" In such an atmosphere of urgency and fear, environmental safety, like the health of Hanford workers and residents of nearby towns, was secondary. In Hanford's first decade alone, billions of cubic meters of radioactive gases went into the air during regular venting of flume gases, sowing the winds with particulate plutonium, iodine-131, xenon-133, ruthenium-103 and other deadly radionuclides, which contaminated plants, fruits and vegetables for hundreds of miles downwind and accumulated in the animals that ate them—pheasants, mule deer, cows, humans. The approximately two million people who lived south and east of Hanford during its peak pollution years are known today as "downwinders," since the heaviest doses from the smokestacks followed the prevailing winds. Still more radiation went into the Columbia, whose waters, after cooling the reactors, stood for a few hours in retention basins to allow some of the short-term radiation to dissi-pate, and were then pumped back into the river, with a radioactive burden of nep-tunium, chromium, phosphorus and arsenic.

The worst waste of all went into the ground: 710,000 cubic meters of solids and a half trillion gallons of liquids that were simply dumped or injected into the soil, in a labyrinth of pits, wells, trenches, cribs, burial grounds and French drains. Other deadly materials were shipped here, from around the country: spent nuclear submarine engines as big as trailer homes, the radioactive corpses of 828 beagles killed during experiments at the University of California, Davis, an ambulance buried whole after it delivered the victim of a radiation accident to a local hospital, and countless other odds and ends are interred at Hanford. About sixteen hundred soil dump sites have been identified, and many more probably exist. Some of the deadliest material was pumped into 177 underground tanks, which today contain some fifty-six million gallons of radioactive, superheated, hypertoxic waste. Most of the tanks were filled so long ago that no one knows their exact contents. As a 1997 study of tank composition put it, "Hanford waste tanks are, in effect, slow chemical reactors in which an unknown but large number of chemical (and radiochemical) reactions are running simultaneously. Over time, the reaction dynamics and com-positions have changed and will continue to change."

"People call their contents 'poorly characterized,'" Carpenter says, "which basi-cally means, 'Who the fuck knows what's in there?'" Everyone agrees, however, that their concentrated slurry of isotopes, heavy metals, acids and solvents is so deadly that one liter from certain tanks, properly distributed, would kill everyone in North, Central and South America. Some tanks contain dimethyl mercury, one of the strongest known neurotoxins—according to the Washington state Clean Air Act, permissible emissions of dimethyl mercury, in micrograms per cubic meter of air, are expressed as a decimal point followed by 99 zeros, then a 1. Dimethyl mer-cury is believed to be carcinogenic as well, though nobody who has come in contact with it has lived long enough to worry about tumors.

Hanford's tanks are wearing out under the intense heat and radiation of their contents, and those contents are leaking into the soil. A total of 149 of the tanks are single-shelled carbon steel tanks built between 1943 and 1964, with an expected design life of twenty years; at least 67 of these are termed "confirmed leakers," while many others are "assumed leakers" or of "questionable integrity." Twenty-eight double-shelled tanks, each of which holds up to one million gallons of material, were built underground between 1968 and 1986 to replace some of the single-shelled tanks and hold the most dangerous wastes at Hanford. These, too, are starting to fail. The first double-shelled "confirmed leaker," AY-102, was reported by a worried tank worker, Mike Geffre, in 2011, but the leak was denied by the DOE and its contractor that operates the tank farm, Washington River Protection Solutions (WRPS), for over a year. The DOE eventually admitted that three to five thousand gallons of liquid waste had escaped the tank's inner shell, but blamed the leak on an isolated construction flaw that made this tank an "outlier." Further investigation revealed that six more double-shelled tanks had the same flaw, and that thirteen additional tanks had other defects that could shorten their life span. On April 17, 2016, radiation alarms went off on another double-shelled tank, suggesting a leak into the annular space between its inner and outer shells. Though WRPS and DOE managers have denied that any new waste has escaped, blaming historical contamination of the annulus, not everyone is convinced. "This is catastrophic," former tank farm employee Mike Geffre told Seattle's *KING 5 News*, shortly after the alarms went off. "The double shell tanks were supposed to be the saviors of all saviors." The next potential disaster surfaced on May 19, 2017, when workers detected radiation levels three times above normal between the walls of yet another double-shelled tank. Video images show extensive debris, though so far no liquid. The DOE is investigating.

Clearly, the last line of defense against the deadliest radioactive waste in the Americas is failing. "Tanks are leaking and have been known to be leaking since the 1950s," says Carpenter, "though no one knows how much they've been leaking, because the DOE and its tank farm contractors have avoided testing to find out." The DOE estimates that one million gallons has already leaked from the tank farm; other experts say the leakage is probably ten times higher. These millions of gallons of leaked high-intensity waste, together with the waste at Hanford's numerous dump sites, are sinking into the soil at different speeds, creating plumes of toxicity that billow downward and outward beneath about eighty-five square miles of Hanford terrain. Some plumes have reached groundwater, most of which flows into the Columbia River; chemical and radioactive materials have already entered the river at numerous points, and have lit up whales and oysters in the Pacific Ocean some three hundred miles downstream. If the plumes are not halted, far worse will come. The Columbia is the largest river in the West, irrigating millions of acres of farmland and orchards, and supplying drinking water to cities and towns along its course. It also flows through Portland, Oregon.

Leaking waste is Hanford's ongoing, slow-motion catastrophe, but other cataclysms could happen in seconds. According to a number of third-party expert reports, several decrepit structures holding large caches of radioactivity are susceptible to nuclear accidents which would threaten people across the Pacific Northwest. The Canister Storage Building, built in the 1970s, holds spent reactor fuel containing a ton of plutonium in each of its 220 closely spaced steel pipes. Hanford insiders call this the "Roman Candle Storage Building," because a failure in the facility's cooling system could lead to radioactive fireworks. Still more menacing is the Waste Encapsulation Storage Facility, built in the early 1970s, which consists of several large, steel-lined concrete basins that are filled with water and hold 1,936 capsules of cesium-137 and strontium-90. The capsules have a total radioactivity of 120 million curies, far more cesium and strontium than was released during the Chernobyl disaster, and their extreme heat and radiation are devouring the cement-containing walls that hold them. These structures, which one technician described to me as "1970s concrete swimming pools," aren't earthquake compliant (though Hanford is a high-risk seismic zone) and are susceptible to a series of events—a wildfire on the tinder-dry grassland, volcanic ashfall from one of the eleven active volcanoes in the nearby Cascade Range, or an extended power or water outage—which could cause the strontium and cesium to overheat, catch fire underwater, and release massive quantities of deadly isotopes into the atmosphere. Further serious threats at Hanford include a potential fire in the Central Waste Complex, a blaze in the submerged sludge in K Basins, and a collapse of parts of the tottering PUREX (Plutonium Uranium Extraction) facility, weakened by decades of radiation.

But the most likely and lethal disaster at Hanford is widely believed to be an explosion in the tank farms. The contents of many tanks are undergoing a number of poorly understood chemical and physical reactions, often at extreme heat, which cause them to periodically belch gases from their depths. These gases include hydrogen, which is highly flammable—even in small quantities, it can cause dramatic explosions, especially when combined with nitrates and ammonia, which many tanks also contain. Most of the hydrogen bubbles out gradually and is discharged by the tanks' ventilation system. But viscous slurries or hard crusts several feet thick have formed at the surface of some tanks, which can trap hydrogen until it reaches potentially explosive concentrations. Some technicians worry that such a tank could undergo a Fukushima-style hydrogen blast, propelling large quantities of radioactivity into the atmosphere. (In 2011, hydrogen gas explosions blew the tops off Fukushima's spent fuel pools, spewing radiation into the sea and sky.) For two decades, tank SY-101 was nicknamed the "burping tank" for the hundreds of cubic feet of hydrogen at a time that it released, which never exploded, but only for lack of a spark. "We aren't in control of the tank," the Hanford deputy manager, Phil Hamric, observed in 1992. "It's kind of in control of us." SY-101 was partially neutralized in the late 1990s, but since then, more tanks have begun to burp. The tanks are interconnected by networks of pipes, so a blast in one could drive superheated air into neighboring tanks and trigger further explosions, the so-called ammo dump effect. Given that double-shell tanks may contain two million curies of radioactive waste—something like 15 percent of the radiation released at Fukushima—an ammo dump explosion in the Hanford tank farms would be devastating. Likewise, since the constant intervention by some ten thousand site workers is required to prevent many volatile facilities from overheating, catching fire, melting down or exploding, and since most major disasters would make significant parts of the site inaccessible to those workers for months or years, one serious problem at Hanford could easily turn into a knock-on apocalypse.

Why doesn't everyone in America know about the Hanford Nuclear Reservation and its enormous risks? We've all heard of Los Alamos, where Oppenheimer and Fermi and other outsize brains invented the atom bomb. But Los Alamos was a fast-paced, sexy story glistening with the pixie dust of genius, a meeting in the New

Mexico desert of beautiful minds who quoted John Donne and the Bhagavad Gita as they worked out the theory of a nuclear explosion, tested it in one triumphant blaze at Alamogordo and walked away. Hanford is where those cerebral theories became prosaic, toxic realities, under rigorous military-industrial control. The combination of national security, industrial secrecy and relentless hit-the-numbers urgency has always set the tone at Hanford. During World War II this approach was justified, compellingly, by fears that Nazi physicists led by Kurt Diebner and Werner Heisenberg were building a nuclear weapon of their own, a race the Allies needed to win. "We would have to move ahead with the utmost speed," General Leslie Groves, the project's director, wrote years later in his memoir of the war, *Now It Can Be Told*. "Chances would have to be taken that in more normal times would be considered reckless in the extreme." As Hanford was a hub of the Manhattan Project, its security classification was higher than Operation Overlord, the Normandy invasion. In March 1943, the US Army and its largest explosives contractor, DuPont, began what became one of history's great industrial achievements. They evicted three hundred people from their hardscrabble farms and orchards along the Columbia, bulldozed the towns of Hanford and White Bluffs, and raised a work camp of tents, barracks and hutments for forty thousand men and women, with eight mess halls, each the size of a football field, that every day prepared and served 2,200 loaves of bread, 120 tons of potatoes, 144,000 pork chops and 7,200 pies, and 12,000 turkeys on Thanksgiving Day. They designed and built the B Reactor, the world's first nuclear reactor, in thirteen months, and less than a year later had produced enough plutonium to arm Fat Man. Secrecy at Hanford was so extreme that only 1 percent of the workforce knew they were making an explosive device at all, and rumors raced through the site. People spoke of the glowing yellow slugs of metal dropping out the back of the reactors, and speculated that scientists had finally solved alchemy's supreme riddle: they were turning lesser metals into gold, to fund an Allied victory. Only after a mushroom cloud rose over Hiroshima were people at Hanford told that they were making atomic bombs.

World War II ended, but the urgency, secrecy and strict authoritarianism continued at Hanford, during the long, enervating decades of the Cold War. The Atomic

Energy Commission (and later the Department of Energy) teamed with a series of the nation's largest engineering and construction firms as the government's prime contractors—after DuPont came General Electric, then Westinghouse, Rockwell, Fluor, and today, Bechtel, along with Washington River Protection Solutions (WRPS), which runs the tank farms—to control every aspect of work and life at Hanford. Oddly enough in a place that claimed to champion capitalism and democracy against the Communist aggressors, free enterprise at Hanford was strictly limited. For the first fourteen years, Richland residents could not own land or their own homes, and the town itself remained unincorporated. Prime contractor DuPont chose the original size and location of houses; its successor, General Electric, determined the siting of stores and set their rents. GE employed the firemen, garbagemen and librarians at Richland, as well as nearly fourteen hundred undercover and uniformed policemen, who, together with FBI agents and military counterespionage operatives, kept close watch over the community, intercepting phone calls, scanning mail, eavesdropping on conversations in bars and restaurants, and carrying out surveillance on any locals who raised suspicions. LOOSE TALK: A CHAIN REACTION FOR ESPIONAGE, read one billboard into the facility, where the technologies being used and the amount of plutonium produced were state secrets. The plant's pollution was itself a secret: military and corporate leaders worried not only that the quantity and nature of the waste might tip the Russians off to how many bombs America possessed, but also that workers and the general public might panic at news of all the radioactivity they were breathing, drinking and eating. Hanford leadership repeatedly stated that "not one atom" had escaped the facility, and that Hanford was "as safe as mother's milk." General Electric ran advertisements in major magazines above the company slogan, "You can put your confidence in General Electric," describing how GE scientists at Hanford were feeding radioactive iodine to sheep and salmon to determine its health effects. "Even the maximum dose of radioactive material, it has been found, has very little effect on the sheep," one ad announced reassuringly, adding that a person would have to consume a hundred pounds of "hot" salmon at a sitting to "absorb a noticeable amount of radioactive material."

Meanwhile, corporate and government researchers were performing a series of classified radiation experiments that told a different tale. In addition to sheep and salmon, they tried out radioactive isotopes on a range of algae and plants, and fed them to crustaceans, pygmy goats and miniature pigs, stray dogs, and alligators. (At least one hot alligator escaped its Hanford keepers and vanished into the Columbia.) Researchers secretly harvested wild animals from the Hanford reservation and studied their corpses for radiation damage, and posed as agriculture and school inspectors to surreptitiously measure the radiation levels in livestock on nearby farms, in milk at local dairies, and in local schoolchildren. Scientists discovered, in contrast to comforting public proclamations, that radioiodine ravaged the immune system of salmon and caused the "virtually complete destruction" of the thyroid glands of sheep. Iodine-131 was a particularly deadly radionuclide because it concentrated in the thyroid glands of everything that ate it, growing in concentration as it moved up the food chain and creating an ever larger risk of thyroid cancer and other ailments. At Hanford, "mother's milk" and cow's milk alike were often laced with iodine-131, and were dangerous to children.

Some nuclear researchers at Hanford performed more or less intentional human experiments. On the night of December 2, 1949, at the orders of a high-ranking official whose name remains classified to this day, Department of Defense officials and GE employees intentionally released as much as 12,000 curies of highly radioactive iodine-131 into the atmosphere, 600 times more than the quantity released during the Three Mile Island disaster, together with 20,000 curies of xenon-133. This test, eventually called the "Green Run" because it involved the use of highly radioactive "green" spent reactor fuel that had not, as normally happened, been cooled for several weeks after leaving the reactor, was apparently done to test equipment that would be used to detect similar emissions in Russia, in order to quantify the Soviets' nuclear capabilities. The Green Run contaminated water and food sources all the way to Los Angeles. At the prompting of Manhattan Project leaders Robert Oppenheimer and Stafford Warren, federal, corporate and university scientists and physicians performed more targeted experiments, administering Hanford plutonium and other radioactive materials to unwitting human guinea pigs. In 1945, scientists at Berkeley injected housepainter Albert Stevens, identified in top-secret records as CAL-1, with 858 times the normal lifetime exposure of plutonium. They initially believed Stevens had terminal cancer, but were able to study his radioactive urine and feces for a number of years, because his tumor turned out to be benign; they published a paper about the experiment, titled "A Comparison of the Metabolism of Plutonium (Pu238) in Man and the Rat." Other victim-participants in these experiments included CAL-2 (Simeon Shaw, a four-year-old Australian boy with bone cancer), CAL-3 (Elmer Allen, a thirty-six-year-old black railroad porter), CHI-1, CHI-2 and CHI-3 at the University of Chicago, and more at the University of Rochester. Researchers at a prenatal clinic run by Vanderbilt University gave 829 pregnant women, preselected to be poor and white, regular doses of radioactive iron, to determine the percentages of that iron absorbed by mother and fetus. During the 1960s, researchers at Seattle's Pacific Northwest Research Foundation used over a million dollars in federal grants to irradiate the genitals of 131 inmates in Washington and Oregon state prisons, to study the effects of radiation on fertility. MIT researchers fed 74 boys interned at the Walter E. Fernald State School, a institute for children with developmental disabilities, radioactive iron and calcium in their oatmeal and milk. Scientists at the University of Tennessee's College of Medicine injected 7 newborns, 6 of whom were black, with radioactive iodine, in one of five such studies conducted in different parts of the nation on 235 newborns and infants. In all, researchers administered doses of radioactive materials to about 16,000 people, in experiments that—as Berkeley MD and researcher Joseph G. Hamilton, a senior radiation biologist at the Atomic Energy Commission, observed in 1950—had "a little of the Buchenwald touch."

These tests were kept secret for decades. The Green Run wasn't revealed until 1986, when the Chernobyl disaster and the growing antinuclear movement prodded the DOE into greater openness, though important details of the test remain classified. The general public didn't start to learn about the sixteen thousand human guinea pigs until late 1993, when investigative journalist Eileen Welsome published the first of a series of three articles in the *Albuquerque Tribune*, which helped force a formal government investigation, and extensive reports/confessions published by the DOE, the DOD and other agencies in subsequent years. Likewise, it wasn't until 2000 that the DOE admitted that its own workers, at Hanford and other nuclear weapons facilities, had been exposed to radiation and chemicals that cause cancer and death. As far as we know, human radiation experiments ended in the mid-1970s. Wrongs of this magnitude, one assumes, were possible and could have remained hidden so long only because of the fear, paranoia and secrecy of the Cold War era. But another kind of human radiation experiment is still being carried out at Hanford, on workers at the tank farms—workers like John Swain, the skipper of our craft on the Columbia River.

Plutonium hasn't been produced at Hanford since 1987, and attention there has shifted from building nuclear weapons to cleaning up after them. Yet the atmosphere of secrecy and government-corporate control remains. Today it serves mainly to keep Hanford's abuses—the vast environmental damage and risk of nuclear disaster, the widespread and ongoing harm to Hanford workers, the decades of staggering mismanagement and repeated, colossal thefts of taxpayer dollars—from coming to light. Hanford is a textbook case in how corporate short-termism and profit motive, regulatory capture and fraud as a business model can be concealed from the general public, for decades, behind the gleaming but by now irrelevant shield of national security. "There's still this attitude from the Cold War, among Hanford insiders, that we are the only people qualified to know about this stuff," Tom Carpenter says, "and that the public shouldn't be told—in fact that it would panic if it knew. Well, frankly, I think people should be panicking, and it's urgent that they know what's happening here." He looks out across the river at the tan landscape with its luminous gray monuments. "It's crazy. The corporations get more and more brazen, the DOE gets more and more complacent. About $45 billion has been spent out here on cleanup, plus or minus a billion, and another $110 billion needs to be spent—though at this rate, the total is probably two or three times that, really. The place has become an ATM in the desert, just a giant teller in the desert for corporations. When does the account run dry?"

Historically, nuclear energy has been a hotbed for whistleblowing, because it exhibits many of the key whistleblowing triggers: the same cult of secrecy and security that exists in its close cousin, nuclear weapons; an enormous potential for public harm; and plentiful public funds at high risk of fraud and abuse. Some of America's first nationally known whistleblowers worked in nuclear power. In 1974, Karen Silkwood revealed widespread wrongdoing at the Kerr-McGee (later Cimarron) nuclear fuel plant in Oklahoma, and later died in a mysterious car accident that some observers believed was murder. In 1976, the so-called GE Three, a trio of experienced nuclear engineers at General Electric, resigned from the company in protest and denounced, to Congress and the press, how nuclear power, like nuclear weapons, represented, as one of them put it, "a serious danger to the future of all life on this planet." (The men served as expert consultants for the popular 1979 film *The China Syndrome*, which presaged with uncanny accuracy the partial meltdown at Three Mile Island that took place twelve days after the film was released.)

Carpenter is the institutional memory of Hanford. He got his start in nuclear safety at the age of twenty-one, in 1978, shortly before the Three Mile Island disaster, when he attended a direct action rally at the Rocky Flats nuclear weapons facility near Denver, Colorado. There he heard Daniel Ellsberg speak and Allen Ginsberg recite his "Plutonian Ode," and narrowly escaped arrest when the Denver police swept up several hundred protesters. Carpenter returned home to Cincinnati and formed a group to oppose the Zimmer nuclear power plant being built there. When his name appeared in the news, he was contacted by whistleblower electricians, welders and quality assurance employees at the plant, and then by Tom Applegate, a young private detective who had been hired by plant owners to infiltrate the employees and find reasons to fire them. Instead of spying on workers, Applegate compiled the information they gave him on faulty welds, time card fraud, falsification of documents, violation of federal safety rules, and other serious violations at Zimmer. Carpenter had held several press conferences to publicize these same revelations, each of which had been dismissed out of hand by the Nuclear Regulatory Commission (NRC), though neither the commissioners nor agency investigators had actually spoken with the whistleblowers who'd made them. Determined that the same wouldn't happen to Applegate and his explosive disclosures, Carpenter drove the private detective to Washington, DC, in his girlfriend's VW bug, Applegate with a loaded .357 Magnum in his lap. "Karen Silkwood's death was in the news again, and Applegate was paranoid that we'd be attacked or driven off the road," Carpenter remembers. The two men spoke with a number of nuclear and environmental defense groups, including NIRS (the Nuclear Information and Resource Service) and several organizations founded by Ralph Nader, before finding their way to the Government Accountability Project, where they met Tom Devine.

In a joint venture with GAP, Carpenter worked closely with Devine to represent fifty Zimmer whistleblowers and channel their revelations to the appropriate members of Congress, the press and the NRC, as well as to prosecutors. As a result, the Zimmer plant was scuppered shortly before its potentially disastrous power-up. Carpenter soon entered law school in DC, where he interned at GAP, working on further landmark nuclear whistleblower cases, including another Cincinnati-based crisis, this time involving the DOE, at the Fernald uranium enrichment plant. He testified at congressional hearings and appeared in "The Bomb Factory," an episode of ABC's *20/20* that was the first major TV exposé of the nuclear weapons industry. After the show aired, Carpenter got a call from Casey Ruud, a safety auditor at Hanford who had discovered plutonium leaks, nuclear explosion hazards and other serious safety violations by his employer, Rockwell International. More and more whistleblowers called Carpenter, and in 1992 he moved to Washington state to work full-time on Hanford. He's been here ever since, and now heads Hanford Challenge, a nonprofit organization based in Seattle that defends whistleblowers and injured employees at the site, and advocates for environmental safety and corporate transparency. He has defended or advocated for over a hundred Hanford whistleblowers in legal actions and in court, and has had extensive dealings, more or less secret, with about five hundred more. In the process, Carpenter has become a nuclear meta-whistleblower in his own right, and regularly denounces wrongdoing by contractors and government agencies working at Hanford, to the media, in the courts, and before Congress.

Hanford, the biggest nuclear facility in America, has produced more whistleblowers than any other site on earth. Carpenter says there are two principal types of whistleblowers here: visionaries and details people. The visionaries are typically nuclear engineers, auditors and other highly trained professionals with decades of experience in their field. "They understand the big picture, and realize they're see-ing systemic issues that no one else is quite seeing: this plan, if allowed to go for-ward, is not going to operate as advertised. In fact, it's going to kill a lot of people. They persist and are a real pain in the ass, and they're hard to satisfy, and they usually become big victims. But they go into whistleblowing with their eyes wide open, and do what they do because they feel, 'This is bigger than me, so whatever happens to me, I'm going to make a difference out there.'" Such figures are widely known in the Hanford community, and are either admired or reviled, depending on whom you ask.

Carpenter's quintessential visionary whistleblower is Ed Bricker. In the late 1980s, Bricker was compelled to blow the whistle by the death of a childhood friend, which he had helped cause: following the orders of his superiors, and against his better judgment, Bricker failed to reconnect a safety alarm on a crane, and weeks later it crushed his friend. "Ed had to go to this guy's funeral, and his family with his kids were there," Carpenter remembers. "And he felt like it was his fault—that he could have prevented it if he'd only had the spine, the backbone, to stand up. He determined at that point that he was going to stand up and be forceful about safety."

Bricker would have plenty of chances to do so. He worked as a nuclear process operator in the vast, mazelike Plutonium Finishing Plant, piping plutonium slurry from one area to another within the facility. He reported a series of hazards to his superiors, including "misroutings" during which he and his colleagues, relying on error-strewn blueprints, had piped plutonium to the wrong place—and sometimes simply dumped it on the ground outside. In August 1986, Bricker was helping to clean up one such plutonium spill, near a road that Booth Gardner, then governor of Washington, was scheduled to use during a bus tour of the Hanford site. Before the bus arrived, Bricker and his fellow workers were instructed to remove the high-radiation signs and ropes that blocked the road, and to replace them after the bus had passed. Driving a vehicle through an area known to be contaminated with plutonium will likely spread radiation for miles. Bricker reported this incident to a congressional investigator, and it made national news.

He was elected a steward for one of the workers' unions, and began communicating safety infractions to Congress and the press which his colleagues were afraid to report. This made Bricker unpopular with Rockwell, the prime contractor at Hanford, and with Westinghouse, Rockwell's successor. A Department of Labor investigation revealed a concerted effort by Rockwell and Westinghouse managers to turn Bricker's bosses and fellow workers against him. One of his former personnel managers, who had tried to fire Bricker, later told Labor Department investigator John Spear, "I'm surprised one of the guys hasn't killed him by now."

They tried. During one cleanup operation deep in a highly radioactive area of the Plutonium Finishing Plant, in what Hanford insiders call "one sniff, you're stiff" conditions, Bricker was working in a full radiation suit with supplied air, when his air regulator, which his coworkers had attached for him, came loose. "It was absolutely sabotage, there is no question about that," says Carpenter. "Ed managed to make it out of there holding his breath, but guess what? No investigation, nothing happened. There should have been an FBI investigation into a criminal assault on a whistleblower, but instead, people were like, 'Yeah, he got what he deserved.'"

After Bricker contacted Carpenter for legal help, both men noticed that an unmarked van appeared regularly near Bricker's house, and heard a strange echo during their phone conversations. "I would go to Ed's house and this van would show up," Carpenter remembers. "And they would send an agent with this little earpiece in his ear to walk back and forth in front of his house. It was overt. We would go out and take his picture, and he'd run. It was a joke!"

Through legal discovery, John Spear eventually obtained four fat ring binders' worth of documents from the security operation, code-named "Special Item—Mole," designed to spy on, contain and neutralize Ed Bricker. The operation, run by former Air Force counterintelligence officer Whit Walker, targeted Bricker for having cooperated with Congress about wrongdoing at Hanford. The file contained lists of Bricker's known associates, his habits, his memberships. Since nothing in his background provided much leverage—Bricker was a strict Mormon, who neither drank nor danced—several of his friends in the plant were investigated, too, and

REAPING THE NUCLEAR HARVEST

those with vulnerabilities were blackmailed into informing on Bricker, searching his mail, and wearing a wire when they spoke with him. Bricker received scathing performance reviews and was sent for a psychological-fitness-for-duty examination. Eventually, through a subpoena in a whistleblower case, Tom Carpenter even got his hands on the purchase order of the mysterious van he and Bricker had seen. He still has it on the bulletin board in his office. It reads: "Tactical command investigation van: Rockwell Security Projects, 1987, purchased an unmarked window van which is equipped with surveillance equipment, emergency lighting, radio communications, and is completely self-contained. The criminal investigations unit requires a mobile unit equipped to handle sensitive investigations, and to conduct surveillance as necessary, to support customer-directed activities."

"Ed was unusual as a whistleblower," Carpenter concludes. "He was a young guy, he had little kids. He just didn't feel he had a choice anymore, after the death of his friend in that crane accident. He was bound by his moral conscience, and had an internal compass that said he had to do this. But he got death threats, his wife got death threats, all kinds of things happened to him. Not too many people are up for that."

The second group of whistleblowers Carpenter mentions, the details people, are lower-profile Hanford employees who focus on a specific problem, often a potentially deadly situation they encounter at work. They typically remain anonymous if they can, to preserve their careers. Some work for contractors, some for the DOE and other government entities. Some are secretly wearing Geiger counter transmitter devices under their radiation suits, which beam out information on Hanford's hotspots to Carpenter. He has about fifty anonymous whistleblowers on the inside at Hanford. In crisis moments, which occur every few months, he sometimes gets a dozen calls a week from these secret sources.

Other whistleblowers use their names, though regretfully. One such source is Paula Nathaniel, an industrial chemist who worked for Westinghouse to monitor 101-SY, the highly volatile tank that was burping large quantities of hydrogen. During one of her night shifts in October 1990, she saw a radiation technician light a cigarette, though smoking was strictly prohibited by site protocol (and by common sense, near a tank known to be burping hydrogen). Nathaniel objected, but the rad tech continued smoking. Nathaniel reported the incident in her shift report, but her supervisor criticized her for having put the complaint in writing, which he said might cause bad publicity if read by the press. He demanded that Nathaniel change her report; when she refused, she was fired. "She called us up in tears," Carpenter remembers. "And right afterwards the van showed up. Her apartment was ransacked, she was followed, she felt like she was almost run off the road, the whole thing. Her reaction was, 'I can't do this. I'm not built for this. I don't want this trauma. I'm young, I want my career, I want to have kids. This is stupid.' We represented her, we won her case, by which time she was all the way across the country, as far away from as she could get from Hanford, and wanted nothing more to do with any of it. And I think that's the normal reaction most people would have: 'I'm not up for this.' Only people later in their careers, or who are made of something different, have any interest in doing something public, in taking a stand, whatever the consequences."

Representatives of Carpenter's two Hanford whistleblowing types are here in the boat with us during our river cruise of July 25, 2015. John Swain, our skipper, formerly worked in the tank farms. On August 17, 2003, he and a team of coworkers were transferring waste from one of the most dangerous and unpredictable tanks, C-106, when a blast of unknown chemicals vented from the tank's headspace. Swain speaks haltingly because, according to his doctors, he suffered permanent cognitive, neurological and lung damage that day. Walt Tamosaitis, a barrel-chested, seam-faced sixty-six-year-old PhD nuclear engineer, a forty-year veteran at some of America's largest nuclear facilities, voiced his concerns—shared by many other experts and expressed by at least three other whistleblowers—about mismanagement and consequent risks of explosion at the massive Waste Treatment Plant (WTP) at Hanford. He, too, discovered that DOE managers and the WTP's prime contractor, the engineering giant Bechtel, were in lockstep against him. Like most whistleblowers at Hanford, Swain and Tamosaitis sought help from Tom Carpenter.

Carpenter is a born storyteller, whose tales capture both the menace and the

Strangelovean absurdity of Hanford. He starts with one about a freewheeling physicist and oceanographer named Norm Buske.

"Some time ago, Norm discovered a number of hot tumbleweeds. Turns out that
the plant, being highly adapted to dry environments, can send a taproot down as
far as seventy feet into the soil to find moisture. But a lot of groundwater at Hanford is radioactive. When the tumbleweeds suck up this groundwater, they become
radioactive—hot enough to harm people, but even more harmful when they cut
loose from their taproots, as they periodically do, and roll across the landscape spin-
ning out radioactive seeds. Jackrabbits love tumbleweeds, and jackrabbits that eat
hot tumbleweeds and hot tumbleweed seeds become hot jackrabbits. Coyotes eat
those jackrabbits, and sure enough: hot coyotes. People were running Geiger coun-
ters over rabbit and coyote turds. It was pretty crazy."

Carpenter's dark brown eyes beneath his snowy hair look concerned, but the
corners of his mouth in his white beard twitch slightly with what might be repressed
mirth. "So, the Hanford authorities decide to tackle the radioactive tumbleweed
problem. Two teams hop into trucks and head out in search of hot tumbleweeds.
The lead team identifies the problem plants with a Geiger counter and marks them
with pink spray paint. The second team follows, uprooting the pink tumbleweeds
with big tongs and lowering them carefully into insulated fifty-five-gallon drums. So
far so good: the teams are dealing with the hot tumbleweeds."

Walt and John listen silently, but they're already smiling. This is obviously a classic Hanford story, and they know how it ends. Or maybe all Hanford stories end
the same way.

"Trouble is," Carpenter continues, "it's a lot easier to spray paint tumbleweeds than
it is to uproot and stow them. The paint crew zooms ahead, leaving more and more
painted tumbleweeds. The pickup crew is falling farther and farther behind. Then a
big wind blows up, as it often does here in the high desert. All those pink, radioactive
tumbleweeds tear loose and blow all across the landscape. Some of them end up in the
middle of the nearby towns: Richland, Pasco, Kennewick. People look out of their
windows and see the pink tumbleweeds rolling down the street, and they wonder,
'What's up with the pink tumbleweed?' Kids go chasing after them. It's a new game."

We all picture the scene, goofy and futuristic and more than a little deadly. Carpenter looks at us for a moment, deadpan. Then he tosses back his head and emits a high, loon-like hoot of laughter that's loud even over the engine noise. The boat rocks as we all roar with him.

"And the official reaction at Hanford?" Carpenter concludes, when he has caught his breath and wiped away the tears. "Do the managers race around grabbing up those hot pink tumbleweeds? Do they double up on the crews charged with collecting them? No, of course they don't. They do what they always do at Hanford. They made like ostriches, and pretended the problem didn't exist. They shut down Project Tumbleweed. Stopped testing, spraying or collecting those troublesome plants. Don't ask, don't tell."

Carpenter points out the dark green mulberry bushes growing along the riverbank, and says Norm Buske also found that some of them were contaminated with strontium-90. To make the problem more comprehensible for politicians and the general public, Buske picked some ripe mulberries, made radioactive mulberry jam with them, put it in jars with radiation hazard labels, and sent it to Energy Secretary James Watkins and Washington governor Booth Gardner, with a cover note reading, "This mulberry jam is a token of the future hazard of unidentified, uncontained and unmanaged radioactivity at Hanford." Buske was threatened with prosecution for felony charges, including terrorism, but was eventually cleared. He made more jam. In response, Hanford workers cut down the bushes and poisoned their roots with herbicide. There are still hot mulberry bushes growing along the Columbia, a little farther up the bank; Carpenter points out a pair in the K Basin, twenty yards back from the river. "You can go pick fruit and leaves off those trees, and they give off a dose," he says. "Birds that eat there are probably not going to be very happy."

The stories keep coming. Carpenter tells how environmental scientist Marco Kaltofen discovered surprising quantities of plutonium in squawfish, an invasive, bottom-feeding predator that is also known by the more politically correct name of "Minnesota minnow-catcher." Kaltofen asked Hanford health and safety managers what levels of plutonium they were finding in the fish, and they replied that they weren't finding any plutonium at all.

"Really?" Kaltofen replied. "Can I see your data?"

Whereupon the Hanford officials admitted that they had found no plutonium in the squawfish for a simple reason: they had not tested for plutonium in the squawfish.

"Seriously?" Kaltofen responded. "You have a monster multibillion-dollar budget and you don't test, I have a multithousand-dollar budget and I get it done?"

Nor did the managers ask to see Kaltofen's findings. "That's maybe what bothers me the most," says Carpenter. "They ought to be telling Marco, 'Wow, can we see *your* data?' These people are in charge of detecting pollution hazards at America's most polluted site. They should be bloody curious!"

According to Steven Blush, an independent researcher and former DOE official with extensive knowledge of DOE operations at Hanford, contractors have known about the danger of hydrogen buildup in the tanks since 1977, perhaps earlier, but didn't inform the DOE until 1990. The timing may have had something to do with the revelation the year before, by a dissident Soviet agronomist, that two decades earlier, at the Mayak facility in the Ural Mountains that is the Russian equivalent of Hanford, a tank containing high-level nuclear waste exploded with the force of about 100 tons of dynamite, spreading cesium-137 and strontium-90 over several hundred square miles, killing thousands with radiation sickness and cancer, and forcing the permanent abandonment of several dozen villages and towns. While the DOE downplayed the risk of a similar tank explosion at Hanford—essentially on the logic that such an explosion had never happened there before, so it wasn't likely to happen in the future—it did install gauges and automatic vents to try to clear the tanks' headspace when the hydrogen reached 25 percent of the minimum lower explosive limit. Over the years the gauges started to break down, however, and were not repaired. In 2013, the Defense Nuclear Facilities Safety Board (DNFSB), the independent body created by Congress in 1988 to oversee the DOE's military-related nuclear operations, wrote a sharp warning about this threat and demanded swift remedial action. Senior Oregon senator Ron Wyden, one of the best-informed and most persistent critics of the DOE-contractor cabal at Hanford, wrote a toughly worded letter with similar demands. Hanford officials promised to fix the problem by 2016. They didn't.

Instead, they removed the hydrogen gauges. Tom Carpenter, a connoisseur of the Hanford bureaucratic mind-set, says this was to avoid being held accountable for explicit errors: "What you can't see can't hurt you." He shrugs. "Except of course, it really can. A hydrogen explosion can hurt you." In June 2015, Carpenter read in a field report on the tank farm—passed to him by a confidential whistleblower—that tank C-102 was at 97 percent of its lower flammable limit. "Forget the cleanup! They're going to blow the whole damn place up!" Carpenter isn't smiling anymore. Nobody in the boat is.

He glares out over the river. "These things happen over and over and over again," he says. "People in charge of cleanup have no transparency, no accountability, and that's how they want things. Safety is a marginal consideration for them. Reality is simply not their game. It's all about perceptions."

The tank farms are a uniquely dangerous work environment, not only because the substances are so deadly, but also because they are so poorly understood. The fifty-six million gallons of waste contain some eighteen hundred different chemicals, but no one knows exactly which is where: the World War II and postwar-era documentation for many tanks is unreliable, and their composition changes constantly because of the chemical and physical reactions they are undergoing. The effects on human health of the overwhelming majority of chemicals present in the tank farms have never been studied, and have no established occupational exposure limits. Which means that a doctor trying to analyze and treat a worker after an exposure is typically flying blind.

Most of the time, workers suffer no apparent consequences, but when the tanks vent vapors in large quantities—which can happen after the tank waste has been disturbed, or during a change in the weather—some have been badly, and permanently, injured.

Over the decades, the DOE and the series of contractors in charge of managing the tank farm have consistently denied any causal link between tank farm vapors and the medical harm that workers have suffered. They claim that their own measurements of the chemicals in the tank farm atmosphere have shown that the air is safe to breathe, and that workers are feigning their injuries, perhaps at the instigation of groups like Hanford Challenge. This position is getting harder and harder to maintain. Tallying the number of workers affected is complicated, of course, by the sweeping governmental and corporate secrecy at Hanford, but several authoritative reports agree that the number of workers affected is in the hundreds. Working on the basis of public records, Robert Alvarez, a senior Energy Department official during the Clinton administration, has counted at least 350 documented cases of vapor injury since 1957. But the problem is probably far worse. At a hearing in August 2016, union worker safety representative Don Slaugh, referring to internal data, testified that between November 2009 and January 2016 alone, about 380 workers had reported vapor-related injuries. Since 1992, thirty major studies performed by panels of experts in nuclear waste, environmental health, toxicology and industrial hygiene, by the Government Accountability Office, and by the DOE's own inspector general have identified serious health hazards at Hanford, and glaring inadequacies in the safety culture.

Another investigation of the tank farm vapors, probably the most authoritative to date, began in the spring of 2014, after dozens of workers had suffered vapor exposures. WRPS and DOE commissioned a team of nationally recognized experts in occupational health, environmental engineering, toxicology and industrial hygiene to study the problem. Their findings were published in October 2014 as the *Hanford Tank Vapor Assessment Report* (TVAR), which reached three major conclusions: First, that the evidence "strongly suggests a causal link between chemical vapor releases from Hanford waste tanks and subsequent adverse health effects" in Hanford tank farm workers. Second, that the methods used to monitor vapor exposures were utterly inadequate, because they were designed to detect chronic, long-term exposures using eight-hour weighted averages, while most workers are actually harmed by sudden, concentrated doses of chemicals. And third, that "the ongoing emission of tank vapors, which contain a mixture of toxic chemicals, is inconsistent with the provision of a safe and healthful workplace free from recognized hazards." In the opinion of this group of experts, in other words, nobody should be working in an environment as dangerous as the Hanford tank farms.

Many workers have probably been harmed by vapors but have chosen not to report them. Workers who complain of health problems are often branded as malingerers, both by management and by their own coworkers, and are denied the overtime pay that many depend on. Until recently, workers in the Hanford tank farms were neither required nor encouraged to use supplied oxygen on the job; many managers objected that oxygen equipment was expensive and slowed the work.

John Swain was working with his colleague Mike Armstrong in the tank farms on August 17, 2003, supervising the transfer of waste from C-106, when he suddenly caught a strong, strange odor, which he has never been able to describe. He moved away from the tank as fast as he could; by the time he reached the shift office, he was vomiting, and subsequently developed severe breathing problems, swelling and drooping of the left side of his face, spiking blood pressure, numbness, and uncontrollable twitching. On-site medical personnel and contractor managers assured him that nothing had happened, and urged him to return to work. Instead, Swain sought an unbiased opinion at Harborview Medical Center in Seattle, the nationally recognized teaching hospital of the University of Washington; doctors there determined that he had lost 40 percent of his lungs' capacity to process oxygen, and diagnosed him with reactive airways dysfunction syndrome (RADS). Harborview doctors also instructed him not to return to the tank farms, telling him, "Next time you might not be so lucky." Other specialists subsequently diagnosed him with toxic encephalopathy (brain damage caused by toxic chemicals) and peripheral neuropathy—nerve damage—in his lower extremities, particularly on his left side. Since the episode his symptoms have improved, he says, but he still stutters and is subject to sudden fainting spells and respiratory arrest, which can be triggered by something as apparently innocuous as an unfamiliar cologne or deodorant. "I can't smell them, because I lost my sense of smell in the accident," he says matter-of-factly. "But my left cheek will start tingling, and I know it's time to get the hell out of there."

Nevertheless, Swain's employers, worker safety representatives, DOE staff and even fellow employees of the tank farm workers' union continued to insist that tank vapors had nothing to do with his symptoms—or to claim that he had invented them. So Swain contacted Tom Carpenter. In previous vapor exposure cases, Carpenter had encountered a disturbing pattern of local health officials, many of whom were employed by the contractors, concealing or modifying documentation of injuries or diagnoses in order to minimize the number of "recordables"; sending affected workers back to the tank farms immediately; and recommending psychological examinations for those who insisted that their illnesses were work-related. Fortunately, Swain's condition was verified by several medical specialists, including his doctor in Richland, John Intradolta, who refused to sugarcoat their assessment of Swain's condition to suit the contractor. Knowing that documentation of vapor incidents often disappeared, Swain had also obtained originals of key records from his case, including the event report of the vapor release on August 17, 2003, and the chemical readings taken by an industrial hygienist at tank C-106 two hours after his exposure. Despite continuing denials by the contractors and the DOE, he and Hanford Challenge managed through several years of administrative warfare to secure a workers' compensation settlement, and even a letter of apology from the president of the tank farm contractor. (The terms of Swain's settlement forbid him from naming his employer, but CH2M Hill was the prime contractor of the tank farms in 2003.)

"The contractors fight anything that slows the work down or costs extra," says Swain. "I could take you out there and show you people going through the same stuff I am. Ninety-five percent of people don't raise their voices because they gotta have that paycheck. They saw what the company does if you write too many PERs [problem evaluation reports]—you lose your overtime, get laid off. So they don't ask for oxygen. They just suck it up."

In September 2015, Washington state attorney general Bob Ferguson, along with Hanford Challenge and a local plumbers' and steamfitters' union, brought lawsuits against the DOE and its current tank farm contractor, WRPS, alleging that their handling of waste in the tank farms represented "an imminent and substantial endangerment to human health or the environment." In a press release following the lawsuit, Ferguson said, "For years, Washington workers have been exposed to noxious fumes and chemical vapors as they clean up the federal government's nuclear site at Hanford. Enough is enough. The health risks are real, and the state is taking action today to ensure the federal government protects these workers now and in the future."

In response to the suit, the DOE and its contractor doubled down, not only denying that workers were being harmed, but actually reducing the worker safety requirements in the tank farms. In July 2016, the attorney general, denouncing the "culture of indifference" to worker safety at Hanford, filed a motion for injunctive relief to force the DOE and its contractors to take immediate action to protect workers. The DOE and WRPS continued litigating.

And why not? In court, the DOE, like other federal departments in their legal affairs, is being represented by DOJ attorneys. WRPS is represented by the Summit Law Group, a leading Seattle law firm, whose fees are being paid, per the contract with the DOE, by the DOE—that is, by taxpayers. Which means that the Hanford tank farm workers who have been injured by vapor releases—injuries whose existence the DOE and the contractors continue to deny—are paying the legal fees of their opponents. Downwinders are in the same position, with even fewer resources. "There are no definitive studies to prove that downwinders were harmed by Hanford's decades of radioactive releases," Carpenter says, "mainly because the burden of proof in that kind of epidemiological study is so high. You can't study tens of thousands of people. You can always blame their thyroid cancer and other health problems on other factors. Fuck, they couldn't even prove definitively that problems happened at Love Canal, where you could pretty much light water from the faucet on fire! The DOE and its DOJ lawyers settled those cases out for peanuts— most in the tens of thousands of dollars. And they took their time, grinding people down. The original population of downwinders in the suit started at three thousand, but by the end was down to fifteen hundred, because the others had died. About $100 million was paid by taxpayers to fight the suits. You'd think that money would have been better spent helping the sick people. But that's not the way we do things in America. What a country!"

Living next to Hanford might seem precarious to outsiders, but most people I've met in Richland don't appear to mind. Since 1943, when the Army and DuPont built those reactors and factories in the desert across the Columbia, the town has thrived

on the steady flow of atomic cash they produced, which the *Spokesman Review*, published in nearby Spokane, has called "the river of money" and historian Rodney Car-
lisle has dubbed "nuclear pork." Two billion tax dollars flow into Hanford each year,
and much of it fans rapidly out into the community. Ten thousand people work on
the Hanford Nuclear Reservation, where each job creates three more in the community. Salaries at Hanford start at $45,000 and rapidly reach six figures; this disposable
wealth buys boats, cars, dinners at local restaurants and goods at fancy stores. While
the rest of the state was in an economic downturn in 2008, 2009 and 2010, the cities
of Richland, Kennewick and Pasco, which call themselves the "Tri-Cities," were
thriving. "The leaking tanks, the threat of explosions and criticality—that all fades
into the background," says Tom Carpenter. "You develop a certain mind-set. You
need to be 'Hanfordized.' You just gotta put on the blinders and pop in the mouth-
piece, only focus on certain things, only hear certain things, and certainly don't say
the wrong things. And if you do all that, you're gonna get along just fine out there."

During the Cold War, aware of its leading role in the arms race against the Soviets, Richland referred to itself, with a strange blend of futurism and Old West
pride, as "the Atom-bustin' Village of the West," and held a yearly summer parade
known as the "Atomic Frontier Days." The disasters at Three Mile Island, Chernobyl and Fukushima dimmed Richland's atomic smile a tad, but the town still
recognizes its debt to the bomb, and seems unrepentant about the destructive force
it helped unleash on the world. To this day you can order a "Meltdown" mushroom
burger or a "B-52 Stratofortress" burger at Bombers Drive Thru, drink a pint of
Plutonium Porter or Heisenberg's Heavy Water WeizenBock at the Atomic Ale
Brewpub & Eatery, and enjoy Neutron Night at the Atomic Bowl bowling alley.
The sports teams at local Richland High School call themselves the Bombers, and
their uniforms sport a billowing orange mushroom cloud—the school's Facebook
page proclaims they're "Proud of the Cloud," and home crowd cheers include,
"Nuke 'em! Nuke 'em till they glow!" (General James Mattis, the former secretary
of defense, who as head of the Marine logistics command at Quantico was Franz
Gayl's antagonist, grew up in Richland, and was a Bomber at Richland High, then
called Columbia High.)

Ultimately, the Tri-Cities resemble an outsize version of the company town that once existed throughout America, anchored by a big mine or lumber mill, a steel plant or automobile factory. Here the local industry is nuclear cleanup, and boosters are always calling for more money to run it. "The town doesn't care about delays or cost overruns at Hanford, so long as the money comes," says Tamosaitis. "The town resists the government shutting anything down—they all rally around the contractors to keep the money coming." Before he became a whistleblower, Tamosaitis was at home in this world. "I was a company man. I'd worked twenty years for DuPont, another twenty-two more at URS [a major contractor at the WTP, now owned by Aecom]. When I started working, the attitude was like the words from that Tennessee Ernie Ford song, 'Sixteen Tons': 'I owe my soul to the company store.' You hired on, you were loyal to the company and they were loyal to you. Life went on. So I had no backup plan for what happened here at Hanford."

The day after our cruise on the Columbia River, I met Tamosaitis at his home in Richland, where he's expanded the garage into a two-story workshop to restore vintage cars. He was wearing a white Tyvek jumpsuit, and a white headband to keep perspiration out of his eyes in the summer heat. His hands were too greasy to shake, so he held out a meaty fist for a bump, then walked back to his workbench, picked up a razor blade, and continued gently teasing apart a stack of bronze shims, each a thousandth of an inch thick, that he was using to seal a Babbitt valve on the crankshaft of the glossy Ford Model A he was restoring. He added one slender shim at a time to the valve, reassembled it and turned the engine over to test the seal. If it failed, he stripped the valve down again, feathered in another shim, reassembled it and cranked up the engine again. And again. And again . . . as many times as required. As he worked, his thick fingers testing and teasing the metal with antenna-like delicacy, he spoke in a low, steady, almost trancelike voice about his job at the WTP.

In their classic study *The Whistleblowers*, sociologist Myron Glazer and historian Penina Glazer examined the lives and careers of sixty-four whistleblowers and found that most were conservative people devoted to their work and their organizations, who had happily followed familiar bureaucratic protocols until the day that their superiors asked them to violate their own professional or ethical standards. Walt Tamosaitis fits this mold. Country western music plays from a small radio on a shelf in his shop, at the same high volume as the Fox News shows running continuously on the television upstairs. His fridge wisdom includes quotes from George W. Bush on praying for powers equal to your tasks, and Mother Teresa on the power of love. (He also has quotes from Thoreau and Martin Luther King, recurrent voices of inspiration among whistleblowers I've met.) He and wife Sandy are devout Catholics. When he testifies before the Senate, he wears dark three-piece suits with narrow pinstripes, suspenders, and an American flag pin in his lapel. He refers to the United States as "our Country," with an emphasis that suggests he spells the word with a capital C.

Tamosaitis also fits the profile of many historic whistleblowers, at Hanford and elsewhere, in being a successful, highly qualified professional with a strict, internalized code of procedure and the self-confidence required to stand up for their views. In fact, like Ernie Fitzgerald and several whistleblowers I've interviewed, Tamosaitis dislikes the term "whistleblower" (he prefers "person of conscience"). "It was just a matter of doing my job as a nuclear engineer right." A central responsibility of that job, he said, is placing public welfare first. He saw the problems he encountered at Hanford as symptoms of the rise of short-termism, selfishness and cheating in American society. "Look at how Americans used to do things," he said. "We built the B Reactor in thirteen months, without a clear plan. DuPont took one dollar for their work, because it was wartime. Now companies just waste time and milk as much money as they can, with no sense of public service. Cheating is so widespread in our culture—the Atlanta Falcons pipe in crowd noise to distract their opponents, the New England Patriots deflate their footballs. Obama and Michelle take separate planes to Los Angeles on the same day, and waste taxpayer dollars. Even Barnum & Bailey circus has whistleblowers! Everything is about serving our near-term needs, and 'What can I do for me today?'"

Though he was retaliated against and fired from the WTP for reporting sweeping safety concerns—concerns shared by numerous other experts, and ultimately vindicated by his whistleblower lawsuits—he said he remains a believer in the project, which is the answer to Hanford's most pressing question: What to do with the fifty-six million gallons of high-level nuclear waste? "We need the WTP," he said firmly. "Just so long as it's built right."

The WTP, Tamosaitis explained, is the largest construction project in the Americas, and will be the biggest waste treatment facility in the world. It will immobilize Hanford's tank waste and make it more easily disposable, using a technique called glassification. The waste will first be piped out of the tanks into the Pretreatment Facility, where it will be separated into high-level and low-level waste, depending on its radioactivity, and then sent either to the High-Activity Waste Facility or to the Low-Activity Waste Facility. In both areas, the waste will be mixed with glass-forming silica, heated to 2,100 degrees Fahrenheit and poured into steel canisters. Once they've cooled, these steel-encased glass logs will be easily transportable, and will be shipped to a deep geologic storage facility, perhaps Yucca Mountain in Nevada, where, far underground, their remaining radioactivity will dissipate over the millennia. The glassification technique has already been used successfully to deal with nuclear waste at the Savannah River nuclear facility in South Carolina, where Tamosaitis worked before he came to Richland. His previous successes there made him a natural choice to lead the WTP project. In March 2003, he moved to Hanford and soon led the new plant's Research & Technology (R&T) program for URS, which as the main subcontractor on the WTP is in a fifty-fifty profit-sharing partnership with the prime contractor, Bechtel. (URS was acquired by Aecom Technology in 2014.) Tamosaitis and his R&T team were responsible for identifying and solving technical problems that might prevent the facility from running safely and well.

They had plenty to do. Not long after Tamosaitis arrived at Hanford, a congressional hearing and a GAO report sharply criticized the delays and skyrocketing costs at the WTP, which it blamed not only on the project's technical complexity, but also on Bechtel's poor cost and safety estimates, and on the DOE's inability, or unwillingness, to keep its contractor honest. As a result, then Secretary of Energy Samuel Bodman commissioned a detailed technical review of the plant, which Tamosaitis would lead, drawing on the expertise of both his own team at URS and over fifty outside consultants at universities and major laboratories—the most expert group of scientists and process engineers in the world on the technologies to be employed by the WTP. In early 2006, they produced what came to be called the "Best and Brightest" review, which identified twenty-eight design problems at the WTP, seventeen of which they considered serious. Tamosaitis's R&T team and others set to work to resolve those problems; by late 2009, all but one had been marked "closed."

The term "closed" was actually administrative jargon used by contractor executives, which simply meant that a problem had been removed from the "open" list, not that a solution had necessarily been found. "Bechtel uses the word to mean that they plan to work on an item in the future, even when they have no clue how to fix it," Tamosaitis explains. "In their business-speak, they call this 'providing the plan for the plan.' By marking things 'closed,' they give the perception of progress, and can continue to collect their award fees and funding." Classifying problems as closed was a prerequisite for receiving milestone payments.

The last "open" problem was the thorniest of all: proper mixing of the waste, which is a heterogeneous jumble of gases, liquids and solids with a wide range of textures: steam, soup, ketchup, wet sand, peanut butter, chunks of ice. Slurping this concoction out of the tanks and piping it through the various phases of the treatment process, while keeping it thoroughly mixed, was one of the most complex technological challenges at the WTP—and one of the most vital to solve, since if plutonium or uranium particles settled out of the mixture they might go critical, causing a fire, an explosion, or an uncontrolled nuclear reaction. Alternatively, hydrogen bubbles might coalesce and detonate, launching tons of America's most deadly substances into the wind. During the glassification process, if improperly mixed waste were blended with molten glass, a steam explosion in the melter could blow up the plant.

In short, the success of the entire WTP project hinged on proper mixing. On October 2, 2009, the contractors and DOE appointed Tamosaitis to tackle the mixing problem, which they code-named "M3." Top managers at the WTP instructed Tamosaitis to take a "kitchen sink" approach to M3: an all-out attempt using extensive analysis, testing with mockups, and further consultation with outside experts. The DOE set June 30, 2010, as the date by which the mixing issue should at least be marked "closed," if not fully resolved, and established a $6 million milestone payment to incentivize Bechtel to meet this deadline. An additional $50 million in congressional funding for the project was also made contingent on closing M3 by that date. The bonus fuse had been lit.

And so began another chapter in the long, sad story of the WTP, with its elaborate rituals of dominance and submission between Bechtel and DOE, which demonstrates yet again what happens when a powerful contractor with an extreme
bonus culture meets a captured regulator that has itself bought into the incentives
system, in close proximity to colossal amounts of Other People's Money. Decade
after decade, the DOE has paid out 90 percent of its budget, currently about $31
billion, to contractors. At Hanford and other sites of nuclear research and cleanup,
contractors outnumber DOE engineers by 100 to 1; true to Ronald Reagan's now
time-honored prescription of self-regulation, the DOE follows a "least interference"
policy and performs no active oversight of its contractors. You can already guess
how well this approach works. Since 1990, the DOE's management of major nuclear contracts has been on the GAO's High Risk List for fraud, because, as the
GAO wrote succinctly in that year, "DOE's record of inadequate management and
oversight of contractors has left the department vulnerable to fraud, waste, abuse,
and mismanagement."

Most DOE contracts are noncompetitive, and are typically written in a form
known as project management, which establishes work milestones and pays bonuses upon their completion. This supposedly aligns the interests of the contractor
with those of the government and of the general public, and ensures that everyone
finishes the project as swiftly as possible. In reality, DOE incentives create a bonus
fixation among its contractors that often ends in a headlong race for money, at the
expense of professionalism and ethics. What's more, Bechtel and URS, with the
DOE's blessing, were building the WTP with the same "fast-track design-build"
approach often employed by defense contractors when manufacturing aircraft,
warships and other complex, high-priced weaponry (the Lockheed F-35 is another
infamous example). Instead of designing the plant first and then building it, Hanford contractors started building while the design was still evolving. In principle,
this approach allows new technological advancements to be added to the initial
design, keeping it cutting-edge. In practice, building and designing on the fly often
leads to waste, or worse, as contractors make a series of expensive "change orders"
to the original plan.

"There's a saying that's famous among Hanford contractors, about the dinghy and the yacht," Walt Tamosaitis told me. "The dinghy is your original bid, and the yacht is what you eventually build through change control." Though most experts at Hanford agreed that the WTP could not be built for less than $6 billion, and another group had bid $15 billion, in 2000 Bechtel promised to complete it for $4.3 billion, in seven years. Having won the contract, Bechtel ramped up the plant's final cost through change orders, even as the completion date slid. By 2006, the WTP's price tag had nearly tripled, to $11 billion, and the completion date was 2017. By 2012, its price tag had grown to $13.4 billion, and by 2016 to $16.8 billion. Current estimates now price the WTP at somewhere between $25 and $30 billion, with completion in 2039—or perhaps 2047. "Bechtel has no incentive to build the WTP right, or even to finish it," Tamosaitis said.

A new phase in the WTP debacle began in January 2010, with the arrival of Bechtel senior manager Frank Russo. Russo came to Hanford from Lawrence Livermore National Laboratory, the historic nuclear research facility that was privatized and turned over to Bechtel management in 2008. "Bechtel promised the Bush administration that they could save $50 million a year," says Gary Gwilliam, a California employment lawyer. "As soon as Bechtel took over the lab, they started planning firings to cut costs. The man who led those firings, Bechtel's hatchet man, was Frank Russo." Russo oversaw the termination of 440 senior career scientists and other employees, many of whom had worked at the laboratory for decades; most were confronted by staff and security guards at their desks, watched closely while they collected their belongings, and then escorted off the premises. "I was treated like a common criminal," remembers Marian Barazza, an administrator of thirty-eight years who was left crying in the parking lot. According to Gwilliam, who won a wrongful-termination lawsuit settlement of $37.5 million from Bechtel on behalf of 130 Livermore employees, Russo and his Bechtel associates claimed to be acting under orders from the DOE to cut costs at the laboratory, while actually acting to increase the firm's profits. "After several months, when the firings were done and the costs were cut, Frank Russo moved on," Gwilliam remembers.

Soon after Russo's arrival at Hanford, Walt Tamosaitis says, the atmosphere at the WTP changed abruptly. Russo replaced several top WTP engineers, at both Bechtel and URS, and modified Tamosaitis's chain of command to have him report to a Bechtel manager, Mike Robinson. Russo also brought in new DOE managers, including Dale Knutson, who was named WTP federal project director. Russo assumed direct personal authority over all technical aspects of the project, including the troublesome mixing problem. "With all the high-level engineers that Bechtel had at their disposal, this was a strange choice," Tamosaitis says flatly. "I'm sure Frank Russo is a very good manager. But he has a BS in political science. He's not an engineer. He's not a scientist. Mixing was a scientific question. A tough scientific question."

From the outset Russo's primary goals appear to have been financial, not technical. He stressed that the team's central mission was to close the mixing issue by June 30 and thereby secure tens of millions of dollars in funding. Emails produced in litigation reveal that Russo exerted considerable pressure on senior contract management and the DOE. After Tamosaitis raised engineering concerns, Russo wrote a senior DOE official, Ines Triay, "I will send anyone on my team home if they demonstrate an unwillingness or inability to fulfill my direction." He later wrote to Bechtel vice president David Walker and president Scott Ogilvie, stressing the urgency of closing the M3: "Our $50 million is still in play. Declare failure [of M3] and our $50 mil goes away." Russo also suggested that his team could close the M3 issue "if they are willing to take some risk." This is the quintessence of financialism: managers assuming control of a vastly complex technical project and turning it into a high-pressure, money-fueled race against the clock.

But sometimes good science doesn't respect timetables. In mid-March 2010, three months before the fateful deadline, Donald Alexander, the DOE's chief scientist responsible for reviewing the design of the WTP, announced that he'd discovered serious new problems with M3, which could lead to explosions or criticality. Tamosaitis says that Alexander's concerns enraged senior managers at Bechtel and URS, who ordered Tamosaitis to "oppose and kill" them by marshaling contrary opinions from as many PhD scientists as possible. Yet when Tamosaitis checked Alexander's calculations, he found them valid. In a meeting in early April 2010, Tamosaitis said so. This, it later turned out, was the beginning of the end of his career as a nuclear engineer.

Tamosaitis continued to point out technical problems with the mixing problem, and to push for further testing. "I knew that if Bechtel and URS officially declared the mixing issue closed, there would be no further scientific examination of this very serious nuclear safety problem," he told me. Other experts agreed with him. An external team of consulting university scientists hired by the DOE wrote a report that detailed numerous problems with mixing. Senior technical advisers to the project condemned Bechtel's refusal to perform more tests of the mixing system as unrealistic, and even "criminally negligent."

Frank Russo and his allies at Bechtel, URS and the DOE ignored these dissenting voices and forged ahead with the project. Senior URS executive Robert French emailed Bechtel and URS management that "now is the time to push for closure. By the time any issues or concerns are identified, the review group [i.e., the team of university consultants] will have been disbanded and there will [be] no way to reopen it." Tension continued to build about the closure of M3. For his part, Tamosaitis continued to insist that further testing was mandatory, and would probably necessitate substantial design changes.

Matters came to a head on June 30, at a gathering chaired by Bechtel chief engineer Barbara Rusinko that became known as the "Choke on the Cherries Meeting." Tamosaitis had been directed to submit all outstanding technical issues concerning the WTP that he knew of. With input from his team and from outside scientists, he had produced a list of nearly fifty technical problems, most of which concerned mixing and had serious nuclear safety implications. Feeling that this meeting was his last chance to raise concerns, he also produced a list of one hundred additional problems that, though previously marked "closed," he believed were far from resolved. Tamosaitis had a heated exchange with Bechtel's Garth Duncan, who insisted that many of the issues on the two lists had already been resolved. During a lull in the argument, Tamosaitis noticed a bowl of cherries on the table. He asked Rusinko, who had brought them, if he might have one. As Tamosaitis remembers it, Rusinko replied that he might indeed—and that maybe he would choke on them. Tamosaitis interpreted this statement as a veiled threat.

Later that day, Frank Russo announced in an effusive email to the M3 team that the mixing issue had been closed, and that the WTP had cleared its last technical hurdle: "Today is June 30th. A day of reckoning. I reckon you all did extraordinarily well. . . . The outstanding results you achieved as a team could only have happened because each and every one of you worked longer, harder, faster and smarter than any project director has the right to expect. And as previously stated, I expect a lot. You were outstanding in your effort and outstanding in the result. You came through at a time that any other result could have destroyed DOE and stakeholder confidence in the entire WTP project."

Walt Tamosaitis was unimpressed. He forwarded Russo's email to three of the external university scientists with whom he had worked on mixing for the past five years, condemning the decision as having been made over the opinions of highly qualified technicians. He signed off with some vintage Hanford black humor: "Have a big bang on July 4th to celebrate."

At seven a.m. on July 2, shortly after Tamosaitis entered the WTP offices, URS operations manager Dennis Hayes told him to hand over his cell phone, BlackBerry and badge, and said that he was being removed from the WTP project at Frank Russo's order. Tamosaitis was escorted to the front door and told to leave the premises immediately, not to speak with anyone in the office, nor to return. "I felt like the man with no country. 'What just happened there?' 'Where do I go?' 'What do I do?'"

Though Tamosaitis had been removed from WTP, at least for the time being he was still a URS employee. He was instructed to report for work at the main URS building in Richland, where he was assigned a workspace in the basement, beside the janitor's closet and next to two large photocopiers that were so noisy that Tamosaitis brought earmuffs from home. He had no phone and no chair, and had to jury-rig a desk by laying a shelf across two cardboard boxes. He referred to this makeshift den as his "mole hole." There he persisted for sixteen months, without meaningful work, isolated from other URS employees. One February afternoon his wife called on his cell phone to ask why he was still at work. "Don't you know it's snowing like crazy outside? They have sent everyone home," she said. He went upstairs and found the office empty, the lights off, the doors locked.

As Tamosaitis retold the story to me four years later, he tried to laugh about it. "I thought maybe the Rapture had come," he said with a forced grin. But clearly the humiliation still stung. "I didn't know who I reported to, or what my job title was," he continued, his head slightly canted, his chin raised and lower lip jutting, assessing whether I could fathom quite how painful this kind of treatment would be for a lifelong company man. "I wasn't invited to any meetings, and when I'd go to one, people would sit around in silence looking at me until I left." He gestured impatiently at the sleek Ford Model A he was rebuilding. "Hobbies are fun, until you start doing them full-time. I worked with the same intensity as I do on these hot rods, to make everything perfect. Work was my calling—I lived to work. They took away from me what I cared most about. One day I was a top engineer, leading an office with a budget of $700 million; the next day I was down in the mole hole sitting on a cardboard box."

Down in the basement with his earmuffs on, Tamosaitis chewed over what had happened to him, but couldn't digest it. He had flashbacks of the scene of his dismissal. He remembered the click of the security door closing behind him for the last time, the shock on the faces of his wife, daughter and son-in-law when he showed up unexpectedly at home and told them he'd been fired. He thought about what his company was doing to him. "I saw that URS had a twofold strategy," he told me. "First, they were trying to wear me down so I would quit and go away. Second, they were sending a clear signal to every other employee: 'Don't do what Walt did! If we did this to a manager of forty-four years, just think what we'll do to you.'"

Tamosaitis thought a lot about those other employees, including the members of his former R&T team on the WTP project, and what they must be thinking. "I had always told my people that nuclear safety was a job with unique and serious responsibilities, where they should always be asking themselves four questions: Question One, What was the right thing to do? Question Two, Were they going to do it? Question Three, Would they defend doing the right thing—would they stand up and tell people what they were going to do? And Question Four, Did you answer 'no' to any of the previous questions? If so, go back to Question One."

Gradually Tamosaitis concluded that the time had come to practice what he'd preached. "The more I thought about what had been done to me, the more I realized I couldn't face my former workers and admit I wasn't fighting back—doing the right thing, and then standing up for it. I wanted them to know this wasn't how you manage an important project like the WTP. More important, I wanted to make sure that what was happening to me didn't happen to anybody else." For the first time in his life, he began to think about reporting serious technical concerns outside the tight circle of contractors and the DOE. He knew the risks he was running, and says that he might never have acted if this crisis had happened earlier in his career. "I was lucky that I was about sixty-two when it all started," he told me. "I was near Medicare, Social Security. But if I'd been thirty-eight, knowing what I know now about how whistleblowing works. . . ." His voice trailed off. "Where do you draw the line, even when that means losing everything?"

Eventually, Tamosaitis drew his line. He began a detailed letter to the Defense Nuclear Facilities Safety Board, the independent executive-branch organization that oversees public health and safety at DOE nuclear facilities, in which he laid out his concerns about the WTP. He met with two managers of the DOE Employee Concerns Program. One said that she had never heard of such a blatant case of workplace retaliation; the other said he felt that their office wasn't in a position to handle his situation, and suggested that he contact someone outside Hanford: Tom Carpenter. Tamosaitis called Carpenter at his office in Seattle, identified himself, explained his situation, talked about the letter he was writing to the safety board. "It was an awkward conversation," Tamosaitis remembers. "I said I didn't know who to talk to, or where to turn."

"Stay where you are—I'll be right there," Carpenter replied. He rose from his desk, walked out to his car, and drove across the Cascade Mountains to Tamosaitis's house in Richland. "When Walt called me, I recognized this as one of those rare occasions when something really important comes along. From what he had to say, from his title, I knew right away this was big. I speak with a lot of whistleblowers, but very few people as senior as Walt have ever blown the whistle at Hanford. And he was going to decide within twenty-four to forty-eight hours what he was going to do. If he doesn't have a good picture of it, he's likely to say he can't take this on. But if he has allies, maybe he will." Carpenter told Tamosaitis that he strongly supported his plan to alert the safety board, and connected him with Jack Sheridan, a Seattle lawyer and former colleague at GAP, who specialized in defending whistleblowers.

Within weeks, all hell broke loose at Hanford. In response to Tamosaitis's July 16 letter, the safety board, led by its principled and energetic chairman, Peter Winokur, began a formal investigation into his accusations. In October 2010, Winokur chaired hearings in Richland, both public and closed, to explore design and safety concerns at the WTP. The board issued a report in June 2011 that lambasted both the contractors and the DOE for suppressing technical dissent at Hanford and intimidating employees who wanted to report legitimate safety concerns. In January 2012, the DOE's own enforcement office released a report severely condemning the "broken safety culture" at the WTP and finding that many DOE and contractor employees alike feared retaliation for raising safety concerns.

After Tamosaitis spoke up, other senior whistleblowers began to come forward. On August 23, 2012, Gary Brunson, the director of the DOE's Engineering Division at Hanford, wrote a terse memorandum to the acting federal director of the WTP, Scott Samuelson, listing thirty-four serious problems with Bechtel's work at the facility, which in his view indicated that "Bechtel National Inc. is not competent to complete their role" at the WTP and should be removed from its leading position at the plant. A few months later, Brunson wrote a letter to Energy Secretary Steven Chu, in which he provided evidence of systemic wrongdoing by the contractor and issued a "stop work" order, an official procedure by which a senior manager at a nuclear site can halt any activity that he or she believes to be a threat to human safety or the environment. Senior Hanford nuclear engineers David Bruce and Murray Thorson also expressed their concerns about the WTP publicly. "This sucker is not going to run as currently designed, plain and simple," Bruce told the *Seattle Weekly* on February 21, 2012, "and a heck of a lot of people around here know it but are too afraid to speak up."

In late 2012, Steven Chu halted all work at the WTP and opened an investigation. The DOE's own inspector general criticized the department for ignoring persistent technical problems. Soon after, the GAO issued a report condemning both the technical and the management decisions made by contractors at the WTP, and the DOE itself for paying Bechtel "incentive fees for meeting specific project objectives even as the project's costs and timelines balloon far beyond the initially planned goals."

Once Walt Tamosaitis had decided to speak out, like a good engineer he did his whistleblowing work thoroughly. He testified twice before Congress, spoke to countless reporters, appeared on Rachel Maddow's show and on the cover of *Newsweek*. He sued URS, Bechtel and the DOE for whistleblower retaliation and wrongful termination. Tamosaitis's work seemed to produce results. In May 2013, Obama appointed a new Energy secretary, Ernest Moniz, who, during his confirmation hearings, promised to meet with whistleblowers at Hanford. That June, Moniz visited Hanford and spoke with Walt Tamosaitis and five other whistleblowers, in a supposedly confidential meeting. On September 20, Moniz issued a new Safety Culture policy, which stated that the DOE "will pursue a safety culture built on an environment of trust and mutual respect, worker engagement and open communication, an atmosphere that promotes a questioning attitude with effective resolution of reported problems. . . . Federal, laboratory, and contractor workers have the right to identify and raise issues that affect their safety and health or that of their co-workers openly, and without fear of reprisal."

Twelve days later, URS fired Tamosaitis. The company claimed that Tamosaitis's position had been eliminated not in retaliation but as part of a "reduction in force." Four of the other five whistleblowers who met with Moniz were also terminated or forced out. Tom Carpenter learned that, contrary to his explicit agreement with DOE headquarters, they had communicated the names of the whistleblowers to the local DOE office, which promptly passed them on to the contractors. Neither Moniz nor any other senior DOE official made any public protest of the firings. "The department's silence here can only be interpreted by contractors as approval," Tom Carpenter says. "In case anyone was still wondering who was in charge out on the Hanford Nuclear Reservation, the Department of Energy or the contractors, there's your answer."

During litigation, an email string between contractors and DOE executives emerged that shed additional light on why Tamosaitis had been terminated from the WTP project so abruptly, and how the project was being managed.

Somehow Tamosaitis's "big bang" email had reached Dale Knutson of the DOE, who forwarded it to Frank Russo of Bechtel. "If this shows up in the press we will be sticking to our previous comment," Knutson told Russo, evidently referring to earlier statements that all was well at the WTP. "Walt does not speak for DOE."

Knutson also told Russo to "use this message as you see fit to accelerate staffing changes," as well as to "color" his conversations with other Bechtel managers.

Russo, in turn, forwarded Knutson's email note to Tamosaitis's boss, William Gay at URS, with the curt comment, "Walt is killing us. Get him in your corporate office today."

Gay replied: "He will be gone tomorrow."

As Gay promised, Tamosaitis was fired from the WTP the next day. During litigation, Dale Knutson stated under oath that he had not directed Bechtel or URS to "take any specific actions" in relation to Tamosaitis, but this sworn statement appears at odds with the email string of July 1, 2010, as well as with the comment by William Gay about Tamosaitis's termination, which he wrote in an email of July 5, 2010: "This action was initiated by Dale Knudsen [sic] probably not knowing the sensitivity."

A July 28 email string between Russo and several of his senior Bechtel colleagues further revealed the extent to which Bechtel and DOE coordinated Tamosaitis's dismissal from the project and their subsequent PR posture about it. Russo's boss, David Walker, observed that he had spoken with Ines Triay, the senior DOE official at Hanford who had originally requested Russo's transfer to the WTP. Walker said that Triay felt that the technical difficulties at the WTP as well as the investigation by the safety board would eventually be resolved. "Need to be sure 'Hill' [i.e., Capitol Hill] get covered and protect the $50 million," Walker concluded.

Russo, for his part, reported speaking with Triay, Knutson and Deputy Secretary of Energy Daniel Poneman and affirming that they understood Bechtel's handling of the Tamosaitis situation, though they weren't happy with URS. "DOE can't be seen as involved," he added.

On July 24, 2015, the evening before my boat trip on the Columbia River, I met Donna Busche at the Barnard Griffin Winery in Richland. The hot, dry weather here in the rain shadow of the Cascades, combined with the long summer days and cool nights and mineral-rich loess soils along the Columbia River, produces superb wines, and vineyards have flourished there for the last thirty years—tens of thousands of acres of vineyards line the river. We drank a glass of big, bruising Cabernet Sauvignon. Then we drank another.

Tom Carpenter calls Busche a "force of nature," and I see why. She is a compact, muscular woman of fifty-two, with bright, wavy, stainless-steel-colored hair cut in a bob, restless green eyes and a nonstop verbal ebullience, which she attributes to her maternal relatives, from Perugia in central Italy. (Perhaps her precision and toughness come from her father, who was Czech, though she can't say for sure, because she never met him.) She was raised on the Gulf Coast of Texas, and earned her nuclear engineering degree at Texas A&M, and her accent strengthens as the wine takes hold. She seems to be enjoying herself even when she describes her five years of whistleblowing and the vicious retaliation she's had to endure at Hanford. Things have finally started to go her way.

Busche joined URS and went to work on the WTP in March 2009, shortly before Walt Tamosaitis was removed from the project. She was the manager of environmental and nuclear safety, one of a small group of "listed personnel" who could not be fired without explicit DOE approval. She reported to William Gay, the senior URS manager who was also Walt Tamosaitis's boss. Her job was to ensure, on behalf of the contractors and the DOE, that every procedure performed and piece of equipment installed at the WTP met the stringent technical, safety and environmental requirements for nuclear facilities set by federal and state law. She also had to maintain exhaustive documentation for every aspect of the WTP, verifying its compliance with nuclear and environmental safety standards. At first, when she found a problem, she felt that she was able to raise and resolve it with Bechtel, URS and the DOE, just as her job required. In early 2010, however, with the arrival of Frank Russo and the major management changes at the plant, the support for her work disappeared. "Within weeks, the focus at the WTP shifted from nuclear and environmental safety compliance to meeting deadlines at all costs, regardless of quality or safety," she remembers. "At that point, I stopped being a valued team member, and became a roadblock to be overcome in whatever way necessary."

Managers from Bechtel and URS began ignoring or circumventing her directives, or simply refusing to comply with them. During the fateful "Choke on the Cherries Meeting" on June 30, 2010, she saw how dysfunctional the workplace had grown. She recalls the tension in the room as Tamosaitis, exhausted after working a series of sixteen-hour days to prepare for the meeting, engaged in an escalating argument with Garth Duncan about his two lists of unresolved technical problems. She remembers Barbara Ruskinko's comment to Walt Tamosaitis not as a veiled threat, but an attempt to ease the mood at a stormy meeting with a touch of irony.

"Walt and Garth were just going at it—there was a whole lot of testosterone flying around that room. And I said to myself, 'Oh well, we're not getting anything done today.'" To pass the time, she picked up one of Tamosaitis's lists. The ongoing squabble faded rapidly into the background of her consciousness. "I just sat there dumbfounded. I thought to myself, 'Holy crap! This project is way, *way* worse than I thought.'" She read the other list and saw more problems. The seriousness of the technical concerns that Tamosaitis and his team had raised meant that Busche, as manager of environmental and nuclear safety, was legally obligated to conduct a thorough "hazards review." After Tamosaitis and Duncan had finished arguing, Busche said this to the assembled managers at the meeting. Rusinko agreed, so long as the review remained "quick and short." Actually, Busche countered, to be effective, her review would need to be long and extensive. Rusinko repeated, "Make it quick and short." A few days later, after Tamosaitis had been banished to his basement purgatory in Richland, Bechtel technical director Greg Ashley told her that now that Tamosaitis had been removed from the project, she no longer needed to do a hazards review on his lists of concerns. Busche disagreed.

She explained her position to me like this: "If you're an executive, your job is to bring in quarterly earnings. But for me it's different. I hold a professional engineering license, which legally obligates me to investigate certain things. By signing some documents, like environmental dangerous waste permits, I'm personally certifying that the procedure is safe, under penalty of jail. I'm not going to jail just because some idiot manager is in a hurry!" She looked at me sharply, as if I had suggested otherwise. "Also, Rule 10 CFR 820 concerning DOE nuclear activities says that if you know something, you have to report it. Procedural Rule ten, Part eight-twenty, of the Code of Federal Regulations," she repeated, as if explaining something to a slow learner. "Like I say, I'm a rules girl."

She sat back, sipped wine. "Look," she said, breathing out, "I have an affinity with black-and-white situations. I'm uncomfortable with gray areas. So there was really no choice for me. And besides"—here she shrugged and looked wonderingly skyward—"you just can't light up the desert with radioactive waste. It's not okay. *It's . . . just . . . not . . . okay.*"

From that moment on, Busche experienced the same kinds of workplace retaliation as Tamosaitis had. Fellow managers countermanded her safety and compliance orders, bosses publicly berated her. She had already seen, earlier in her career, how contractors and DOE staff could treat a "rules girl." In 1998, while working for a contractor at Rocky Flats, a former nuclear weapons production area being cleaned up by DOE and private contractors, she says that she was directed by Shirley Olinger, a DOE official at the facility, to change the radiological consequences in a safety analysis. Busche objected that in order to do this, by law she would first have to update the safety analysis documentation, to explain why the nuclear control strategy had changed; according to court papers, "Ms. Olinger insisted that Busche implement the directed change without any technical justification," which Busche saw as a violation of a nuclear safety requirement. She reported this incident to senior DOE management at the site, and soon after learned from her contracting supervisor that Olinger wanted to have her removed from the project. (She left Rocky Flats soon after.) Similarly, Busche was working as chief nuclear engineer and manager of nuclear safety at the Waste Isolation Pilot Plant in Carlsbad, New Mexico, in June 2008, when a drum of transuranic waste arrived at the facility that was more radioactive than the facility was allowed to accept, requiring her and colleagues to file a technical safety requirement violation report. About three months later, she says, she was asked by senior DOE manager Dave Moody and senior URS manager Farok Sharif to rescind this report. When she refused, she was removed from her position and reassigned to Hanford.

Shortly after Walt Tamosaitis wrote his letter to the DNFSB, the board subpoenaed Busche to testify at its October 2010 hearings. Here, she says, the DOE turned on her once again. Her testimony contradicted the department's stated position concerning risk analysis, as well as statements by DOE, Bechtel and URS managers about the risk of hydrogen explosions at the WTP, and the likely dose of radiation that would be released in the event of an accident at the facility. While testifying, she used a system of note cards to communicate with her staff, who supplied details in areas where they had superior knowledge. Busche says that Shirley Olinger, with whom she'd already clashed at Rocky Flats back in 1998 and who was now the DOE site manager at Hanford, began censoring the note cards Busche received from her staff. After the first day of testimony before the safety board, in a room filled with URS employees, Busche remembers, the DOE's assistant secretary for environmental management, Ines Triay, publicly criticized her for her testimony, saying that if her "intent was to piss people off, [she] did a very good job." (The following day, Busche says, both Frank Russo of Bechtel and William Gay of URS asked her if she could "provide a different answer" to questions she'd answered during the hearing, which she understood to be a request to change her testimony. She refused.)

After the hearings, retaliation intensified. URS and Bechtel employees began to circumvent her and work directly with her subordinates. Her URS boss, Mike Coyle, told her to stop putting technical and safety issues in writing to him, and only to report them verbally, evidently to avoid written records that would require remedial action. In July 2011, a consultant hired by URS, John Parker Stewart, interviewed Busche about her work at the WTP, and questioned forty of her co-workers about her behavior. Stewart's notes, obtained in discovery, consisted of five pages of bullet points teeming with scare quotes, exclamation points and underscores, evidently compiled as a laundry list of criticism for her employer to use against her. His observations about Busche include:

- Must never manage others!! (This is imperative!)
- Must be in control of everything—always!
- Shames, belittles, demeans her own people constantly—especially in open meetings.
- Has positioned herself to be a literal bottleneck of all processes for the project.
- She reminds one of J. Edgar Hoover in her sociopathic paranoia—having meticulous records & files on "everyone."
- She relishes control, authority & power.

Stewart also alluded to Busche's difficult childhood, her love of her stepgrandchildren, and her desire to remain in the Tri-Cities area. He closed with a series of recommendations:

- She must be removed ASAP from her current position.
- She must not be in a position of supervising anyone.
- She must not work at Hanford.
- She must have no authority.
- The status quo is not an option. She is a lit fuse that could explode at any moment. (A second whistleblower incident could shut down WTP—a disaster for URS!)
- Money alone is not a motivator. She cannot be bought.
- Strong males trigger her & arm her for battle. Weaker males she walks on. She trusts no one except her husband. (Her early life explains why.)
- Her version of her sense of honor, purpose & integrity are essential to satisfy/ placate her.

Like many whistleblowers, and would-be whistlers who never actually blow, Donna Busche realized she had reached the moment of truth or silence. "I'd seen what happened to Walt. I knew that speaking out would be the death of my career. I just didn't want to make the decision." She consulted a former boss, a distinguished veteran of the nuclear Navy. "Without telling me what to do, he reminded me that my job was to hold the line—to hold it firm." Many days she came home from work emotionally exhausted. One evening, she walked into the house and burst into tears. Her husband, Jim, handed her a double Crown Royal whiskey and said, "Look, you're not a crier. You need to shit or get off the pot. Just do the right thing."

"Jim has been a trooper throughout this whole process," Busche says. "He's been my guardian angel. Because that's another angle of the personal side of being a whistleblower: bad stuff doesn't happen just to you. Everybody in my inner sanctum has to live this hell." In the end, she called Tom Carpenter, hired a lawyer, and filed a lawsuit with the Department of Labor against URS and Bechtel, under a law that prohibits retaliation against whistleblowers in the nuclear industry.

Retaliation continued nonetheless: exclusion from meetings, a corrective action letter, an employee concern investigation, written warnings from bosses about her "performance issues" and her failure to complete actions on time. She persisted in identifying serious problems with key aspects of WTP, and with the documentation that certified the plant's quality and safety. These were ignored by her colleagues, who instead, in a report to DOE and other Hanford stakeholders, blamed Busche herself for the safety problems at the WTP. In February 2014, she was fired for what the company called "unprofessional conduct."

Nevertheless, bad news about the WTP continued to roll in for the DOE and its contractors. It became increasingly clear that the fundamental technological flaws identified by Donald Alexander, Walt Tamosaitis, Gary Brunson, Donna Busche and others, far from being chimeras invented by disgruntled employees, were serious technological roadblocks that might halt the entire project or cause it to malfunction once complete. Moreover, since Donna Busche's work of documenting quality standards at the WTP had been stonewalled for months, the plant's quality was now "indeterminate"—contractors could not demonstrate that their designs or materials were to code for high-level radioactive waste. An anonymous whistleblower sent Carpenter a confidential draft report on the Low-Activity Waste Facility, a major processing area of the WTP, prepared by a panel of external experts, which identified 362 design vulnerabilities that threatened to delay or derail the plant—although the DOE had recently informed the State of Washington that the facility had no known technical problems. Speaking of this unnamed whistleblower, Carpenter explains: "That person said, 'The conditions here are horrendous. Because of that, I'm making sure you have this report. But I'm terrified for my job, so I'm not going to say what my name is.'" Donna Busche agrees. "There are so many people on the inside at Hanford who have begged me to surface their issues, because they're afraid to step forward themselves. They've seen what happens to whistleblowers here. The safety culture is worse than ever."

Meanwhile, Busche and her husband and their two boxers continued to live in Richland, only three miles from the nearest Hanford facility. "I bought a house as close as I could get to Hanford, because I was so gung ho and committed to the project," she recalls at the winery. "So now I live in a neighborhood with four Bechtel employees, three Aecom people, all the other contractors. One of the people I fought with every day at work lives three doors down, another lives just around the corner. I'm on the Columbia River, and there's a river trail where I bump into those people every day when I go running." She turns up her Texas drawl. "'How y'all doin'?' I say. 'I'm doin' great,' they say.

"A few people thank you, say they're glad you did this, that you're making this a better place. But a whole lot of people give you the visceral, angry treatment. My husband gets shunned at the country club; some of his friends are downright nasty to him. It's like I'm somehow impacting their livelihood by reporting serious safety violations. They seem to be saying, 'What's wrong with her? Why is she doing this? She had a great job, and then she stopped the money. And why is she trying to screw with my cushy job at Hanford?' I feel like saying, 'Uuuh, you do understand that the plant was not being built safely, right? Are you really asking me that question?' They're just following the contractor's press releases, which say, 'Take your news from us: that Vit Plant [another name for the WTP] is gonna work someday.' Well, no it's not. That plant is an embarrassment to the Department of Energy. It is very broken, and I live here. Here's the only thing that allows me to sleep at night: They're so incompetent that the plant won't ever operate. So it won't blow up."

After she spoke out at Hanford and was fired by URS, Busche's job prospects dried up. Successful female nuclear engineers were in short supply: before blowing the whistle, she had regularly received calls from headhunters. Afterward, the calls stopped. She contacted a former colleague at Fluor, where she'd worked in the past, who told her frankly, "We'd love to have you here, but you chose a different path. It wouldn't be wise for us at this time." She phoned her network of friends and acquaintances in the Tri-Cities, but no openings appeared. "People generally seemed to think that, as a whistleblower, I was a troublemaker, a difficult person. 'Why hire someone like that?'" She also found that nuclear whistleblowers weren't always welcome, even in Congress. In March 2014, Missouri senator Claire McCaskill called Busche and Tamosaitis to testify on the WTP debacle, along with senior managers from Bechtel, URS and the DOE, before the Homeland Security Committee's Subcommittee on Financial and Contracting Oversight. However, the subcommittee's ranking Republican member, Senator Ron Johnson, blocked their invitation, claiming that it had come too late for the committee members to prepare—a transparent favor to the contractors and the DOE, who were able to speak unrebutted by the people who had revealed their fraud, waste and abuse. Bechtel's steady attention to "the Hill," its relentless lobbying and campaign contributions and messaging through its DOE surrogates, had apparently paid off again.

"McCaskill set up a 'non-hearing hearing' with Walt and me, before the real hearing with the contractors," Busche remembers. "So we got to fly out to Washington, DC, on our own dime, and talk to each other for a while, which was quite an honor. But I did learn another lesson in just how broken the system is for whistleblowers. While I was speaking, there was a wall of suits behind me—you can see them on C-SPAN. Those are the thousand-dollar-an-hour boys retained by Bechtel and URS. Who pays them? The DOE does. Meaning, the taxpayer does—you and I do. The DOE refunds contractors for their legal expenses against me, using my tax dollars." She shakes her head, and starts looking for a waiter to bring another glass of wine. "If I ever manage to get a settlement out of these guys," she says, as she cranes her neck and gestures, "I'll be sending a big chunk of it back, by writing a fat check to the IRS."

Senator McCaskill expressed outrage at this state of affairs in a letter to Secretary of Energy Moniz, pointing out that the DOE might be incentivizing contractors to engage in protracted litigation against whistleblowers by picking up their legal bills. Subsequent research by McCaskill's staff revealed that, merely to prepare for the 2014 hearing with McCaskill, the contractors had racked up $650,000 in legal fees, and that they'd already spent 3.5 million taxpayer dollars fighting Tamosaitis and Busche in court. But Donna Busche saw a deeper dodge. "In preparing for my trial, I FOIA'd a lot of documents. What I found out is that the clause about DOE paying the contractors' legal fees is actually in the federal acquisition regulation. Everyone on that stage was acting like it's a big surprise: 'What do you mean, it's in the contract? What do you mean, we pay those fees?' But Senator McCaskill isn't stupid. Her staff would have told her that. So I say, 'Shame on you, Senator McCaskill, for farcin' that crap!'"

What happened—and continues to happen—at the WTP is a scene that has repeated itself countless times in countless DOE facilities, part of an MO that has made billions for major government contractors like Bechtel, while fleecing taxpayers and leaving serious nuclear threats unresolved. Anyone who really believes that private sector entities are more efficient and trustworthy than government agencies should take a careful look at the WTP, and at Hanford in general. "I can tell you from the training I got when I was a young corporate wannabe, at Fluor, and then at URS," Donna Busche says. "These big contractors all have the same business model. They always go after large DOE and DOD contracts, because those mean steady earnings per share. Instead of a standard construction job where you go and build a strip mall, which you know will be a $4 million and eighteen-month thing, these contracts are huge. They last ten years, you have zero capital investment, and you get to bill the government overhead, which gives you seed money to go out and bid new jobs. Anybody else, even a Microsoft, has capital costs, the cost of doing business, but not if you have these big contracts. From the corporate standpoint, when you're publicly traded, this is exactly the business model you want. What this has bred over time is that you literally don't have to perform, and you still get paid. So everybody's salary gets paid, their bonuses get paid. They may get a little less award fee if they do a bad job, but the stuff they report to Wall Street still gets taken care of. They're excellent at what they've done. They've learned how to be the corporate welfare of America—and they convince themselves it's okay! They're like China: they're playing the long game. They probably already have their next $30 billion project lined up. And if they get hit with an occasional fine or lawsuit, they just charge it to their shareholders, or build it into their unit rates, which you can never see, and just steal it back. You don't even know."

Ultimately, she says, contractor executives are playing a game that is scored exclusively in dollars. "These people are very enamored with their financial status, and so is everyone they spend time with—they're enamored with big money. So a little city manager who's got a part-time gig and works at Hanford is thrilled when they get to say, 'I'm hanging out with the board of directors.' It's a joke! I'm like, these people put their pants on one leg at a time, just like you do. But no, they're glamoured by the money. Our whole society is like that. Who thinks the Kardashians are news? They aren't news, they're sad. But our whole society holds these people in high regard, just because they can sing. And some of them can't even sing."

Hanford is the perfect crime, a self-licking ice cream cone of military-industrial-congressional corruption, a fraud so immaculate that the regulators help you to commit it, the taxpayers pay your legal bills, and the DOJ is on your side. Hanford showcases all of the dynamics of corruption that we've observed, grown rank in the hothouse of Cold War secrecy that's been obsolete for thirty years. Here we see financial managers who hold sway over nuclear scientists and engineers, gobbling up milestone payments rather than doing the work right, or doing the work at all. We see hundreds of human lives harmed in the tank farms, human lives endangered in the millions by the threat of a nuclear disaster that could taint the whole upper left-hand corner of the United States. Yet despite decades of human harm, waste, fraud and abuse, Hanford's culture of impunity remains intact, because the would-be regulators at the DOE and the EPA, but also at the state and local levels, are part of the game, and look silently away as the billions roll into the Tri-Cities, a river of money as broad and deep as the Columbia, flowing into an ocean of taxpayer trillions swallowed by the Bechtels and the Lockheeds of our land year on year, decade after decade. *Our* trillions, that should be spent to clean up the waste at Hanford, but also to cure our sick, teach our children, feed our hungry, pave our streets. Trillions that slip, instead, into the pockets of corrupt contractor millionaires and their government accomplices, because there are too many deal makers and team players and too few whistleblowers, too many wolves and sheep and not enough sheepdogs.

The same ugly pattern has recurred at Hanford for generations, and when a rare whistleblower dares to name it, the contractors lie to the press about him, lie to investigators, lie under oath to the courts and to Congress, knowing that the DOE and the DOJ have their backs, nobody will check their lies, and even if they do, ultimately nobody will punish them. They lie and they lie, until, at a silent signal that all players in the game understand, they settle the charges, cut a check, and move on, writing off the settlement charge against their taxes and billing legal costs to the government, or building it all into their next fraudulent government contract. Because one thing is certain: the fraud will go on. The DOE will continue to sign contracts with the same contractors and do their bidding, pretending to regulate while aiding and abetting, swearing zero tolerance for whistleblower retaliation while whispering their names to the contractors, laughing behind their hands while whistleblowers twist in the wind. Congress holds hearings, shows its outrage at the behavior of the contractors and their government facilitators, yet Congress continues to send them our billions, because a goodly portion of those billions are kicked back to Congress as campaign contributions, votes, nuclear pork.

Meanwhile, as the money disappears and no cleanup happens at Hanford, the clock is ticking. Each day, every hour that passes, radioactive waste seeps deeper into the soil beneath the tank farms, poisons more groundwater, taints the Columbia, sweeps into the Pacific. The World War II–era buildings crumble under their own weight and radiation, pipes and valves and motors and compressors run to failure; hydrogen gathers in headspaces. Report after report is written, by the GAO, by teams of outside experts, by the DOE's inspector general, by federal and state investigators. *Train Wreck Along the River of Money* was written in 1995, by Steven Blush and Thomas Heitman, two experienced former DOE officials charged by Congress to tell the truth about Hanford. Their detailed, scathing report brings no significant change, save for Blush and Heitman, who as a reward for their honesty are blackballed from future work in nuclear energy. More reports are written in 2005, in 2009, in 2011, in 2013, in 2014, in 2016, in 2017, in 2018, in 2019. Reports cite one another. Journalists extract and publish a few juicy details from each. Lawsuits are filed, litigated, settled. More hearings happen on the Hill. And still the money flows.

Maybe Rick Perry, the Energy secretary appointed by Donald Trump in January 2017, was right, for once, some years back, when he said that the Department of Energy should be abolished. But this will never happen. As Voltaire said of God, if the DOE didn't exist, the contractors would have to invent it, since a more effective way of moving our money into their pockets is hard to imagine. Contracts like the WTP are written by experienced managers and skilled lawyers, with a deep understanding of organizational behavior and of the political currents that run between Washington, DC, and Washington state. In a variation of the financial engineering that Ernie Fitzgerald saw Lockheed perform with the C-5A and that Lockheed continues today with the F-35, the salaries of many federal, state and local government employees at Hanford are paid by the prime contractor, which creates a strong sense of team: if that contractor gets fired, everyone's money stops coming. Of the $690 million allocated each year to build the WTP, $125 million goes to the Office of River Protection, the DOE body that specializes in the Hanford cleanup. Part of that $125 million, in turn, gets peeled off and passed to the Washington State Department of Ecology, also responsible for overseeing the WTP. "You have all this incestuous bullshit going on at the WTP, where the very survival of these federal bureaucracies depends on Bechtel getting that money," Busche tells me during our conversation at the winery. "That's broke! If you ever set up a system to absolutely fail, that's the one."

So perhaps it's not surprising that, after Hanford Challenge issued a formal "stop work" call to the DOE in November 2015 to prevent further waste, fraud and construction of potentially dangerous engineering works at the WTP, no state or local official applauded. "We got several encouraging phone calls and emails saying, 'Thank God someone said it, this stuff clearly needs to stop,'" Tom Carpenter remembers. "But officially, in public, there was silence from the state bureaucracy about what we'd said—dead silence. I mean, they know that there are serious problems, dangerous problems, and they agree with us that those problems need to be fixed. They also agree with what we've done to fix them. But ultimately, they don't want us airing Hanford's dirty laundry, because it might actually sink into Congress's ears that they shouldn't be funding this place, and that's what they're terrorized about: that the spigot would get shut off. It's not just federal officials, it's state and local officials as well. They don't like people criticizing the contractors too vocally, because it might shut off the money."

The revolving door, though nailed shut for Walt Tamosaitis and Donna Busche, continues whirling for people at Hanford who play the game. An insider described it to me like this:

When DOE people at Hanford retire, some go to work for contractors, but a lot more become consultants, and work alongside the very same contractors they've been regulating while at DOE, running interference with their buddies still at

DOE. They're allowed to do that, the day after they retire from the Department. And if anyone at DOE gives them shit, they tell that person, "Look at me, what am I making? Well let me tell you what I'm making—I'm making $8,940 today. And you? You're making a hundred bucks today, maybe two hundred, right? Guess who gets this kind of job? People who play fair with the contractors. I'm not saying that you shouldn't be a hard-ass and catch them when they've done wrong, that's not my suggestion at all. It's just, play fair. The contractors appreciate that." So, if you want a consulting or contracting job at five, ten times the salary that you were making at DOE, you'd better have been nice when you were the DOE person regulating them, or you can kiss that job goodbye. This explains why the DOE is the way it is. Because the contractors know how to reward people, they're vicious, and you always know the DOE brown-nosers who are going to leave their jobs one day, and show up with these contractors the next morning.

The website of Independent Strategic Management Solutions, a Richland-based consulting company that specializes in nuclear engineering and environmental cleanup, teems with former federal and state employees connected with Hanford who are now offering their services to Hanford contractors. These include former DOE managers Dana Bryson, Keith Christopher and Mark Steelman; Nick Ceto, the former head of the Hanford EPA office; Jane Hedges, the former director of the Washington State Department of Ecology; and Debra McBaugh, who worked for the Washington State Department of Health. Last but not least there's Ines Triay, former senior DOE official who played a prominent role in Walt Tamosaitis's and Donna Busche's whistleblowing cases, and whose CV on the site praises how she "defended and acquired $6B in additional funding" for environmental remediation, which resulted in cleanup work that "was accomplished years ahead of schedule and millions of dollars under budget." Founder and president of Independent Strategic Management Solutions is Shirley Olinger, the former DOE site manager (a role her husband also held) who came into conflict with Donna Busche both at Rocky Flats and at Hanford.

Some people dispense with the revolving doors and simply work on both sides of the public-private divide simultaneously. Consider, for instance, Larry Haler, a

Washington state representative who has worked for Fluor, Westinghouse, Rockwell and other Hanford contractors for forty years; at the same time, between 1990 and 2004, he was the mayor or a councilman of the city of Richland. Haler regularly praises Hanford contractors, and downplays problems on the site. (To his credit, Haler recently authored a law to provide compensation for Hanford workers harmed by chemical exposure and, in testimony before the Washington legislature, deplored the lack of a safety culture among Hanford contractors.) Or take Sharon Brown, a Washington state senator for the district that includes the Tri-Cities, who also works for a Hanford subcontractor, and who was instrumental, behind the scenes, in killing the worker health law that Larry Haler had introduced. "Brown epitomizes the undue influence of Hanford on policy in the most gross and direct of ways," one Hanford veteran told me.

It's easy to guess what public servants with private ties to contractors might think of Hanford whistleblowers, but one recent case provides a clear answer. For seven of his ten years as mayor of Kennewick, Steve Young also worked as vice president of Mission Support Alliance (MSA), a Hanford contractor founded by Lockheed and run by other military-industrial-complex players that holds a $3 billion contract with the DOE. In 2013, Julie Atwood, a manager at MSA, was forced to resign after she told company investigators looking into Young's work habits that he regularly performed mayoral duties while in his office at the company, and that he'd created a hostile work environment for women. The day she left, Atwood was put through the usual whistleblower perp walk, pushing her belongings past her former colleagues on a wheelchair. She was later blacklisted by other Hanford contractors, because MSA spread the false rumor that she'd committed accounting fraud. In 2015 she filed a whistleblower retaliation lawsuit against the company; in October 2017, a jury awarded her $8.1 million in damages from her former employer and found that Steve Young had aided and abetted the company's wrongdoing. Young testified at the trial that his being mayor was a significant advantage to both the company and the DOE, and that he actively lobbied in Washington, DC, to bring more money to Hanford. Jack Sheridan, Atwood's lawyer, commented, "Young was so valuable to MSA and to the DOE that when they perceived that Julie had focused a spotlight on him with her report to the investigators, MSA took immediate action to terminate her." (Young later resigned from MSA and stepped down as mayor, though he remains on the Kennewick city council. He and MSA are appealing the 2017 verdict.)

Culturally as well as technically, the DOE is one of the most radically captured of all government agencies—so captured that they often don't even bother to pretend otherwise. DOE officials colluded with Bechtel and URS managers to muzzle and fire Walt Tamosaitis. The Energy secretary met personally with six whistle-blowers in Richland and announced the department's "zero tolerance" rule for whistleblower retaliation, but didn't lift a finger when five of the six were terminated. The DOE's only apparent action in Donna Busche's case was to open a special investigation of her firing, during which Bechtel and URS, citing attorney-client privilege, refused to supply DOE inspector general Gregory Friedman with several thousand documents and emails, to which he was entitled according to the terms of their contracts with DOE. After a brief tussle, the DOE and its inspector general gave up. Nothing happened to the contractors. Nothing ever does.

In 2016, after Tamosaitis's and Busche's cases had gained widespread attention, Senators Ron Wyden and Claire McCaskill ordered the GAO to scrutinize the anti-whistleblower culture at Hanford and other nuclear weapons facilities. GAO investigators questioned Sandra Black, director of the Employee Concerns Program at Savannah River Nuclear Solutions, a government contractor at the plutonium production and research facility in South Carolina where Tamosaitis once worked. Soon after, Black was fired, allegedly for speaking with the GAO. Even Wyden, who has defended nuclear energy whistleblowers for decades, seemed shaken. "We thought that we had seen it all," he said at a July 2016 news conference at which he presented the GAO report. "Today, however, it seems that there's a whole new precedent. We're talking about a contractor who was retaliated against for actually helping government auditors investigate retaliation against whistleblowers. . . . It's clear that DOE contractors are going to go to amazing lengths to send a signal to their employees that when you blow the whistle, it is going to be the end of your career." (In February 2017, Savannah River was ordered to reinstate Black and pay her $371,776 in damages.)

Beginning in 2004, under the administration of contracting and outsourcing promoter George W. Bush, America's nuclear weapons research and production complex, which in addition to Hanford includes three national laboratories (Los Alamos National Laboratory, Lawrence Livermore National Laboratory and Sandia National Laboratories) and weapon production and testing facilities (Savannah River Site, Y-12 National Security Complex, Pantex, Kansas City Plant and the Nevada National Security Site), was privatized, shifting decades of scientific research and countless billions of dollars of public resources into corporate hands. Like Hanford, these facilities became "GoCos"—government owned, contractor run. At each site, the contractors who assumed control promised that their private management would significantly reduce costs and improve efficiency. The results, as at Hanford, have been the reverse.

And no wonder. Each of the contractors in charge—Bechtel, Aecom, CH2M Hill, Fluor, Lockheed, Northrop Grumman, Honeywell and Babcock & Wilcox—has a long history of defrauding the DOE and looting tax dollars. POGO's online Federal Contractor Misconduct Database identifies the overall leader as Lockheed, which, as of 2017, held over $51 billion in government contracts, eighty-six instances of wrongdoing and total penalties of $768 million since 1995. Bechtel ranks eighth in contracts, with $453 million in penalties. Aecom is in twelfth place, with $264 million in penalties. Babcock & Wilcox, Honeywell, Fluor and Rockwell are all there, too. And of course, the reported fines represent only the frauds, waste and abuses that were discovered and successfully litigated. As a New York farmer once told me about rats, so, too, for contractor fraud: for every one you see in daylight, there are another five hundred gnawing away in the dark of your granary. Nevertheless, the DOE, the department's semiautonomous National Nuclear Security Administration (NNSA), Congress and the American people continue to allow these corporations to run these vital, valuable, extremely dangerous facilities, where they transparently pursue not the national interest but their own profit.

Hanford-style boondoggles, waste and outright fraud are common at all of the other nuclear facilities that the DOE oversees. At Savannah River, the Mixed Oxide (MOX) Fuel Fabrication Facility was originally expected to cost $1.4 billion and be completed in 2004. The budget rapidly ballooned to $17.2 billion, while the expected completion date slid to 2048. In 2016, the DOE proposed to cancel the MOX program, but was stymied by advocates in Congress, particularly South Carolina senator Lindsey Graham, who authored legislation that required the DOE to continue building the MOX facility. Finally, in late 2018, after consuming about $7.6 billion, the unfinished project was terminated. The Y-12 facility in Oak Ridge, Tennessee, run by Bechtel, Booz Allen and others, boasts the Uranium Processing Facility (UPF), whose original price tag skyrocketed thirty-two-fold, from $600 million to as much as $19 billion, before the project was abandoned as technologically obsolete. The security system at Y-12 was so advanced that, in 2012, an eighty-two-year-old nun and two other antinuclear activists cut through fences, skirted sensors and cameras, and entered a storage facility containing bomb-grade uranium, which they spray painted with antiwar slogans and festooned with crime-scene tape. What a team of technically savvy terrorists or criminals might have done in their place doesn't bear thinking about.

The nuclear laboratories are likewise the scene of gargantuan contractor-led swindles. When Livermore Labs was privatized under Frank Russo's supervision, members of the management consortium (which include Bechtel and Aecom) promised all of the familiar benefits of private sector management: increased efficiency, transparency and contractor accountability, leveraging industry expertise, and above all, cost reductions. In reality, scientific productivity and morale at Livermore are widely reported to be in free fall, while management costs have increased by $40 million annually. "The privatization of Livermore created the Holy Grail of unaccountable profiteering," write Roger Logan and Jeffrey Colvin, former and current scientists at the laboratory. "Not just a for-profit monopoly, but a taxpayer-funded for-profit monopoly. If ever there was a case of privatization gone bad, this is it."

Los Alamos National Laboratory, also run by Bechtel and Aecom, has seen a similar trend; its director, who earned $348,000 before the privatization, now makes $1.5 million. But Los Alamos has experienced far more tangible problems as well. In February 2014, a fifty-five-gallon drum of transuranic waste caught fire and exploded in an underground repository, contaminating twenty-two workers with radiation, and shutting the only US deep geologic disposal site for nuclear waste for the foreseeable future. Repairs are expected to cost $550 million. According to a DOE report, the accident occurred because contractors changed the waste disposal procedures without following department guidelines (instead of the inert clay they should by protocol have used to pack the radioactive material, they'd substituted cat litter), and failed to ensure that these procedures were properly documented, reviewed and approved—the same problems, among others, that Donna Busche reported at the WTP. In a highly unusual show of character, the DOE called this fiasco a "first-degree performance failure" and reduced the incentive it paid to Bechtel, Aecom and the other members of their merry band from the $63.4 million they expected to earn to a measly $6.25 million.

Contractors caused a massive radiation accident through gross error, which harmed workers and will cost taxpayers at least half a billion dollars to fix. So why is the DOE still paying them? Why not charge them the $550 million repair costs instead, and add a massive fine for misconduct? What about investigating them criminally and civilly, and throwing the responsible managers in jail? But this is not the department's style. "There has been little accountability for literally hundreds of fiascos and goofball management decisions," observes Greg Mello, a hydrogeologist and former hazardous waste engineer for the New Mexico Environment Department, who has scrutinized operations at Los Alamos since 1984. "A lot of people can get rich while doing very little work at a federal nuclear weapons laboratory."

The DOE site manager at Los Alamos until shortly before the explosion occurred was Kevin Smith. Smith was promoted to a new post: head of the DOE's Office of River Protection at Hanford, which oversees the Waste Treatment Plant and the 56 million gallons of high-level nuclear waste in the tank farm. At Hanford he instituted an aggressive lockdown on information, presided over continuing worker harm in the tank farms and created one of the most chilled environments against whistleblowers that longtime Hanford observers can remember. Smith retired in late 2017, but the chilled environment persists—and silencing whistleblowers in nuclear facilities is widely recognized in the industry as an effective way to cause nuclear accidents.

Of the many contractors in the nuclear power, weapons and cleanup business that dupe the US government, the DOE and the American taxpayer, Bechtel is the most experienced. What Walt Tamosaitis and Donna Busche saw the company do, and what the company did to them, it has done many times before in its storied history, at Hanford and elsewhere.

To see just how well established the routine of financialism, contract "nourishment" and whistleblower retaliation is at Bechtel, and how the three processes reinforce one another, let's return to March 28, 1979, and America's first major nuclear accident, the partial meltdown of a reactor at Three Mile Island. Bechtel was chosen to conduct the cleanup operation. At the time, Bechtel had been a powerhouse in Washington, DC, for decades, having built major railroads, pipelines, refineries and dams, and then Liberty ships during World War II. Its president, Stephen Bechtel Sr., and his close business ally John McCone played golf with Eisenhower during and after the war—their company would almost certainly have been one whose "unwarranted influence" over government he had in mind when he made his military-industrial-complex speech in 1961—and had pioneered the cost-plus contract. McCone, who later led the CIA, described their government contracts in a 1943 interview with *Fortune* magazine: "Every six months, we estimate how much work we expect to do in the next six months and then we get a fee of five percent of the estimated amount of work regardless of how much work we actually do turn out."

After the war, the company continued with engineering megaprojects, now including nuclear reactors. By the time Reagan was elected in 1981, Bechtel had begun securing major contracts with the newly created DOE to clean up the nation's nuclear weapons sites. Reagan named former Bechtel managers to key positions in his cabinet: George Shultz, president of Bechtel, became secretary of state; Caspar Weinberger (he of the $640 toilet seat), Bechtel vice president and general counsel, was named secretary of defense; and W. Kenneth Davis, the company's vice president for nuclear development, became deputy secretary of the DOE (and the de facto head of the department). Not surprisingly, Bechtel secured the

$1.5 billion contract with the DOE to fix Three Mile Island. Two other organizations were present on the site—General Public Utilities, the operator of the plant, and the NRC, which was formally required to review and approve every phase of the cleanup—but Bechtel became the unquestioned leader of the project. Since the Three Mile Island disaster hurt the public image of civilian nuclear power, an industry that had become a major profit center for Bechtel, the company was determined to complete the cleanup as swiftly as possible.

Bechtel's senior startup engineer on the site was Rick Parks, who began work at Three Mile Island in 1982. As with Donna Busche at Hanford forty years later, Parks's job was to ensure that all work performed during the cleanup followed strict protocols prescribed by the NRC for the nuclear industry. He reported to Larry King, director of site operations, and worked alongside Ed Gischel, plant engineering director. Parks had distinguished himself in the nuclear Navy, where he graduated near the top of his class and then served as an instructor. Born and raised in Qulin, a poor village in rural southeast Missouri, he speaks with a deep country accent and a flow of obscenities one often hears among military veterans. When he started at Three Mile Island he was thirty-two, a hard-charging executive in what seemed to him a thrilling new industry of the future. Despite the partial meltdown, he remained a believer in atomic energy. "I thought at the time that nuclear power was the answer to all of America's energy needs. To me, the production of power and the operation of nuclear reactors—it was kinda Buck Rogers stuff. I wanted to be part of it. That job with Bechtel was a dream job for me. My career was really taking off. I loved the people I was working with, I loved the work." Parks also needed this job: his ex-wife had recently died in a car accident, leaving him to raise their five- and nine-year-old sons alone. "When I was young and dumb and full of cum, money drove most of my decisions. But when the boys' mother died, that really made me think about things differently. When I was responsible for them, it quit being so much the pursuit of money, and instead became trying to find a stable environment for them."

Despite his original enthusiasm, Parks soon began to notice problems in the work culture at Three Mile Island. First, he says, Bechtel seemed to be trying to extract maximum profit from each task. "Everything was about money. It wasn't about hurrying up and getting stuff done, it was more like 'How much can we milk out of this?'" When the money that the DOE had allotted for a given phase of the job ran out, however, the mood changed. "The only time it became a hurry was when they'd spent all the money and had not accomplished the milestone objective. So you couldn't get more money until you had that little tick mark, saying, 'Okay, this objective is completed.'"

Instead of creating an integrated, global plan for the project, the DOE contract established a series of achievement milestones along a tight timeline. DOE would only disburse money for the next milestone once the previous milestone had been completed. When a milestone loomed, Parks watched the company rush to meet objectives and collect fees, often by cutting corners on NRC procedures, following streamlined corporate procedures instead. "There seemed to be a marked tendency to bypass the administrative procedures that had been developed to ensure against mishaps," observes Stephen Unger, an industrial engineer who later analyzed the problems with the Three Mile Island cleanup. "While strict adherence to such procedures may seem to be a picayune matter, in a complex system such as a nuclear power plant, seemingly minor errors can have drastic consequences." Corner cutting became so commonplace that Parks, like his boss Larry King and his colleague Ed Gischel, believed that the NRC was tacitly approving them, out of deference to Bechtel. Although the three men saw that they were being circumvented on significant decisions, they still felt legally and ethically responsible for the outcomes of those decisions.

The decisive—and most dangerous—phase of the cleanup, the head lift, was swiftly approaching. During this procedure, the reactor vessel would be opened, and its contents, about 200 tons of highly radioactive fuel rods and debris from the meltdown, would be removed. Bechtel's plan was to use the facility's polar crane, the enormous four-legged lifting device housed inside the reactor building, to lift away the 150-ton steel reactor head and the four 40-ton concrete "missile shields" that covered the vessel. But the crane hadn't been used since the 1979 meltdown, and Parks, King and Gischel all feared it had been damaged during the incident; if the crane failed during the head lift, it might drop a heavy load into the vessel and cause another nuclear disaster. (In a later affidavit, Gischel stated his belief that such an accident could have triggered a full meltdown, and necessitated the evacuation of New York, Philadelphia and Washington, DC.) The three men insisted that the crane be thoroughly load-tested and recertified before use, as NRC protocols required. Their Bechtel superiors argued that this was a waste of time.

Eventually Parks nixed the plan, citing, like Donna Busche, the Code of Federal Regulations. "According to 10 CFR 50.55, I had to reject it. Which I did. And man, you'd have thought I'd just raped their ten-year-old daughter. They went ballistic."

An investigator arrived from San Francisco to grill Parks about his behavior on the site and after work. "I knew the fix was in," Parks says. "I'm a dumb ol' country boy but I wasn't born stupid. Anytime they bring in a company investigator, it's to create a record that they can stand on to justify what they're about to do to you." Larry King and Ed Gischel were also investigated. King was soon accused of a conflict of interest with a consulting company he had formed, while Gischel was ordered to undergo a psychological-fitness-for-duty examination, and was later transferred to another job.

As Parks entered the plant soon after, a friend of his, Ed Kitler, told him that Bechtel was furious. "He asked me, what was I doing? Did I realize who I was messing with? Don't you know how big they are? It's like dealing with the US government. Just shut your mouth and sign off on this." Kitler, evidently not having done his homework, also warned Parks that his ex-wife had contacted Bechtel for help in gaining custody of their children. "And I'm like, 'Really? Hmmm, damn. How's she going to do that, from the grave?' I took that as a warning."

Soon after, when his van failed to start, Parks reached down beside the driver's seat for a tool kit and felt something soft and crinkly. It was a baggie of marijuana that someone had planted there. He disposed of it. The next morning, the guards at the entrance to the Three Mile Island plant subjected his van to a thorough search—something they'd never done before. "I'm thinking, 'What the hell is goin' on with me? This is like stuff you see on some cheap B-grade movie.'"

Still, Parks did not want to blow the whistle. "I finally had things set the way I wanted," he remembers. "A great job, good pay, people were happy, I was happy. I didn't want to rock the boat, hell no!" Morally as well as professionally, however, he felt he had no choice.

Parks began to copy documents, to prove the violations he was observing. He contacted GAP, a new organization he'd learned about from an antinuclear activist neighbor, and drove to Washington one Friday evening after work to meet with Tom Devine and his colleagues.

"Three things were clear immediately," Devine remembers. "First, behind his country boy mask, Rick was a strong, smart, shrewd survivor with moral values that couldn't be breached. Second, Bechtel was so threatened by him that he had to be on to something. Third, with the head lift scheduled for the following Wednesday, there was no time to lose." Over the objections of Parks, King and Gischel, Bechtel still planned to use the potentially defective crane to raise the reactor head.

With only days to go before the head lift was scheduled to be performed, Parks and Devine worked day and night through the weekend to prepare his fifty-six-page sworn affidavit, which they filed that Monday as part of a whistleblower retaliation lawsuit. They also shared the affidavit with Congress and the media; Congress announced it would hold hearings into the matter. Finally, Bechtel postponed the head lift. GAP's strategy had produced a reprieve.

When Parks returned from DC, he discovered that his apartment had been broken into. Nothing of value had been stolen—there was cash untouched on his bedside table, and his guns and television were still there—but his filing cabinet had been rifled. "That's when I sent my sons out to my brother's farm in Kansas. The more stuff happened to me, the angrier I got. I thought, 'This is bullshit. You've got me backed into a corner, and I'm gonna come out swingin'.'"

Parks contacted the FBI, and began to brief a special agent assigned to the case, explaining technical papers from the Three Mile Island cleanup that would later be used in a grand jury investigation. "I would go to his house and go over documents, and explain their significance. Because nobody was assisting them and the grand jury to understand those documents. God knows the NRC wasn't explaining what they showed. Why should they? They wanted to hang us!"

Bechtel suspended him from work. "I'd broken the unwritten law." Parks laughs.

"I was the aberrant redheaded stepchild. I'd spoken outside the company." Many other engineers at the facility agreed with his assessment of the situation, he says, but refused to speak publicly for fear of the kind of retaliation they'd already seen him, King and Gischel suffer.

Parks and King testified before the House Committee on Interior and Insular Affairs about the problems with the cleanup. Parks remembers watching Bechtel lawyers walk to various members of the committee and hand them a list of questions they wanted the congressmen to ask. One who received the list was a freshman Republican representative from Arizona, John McCain. "McCain was confrontational and aggressive in his questioning," Tom Devine remembers, "and did everything in his power to discredit Bechtel's critics."

An NRC investigation confirmed that serious violations had occurred during the cleanup, which could have produced major public safety risks. But the penalties that the NRC proposed came years later, and were absurdly low—much like the wrist-slap punishments that the DOE gives its own contractors today. "This paper-tiger performance will do little to deter employers from retaliating against other responsible engineers in the future," Stephen Unger writes. Bechtel transferred Parks across the country, to a coal gasification plant in the middle of the Mojave Desert, then fired him six months later. Jobless but determined to pay GAP for their legal help, Parks went to work for them as an investigator.

In *Moral Mazes*, his classic analysis of the corporate and bureaucratic mind, sociologist Robert Jackall explains that the Three Mile Island cleanup ended in wrongdoing because, at the highest levels, managerialism had trumped science, and bureaucracy had overwhelmed ethics. (Jackall used pseudonyms: "Joe Wilson" is Larry King.)

> Bureaucracy transforms all moral issues into immediately practical concerns. A moral judgment based on a professional ethic makes little sense in a world where the etiquette of authority relationships and the necessity for protecting and covering for one's boss, one's network, and oneself supercede [*sic*] all other considerations and where nonaccountability for action is the norm. . . . Top management always exerts pressure on subordinates, and subordinates on themselves, to do

what they believe has to be done. There are, in fact, few more effective legitimat-
ing rationales in the corporate world than the invocation of one's authoritatively
approved "goals," "objectives," or "mission." . . . [Many managers feel that] authority has the prerogative to resolve technical disputes. Whether Wilson liked it
or not, Bechtel had won the power struggle and they had the right, that is the
power, to call the shots on the cleanup. One has to bend with prevailing winds.
One can be beaten even when one is "right"; therefore, these managers stress that
whether Wilson was right or not was irrelevant. What mattered was that key
authorities decided that Wilson and his engineers were "wrong."

Jackall was describing malfeasance that took place in Pennsylvania in the early
1980s, and the managerial mentality that produced it. Yet he accurately describes
the corporate and governmental deviance that's happening at Hanford as you read
this.

Sociologist Edwin Sutherland coined the term "white-collar crime" in 1939, to
challenge the widely held assumption that the only true criminals were burglars,
muggers, murderers and other violent, blue-collar thugs. Sutherland suggested that
crimes and other deviant behavior by wealthy business executives were widespread
and rapidly increasing, and that such people actually caused far more social harm
in the aggregate than street criminals. He also argued that while society deals with
violent offenders in a highly visible way, through the criminal justice system, it
handles white-collar criminals predominantly through lower-profile regulations
and civil legislation that escape public attention. "In many periods, more important
crime news may be found on the financial pages of newspapers than on the front
pages," Sutherland said. He warned against normalizing white-collar crime, which
he considered a dangerous trend.

Sutherland's warnings were prescient. In fact, to this day crime by corporations
does much more harm than the working-class kind. "Just a couple major corporate
crimes add up to far more money damages, violence, and deaths than all the bur-
glaries and robberies and homicides in the United States each year," says Russell

Mokhiber, editor of the *Corporate Crime Reporter*. Data compiled by David A. Anderson, the distinguished scholar of crime and its social consequences, suggests that the economic costs of corporate crime may be as high as $800 billion per year—more than twice those produced by blue-collar crime.

Corporate crimes are often considered "victimless," but this is inaccurate. Air and water pollution, mine safety violations, overmedication with opioids and unnecessary spinal surgeries all have explicit victims. More broadly, crimes that siphon off public funds, particularly in times of financial duress, make victims of us all, harming everyone who suffers from the resulting shortfall in taxpayer dollars—everyone who dies in an overcrowded ER waiting for treatment, drinks lead in water or dies in a bridge collapse. As Edwin Sutherland pointed out, such crimes harm not just individuals but nations as a whole, because they destroy our trust in equal justice and opportunity, and in the social contract itself.

Despite Sutherland's warnings, we persist in viewing corporate crime as an inevitable part of the financial news, and increasingly idolize its perpetrators. Our ability to see executives as dangerous offenders is often diminished by their glamour, to which judges, prosecutors, journalists and others charged with detecting and punishing their crimes are not immune. Over time, many of us stop seeing much financial wrongdoing as wrong at all, shrugging it off as part of the corporate game. In fact, as we've observed, some distinguished economists, policy makers and business school professors actually try to argue corporate crime out of existence. At the same time, the Supreme Court has steadily reduced the set of corporate acts that can be considered illegal. Over the last two decades, the court has gutted federal laws dealing with bribery, influence peddling and campaign finance by applying a definition of corrupt behavior that fits homo economicus, but not homo sapiens. In 1999, the court overturned the fraud conviction of an almond company that had showered the secretary of agriculture with gifts shortly before his department made two major policy choices that affected the company's interests; the majority decision, written by Antonin Scalia, declared that only the explicit gift of money for a subsequent official act was illegal. "The opinion shows a lack of understanding of the corrosive power of gifts and subtle influence," writes constitutional scholar Zephyr Teachout; "the Court suggests that using money to influence power through gifts

328 CRISIS OF CONSCIENCE

is both inevitable and not troubling." In a 2010 ruling that largely voided the fraud conviction of Jeffrey Skilling, Enron's notorious CEO, the Supreme Court essentially narrowed honest services fraud to quid pro quo bribery and kickbacks. Similar thinking was applied to campaign finance in the *Citizens United v. Federal Election Commission* decision of 2010 and *McCutcheon v. Federal Election Commission* of 2014, which continued the court's program of deregulating the US electoral system. "We now conclude that independent expenditures, including those made by corporations, do not give rise to corruption or the appearance of corruption," stated Justice Anthony Kennedy sonorously for the majority in *Citizens United*, adding that "the appearance of influence or access, furthermore, will not cause the electorate to lose faith in our democracy." Kennedy and his fellow conservatives on the court seemed to have forgotten that the sweeping campaign finance and anticorruption laws passed after Watergate, which they had dismantled, were passed explicitly to restore public faith in a democratic system that Americans feared was being corrupted by secret corporate wealth. In the same way, the court as a whole has evidently lost sight of the Framers' strong conviction, as expressed in the emoluments clause of the Constitution, that gifts to public servants are a powerful corrupting force.

The court's equation of free speech, the supreme democratic good, with money has been used to overturn convictions for off-label marketing of prescription drugs and for securities fraud; in both cases, defense lawyers successfully argued that these actions were protected by the First Amendment. In April 2016, after former Virginia governor Bob McDonnell was convicted of fraud for accepting gifts, loans and rides in a Ferrari in return for favors to a local businessman, McDonnell's attorneys argued on appeal before the Supreme Court that "paying for 'access'—the ability to get a call answered or a meeting scheduled—is constitutionally protected and an intrinsic part of our political system." The Supreme Court agreed, and unanimously overturned McDonnell's conviction.

So it's official: the US government's day-to-day operations are now on sale to the highest bidder, because any other approach would interfere with democracy in America. This is naturally welcome news to corporations, which no longer have to disguise their donations, but can make them overtly. In this environment, employees of corporations would be forgiven for finding moral behavior to be unnecessary, maudlin or downright immoral in many business contexts. If all this has an Orwellian ring, it's because corporations, in the gulf between their publicly stated missions and their real agendas, often create a distinctly Orwellian atmosphere. After resigning from a Fortune 500 healthcare company in 2014, one whistleblower I interviewed filed a false claims case against his firm but continued to socialize with a few of his former colleagues who still worked there. The company's hard-driving, cultlike culture often came up in their conversation. During lunch with one friend, a vice president at the firm, the whistleblower mentioned that he'd recently reread *Animal Farm*, and said that the book reminded him of their company.

The VP perked up. "Oh yeah, it's exactly like that! The rules written on the barn door are totally different from what's really going on behind the scenes." He paused, then added, "At least it's nice, though, when you make it into the farmhouse, and you're sleeping in the beds with the pigs."

In 1939, Justice William O. Douglas observed, "One aspect of modern life which has gone far to stifle men is the rapid growth of tremendous corporations. Enormous spiritual sacrifices are made in the transformation of shopkeepers into employees. . . . The disappearance of free enterprise has led to a submergence of the individual in the impersonal corporation in much the same manner as he has been submerged in the state in other lands." Two decades later, at the height of the Cold War, Robert Wood, longtime CEO of Sears, Roebuck and Company, and a former general in the US Army, told a gathering of managers, "We stress the advantages of the free enterprise system, we complain about the totalitarian state, but in our industrial organizations, in our striving for efficiency, we have created more or less of a totalitarian organization in industry—particularly in large industry." Robert Jackall describes how the extensive bureaucracy within which managers, salesmen and other functionaries in large, hierarchical organizations learn to operate shapes their consciousness, by regimenting their lives, inculcating goal-oriented habits of mind, and engendering an almost reverential respect for the rules, procedures and social contexts of their firm.

Top managers, Jackall writes, must be adept at doublethink and doublespeak and learn to treat morality, like truth itself, not as an absolute, but as socially constructed. "What is right in the corporation is not what is right in a man's home or in his church," the business executive told him, but "what the guy above you wants from you." Corporate bureaucracies, Jackall explains, tend to diminish a sense of individual responsibility for wrongdoing, particularly among higher-level executives, who are carefully shielded from blame. Among the basic rules of bureaucratic life, Jackall includes: "You tell your boss what he wants to hear, even when your boss claims that he wants dissenting views," and "Your job is not to report something that your boss does not want reported, but rather to cover it up."

It's easy to see why tone at the top is such a powerful driver of wrongdoing in large, hierarchical firms of this kind, and why whistleblowers, outspoken and often unwilling to shield their superiors from blame, are anathema there. The people who thrive in such worlds are often what David Riesman called "other-directed," guided less by goals or standards of behavior they learned from their society than by the actions, tastes and aspirations of their peers; such people, Riesman said, have a deep need for group approval. Whistleblowers I've met, by contrast, seem to fit better with Riesman's tradition-directed or inner-directed groups, whose behavior is guided by ancient rules of conduct or by a highly developed personal conscience. While the successful managers Jackall describes are utilitarians, for whom morality is fluid depending on whether an act benefits the greater good (in this case, the firm), whistleblowers tend to be deontologists or virtue ethicists, whose morality is determined by relatively clear-cut conceptions of ethical norms or individual virtue—the Golden Rule, or what Jesus would have done in their place.

Large corporations, in divorcing the conscience of the individual from the rationales of the group, often create an ideal environment for authorization, routinization and dehumanization, Herbert Kelman's three drivers of crimes of obedience. Authorization takes place through the messages of senior management, particularly the CEO. In *The Seven Signs of Ethical Collapse*, Marianne Jennings identifies the charismatic chief executive running a high-pressure organization according to his own personal whims as one of her seven red flags for fraud. When senior managers intentionally turn their firm into a "control fraud," in Bill Black's term, they may be conscience-free sociopaths, yet many managers even in fraud-riddled organizations believe they are fulfilling their fiscal, legal and regulatory responsibilities. "It's not that executives themselves are corrupt," Gary Rogers, billionaire entrepreneur and former head of the Federal Reserve Bank of San Francisco, told me. "I don't know any individuals in business who are really corrupt. It's the system itself that is corrupting." Noam Chomsky concurs: "When you look at a corporation, just like when you look at a slave owner, you want to distinguish between the institution and the individual," he said in a 2003 interview. "So slavery, for example, or other forms of tyranny, are inherently monstrous, but the individuals participating in them may be the nicest guys you could imagine. Benevolent, friendly, nice to their children, even nice to their slaves, caring about other people. I mean, as individuals they may be anything. In their institutional role they're monsters because the institution is monstrous."

If executive charisma and corporate prestige help authorize many employees to commit harm on their organization's behalf, the firm's bureaucracy also helps to routinize and dehumanize that harm. Carrying out repetitive, ritualized, highly circumscribed tasks, often reduced to numbers, tends to divorce these tasks from their real-world impact in the employees' minds. Balance sheets and Excel spreadsheets have a remarkable capacity to mask faces and personal suffering. Duties that produce a gradually escalating level of harm can give rise to the "slippery slope" phenomenon, or what philosopher Sissela Bok has called "psychic numbing": some employees do not clearly perceive incrementally more injurious actions as wrong, or, already feeling complicit in the wrongdoing, are reluctant to declare it blameworthy.

Money incentives, like bonuses for meeting specific financial targets, provide an effective way to turn a crime into a transaction, by creating a perverse feedback loop that Harvard behavioral ethicist Max Bazerman has called "goals gone wild." A striking illustration of this concept was provided by Franklin Raines, former head of Fannie Mae, in a 2003 interview with *BusinessWeek*. Commenting on a recent financial scandal on Wall Street, Raines said, "Investment banking is a business that's so denominated in dollars that the temptations are great, so you have to have very strong rules. My experience is where there is a one-to-one relation between if I do X, money will hit my pocket, you tend to see people doing X a lot. You've got to be very careful about that. Don't just say: 'If you hit this revenue number, your bonus is going to be this.' It sets up an incentive that's overwhelming. You wave enough money in front of people, and good people will do bad things." Yet Raines himself helped create precisely this situation in 1999, when he made bonuses at Fannie contingent upon reaching a specific earnings-per-share figure, 6.46. The head auditor at Fannie, Sampath Rajappa, told members of the audit team that they had a "moral obligation" to meet Frank Raines's goal. "By now every one of you must have 6.46 branded in your brains. You must be able to say it in your sleep, you must be able to recite it forwards and backwards, you must have a raging fire in your belly that burns away all doubts, you must live, breathe and dream 6.46, you must be obsessed on 6.46. . . . After all, thanks to Frank, we all have a lot of money riding on it." Threats give "goals gone wild" even greater gravitas: hit your numbers and you win a big bonus, miss them and you're fired. Don Blankenship, the tyrannical former chief executive of Massey Coal, forced his managers to fax him hourly production results from the mine face, and terminated out of hand those who failed to fax on schedule—part of a reign of terror that resulted in a corporate culture riddled with safety failures and the deaths of dozens of workers.

Donna Busche is right: Bechtel is playing the long game. They can outwait and outspend any regulator or whistleblower who objects to their business practices. They can outlast and out-lobby Congress itself, and the few legislators who fail to play along: politicians come and go, but Bechtel abides, with its countless friends in high places. And though the company's leadership has long favored the minimal-public-sector, zero-regulation goals of the reactionary right—Bechtel along with the Kochs were major funders to Americans for Tax Reform of Grover Norquist, who famously proposed to cut government so severely that he could drown what remained of it in a bathtub—nevertheless, the federal government and its endless flow of tax dollars are the company's lifeblood. As Sally Denton, in her recent history of the company, observes, "Despite its fiercely antiregulatory, antigovernment stance, the Bechtel family owes its entire fortune to the US government, dating back to its first Depression-era construction projects in the western United States."

The company is notoriously secretive—former CEO Stephen Bechtel Jr. once reportedly declined an interview request from *Newsweek* with the observation "There's no reason for people to hear of us. We're not selling to the public." Yet the money the company earns in its gigantic public works projects comes in large part from taxpayers. Increasingly, too, its work not only concerns the public, but endangers its survival.

In fact, the game Bechtel and their fellow nuclear contractors are playing goes far beyond nuclear cleanup and the management of nuclear laboratories, and now encompasses another lucrative business, which Jonathan Alan King, a molecular biologist at MIT and close observer of nuclear proliferation, has called "privatizing the apocalypse." Just how deep their designs, how wide their reach, is demonstrated by a masterful piece of bipartisan theater performed over the last decade. Under George W. Bush, Bechtel, Lockheed and a handful of other major engineering and defense contractors gained control of US nuclear laboratories and weapons sites. The election of Barack Obama in 2008, however, seemed to signal a change. In one of his first speeches as president, delivered in the symbolically powerful city of Prague on April 5, 2009, Obama announced: "So today, I state clearly and with conviction America's commitment to seek the peace and security of a world without nuclear weapons." Obama explained that he intended to "put an end to Cold War thinking" by reducing the role of nuclear weapons in the national security strategy of the United States. Soon he and the new Russian president, Dmitry Medvedev, began crafting a far-reaching arms treaty they called "New START," their blueprint for a nuclear-free world. Largely on the basis of his visionary promise of disarmament, the Norwegian Nobel Committee awarded Obama the 2009 Peace Prize, citing his "vision of and work for a world without nuclear weapons."

What happened next is all too typical of the Obama presidency. Ostensibly in the service of his nuclear reduction agenda, Obama began a highly visible alliance with four old-school members of the military-industrial complex that had created America's nuclear arsenal: George Shultz, Henry Kissinger, retired Republican senator Sam Nunn, and former defense secretary William Perry, all Cold Warriors and members of the Hoover Institution, a conservative think tank headquartered at Stanford University. The men, who called themselves the "Gang of Four" (and whom the press dubbed the "Four Horsemen of the Apocalypse"), had written a series of high-profile op-eds arguing for a radical reduction in the US and Russian nuclear arsenals. Nuclear weapons and the doctrine of deterrence, they said, were part of a Cold War mentality that had become obsolete with the demise of the USSR; nuclear weapons and Cold War thinking now posed a growing threat to world survival, both because of the proliferation of weapons to other countries, and because the United States' own Cold War–era arsenal was becoming dangerously decrepit.

Obama needed such alliances with right-wing leaders: in order to marshal sufficient votes to pass his signature New START treaty with the Russians, the vital first step toward his Nobel Peace Prize–winning vision of a nonnuclear world (and the first major political battle of his presidency), he had to persuade a group of highly skeptical war hawks in Congress, led by Senate minority whip Jon Kyl, to go along. Bechtel and the other managers of the DOE's nuclear facilities lobbied Kyl and other key Republicans, and convinced them to vote for the treaty only in return for what Kyl and Mitch McConnell, in a letter to Obama of December 2009, called "a significant program to modernize our nuclear deterrent"—$85 billion over ten years to upgrade obsolete weapons and delivery systems.

This is the devil's bargain that Obama struck to secure support for his treaty and win his Peace Prize. His nuclear rhetoric gradually pivoted through 180 degrees, from the "abolition" of US nuclear weapons to its "modernization," and eventually to a sweeping remake of the entire US nuclear arsenal, with a new ICBM, strategic bomber, missile-carrying submarine, air-launched cruise missile, and other nuclear goodies, at an estimated price of $1 trillion over thirty years. Shultz and his fellow Horsemen have gone silent about their dream of a nuke-free world. Perhaps they have grown disheartened. Or perhaps their real mission has been accomplished.

"All these systems are in the early stages of development," says Chuck Spinney of the new missile, bomber, submarine and other planned defense systems. "And knowing how things go at the Pentagon, that one-trillion-dollar number is just a 'buy-in' estimate, which deliberately understates future costs while overpromising future benefits. The money for all of these programs is only starting to flow. As it builds to a torrent over the next decade, the flood of subcontracting money and jobs in hundreds of congressional districts will guarantee that the entire nuclear spend-up acquires a political life of its own. The taxpayer will be burdened with yet another unstoppable behemoth."

President Obama and his team knew just the people to whom to entrust this vital work: insiders who understand how to play the game on both sides of the imaginary public-private divide, who will never betray its institutional hypocrisy because they personify it. Ashton Carter, whom Obama appointed secretary of defense in 2015, had worked for the Pentagon as its top arms buyer and science adviser, consulted and lobbied for arms contractors, and advised financial companies that invest in defense technology. Often he performed several roles at once: in 2008, while serving on a State Department advisory board on missile defense, Carter provided paid technical advice to Raytheon, manufacturer of the Patriot missile and other billion-dollar missile systems; two years later, as undersecretary of defense, in a *Wall Street Journal* op-ed, Carter called another Raytheon missile an "essential element" of the nation's missile defense system. Another paradigm Obama defense revolver was Frank Klotz, sworn in on April 17, 2014, as head of the National Nuclear Security Administration. Klotz had retired from the Air Force as lieutenant general in 2011, founded a defense consultancy, and begun helping Bechtel win bids to manage a number of nuclear facilities, including the colossally wasteful Uranium Processing Facility at Y-12. When he became head of the NNSA, Klotz obtained an ethics waiver allowing him to continue to work for Bechtel. (The waiver cites "the critical services that Bechtel provides the Department with respect to national nuclear facilities.") Just two weeks after putting on his new NNSA hat, Klotz appeared before Congress to request more money for the Uranium Processing Facility and Bechtel. When Washington decided that the NNSA itself needed reforms, the pattern continued. The grandly titled Congressional Advisory Panel on the Governance of the Nuclear Security Enterprise is a Who's Who of nuclear insiders, cochaired by Norm Augustine, former chairman and CEO of Lockheed Martin, and Richard Mies, a former Navy admiral and a director of Babcock & Wilcox. Given their career paths and their past, the reforms they proposed were predictable: to reduce the influence of the DNFSB, whose reports on nuclear mishaps had caused public alarm, and cut DOE staff charged with evaluating contractor performance and compliance. In October 2017, Klotz proposed to stop making safety reports public, while Sean Sullivan, Republican chair of the DNFSB, secretly advised the Trump administration to abolish the board altogether.

Such nuclear sleight of hand doesn't merely promise more waste and theft of taxpayer trillions. The same folks who are now busily "modernizing" the nuclear arsenal are also helping to plan how to use it. In fact, as nuclear modernization becomes the new defense mantra, the venerable doctrine of mutually assured destruction refined by Cold War technocrats, widely credited with preventing nuclear war by ensuring it would be so cataclysmic that no country would dare to begin one, is being replaced by a more open-minded exploration of how nuclear weapons might actually be used in warfare, complete with a gleaming new set of smaller-scale tactical nuclear weapons being developed for real-world battle scenarios. Donald Trump has reinforced this message of offensive nuclear expansion, by rejecting the New START treaty with the Russians as "a bad deal," urging an upgrade of the country's nuclear arsenal, and repeatedly suggesting he might actually use nuclear weapons. Chuck Spinney, like many experienced defense analysts, sees the growing influence of arms makers and their allies on American defense policy and foreign policies as a serious threat to world peace. "As more and more money flows into nuclear modernization, members of the military-industrial-congressional complex will have more power in shaping official threat assessments, alliances, treaties and US force deployments. And will the Russians interpret all this spending and rhetoric as a plan to actually fight and win a nuclear war?"

Let's close this chapter with a quick Military-Industrial-Congressional Complex Quiz. What do these seven people—Riley Bechtel, George Shultz, Henry Kissinger, William Perry, Sam Nunn, James Mattis and William Frist (the former senior executive at the Columbia/HCA hospital chain)—have in common?

Obviously, their life trajectories intersect at many points. The first six men share deep ties to the military-industrial-congressional complex and to the nuclear weapons industry. Shultz, Kissinger, Perry and Nunn are the Gang of Four who pushed the nuclear nonproliferation-turned-modernization project. Bechtel, Shultz and

Mattis, too, have long-standing links to Hanford, where Bechtel Corporation has contracted for many years. But all seven people share a more explicit bond: until recently, they were on the board of Theranos, the blood-testing biotech firm founded by Elizabeth Holmes. (Most resigned or moved to "adviser" roles when the company fell on hard times.)

It is interesting to speculate about the precise nature of the expertise that these seven gentlemen offered. Clearly it had nothing to do with blood testing or biotech. (Frist is an MD, but in recent decades has practiced more politics than medicine.) All would have provided prestigious, though perhaps dated, contacts in Washington, which may have made attracting big-name investors easier. Bechtel and Frist, in particular, also have extensive experience dealing with, outmaneuvering and neutralizing regulators, prosecutors and lawmakers, both in the normal course of their business and while fighting off major lawsuits against their firms—all skills that, it turned out, Theranos needed.

In certain instances, however, their expertise and influence may have been useful to Theranos in more practical ways. Hypothetically, if you wanted to run a pilot project in the US military, to test a medical device on soldiers that perhaps wasn't passing muster at the FDA, whom would you want on your team, to make sure no DOD official raised niggling problems? James Mattis, the "Warrior Monk," might be a good choice. In fact, emails exchanged in 2012 by Mattis and Holmes and later published in the *Washington Post* suggest how this might have played out. In June 2012, not long after meeting Holmes, Mattis, then head of US Central Command in Afghanistan, expressed his interest in trying out Theranos's blood-testing technology in the battlefield—evidently a project the two had discussed previously. "I've met with my various folks and we're kicking this into overdrive," Mattis wrote Holmes. "I'm convinced that your invention will be a game-changer for us and I want it to be given the opportunity for a demonstration in-theater soonest."

Two months later, however, Holmes wrote Mattis with a problem. A military regulatory and compliance official who was evaluating Theranos's blood-testing technology for use in the military had contacted the FDA, and learning that the agency had not approved a central component of the company's product, had opened a formal inquiry. Holmes asked Mattis to intervene to correct the reviewer's "blatantly false information" that the company's technology did not comply with FDA regulations. "I would very much appreciate your help in getting this information corrected with the regulatory agencies. Since this misinformation came from within DoD, it will be invaluable if this information is formally corrected by the right people in DoD."

Within hours, Mattis emailed military officials to ask how they could "overcome this new obstacle." "I have tried to get this device tested in theater asap, legally and ethically," Mattis wrote. "This appears to be relatively straight-forward yet we're a year into this and not yet deployed."

In a later statement to the *Washington Post,* Theranos claimed that the military wanted to adapt the company's blood-testing technology to a battlefield environment, a pilot project that would not have required standard regulatory approval. The *Post* added, "But the military reviewer's concerns apparently were broader than that project and foreshadowed Theranos's current problems with the FDA." In fact, after a series of explosive articles by John Carreyrou in the *Wall Street Journal* revealed grave doubts about the viability of the firm's core technologies, Theranos came unraveled. In July 2016, Holmes was barred from the medical-laboratory industry, because regulators determined that her company's testing practices put patients at risk. She and Theranos president Ramesh "Sunny" Balwani have since been charged with "massive fraud" by the Securities and Exchange Commission, and in June 2018 were indicted by a federal grand jury on conspiracy and wire fraud charges.

In May 2013, Mattis retired from the Marine Corps. Three months later he joined the board of Theranos, along with other boards, including General Dynamics. According to disclosures made when he became Trump's secretary of defense in 2017, he earned $150,000 as a Theranos board member. Not as much as the $242,000 salary and $900,000 in stock and options that, according to SEC filings, he received from General Dynamics, but still better than a poke in the finger with a Theranos stick.

It may be going too far to suggest that having people like this on your board would provide your company with expertise in successfully neutralizing whistleblowers, though some of them have already appeared in this book attempting to do just that: Kissinger as archenemy of Daniel Ellsberg, Mattis as one of Franz Gayl's MRAP nemeses, and Bechtel's company triggering, and then attempting to crush, numerous acts of whistleblowing during its nuclear cleanup boondoggles. Yet George Shultz, ever the Bechtel man, has recently demonstrated that he knows the corporate whistleblower drill, in the way he dealt with his own grandson, Tyler Shultz, who worked at Theranos. Tyler, whose job entailed verifying the accuracy of certain blood tests the company was performing, eventually blew the whistle on Theranos to New York state regulators in April 2014, because he believed that his company was manipulating test results. He later became a confidential source to *Wall Street Journal* reporter John Carreyrou, whose exposés helped prompt the firm's collapse. (Carreyrou recently told the Theranos story at length in his book *Bad Blood*.) Tyler Shultz, who is now twenty-nine years old, says he ultimately became a whistleblower to safeguard the health of patients, which he believed might be endangered by incorrect test results, as well as to protect his grandfather's reputation.

As most whistleblowers do, Tyler Shultz first tried to air his concerns internally. He met with company founder Elizabeth Holmes in early 2014 and expressed concerns about the technology. Holmes referred him to company VP Daniel Young, in charge of biostatistics, but Young's explanations failed to satisfy Tyler. On April 11, 2014, he emailed Elizabeth Holmes that Theranos had doctored research and ignored failed quality-control checks. Holmes forwarded this letter to Balwani, who rejected Tyler's assertions as scientifically and mathematically baseless, adding that he'd only bothered to respond to them at all out of respect for Tyler's famous grandfather. "Had this email come from anyone else in the company, I would have already held them accountable for the arrogant and patronizing tone and reckless comments," Balwani wrote.

Tyler resigned on April 15; as he left work, he received a frantic call from his mother, who reported that Holmes had called George Shultz and delivered a warning: his grandson would "lose" if he started a vendetta against Theranos. "Stop whatever you're about to do!" his mother told him.

After he spoke confidentially with Carreyrou, Tyler Shultz learned from his grandfather that Theranos suspected him of being a whistleblower. He asked his grandfather if they could meet and talk, without lawyers present, and George agreed. During a meeting at his house, George asked his grandson to sign a one-page confidentiality agreement to reassure Theranos. When Tyler agreed, George informed him that two Theranos lawyers were waiting upstairs with the agreement. Two partners at the law firm of Boies, Schiller & Flexner came downstairs; one handed Tyler the document, together with a temporary restraining order, a notice to appear in court and a letter signed by David Boies, chairman of the law firm and a famous litigator, that claimed that Tyler had leaked Theranos trade secrets. Tyler refused to sign the agreement, and the lawyers eventually left.

"Fraud is not a trade secret," Tyler Shultz told Carreyrou later, after he had decided to speak publicly about wrongdoing at Theranos. "I refuse to allow bullying, intimidation and threat of legal action to take away my First Amendment right to speak out against wrongdoing." He said he hoped his grandfather would cut ties with Theranos once the company's practices became known. Tyler and his parents have spent over $400,000 in legal fees to defend him from Theranos. (George Shultz later resigned from the company's board and initially refused to speak to his grandson, though at a family gathering in spring 2018, George admitted that Tyler had been right all along, and called him a hero.)

John Phillips told me that with the first signs of trouble at Theranos, he had recommended David Boies to Elizabeth Holmes as a useful ally in turning the company around. Boies became a director at the company; his law firm began sending letters to employees that threatened lawsuits if they disclosed confidential information, and also sent a twenty-three-page warning to the *Journal* not to publish Carreyrou's first article. Boies's strong-arm tactics at Theranos, which he left in November 2016, may not have been an anomaly; he also hired Black Cube, a corporate-intelligence company run largely by former Israeli intelligence officers, on behalf of another of his clients, Harvey Weinstein, to gather information from an actress whom Weinstein had allegedly raped, and to block a *New York Times* reporter's efforts to write about the case.

These people all know one another. They all work together, in secret, with great determination. But whether they are wearing a Bechtel pin or an American flag on their lapel, for all their resonant talk of God and country, of security and freedom and the American way, their interests rarely coincide with those of the nation, or with the common good. Their true objectives are invariably their own financial gain, or some conception of power that facilitates it. They appropriate for their own purposes landscapes, work, associations and knowledge that were once assets of the nation, public goods that have inexorably become their private property.

Lately there has been some good news at Hanford. In August 2015, Walt Tamosaitis won a $4.1 million settlement in his OSHA case against Bechtel and the DOE. We know the exact figure because he refused to sign a confidentiality agreement. "I want people to know that I won and how much I won by," he says. "I wanted to send a signal, that whistleblowers can win." (His settlement seems a little less impressive when you consider that 40 percent went to his lawyer, and 40 percent of what was left went to the IRS.) Not long after, Donna Busche successfully settled her OSHA case; she signed a confidentiality agreement and can't discuss the suit's outcome.

Finally, in November 2016, Walt, Donna and Gary Brunson won a $125 million settlement in a False Claims Act suit against Bechtel and URS. In their complaint, they accused the companies of knowingly charging the DOE, for over thirteen years, for materials and services that failed to meet rigorous standards for nuclear facilities, and further for illegally spending tax dollars to fund a multiyear lobbying campaign designed to convince Congress to pay the company even more money. Though all three signed a confidentiality agreement and could not talk with me about the case, their complaint is replete with substandard flow-indicator rotameters, hot-cell monorail airlocks, sacrificial heater element assemblies, and other systems and components they say Bechtel and URS skimped on while building the WTP—gear you've probably never heard of, but would learn more about in a hurry if their failure had caused the WTP to explode. Their charges remain allegations, naturally, because as part of the settlement agreement, Bechtel and URS got to deny them all. Nevertheless, in March 2018, the Department of Energy wrote an uncharacteristically blunt letter to Bechtel, demanding to know why the essential quality documentation for large amounts of structural steel used to build the WTP was missing, and the documentation for rebar, piping and other materials was of dubious value. The DOE called these omissions, which Donna Busche and Walt Tamosaitis began blowing the whistle on back in 2010, a "potentially unrecoverable quality issue," meaning that the entire multibillion-dollar facility may have to be scrapped.

In January 2016, the GAO published another blistering report, condemning contractors for rampant, unlawful whistleblower retaliation and the DOE for failing to hold the contractors accountable. Meantime, in the lawsuit that Hanford Challenge and the Washington state attorney general brought against the DOE and WRPS on behalf of tank farm workers, the presiding judge, Thomas Rice, rejected the age-old rationale of the DOE and its contractors, that workers never suffered harm in the tank farms, as "belied by the record." "The Court does not deny that vapor exposures have occurred or that employees have experienced serious vapor-related illnesses," Rice said, in a historic pronouncement. The DOE and WRPS settled the suit in September 2018, agreeing to install protective ventilation and alarm systems and to reimburse Washington state and Hanford Challenge $925,000 for legal costs.

Despite a handful of legal victories, however, little has changed at Hanford. WRPS is still the prime contractor in the tank farms, and continues to enjoy the public support and legal funding of the DOE. The DOE and WRPS paid their opponents' lawyers in the recent case, but gave nothing to sick workers. Bechtel and URS may have lost, or rather, *settled*, their suits with Walt Tamosaitis, Donna Busche and Gary Brunson, but Bechtel is still the prime contractor at the WTP, and still pulls in its $690 million a year, though the project is largely dead in the water.

Since a major component of the WTP, the Pretreatment Facility (PTF), which should have treated low-activity waste, is stalled, contractors and the DOE have begun to build a new facility to process this waste known (apparently without intentional irony) as "DFLAW" (Direct Feed Low-Activity Waste). Donna Busche prefers to call it the "Shiny New Facility." "It's being built by the same people, with the same defective safety standards and documentation, as the Vit Plant," she says. "Do you have confidence that they'll build it right? It will be interesting to see how it works out." (The GAO shares her skepticism.) Elsewhere, the fraud rolls on. In February 2019, the DOJ announced a false claims suit against Lockheed Martin, MSA and other contractors, which it contends lied to the DOE on their $3 billion contract. "Fraud, corruption, and self-dealing at Hanford will simply not be tolerated," one DOJ attorney said. "The Department of Justice will work tirelessly to ensure that public funds are used for the important purposes for which they are intended," another added. Lockheed and the rest insist they are innocent, and say they will contest the charges vigorously—no doubt with taxpayer money.

Meanwhile the waste problem that the WTP is supposed to resolve grows more serious every day, as numerous tanks continue to leak. In time they all will, unless their waste is pumped out and properly disposed of. On June 4, 2018, Trump's DOE proposed to deal with sixty-six thousand gallons of high-level nuclear waste not by cleaning it up, but by reclassifying it as low-level waste, pouring concrete over it, and forgetting it. (If successful, this may become the Trump administration's approach to dealing with the rest of Hanford's high-level waste.) That same month, more workers were exposed to potentially harmful vapors, and radioactive dust was detected at the homes of other workers.

Hanford's World War II–era facilities are disintegrating: on May 9, 2017, a twenty-foot section of Tunnel #1 collapsed at the labyrinthine, largely subterranean PUREX facility. A state of emergency was declared at Hanford, several hundred workers took shelter, and the FAA prohibited flights over the area. Not that this event surprised anyone. A 2015 report by independent experts identified a collapse in this tunnel as one of many likely accidents waiting to happen at Hanford: "The timber walls and ceiling of Tunnel #1 will also continue to weaken and possibly collapse causing a . . . release of contaminants."

The general atmosphere toward safety, openness and whistleblowing at Hanford, as at other nuclear facilities, has deteriorated further. Peter Winokur was ousted as chair of the DNFSB, and according to Tom Carpenter, the board is no longer the force for good it was under him: "There is nobody left on the board— save one, Jesse Roberson—that's worth a shit. None of them are safety advocates, none of them have any history or awareness of safety culture." When an anonymous whistleblower sent them the damning report on the LAW facility, detailing countless safety problems, they never responded, Carpenter says. Contact between Hanford officials and the outside world has been sharply curtailed by DOE managers, who cite ongoing litigation as a reason for not revealing what is happening inside the facility. The Trump administration has only heightened this lockdown environment: one of the new president's early directives forbade personnel at the DOE (and other government offices) from communicating departmental information to outside persons, effectively a gag order that many observers believe violates whistleblower laws. In February 2017, ostensibly as part of his regulation-cutting drive, Trump announced the removal of civil penalties against nuclear contractors who retaliate against whistleblowers.

CHAPTER 6

Money Makes the World Go Round

At its heart, therefore, the financial crisis was a breakdown in the rule of law in America.

James Galbraith, statement for the Senate Committee on the Judiciary, Subcommittee on Crime and Drugs, May 4, 2010

And I sincerely believe with you, that banking establishments are more dangerous than standing armies.

Thomas Jefferson, letter to John Taylor, May 28, 1816

On November 3, 2007, Richard Bowen, a chief underwriter at Citigroup, the world's largest financial institution, sent an email to Robert Rubin, senior member of the bank's Executive Committee, as well as to its CFO, chief risk officer and chief auditor, with the subject line "URGENT—READ IMMEDIATELY—FINANCIAL ISSUES." In the message, Bowen described the "breakdowns of internal controls and resulting significant but possibly unrecognized financial losses" he knew to exist at Citi, and urgently requested a high-level investigation to fix these problems, before they bankrupted the bank. Rubin and the others ignored Bowen's warning, much as Bowen's immediate bosses had been ignoring him for the previous two years. Only months later, the bomb he warned of detonated, blowing up Citigroup and joining a chain reaction that devastated the US financial system.

At last count, the 2008 financial crisis has cost American citizens and taxpayers some $24 trillion. Tens of millions of Americans lost their jobs, and many remain out of work or chronically underemployed. Tens of millions lost their homes and automobiles in foreclosure, saw their household finances and home equity ravaged and their retirement savings disappear. In some municipalities that invested heavily in the toxic financial products at the heart of the crisis, schools, hospitals, roads and other basic infrastructure were crippled and entire neighborhoods were largely abandoned. Homelessness, drug abuse and suicide spiked; in some parts of the nation, average life expectancy fell below that of Bangladesh. A cloud of hopelessness and impending disaster still hangs over many communities. The 2008 financial crisis was, in many ways, a far more devastating attack on the American homeland than 9/11.

Richard Bowen grew up in the 1950s in the West Texas towns of Seminole, Abilene and Sundown, where his father was an oilfield engineer. As a boy he spent a lot of time outdoors, riding his bike and hunting in the broad, hot, empty landscape, or tinkering with electronics in his father's workshop. His parents were warm, but strict. "There was no shortage of discipline in my family," he says. "There was really no question of right or wrong. When I misbehaved, I got spanked, or got an old-fashioned tanning with a belt." Bowen's voice is deep and melodious, a polished public speaker's voice with a mild Texas twang—the voice of a trial lawyer, a judge, a preacher—but he answers questions carefully, methodically, like an accountant. "I've been accused, if asked what time it is, of telling you how to build a watch," he says.

When he was ten, his family moved to Highland Park, an affluent neighborhood in Dallas. Weeks later, Bowen's father suffered a major stroke, the first of a series, which severely impaired his speech and his ability to work. In Dallas, Bowen missed the presence of nature and the sense of community that he'd enjoyed in West Texas. He also missed his father, who was unable to continue leading the local Boy Scout troop. The family stopped attending the Methodist church they'd belonged to.

After high school, Bowen enrolled in electrical engineering at Texas Tech. He enjoyed fraternity life, and when the head of the department said that real engineers needed to focus on their work, Bowen "told him to stick it" and transferred to mechanical engineering. He was planning to join the Air Force, anyway. His father had fought in World War II, his grandfather in World War I, and his great-grandfather in the Civil War, and Bowen, who'd been in ROTC since high school, was determined to follow in their footsteps. "I was going to be a navigator in a B-52," he says ruefully. "I was going to go bomb the hell out of Vietnam." But just before graduation, his life was upended once again, when he tore ligaments in his knee, meaning he couldn't pass the Air Force physical. Within weeks, his father suffered another stroke. "My whole world just sort of crumbled," Bowen remembers.

He returned home, to help his family survive. Gradually he made another plan: to complete his engineering degree at Texas Tech, then get an MBA. First, though, he decided to learn finance. He joined Republic National Bank in Dallas, where he entered the credit training program. He was several years older than his peers, but made up for lost time with a string of promotions. In 1980, he was named CFO of First National Bank of Oklahoma City, then the largest publicly traded bank holding company in Oklahoma. Here Bowen had a front-row seat on the first major financial collapse and bailout in the United States since the Great Depression: the savings and loan crisis. Another bank in Oklahoma City, Penn Square, was making highly speculative and poorly documented loans to oil and gas companies, on the tail end of an oil boom that by 1982 was swiftly becoming a bust. Sensing trouble, Bowen put all his bank's dealings with Penn Square on a cash basis. Sure enough, Penn Square folded. Bowen's precautions had saved his bank many millions of dollars in losses.

After Penn Square's collapse, Bowen began warning his colleagues that their own bank was exposed to similar risks. "The people at my bank were very smug. 'Those people at Penn [Square], they weren't professionals—they didn't know the energy industry,' they'd say. '*We're* the professionals.' But we were swimming in the same pool they swam in." At loan committee meetings, Bowen began to vote against risky loans, and as CFO, he put numerous loans on a nonaccrual basis, which reduced the bank's exposure but also cut its profits. His caution earned him the nickname "Chicken Little" and the ire of the bank's chairman. When federal examiners reviewed the bank's dealings in 1983, Bowen shared his concerns with them; in their report, they condemned all of the executive management except for him. Shortly after, Bowen was fired—and not long after that, First National Bank of Oklahoma City collapsed. It was one of the biggest bank failures in a quarter century, caused largely by the kinds of bad loans that Richard Bowen had been warning about. "So that was my first experience with whistleblowing," he says. "I didn't know that's what you called it, by the way. That was my job, and I was just trying to do it. I didn't have a word for it at Citi either. The first time I saw the word 'whistleblower' applied to me was after I testified before the congressional commission."

Bowen continued his career in banking, developing particular expertise in credit and mortgage lending, and in 2002 joined CitiFinancial Mortgage, part of the sprawling Citigroup empire. Here again he steadily climbed the corporate ladder; in 2006, after a sweeping reorganization at the bank that consolidated all mortgage lending operations into one management area, he was named senior vice president and business chief underwriter, a major promotion, with a staff of 220 underwriters and responsibility for ensuring the quality of what by then was $90 billion a year in residential mortgages. Citi did not originate these mortgages itself, but bought them from other mortgage companies like Countrywide and Wells Fargo, combined them into pools and resold these pools to government-sponsored enterprises (GSEs) like Fannie Mae and Freddie Mac, or to mortgage securitizers, which included leading Wall Street banks. The GSEs and securitizers, in turn, bundled them into a range of financial instruments, including collateralized debt obligations (CDOs), which they resold, often with a triple-A rating from a credit rating agency, to a wide range of investors—federally insured financial institutions, city and state governments, pension funds, universities, hospitals and religious charities. Bowen's team was responsible for verifying that the mortgages Citi bought and resold—the foundation on which the value of CDOs and other securities ultimately rested—met the bank's credit guidelines. Loan recipients had to prove they had the income, collateral and other characteristics that would make them good credit risks, as well as satisfying further requirements imposed by government entities like the Federal Housing Administration. When Citi resold these mortgages to third parties, it guaranteed with a series of representations and warranties that the loans met all of these criteria.

Soon after his promotion, Bowen began to make disturbing discoveries about the mortgages Citi was buying and selling. Examining sample loans from the enormous pools of mortgages the bank had bought, he found that a substantial number failed to meet the bank's credit guidelines. The files on other mortgages were missing essential documentation, like proof that the applicants earned anything like the salaries they'd claimed, or that they actually had jobs at all. Though the bank's maximum allowable level of defective loans in such pools was 5 percent, the industry standard, 60 percent of the loans Bowen examined from the year 2006 were defective. This was no fluke, he found: by 2007, the defect rate had climbed to 80 percent. Citi continued to sell these loans with the same reps and warranties.

Trying to understand why his bank was buying so many bad loans, most of which seemed likely to default, Bowen visited bank offices around the country. Time and again, he found that executives had approved bad mortgages over the strong objections of their underwriters, who actually knew the loan documentation. "Frontline employees were telling me one thing, but their boss was telling me something completely different," he remembers.

There were two simple causes of this apparent paradox: perverse incentives and moral hazard. Just as perverse incentives could drive the sales of potentially harmful medication or the construction of out-of-code nuclear facilities, at Citi, the salaries and bonuses of employees throughout the bank were set not by loan quality, but by the sheer number of loans processed and resold. Moral hazard entered the equation when Citi executives, knowing that the bank was immediately reselling their defective loans to investors, could reassure themselves that it faced no harm from defaults. Richard Bowen instead felt that this practice created major liabilities. "If the defects were discovered, the people we sold mortgage-backed securities to could demand that we buy them back, creating multibillion-dollar losses for us," he remembers thinking.

Bowen alerted his boss, Owen Davis, who was alarmed. In emails, weekly reports, and committee meetings, the two men warned their colleagues that these defective mortgages were a mortal threat to their organization. By mid-2007, the housing market was in steep decline, and people began to sense just how toxic the mortgages underpinning mortgage-backed securities might be. Nevertheless, the volume of bad loans that Citi bought and sold continued to rise, and upper management appeared unconcerned. In July 2007, Citibank CEO Chuck Prince famously said, "As long as the music is playing, you've got to get up and dance. We're still dancing." He was talking about loans for risky leveraged buyouts, but the money dance in the subprime mortgage arena—expectations over reality, volume over value, and willful blindness to risk and to outright fraud—was the same.

In fact, the bank began punishing those few employees who refused to dance. Owen Davis was stripped of nearly all of his operational responsibilities, and soon accepted an early retirement package. Bowen didn't relent. "I was not a visionary," he says. "I didn't predict the 2008 financial crisis. I didn't dream that Citigroup would fail and have to be bailed out three times. But I did see a serious threat to the bank, right there in my department, and I figured that if I jumped up and down and screamed enough, someone would get it." He confronted the chief risk officer of subprime lending, far senior to him on the corporate ladder. "His response was that I was only picking up technical exceptions to the policies, and that these mortgages would never actually default."

Bowen never had an "aha" moment, a sudden realization that the fraud he was witnessing was part of the business model of his bank. "It was sort of a slow dawning, that people weren't listening because they didn't want to hear. That this wasn't going to change." Gradually his superiors pared back his responsibilities, as they had done to his former boss.

By the beginning of November 2007, home sales were plummeting, foreclosures were soaring, the mortgage-backed securities market was in disarray and the subprime market had collapsed. Countrywide, the largest mortgage lender in America, teetered on the edge of bankruptcy. All those bad loans lurking in the books of his bank—and of their clients—weighed on Bowen's mind. At this critical juncture, he attended a conference on corporate governance in Dallas. The keynote speaker was Michael Oxley, the Republican senator from Ohio and cosponsor of the Sarbanes-Oxley (SOX) Act of 2002, passed in response to the spate of corporate fraud scandals including Enron and WorldCom. Oxley reminded his audience that his law required the CEO and CFO of every public company to certify that their quarterly and annual reports were accurate and complete, and that their firm had adequate internal controls to ensure these represented a faithful picture of its financial health.

"I was very inspired by that talk," Bowen remembers. "I saw it was directly related to my situation." The next day, he read in the morning papers that Citigroup had scheduled an emergency board meeting for November 4, during which Chuck Prince was expected to resign because of the bank's losses in mortgage-related investments. Robert Rubin would likely step in as chairman.

Bowen saw that the leaders of Citi, who were responsible for signing off on the bank's financial statements according to SOX, would be discussing the future of their organization at this meeting. "Hell, I need to get what I know to New York!" he remembers thinking. "The board of directors needs to understand how bad things are—that our accounts aren't accurate, and our internal controls just aren't there!"

So on November 3, Bowen sent his fateful email to Rubin and the others. He included his cell phone number, and the words "Please call me." He waited all weekend, and all day Monday. At last, on Tuesday, the general counsel of the Global Consumer Group phoned him to say, as Bowen summarizes the message, "We got your email, we're taking it seriously, we're looking at it. Don't call us, we'll call you."

After several more weeks of waiting, Bowen emailed the general counsel again. "You need to know the details behind this," he wrote. "There are risks to the company." Late in December he wrote again. "Please! You have got to understand what's happening. I need to give you details you can look at."

Time dragged on, and still no senior executive contacted Bowen. Citigroup completed its year-end financial report, senior bank officers signed the SOX certifications, the bank submitted its year-end accounts. Gradually Bowen had another insight. "They didn't want to know the details, so they could sign off on the Sarbanes-Oxley certification," he says today. "They did not want to know specifically that they were broke."

Early in the new year, Citigroup dealt swiftly with Bowen. His superiors cut his staff of underwriters from 220 to 2 and stripped him of all significant responsibilities; in February he was placed on administrative leave. Bowen was going through a series of hardships in his personal life at the time. His son underwent brain surgery. A member of his extended family committed suicide with a handgun, and Bowen had to clean up the aftermath. Bowen's mother-in-law moved into their home under hospice, and died in their bedroom. In April 2008 he nevertheless managed to file a Sarbanes-Oxley whistleblower suit—Michael Oxley's pioneering law also offered some protections to whistleblowers—against Citigroup, claiming that the bank had retaliated against him for sending his momentous email. In the meantime, he continued to blow the whistle—and to suffer retaliation. Despite a confidentiality agreement with Citi he'd signed when he joined the bank, Bowen could still testify under oath; in July 2008, he was interviewed for two days by Securities and Exchange Commission investigators, to whom he provided over a thousand pages of evidence of the fraud he had witnessed. He detailed the abuses he'd seen at the bank, and his repeated attempts to fix them. The investigators assured Bowen that they would pursue the matter vigorously.

By October 2008, the frantic music to which Chuck Prince and the bank's other leaders had been dancing went silent. Citigroup was bankrupt, its $2 trillion balance sheet and $1.2 trillion off-balance-sheet "assets" crippled by terrible financial bets—in particular the toxic mortgages that Bowen had repeatedly warned about. On October 28, the US Treasury, deeming Citi too systemically important to fail (the collapse of the far smaller Lehman Brothers a month earlier had rocked the economy), injected $25 billion in taxpayer money into the bank. The hemorrhage continued; by November, the bank's stock had lost almost 90 percent of its value, and Citi fired 52,000 employees. The US Treasury gave Citi another $20 billion transfusion, while the FDIC guaranteed $306 billion of its questionable mortgage assets and assorted other types of toxic debt. The Federal Reserve pumped a staggering $2.5 trillion in near-zero-interest loans into the bank between 2007 and 2010—an operation that remained secret until journalists at Bloomberg forced the Fed to reveal it with FOIA lawsuits. This was the largest bank bailout in US history. American citizens paid with their tax dollars for the excesses, willful blindness and malfeasance of Chuck Prince, Robert Rubin and the other heads of Citigroup. The US government, which now owned 36 percent of Citi's common stock, was firmly focused on the expectations market—propping up public confidence in the bank and shoring up its share price.

After the bailouts, the SEC seemed to lose interest in Richard Bowen. They halted their investigation of Citigroup and sealed Bowen's testimony, together with the documents he had given them, which the commission has refused to release ever since, claiming they contain confidential competitive information. "I guess even those fraudulent reps and warranties to mortgage-backed securities that I gave

them, which I'd saved off the internet, are 'confidential Citigroup trade secrets,'"
Bowen says. For his part, Bowen reached a settlement with the bank in January 2009,
under which he signed a strict nondisclosure agreement and received a severance
package of less than $1 million. His promising career, his $200,000-a-year salary and
his pension were gone.

In May 2009, Congress formed the Financial Crisis Inquiry Commission (FCIC),
a panel of ten politicians, attorneys, economists and public servants charged with
identifying the root causes of the 2008 collapse. The FCIC was created on the model
of the Pecora Committee, formed in 1932 by Congress to investigate the origins of
the Great Depression and named after its leader, New York prosecutor Ferdinand
"Ferd" Pecora, whose relentless grilling of the leading bankers of the Gilded Age laid
bare the wrongdoing by Wall Street banks that had triggered the crash of 1929,
crippled the US economy, and put a quarter of American workers out of their jobs.
Pecora's hearings popularized the term "banksters" to describe the financial gang-
sters of Wall Street who had robbed the American people through their tax-evasion
schemes, lavish paychecks and sales of dubious securities to unsuspecting investors.
Senior government officials, including the newly elected president, Franklin Delano
Roosevelt, championed Main Street over Wall Street. In June 1933, the cigar-
chomping Pecora appeared on the cover of *Time*; in his memoir, *Wall Street Under
Oath*, he wrote that dragging the banksters' secret deeds into the sunlight was the
best way to halt them: "Legal chicanery and beneficent darkness were the banker's
stoutest allies."

The Pecora Committee's public censure of venerated financiers led to the rapid
passage of the 1933 Glass-Steagall Act, which separated commercial and investment
banking, and to the formation of the SEC to serve, in Pecora's words, as the police-
man at the corner of Wall Street. Now, in February 2010, Pecora's would-be successors interviewed Bowen by phone and asked if he would testify about his experiences.
He knew this would mean direct conflict with Citigroup and its army of lawyers.

It was at this troubled moment in his life, during an Ash Wednesday service at
his church in Dallas, that Bowen had a vision. Bowen is a devout Christian, but was
initially reluctant to describe how his faith had shaped his whistleblowing. "I don't
want to be painted with the brush of the religious zealot, which would detract from

my message about wrongdoing by the banks," he told me. Eventually he agreed to discuss it. "The Lord guided me in this, day to day, minute to minute," he says matter-of-factly of how he became a truth teller against Citigroup. "He wants there to be lessons from this story."

As Bowen sat in his pew with his eyes closed, praying for guidance in how to handle his conversations with the FCIC, all the tension and fear suddenly vanished, leaving him with a deep sense of calm. In his diary that night, he described what he experienced next:

> I felt myself sitting on a seat held securely, moving very quickly through the dark, with all sorts of things coming at me from all directions. But before the fire, the dragons and other things could touch my chair, it moved quickly from side to side or up and down, and avoided them, all the while moving faster and faster. And I heard this voice saying "Hold on, I have you, we are going to accelerate."

"'Accelerate'? I'm not sure that's biblical!" Bowen chuckles today. "But that's what the Lord said." He explains that the abiding sensation he had from the vision, whose full significance took him some time to decipher, was that of riding through a carnival scare house, in a seat on rails: "All sorts of things jumping out at you and trying to harm you and scare you, but you know it is only a ride, and you will be safe."

The next day, sure enough, events began to accelerate. The FCIC asked Bowen to travel to Washington as soon as possible; on February 27, accompanied by his two lawyers, he spoke for four hours with commission investigators, and briefly with Bradley Bondi, the commission's deputy general counsel. He described his experiences at Citi, and how he'd repeatedly warned that bad mortgages represented an existential threat to the bank. Members of the commission said his testimony was "compelling," and that they might ask him to testify in future public hearings.

Soon after, as he sat in his office at home and prayed, another vision came, which he again recorded in his diary. He again saw himself moving through the darkness as before, but then emerging into a beautiful sunlit day and coming to rest in a grassy meadow ringed by trees. He sensed that this peaceful place would be the site of a great battle, which he would fight alone, against a powerful enemy.

Nevertheless, he felt that God had prepared him for this battle; he also understood that his whistleblowing experiences in Oklahoma, decades before, had been part of this preparation. His feeling of a divine calling to reveal what he had seen at Citi grew even stronger. "This battle will not be waged with swords and spears, but rather with words—the words of my story," he wrote in his journal.

Later that week, he learned that he would likely be called to testify at the public FCIC hearings. During a series of conference calls, commission staffers, referring to investigative reports they had read about him, questioned him extensively about events in his background, some of which had occurred in high school. (Bowen later learned that someone had hinted to the commission of the existence of embarrassing facts in his past, which would destroy his credibility if he were called as a witness.)

On March 14, while in church with his wife and father, he had his third and final vision. That evening, he wrote in his journal: "Although I didn't hear the Lord during my prayer, I did see myself again in that meadow on a beautiful day, and I knew that the enemy was just out of sight, and that I was going to be unafraid in engaging the enemy in battle. I knew that this was what I was sent there for, and I was going to be unwavering in fighting the enemy. And I praised and thanked the Lord for selecting me for this important mission."

"After that, I will never be afraid of anyone or anything again," Bowen says today. "I don't care what the circumstances are. Fear is just not in my being anymore."

The following day, he received a letter from the FCIC calling him to testify at the open hearings. "They told me to write what I'd told them in our closed-doors meeting in Washington and what I had told the SEC, and said I had thirty pages to do it in," Bowen says. He prepared his written testimony with the help of his Dallas-based lawyer, Steven Kardell, and couriered it to the commission on the morning of March 29.

Yet almost immediately, Bowen says, the FCIC began pressuring him to change his testimony. In a March 30 email, Kardell informed him that, while the commission insisted it didn't want to influence his testimony, deputy general counsel Bradley Bondi "thinks that the way it's written now, Citi will declare war on both you and the FCIC, and it will primarily consist of an effort to discredit you." Kardell wrote that Bondi suggested making "substantial changes" to his testimony, and cutting it by ten pages. Through his lawyer, Bowen learned that the FCIC wanted him to remove instances of alleged wrongdoing that he had chronicled in his testimony, much of which the commission had specifically asked him to describe. In a March 31 email, Kardell wrote that he had the impression that the revisions were "nonnegotiable." Kardell also mentioned that the FCIC was "catching some serious, serious heat" from Citi, and that Bradley Karp, managing partner at Paul, Weiss, one of the white-shoe law firms that represented the bank, had become involved in Bowen's case. Kardell said that Bowen might be removed as a witness.

What had caused this sudden change of heart at the commission? Bowen believes it was the headline news on March 29—the day he submitted his testimony—that the US Treasury was planning to sell 7.7 billion shares of Citigroup stock, which the Obama administration touted as a profit for taxpayers of about $7 billion. This would be a major public relations coup for Obama's handling of the financial crisis . . . assuming, of course, that Citi's share price didn't collapse in the meantime. Bowen's news about high-level wrongdoing at the bank was unwelcome.

Bowen was faced with a choice. He says that being forced to cut back his testimony felt like a "violation," yet testifying before the FCIC was the only way he could circumvent his nondisclosure agreement with Citigroup and make at least part of his story public. "Otherwise the bank would have come after me and ruined me, as they have come after and ruined others. I really couldn't put my family at risk." After a long night of soul-searching and prayer, he made the requested changes to his testimony.

Bowen testified before the FCIC on April 7, immediately after Alan Greenspan and a day before Robert Rubin. He read a watered-down script and sat through the Q&A session that followed, during which the commissioners seemed to him to avoid any hard-hitting questions. They never really asked about his email to Rubin and the other directors of Citigroup. Bowen's original sworn testimony, together with all the materials he'd provided the commission and his earlier statements to the SEC, were sealed and sent to the National Archives, where they remained confidential for five years.

In a meticulous piece of investigative reporting published by the *New York Times* in September 2013, titled "Was This Whistle-Blower Muzzled?," financial journalist

William Cohan captures the internal dynamics at the FCIC that explain how lawyers representing Citigroup, together with members of the commission, may have helped engineer changes to Bowen's testimony, and then had that testimony safely sealed away. Kardell, Bowen's lawyer, told Cohan he believed "there's no question that Richard was censored." Bondi, the former deputy counsel, strenuously rejected the notion that the FCIC had been pressured to change Bowen's testimony, or that the commission had pressured Bowen. Bradley Karp, Citigroup's lawyer, while agreeing that he had spoken regularly with Bondi about his client's business before the FCIC, also denied that his firm had persuaded the commission to silence Bowen. "We represented and defended Citi," he wrote Cohan. "And I am certain that the F.C.I.C. would confirm that." Angelides told Cohan he didn't believe that Bowen had been censored, though he conceded that the Wall Street banks "and their phalanx of attorneys were putting enormous pressure" on the FCIC "every day of every week with every witness," and attempted "to discredit people who were testifying against their interests."

Consider this for a moment. Why should a "phalanx" of Wall Street attorneys like Bradley Karp have been present at the Financial Crisis Inquiry Commission, an investigative body formed by Congress to get to the bottom of the worst economic disaster since the Great Depression, much less pressure commissioners or discredit witnesses? And where, conversely, was the army of lawyers to represent and defend the interests of the American people? The contrast with the Pecora Hearings, during which Pecora publicly pilloried bank presidents and taught the nation how they had caused the Great Depression, is stark.

"That's the reality behind these commissions—there's a lot that goes on behind the scenes," says Richard Condit, a former GAP attorney who represented Richard Bowen after he testified at the FCIC. "We're led to believe that this blue ribbon panel of highly capable, highly ethical, law-abiding individuals have looked objectively at these events, and have come out with some objective conclusions that we can all use to move forward, to make sure this doesn't happen again. That's what we think, until someone like Richard Bowen blows the whistle on what really goes on. Well, the reality is that lawyers for all the power players were called in, and were all over this stuff in the background, to try to limit, to try to dissuade, even going to the point of threatening, so that people on the commission would back off or narrow their focus. Why, otherwise, would the FCIC seal Richard's testimony in the National Archives for five years, when we, the American taxpayers, spent millions of dollars for this commission to bring the truth about the financial crisis to light?"

The FCIC concluded its work in the kind of partisan split that has become the norm in Washington. The Democratic members issued a fact-rich report that identified several causes of the 2008 crisis, including major failures of corporate governance and risk management, poor regulation and supervision, as well as systemic ethical breakdowns on Wall Street and the banks' pervasive use of derivatives and off-balance-sheet entities. Republican commissioners, by contrast, shifted the blame for the crisis away from the major banks. They voted to exclude from the report the words "deregulation," "shadow banking," "interconnected," "credit default swap" and even—yes—"Wall Street." When this move failed, they wrote two dissenting reports of their own. The report by Commissioner Peter Wallison, a Reagan Treasury official who for the previous two decades had worked at the American Enterprise Institute, a right-wing think tank that urges smaller government, blamed the entire crisis on the US government's drive to increase home ownership through the sinister socialist vehicles of Fannie Mae and Freddie Mac, which, Wallison claimed, had destroyed underwriting standards and forced banks to make bad loans just to remain competitive.

In 2009, having helped to crash the economy with deregulations he'd pushed as secretary of the Treasury and profited from at Citi, Robert Rubin returned to Washington to help fix what he'd broken. Barack Obama placed a number of Rubin protégés in other key economic posts: Lawrence Summers and Gene Sperling as successive directors of the National Economic Council, Jack Lew as Treasury secretary, Sylvia Mathews Burwell as head of the Office of Management and Budget, and Michael Froman as a senior White House economic adviser.

Doors also revolved at the FCIC. In December 2010, even before the commission issued its final report, Bradley Bondi became a partner at Cadwalader, Wickersham & Taft LLP, a leading adviser to major financial institutions including Citigroup. Bradley Karp continued to defend Citi in a raft of lawsuits that the bank faced in subsequent years.

Since the FCIC hearings, in fact, Citi has given Karp and his peers plenty of business. In October 2011, the bank settled a suit with the SEC for $285 million alleging that it misled investors in a $1 billion financial product, packing it full of weak assets and then betting against it. In February 2012, Citi paid $2.2 billion in the nationwide settlement of bank foreclosure fraud. That August, the bank settled a class action lawsuit for $590 million over claims that it vastly understated its exposure to subprime debt from shareholders. Between July and October 2013, Citi paid Fannie Mae and Freddie Mac nearly $1.4 billion for having sold them toxic mortgages. In July 2014, the bank paid $7 billion for its sale of toxic mortgage products before the financial crisis; the DOJ called the bank's behavior "egregious" and said it had "contributed mightily to the financial crisis that devastated our economy." In November 2014, the bank paid over $1 billion to settle civil charges for its part in another massive fraud scheme, the manipulation of foreign currency; six months later it paid another $1.3 billion for criminal foreign currency rigging, and a unit of the bank pleaded guilty to a felony charge. In July 2015, the Consumer Financial Protection Bureau ordered the bank to pay $733 million in consumer relief for illegal credit card practices. In May 2016, Citi paid $425 million to settle a Commodity Futures Trading Commission (CFTC) lawsuit alleging its participation, from 2007 to 2012, in yet another colossal market manipulation scheme, this time involving the rigging of interest-rate benchmarks such as ISDAfix. A year later, it settled with the DOJ for massive money-laundering violations by its Mexico operation, Banamex. In 2018 alone it settled violations involving the Bank Secrecy Act, the Truth in Lending Act and foreign commerce laws; deficiencies in mortgage servicing, trader mismarking, proprietary trading, trading in dark pools, bankruptcy procedures and the handling of certain American Depositary Receipts; and involvement in fraudulently induced loans and manipulation of the SIBOR interest reference rate. In 2018, Citi paid nearly half a billion dollars for its various alleged wrongdoings; in monetary terms, this was a good year for the bank.

Several of these lawsuits against Citi referenced evidence of defective mortgage underwriting provided by Richard Bowen, though Bowen's help has never been acknowledged by the DOJ, the SEC or other government bodies. Of particular relevance to his experiences at Citi was a False Claims Act suit that the bank settled in 2012 for over $158 million, brought by relator Sherry Hunt, who had worked for Bowen. Hunt alleged that the bank had defrauded the Federal Housing Administration by certifying thousands of unqualified mortgages for FHA insurance, through at least March 2011. Uncharacteristically, CitiMortgage conceded that some of Hunt's accusations were true: in the settlement, CitiMortgage "admits, acknowledges and accepts responsibility" for misleading the US Department of Housing and Urban Development and FHA into insuring risky home loans, causing substantial losses. The DOJ's press release describes how the relevant business units "were instructed to apply 'brute force' to pressure quality control personnel to reduce or downgrade their findings of defects, and to challenge all adverse findings by the quality control unit in an effort to drive down the defect rates. These practices caused a systemic breakdown of CitiMortgage's quality control program."

All of which is what Richard Bowen had reported at Citi five years before. Hunt's case shows that long after the 2008 crash, after the trillion-dollar taxpayer-funded bailouts and loan guarantees had rescued Citi from self-inflicted bankruptcy, some senior managers continued the same fraudulent practices that had just crashed the bank—in effect robbing taxpayers twice. This matches what other former employees have said about Citi. When the financial crisis hit, Chris Arnade, who traded bonds at the bank, says it was obvious that Citi and other major banks had seriously damaged the US economy. "I thought, 'Wow, we fucked up!' And I figured that in ongoing conversations over the next five years, other people would say, 'Yeah, we fucked up, let's figure out how to do it right.' But they didn't. They doubled down."

In March 2016, the five-year embargo on Bowen's testimony expired, and his original testimony was released, along with the bombshell announcement that, back in 2010, the FCIC had referred Robert Rubin and other Citi managers to the DOJ for investigation, on suspicion of having misled investors by misstating Citi's financial condition. Some close observers have speculated that top DOJ leadership intentionally failed to communicate this referral to prosecutors who could have acted on it. "I've had four different AUSAs tell me they never saw anything [about Rubin] from the Congressional Commission," Bowen says. His former lawyer at GAP, Richard Condit, agrees. "The whole notion of a referral seems very suspicious to me. Did it happen with an agreement from Justice people that they wouldn't look into it? I suspect that those in power in the commission saw that Rubin was obviously not going to be low-hanging fruit, and they felt they'd be tilting at windmills to pursue it. That's putting this matter in as positive a light as possible. Another way to interpret the facts here is that they seem to indicate that Robert Rubin was being protected."

Despite all the uncertainty, two points are clear. First, no senior official, at Citi or any other major Wall Street bank, was ever prosecuted for the massive wrongdoing that caused the 2008 financial crisis. And second, in a related vein, five years—the period of time for which Bowen's original testimony was kept confidential in the National Archives—is the statute of limitations for fraud under SOX. Other government agencies have likewise appeared to put Citi's interests over those of the general public. True, the SEC did eventually sue Citi for selling a made-to-fail CDO to investors while shorting the same instrument themselves. (Court papers revealed veteran Citi traders privately calling the assets contained in the CDO "horrible," "dogsh!t," and "possibly the best short EVER!") But the figure that the SEC asked from the bank, $285 million, was so ludicrously low—investors had lost somewhere between $700 million and $843 million in the transaction—that the presiding judge, Jed Rakoff, refused to confirm the settlement, observing that the deal, which would have remained secret, was "neither fair, nor reasonable, nor adequate, nor in the public interest." The SEC, he wrote, has a statutory duty "to see that the truth emerges; and if it fails to do so, this Court must not, in the name of deference or convenience, grant judicial enforcement." In an amicus brief, nineteen distinguished securities law scholars, including Lynn Stout, agreed with Rakoff. The collective reasoning of Rakoff and the scholars was rejected on appeal by the Second Circuit, which stated, "Trials are primarily about the truth. Consent decrees [i.e., settlements] are primarily about pragmatism."

Other government entities have shown Citi the same deference. When the DOJ has gone after the bank for selling toxic mortgages, laundering money in Mexico likely linked to narcotraffickers, and other serious offenses, it routinely offers the bank non-prosecution agreements and anodyne statements of fact in return for financial settlements, instead of serious fines, searching revelations of wrongdoing,

and prosecution of the senior bankers who either planned these frauds or should
have prevented them. Testifying before the Senate Judiciary Committee in March
2013, Attorney General Eric Holder finally said aloud about Citi and other top
banks what the DOJ had been thinking since long before the 2008 collapse: "I am
concerned that the size of some of these institutions becomes so large that it does
become difficult for us to prosecute them when we are hit with indications that if
you do prosecute, if you do bring a criminal charge, it will have a negative impact
on the national economy, perhaps even the world economy. And I think that is a
function of the fact that some of these institutions have become too large." Richard
Bowen's experiences with Citi mirror Holder's concerns about major banks' being
too big to fail, or to jail. "Investigators at the SEC and the DOJ took no action
on the extensive evidence provided to them," Bowen says. "An independent congressional commission forced me to change my testimony, which is illegal. I see
all this as evidence of corruption, private and public, at the highest levels of this
country."

Now seventy-two, Bowen teaches accounting at the University of Texas at Dallas, and speaks widely about business ethics and his experiences in an organization
sliding down the slippery slope into fraud. He says his sense of mission remains as
strong as ever, not only to call out fraud by his bank, but to denounce what he sees
as the wider corruption of the financial system in America, which he believes represents an existential threat to the nation. "The so-called 'too big to fail' banks have
a stranglehold on this country. They control the regulatory process, they control the
legislative process through money and the revolving door. They took this country
down the tubes in 2008, and will do it again unless we stop them." With the help
of Michael Termini, an attorney at GAP, he is calling for a congressional investigation into the FCIC's modification of his testimony. "This is an opportunity to wake
this country up," he says. And Bowen clearly believes that America needs an awakening. "Before I give every talk, I pray that the Lord be in the heart of everyone who
hears it, and help each one of them to learn whatever lessons are most appropriate
for them." In January 2016, he and three other financial whistleblowers founded
Bank Whistleblowers United, an advocacy group that aims to underscore the

existential threat that bank crimes pose to the nation, and increase public support for insiders who report these crimes.

Near the end of our most recent phone conversation, Bowen said, "History tells us that the collapse of every great civilization began with erosion of moral values." His voice was resonant, as I imagine it is when he preaches at his church in Dallas. Then he paused, so long I was afraid the line had gone dead. When he spoke again, he sounded like a different person. "Look, I've got four grandkids," he said in a low, broken voice. "I've got to say this without tearing up. I'm worried sick about them, if we don't stop this corruption. And I'm worried sick about everybody in this country."

"What happened to Dick Bowen at Citi was like that *Far Side* cartoon of the cow lying on the psychiatrist's couch," says Bill Black, professor of economics and law at the University of Missouri–Kansas City. "The cow is saying, 'Maybe it's not me. Maybe it's the rest of herd that's gone insane.' In fact, Dick wasn't crazy. His herd had turned criminal."

Black, like Bowen, knows firsthand how banks can become offenders. In addition to his expertise in economics and law, he holds a doctorate in white-collar criminology—he testified before the FCIC on how financial fraud caused the 2008 financial crisis—and worked during the savings and loan crisis as a senior executive and litigator at a series of regulatory bodies, including the Federal Savings and Loan Insurance Corporation, which, until its dissolution in 1989, insured deposits at S&L institutions in the US, also called "thrifts." Like Bowen, Black recognized that financial fraud was spreading like Ebola through the thrift system, while countless other people ignored the disease, denied its existence or celebrated it as a visionary business practice. Unlike Bowen, however, Black was able, through determined and sometimes audacious whistleblowing, to teach key Washington lawmakers and the general public how this fraud worked, and why it threatened the economy. The popular understanding and outrage created by Black and his allies forced politicians, regulators and prosecutors to intervene: hundreds of bankrupt thrifts were shut down, and over a thousand crooked bankers were convicted on felony fraud charges. These decisive actions vastly reduced the harm that taxpayers ultimately suffered in the S&L crisis. Black is still amazed by the contrast with the aftermath of 2008, when the economy was brought to its knees, taxpayers paid tens of billions to bail out miscreant banks, and no senior banker was prosecuted.

Bill Black is big, red-bearded, voluble and angry—voluble and angry because, since the S&L crisis, he's been a financial Cassandra. Well before the 2008 crash, he recognized the frauds being perpetrated at Citi and other major banks, because he'd seen them in the 1980s. Despite his expertise and successful track record in the S&L crisis, he never again found a job as a bank regulator or examiner, and so could not help avert the vastly larger economic disaster of 2008. For all the devastation that the banks wrought in 2008, he says, to this day few people comprehend the criminal nature of their acts—or the myriad frauds they're still committing.

Black emphasizes that whistleblowers are essential to holding financial fraudsters accountable. "Senior bank executives like Richard Bowen who turn whistleblower can provide prosecutors with the highest-quality evidence," he says. "They can not only explain the day-to-day mechanics of the fraud, as highly credible fact witnesses, but can also demonstrate mens rea on the part of the higher managers who orchestrated that fraud." Giving bank insiders a bigger megaphone is why Black, Bowen and two other financial whistleblowers—Gary Aguirre, a former SEC attorney who blew the whistle on the commission and on a leading hedge fund, and Michael Winston, once a senior manager at the notorious mortgage mill Countrywide—formed Bank Whistleblowers United. The four speak at conferences, serve as expert witnesses in lawsuits and testify before Congress, tirelessly repeating two central messages. First, that the main cause of the 2008 financial crisis was massive financial fraud by the major banks. Second, that the United States government and the American people are failing to fix—or even to face—this fraud, which makes another, even more severe financial crash inevitable, and endangers the US democratic system itself.

Finance is whistleblowing's new frontier. Over the last fifteen years, more major whistleblower laws have been written in finance than in any other industry. Insiders are essential to unmasking wrongdoing in the highly technical and secretive world of banks, hedge funds and other financial institutions. "The financial whistleblowers I've worked with are smart, successful, independent people who provide information straight from the heart of the fraud," says Erika Kelton, the attorney at Phillips & Cohen who first used the False Claims Act against Wall Street banks in a case in 1999 and has been an innovator in financial whistleblowing ever since. "They are quintessential insiders, in areas where sometimes only a handful of people know how to interpret the data, or understand the fraud schemes in the first place. They make powerful and convincing witnesses." In the aftermath of the 2008 financial collapse, New York prosecutor Preet Bharara, New York Federal Reserve Bank chair William Dudley and Attorney General Eric Holder all publicly called on honest finance employees with knowledge of crime to step forward, and for increased whistleblower bounties and protections to encourage them to do so. New whistleblower support groups including Bank Whistleblowers United, Whistle Blow Wall Street and Elizabeth Warren's Take On Wall Street have been formed to improve accountability in the financial sector through whistleblowing.

In fact, whistleblower revelations have been central to many of the major legal actions by the DOJ, the SEC, the CFTC and other entities against financial institutions. Bank whistleblowers have also prompted major improvements in national and international law concerning banking and whistleblowing. The revelations of Bradley Birkenfeld, a former wealth management banker, of a systematic tax evasion scheme by his employer, the Swiss bank UBS, triggered changes in the US federal tax code and an overhaul of the venerable, secretive and notoriously criminogenic Swiss banking laws. From 2013 to 2018, Howard Wilkinson, a longtime head of the Baltic trading desk for Danske Bank, repeatedly informed his superiors of what turned out to be some $234 billion in suspicious transactions processed by the Danish bank, much of which apparently involved money laundering. In September 2018, news of the transactions was leaked anonymously to a Danish paper, perhaps by Wilkinson; his name was then leaked to the press, evidently by other Danske employees. On November 21, 2018, Wilkinson testified before the European Parliament, on the problem of money laundering and on the weakness of whistleblower protection in Europe; in March 2019 the EU approved a new directive to protect whistleblowers who reveal money laundering, tax evasion and a range of other crimes. "The EU Directive is a step in the right direction," says Wilkinson's attorney, Stephen Kohn, "but Europe must do more to protect whistleblowers, and needs to implement a reward-based structure modeled on US law." Even when their initial attempts to correct misconduct fail, financial whistleblowers can help write better laws. In 1998, "Mr. ABC," an anonymous whistleblower represented by Erika Kelton who still works at a Wall Street investment bank, filed the first of several tax claims, to inform the IRS of numerous off-balance-sheet shell companies being used by Enron with the blessing of its accountant Arthur Andersen, to conceal hundreds of millions of dollars in debt. (The IRS took no action, and Enron collapsed three years later, when news of its secret debt became public.) Mr. ABC later urged the Senate to institute an IRS whistleblower office, which it did in 2006 after a determined effort by Chuck Grassley. Starting in 2000, eight years before Bernard L. Madoff Investment Securities LLC cratered with $65 billion in losses, the independent forensic accountant Harry Markopolos repeatedly warned the SEC that Madoff's returns were mathematically impossible, and had to be fraudulent. Markopolos's attempts to sound the alarm, though fruitless, later contributed to the formation of whistleblower offices at the SEC and the CFTC, under the Dodd-Frank financial reforms of 2010.

These new offices have received skyrocketing numbers of whistleblower reports, successfully litigated many cases and distributed multimillion-dollar payouts. Unlike FCA relators, whistleblowers under the IRS, SEC and CFTC programs can maintain their anonymity—the data they supply are usually enough to unmask fraud without their having to validate it with their identities. More recently, anonymous financial whistleblowers have revealed details of major offshore tax evasion schemes. The so-called Panama Papers whistleblower supplied nearly 3 terabytes of files to the *Süddeutsche Zeitung*, a German newspaper, that documented how the Panama-based law firm of Mossack Fonseca had created almost 215,000 offshore shell companies, many of which had been used to facilitate tax evasion and money laundering by a long list of international criminals, oligarchs, and heads of state. This data has since led to a string of investigations and prosecutions in over eighty countries, the recovery of more than $1.2 billion from tax evaders, and the arrest of founding partners Jürgen Mossack and Ramón Fonseca Mora. (Subsequent anonymous leaks to the *Süddeutsche Zeitung* and the International Consortium of Investigative Journalists concerning similar tax evasion schemes have been dubbed the "Paradise Papers," "Bahamas Leaks," "Offshore Leaks," "Swiss Leaks" and "Luxembourg Leaks.")

Finance insiders have revealed how their banks did business with some of the world's worst criminal organizations. In 2006, Martin Woods, then a senior anti-money-laundering officer at Wachovia Bank (which became part of Wells Fargo in 2008), learned that hundreds of millions of dollars were flowing into his bank from Mexican *casas de cambio*, exchange houses typically used by tourists to change traveler's checks; Woods, a former narcotics cop in East London, discovered that Wachovia was laundering money for the Sinaloa drug cartel, one of the world's most deadly criminal organizations. After his superiors refused to act on his repeated warnings, he resigned from the bank and notified the DEA. Wells Fargo eventually paid a $160 million settlement. (Since then, of course, Woods has been unable to land another job in banking.) Whistleblower Everett Stern at HSBC, the British bank, helped document his bank's laundering of money for narcotics traffickers, arms dealers, terror groups and rogue states. Much of this criminal activity had been going on for decades, and business arrangements were smooth and mutually profitable: the lead prosecutor in the case explained that cartel members would arrive at HSBC branches in Mexico and "deposit hundreds of thousands of dollars in cash, in a single day, into a single account, using boxes designed to fit the precise dimensions of the teller windows." Deutsche Bank equity traders have been caught, and their bank fined $630 million, for using sham "mirror trades" to move $10 billion in rubles from Russia into offshore accounts for anonymous customers, "in a manner that is highly suggestive of financial crime," a British regulator observed. The $234 billion in suspicious Danske Bank funds, most of which came from Russian nationals (including some with direct ties to the Putin family), flowed through the bank's Baltic affiliate into the wider financial system with the help of correspondent banks widely reported to have been Deutsche Bank, JPMorgan, Bank of America, Citigroup and Swedbank. "Banks that launder money are parasitic organized crime groups," says Martin Woods. "People who forget the criminal nature of money laundering need to remember that the banker's finger is right there next to the killer's, on the trigger of the gun. They need to see the tight correlation between banks that launder money and the tens of thousands of Mexicans murdered by the cartels over the last few years."

When they weren't laundering drug or terror money, many leading banks were systematically rigging the global economy. In December 2016, Deutsche Bank settled a lawsuit for manipulating the silver and gold markets, in which traders exchanged lurid text messages with peers at UBS, HSBC and other banks (though charges against those banks were later dismissed). Goldman Sachs, Morgan Stanley and JPMorgan had already been excoriated by a Senate investigation into their secret attempts to corner the market in commodities like aluminum, crude oil, coal and uranium. These and other major banks have also been caught rigging foreign exchange benchmark rates, ISDAfix, EURIBOR, SIBOR and other seemingly arcane acronyms that are actually central levers of our daily lives and financial well-being. Barclays, Deutsche Bank, UBS, Citigroup, JPMorgan, the Royal Bank of Scotland and others have paid major settlements or fines for rigging LIBOR, the "London interbank offered rate," a primary benchmark for global lending that influences somewhere between $350 and $500 trillion financial instruments worldwide. LIBOR helps to determine the rates we pay for mortgages, auto loans, student loans, credit cards and much else. (In a lawsuit against Bank of America, the City of Philadelphia stated that the LIBOR manipulations had "cost state and local governmental entities hundreds of millions or even billions of dollars, depleting treasuries, ruining budgets and hindering the delivery of public services.") SEC commissioner Kara Stein described the activity of one of the co-conspirators as follows: "Deutsche Bank's illegal conduct involved nearly a decade of lying, cheating, and stealing. This criminal conduct was pervasive and widespread, involving dozens of employees from Deutsche Bank offices including New York, Frankfurt, Tokyo, and London. . . . It was a complete criminal fraud upon the worldwide marketplace."

These bank cartels were thumbing the scales at the very time that millions of American families, businesses and communities were already reeling from the 2008 financial crisis that those same banks had helped to create. And their market rigging is ongoing. Most big banks engage in high-frequency algorithmic trading and participate in vast, secret exchanges known as "dark pools," two practices that effectively make stock trading by individuals obsolete. These massive manipulations reveal the absurdity of the dogma of perfect markets, transparent competition and free enterprise that banks and their lobbyists invoke to argue against government regulation of their industry.

Wrongdoing by household-name megabanks is not merely acute, but recidivist. We've already reviewed Citigroup's rap sheet, much of which was committed while the bank was running on bailout money provided by its primary victim, the American taxpayer. Bank of America likewise boasts an impressive range of wrongdoing—bilking seventy-three thousand military personnel; taking illicit fees from the unemployment checks of jobless workers; soaking municipalities, unions, pension funds and school districts; and committing other illegal acts, of which, since 2006 alone, at least eighty have been identified, litigated, and safely settled out. JPMorgan has committed so much fraud that two New York attorneys created a website, JPMadoff.com, to help people keep up with the bank's exploits, which include victimizing veterans, municipalities, pension funds, credit card users and the bank's own employees, as well as three felony convictions for facilitating Bernie Madoff's Ponzi scheme and manipulating foreign currencies—seventy-one major legal actions since 2006, $38.9 billion in settlements paid.

This isn't really news. Back in 2011, the *New York Times* published a list of repeat-offender banks that had been caught violating a law against fraud, signed an agreement with the SEC promising not to do so again, and then turned right around and violated another antifraud law—and signed yet another empty promise to behave. The list includes AIG, Bank of America, Bear Stearns, Deutsche Asset Management (a subsidiary of Deutsche Bank), Credit Suisse, Goldman Sachs, JPMorgan Chase, Merrill Lynch, Morgan Stanley, UBS and Wells Fargo. Between 2005 and 2011 alone, the *Times* noted, the securities unit of Bank of America had agreed four successive times not to break one major antifraud law, and another four times not to violate another.

In the eight years since that article was published, each of these organizations has racked up more fraud charges and settlements. In May 2015, for example, five of the usual suspects—Citicorp, JPMorgan, Barclays, UBS and the Royal Bank of Scotland—pleaded guilty to felony charges of rigging yet another several-hundred-trillion-dollar market, in fact the biggest and most liquid of them all: the foreign exchange spot market. The banks admitted doing so between 2007 and the end of 2013, and agreed to pay cumulative criminal fines of over $2.7 billion. While announcing the "resolution" of this case that actually resolved very little, Leslie Caldwell, then head of the DOJ's Criminal Division, described one of the perps as follows: "UBS has a 'rap sheet' that cannot be ignored. Within the past six years, the department has resolved criminal investigations of UBS three times, resulting in non-prosecution or deferred prosecution agreements. UBS also has entered into civil and regulatory settlements on multiple occasions within the past few years. Enough is enough." Caldwell's irritation was comprehensible. The DOJ, thanks to Bradley Birkenfeld, had already caught UBS's tax evasion scheme in 2009. It had nabbed the bank again in 2012 for manipulating LIBOR, and allowed it to sign a deferred prosecution agreement, which contained the conventional promise never to break the law again. Yet here UBS was once more rigging interest rates and riling a DOJ prosecutor. Leslie Caldwell was wrong about one thing, though: Enough was not enough. Since then, UBS has been the target of more investigations, and has scored more settlements, including a February 2019 fine (which UBS is appealing) of $5.1 billion assessed by a French court, which found the bank guilty of money laundering and illegal client solicitations. UBS, together with Credit Suisse and Deutsche Bank, is being scrutinized for possible tax evasion as a result of the Panama Papers revelations; HSBC, which the Papers revealed had set up over 2,300 shell companies for wealthy clients, says it expects to pay $1.5 billion to settle related tax evasion and money-laundering charges.

The wrongdoing of the major banks is massive and repeated—and the bankers often seem to revel in it. Traders involved in LIBOR and interest-rate rigging called themselves the "Cartel," the "Mafia," the "Bandits' Club" and the "players." After one trader was inducted into the Cartel, a co-conspirator told him, "Mess this up and sleep with one eye open at night." Another trumpeted: "If you ain't cheating, you ain't trying." An air of impunity also prevails in bank boardrooms. In 2014, the year after JPMorgan paid $20 billion in fines, penalties and settlements for a range of misconduct, the bank's directors doubled CEO Jamie Dimon's pay to $20 million, thumbing their noses at prosecutors, regulators and lawmakers. After HSBC paid $1.9 billion in 2012 to make its money-laundering-for-narcos-and-terrorists charges go away—$1.9 billion being less than five weeks' worth of pretax profits at HSBC in that year—it promoted Paul Thurston, the head of the bank's Mexico division for part of the period that the scheme was in operation, to chief executive of retail banking and wealth management, while the bank's chair almost the entire time, Stephen Green, Baron Green of Hurstpierpoint, became the British minister for trade and investment.

But who can blame bankers for behaving as if they can't be touched, when the evidence is they won't be? The LIBOR fraud by UBS that had so irritated prosecutor Leslie Caldwell in 2015 came after another massive and egregious fraud in 2012, which came after another massive and egregious fraud in 2009. You'd have thought a third strike would finally have resulted in a serious punishment, but no: the bank got off with a guilty plea, the promise to create an "institution-wide compliance program," and yet another fine, which, like all the others, would ultimately be paid by shareholders or written off on the bank's taxes.

How the DOJ justified its handling of UBS in 2012 is revealing. "In the world today of large institutions, where much of the financial world is based on confidence, one of the things we want to ensure," said Lanny Breuer, then head of the Criminal Division, during a press conference, "[is] that counter-parties don't flee an institution, that jobs are not lost, that there's not some world economic event that's disproportionate to the resolution we want." The goal, he said, "is not to destroy a major financial institution." His boss, Eric Holder, the attorney general, chimed in: "The impact on the stability of the financial markets around the world is something that we take into consideration. We reach out to experts outside of the Justice Department to talk about what are the consequences of actions that we might take." These were presumably the same sorts of experts that Breuer had reported paying close attention to in a speech he gave two months earlier to a gathering of New York City lawyers: "We are frequently on the receiving end of presentations from defense counsel, CEOs, and economists who argue that the collateral consequences of an indictment would be devastating for their client. In my conference room, over the years, I have heard sober predictions that a company or bank might fail if we indict, that innocent employees could lose their jobs, that entire industries may be affected, and even that global markets will feel the effects." No doubt some of those presentations also came from once and future bankers at Treasury and the White House.

What happened next, of course, was that UBS broke the 2012 non-prosecution agreement it had signed with Breuer and Holder, containing the de rigueur pledge of no further law-breaking. But perhaps the most interesting act in this whole theater of justice came when, after being nailed for criminal violations of LIBOR, some of the aggrieved parties—which included the City of Baltimore and the Firefighters' and Police Benefit Fund of New Britain, Connecticut—brought a class action suit against UBS and the other big LIBOR fraudsters, to recoup the financial losses that the market rigging had caused them. The banks were represented by the usual phalanx of white-collar defense lawyers, including a team from Covington & Burling, where Eric Holder and Lanny Breuer had worked defending banks, pharmaceutical multinationals and other white-collar fraudsters before shuffling around the table to run the DOJ. In March 2013, the attorneys for the banks persuaded a federal judge to throw out the charges on the spurious grounds that LIBOR wasn't a competitive market—never mind that several banks had already dealt with related charges by paying major settlements to the DOJ. By then, Breuer had already left the DOJ and returned to his alma mater, Covington. Not long afterward, Eric Holder, too, finished his detail at the DOJ and moved back into the corner office that Covington had reserved for him.

The same Kabuki drama took place with HSBC, which, after being denounced in 2012 for putting its money-laundering expertise at the service of the Sinaloa Cartel, rogue states and potential terrorists, won a deferred prosecution agreement and paid $1.9 billion but was not criminally indicted, again because of Eric Holder's concerns about "collateral consequences" of prosecuting the bank. HSBC proceeded to ignore some of the corrections stipulated in the agreement and to push back against others, earning it an official reprimand from the DOJ (though no punishment). Subsequently, HSBC whistleblower Hervé Falciani made available to law enforcers over 100 gigabytes of bank files containing details on a hundred thousand wealthy tax evader clients, some linked to narcotrafficking, terrorist financing, arms dealing and blood diamonds. (HSBC says Falciani stole the data in order to sell it; although his motives have been questioned, his files have caused HSBC to pay substantial fines to France, Belgium, the UK and other national governments.) The DOJ nevertheless did not revoke the bank's deferred prosecution agreement—an omission so striking that the House Financial Services Committee opened an investigation, which concluded that Holder had improperly overruled the recommendation of line attorneys to criminally prosecute the bank, and had then misled Congress about his motives and impeded a congressional investigation into the matter. Again, given the opinions Holder had previously expressed to Congress, his lack of action against HSBC is unsurprising. If the chief prosecutor of the United States says that he can't or won't prosecute big banks, he has not only acquiesced to bank fraud but also tacitly admitted the failure of "equal justice under law" as a premise of American democracy.

But all of these schemes were small beer, compared to the largest, longest-running and most devastating bank crimes in recent memory: the mortgage frauds that triggered the 2008 financial crisis, which Richard Bowen witnessed up close at Citi. All major Wall Street banks eagerly inflated the toxic mortgage bubble at the heart of the crisis. Their allies have long argued that the 2008 collapse was caused by many factors—the government's policies pushing home ownership, lax regulators, the complicity and corruption of GSEs like Fannie and Freddie—and that the banks, hedge funds and other financial operators were merely behaving aggressively, not fraudulently. Yet over the past decade, as lawsuit after lawsuit against the banks has ground through litigation and revealed endless examples of extreme misconduct, such arguments have sounded increasingly hollow. They are like blaming a burglary on a homeowner who forgot to lock her windows and doors, rather than on the thief who robbed her.

Numerous finance whistleblowers have revealed their banks' role in various phases of the long assembly line of crime that created the Crash, from appraisal fraud, liar loans and other chicanery when the mortgages were signed; to the gutted underwriting, faked reps and warranties, and other lawbreaking of the kind that Richard Bowen saw as the loans were bundled; to successive phases of slicing, resale

to investors, stealth shorting and much else carried out on Wall Street. Employees
at the major banks recognized fraudulent schemes like those that Bowen witnessed,
and, after alerting their superiors, reported them to authorities. Sherry Hunt did so
at Citi. Securities lawyer Alayne Fleischmann blew the whistle on what she called
"massive criminal securities fraud" in JPMorgan's mortgage business. Edward
O'Donnell, Eileen Foster, Kyle Lagow and Michael Winston called out the toxic
mortgage exploits of Countrywide and Bank of America, which bought Countrywide and continued much of that firm's wrongdoing. Many more financial truth
tellers stepped forward.

When the bad mortgages began to default, the banks launched another crime
spree. Just as they had sold misleading or false mortgages to borrowers, sometimes
using forged, robo-signed documentation, so they now began to foreclose on delin-
quent borrowers by cobbling together more fake mortgage documents. As Arthur
Wilmarth, professor at the George Washington University Law School and veteran
critic of Wall Street malfeasance, remarked in a 2015 interview, "You had systematic fraud at the origination stage, then you had systematic fraud at the securitization stage, then you had systematic fraud at the foreclosure stage. At what point do
we consider these institutions to have become effectively criminal enterprises?"
Wilmarth was specifically describing Citigroup's behavior before, during and after
the 2008 meltdown, but his words apply to nearly all major banks that wrote and
foreclosed on mortgages in those years. A searching 2011 investigation by Reuters,
"The Watchdogs That Didn't Bark," chronicled perjury, forgery, obstruction of justice, and illegal foreclosures by the five largest servicers, Ally Financial Group,
Bank of America, Citigroup, JPMorgan and Wells Fargo. "I think it's difficult to
find a fraud of this size on the US court system in US history," Raymond Brescia,
an expert in the legal and policy implications of financial crises at Albany Law
School, told Reuters. "I can't think of one where you have literally tens of thousands
of fraudulent documents filed in tens of thousands of cases."

Whistleblower denunciations have helped the US government to reach scores of
legal settlements, including some of the largest in history, to resolve charges of
various flavors of mortgage fraud committed before, during and after the financial
crisis. Wells Fargo paid $2.1 billion to the US government, Morgan Stanley paid

$3.2 billion, Goldman Sachs paid $5.1 billion, Credit Suisse paid $5.3 billion, Citigroup paid $7 billion, Deutsche Bank paid $7.2 billion, JPMorgan paid $13 billion and Bank of America paid $16.7 billion. Though the banks were routinely able, in their settlement agreements, to purchase the right to deny wrongdoing, it's safe to assume that enormous banks defended by armies of top lawyers would not part with record amounts of their own money without having been caught committing record amounts of fraud. But again, none of the bank executives who drove this fraud were ever charged, or lost a dollar of the bonuses they received for carrying it out. Many, in fact, were promoted or, at worst, began a prosperous retirement. Icons of the 2008 collapse like Angelo Mozilo of Countrywide and Dick Fuld of Lehman Brothers, who as CEOs drove their firms straight to cataclysmic bankruptcy that crushed their investors, their clients and the economy, left banking with substantial personal fortunes, and their hubris intact.

If these settlements don't represent real punishment for the banks, they likewise fail to acknowledge the suffering of their victims, whose lives were upended or destroyed by the 2008 financial crisis. For millions of Americans, the storm that broke eleven years ago is still raging. "The 2008 crisis devastated employment in America," says Dennis Kelleher, head of Better Markets. "The US economy now offers fewer jobs, lower pay, worse benefits, and less security than at any time since the Great Depression." While the rate of unemployment has returned to pre-crisis levels, official figures conceal the reality of a job market still reeling after 2008. Almost 40 percent of people of working age without jobs are "discouraged workers," who have given up looking for work and are therefore, absurdly, not counted as unemployed. Broad statistics, however, fail to convey the human suffering that financial crimes cause.

Consider the case of *Erik and Renée Sundquist v. Bank of America*. "Franz Kafka lives," wrote Christopher Klein, a judge in a federal bankruptcy court in Sacramento, California, in his March 2017 opinion on the Sundquist case. "He works at Bank of America."

The 2008 collapse forced Erik and Renée Sundquist to close their construction and development businesses. To economize, they sold their house in Sacramento and bought a smaller one in Lincoln, California, paying down $125,000 and taking out a $587,000 mortgage. The note and deed of trust was bought up by Country-wide; Countrywide was soon taken over by Bank of America, the bank that serviced the Sundquists' loan throughout their ordeal. Judge Klein, in his opinion, explains how Bank of America, after convincing the Sundquists to miss several payments in order to qualify for a mortgage modification, began an extended game of cat and mouse, urging them to request twenty separate mortgage modifications, each of which the bank lost, declared insufficient or declined, while at the same time proceeding with the foreclosure of their house. The Sundquists eventually declared chapter 13 bankruptcy, which automatically invoked a stay of foreclosure, but Bank of America's foreclosure proceedings continued anyway, illegally. Klein describes how the bank's agents "lurk[ed] about the Sundquist home. Without identifying themselves, they staked out the premises, tailed the Sundquists, knocked on doors, knocked on windows, and rang doorbells, all to the terror of the Sundquist family." Wanting to shield their ten-year-old twin sons from this on-slaught, the Sundquists abandoned the house over Labor Day Weekend 2010 and moved into a small rental apartment. Bank of America foreclosed on the house, again illegally; ripped out major appliances, carpets and window coverings; and allowed the front lawn and shrubbery to die, creating an eyesore for which the local homeowner association charged $20,000. Bank of America refused to pay this penalty, and moreover demanded that the Sundquists pay all mortgage and maintenance expenses for the six-month period when the bank held title to the property.

The Sundquists had been elite athletes, Erik a member of an NCAA national championship soccer team, Renée an Olympic skater. Klein describes what Bank of America's predations did to their physical and mental health. Renée Sundquist "descended to depths of emotional despair during the six years between Bank of America's illegal foreclosure . . . and the time of trial. In the later stages of that ordeal, she reacted to the doorbell by hiding under the clothes hanging in her closet, developed suicidal thoughts, and responded to written communications from Bank of America by cutting herself with a razor and bleeding all over the bathroom." Erik Sundquist attempted suicide and developed chronic back pain that prevented him from most kinds of exercise; he was on opioids and steroids, while Renée was taking medications for stress, depression and chronic migraines.

Near the end of his order, Judge Klein speculated on why things had gone so wrong for the Sundquists—and how Bank of America could have committed this misconduct with such cool self-assurance. "It is apparent that Bank of America's strategy regarding the Sundquists has been infused with a sense of impunity," Klein wrote. "The reasons for this attitude of impunity no doubt are complex and overdetermined. The governmental regulatory system has failed to protect the Sundquists. Bank of America held out the Comptroller of the Currency as a source of redress, but that turned out to be a chimera. The Consumer Financial Protection Bureau was thwarted by Bank of America's bald-faced lie that there was no pending litigation with the Sundquists and that there were no litigation papers that could be sent to CFPB." Klein made clear that the arguments routinely adduced by banks, economists and other free marketeers to excuse flagrant fraud and criminal behavior by financial institutions—the rogue employees, senior management out of the loop, or the shareholder value mantra—carried no weight with him. Klein observed that Bank of America was a repeat offender in the mortgage fraud business, listing several major settlements in what he calls "a long rap sheet of fines and penalties in cases related to its mortgage business."

He also stresses that the bank's repeated and "astonishingly brazen" wrongdoing was carried out at the orders of senior management: "It is apparent that the engine of Bank of America's problem in this case is one of corporate culture. The evidence is replete with so many communications from the office of Bank of America's Chief Executive Officer that the oppression of the Sundquists cannot be chalked off to rogue employees betraying an upstanding employer. This indicates that the engine is driven by direction from senior management. Nor can Bank of America hide behind some alleged fiduciary duty to a third-party investor that constrains its ability to do the right thing. Bank of America owned the Sundquist mortgage for its own account." In fact, Klein writes, when the office of the CEO lied to the CFPB that no foreclosure had occurred, and that the bank was not in litigation with the Sundquists, Bank of America's offenses became criminal.

In the end, Judge Klein fined Bank of America $46 million in damages, to be paid primarily to organizations that protect mortgage holders from similar trauma. (The bank later offered to pay the Sundquists several million additional dollars on the condition that Klein's opinion be expunged, which the angry judge rejected as "a naked effort to coerce this court to erase the record.") But this "happy ending" to the Sundquists' ordeal, at least in court, is one shining exception in a wilderness of abuse. Countless other victims, without the knowledge or resources to pursue their cases, were simply silenced.

Whistleblowers in the banking industry rarely fare better. Most encounter crushing retaliation and legal intimidation by their organization, and are typically banned for life from the field. "There is a wall of silence around fraud in the financial sector, and those who break it are excluded more ruthlessly than in any other industry I know," says Erika Kelton. Government officials can be unsympathetic as well. HSBC banker-whistleblower Hervé Falciani, who revealed criminal money-laundering activity by his employer, was sentenced in absentia in Switzerland to five years in prison for industrial espionage. Antoine Deltour and Raphaël Halet, former accountants at PricewaterhouseCoopers who in 2014 revealed a sweeping tax avoidance scheme by some 350 multinational corporations headquartered in Luxembourg, were criminally prosecuted (the journalist who published their revelations was also indicted). Bradley Birkenfeld, though enabling the US government to recover billions in unpaid taxes by blowing the whistle on UBS, spent thirty months in prison for allegedly omitting names from the list of tax evaders he supplied to US authorities. (He later received a $104 million award from the IRS whistleblower program.) Whistleblowers nonetheless rely on government support, since the qui tam mechanism that enables FCA whistleblowers to prosecute their suits on their own behalf is absent in IRS, SEC and other financial whistleblowing, meaning the government must take the lead in their cases. Yet as Richard Bowen discovered, the government frequently sides with the banks. Like him, many financial whistleblowers end up blowing the whistle not only on their firms but on financial regulators as well. Carmen Segarra, an attorney at the New York Federal Reserve, called out a shady transaction between Goldman Sachs and Banco Santander, and subsequently blew the whistle on the New York Fed itself when it closed her investigation and fired her. And though prosecutors like Eric Holder and Preet Bharara claim to encourage financial whistleblowing, all too often they have failed to act on whistleblower information they have received, or even to acknowledge the vital contributions of whistleblowers in cases they have prosecuted successfully.

Bill Black believes that, deep down, the DOJ dislikes and mistrusts whistle-blowers. The truths that whistleblowers tell, he says, don't fit the DOJ's narrative of the financial crisis, and draw unwelcome attention to the department's own failure to prosecute the individuals who caused it.

"One of the first rules of criminology is that organizations, like fish, rot from the head," Black says. "You won't find pervasive fraud at a bank unless the people at the very top—Robert Rubin and [CFO] Gary Crittenden at Citi, for example—are at a minimum turning a blind eye, and far more often structuring the fraud. Dick Bowen handed the DOJ a perfect case against Citi's senior officers. So did other senior whistleblowers at the other banks—Alayne Fleischmann at JPMorgan, Edward O'Donnell at Bank of America, and on and on. But the DOJ under both [George W.] Bush and Obama never welcomed financial whistleblowers, and never thanked them, because in reality, they never intended to prosecute senior bankers in the first place."

Though many finance leaders show little concern for their customers, and outright hostility to whistleblowers, you'd assume they would scrupulously preserve the reputation of their firm, and their own good name as honest entrepreneurs. Bill Black saw through this myth thirty years ago, and wrote a book to debunk it: *The Best Way to Rob a Bank Is to Own One*. While poring over the accounts of hundreds of thrifts that had failed during the S&L crisis, he realized that much lawbreaking hadn't been an oversight, but a central part of the business plan. If C-suite managers unencumbered by basic ethics are able to earn large bonuses based on the volume rather than the quality of their business, Black explains, their short-term personal financial incentives are often diametrically opposed to the long-term health of their banks. Countless S&L executives he examined had transmuted their apparently legitimate—and often illustrious—enterprises into fraud vehicles, and enriched themselves while destroying their firms. Black terms this practice "control fraud."

Here's how a popular version of this fraud works in banking. Corrupt bank managers write massive quantities of bad loans, which fuel rapid growth in their institutions and enormous (though imaginary) profits in the short term. Such short-term profits produce equally enormous (and very tangible) income for the managers. Not too long down the road, of course, the bad loans default and the banks fail, but by then the crooked CEOs and their cronies have tucked away sizable personal fortunes. "For managers with a strong stomach for fraud, this was a much safer course to personal wealth than taking honest business risks, which might or might not pay off," Black remembers. "If they'd been honest risk takers, we'd have seen some big winners and some abject losers. Instead, everybody who followed the recipe won big, in terms of personal wealth, though of course their S&Ls all failed catastrophically." The longer they can conceal the growing hole in their accounts, the larger their fortunes become. Hence having lax accounting standards, limited regulations and few regulators peering into their books is vital to the success of the scheme.

Black explains that the S&L crisis, like many financial crime waves, was preceded by what he calls the "3 Ds": periods of deregulation, de-supervision, and de facto decriminalization. The deregulation phase began in 1980, when Congress, noting the soaring indebtedness of S&Ls due to rising inflation, reduced oversight of thrifts by passing a series of measures that culminated in the 1982 Garn–St Germain Depository Institutions Act. Ronald Reagan called this law "the most important legislation for financial institutions in fifty years," adding with a Trumpian flourish, "I think we hit the jackpot." It was an apt metaphor: Reagan had started US finance down the road to casino capitalism, with its attendant espousal of debt as a blessing and its blind faith in the self-regulatory power of markets, in volume over value and growth over health. Long before the repeal of Glass-Steagall, Reagan-era deregulation like Garn–St Germain enabled S&L institutions to gamble with savings accounts insured by the US government (and therefore backstopped by the American taxpayer). Lawmakers also began dismantling New Deal–era restrictions on mortgage lending and consumer credit, written by people who had lived through the devastation caused by Gilded Age risk taking and were determined to prevent another Great Depression. American financial institutions and households alike were allowed—indeed encouraged—to grow beyond their means by radically increasing their own leverage. Household savings fell, and household debt skyrocketed, as did indebtedness by businesses and banks, all driven by irrational exuberance and the rock-bottom interest rates pushed by Alan Greenspan's Fed. American finance had become a pyramid scheme. A series of bubbles and bursts predictably ensued.

The new Garn–St Germain Act permitted S&Ls to participate in a host of risky ventures previously forbidden to them, including writing commercial loans and adjustable-rate mortgages, and investing directly in real estate. At the same time, permissive new accounting standards were introduced, which helped many a crooked manager camouflage, at least temporarily, his thrift's ballooning debt load. S&Ls also gained new access to deep pools of Other People's Money, when, in 1981, the industry's powerful lobbyists surreptitiously increased federal insurance on thrift deposits from $40,000 to $100,000 per account, putting the US taxpayer on the hook for far larger S&L failures. To deregulation Congress added de-supervision, by reducing the number of bank supervisors, FBI agents and prosecutors assigned to the S&L industry, even as the assets of S&Ls grew from $686 billion to $1.1 trillion in just three years. By 1989, a third of these had collapsed, and a taxpayer bailout was imminent.

"I spent a lot of my time working as a coroner," Black says. He and his staff performed forensic autopsies on a series of failed institutions, looking for the causes of their collapse, and of the larger S&L crisis itself. They soon recognized a characteristic pattern of conduct at many thrifts, what Black calls a "fraud recipe." Within two years of deregulation and de-supervision, many institutions began to make strikingly bad loans at a premium yield, gutting their own underwriting procedures and internal controls, and setting aside absurdly inadequate provisions for future losses on bad loans. "These were the 'tells,' in the poker sense, that a thrift was engaged in fraud. They were the early-warning system, because they told us as regulators that a thrift was a fraud scheme and should be halted or shut down, even while it was recording record profits . . . at least on paper."

Making such loans intentionally was unprecedented in the industry, for good reason: thrifts that wrote bad, unprotected loans were sure to fail. But as Nobel Prize–winning economists George Akerlof and Paul Romer observed in their 1993 article on the S&L crisis, "Looting," many thrifts had a "total disregard for even the most basic principles of lending: maintaining reasonable documentation about loans, protecting against external fraud and abuse, verifying information on loan applications, even bothering to have borrowers fill out loan applications." With a note of wonder, Akerlof and Romer noted that the heads of such S&Ls "acted as if future losses were somebody else's problem. They were right." (Richard Bowen was similarly amazed at Citi fifteen years later.)

Black and his colleagues also saw how fraudulent S&Ls created their own ecosystems of lawlessness, by bribing or suborning auditors, appraisers, lawyers and other professionals they needed to carry out their frauds. In such an environment, corrupt actors played ball and prospered, while principled professionals refused and were ejected from the field. "When fraudulent firms gain a competitive advantage, bad ethics drives good ethics out of the marketplace," says Black. "That is exactly what we saw in the S&L industry after deregulation: with such powerful incentives to defraud and so few real deterrents, the industry became criminogenic, punishing not only their customer-victims, but also the honest CEOs who wouldn't cheat, but couldn't compete with the cheaters." Only the rule of law—not free market forces—can break the fraud cycle.

Black witnessed particularly flagrant criminality in Texas, California, Arizona and Florida, where legislators had started removing state-level regulations on S&Ls even before major federal deregulation began. He found yachts and private jets and fleets of Rolls-Royces, corporate debauches in Las Vegas and Europe, and high-priced prostitutes at board meetings, all financed by the banks' toxic loans and corrupt deals. Don Dixon, owner of a particularly heinous S&L called Vernon Savings & Loan, used his depositors' funds to buy himself a ski chalet in Colorado and a beach house in San Diego, and a $2.6 million 112-foot yacht called *High Spirits* where he entertained, sometimes with call girls, influential politicians including the Texas Savings and Loan commissioner, Linton Bowman; Speaker of the US House of Representatives Jim Wright, another Texan; and former House whip Tony Coelho from California. Dixon was the ringleader of a group of corrupt S&L operators Black called the "Texas 40," who colluded to conceal one another's fraudulent accounts. When Black and his colleagues at the Federal Home Loan Bank Board moved to shut down Vernon, Dixon's strategic deployment of sex and boats paid off. Jim Wright supported Dixon and attempted to block Black's takeover of Vernon. Wright ticked off the third D in Bill Black's control fraud recipe, de facto decriminalization, by portraying Dixon as an innocent businessman being unfairly restrained by government bureaucrats like Bill Black, and not the lurid con man that he was.

Wright's actions prompted Black's first act of whistleblowing. He told the *Washington Post* about Don Dixon's assorted shady dealings, and described for the *New York Times* Wright's repeated obstruction of the Bank Board's management of the S&L crisis: "For the first time, in the F.S.L.I.C. we are seeing recurrent attempts to use political influence to prevent F.S.L.I.C. from taking effective enforcement action against hopelessly insolvent thrifts," Black said in the *Times*. "Such interference from influential, powerful members of Congress will increase F.S.L.I.C.'s losses." Black's views were borne out when, in March 1987, Vernon went into federal receivership with $6 billion in bad loans, and required a $1.3 billion taxpayer bailout. Dixon was convicted of twenty-three counts of bank fraud and sentenced to five years in prison; Wright's political star began to wane.

In June 1987, Black was called to testify before the House Banking Committee, chaired by Fernand St Germain, author of the deregulation bill that had set the stage for the S&L scandal. Black had prepared a written statement in which he described how Jim Wright had hindered the Bank Board's work in winding down troubled S&Ls, and debunked the popular belief that most S&L insolvencies had been caused by an economic downturn, demonstrating instead how their demise had been due to mismanagement and malfeasance. St Germain and Wright tried to muzzle Black by canceling his testimony at the last minute, so Black told his story to several national newspapers. Wright repeatedly pressured Black's bosses to fire him, but they refused. In May 1989, Wright resigned from Congress after an external investigation concluded that he had committed serious improprieties in his dealings with the S&L industry, and a separate House Ethics Committee report found that he had violated House rules sixty-nine times.

Black's most formidable and picturesque opponent was Charles Keating, head of Lincoln Savings and Loan in Irvine, California, who, thanks largely to the efforts of Black and his colleagues, has gone down in history as a paradigmatic white-collar criminal, and not as the financial visionary he and his allies claimed. Keating, who died in 2014 at the age of ninety, was a champion swimmer and an Eagle Scout, widely known in Washington circles as "Mr. Clean" for his overt Catholic piety and his energetic antipornography campaigning. Keating also engaged in the kind of bank fraud and plunder of the public treasury that characterized the S&L scandal at its worst. He bought Lincoln in 1984 with the help of Drexel Burnham Lambert, which raised $56 million for him with the sale of junk bonds; in return, according to journalist James Stewart, Keating absorbed other junk bond issues that Michael Milken couldn't sell elsewhere, becoming one of several "captive" S&Ls whose depositors' cash helped maintain Milken's unrivaled (and deceptive) reputation for success in placing his debt. Keating also "invested" his depositors' funds in raw desert land and other high-risk development schemes, and speculated with it on foreign exchange markets. Within three years, most of these wagers had failed spectacularly, but by then Keating had become a rich man. "Always remember," Keating's marketing manual for selling junk bonds exhorted his sales force, "the weak, meek and ignorant are always good sales targets." To victimize one particularly vulnerable demographic, elderly widows, he recruited a team of fresh-faced, impeccably groomed young salesmen who, while playing the part of the ideal grandson, bilked grannies of their retirement savings. In all, Keating persuaded twenty-three thousand of his S&L customers to transfer their savings from federally guaranteed bonds to uninsured junk bonds, which became worthless when Keating's firm went bankrupt.

Keating campaigned for further deregulation of the S&L industry, and for special exemptions for Lincoln, hiring economists to serve as lobbyists and to vouch for his thrift's financial health. One of them was Alan Greenspan, the future Federal Reserve chairman, who at the time ran an economic forecasting firm. In 1984, Greenspan wrote a position letter to Bill Black's Bank Board, stating that savings and loan deregulation "was working just as planned," and that the board should stop worrying so much about junk bonds and other risky investment techniques.

Greenspan elsewhere pronounced Lincoln a "financially strong . . . vibrant and healthy" institution that posed "no foreseeable risk" to the FSLIC; and called Keating and his staff "seasoned and expert in selecting and making direct investments." Keating also retained Lexecon, the economic consultancy founded by University of Chicago professors Richard Posner and Daniel Fischel. Lexecon, like Greenspan, vouched for Lincoln, calling it "sound" and "safer than comparable thrifts."

Having seen how trenchantly Black had dealt with Dixon and the Texas 40, Keating went after him with a vengeance. In an all-caps memo to his chief Washington lobbyist, Jim Grogan, Keating wrote, "GET BLACK . . . KILL HIM DEAD." Grogan set a law firm and two private detective agencies to dig into Black's past. Keating also made large campaign contributions to influential politicians, whom he expected to help him keep S&Ls, and Lincoln in particular, free of vexing regulators like Bill Black. Among his champions were five US senators who eventually became known as the Keating Five: John McCain, Dennis DeConcini, Donald Riegle, John Glenn and Alan Cranston. On April 9, 1987, when the Lincoln house of cards had already begun to collapse and the Bank Board was actively investigating Lincoln, the Keating Five summoned Black and three fellow bank regulators to a meeting in Washington and urged them to halt their investigation, as well as to ease their restrictions on the thrift's business. The board was eventually forced to comply, which allowed Keating to spin out his fraud and expand his debts for another two years, greatly increasing the ensuing taxpayer bailout. Black kept meticulous notes of the meeting, and his record of the five senators' ill-informed bullying of regulators on Keating's behalf formed the basis of a Senate ethics investigation.

In 1989, for all Keating's political influence, Lincoln went bankrupt, necessitating a $3.4 billion bailout, the largest in history at the time. Two years later, in part thanks to Bill Black's expert testimony, Keating was convicted in the Superior Court of California on seventeen counts of fraud, racketeering and conspiracy; Judge Lance Ito gave him ten years in prison, paraphrasing Woody Guthrie in his sentence: "More people have suffered from the point of a fountain pen than from a gun." Keating was also convicted in federal court on seventy-three counts of fraud, racketeering and conspiracy, sentenced to twelve and a half years in jail, and ordered to pay over $120 million in damages and restitution. (Four years later, an appeals court overturned both Keating's state and federal convictions on technicalities, and he pleaded guilty to lesser charges.)

Bill Black's whistleblowing, coupled with his investigative work on bank fraud, ultimately helped to halt the S&L crisis before it ballooned to a size that might have smothered the US economy. He and his allies also ensured that numerous S&L heads were prosecuted for fraud and sentenced to prison. Why, I ask him, have Richard Bowen and other bank whistleblowers not had a comparable impact on the financial fraud that caused the 2008 crisis?

First, Black says, he enjoyed widespread support among colleagues and superiors, which made him a more effective whistleblower. "Without that support, whistle-blowers can become terribly isolated, and are more easily silenced. If I hadn't been surrounded by people who thought like I did, I might not have survived." Second, he was able to become a meta-whistleblower, and to explain to an extensive audience why the business dealings of Dixon, Keating and the others weren't inspired entre-preneurialism or even risky business, but audacious fraud that harmed millions of employees, depositors, investors and taxpayers. And third, Black stresses the impor-tance of the tight coordination that regulators established during the S&L crisis with investigators and prosecutors. He and his colleagues referred thirty thousand instances of suspected bank fraud to state and federal prosecutors, and drew up a list of the hundred worst fraud schemes as teaching paradigms. Their expert bank exam-iners trained FBI agents and prosecutors how to recognize the control fraud "tells." The results were striking: cases spearheaded by Black had a 90 percent conviction rate, perhaps the highest in history against elite financial criminals.

The thousands of press conferences generated by these prosecutorial successes became teaching moments, when regulators, investigators and the DOJ could edu-cate the media about the fraud that had caused the S&L crisis. The media, in turn, explained it to the American people. Black sums up the process:

Each successful case had an indictment, an arrest, a trial, a conviction and a sentencing hearing, and these became a drumbeat in the press. Americans heard in clear, understandable English what the fraud scheme was, how it enriched specific wealthy and powerful people, and which politicians they were cozy with. After about the twentieth case, you get broad recognition. People start to say, "Wait a minute, this fraud scheme sounds a whole lot like the nineteen prior fraud schemes! This is not anomalous. . . ." They see this isn't just risk-taking or sharp operating, it's sleazy, it's fraud, it's incredibly damaging, and they're going to have to pay for it. . . . It's really a fundamental message, asking people to reappraise how they look at the world, in a way which we can prove against the best criminal defense lawyers in the world. That's how you change a nation.

Black remembers when Congressman Frank Annunzio, an S&L booster, started wearing a large button saying JAIL THE S&L CROOKS. "He was one of the sleaziest members of the House, a guy who was in the pocket of Charles Keating," Black says. "When he started wearing that button, we knew we'd won."

No one in Congress wore a JAIL THE WALL STREET CROOKS button after 2008. The vastly larger scale of the latest crisis became a gun that banks and their government allies held to America's head: Rescue Wall Street, the lifeblood of the nation's economy, we were told, or the economy dies. As was not the case in the S&L crisis, former bankers now controlled many areas of US financial policy, and enjoyed far greater political and economic influence than regional players like Keating and Dixon could muster. The fundamental causes of the crisis, too, were harder to grasp. Liar loans and other early scams were simple enough to comprehend, although most Americans had no idea how widespread they had become. But the financial instruments that amplified the 2008 disaster exponentially—the complex derivatives that multiplied risk and concentrated like radioactivity in systemically important nodes of the economy—were obscured by a welter of acronyms and financial jargon that few laypeople followed.

But perhaps most harmfully, despite the proof supplied by several thousand court cases that runaway control fraud had caused severe economic harm during the S&L crisis—and despite the almost comical misreading of the thrift industry by prominent economists like Alan Greenspan and Daniel Fischel—the neoliberal narrative of self-regulating markets remained intact. Greenspan, Fischel and their law and economics peers continued to deny (often for substantial fees) that fraud had caused the S&L crisis, or that ringleaders like Keating were criminals. Instead, they blamed the crisis on external economic shocks, or on bad regulations.

A few influential economists supported Black's straightforward, midwestern, man-in-the-street, whistleblower-style interpretation that Keating and the rest were old-fashioned grifters, and that behaving ethically, by not treating your investors or customers like ignorant dupes, isn't irrational, but is the only acceptable way to do business. Yet as George Akerlof and Paul Romer have observed, "Many economists still seem not to understand that a combination of circumstances in the 1980s made it very easy to loot a financial institution with little risk of prosecution." In fact, numerous distinguished economists simply denied—and continue to deny—the existence of financial fraud.

With free-market fundamentalism increasingly influential among Democrats as well as Republicans, Bill Black's victories during the S&L crisis proved short-lived, and the lessons of that crisis were lost. The relative independence of the Bank Board, which had enabled Black and his colleagues to fight crucial political and economic battles, was lost when George H. W. Bush disbanded the board and folded it into the Office of Thrift Supervision (OTS), part of the Treasury. Bill Clinton cemented the alliance between the Democratic Party and Wall Street by making former Goldman Sachs cochairman Robert Rubin his Treasury secretary. A remarkable number of prominent economists, business school professors, financiers, CEOs, regulators, officials at the Treasury and the Federal Reserve, and politicians of both parties ignored the lessons of the S&L crisis, denied the existence of control fraud, and maintained that self-regulating free markets operating with efficient contracts and peopled by rational self-maximizers would prevent serious future economic shocks.

Alan Greenspan, true to his neoliberal roots and the libertarian dogma of his close personal friend Ayn Rand, remained violently opposed to financial regulation, and his nomination by Ronald Reagan to head of the Federal Reserve—reconfirmed by George H. W. Bush, Bill Clinton and George W. Bush—gave him a powerful new platform for his deregulatory zeal. Though he admitted having been "distressed," "embarrassed" and "thoroughly surprised" by the bankruptcy of

Lincoln Savings and Loan, which occurred shortly after he had pronounced it to be in excellent financial health, Greenspan concluded that mismanagement, not fraud, had caused its demise. Seven years later, the still more self-assured Maestro told Brooksley Born, the chair of the Commodity Futures Trading Commission, that since markets self-corrected to prevent fraud, antifraud laws were unnecessary. He reputedly browbeat any member of his Federal Reserve Bank staff who disagreed.

Greenspan found strong allies in Robert Rubin and in Rubin's protégé Lawrence Summers, two Democrats who together continued the work that Ronald Reagan had begun, aggressively cutting the financial world free of government control, which, according to their doctrine, would allow the market to work its special magic at maximal efficiency. They winked at the illegal merger of Citibank with the financial conglomerate Travelers Group, which violated the Glass-Steagall Act. Then they repealed Glass-Steagall, opening the door to more such systemically intertwined, too-big-to-fail financial institutions. Senator Phil Gramm, a driving force behind the repeal, fought ferociously against the regulation of derivatives, then took his post-government reward as a derivatives czar at UBS; his wife, Wendy Gramm, chair of the CFTC, explicitly exempted energy derivatives from federal regulation, then six days later left government to become a director at Enron, a leading trader in energy derivatives. When Brooksley Born persisted in urging the regulation of derivatives, in June 1998 Rubin publicly denounced her initiative as a threat to the financial system and asked Congress to strip the CFTC of its authority to regulate derivatives. Congress complied.

Just months before Glass-Steagall was officially repealed, Robert Rubin turned over the helm of Treasury to Larry Summers, and revolved to the board of Citigroup, the megabank that his deregulatory fervor had helped bring into being, where he reportedly earned $126 million over the next decade. Here, on November 3, 2007, he received the anguished email that marked the beginning of Richard Bowen's whistleblowing.

In the years after the S&L crisis, the Three Marketeers and their allies prosecuted a full-blown program of deregulation, de-supervision and de facto criminalization. There were several dress rehearsals for the 2008 catastrophe, each of which reinforced the validity of Black's control fraud model. Enron's wunderkind financiers

Kenneth Lay, Jeffrey Skilling and Andrew Fastow, under hands-off, revolving-door directors like Wendy Gramm, collaborated with JPMorgan, Citi and other major banks to build a vast network of special-purpose entities to commit accounting fraud, hiding billions of dollars in debt and evading taxes; when Richard Spillenkothen, the Fed's leading supervisor, asked to brief the Fed board on the major role of the banks in these vehicles, Greenspan and his apparatchiks angrily refused. Other accounting scandals of the early 2000s—WorldCom, Tyco, HealthSouth, Adelphia and others—were further control frauds, whose proliferation supported Black's contention that control frauds can become epidemics that corrupt entire industries.

Black watched the run-up to 2008 with a dawning sense of déjà vu, seeing many of the same fraud "tells" he'd seen during the S&L crisis. He also noted major differences in the way regulators, investigators, prosecutors, politicians and the general public reacted to the growing evidence of fraud in the mid-2000s.

Like the S&L crisis, 2008 began with a bout of deregulation, which led to the mass entry into the market of a range of unscrupulous opportunists. Mortgage originators colluded with or suborned property appraisers to artificially inflate house values, and pumped out an ever-growing stream of defective and downright fabricated loans, which they sold to bigger banks and securitization firms. The behavior that Richard Bowen observed at Citi was widespread at other banks, which routinely bought such loans knowing they were fraudulent, but didn't care, because they were swiftly bundling them and reselling them as mortgage-backed securities to investors. Investments got further and further from the underlying foundation of the mortgages they were based on, as banks repackaged mortgage-backed securities into CDOs, sliced them into tranches with different risks, and sold these to still other investors. When the supply of "real" mortgages ran out, bankers created "CDO squareds," composed entirely of other CDOs, and concocted synthetic CDOs not based on real home loans at all, but on predictions about how those loans and other mortgage-related products would perform in the future. Each transaction created fat fees and trading profits for intermediaries, which drove enormous, largely artificial demand from securitizers on Wall Street for still more mortgage-related products. As the FCIC investigators later observed, "each new layer brought in more investors wagering on the mortgage market—even well after the market had started to turn. So by the time the process was complete, a mortgage on a home in south Florida might become part of dozens of securities owned by hundreds of investors—or parts of bets being made by hundreds more."

Despite all of this opacity, some observers had known for a decade about rampant fraud in the mortgage industry. In September 2004, Chris Swecker, the FBI's assistant director for investigations, warned that mortgage fraud, whose growth he had witnessed since 1999 as a special agent in the field, had the "potential to be an epidemic . . . that could have as much impact as the S&L crisis." Suspicious Activity Reports (SARs), filed by financial institutions with the Treasury to flag transactions that appear likely to be connected with financial crimes, grew twenty-fold between 1996 and 2005, from 1,300 to 26,000. By 2009, the number of SARs had reached 67,507. The mortgage industry itself winked at the fraudulent nature of the loans being produced, which involved little or no verification of the applicants' stated income, openly using terms like "liar loans," "no doc loans" and "NINJA loans" (an acronym for "No income, no job, no assets"). Research by Credit Suisse estimated that 49 percent of all mortgages written in 2006 were liar loans; an investigator for the Federal Reserve Board put the number at 66 percent in 2003. The Mortgage Bankers Association warned that such loans were "open invitations to fraudsters. It appears that many members of the industry have little historical appreciation for the havoc created by low-doc/no-doc products that were the rage in the early 1990s. Those loans produced hundreds of millions of dollars in losses for their users."

Nevertheless, Washington leaders continued to deregulate the financial industry, and added substantial de-supervision in the name of unleashing capital markets from unnecessary bureaucratic burdens. The Fed, under Greenspan and his protégé Ben Bernanke, was, as Black says, "so passionate in its hatred for regulation, supervision, enforcement, and prosecution, and so dogmatic in its faith in 'markets' and the inherent sainthood of financial CEOs, that it fought an unholy war against its own supervisors." Mortgage fraud investigators were hampered by funding cuts and staffing reductions. The FBI, for instance, had only 120 agents detailed to mortgage fraud investigations, and Swecker's repeated requests for additional funding were refused or obstructed by superiors at the FBI, the DOJ, or by the White

House Office of Management and Budget. Swecker proposed the creation of a national task force against mortgage frauds, a big-picture group aimed at tackling not only the fraudulent lenders but their vital co-conspirators, the credit rating agencies and external auditors. Then Attorney General Michael Mukasey refused, dismissing mortgage fraud as "white-collar street crime."

State government officials and consumer advocates, alarmed at the rising tides of mortgage fraud, predatory lending and home foreclosures that began to devastate local communities, begged the Fed to create rules to help limit the damage. The Fed had the statutory authority to forbid liar loans altogether, but Greenspan did nothing. When some state attorneys general attempted to rein in the misbehavior within their states, free-market federal bureaucrats at the OTS and the Office of the Comptroller of the Currency (OCC) sided with the banks, issuing rules preventing the states from interfering with the consumer practices of nationally regulated banks and thrifts. These regulators made no secret of which side they were on. At a press conference in 2003, as the mortgage fraud bonfire was reaching white heat, OTS director James Gilleran posed for a group photograph holding a chain saw over a stack of paper symbolizing government regulation, together with FDIC vice chair John Reich and the heads of three of the largest bank lobby groups, each of whom held pruning shears. The FDIC included the photo in its 2003 annual report, with the observation: "As a former community banker, Vice Chairman Reich understands bankers' concerns regarding the extent of regulatory burden, and believes that, with the assistance of bankers, meaningful changes can be made." The OTS was funded by fees from banks it regulated, which included such notorious mortgage factories as Countrywide, Washington Mutual and IndyMac Bancorp; it referred to its regulated entities as "customers," and its stated mission was to let them "operate with a wide breadth of freedom from regulatory intrusion."

Predictably, when the Supreme Court entered the fray in 2007, it did so to ensure that fraudsters could continue to fly under the regulatory radar, by ruling that Wachovia Bank, a repeat mortgage offender, did not have to abide by state law because it fell under the sole supervision of the OCC. Prentiss Cox, a former Minnesota assistant attorney general who smelled the rot early and pushed for state action to head off mortgage fraud, blasted the federal bureaucrats: "Not only were they negligent, they were aggressive players attempting to stop any enforcement action. . . . Those guys should have been on our side."

In such an environment, the tight coordination between bank regulators, examiners, investigators and prosecutors that Bill Black had enjoyed melted away, or was actively dismantled. Chris Swecker told the FCIC that he'd never had contact with a bank examiner during his tenure at the FBI—a drastic change from the days when Black and his fellow examiners trained special agents and consulted with them on how to make their own SARs more effective. The entire criminal referral process, essential to zeroing in on fraud during the S&L crisis, broke down: bank regulators no longer had a mechanism for sending cases of flagrant fraud to prosecutors and the FBI. The thirty thousand criminal referrals of executives during the S&L crisis dwindled in the aftermath of 2008 to a handful.

In an attempt to compensate for their understaffing and lack of expertise, investigators and prosecutors began to receive coaching from the opposition. In 2007, the FBI entered a cooperative agreement with the Mortgage Bankers Association, an influential lobbying group for the banking industry that represented the very firms that had created and profited from the 2008 financial crisis. At the association's urging, the FBI began pursuing small-time mortgage originators, often of foreign descent, rather than following Chris Swecker's plan of moving up the food chain to investigate the large banks that had masterminded the fraud. Benjamin Wagner, US attorney for the Eastern District of California and head of the DOJ's mortgage fraud unit, either did not understand or refused to accept the control fraud model. "It doesn't make sense to me that they would be deliberately defrauding themselves," Wagner said of banks making bad loans. Bill Black shakes his head: "He bought into the storyline that the perps themselves handed him!"

Without educated investigators or a steady stream of prosecutions, Black says, no clear media story could emerge from the 2008 crisis, as it had during the S&L fiasco. "There was no drumbeat, no opportunity to explain to Americans how the 2008 collapse had occurred, who had done it, and which politicians they were paying off." Without this popular understanding, he says, politicians who protected the interests of the financial industry—modern-day equivalents of the Keating Five—continued, and continue to this day, to side with the perpetrators (who typically contribute generously to their campaigns), instead of helping the millions of Americans whose lives were devastated by the crisis. Congress was never shamed into denouncing Wall Street wrongdoing, as happened during the S&L crisis. On the contrary, Wall Street and its allies helped Congress design the bailouts that kept the banks afloat, and shape the subsequent legislative and regulatory response to the crisis.

Whereas Franklin Delano Roosevelt had urged a tough response to Wall Street crime after the Great Depression, passing Glass-Steagall, founding the SEC, defying Wall Street speculators—"I welcome their hatred"—Barack Obama, who was elected on a promise of "Change You Can Believe In" and a wave of popular anger at Wall Street, sided with his biggest campaign donors, the banks. Shortly after his election, Obama summoned the CEOs of America's thirteen leading bankers to the White House. The meeting was widely portrayed in the press as a stern dressing-down, with Obama telling the bankers that he was the only thing that stood between them and the pitchforks of the angry American people. Years later, however, one of the bankers told Pulitzer-winning journalist Ron Suskind how the conversation in the Oval Office had actually gone. "You guys have an acute public relations problem that's turning into a political problem," Obama told them. "And I want to help." The banker recalled a palpable sense of relief after the meeting. "The president had us at a moment of real vulnerability. At that point, he could have ordered us to do just about anything and we would have rolled over. But he didn't—he mostly wanted to help us out, to quell the mob."

Bill Black agrees. "Obama did not come in seeking fundamental change. In fact, he said that he rejected the FDR model, that he wasn't going to do anything equivalent. That the world was all about compromising on the margin, and that's what 'serious people' do. That's why the bank whistleblowers are so threatening. They reveal the sweeping corruption of the system, something you can't fix with marginal change, only with radical change, real justice.

"There's a chicken-and-egg problem about outrage," he continues. "People can only be truly outraged about things they understand. So at this point, there's a huge chunk of America that understands something—that the system is rigged. Which is true. But people would be vastly more outraged, and their outrage would be vastly more powerful, if they understood *how* the system was rigged. How it was rigged in multiple ways, by people who are wealthy and powerful, working with top politicians who are wealthy, powerful and venal. Fostering that knowledge, spreading that outrage, is how you get fundamental change."

Accepting Wall Street's modus operandi as part of the ineluctable movement of the markets, Black says, means endorsing the corruption of entire professions that helped first to rob, and then to hoodwink, the nation: real estate appraisers, notaries, accountants, lawyers, regulators, consultants, and above all bank executives. It means giving the culture of sales and marketing precedence over the culture of honesty, the expectations market over the reality market, the world of creative accounting and financial engineering over straightforward bookkeeping based on real products, hard dollars, and common sense.

The transformation of many major US banks from aggressive, self-serving but basically conservative organizations to the reckless speculators and recidivist fraud vehicles they are today began in the early 1990s, and accelerated with the repeal of Glass-Steagall in 1999. Over this period, the activities and ethical norms of Wall Street banks changed, in ways that both reflected and contributed to broader social shifts toward the short-termism, amorality and winner-take-all mentality that are implicit in modern neoliberalism. At the same time, shifts in bank regulations and ownership structure were opening up large new reservoirs of wealth for investment bankers to speculate with.

When I began work at Goldman Sachs in 1990, as an associate in the mergers and acquisitions department in London, I was taught that the banker-client relationship was sacred. John L. Weinberg, an ex-Marine who'd served in combat in the Pacific in World War II and come under arms again during the Korean War, was still chairman, and his big, beefy, sometimes slightly slovenly demeanor stood in marked contrast to the new generation of sharp-dealing suspenders-and-pinstripes bankers like the one Michael Douglas played in the 1987 film *Wall Street*, and like Michael Milken and Ivan Boesky truly were. In an interview that ran shortly before I joined the bank, Weinberg said he preferred to keep a low profile, noting that whales got harpooned only when they came to the surface to spout air. His golden rule, frequently repeated at Goldman, was "Be long-term greedy": form lasting relationships with your clients, treat them well, and sooner or later they will make you rich. When faced with the choice of keeping his word to a client and losing money, or betraying them and profiting, Weinberg never hesitated. After the Black Monday stock market crash of 1987, Weinberg decided that Goldman would continue its role in the partial privatization of British Petroleum on behalf of the UK government, though he knew the bank would suffer massive losses. (In fact, Goldman lost $100 million, the largest underwriting loss the bank had ever experienced.) "It's expensive and painful, but we are going to do it," Weinberg was later quoted as saying about the deal, "and those of you who decide not to do it, you won't be underwriting a goat house. Not even an outhouse."

Weinberg taught this devotion to clients by example. After his father, Sidney Weinberg, retired from Goldman, long-term client General Electric dropped the bank. So young John visited GE, every month for twelve years, until they hired him back. During my time at Goldman, I heard similar stories of senior partners making their names by camping humbly on the doorsteps of prospective clients. The bank never worked on the opposite side of a transaction from one of its clients, or took part in hostile takeovers. Veteran banker Raimund Herden, my colleague in mergers who left Goldman in 2001, sums up the bank's philosophy at that time regarding long-term relationships with clients. "When an advisory banker chases a deal, sometimes it takes a year or two before that deal actually materializes. You have to invest in the relationship, you have to raise the idea with different permutations, come back to the client again and again to answer questions. You sometimes take deals with that client that are less profitable, just to get into a relationship that pays off maybe five, six, seven years down the road."

Wallace Turbeville, another of my colleagues in London, was a senior banker in the structured finance group that helped fund roads, power plants and other infrastructure projects. "My work was inherently long term," remembers Turbeville. "Even when you weren't making a lot of money in that area, compared to other financial areas, in terms of relationships, contacts, the whole John Weinberg approach to life, you would really want to be involved in it, because of how impor-

tant it is at all different levels: in terms of dealing with corporate and political leaders, and just being involved with the fabric of cultures. In the long term, those kinds
of relationships and the kind of favor that you generate—you as a banker participating in the creative life of society—is a good thing, right? Eventually that will
come back to you, you'll make money from it. That's what Weinberg would say."

Another reason for Weinberg's conservatism was that his own money was at risk:
Goldman was still a private partnership, and deals that turned sour threatened the
personal fortune of each partner. Also, the bank was still small enough and the
management structure lean enough that wrongdoing was hard to hide. Chris Arnade, who worked for twenty years as a bond trader on Wall Street, remembers the
atmosphere in 1993 when he joined Salomon Brothers, which would soon become
part of Citi but still operated like a partnership, with a relatively flat organizational
structure. "Each employee had that sense of ownership that made them act more
cautiously, feel more personally responsible. There was always a culture of risk-
taking, but it was tempered by the fact that you had money on the line, money that
belonged to you and to everybody around you." Before he put on his first big trade,
he was required to speak with the second-ranking banker at the firm. "I had been
there six months, and already I was talking to one of the very top people. There
were only three levels—three people—between me and CEO." Three weeks later,
the same senior manager buttonholed him about the trade. "I was riding in the elevator with him, and he said, 'I don't think your trade is working out very well.' The
point was that it was his money, so he was paying attention."

This was the investment banking ethos—hard-driving but cautious and client-
centric—that I saw at Goldman between 1990 and 1992. But change was in the air.
Goldman's competitors had already gone public, which gave them vast pools of
capital for their deal making, and some in finance felt the bank's small size made it
less competitive. At the same time, Goldman traders began to take huge, highly
profitable positions in commodities. In August 1990, Weinberg retired as senior
partner of the firm; one of the two cochairs named to replace him was Robert
Rubin, head of Goldman's trading and risk arbitrage activities. (Henry Paulson, the
future Treasury secretary, was the cohead of investment banking at the time.) Thus
began the precipitous rise of the trader at Goldman and throughout Wall Street.

Soon traders were making most of the bank's profits, as Wall Street shifted its focus from longer-term work like advising and funding new businesses to more lucrative activities like trading derivatives, and making proprietary deals with the bank's own money.

This shift from banker to trader caused a cultural upheaval at Goldman. Herden remembers that when he left the firm, some 90 percent of the profits in the Frankfurt office were made by traders selling derivatives and other sophisticated financial instruments, yet the head of the office was from mergers and acquisitions, a department that at the time was barely breaking even. "When you're a trader, and people show up in the newspaper as leading the firm and giving interviews, and they represent a completely different side of the firm which is making a lot less money, it creates friction." Soon Goldman fixed this disconnect: Lloyd Blankfein, a former gold trader, became the new global CEO, and another metals trader, Gary Cohn, became president.

Traders and bankers have a fundamentally different attitude toward their clients. Technically, in fact, traders don't have "clients" at all, but "counterparties"—the entities on the other side of their transactions, with whom they buy and sell. "With a client, you work collaboratively, over time, to create a new thing—a new venture or a new capital instrument," says Wally Turbeville. "A counterparty is somebody you agree to a price with, really quickly, and then the transaction stops." Speed is vital in closing the transaction, both to lock in a position, and because the banker normally earns fees on each trade, and is therefore incentivized to make as many trades as possible. Traders have little or no personal interaction with counterparties, who are often anonymous: traders typically don't even talk to them on the phone, but communicate by instant message. Their "cooperation" is skewed by an inherent conflict of interest: in order to take profits out of a position, the trader has to buy low and sell high, meaning he needs to ensure that his counterparty is buying high and selling low. From the trader's perspective, a counterparty can look a lot like a mark.

For that matter, traders typically don't have much interaction with their colleagues or bosses, either. "In trading you don't really have teamwork," says Herden. "Nobody talks to you and says, 'Ah, great job!' You have one guy who pays you at the end of the year, and that's why he's important. You don't sit down with people. You sit at your screen and you trade, and at the end of the day you either made money or lost money. It has some aspects of the video game. And gratification is largely based on money."

Turbeville tells the story of a trader at a firm he went to visit, who had taken a heavy dose of Ritalin to increase her concentration, and passed out on the trading desk while he was there. As she slumped forward onto her keyboard, she inadvertently pressed a key that caused her to buy a massive position. "The other traders rushed over and pulled her off. Then one of them realized she had taken on this giant position. They left her lying on the floor while they unwound the position. Then they called the ambulance."

"You can't have too much empathy," says Arnade, himself a former trader. "It's not surprising to me that a lot of traders have traits of autism, or Asperger's." Arnade laughs. "That lack of social skills kinda works. It filters out the distractions that the things you're doing are about people. That they have human consequences."

Traders are living examples of homo economicus, embodiments of the chill, numeric, often predatory agent who, according to the neoliberal worldview, populates competitive markets. Money, the universal fuel of markets, is their sole metric of success. Their inherently zero-sum worldview crystallizes in the initialism IBGYBG ("I'll be gone, you'll be gone"), a verbal shrug that traders made to one another in the run-up to 2008, when sealing a deal that they knew would generate instant profits for them, though meaning likely disaster for their counterparties somewhere down the line. In this landscape of vanishingly short time horizons and every man for himself, traders feel no social responsibility. "They don't even know what 'social responsibility' means," Turbeville says. "They would deny it even exists. The trader's approach to things is corrosive of a sense of common good and of working toward creating things together. That's how Wall Street operates now. And we as a society are taking our cues from them. We've lost the capacity to understand that there's value beyond what's quoted on a screen. More and more, value is simply determined by a trader sitting in front of that screen."

Another key cause of Goldman's—and Wall Street's—ethical decline was the transition from private partnerships to publicly traded companies, which at Goldman, the last major private holdout, came in 1999. We've already seen in other industries how the availability of enormous reserves of Other People's Money—in this case belonging to shareholders—can desensitize managers to risk, and encourage fraud. Chris Arnade saw this happen at Citi: "Early on, people said, 'We own this firm, and all my money is in it. So let's not let it fuck up.' When the banks went public, the attitude was basically, 'Well, how much is my bonus this year, and I'm out of here.' At first we had a shared responsibility to better the firm; and in the end, we had a shared responsibility to financially rape the firm." The publicly quoted banks grew rapidly, often through acquisitions; soon the sheer size of megabanks like Citigroup and JPMorgan made them vastly harder to manage—and to keep employees honest. Early in his career Arnade reported to a top executive on every trade; by the end of his career at Citi, he says, "I couldn't even count the number of lawyers between me and the CEO, or the various paths to get there. I could basically make up my own risk limits, if I wanted to." The repeal of Glass-Steagall, and the breakdown of the firewalls between commercial and investment banking, not only allowed traders to make speculative bets with government-guaranteed depositor money, but soon infected the staid, conservative world of commercial banks with the risk-loving habits of Wall Street traders.

Once banks went public, too, the shareholder value mantra added gasoline to the fire of speculation. "Managers started measuring what's good for shareholders by their quarterly profit statements," says Turbeville. "Which was natural, because traders had taken control of all the firms, and the traders think in terms of short-term profits. This, in turn, facilitated the mentality that what was good for shareholders was just good, by definition—a mentality that has justified all kinds of wrongdoing." And naturally, the wheels of such thinking were greased by the powerful self-justifying force of cash: the dizzying payoffs available on Wall Street, where a hedge fund manager can take home $2 billion in one year, dwarf all other industries. Wall Street bonuses create a goals-gone-wild culture in which, as Lynn Stout predicted, some people appear willing to do anything to hit their numbers and join the financial elite—all the more when society itself applauds their escapades as the triumph of capitalism.

I left Goldman, and finance, in 1992, and didn't think much about banking for years. Now and then I'd see the former heads of my bank taking top financial jobs in Washington, and imagine the mind-bending conflicts of interest this entailed. I watched Robert Rubin go to Treasury to shape and deregulate the economy as a banker would, then revolve back into banking at Citi to reap what he had sown. I saw Hank Paulson, who as chair of Goldman had taken on an enormous inventory of toxic mortgage-related securities before the 2008 collapse, slide over to Treasury and temporize as the bank unwound them and cashed in on its huge bets against the housing market, letting Lehman fail but rescuing AIG, the insurer of Goldman's bets, thus enabling Goldman bankers to collect their bonuses through TARP's (Troubled Asset Relief Program) back door, even when their bank itself required a bailout. But it wasn't until I listened to the congressional hearings and read the court cases in the aftermath of 2008 that I realized how fundamentally the ethos of investment banking had changed, and how the trader-mind of Wall Street had stoked the financial crisis. As the housing bubble burst and the economy came unstuck, Goldman Sachs traders bragged in internal emails and memoranda how they'd sold made-to-fail securities—"shitty deals," "crappy deals," "pigs," "monstrosities"—to unsuspecting clients/counterparties, whom they called "muppets." While vigorously promoting these worthless securities to clients as sound investments, Goldman traders had secretly sold them short.

"You are betting against the very security that you are selling to that person," Michigan senator Carl Levin, a former federal prosecutor, said to Goldman CEO Lloyd Blankfein during a Senate hearing in April 2010. "You don't see any problem?"

"I am not troubled by the fact that we market-make as principal," Blankfein replied, "and that we are the opposite—when somebody sells, they sell to us, or when they buy, they buy from us." In an interview with Charlie Rose a month later, Blankfein said, "We're like a machine, that lets people buy and sell what they want to buy and sell. That's not the advisory business. That's just a facility for market making."

Blankfein's statement is false on multiple levels. In a technical sense, in key CDO deals Goldman acted not just as a market maker but as a "placement agent," which under banking rules and federal securities laws has a fiduciary duty to reveal material information to clients to whom it recommends investments. (The fact that the bank believed a security would fail, and was betting large sums of bank money on that outcome, could be considered "material.") But in a broader sense, free markets are predicated on transparency—that all participants know what is being bought and sold. Goldman traders who had put the deals together knew, as their customers did not, precisely what was inside those ticking time bombs: ultimately the same sorts of no-doc, zero-down-payment mortgages that Richard Bowen had futilely fought against buying at Citigroup, before his bank, like Goldman, wrapped them all up with pink bows and sold them on to some more or less unsuspecting counterparty/schlub. Strip away the trader talk about markets, liquidity and leverage, and these deals are fraud in its most essential form, in securities or anywhere else.

I also read the names of plaintiffs in the class action suits against Goldman—retired schoolteachers in Arkansas, public workers in West Virginia, plumbers and pipefitters elsewhere—which suggested the kinds of people whose pensions had been decimated by the bank's exploding securities. But I also knew that many of the traders involved never thought about the money as having come from real people. They'd seen these transactions as numbers on a screen, successive rushes of free-market adrenaline, poker chips in the high-stakes game to which they'd reduced the world . . . a game that they were winning. Since then, Goldman has made the headlines with more wrongdoing, most recently the so-called 1MDB scandal, in which the bank played a leading role in raising $6.5 billion for the Malaysian government's economic development fund, of which prosecutors say over $2.7 billion was siphoned off by corrupt officials, including the former Malaysian prime minister Najib Razak. In August 2018, Tim Leissner, one of the chief Goldman bankers in the affair, pled guilty in a Brooklyn court to conspiracy charges of violating the Foreign Corrupt Practices Act and money laundering. (Leissner paid bribes and kickbacks to Malaysian officials to secure Goldman's role in running 1MDB, laundering the money through shell companies.) During his plea hearing, Leissner stated that his conspiracy was "very much in line" with the bank's "culture to conceal facts from certain compliance and legal employees." (The bank, which made almost $600 million from the 1MDB transaction, has blamed the corruption on Leissner and a few other bad apples.)

In retrospect, Goldman's turn to the dark side shouldn't have surprised me. The twin transitions of banker to trader and partnership to public company probably made it inevitable. More broadly, a substantial body of research has shown that beyond a certain level of development in the financial sector, banks that initially stimulated commerce by loaning to firms that produce goods and services, and by helping individuals to buy houses and cars, concentrate, as they grow larger and more powerful, on rent-seeking instead, and thus begin to stifle real economic activity, a process economist Michael Hudson calls "killing the host." Many academic studies show that Wall Street banks transitioned from economic proponent to parasite in the early 1990s. The costs of financial intermediation in the United States, between 1.3 and 2.3 percent of assets for most of the last century, are now at 9 percent, despite a steep rise in technology during that period, which should have reduced financial costs. The reason for this, says Thomas Philippon, an economist and professor of finance at NYU's business school, is a massive increase in trading by the banks, now "many times larger than at any time in previous history." Investment magnate John Bogle agrees, estimating that 99.5 percent of stock market activity is in short-term speculation—bankers buying and selling financial instruments with other bankers—while only 0.5 percent actually creates capital. "But it is only capital formation that adds value to our society," Bogle writes. "Trading, by definition, subtracts value." Finance also takes a growing and outsize share of the profits of American business: while banks earned 10 to 20 percent of all corporate profits for most of the twentieth century, in the run-up to the 2008 crisis their share rose to 40 percent, and they still earn 25 percent of all corporate profits in the United States, though offering only 4 percent of American jobs.

A recent analysis by Gerald Epstein and Juan Antonio Montecino, economists at the University of Massachusetts, Amherst, attempts to quantify the economic drain caused by the financial hypertrophy of the US economy. From 1990 through 2005 alone, they peg the cost of excess pay and profits, including the sale of excessively complex and risky products, government subsidies and bailouts, outsize fees and outright fraud, at some $3.6 to $4.2 trillion, and the cost of diverted resources from productive economy (the excessively large finance sector absorbing too many skilled workers, starving businesses and households of credit, and imposing a mindset of short-termism on commerce) at $2.6 to $3.9 trillion, for a total of $6.3 to $8.2 trillion that Wall Street is skimming off our economy—without even considering the tens of trillions lost in financial crises like that which occurred in 2008.

Fraud has metastasized in finance for the same reasons it has spread in other industries, accentuated by certain intrinsic aspects of Wall Street. The supremacy of numbers, the tidy beauty of spreadsheets and financial statements, the layered nature of financial instruments and the numerous intermediaries often involved in large financial transactions all allow bankers and traders to dissociate themselves from the ultimate victims of their actions, those teachers and pipefitters whose money gets hoovered into dubious deals. Secrecy surrounding data, client information and proprietary financial schemes, as well as the extensive use of nondisclosure agreements and confidentiality policies to prevent employees from revealing wrongdoing, can create an atmosphere where fraud thrives. The sense shared by many Wall Street denizens of being part of an elite team, a Band of Brothers who can do no wrong, accentuates this criminogenic atmosphere. And since money is a perilously psychoactive substance, it's hardly surprising that in finance, where money is the primum mobile and raison d'être, the temptation to cheat is strong, especially as short-termism and the cult of money grow and counterweights to wrongdoing, like devotion to clients and professional ethics, melt away.

Two extensive surveys of the financial services industry in the United States and the UK, performed in 2012 and again in 2015, suggest how fraud has become normalized on Wall Street: 47 percent of respondents in 2015 believed that their competitors had likely engaged in unethical or illegal activity to gain an edge in the market—up sharply from 39 percent in 2012. And 34 percent of respondents in 2015 knew about or had personally witnessed wrongdoing in their workplace, with nearly a quarter saying they themselves would break insider trading laws, if sure they would not be caught. A team of researchers at the University of Zurich argue, based on empirical research at a major bank, that "the prevailing business culture in the banking industry favours dishonest behaviour," because norms of behavior in banking no longer encourage people to feel they should be honest, or lead them to expect that other industry participants are behaving honestly. In fact, Luigi Zingales, finance professor at the University of Chicago business school, points out that such norms are part of a basic finance course, and are taught to every MBA candidate. "We teach our students how to maximize the tax advantage of debt and how to exploit any arbitrage opportunity. Customers are often not seen as people to respect, but as counterparties to take to the cleaners. . . . If the only goal is enrichment, there is a risk that abuses and fraud become not a distortion, but a continuation of the same strategy by other means."

Wall Street banks are helping to spread financial fraud into many other industries, as we've seen, by fueling the corporation's increasing obsession with short-term profits and financial engineering. To build a firm's share price, which in turn boosts bonuses, top industry managers are spending ever more time wooing analysts, and less time creating new products or services. The metrics they follow, which finance scholar Clayton Christensen has called the "Doctrine of New Finance," involve not real wealth or corporate health, but ratios of profit to capital or profit to assets employed; particularly in the short term, it's almost always harder to increase the numerator (profits) than to reduce the denominator (costs), so many executives concentrate ruthlessly on paring back R&D, firing workers and selling off assets, rather than making new investments that, in a longer time horizon, might materially improve the company and what it makes or does. They engage in various forms of balance sheet manipulation and creative accounting, which comes naturally to many CEOs, who, true to Robert McNamara's vision, are trained in finance, not in the operations of their specific industry, and are following the managerialist model they learned in business school. "Today many American corporations are managed more like hedge funds than operating companies," says Wally Turbeville. "They're behaving like hedge funds with a particular exposure to one business."

One of the favorite methods companies use to increase their share price is to buy large quantities of their own stock, often with borrowed money. As the elementary law of supply and demand predicts, the share price increases as a result, which pleases major shareholders as well as C-suite managers who own lots of stock and whose incentive pay is linked to the firm's share price. But the company itself is typically left deeper in debt, and drained of the cash it could have used to hire and train skilled workers, build laboratories or factories, or invent and design new products. Ernie Fitzgerald would instantly have recognized this exercise as a self-sucking cow—a short-term, shortsighted gain that undermines long-term prosperity. Stock buybacks have become a pandemic. Until 1982, the SEC prohibited them as a form of market manipulation by corporate insiders. But then Ronald Reagan appointed stockbroker John Shad to lead the SEC—the first Wall Street executive to head the commission since it was founded in 1934—and Shad obligingly legalized buybacks. The SEC made another key rule change in 1991; previously corporate executives, like other major shareholders, were required to hold shares they'd received by exercising their stock options for six months, but henceforth they could sell them off immediately. Corporate insiders were now free to rig their own stock through buybacks, and instantly monetize their manipulation.

Not surprisingly, public companies have since spent many trillions of dollars in share repurchases—over $4.3 trillion since 2009, and more than $1 trillion in 2018 alone, after the Republican corporate tax cut of December 2017 gave businesses more money to "invest." Beyond weakening corporate America, stock buybacks and other market manipulation schemes have serious consequences for US society. William Lazonick at the University of Massachusetts, Amherst, a leading critic of buybacks, has shown their major role in increasing income inequity and destroying middle-class jobs. Share compensation packages and ballooning stock prices, bolstered by buybacks, have created an enormous gulf between CEO and average worker pay, as money flows out of productive enterprises and into a few pockets. To finance those share buybacks and C-suite pay packages, companies shed jobs, and cut training and opportunities for the workers who remain. Wages for the top 1 percent of earners have soared 157 percent since 1979, and for the top 0.1 percent a staggering 343 percent, while the bottom 90 percent has grown just 22 percent. (The top 0.1 percent now owns as much wealth as the bottom 90 percent.) Worker pay has lagged increasingly behind productivity since the early 1970s, and upward mobility, the premise for the American Dream, is disappearing. The division of the spoils is the same on the stock market: stocks have been on the rise for ten years, the longest bull market in US history, but the $20 trillion in value this has created has gone disproportionately to the top 10 percent of wealthy Americans, who own 84 percent of all shares.

As Bill Black suggests, most Americans have yet to understand, much less to reject, what the banks have known for years: that the crisis of 2008 and its aftermath represented, in economist James Galbraith's words, "a breakdown of the rule of law in America." In an essential article written in 2009, Simon Johnson, a former senior economist at the International Monetary Fund, calls the 2008 financial crisis a "quiet coup." Johnson writes from decades of experience with similar economic crises in Ukraine, Russia, Thailand, South Korea, Indonesia and other emerging nations, brought on by powerful elites, particularly in finance, who had made too many poor investments when their economy was booming. When the inevitable crisis came, the governments typically tried to spare these oligarchs, who enjoyed considerable political influence, by forgiving their debts or giving them tax breaks. "Meanwhile, needing to squeeze *someone*, most emerging-market governments look first to ordinary working folk—at least until the riots grow too large," Johnson writes. But the IMF knew that to end the crisis and right its economy, the nation ultimately had to rein in its oligarchs, and above all to wrest "control of the banking system from the hands of the most incompetent and avaricious 'entrepreneurs.'" This is what Bill Black and his fellow regulators and prosecutors helped do during the savings and loan crisis.

The United States was in just such a predicament in 2008, Johnson explains, but since it doesn't consider itself a third-world nation, it failed to take the necessary medicine. Instead, it turned for treatment to the same snake oil salesmen who had caused the crisis: the financiers, who he notes "are now using their influence to prevent precisely the sorts of reforms that are needed, and fast, to pull the economy out of its nosedive. The government seems helpless, or unwilling, to act against them." Americans and their government, together with Nobel Prize–winning economists and Federal Reserve pundits, continue to accept the "cult of finance" and the "faith in free financial markets" as essential to US growth and prosperity. "In a society that celebrates the idea of making money, it was easy to infer that the interests of the financial sector were the same as the interests of the country—and that the winners in the financial sector knew better what was good for America than did the career civil servants in Washington."

Wall Street's knowledge of its own impunity, proven in the aftermath of 2008, has devastated ethics in the finance industry. It explains the banks' business-as-usual attitude to fraud, and their cost-of-doing-business approach to lawsuits and settlements. An Arab American financier who has worked both on Wall Street and in the Middle East explained the situation to me like this: "Wall Street turned corrupt after the financial crisis, when the banks realized they would get away with it—that they could get away with anything. What in other countries we call baksheesh, or corruption, is legal and organized in the US, so you can shovel big money to influence outcomes." In fact, the crisis has been a boon for too-big-to-fail banks. Since 2008, they have grown even bigger and more indispensable; the top five banks now hold nearly half the assets of the entire US banking industry, and a stunning 94 percent of derivatives, valued at about $104 trillion. Just as banks that sold impossible mortgages to countless borrowers swooped in and took the properties back when their owners defaulted, so private equity firms—newspeak for the leveraged buyout shops of Michael Milken's heyday—have preyed on municipalities crippled by the implosion of their Wall Street portfolios, buying up ambulance companies, fire departments, waterworks, sewers, schools, bridges, highways and other erstwhile public goods at bargain prices, and hiking rates to customers and slashing budgets (and payrolls) to ensure they generate Wall Street–size returns. These organizations, cut to the bone by privatization, default far more often than their public sector counterparts, which leaves their communities without essential services. When this happens, private equity players, who have taken their fees up front, shrug and move on.

Wall Street impunity causes harm far beyond the economy, eroding trust in politics and the judicial system, and undermining the feeling among many citizens that they are taking part in a shared national project. Wall Street's extralegal status has deepened the widespread popular perception of the rigged game, as it accelerated long-term trends that distanced rich from poor, leaving most wealthy people untouched by the 2008 crisis in the medium term—their financial assets regained value—while less wealthy Americans were out of a job, a house, a life. More than at any time since the Gilded Age, Americans in different socioeconomic groups are living separate lives—geographically, socially, educationally, psychically.

In *Capital in the Twenty-First Century*, economist Thomas Piketty has observed that some 60 to 70 percent of the top 0.1 percent of wage earners from 2000 to 2010 were managers, while less than 5 percent were famous public figures like film stars or athletes. "In this sense, the new US inequality has much more to do with the advent of 'supermanagers' than with 'superstars,'" Piketty writes. In fact, Wall Street deal makers *are* superstars in America today. We admire their savvy, ruthlessness and calculation; we put their names on distinguished universities; we read their op-eds in major newspapers and see their unimaginable wealth as the quintessential American success story. Instead of rags to riches, the new social narrative spread by finance is every man for himself, and devil take the hindmost. Hedge fund managers are traders, the ultimate zero-sum value extractors and maximizers of their own utility. They thrive on market volatility—the very thing that makes long-term building of value harder—and can profit whether a stock goes up or down, so long as it moves. Indeed, as author Roger Martin has shown, because of the way their stock option payments are made, many CEOs make more money during volatile periods, and actually profited from the 2008 financial crisis. No wonder "creative disruption" has become a management mantra.

Consider the worldview of one trader, Ray Dalio, CEO of Bridgewater, the world's biggest hedge fund. Dalio, who earned $2 billion in 2018, has codified his philosophy of life and business in a couple hundred "Principles," which he distributes to his employees. (Excerpts of this document were leaked by the website Dealbreaker in 2010; the version that Dalio published in 2018 is substantially different.)

When a pack of hyenas takes down a young wildebeest, is that good or evil? At face value, that might not be "good" because it seems cruel, and the poor wildebeest suffers and dies. Some people might even say that the hyenas are evil. Yet this type of apparently "cruel" behavior exists throughout the animal kingdom. Like death itself it is integral to the enormously complex and efficient system that has worked for as long as there has been life. It is good for both the hyenas who are operating in their self-interest and the interest of the greater system, including those of the wildebeest, because killing and eating the wildebeest fosters evolution (i.e., the natural process of improvement). In fact, if you changed anything about the way that dynamic works, the overall outcome would be worse.

"I believe that self-interest and society's interests are generally symbiotic," Dalio writes later in the text. "That is why how much money people have earned is a rough measure of how much they gave society what it wanted." Dalio's credo captures the ethos of homo economicus, and the social Darwinian world without conscience that so troubled Lynn Stout. Be a hyena, and pull down as many wildebeests as you can, he tells us, for that is the law of the jungle in which we live. Suppress all sensation of the human harm you do through the knowledge that your victims are legitimate prey, who indeed should thank you for your predation, because it helps them to evolve.

The control of wealth over politics has grown increasingly naked and unapologetic. Even self-described liberal politicians no longer trouble to disguise their ties of cash, friendship and common worldview with the barons of finance. Barack Obama matter-of-factly took his largest campaign contributions from Wall Street, and chose Wall Street bankers and lawyers to re-regulate the industry after 2008, with the predictable result that nothing changed. Now, in retirement, he accepts $400,000 speaking fees from Wall Street banks and kite surfs with billionaires, bounties that smack of payment for services rendered. Donald Trump, having railed against Goldman Sachs's outsize power in previous administrations, literally surrounded himself with Goldman bankers, including some of the worst financial predators to create, and then exploit, the 2008 crisis. Gary Cohn, Trump's first senior financial adviser, was the trader who oversaw Goldman's mortgage business in its most toxic phase; his name appears in congressional reports and investigations of 2008 countless times, often in association with dubious banking practices. Secretary of the Treasury Steven Mnuchin, another Goldman banker, made one fortune flogging the mortgage-backed securities that brought down the economy, and another as the "Foreclosure King," ruthlessly—and sometimes illegally—repossessing the homes of tens of thousands of Americans much as Bank of America did to the Sundquists. Secretary of Commerce Wilbur Ross likewise became a billionaire on the backs of distressed homeowners, with the extensive use of robo-signing and other illicit practices. (The commander in chief himself, in ads for Trump University, proclaimed that "investors nationwide are making millions in foreclosures . . . and so can you!")

That such people have been able to rise to the top of the political heap after bringing down the US economy, and are now "regulating" their own industries, is a measure of our failure to rein in Wall Street after the 2008 crash. It's as if we have come to accept in our society the existence of an aristocratic class that is fundamentally at odds with the traditions of American egalitarianism. Abroad, we stigmatize the lawless, cronyistic abusers of the common good in Russia as "oligarchs," but at home we idolize them as "billionaires," acquiescing in their power to shape laws, regulations, the tax system, and countless aspects of our society.

This gradually consolidating control of the economic elites over the financial system helps explain why bank whistleblowers have gotten scant traction, triggered no arrests or convictions of top bank fraudsters, led to no lasting regulatory changes: the hyenas, wolves and foxes, the people who consider predatory fraud not only clever business but socially desirable, have been set to guard the henhouse. Inside the government itself, thanks to the growing influence of Wall Street and its allies, people like Bill Black are no longer welcome, despite—or rather, because of—their experience as bank regulators and litigators during one of the most successful periods of elite white-collar crime prosecutions in US history.

Gary Aguirre was born in San Diego in 1940 and grew up with his grandparents Pearl Robbins from Texas and Rafael Espiridion Guarneros—"Pop"—a former captain in the Mexican cavalry and prizefighter who fought under the ring name "Slippery Guarneros." Life had been hard for Pearl and Rafael, as they raised Gary's mother and her four siblings during the Great Depression, and grew harder still when Pearl, in her late thirties, contracted polio and was paralyzed from the waist down. When the war came, their sons enlisted and served in the Pacific, while Pearl and Pop converted the family home into a boardinghouse, which quickly filled with "Rosie the Riveter": women who worked at the warplane factories that were concentrated in San Diego. Pop was the block captain, responsible for ensuring that all lights on the block were turned off during air-raid drills.

Aguirre idolized his grandfather, who was a humble man devoted to his family, but who also had the fearlessness of a fighter. Aguirre remembers that once, when Pop had an abscessed molar, he extracted it himself, with a pair of pliers, because he felt that the family could not afford a dentist. To help make ends meet, Pearl designed and fitted hats for wealthy suburban women; while they waited for her in the car, Pop told Gary of his adventures in the Mexican cavalry fighting Pancho Villa. Sometimes Gary's classmates asked him about the dark-complexioned older man who walked him to school each morning. Was he Japanese?

Aguirre went to law school at Berkeley, in part because he saw that his grandparents felt intimidated, not protected, by the law. "I believed that knowing the law gave you the ability to maneuver through society and through the world," he says. There he witnessed the growing protests against the Vietnam War, which made him further consider how an attorney should balance the pursuit of his career with the duties to society implicit in the legal profession. He watched classmates risk arrest by participating in antiwar rallies. He began to read about Vietnam, and soon joined the protests himself, having come to the conclusion that "we were on the wrong side of history." Years later, when Aguirre had the opportunity to drive Arthur Schlesinger, former adviser to President John F. Kennedy, to a conference, he asked Schlesinger why the United States had gotten entangled in Vietnam, when the historians Aguirre had read had warned in advance that this would be a mistake. "We didn't read the books," Schlesinger told him.

After graduating from law school, Aguirre joined a major San Francisco law firm, where he spent most of his time in the basement of one corporate client, combing through documents to locate evidence of their securities frauds. He quit after a year and joined a public defender's office that had just opened in the low-income county of Fresno. After two weeks on the job, he had his first superior court jury trial. "It was a baptism by fire, and a complete disaster," he says, shaking his head. "But there is no better learning experience. Jury trials give you immediate feedback, and juries don't get it wrong—they help you face reality."

Later, in private practice, he represented homeowner associations against build-

ing materials and construction companies that were turning out shoddy and sometimes dangerous work. He soon realized that the laws governing home, condominium
and cooperative development in California were hopelessly vague, and began researching their history. "I wanted the ability to see the problems and the matrix
with the solutions—to understand the original problems from which the legislative
solutions had grown," he says. With this deeper understanding, he helped to draft
the Davis-Stirling Act of 1985, which substantially improved the rights of state
homeowners. Subsequently he won ninety-four consecutive cases involving the act,
resulting in over $200 million in recoveries on homeowners' behalf.

By 1995, however, he'd had enough. "I'd started out doing law for the underdogs, but in later years I watched the whole class action practice get ugly. It
became more about lawyers losing sight of people, doing a lot of lawyering and
lining their pockets." So Aguirre left the law, moved to Spain, and married a
Spaniard. But in 2000, he saw Theodore Olson, who'd been one year ahead of him
at Berkeley, arguing *Bush v. Gore*, the suit that determined who the next president
of the United States would be. Aguirre immersed himself in the case, reading up
on the key points of the law and the judges' backgrounds. "It was as if someone
had retained me on the case," he says. His wife, María, noticing his fascination,
observed, "Seems to me that you haven't gotten lawyering out of your system yet."

So at the age of sixty-one, Gary Aguirre returned to law school, this time at
Georgetown. Initially he'd intended to do human rights law, but he soon discovered there was little that an American lawyer could do in this area apart from writing letters to the United Nations. "It was like playing canasta—too academic, too
passive. You're pleading with the UN to intervene, and I don't plead well. I present
a case: 'These are the facts, this is the law, what do you think?'" He also applied the
"trim tab" theory of Buckminster Fuller, whom he'd admired throughout his life:
identifying those small, pivotal features in a situation that, like the rudder on a
supertanker, can with a tiny adjustment produce a major change in direction of the
whole. "In deciding what you are going to do with your life, the idea is to find the
trim tabs that alter the course of things. I myself was looking to be a trim tab, where
I could make a difference."

At that time, in the early 2000s, Enron, Tyco, WorldCom and other major accounting scandals were breaking and securities law was rapidly evolving. Aguirre had already done some securities litigation immediately after Berkeley, and had managed his own investments since his retirement, which taught him how vulnerable people were when they made investment decisions based on what companies filed publicly with the SEC. Aguirre decided to specialize in securities law. He took the same historical approach he'd used while crafting new homeowners' legislation in California. "I thought you should immerse yourself in how the law evolved, and understand the problems that the laws were written to deal with." He studied the work of Ferdinand Pecora, reading thousands of pages of transcripts of Pecora's examinations of leading financial figures, and his staff's exhaustive analyses of the American banking system. "Pecora was a good example of a trim tab," Aguirre says. "He was the critical player at the critical moment. The public had gone through four years of pain, and was totally frustrated. And up steps this Italian American— J. P. Morgan once called him a 'dirty little Wop'—who was more than a match for J. P. Morgan under cross examination, addressing him in a gentlemanly and articulate way yet dissecting him, with no reluctance at all to go straight for the jugular."

In his law school honors thesis, Aguirre described how Pecora's securities laws of 1933 and 1934 had progressively been blunted by a series of Supreme Court rulings that began in 1974, shortly after Justices Lewis F. Powell and William Rehnquist joined the court. (In a trenchant dissent, Justice Harry Blackmun characterized one such decision as showing "a preternatural solicitousness for corporate well-being and a seeming callousness toward the investing public quite out of keeping . . . with our own traditions and the intent of the securities laws.") Aguirre wrote that the Supreme Court had "defined a zone of conduct beyond the reach of antifraud provisions," from which "investment banks, accountants, and lawyers could earn large fees helping public companies cheat their investors." "In the shadows of this lucrative zone, a fraud-free zone," he continued, "Citibank, J. P. Morgan, Arthur Andersen, and others allegedly nurtured Enron's conversion from a quasi-viable company to a full-blown Ponzi scheme."

He concluded his thesis with Pecora's own words, which seemed to foretell the fraud-fueled bankruptcies of Enron, WorldCom, Tyco and other scandals of the early 2000s.

> Under the surface of the governmental regulation of the securities market, the same forces that produced the riotous speculative excesses of the "wild bull market" of 1929 still give evidences of their existence and influence. Though repressed for the present, it cannot be doubted that, given a suitable opportunity, they would spring back into pernicious activity.
>
> Frequently we are told that this regulation has been throttling the country's prosperity. Bitterly hostile was Wall Street to the enactment of the regulatory legislation. It now looks forward to the day when it shall, as it hopes, reassume the reins of its former power. . . .
>
> The public, however, is sometimes forgetful. As its memory of the unhappy market collapse of 1929 becomes blurred, it may lend at least one ear to the persuasive voices of The Street subtly pleading for a return to the "good old times."

Pecora got only one thing wrong: it would be the Supreme Court, more than the public, that would warm to the message that the antifraud provisions were "throttling the country's prosperity." When the court dismantled those laws, the riotous speculative excesses returned just as Pecora had predicted.

"The collapse of the financial markets in 2000 was its own doing, the bursting of a bubble that began to form in 1995," Aguirre wrote. "One year before that bubble began to inflate, [the] Central Bank [ruling by the Supreme Court] declared the fraud-free zone open for business. Attorneys, accountants, and banks could help public companies cheat their investors and not worry about pesky lawsuits."

At the suggestion of Mark Kreitman, one of his professors of securities law, Aguirre joined the SEC in September 2004, as a senior counsel in the commission's Enforcement Division, which investigates violations of federal securities laws and prosecutes civil suits and administrative proceedings. In his first month at work, he received the case of a lifetime.

Pequot Capital Management, formerly the world's largest hedge fund, was run by Arthur Samberg, a Wall Street legend, whose fund had posted a near-miraculous average return of 17 percent over its twenty-two years. Aguirre began to understand the reasons for Art Samberg's success when he saw that on July 2, 2001, Pequot had suddenly begun buying the stock of a little-known finance company called Heller Financial. In just over three weeks, Samberg spent about $36 million to buy 1.1 million shares of the company, and attempted to buy 4 million more. In the same period, he also shorted the stock of General Electric. When GE announced its acquisition of Heller on July 30, Heller's stock spiked and GE's dropped—the normal pattern in corporate acquisitions. Samberg liquidated his positions, earning about $19 million. Yet in reviewing Samberg's emails, calendar, memoranda and other documentation, Aguirre saw no evidence that Samberg had contacted Heller or done any market research on the company.

What Aguirre did see was a phone call between Samberg and John Mack, a veteran Wall Street banker nicknamed "Mack the Knife" for his brutal management style; Mack had recently been named the CEO of the investment bank Credit Suisse First Boston (CSFB). On the next trading day after that call, Samberg had started buying Heller. It turned out that Credit Suisse, CSFB's parent, was representing Heller in its negotiations with GE. When Mack and Samberg spoke, Mack had just returned from three days of meetings with the Credit Suisse hierarchy in Zurich. What's more, Mack had previously been the CEO of Morgan Stanley, the bank that was representing GE, the potential buyer.

Aguirre went to the NYSE and the National Association of Securities Dealers (NASD) to search for a similar pattern in Pequot's previous investments. "I was doing what I'd have done at the public defender's office," Aguirre says. "I was looking to see if Pequot had priors." In fact, Heller trades were one of at least seventeen sets of suspicious transactions, which also involved Microsoft, AstraZeneca, and Par Pharmaceutical, that the NYSE and the NASD had reported to the SEC, though the SEC at that time had no mechanism for recording such reports. "This hedge fund comes up constantly on our radar screen—they're way too lucky," one NYSE official told him. "We keep sending these referrals over to the SEC, but nothing happens." Veteran SEC attorney Hilton Foster, an insider trading expert, told Aguirre that he'd tried to catch Pequot out some years before, and though he'd failed, he considered them "perennial insider traders."

The deeper Aguirre dug, the dirtier Pequot looked. He questioned Samberg about why he'd bought Heller stock; the hedge fund leader rattled off six answers, all of which, Aguirre learned later, had been "spoon-fed" to him by his lawyers before the interview. Aguirre found another case in which Samberg had hired a Microsoft employee, David Zilkha, and asked him for inside information on the company's third-quarter earnings. Microsoft had been performing poorly in the United States, and the company was widely expected to miss its already reduced earnings and revenue estimates. In reality, sales of the company's recently introduced new operating system were booming, and the company's US performance was sharply up, which had led the company to revise its economic forecast upward—but nobody outside the company should have known this yet. As in the Heller case, immediately after a series of communications with Zilkha, Samberg bought 3.4 million shares of synthetic Microsoft stock and held on to 1.5 million more, which made him $32.1 million in profit when, contrary to market expectations, the company announced surprisingly high earnings two weeks later. Aguirre also learned that, on the same night that Samberg and Mack had their conversation, Samberg promised to include Mack in an exclusive Pequot transaction code-named "Fresh Start," which swiftly earned over $10 million for Mack. "This sounded an awful lot like quid pro quo," Aguirre remembers thinking. "It didn't take much in the way of brilliant analysis to conclude that we had to take Mack's testimony."

He assembled the emails and other evidence against Pequot, Samberg and Mack in a fat ring binder and showed it to his supervisor, SEC branch chief Robert Hanson, and to Hanson's boss, Assistant Director Mark Kreitman. The two men were so struck by Aguirre's account that they told him to take it to the FBI and the US Attorney for the Southern District of New York, for them to start a parallel criminal investigation. Kreitman gave Aguirre a photo of Perry Mason, the fabled criminal defense attorney played by Raymond Burr on television, to commend his sleuthing skills. "I was on top of the world," Aguirre remembers. "The SEC had never done a major case against a hedge fund before, but my supervisors were stoked about the case." He received a merit pay increase in June 2005, and in his performance evaluation, Hanson wrote, "Gary has an unmatched dedication to this case (often working well beyond normal work hours), and his efforts have uncovered evidence of potential insider trading and possible manipulative trading by the fund and its principals. . . . He has consistently gone the extra mile, and then some."

Only days later, the investigation hit a sudden snag. On June 23, shortly after the news broke that John Mack was being considered by Morgan Stanley to resume his old job as CEO, Aguirre received a call from the bank's head of regulatory affairs, Eric Dinallo, asking whether the SEC was proceeding against him. "Because if you proceed against Mack, we are going to have a problem in having him step in as CEO," he told Aguirre. The bank retained the noted Wall Street law firm Debevoise & Plimpton to perform due diligence on Mack; on June 26, Mary Jo White, an influential white-collar defense partner at Debevoise and former senior prosecutor at the Southern District of New York, sent an email marked "URGENT" to the head of the SEC's Enforcement Division, Linda Thomsen, demanding that Thomsen call her that same day.

After consulting with Paul Berger, her associate director of enforcement (and Kreitman's boss), but without speaking with Aguirre though he was the attorney in charge of the investigation, Thomsen returned the call. The SEC had no compelling evidence of wrongdoing by Mack, she told White: there was "smoke there," she explained, but "surely not fire." In a separate conversation with the compliance director of Morgan Stanley, Paul Berger revealed, against normal SEC procedure for the release of nonpublic information, that his agency's evidence against Mack consisted primarily of emails between Mack and Samberg, which contained no proof of wrongdoing.

That same day, when Aguirre asked Hanson for permission to subpoena Mack— the next logical step in his investigation—Hanson declined, citing Mack's "very powerful political connections." Hanson later explained his refusal to allow Aguirre to question Mack by observing that Mack's lawyers had "juice," and could access the leaders of the SEC. In fact, Mack and Morgan Stanley had the influential Mary Jo White on their side, as well as former SEC enforcement director Gary

Lynch. Pequot had juice of its own, including former enforcement head Stanley Sporkin and former SEC commissioner Irving Pollack, which it had already used: in January 2005, as Aguirre's investigation of Pequot took shape, the company's lawyers had met with Stephen Cutler, then the SEC enforcement director, in a meeting to which Aguirre was not invited. Shortly afterward, Aguirre was ordered to narrow the scope of his investigation.

The idea that he was being prevented from questioning a key witness and suspected insider trading tipster because of that person's political clout struck Aguirre not only as outrageous, but as ominous for his future with the SEC. "I'd issued seventy subpoenas in the case at that point, with never a pushback on anything," he says. "I thought to myself, 'Ah, okay, this goes all the way to the top. I didn't come here to fix the SEC. It's time to move on.'"

But when he told his wife that he intended to resign, she asked, "How are you going to feel about yourself in five years?" A close friend at the SEC, whom Aguirre had told about the case, observed that if Aguirre left at that point, the entire investigation would disappear. Aguirre also thought about the oath he'd taken when he joined the SEC, to enforce the securities laws of his hero Ferd Pecora without bending to political bias. He realized that if he didn't take a stand, he'd feel complicit in the corruption of those laws.

"So without really knowing how far I'd go, I decided to take things up just one notch," Aguirre remembers. He told Paul Berger what Hanson had said about not subpoenaing Mack because of his political influence. Berger was outraged—not at Hanson, but at Aguirre for indirectly accusing Berger of political favoritism.

"I'm not accusing you of anything," Aguirre remembers responding. "I'm just telling you what Bob said."

"If he'd called Bob in to ask just what he'd meant by that statement," Aguirre says, "then the rest of my story might have had a very different conclusion." But Berger asked for no explanation from Hanson. Instead, he and Robert Hanson attempted to modify Aguirre's positive performance evaluation, which had already been approved along with a merit pay raise, by the Enforcement Division. Berger also confirmed that the SEC would not subpoena John Mack.

So Aguirre escalated his battle one more degree. He wrote a series of memos laying out the evidence that suggested Mack was the tipster; he marshaled the emails, phone calls and other communications that made clear why questioning Mack was essential for the investigation. "I showed how the evidence trail led straight to his door." His superiors at the SEC responded with a series of objections, and a continued refusing to question Mack. "Their answer was always 'No,'" Aguirre remembers. "They asked, 'Where's the motive?' Well, Samberg arranged for Mack to triple his $5 million investment. So then they found another objection, and when I answered that one, they had another objection, and that went on a while. And finally, I took the cat-and-mouse game to the head of the Enforcement Division, Linda Thomsen. And that's when they said, 'Gary, why don't you go on vacation, and when you get back we'll vet your facts. And if you're right, we'll take his testimony.'"

Aguirre went home to San Diego and spent two weeks unwinding on the long golden crescent of South Mission Beach. While sitting on the sand on September 1, the last day of his vacation, he received a phone call from Kreitman, who announced that he was being fired for insubordination. During his absence, his supervisors, at Berger's suggestion, had written a supplementary performance evaluation—an unprecedented document. Whereas the original evaluation had recognized Aguirre's "unmatched dedication," the new evaluation criticized him for being "resistant to supervision," for expressing "resentment at what he inaccurately perceives as attempts by his supervisors to thwart his success," and for his lack of awareness of institutional protocol, which had caused a defense lawyer to object to his conduct.

Aguirre's termination memorandum described his "demonstrated inability to work effectively with other staff members and unwillingness to operate within the Securities and Exchange Commission (SEC) process." In short, as his colleagues stated on several occasions, Aguirre was a "loose cannon"—a term that, Senate investigators later observed, is often applied to individuals who are "unwilling to look the other way when it comes to evidence of misconduct or mismanagement," and who are consequently targeted for retaliation. The memo was initialed by Paul Berger. The SEC soon closed its investigation into Pequot. At the same time, the commission also dropped seventeen other investigations of Pequot and its portfolio managers for possible insider trading.

But the SEC had chosen the wrong man to bully. Aguirre wrote two detailed letters to SEC chairman Christopher Cox, explaining his concerns that the Pequot investigation was being obstructed, and naming other experienced SEC employees who shared his suspicions about Pequot's trades: "Staff who worked on this matter from the beginning—Hilton Foster, Eric Ribelin, Thomas Conroy, and I—believe that PCM [i.e., Pequot] engages in an institutionalized form of insider trading that corrupts the financial markets." This formal charge triggered an investigation by the SEC's inspector general. Aguirre contacted GAP, and GAP attorney Joanne Royce introduced him to Chuck Grassley, ranking member of the Senate Finance Committee, whose staff questioned him extensively. He wrote an eighteen-page letter to Senators Chuck Hagel and Christopher Dodd on the Senate Subcommittee on Securities and Investment of the Committee on Banking, Housing and Urban Affairs, which someone on the Banking Committee leaked to the *New York Times*; the leading financial journalist Gretchen Morgenson wrote a major story that appeared on June 23, 2006, questioning the legitimacy of the SEC's Pequot investigation. Senators Chuck Grassley and Arlen Specter opened an investigation that lasted for eighteen months.

The SEC struck immediately—not against Samberg or Mack, of course, but against Aguirre. The commission threatened several times to prosecute him for violating the criminal theft statute, 18 USC 641—one of the laws under which Edward Snowden and Chelsea Manning would later be charged—claiming he had illegally kept his work notebooks, and ordering him not to hand them over to the government. (In fact, he'd had them with him in San Diego when he was abruptly fired, and was fully entitled to communicate with Congress about them; two years later, via a FOIA request, he received internal memos showing that the SEC had known this legal ploy was illegitimate, but had made it nonetheless.) The SEC opened three investigations against Aguirre, accusing him, without evidence, of hacking, of illegal entry into the SEC after his termination, and of taking too much vacation time. The SEC inspector general closed his investigation in under two months, with a terse denial of Aguirre's claims. The SEC's Office of the General Counsel planned and executed a media attack to portray him as "a basket case former employee," and had former SEC senior officials deny on national news that politics could sway investigatory decisions at the commission. The commission leaked materials to the *New York Times* in an attempt to discredit Aguirre, though the *Times* declined to print them.

Using tactics reminiscent of the Pentagon's assault on Ernie Fitzgerald, the SEC sued Aguirre to recover his confidential communications with the Senate. Aguirre remembers the DOJ letter demanding, on the commission's behalf, that he turn over all information he had provided to Congress. "I had to retain a lawyer and fight them over that, too. The Senate told the DOJ to back down, and the DOJ responded, 'No, we're representing SEC, and we're going to sue this guy to get the records back.' Grassley and Specter prepared a motion on the floor of the Senate, saying that if the DOJ didn't stop, the Senate counsel would intervene on the other side. We almost had US vs. US." The DOJ eventually relented.

The onslaught lasted four years, a period of intense stress for Aguirre and his family. "When the government comes after you, threatens you with criminal prosecution, sues you, opens multiple investigations, it causes great anguish," Aguirre says. "And knowing that you've done nothing illegal—that the government itself is behaving illegally and abusing its authority—makes it even worse." His case took a heavy toll on his family. His wife, who was pregnant with twins, developed pre-eclampsia, and their daughters were delivered in an emergency cesarean section, two months premature. "Everything was happening at the same time," Aguirre remembers. "Knowing what I know now, I probably wouldn't choose that path."

Gradually, however, the momentum shifted in his favor. Grassley and Specter subpoenaed his entire chain of command, from Hanson up to Linda Thomsen. In January 2007, they delivered their interim conclusions on the floor of the Senate, stating that the SEC's investigation of Pequot had been "plagued with problems"; that the commission's firing of Aguirre was "highly suspect"; and that the SEC's inspector general's investigation was "fatally flawed." "Taken together," Grassley concluded, "these findings paint a picture of a troubled agency that faces serious questions about public confidence, the integrity of its investigations, and its ability to protect all investors, large and small, with an even hand. The SEC should have taken Mr. Aguirre's allegations more seriously and very seriously. Instead, it does like too many agencies do when under fire: it circled the wagons and it shot a whistleblower—an all too familiar practice in Washington, DC."

The SEC inspector general, Walter Stachnik, resigned, and Cox ordered his successor, H. David Kotz, to perform a new investigation of the commission's handling of the case, as well as of the first IG probe. The SEC reopened the Pequot investigation, and though Aguirre's superiors had all insisted that it was unnecessary to question Mack, they now did so, on August 1, 2006—one day after the statute of limitations on all potential charges against Mack had expired. On November 30, 2006, the SEC closed the Pequot case again, without any finding of wrongdoing.

So Aguirre, now a private citizen, took over the investigation. Using repeated FOIA lawsuits, during which he convinced a federal judge that the SEC's handling of the case had been improper or illegal, Aguirre extracted his own Pequot findings page by page from his former employer, and continued the sleuthing he'd started at the commission. "By mid-2008, it was as if I was back at the SEC. I had all of my investigation files. I was still hopeful of making a case against Pequot. Then, in November, I got a phone call. It was just like a movie."

"Mr. Aguirre, I'm sorry I cannot disclose my identity to you," a man's voice said, "but I would like for you to know that David Zilkha, the person you suspected as being the tipper in Microsoft, is being paid off $2.1 million by Art Samberg." The caller said he had been following Aguirre's whistleblowing drama against the SEC and Samberg, and believed that Aguirre was the right person to receive this information. "I'll call you later," he said abruptly, and hung up.

In a subsequent phone conversation, the anonymous informant advised Aguirre to look into a divorce case that had been heard before the Connecticut Superior Court, where he'd find proof of the payoff. The tip was correct. David Zilkha and his former wife, Karen Kaiser, were fighting a bitter legal battle for custody of their two children; Kaiser's lawyer had discovered that Zilkha, who had been fired from Pequot after working at the hedge fund for only seven months, had sued the company for wrongful termination. Samberg, without admitting culpability, had agreed to settle Zilkha's employment suit out of court for $2.1 million; on April 30, 2007, Samberg paid Zilkha the first $700,000 installment of this settlement. In the wrongful termination suit, Zilkha stated that the payments from Samberg were in compensation for the fact that he had "conveyed to Samberg that [Microsoft] would meet or exceed its earnings estimates" before the estimates were made public—a confirmation that they had engaged in insider trading. Zilkha's statement and the money from Samberg had remained confidential until they were brought out by the divorce proceedings.

The anonymous caller had more to say. Several weeks later, he told Aguirre that he had David Zilkha's hard drive from 2001, and offered to search it for evidence of insider trading. From his original investigation at the SEC, Aguirre knew that Samberg had asked Zilkha for information on Microsoft financial performance on April 6, 2001, which would be made public thirteen days later, and that Samberg began buying Microsoft stock on April 9. Since June 2005, Aguirre had postulated the existence of material, nonpublic information being passed by Zilkha to Samberg sometime between those two dates, but none of the emails or other documents that Zilkha, Pequot or Microsoft had turned over in response to SEC subpoenas had contained evidence of such information. Aguirre asked the caller to look for emails between April 6 and 9.

Three weeks later, the anonymous whistleblower said he'd found an intriguing email chain from April 7 and 8.

On April 7 at 11:37 p.m., Zilkha sent Mark Spain, his fellow Microsoft executive, friend and next-door neighbor, an email with the subject line "Re: Any visibility on the recent quarter?" "Hey there, have you heard whether we will miss estimates?" the message read. "Any other info?"

Spain replied on April 8 at 11:08 a.m.: "March was best March of record. Made up the shortfall in us sub. w2k pro major contributor. on track for revised forecast." In plain English, Spain was saying that Microsoft had had its best March financial results in the company's history; that its US subsidiary had improved its earlier disappointing performance; that its new operating system, Windows 2000 Pro, was selling very well; and that the company would probably announce better than expected financial performance.

"That was the smoking gun I'd been looking for," Aguirre says. "I couldn't have asked for better evidence if I'd drafted that email myself. It contained four items of material, nonpublic information about why Microsoft's earnings and revenues would be a positive surprise when publicly announced."

On January 2, 2009, Aguirre wrote a letter to SEC commissioner Christopher Cox, in which he laid out this new evidence, which Zilkha had omitted, intentionally or not, when he turned over documentation in response to the SEC subpoena. Aguirre showed how the SEC enforcement division had mishandled this case, and argued that Samberg's payments to Zilkha represented "the quid pro quo for Zilkha's withholding crucial evidence during the SEC, US Attorney, FBI and Senate investigations relating to Pequot's trading in Microsoft securities." He concluded the letter by requesting that the SEC again reopen its Pequot investigation, and refer Samberg's payment of $2.1 million to Zilkha to a federal prosecutor as possible evidence of witness tampering, bribery and other crimes. This, too, received extensive coverage by Gretchen Morgenson in the *New York Times*.

With the momentum of Senate hearings, IG investigations and the press behind him, Aguirre's latest "smoking gun" finally prodded the SEC into action. The commission reopened the Pequot case, and in 2010 Samberg rapidly settled fraud charges by paying $28 million in fines and disgorgement accepting a lifetime ban on investment advisory. Soon after, he closed Pequot. Karen Kaiser and her second husband, Glen Kaiser—who had been Aguirre's anonymous caller—received $1 million from the SEC as a reward for supplying crucial information in the case. And in June 2010, with the help of his lawyers at GAP, Aguirre won a $755,000 settlement from the SEC for wrongful termination, the largest such settlement in history.

But the story of Aguirre's whistleblowing did not end there. His denunciation of Samberg and the SEC grew into a detailed denunciation of systemic lawbreaking in the US financial system, just as that system was imploding. He testified repeatedly before the Senate between June 2006 and September 2008. Trying to make the most of his fleeting authority and political access as a successful whistleblower, he wrote letters to SEC leadership and prominent members of Congress, delivered keynote addresses at financial conferences, and gave numerous interviews, all driving home the same messages. He showed how hedge funds were engaged in systematic illegal activity like insider trading and market manipulation; he pointed out the weakness and subservience of the SEC to Wall Street; and he argued, quoting Pecora, that the SEC's failure to enforce securities laws was allowing Wall Street to re-create the conditions that had caused the 1929 crash. In late 2007, he predicted that the excessive leverage and runaway fraud in the banking sector, if not halted, would cause another global financial crisis. One month before the collapse of Bear Stearns, the first major casualty of the crisis, he warned that the nation's banks, especially Bear Stearns, were at severe risk because of their massive off-balance-sheet exposure to subprime debt and credit default swaps. After the financial crisis hit and TARP was being debated in Congress, Aguirre wrote senior congressmen to denounce the bailout as "Main Street's gift to Wall Street"; his projections of the staggering costs of the operation were cited on the floor of the House.

Some of his meta-whistleblowing brought positive change. After he told Congress in 2006 that hedge funds were systematically using insider trading as a business model, in both the United States and the UK, the SEC and prosecutor Preet Bharara at the Southern District of New York began a crackdown on insider trading in hedge funds, bringing numerous indictments and a series of successful prosecutions against high-profile hedge funds, including an eleven-year prison sentence for Galleon Group's Raj Rajaratnam, and a $1.8 billion fine for SAC Capital's Steve Cohen, who was also banned from securities advising for two years.

Yet on the whole, Aguirre says, his warnings about the impending crisis of 2008, whose causes paralleled those of the crash of 1929, were ignored. "If the SEC had gotten Pequot right, and filed suit against that company and its tippers in 2005 or 2006, the commission would have sent a strong message to Wall Street at a critical moment: we go after the big fish, too. Instead, the commission did everything it could to avoid conflict with captains of industry like Samberg and Mack, and retaliated against its own employee when he had the temerity, with a handful of smoking guns, to go after them." At the same time, he says, the commission vigorously, often mercilessly, pursues small offenders. In the Pequot case, for example, SEC investigators eventually found that a low-level employee at General Electric and a Taiwanese kung fu instructor, working together, had made a suspiciously deft $150,000 from sales of GE and Heller shares. The two were prosecuted and received prison sentences—fifteen months for the GE employee, eight months for the kung fu master—as well as having to disgorge all their earnings from the transaction.

"This happens because people at the SEC are given two conflicting goals," says

Aguirre. "You need to provide statistics to show that the SEC is doing something. But on the other hand, you are not to pursue anybody who has real influence on Wall Street. So how do you do that? By overzealously prosecuting the small fry, who are basically weaponless, vulnerable, and you bring the full power of the federal government down on them." He describes similar cases in which the SEC prosecuted small parties—a teacher in Chicago, a "hedge fund" that actually was an unregistered Vietnamese family—for trivial abuses. Other SEC officials agree that the SEC has an absurd dual standard of justice. In his retirement speech on April 2014, longtime SEC trial lawyer James Kidney condemned the commission for "picking on the little guys." It "polices the broken windows on the street level and rarely goes to the penthouse floors," he said.

Kidney and Aguirre both feel that this deference to influential financial groups results, in large part, from the revolving door with Wall Street law firms, and the profound conflicts of interest it creates. "If someone is very aggressive at the SEC, and wants to bash down the front door of Morgan Stanley with a pack of German shepherds that haven't eaten for a week, you're not going to be welcome at Wilmer-Hale, and JPMorgan is not going to hire you as general counsel," Aguirre says. Senior SEC staff are responsible for the conduct of the people below them, he explains, and for preventing any of them from "going rogue" by investigating too aggressively. "Failure to control your troops will burn you when you leave the SEC and move to private practice." Aguirre says he would remedy this situation by barring all SEC employees from working in the financial industry for five years.

James Kidney agrees. "The revolving door is a very serious problem," he said in his retirement speech. "I have had bosses, and bosses of my bosses, whose names we all know, who made little secret that they were here to punch their ticket. They mouthed serious regard for the mission of the commission, but their actions were tentative and fearful in many instances. . . . The attitude trickles down the ranks. Combined with the negative views of the civil service promoted by politicians and the beatings we take from the public, it is no surprise that we lose our best and brightest as they see no place to go in the agency and eventually decide they are just going to get their own ticket to a law firm or corporate job punched." Instead of tough enforcement actions against major US firms, the commission prefers to pursue foreign entities with less clout on Wall Street and in DC, thus increasing its enforcement numbers without offending any influential figures. "For the powerful," Kidney concluded disconsolately, "we are at most a tollbooth on the bankster turnpike. We are a cost, not a serious expense."

Aguirre's own case amply illustrates the distortionary effects of the revolving door. The existence of former senior SEC officials in the employ of Pequot and Samberg, Morgan Stanley and Mack apparently intimidated his bosses—or perhaps incentivized them. Paul Berger took a job at Debevoise & Plimpton soon after its head of litigation, Mary Jo White, intervened in Mack's case. A week after he initialed Aguirre's termination, a friend at Debevoise told White that Berger was interested in joining the firm. Within months, White hired him as a partner, commending his "wealth of experience at the SEC and his leadership on many of the SEC's most significant enforcement cases" as "a tremendous asset to our clients." When questioned by Senate investigators, Berger implied that his interest in a job at Debevoise had arisen much later, but his friend's contradictory email eventually emerged. No action was taken against Berger.

Easily the most striking revolving-door figure in Aguirre's story is Mary Jo White, who in 2013 was appointed chair of the SEC. Obama sold her as a tough New York prosecutor who would keep Wall Street in check—"You don't want to mess with Mary Jo," he said. The *New York Times* said that her appointment signaled the administration's "renewed resolve to hold Wall Street accountable"; CBS called her "Wall Street's new sheriff." Predictably, at her Senate confirmation hearing White promised to lead a "bold and unrelenting" SEC that would ensure "that all wrongdoers . . . of whatever position or size, will be aggressively and successfully called to account by the SEC."

In reality, her tenure was a study in revolving-door distortions and severe conflicts of interest. She brought a team of equally conflicted revolvers and Wall Street defense lawyers into the SEC, including another Debevoise partner, Andrew Ceresney, as director of enforcement; Robert Rice, who from 2004 to 2013 was head of governance, litigation and regulation for the American operations of Deutsche Bank, as chief counsel; and chief of staff Andrew "Buddy" Donohue, former managing director at Goldman Sachs, who from 2003 to 2006 had been a lawyer in charge of compliance and regulatory matters at Merrill Lynch, just as Merrill slid into the abyss. White's previous work at Debevoise defending senior bankers at JPMorgan, Bank of America, Morgan Stanley and elsewhere, as well as her husband's ongoing Wall Street defense work—John White, a former director of the SEC's Division of Corporation Finance, was a partner at Cravath, Swaine & Moore—forced her to recuse herself from numerous important SEC investigations, hampering the commission's work. She dragged her feet on imposing rules mandated by Congress; continued to allow wrongdoers to settle without an admission of guilt despite a specific promise to reduce these "no fault" settlements; and continued distributing waivers to recidivist, too-big-to-fail banks whose criminal and civil wrongdoing ought to have disqualified them from certain financial advantages. By June 2015, her performance had revealed itself to be so weak that Elizabeth Warren wrote a scathing thirteen-page letter listing the commitments White had made during her confirmation and then broken in office. "I am disappointed that you have not been the strong leader that many hoped for—and that you promised to be," Warren wrote.

Yet given her background, could we honestly expect anything else from White? Susan Webber, a former investment banker who runs *Naked Capitalism*, the influential financial blog, asked rhetorically: "The SEC's Mary Jo White: A Failure, or Doing Her Real Job?" In February 2017, we got a hint, when White resigned from the SEC and returned to Debevoise as a senior chair. Andrew Ceresney did the same. Their detail to the commission was over, and they were returning to base. "I am thrilled to be coming back home to Debevoise," Ceresney said. "I am excited to rejoin my world-class colleagues to serve our premier clients." White explained that Debevoise "has one of the preeminent white-collar defense practices. It's the core of what I do."

When I asked Gary Aguirre how he had felt when he saw White, whose "juice" had helped to derail his investigation and destroy his career at the SEC, named to head the commission, he shrugged. "She's like a piece of a puzzle that fits perfectly into place. You can't help thinking that these people are actually chosen for their conflicts, for their inability to make real change." He points to Robert Khuzami, who came to the SEC as enforcement director in 2009, after seven years at Deutsche Bank in New York, a bank that was singled out by Carl Levin's Senate investigation, along with Goldman Sachs, as a case study in financial malfeasance in the selling and secret shorting of toxic mortgage-related securities. "Deutsche Bank was ground zero for slimy behavior, which when it exploded gave us the financial crisis of 2008," Aguirre says. "That means that Khuzami, as the bank's general counsel, supervised the attorneys and had oversight on the traders who did all of Deutsche's toxic debt, all their credit-default swaps, their CDOs designed by hedge funds to fail so they and Deutsche could bet against them. So a year after the financial collapse, in 2009, when it's time to really get tough with Wall Street—because those bankers need to be taught a lesson, or they'll just do it again, and burn another $23 trillion—who do they appoint as the Enforcement Director of the SEC? Someone who's so implicated in the collapse that if he's going to do a serious investigation of Wall Street, he'll have to put himself on the list. And we know that's not going to happen." (Khuzami was appointed by another successful revolver, Mary Schapiro, who before heading the SEC had been the CEO of FINRA [Financial Industry Regulatory Authority], the banking industry's self-regulating body, which is staffed and funded by the banks. When Obama tapped her to lead the SEC, the bankers on the FINRA board voted her a $9 million bonus—"a little something to remember them by," financial journalist William Cohan commented.)

Old ties continue to bind. In January 2011, Chuck Grassley received a letter from an anonymous whistleblower stating that Khuzami, after a "secret conversation" with a lawyer friend and former colleague who was representing Citibank, had agreed to spare a high-level banker from a fraud investigation; the SEC subsequently reached an absurdly low, sweetheart settlement with Citibank for its misstatement of toxic mortgage liabilities that Richard Bowen had reported to his board. Grassley passed the letter to the SEC inspector general, who opened an investigation; though the resulting report found no proof of impropriety by Khuzami, it was so heavily redacted that it is hard to interpret. One thing the document did make clear, though, was that the same procedures had occurred here that the SEC inspector general had previously flagged as a major problem in the Pequot case: a high-level official, in this instance Khuzami, passing over the heads of his own line attorneys to deal directly with the senior defense lawyer representing a prominent financial firm. (Khuzami later left the SEC and continued revolving, first to the government, regulatory and internal investigations practice of the law firm Kirkland & Ellis, where he earned $11 million in two years, and then to the Southern District of New York as deputy US attorney, a post he left in March 2019, citing personal reasons.)

Gary Aguirre now works in private practice and represents financial whistle-blowers, some of them at the SEC. One of his clients, SEC lawyer Darcy Flynn, informed congressional investigators that for at least two decades, the SEC had been shredding emails and documents produced during preliminary investigations into major Wall Street banks like Citigroup, Goldman Sachs, Bank of America and Lehman Brothers. Much as Allen Jones discovered at the Pennsylvania OIG's office, and Gary Aguirre found at the SEC when he started looking into Pequot, destroying these documents deprived investigators of potentially vital background information and context, and made it harder for them to connect the dots on large-scale fraud schemes. Khuzami indignantly denied all wrongdoing.

The lack of investigations or incisive action by the SEC against Deutsche Bank, known to be one of the worst actors in toxic mortgage securities in the run-up to the 2008 collapse, remains mysterious. Or perhaps not so mysterious: How many of Khuzami's subordinates would be keen to start an investigation that could lead straight to their director of enforcement? Even before Khuzami's tenure, Darcy Flynn claims, a promising fraud investigation against Deutsche Bank was derailed by the revolving-door behavior of the SEC enforcement director at the time, Richard Walker, who stalled the probe by unexpectedly recusing himself at a critical moment, after which it was swiftly scuttled, to the surprise of many staffers. Months later, Walker resigned from the SEC and resurfaced as the general counsel at Deutsche Bank, where he would mentor Robert Khuzami.

The few tough actions Khuzami took against Wall Street while at the SEC turned out, with hindsight, to look more like smoke screens. The SEC's investigation of Goldman Sachs for its infamous ABACUS 2007-AC1 transaction, for example, produced what initially seemed an impressive $550 million settlement with the bank. Goldman had invented the ABACUS structure, a synthetic CDO that allowed the bank and its clients to target specific assets they wanted to short. The bank made sixteen ABACUS issues in all, the last of which was ABACUS

2007-AC1; in this final incarnation, Goldman didn't invest in the CDO itself, as it had in the past. Instead, it essentially rented the structure to hedge fund manager John Paulson, who had decided that the housing bubble was about to burst and was looking for ways to make money when one of the most hyperinflated parts of the mortgage bubble, subprime mortgages, lost value. Paulson was among Goldman's top customers for assets related to subprime mortgages; he also shorted subprime mortgage instruments in several major deals with Deutsche Bank.

In ABACUS 2007-AC1, Goldman allowed Paulson to handpick a substantial number of the underlying mortgage assets that went into the CDO, and then to bet against it. Paulson naturally chose poor-quality assets, which seemed likely to default in the near future. Knowing that potential buyers would be leery of investing in such a made-to-fail instrument, Goldman hired ACA Management, a widely respected manager of CDOs, to serve as the official portfolio selection agent, and touted them as an honest broker behind the deal—without disclosing that Paulson had actually chosen many of the assets. Goldman sold over $1 billion in ABACUS securities to three unsuspecting investors. Six months later, 83 percent of the mortgage bonds contained in the CDO had been downgraded by rating agencies, and ABACUS 2007-AC1 was essentially worthless. Two of the three investors went bankrupt, and since shorting is a zero-sum game, nearly all of their money went to John Paulson, who pocketed nearly $1 billion, less the fees he paid to Goldman. Khuzami and the SEC sued Goldman and its lead salesman in the ABACUS transaction, Fabrice Tourre, for committing securities fraud and failing to disclose material adverse information to potential investors. The bank agreed to pay $550 million in disgorgement and fines, which seemed a lot for one rotten CDO deal. Eventually, however, sharp-eyed financial journalist Susan Beck discovered that when the SEC settled ABACUS, it quietly dropped eleven other investigations into dubious CDOs underwritten by Goldman. Now $550 million looked like a bargain.

In mid-2016, another skeleton came clattering out of Khuzami's closet, when former SEC lawyer James Kidney, whose retirement remarks had caused a stir, belatedly turned whistleblower and released internal SEC documents and emails concerning the ABACUS investigation to Pulitzer-winning finance reporter Jesse Eisinger. These showed that in Kidney's expert opinion, Khuzami and others had possessed ample evidence to investigate John Paulson and senior Goldman executives involved in the deal, but, much as in the Pequot case, had not done so out of deference to Wall Street power. Instead, like Pequot, they'd focused on the small fry, Tourre, whose incautious emails to his girlfriend and bank colleagues made him an easy target. (Tourre's bosses had been more circumspect, simply writing "LDL"—"Let's discuss live"—when an email conversation strayed into sensitive areas.)

Kidney felt that the SEC should take the testimony of these Goldman executives, and of John Paulson and Paulson's employee Paolo Pellegrini, who had worked on the transaction. "Each of them knowingly participated, as did Goldman and Tourre, in a scheme to sell a product which, in blunt but accurate terms, was designed to fail," Kidney wrote in an October 2009 memo. "In other words, the current pre-discovery evidence suggests they *should* be sued for securities fraud because they are liable for securities fraud." Others at the commission disagreed. Reid Muoio, a longtime SEC lawyer who led the commission's mortgage securities team, emailed colleagues of his concerns about the "devasting [sic] impact our little ol' civil actions reap on real people more often than I care to remember. It is the least favorite part of the job. Most of our civil defendants are good people who have done one bad thing."

Khuzami eventually sided with Muoio and limited the investigation to Tourre. Early in the case, Kidney, who had joined the commission in 1986 when it was capable of pursuing high-profile fraudsters such as Michael Milken and Ivan Boesky, warned a superior that the commission "must be on guard against any risk that we adopt the thinking of those sponsoring these structures and join the Wall Street Elders."

The SEC, in Aguirre and Kidney's time and to this day, exhibits many of the symptoms of a regulator captured by the industry it's meant to police. Its lax oversight of Bear Stearns, Lehman Brothers, and Merrill Lynch, whose 2008 collapse fueled the financial crisis, and its failure to recognize mammoth fraud schemes by Bernard Madoff and Allen Stanford, raised serious questions about how cozy the commission had gotten with the banks. The commission's settlements have been widely criticized as inadequate, obliging to the wrongdoers and uninformative to the general public. In 2009, Judge Jed Rakoff rejected the commission's proposed low-ball $33 million toxic mortgage settlement with Bank of America as "a contrivance designed to provide the SEC with the façade of enforcement," which failed to "comport with the most elementary notions of justice and morality." Four years later he rejected another SEC toxic mortgage settlement, with Citigroup; he condemned the commission for allowing the bank to admit no wrongdoing, and for proposing a toothless settlement that left "defrauded investors substantially short-changed"—a settlement that he asserted the financial world would view as "a cost of doing business." Acting SEC officials have made similar criticisms. Commissioner Kara Stein wrote in a May 2015 memorandum that "allowing these institutions to continue business as usual, after multiple and serious regulatory and criminal violations, poses risks to investors and the American public that are being ignored," adding that the SEC's behavior had "effectively rendered criminal convictions of financial institutions largely symbolic."

Not everyone agrees that the revolving door is a problem. "I was a better US Attorney because of my years representing companies, learning the ways companies think, the way boards think," Mary Jo White said at Fordham School of Law in 2013. Her predecessor as SEC chair, Mary Schapiro, made a related point: "People from the private sector know where the bodies are buried, where the private sector has taken shortcuts or engaged in conduct that is less than exemplary." Even the formidable judge Jed Rakoff himself, one of the most caustic critics of Wall Street misbehavior and regulatory and prosecutorial permissiveness, observes that "most federal prosecutors, at every level, are seeking to make a name for themselves, and the best way to do that is by prosecuting some high-level person." Rakoff himself defended white-collar criminals for years at three major Wall Street law firms, including Debevoise, before joining the federal bench.

Yet substantial evidence bears out James Kidney's observations about the harmful effects on SEC morale of the revolving door with Wall Street, and suggests that the behavior of many SEC attorneys is warped by their future job prospects.

Since 1997, SEC examiners had suspected Allen Stanford, now serving a 110-year sentence in federal prison, of running a Ponzi scheme, but their calls to open an investigation, made repeatedly from 1997 to 2005, were vetoed by the head of the SEC office in Fort Worth, Texas, Spencer Barasch. Then, in 2005, Barasch left the agency to work for Allen Stanford, and attempted to obtain confidential information on the SEC's investigation. After Stanford's fraud became public, Barasch was asked by an SEC investigator why he had done so, even after the SEC ethics office had forbidden him to. "Every lawyer in Texas and beyond is going to get rich over this case," Barasch blurted. "Okay? And I hated being on the sidelines." The SEC inspector general concluded, "This misconduct highlights the dangers of a 'revolving door' environment between the SEC and the private securities law bar."

Consider a less flagrant scenario. Imagine a young SEC lawyer who perceives the atmosphere at the SEC as Gary Aguirre, James Kidney and the GAO have described it, where the attorneys eager to investigate fraud in high places are shouted down, and the rest are just looking to "punch their ticket" and move to a bigger payday on Wall Street. This young lawyer decides to follow the latter path. Now imagine a meeting between this lawyer and a former senior SEC official, who now represents a major bank or hedge fund and is arguing for leniency on her client's behalf. This defense lawyer is wealthy, authoritative, and, well, *senior*: she was once the lawyer's boss's boss's boss; after their meeting, she stops by the commissioner's office to say hello. This person occupies the position that the SEC line attorney wants for himself one day—perhaps even at her same law firm. Perhaps, as Mary Jo White did with Paul Berger, someday she will offer him a job. What will be the tone of their current interaction?

How this works is suggested by former SDNY prosecutor Daniel Richman, now at Columbia Law School (he is the professor to whom James Comey leaked his now famous memos about his conversations with Donald Trump). Richman defended the revolving-door system in a November 2013 interview: "When you hear about a former Assistant U.S. Attorney coming back to the office to talk about an investigation, one could say, 'It's the old-boy network,'" Richman observed. "But those who are closer to the situation see that it's a much more beneficent system. The company chose a former Assistant U.S. Attorney. That shows it's committed to playing by the rules. And that's rewarded."

For most of us, what Richman considers benefits are serious problems. Corruption in such circles is rarely as blatant as a bag of cash, but consists rather in a web of deference, beholdenness and careerist ambitions that legal scholar Lawrence Lessig terms "dependency corruption." It grows from institutional hypocrisy: the belief that following the official, written policies of the government organization is impossible, or at least impractical, and that one must adapt to the game that is *really* being played. All of which is driven, of course, by money. Wall Street lawyers routinely make ten times what they made in government. And in finance, more than most professions, money is the ultimate measure of success. The senior attorneys who move around the table, one day defending banks and the next "regulating" them, are classic examples of Janine Wedel's flexians, those amphibious beings that swim freely between public and private sectors and ultimately transcend both, because their final allegiance is unswervingly to themselves, their careers and the fellow flexians in their networks.

Banks explain the "government service golden parachute" bonuses they offer to senior executives who take Washington jobs as their way of encouraging public service. Jack Lew, the former Citi banker, received over $1 million from his previous employer on joining Obama's Treasury; Antonio Weiss at Lazard was to make $21 million to join the Treasury, before he was blocked by Elizabeth Warren, whereupon Obama opened a back door and made Weiss a presidential appointee, which required no congressional approval. But do organizations with such a steely focus on profits and shareholder value really care about public service? Would they spend so much money without the expectation of a financial return? Sheila Bair, former FDIC chair, wrote in 2014 of such bonuses: "Only in the Wonderland of Wall Street logic could one argue that this looks like anything other than a bribe. Once upon a time, part of the nobility of joining public service was the willingness to make the financial sacrifice. We want people entering public service because they want to serve the public. Frankly, if they need a $20 million incentive, I'd rather they stay away." Or as a crooked S&L head once told Bill Black, "Campaign contributions give the best ROI of any investments we can make."

The argument is also made that US public service needs top talent, and Wall Street produces some of the world's best financial minds. This reasoning fails to account for the susceptibility of human nature to money incentives, especially since, the private sector being the long-term destination for most, Wall Street is typically their ultimate locus of allegiance. Moreover, those who spend any significant time in finance, as in any other influential industry, are subject to cognitive capture; that is, in the words of Berkeley law professor Stavros Gadinis, they become "'socialized' toward that industry's concerns and aspirations, carrying that perspective into their regulatory tasks." Martin Woods, the financial crime expert and former narcotics cop from London who became a bank whistleblower, agrees. "Most people in finance have a hard time seeing rich, prestigious fraudsters in the City or on Wall Street as real criminals," Woods says. "They ask, 'What does a financial criminal look like—a money launderer, a tax evader, an inside trader?' Well, they're rich, their tattoos are spelt correctly if they have any at all, they have crisp white shirts and smart suits and a smile on their face. To most people, they look like the definition of success."

Perhaps the most remarkable example of this increasingly common figure, the master revolver, is former attorney general Eric Holder. Holder has moved repeatedly between the DOJ and his partnership at Covington & Burling, which defends many of the big banks, pharmaceutical companies and other blue-chip recidivists that he was charged with prosecuting while at the Justice Department. Shortly after he resigned as attorney general in September 2014 and returned for the second time to Covington, he told the *American Lawyer*, "This is home for me." In an interview with the *Wall Street Journal*, he added, "I'm going to have the ability to work at the intersection of business, policy, international relations, regulatory schemes, I'm going to have the ability to use all the things I've learned over the years not only domestically but internationally in a way that's going to be fun." Fun, homey and profitable, both for himself and for his clients.

It's easy to see why Holder—widely criticized for failing even to indict a single senior finance executive after the criminal frenzy that caused the 2008 crisis—called Covington "home." Many of his similarly soft-on-finance colleagues at the DOJ were there. He also said that he would decline the offer of a Supreme Court justiceship; judges are referees, Holder said, and "I want to be a player." An event early in his first term of public service, as deputy attorney general under Bill Clinton, suggests what he means. According to a subsequent congressional investigation, Holder attended a dinner in late 1998 to celebrate the merger of Daimler and

Chrysler. He was seated next to a public relations consultant by the name of Gershon Kekst, who, upon learning that Holder worked at "Main Justice," inquired what course of action Holder would recommend if a certain client of his had been unfairly indicted by an overzealous prosecutor. Holder replied that the client should "hire a lawyer who knows the process, he comes to me, and we work it out." He then pointed to a lawyer sitting at another table, and said, "There's Jack Quinn. He's a perfect example."

Kekst represented Marc Rich, a billionaire commodities trader and financier who in 1983, fifteen years before the Daimler dinner, had been indicted by a federal grand jury in New York on sixty-five criminal counts, including income tax evasion, wire fraud, racketeering and trading with Iran during the oil embargo. Knowing he faced up to three centuries in prison, Rich had left the US before he was indicted, and settled in Switzerland, which refused to extradite him. Though some of his companies eventually pleaded guilty to thirty-eight counts of tax evasion and paid $200 million in fines, Rich himself, maintaining his innocence, never returned to the United States to face charges. For years he was on the FBI's Ten Most Wanted Fugitives list.

Kekst followed Holder's advice. He hired Jack Quinn, a veteran Democratic power broker, Bill Clinton's former White House counsel, who was close to Holder. Quinn, Kekst and other members of Rich's legal team began assembling materials to support Rich's cause. They paid $100,000 to two distinguished tax experts, Bernard Wolfman and Martin Ginsburg, husband of Supreme Court justice Ruth Bader Ginsburg, to perform "independent" analyses, which were actually produced exclusively from data provided by Rich's lawyers. The analyses argued that prosecutors had overlooked a US-Swiss tax treaty under which Rich's tax dealings had been legitimate. Kekst consulted Assistant Attorney General William Barr (now attorney general), who advised him not to mount a public relations campaign on Rich's behalf, but to try for a presidential pardon at the end of the Clinton administration. Rich began to distribute millions of dollars in charitable donations to various humanitarian organizations, in return for "letters of support" from those organizations. Rich suggested to the Anti-Defamation League that his prosecution had been motivated by anti-Semitism; the league wrote a letter in Rich's favor, shortly after receiving a $100,000 check, part of a total $250,000 that Rich gave to the organization after he fled to Switzerland. Phil Baum, executive director of the American Jewish Congress, revealed that Rich had approached him with a similar contribution in return for a favorable letter on Rich's behalf. "It was not a contract," Baum explained, "but these things are communicated in more subtle ways. We had reason to hope or expect that if we did this thing, we could probably be the recipient of Mr. Rich's generous recognition of our importance." Baum ultimately declined to write Rich a letter; he received no donation.

Rich also activated his high-level diplomatic and economic connections with Israel, again often making cash contributions to those he approached. Clinton received letters of support from Shlomo Ben-Ami, the minister of foreign affairs; Justice Yaakov Neeman, the minister of finance and former minister of justice; and Shabtai Shavit, the former director of Mossad. Prime Minister Ehud Barak and former prime minister Shimon Peres both urged Clinton to pardon Rich. Rich also persuaded his estranged wife, Denise, a New York socialite and leading Democratic fund-raiser who had close relations with the Clintons, to intercede.

Holder joined the Quinn–Rich axis. First he attempted to arrange a meeting with Rich's prosecutors at the Southern District of New York, who included Mary Jo White. They, however, refused to meet Rich unless he returned to the United States for trial—he was, after all, a fugitive on the FBI's Most Wanted list. So Holder, like Barr, encouraged Quinn to apply for a presidential pardon. Despite consistent DOJ policy to deny clemency to fugitives, and to allow prosecutors to review pardon applications and advise the president on their appropriateness, Holder kept other members of the DOJ in the dark about Rich's maneuverings, while helping Quinn make the most strategic approach to the White House, and suggesting to Clinton aides that he himself favored Rich's pardon.

So do players behave, turning justice into a chess game. During the Senate investigation into the Rich affair, Holder testified that he had been "really struck" by the support Rich had received from Israeli prime minister Ehud Barak, and by the "foreign policy benefits that would be reaped by granting the pardon." Unspoken were the benefits to a rich fugitive and his team of legal lobbyists from Holder's flexian maneuverings—and the returns to Holder himself. Quinn and Holder had cordial relations: Holder had sought Quinn's support before the 2000 presidential election for a potential bid to become attorney general if Al Gore won; soon after Clinton signed Rich's pardon, Holder congratulated Quinn, and asked him to hire two of Holder's former Justice Department aides.

Faced with the public outcry over his role in the affair, which triggered a Senate investigation and a grand jury probe in New York, Holder told the press, "I'm done. Public life's over for me." A few years at Covington & Burling apparently assuaged his concerns, however, and in 2009 he left "home" again, at least temporarily, to rejoin the DOJ as attorney general. Here he continued the practice of arranging back-channel deals with financial high-fliers that once more excluded regulators, prosecutors and the American people from the process, at the expense of transparency and legal equity. He and Jamie Dimon, CEO of JPMorgan, swapped cell phone calls over the details of the bank's toxic mortgage settlement, like two deal guys hashing out a merger. Holder played a similar role with HSBC. After the London-based bank was caught laundering drug cartel money and freely trading, à la Marc Rich, with various nations under US sanction, frontline prosecutors recommended that the bank be criminally indicted. But when Britain's chancellor of the exchequer, George Osborne, expressed his government's concern that such a move might harm the world economy, Holder offered the bank a deferred prosecution agreement instead. A subsequent congressional report found that Holder, his DOJ and the Treasury had "stonewalled" Congress during its investigation into the matter, by failing to deliver some subpoenaed materials and heavily redacting others.

From his eleventh-floor corner office at Covington, Holder looks out toward his old stomping grounds and his former colleagues at DOJ. "When I see something that's happening I say, 'Oh, I wish I was there, they need to be doing this, they need to be doing that,'" he said in a 2015 interview. "I want to call somebody up and make sure that's happening." Then he added, not entirely convincingly, "But you have to fight that." Count on it: Holder is making those calls. That's what players do. That's why Covington hired him.

All this revolving and posturing is part of a larger theater of justice played out between the government and large corporations, which Patrick Burns, former executive director of Taxpayers Against Fraud, calls "the Big Wink." "You see it in finance, in healthcare, in defense, in countless other industries. The US government routinely hammers local grifters, while giving the high sign to corporate predators who steal thousands of times more. Perversely, the more they steal, the less likely any individual is to be prosecuted. If a dentist in Waco, Texas, rips off Medicaid for a million dollars' worth of work he never did, he may be excluded from billing Medicaid for a decade, be fined millions of dollars, lose his home, and get a three-year prison sentence. But if a major pharmaceutical company robs a billion from the state of Texas, through off-label sales of unnecessary, dangerous drugs to children and the elderly, they get the Big Wink from prosecutors and regulators. No one loses their beach house or their freedom, no one loses their job. The only people who are fired when these big cases come down are the whistleblowers who revealed the fraud."

In fact, whistleblowers are one of the few real threats to this closed-circuit game. Since the criminal referral system was dismantled, in fact, Bill Black says that the DOJ's most valuable sources in finance cases are bankers who become whistleblowers. They combine the insider's knowledge with an outsider's commonsense view of honesty and duty and a corresponding lack of deference to hierarchy. Players can't trust them to obey superior orders, can't inveigle them with the promise of future career success or coerce them with the threat of career loss. Perhaps most crucially, players often cannot understand what makes whistleblowers tick—why they would be willing to sacrifice a lucrative future to respect some old-fashioned law or principle. No wonder bosses and colleagues often believe that whistleblowers are insane, and fear them.

The Practicing Law Institute's conferences are among many events at which defense attorneys for major Wall Street banks meet and mingle with acting regulators and prosecutors. Gary Aguirre attended one that took place in November 2010, only months after the SEC had set up its new whistleblower office, as mandated by the Dodd-Frank financial reforms. Defense lawyers in the audience were clearly worried about how the increased support and incentives for whistleblowers might harm their clients. One of the panels Aguirre attended was "The Government Enforcement Agenda," which promised to update participants on the SEC's new powers over banks and hedge funds, including its strategic collaboration with whistleblowers.

The panel contained many familiar faces. The moderator was Mary Jo White, still at Debevoise though soon to be appointed by Obama to lead the SEC. Panelists included Robert Khuzami, SEC enforcement director; Linda Thomsen, former SEC enforcement director, who'd revolved to the leading Wall Street defender Davis Polk & Wardwell; and Preet Bharara, US attorney for the Southern District of New York, protégé of Wall Street ally Senator Chuck Schumer and another widely heralded "Sheriff of Wall Street" who, though the head prosecutor on Wall Street's home turf, had not prosecuted a senior banker for the frauds that caused the 2008 crash. Prosecutors and defense attorneys talked to one another like family, Aguirre says, "with Mary Jo White playing the part of their collective mom." Here is an excerpt from the session transcript:

> BHARARA: *Thank you Mary Jo. I want to . . . first say how pleased I am to be here. To echo what Rob [Robert Khuzami] said that you've spawned all of us, it's almost eleven years ago to the day that Mary Jo White called me and asked me if I would become an Assistant US Attorney. So thank you, Dr. Frankenstein.*
>
> WHITE: *Everything he does right [I taught him]. . . . Everything he does wrong he learned later.*
>
> BHARARA: *I also want to take a moment to applaud Rob, Mary Schapiro, and the entire staff of the SEC for . . . the amazing things they have done over the past year. They are to be commended for thinking creatively, for thinking about all the kinds of ways that they can earn the salary that is paid by the taxpayers. And it has been a real delight to work with all of them. They've done a real service to the country, to the financial community, and not to mention a lot of your law practices.*

Soon a defense attorney named Johnson asks Khuzami about the new SEC whistleblower program, which, along the lines of the FCA, offers substantial rewards for insider information brought to the SEC.

JOHNSON: *Rob, I have a question about the cooperation initiative. Are there . . . Have you found there to be any interference with the typical coordination with US Attorney's offices and parallel investigations as a result of that?*

KHUZAMI: *No. The answer is no. . . . Most defense counsel . . . may well pause before signing up their clients to the SEC without knowing what the Justice Department is doing. And so what it has resulted in, and what we also anticipated, was that there is going to be earlier and more frequent collaboration between us and Justice when an individual wants to sign up with us and, you know, we are going to try to get those individuals answers whether or not there is criminal interest in the case so defense counsel can have as much information as possible in deciding whether or not to choose to sign up their client. But other than that, really it has not proven to be any kind of impediment.*

"I knew this was happening behind the scenes, but I couldn't believe they were saying it publicly," Aguirre remembers. "Khuzami was describing 'collaboration' between the SEC and the Department of Justice, to get bankers 'answers' about what the DOJ might be up to against them, which was strictly against SEC policy and the law. Even more amazing, he was outlining a secret, pay-to-play settlement process for Wall Street players, to make prosecutions go away. The player pays the SEC money, the SEC 'collaborates' with the DOJ, and the DOJ commits to not prosecute the player."

Aguirre suspected that he had observed the results of some of these backroom deals in his own work. During the panel discussion, and in an earlier interview with Reuters, Bharara had said that his office was on the alert for informants who had lied to the SEC. Yet when presented with powerful evidence of lying to federal agents, perjury, obstruction of justice, bribery and blackmail, Bharara's office had taken no action. Was this omission, Aguirre wondered, the result of the kind of "collaboration" Robert Khuzami had described? Shortly after the conference, Aguirre wrote Bharara to remind him of his promise to prosecute those who lied to the SEC. "As I testified before the Senate Judiciary Committee in December 2006," he wrote, "a senior official in the New York Stock Exchange informed me that Pequot and two other hedge funds were at the top of the list of hedge funds suspected of insider trading. If the CEO of such a hedge fund and one of his cronies can lie and bribe their way out of a criminal proceeding for insider trading, which is what the SEC claims Messrs. Samberg and Zilkha have done, and do so with immunity, our nation's capital markets would be more appropriate in a banana republic." He offered to brief Bharara. Bharara never responded.

The new whistleblower programs at SEC and CFTC were and remain a source of great trepidation to business groups, particularly the finance lobby. The American Association of Bank Directors wrote the SEC to deplore the "dual loyalty" that Congress, with these new whistleblower programs, had created for every corporate employee in America: "Employees have a legal duty to serve the best interests of the company they work for and the company's shareholders," yet with the new whistleblower program "they have been deputized and promised huge riches to bypass their companies and report to the government." The American Bankers Association and the Financial Services Roundtable argued for self-regulation in assessing whistleblower charges: "Companies are far better equipped to assess complaints in the context of their particular business and to 'separate the wheat from the chaff.'" A group of companies including Citigroup, JPMorgan, Johnson & Johnson and Pfizer likewise insisted that the SEC permit them to conduct the initial investigations into revelations by whistleblowers at their firms.

They needn't have worried. Self-regulation being the gospel in public and private spheres alike, the SEC, like the DOJ, often allows companies to carry out internal investigations of wrongdoing, including those prompted by whistleblower revelations, and then uses the results of those investigations themselves. The SEC announced in November 2010, "Our staff will, upon receiving a whistleblower complaint, contact a company, describe the nature of the allegations, and give the company an opportunity to investigate the matter and report back."

In response, Chuck Grassley wrote an acerbic letter to the commission, pointing out that its "primary purpose is to protect investors—not internal compliance programs—from potential harm caused by fraud and misconduct," and to insist that the SEC "not throw whistleblowers to the wolves." Given how the SEC handles internal whistleblowers like Gary Aguirre, it's hard to have much faith it will guard outside whistleblowers from the wolves of Wall Street. Since May 2017, the SEC has been chaired by Jay Clayton, a corporate lawyer who spent twenty-two years at Sullivan & Cromwell serving Wall Street banks. In June 2018, Clayton and his SEC proposed to cap larger whistleblower rewards, a move that he said, rather mysteriously, would strengthen the whistleblower program, and that Kara Stein said she feared would weaken it.

Until we start to see this flexian, revolving-door behavior among regulators, prosecutors and the white-collar defense bar for what it really is—not merely ambitious or clever careerism, but corruption, plain and simple—we will never unrig the financial markets, or root out corporate crime. Bank whistleblowers like Aguirre, Black and Bowen are right: unless we can restore basic ethics to the banking industry, the next financial crisis is inevitable—and our democracy itself is at risk.

When Michael Winston was a boy, the license plate on his father's car read HONOR. Winston knew this was more than a word. His father and his two paternal uncles had served in the Army in World War II, and had seen fierce combat in the European and Pacific theaters. Winston remembers his father telling him and his siblings, during long talks at the dinner table, that honor meant both solidity and consistency, which created independence of mind. "He'd say time after time, 'What's right is right, even if nobody else is doing it. And what's wrong is wrong, even if everyone's doing it.' My dad drilled into us the necessity of principles—not just the value but the necessity of principles. It can seem hard to keep your own mind when everyone else is losing theirs. But as long as you know your own mind and know what's right, it's not hard at all."

So when Winston saw a license plate on a sleek silver-blue European sports car that read FUND 'EM, it made him think. He was standing in the front parking lot of the headquarters of Countrywide Financial, the mortgage originator, shortly after joining the firm in mid-2005 to set up a corporate compliance and ethics program. Countrywide had become the largest provider of home mortgages in the world the year before. *Fortune* had just named it as one of its "Most Admired Companies," and *Barron's* had selected Angelo Mozilo as one of its thirty best CEOs in the world.

"What's that about?" Winston asked a man who was standing beside the car. The man stared at Winston for a moment, as if judging whether he was serious. Then he said that the license plate captured Angelo Mozilo's strategy for Countrywide: growing market share rapidly by funding all loans, whether or not the borrowers had the job, income, assets or credit rating to be able to pay them back. "If they can fog a mirror, we'll give them a loan," the man said.

"I knew that Countrywide was the Wild West of financial services, and there were some cowboys here," Winston says today. "That was why they had hired me, to rein in the cowboys. I never imagined that it was the guys at the top who were hatching such an obviously corrupt plot. Silly me!"

Winston had worked for thirty years at a series of Fortune 500 companies, where he had earned a reputation as an authority on organizational succession and business continuity. At Motorola, he had helped the company to retain a healthy culture as its sales grew 500 percent. After earning million-dollar pay packages for several years, he took a leave of absence in 2003 to care for his father and mother, who had been diagnosed with terminal cancer. Countrywide, which had grown at extreme speed over the past few years, recruited him to help ensure its long-term organizational well-being. Succession at the top was a particular concern, since one of the company's cofounders, David Loeb, had retired, and the other, the seventy-year-old Mozilo, was thinking about retirement himself.

At first things went well for Winston. He was promoted twice in his first fourteen months at Countrywide, where he had regular contact with senior management, including president David Sambol. Ethics was a company mantra. Yet Winston was puzzled by certain characteristics of the company. Mozilo had long maintained the same intense emphasis on increasing market share and share price that Richard Bowen was observing at Citi at around the same time. Winston was concerned by the outsize pay packages of executives and board members, and bonuses paid on the quantity of loans sold rather than their quality. "When I was working at Motorola on any given day I couldn't tell you how much I was being paid, and I don't think most of my colleagues could have, either," Winston remembers. "We were all focused on the incredibly important work we were doing, and the money came as a function of that. At Countrywide, I saw the opposite. Financial services firms in general tend to attract people who are less values-driven and more rewards-driven, but at Countrywide the focus on money was extreme, and the things that typically motivate people in healthy organizations—achievement, affiliation, recognition of performance—didn't seem to matter to them. So I was a stranger in a strange land."

As Winston would soon learn, his new company was perhaps the most flagrant subprime mortgage mill in America, which contributed as much as any company to inflating the subprime mortgage bubble and triggering the 2008 crisis. Numerous lawsuits and investigations against the company and its managers—Mozilo was the target of dozens of civil suits and at least one criminal investigation, paid the SEC a $67.5 million settlement and accepted a lifetime ban from serving as an officer or director of a public company to resolve a fraud suit—have revealed Countrywide to be the paradigm for the immorality and illegality that brought the US economy to its knees. In a 2011 interview, Jon Leibowitz, then the FTC chairman, said the company's business model was "based on deceit and corruption, and the harm they caused to American consumers is absolutely massive and extraordinary." Countrywide embodied Bill Black's "control fraud" model: the corporation that senior managers wield as a fraud weapon to enrich themselves, while slaughtering customers, investors, and eventually the firm itself. (The firm collapsed under its debts and was bought in extremis by Bank of America in 2008.) Many of Bill Black's fraud "tells" were on display: the single-minded focus on growth, the gutting of underwriting standards, the use of perverse incentives, and the push to weaken regulation and supervision through overtly corrupt schemes like the "Friends of Angelo" program, which distributed hundreds of highly favorable loans to senior senators, representatives and other government officials.

But all this took time for Michael Winston to see. His first real clash with the company had nothing to do with toxic mortgages, but with an evil-smelling orange vapor that suddenly began emanating from the air ducts in his office in Simi Valley.

The substance, which still hasn't been identified, caused breathing problems, nausea and dizziness to Winston and dozens of others in his office. He repeatedly called attention to the potentially dangerous workplace, but management failed to take corrective action. Instead, in the manner of the bosses at Hanford, they angrily criticized workers who, during one vapor incident, left the building before the end of the workday. Eventually, feeling he had no choice, Winston reported the problems to the California office of OSHA.

The spell was broken, for Winston and his employer alike. As Countrywide began a series of retaliatory acts against him, Winston started to see through the company's rhetoric, and to understand the widespread wrongdoing that was taking place behind the scenes, led by top managers. He became more and more aware of the company's aggressive promotion of NINJA and other defective loans to increase its market share, and how it pushed subprime loans over more conventional loans to increase company profits. He also realized that these schemes had victims: "I began to think about the people who were being enticed to buy property they couldn't afford; the people who owned the property outright who nonetheless were thrown out for failure to pay a mortgage bill they didn't owe; the people who qualified for prime loans but who were scammed into accepting subprime loans, skillfully thrust upon them because they were much higher margin for Countrywide. I saw all this stuff in real time, and objected to it, loudly. And rather than being listened to, I was smacked around."

The crisis came in a meeting in the Countrywide boardroom in January 2007, with senior management led by David Sambol. Not long before, the company had received a report from Moody's, the rating agency, which expressed several concerns: Countrywide's directors had little experience running large public companies, the firm had no credible succession plan in place, and executives' and directors' pay was so tightly linked to share price that it would likely produce an unhealthy focus on growth. Moody's threatened to cut the firm's credit rating, which would devastate its stock price. (In fact, several senior executives, including Mozilo, soon cashed out huge stock positions, shortly before the company's stock plunged.) Winston had been urging management to fix these same problems since he'd joined the firm. "The way Countrywide was being managed, it was like a bus with sixty thousand employees aboard but no driver, careering towards a cliff," he says.

As Winston recalls the meeting in the boardroom, Sambol told him, "You know they can shut us down if we don't get out of this." Winston says Sambol asked him to misrepresent the company's condition to Moody's, and in particular to suggest that Countrywide had already implemented a clear succession plan. Winston refused. "I looked at him and said, 'I know what you want me to do, but I'm not your guy,'" Winston remembers. Today he says: "I'm loyal to my company and to my management, of course, but my principles have a higher standing than their desires. Bosses are just human beings."

The next day he passed Sambol in the hall. "He looked straight through me, as if I didn't exist," Winston remembers. "Then everybody else began to give me that same look." Soon Angelo Mozilo berated Winston for not being a "team player," and urged that he be fired. Countrywide eliminated his management group and his $30 million budget, and canceled each of his leadership initiatives. He was excluded from the sorts of meetings that he'd previously chaired, and was rapidly moved from one office location to another. Finally, on July 31, 2008, one month after Bank of America had completed its acquisition of Countrywide, Winston was terminated. In their conversations with Bank of America executives who were assuming control of the company, he says, his Countrywide superiors gave a disparaging and untruthful assessment of his work, despite his excellent previous evaluations.

Winston filed a lawsuit against Countrywide, Bank of America and several senior Countrywide executives for a range of wrongdoing, including whistleblower retaliation under the California Labor Code. During the extended litigation process, he says, the bank offered him an eight-figure settlement, but he declined, believing that the truth should become public. "I want them to admit what they did, and I want them to promise to fix it—and I want that measured. My attorney told me they'd never agree to that. And my final line to him was, 'Well, then, a $100 million wouldn't settle it.'"

In January 2011, the case went to trial in the Superior Court of California in Van Nuys, before the veteran judge Bert Glennon Jr. The jury heard from a series

of witnesses who attested to the eighty retaliatory actions that Winston said the
banks had committed against him, culminating in his firing by the company's new
owners, Bank of America, at the instigation of his former Countrywide bosses. A
series of senior Countrywide executives also testified—including Angelo Mozilo
and his second-in-command, David Sambol—many of whom were searchingly
cross-examined by Winston's lawyer, Charles "Ted" Mathews, a former deputy district attorney. Some witnesses had changed sides: after Winston named a former
colleague on his witness list, who like Winston had been terminated by Bank of
America, the bank hired her back, whereupon she testified against Winston. Nevertheless, Winston produced so many witnesses in his favor that Judge Glennon
eventually dismissed the last three who were waiting to testify, saying, "This court
and this jury have already heard enough and seen enough."

The jurors agreed. On February 4, after fifteen days of testimony, they ruled 9
to 3 in Winston's favor, and awarded him $3.8 million in damages. "I thought it
was a terrific verdict," remembers Cliff Palefsky, one of the nation's leading civil
rights and employment lawyers. "These are not easy cases. You're fighting big defendants, and I was very pleased. I was hoping it would send a message. I'm a big believer in the deterrent effect of public trials and public verdicts. I know for a fact
that one big public verdict will do more to deter bad conduct than a hundred private arbitrations or secret settlements."

Gretchen Morgenson at the *New York Times*, who wrote several articles about
Winston's case, interviewed one of the jurors, Sam Usher, a former human resources
manager at General Motors. "There was an air of arrogance about them," Usher said
of the witnesses for the defense. "The attorneys for the plaintiff caught most of them
in little lies that cracked their credibility. Meanwhile, Mr. Winston's witnesses had
credibility and the documentation kind of supported his testimony." Judge Bert
Glennon noted in a later hearing, "We had a huge number of witnesses. . . . There
was a great deal of evidence that was provided to the jury in making their decision,
and they went about it very carefully and took their time."

But as countless whistleblowers have discovered, positive verdicts don't always
mean ultimate success. Sixteen months after her first article on Winston's case,
Gretchen Morgenson wrote a story headlined "He Felled a Giant, but He Can't

Collect." She noted that Winston still hadn't received any of his award because of extended legal maneuvers by the bank defendants, which included an appeal before the Court of Appeals of California. Bank of America and its lawyers had deplored Winston's lack of evidence, and criticized the jury for having been "swayed by emotion and prejudice, focusing on unsubstantiated and unsupported statements by plaintiff and his counsel slandering Countrywide and its executives." Juror Sam Usher rejected these claims. "There was no doubt in my mind that the guys at Countrywide had not only done something wrong legally and ethically, but they weren't very bright about it," he said. Evidently drawing on his professional experience in human resources, Usher added, "If somebody in an organization is a whistle-blower, then you not only treat him with respect, you also make sure that whatever he was concerned about gets taken care of. These folks went in the other direction."

On February 19, 2013, the Court of Appeals overturned the jury verdict. In a brief hearing, about which Winston was notified only the day before, a three-judge appeals court panel ruled tersely, "We reverse. Although a jury verdict is entitled to broad deference, Winston's evidence was insufficient to establish Bank of America declined to offer him a job based on impermissible motives."

A number of senior attorneys expressed their dismay at the ruling. "From a constitutional standpoint, juries decide facts, judges decide law," says Cliff Palefsky. "Judges can only get involved in reversing a jury trial when they can say, as a matter of law, that evidence is not enough. Here, anyone reading the appellate decision would see that the court seemed to reweigh the evidence, which is something they're not supposed to do. When you have a case that gets tried for several weeks, and you have motions made to the judge, it's really unusual, and arguably improper, for an appellate court to simply disregard a plaintiff's evidence and determine that there was no evidence to support the verdict. If you look at all of the evidence that was there and presented that would have supported the jury verdict, it really leaves you scratching your head as to what happened here." In an amicus brief filed with the court urging it to reconsider the reversal, Richard Condit, then chief counsel for GAP, cited long-standing precedents in California law that explicitly forbade the kind of intervention the appeals court had just made: "As an appellate court, we cannot usurp the function of the jury and the trial court," read a decision from 1889, "who finally passed upon the weight, effect, and sufficiency of the evidence and the credibility of witnesses, and determine in place of these arbiters of fact the credibility of witnesses and resolve conflicts in proof." Condit concluded that the appeals justices had violated the established legal principle of "leaving matters of credibility, the drawing of inferences, and making judgments concerning the weight of evidence to the jury. Instead, the Court of Appeals nullified the jury's determinations and substituted its assessment of the record for those of the jury and trial judge."

Nevertheless, the Court of Appeals refused to review its decision, and the California Supreme Court declined to intervene. And this time Bank of America acted swiftly in response to the ruling, slapping a $97,000 lien on Michael Winston's house to ensure that the bank recovered its court costs.

Winston's odyssey illustrates several common patterns in whistleblower litigation. Academic studies point to a consistent bias against plaintiffs among appeals court justices, who often pare back damage awards or overturn jury verdicts entirely. "Almost any punitive damage verdict gets reduced," says Cliff Palefsky. Furthermore, appellate justices show a marked bias against whistleblowers. In three decades of testimony before Congress, Tom Devine has chronicled case after case in which appeals courts have distorted the original—and to the untrained eye perfectly obvious—intent of a wide range of whistleblower laws, both government and corporate, in order to find against them. Testifying before Congress in 2009, for example, he observed that in the fifteen years since Congress had strengthened federal whistleblowing legislation, the Federal Circuit Court of Appeals had ruled two hundred times against whistleblowers and only three times in their favor. Devine cited a long list of cases in which the Federal Circuit had narrowed, often with tortured reasoning, the plain language of the law. "Here judicial activism not only has rendered the law nearly irrelevant, but exposes the unrestrained nature of judicial defiance to Congress," Devine said.

Justices at many levels have repeatedly removed legal protections from large populations of whistleblowers—protections that were explicitly written to shield them. Federal district courts have ruled that federal employees don't qualify for the antiretaliation protections of the False Claims Act, despite the act's clear reference to "any employee." Similarly, the Supreme Court pronounced that public servants who made statements in the course of their official duties were not speaking as citizens, and therefore did not enjoy First Amendment protections against disciplinary action by their employers. Continual amendments to whistleblower laws by Congress have been required to correct such judicial misinterpretations.

In this book, pro-whistleblower verdicts reduced or overturned on appeal have been a recurrent theme in many industries, but they are particularly striking in financial services. One such reversal happened in another lawsuit against Bank of America and Countrywide, brought by qui tam whistleblower Edward O'Donnell, a former vice president at Countrywide. In October 2013, a jury in Manhattan found Countrywide guilty of carrying out a fraudulent scheme to sell massive numbers of defective mortgages to Fannie and Freddie, under a standing contract that guaranteed they were "acceptable investments." This program, designed and run by Countrywide vice president Rebecca Mairone, created a streamlined procedure for processing mortgages that Countrywide sold to Fannie Mae and Freddie Mac in 2007 and 2008, known at Countrywide as the "High Speed Swim Lane," or "HSSL," pronounced by insiders as—yes—"Hustle." O'Donnell warned his bosses, including Mairone, that the program was destroying the underwriting process, eliminating previously mandatory steps in the quality assurance checklist, and transferring primary responsibility for approving the loans from quality-focused underwriters to volume-focused and poorly qualified loan specialists who used automated loan-approval software. In short, it was the usual control fraud recipe, with predictable results: defect rates, according to the legal complaint, rose to nine times the industry average. The jury found against Countrywide and Mairone.

The trial judge, the seemingly ever-present Jed Rakoff, wrote in his decision that the HSSL program "was from start to finish the vehicle for a brazen fraud by the defendants, driven by hunger for profits and oblivious to the harms thereby visited, not just on the immediate victims but also on the financial system as a whole." Rakoff ordered Countrywide to pay $1.3 billion in penalties, and Mairone herself to pay $1 million. But in May 2016, a three-judge panel of the US Court of Appeals for the Second Circuit threw out the jury verdict and reversed the convictions of Countrywide and Mairone, finding that the government had not proven intent to defraud at the precise instant that the contracts to sell mortgages to Fannie and Freddie were concluded, making the wrongdoing merely a breach of contract. Think about it for a moment: The Second Circuit reasoned that if you sign a contract promising to sell your client life preservers, and continue selling them life preservers for years while proclaiming how wonderfully buoyant your life preservers are, but at some point secretly start selling them lead-lined vests instead, thereby causing a number of their seafaring customers to drown, this isn't fraud.

Why do appeals court judges tend to rule against whistleblowers, even after juries or trial judges have found in their favor? Aside from the increasing societal reluctance to see white-collar crime as truly criminal that we have encountered at several points in this book, there are structural reasons why judges often find against whistleblowers and in favor of their employers. Robert Vaughn, an acute legal analyst and historian of whistleblowing, observes that courts often favor parties that appear before them repeatedly—like corporations or government agencies—over individuals, like whistleblowers, who typically appear only once; and that repeat players can also benefit when courts are overworked, because delays raise costs that they can more easily pay, and since courts with groaning dockets may tend to adopt interpretations that help resolve claims swiftly. Vaughn also suggests that judges may feel a deep-running uneasiness about the larger social implications of whistleblowers, and, consciously or unconsciously, may construe whistleblower legislation narrowly in order to safeguard organizational efficiency and hierarchy, rather than broadly to guarantee the rights of an individual to dissent. "They may fail to see whistleblower legislation as 'good government' laws, and instead see them more as threats to bureaucracy stability."

Richard Condit says that over his thirty years of legal practice, he has encountered many judges who have psychological biases against whistleblowers. "People who are labeled as whistleblowers often face high hurdles to climb with respect to gaining the confidence [of] or establishing credibility with a judge. In general the courts are upholders of law and order—or they're supposed to be—and a whistleblower at a significant institution, in government or the private sector, often rattles everybody, including the judges themselves, though they wouldn't want to admit it. You see a strong instinctive human desire to reward and appreciate loyalty, and whistleblowing cuts directly against that." Tom Devine agrees. "You don't usually get to be a judge by being an activist, but because you are a pillar of your community. Judges tend to protect the function of offices and of power structures, and whistleblowers are right at the heart of those power dynamics—right at the cutting edge of the divide between reality and propaganda."

The trend of appeals courts' overturning jury trials is part of the broader ascendancy we've noticed, of technocratic fiats eclipsing more transparent and egalitarian forms of adjudication. Take, for example, the disappearance of the jury trial. Historically, trial by jury is one of the central protections of popular self-government against tyranny in America. In the Declaration of Independence, one of the colonists' grievances against King George was that he denied them the right to trial by jury; Thomas Jefferson called the jury trial "the only anchor ever yet imagined by man, by which a government can be held to the principles of its constitution." Nevertheless, Americans have increasingly lost access to a trial by jury, or to the courts in general. The proliferation of the legal settlement, and of deferred and nonprosecution agreements, is a major cause. In a recent essay, Jed Rakoff identifies several other factors, including what he calls the "increasing delegation of judicial powers and responsibilities" by Congress to the internal courts of government agencies, courts that are "run by judges who are selected by, paid by, and subject to review by the administrative agencies themselves," and the ever more frequent use of mandatory arbitration by corporations to shift legal disputes from courts into private tribunals often presided over by arbitrators with strong financial ties to the industries they pass judgment over, who are not obliged to follow rules of evidence or issue a written judgment. The judiciary itself has contributed to the rise of mandatory arbitration; since 1983, the Supreme Court has interpreted the little-known Federal Arbitration Act, passed in 1925 to resolve certain highly specialized kinds of disputes by private arbitration, in an increasingly broad manner that has enabled more and more corporations to deprive their customers and employees alike of their rights to jury trial. In May 2018, in an early decision written by conservative justice Neil Gorsuch, the court ruled that employers may force their employees to settle collective disputes in individual arbitration.

The trend toward mandatory arbitration is particularly marked in finance.

A 2016 report by the Pew Charitable Trusts revealed that from 2013 to 2016 the percentage of the forty-four larger banks that use mandatory binding arbitration clauses rose from 59 to nearly 72 percent; over 90 percent of these banks also employ jury waivers, and many exclude class actions as well. Forced arbitration in financial services is typically done by FINRA, the industry's own self-regulator, or by the American Arbitration Association (AAA), whose members are subject to extreme conflicts of interest. Arbitration is one of the main reasons cited by Rakoff for what he calls a growing belief among Americans "that the courts are not an institution to which they can turn for justice, but are simply a remote and expensive luxury reserved for the rich and powerful."

If the rise of mandatory arbitration and administrative judicial proceedings is bad news for employees and citizens in general, it's a disaster for whistleblowers, for whom access to a jury of their peers is often decisive. Ernie Fitzgerald recognized the dangers of conflicted, non-transparent adjudication systems, which he referred to as "slave courts," yet more and more whistleblowers are funneled there. "The notion of whistleblowing, the very phrase, means you blow the whistle loudly so someone can hear you," says Cliff Palefsky, who has testified before Congress on the threat that mandatory arbitration poses to the justice system. "Allowing companies to force whistleblowers into private, secret tribunals is completely inconsistent with the very concept—it undermines the public policy. If you blow the whistle and no one hears, you're not a whistleblower: you're a sitting duck. If you want to protect whistleblowers, give them access to court. Because nothing good, from a whistleblower standpoint, comes out of private arbitration, from these secret tribunals. It really is an enormous institutional scandal that companies are allowed, unilaterally, to close the courthouse doors to whistleblowers and force them into private conference rooms, with gag orders."

The reversal of the federal jury verdict of fraud by Countrywide and Rebecca Mairone in May 2016 was followed a month later by the DOJ's decision not to charge Angelo Mozilo with civil fraud, either. (Prosecutors had already dropped a criminal investigation.) And the overturning of Michael Winston's emphatic jury verdict by the California appeals court sent shock waves through the whistleblower community. Louis Clark, the executive director of GAP, who has followed the

Winston case closely, says, "Since the appeals court decision, a number of financial whistleblowers have come to us and said, 'I have important things to reveal, but how do I know I won't end up like Michael Winston?'"

Meanwhile, David Sambol was hired by Bank of America to head their mortgage operations, then retired with $28 million in cash and restricted stock. Rebecca Mairone was likewise hired by Bank of America, and then went to JPMorgan, where, ironically, she ran the bank's operations under the government's famously inept program to aid victims of abusive foreclosures. (Mairone, who now goes by her maiden name, Steele, is currently the chief operating officer of Spring EQ, a home equity lender that promises to help homeowners access their home equity faster by replacing lengthy paperwork with a "21st century digital experience"; the company's motto is "Trust in Us.") Despite his many lawsuits, Angelo Mozilo is still a wealthy man; while countless thousands of his former mortgage customers have lost their homes in foreclosure, he lives in a 12,692-square-foot house in Santa Barbara, California. He is the benefactor to private institutions including Gonzaga University, which has a "Mozilo Center" on its foreign studies campus in Florence, Italy. In a 2014 interview, Mozilo denied that either he or his company had ever done anything wrong. Asked for one word to capture the current state of his life, he replied, "Peace."

Michael Winston is not at peace. He is fighting laryngeal cancer, for which he has undergone thirty-six courses of radiotherapy and a dozen surgeries. He has lost his vocal cords and larynx, and now speaks through a prosthetic device implanted in his throat. He can't get a job, and his finances are in disarray. He believes the ruling of the California appeals court was flawed, but his legal options to challenge it are limited. "I firmly believe there's a place in society for a town crier with positive intent, but right now, it doesn't feel like there's much room for me," he says. "Because, where do you go when justice fails? When the courts reweigh your evidence, and eliminate crucial evidence? When you learn that the institutions you've been raised to respect and believe in are harboring the criminals and repudiating the victims?"

Like the other Bank Whistleblowers United members, he believes another financial crisis is imminent if we cannot learn to call fraud by its proper name, and punish white-collar criminals as the criminals they are, above all in the big banks. "Just as in the last administration, when Hillary Clinton described what Wall Street did not as fraud but as 'shenanigans,' we now see the same hypocrisy when Trump talks tough about not repeating the mistakes of the past, yet staffs his cabinet with people who made fortunes in sleazy foreclosures. I was with the Countrywide guys when they were planning their approaches, when they were plotting how to change from somebody who qualified for a prime loan to a subprime loan, and they did it like a SWAT team, like a Navy SEAL team, with such precision and such comprehensive discussions. They planned the fraud, they organized it, they directed it, and they controlled it. It wasn't reckless at all. It was intentional, conscious."

He says that he and his fellow bank whistleblowers Richard Bowen, Bill Black and Gary Aguirre want to banish from the business community firms that systematically victimize the general public. "We've seen far too many people hurt by fraud, and we want to build safeguards into the system which prevent it from happening again. We want to build a compendium of early warning signals, when fraud is getting out of hand. Right now, I'm seeing the same signs I saw before the financial crisis. I see television ads for quick, easy loans with incredibly lax standards for income reporting. 'You need a hundred grand, you need it quick, you have no collateral? Noooo problem!' Where do I recognize that from before? Oh yeah . . . Countrywide. I'm seeing the same stuff happening again, and I fear the same disastrous outcome. I think all of us at Bank Whistleblowers United want to be the Paul Reveres, to tell people, 'Hey, the British are coming, the British are coming, you better watch out!' And if they don't, there's going to be hell to pay."

CHAPTER 7

Ministries of Truth

Liberty cannot be preserved without a general knowledge among the people, who have a right from the frame of their nature, to knowledge, as their great Creator who does nothing in vain, has given them understandings, and a desire to know—but besides this they have a right, an indisputable, unalienable, indefeasible divine right to that most dreaded, and envied kind of knowledge, I mean of the characters and conduct of their rulers.

John Adams, "A Dissertation on the Canon and the Feudal Law," No. 3, 1765

There is very grave danger that an announced need for increased security will be seized upon by those anxious to expand its meaning to the very limits of official censorship and concealment.

John F. Kennedy, speech of April 27, 1961

On February 26, 2015, I had dinner with John Phillips at Villa Taverna, the sprawling Renaissance villa near the Borghese Gardens in Rome that is the official residence of the United States ambassador to Italy. We sat at a round table in the lounge, where a large fire burned on the hearth, glistened on the grand piano and the damasks and brocades of the furniture, and sparkled in the picture windows overlooking the villa's manicured gardens. A member of the embassy staff, in white gloves and a white coat with gold epaulettes, served at table.

Phillips's ancestors were poor villagers from the mountains of Friuli, northeast of Venice, who emigrated to western Pennsylvania in the late nineteenth century, and around 1915 changed their names from Filippi to Phillips. He grew up in Leechburg, in an Italian American community, and in recent decades had visited Italy countless times, so when Barack Obama was considering candidates for the post of ambassador here, Phillips was a natural choice. Of course, it didn't hurt that he was a leading Obama fund-raiser, or that his wife, Linda Douglass, was a White House insider.

Tonight Phillips seemed tense and weary. We briefly discussed his day at work, which like most had been grueling. Since assuming the post, Phillips had told me several times of his determination not merely to be a figurehead ambassador, but to actively draw Italy and America together. This, clearly, was proving a challenge. He was also concerned that his wife, who had left behind a thriving business career and social circle in the United States, was at loose ends.

Then, abruptly, Phillips announced that he was planning to write an op-ed for the *New York Times* about Edward Snowden. "He's not a whistleblower," he said with a disgusted shake of his head. "He's such an *unimpressive* person—a high school dropout, a washout from the military. He's disloyal. And he's done great harm to the United States."

My research on whistleblowing had begun with a chance meeting with Phillips, and an introduction to the False Claims Act into which he had breathed new life in 1986. Since then, studying other kinds of whistleblowing, I'd come to see false claims relators as one species of a far larger genus that included various kinds of government whistleblowers as well; often, from their different viewpoints on the public-private divide, they reported identical frauds. Yet for some reason, intelligence whistleblowers—or leakers, or truth tellers, or dissidents . . . I wasn't even sure what to call them—had initially seemed to me a breed apart, whose secrets had little in common with the fraud, waste and abuse that drove corporate and government whistleblowing. When I eventually interviewed some of them, however, I saw the familiar collision of personal ethics and group loyalty, the same individual actions and systematic organizational overreactions, that I'd seen countless times before. The narratives of Edward Snowden, Chelsea Manning and other national security dissidents fit the pattern of qui tam and government whistleblowing.

Even as a private citizen, Phillips might not have considered Edward Snowden an exemplary whistleblower, but now, as the official representative of the United States president, he was duty-bound to represent Barack Obama's positions in all matters of state. And Obama had condemned national security whistleblowers more harshly than any other president in history.

This seems strange, given Obama's apparent sympathy for whistleblowing as he entered office. In private legal practice before entering politics, he had represented qui tam whistleblowers. A plank of his official "Obama-Biden Plan" for revamping government and restoring the trust of the American people was titled "Protect Whistleblowers." "Often the best source of information about waste, fraud, and abuse in government is an existing government employee committed to public integrity and willing to speak out," his campaign website announced. "Such acts of courage and patriotism, which can sometimes save lives and often save taxpayer dollars, should be encouraged rather than stifled." Obama pledged to strengthen whistleblower laws for federal workers. And the day after taking office in January 2009, in a memorandum to the heads of all government departments and agencies, he proclaimed, "The Government should not keep information confidential merely because public officials might be embarrassed by disclosure, because errors and failures might be revealed, or because of speculative or abstract fears."

As president, he rarely met these commitments. His DOJ resisted whistleblower laws behind the scenes, and often pursued false claims cases tepidly. His DOJ, SEC and other enforcers and regulators failed to crack down on the financial fraud behind the 2008 crisis, often ignoring or even retaliating against bank whistleblowers. But the most extreme breach of Obama's whistleblowing promises occurred in the national security sphere. As veteran newspaper reporter and *Washington Post* executive editor Leonard Downie Jr. observed, Obama seemed unable to conceptualize disclosures about wrongdoing in intelligence and the military—at least those he himself hadn't condoned—as anything but betrayal. "Exposing 'waste, fraud and abuse' is considered to be whistle-blowing," Downie wrote. "But exposing questionable government policies and actions, even if they could be illegal or unconstitutional, is often considered to be leaking that must be stopped and punished."

By the time of my dinner with Phillips, the Obama administration's modus operandi with national security whistleblowers had hardened into a pattern. His DOJ consistently investigated, indicted and prosecuted them under the Espionage

Act, denying them the identity of whistleblowers and the chance to explain their motives to a jury. Ashden Fein, lead prosecutor in the Chelsea (then Bradley) Manning case, repeated the Obama administration's party line when he told the court that Manning "was not a whistleblower. He was traitor—a traitor who understood the value of compromised information in the hands of the enemy."

Now John Phillips was charged with representing this position. Still, the tinge of outrage in his repudiation of Edward Snowden, and that odd word he'd used, "unimpressive," seemed out of character. Over the previous two years I'd met with Phillips perhaps a dozen times; he'd been composed, genial, astute, someone who liked debates and often won them by using reason like a scalpel. Now his arguments seemed blunt, borrowed.

I said that some authoritative observers seemed to agree that Snowden had revealed serious wrongdoing—that a federal judge, Richard Leon, had recently ruled that the NSA's domestic surveillance program probably violated the Fourth Amendment. Phillips seemed irritated. "That's just one judge. He's a very unimpressive person. I don't think he really understands the law."

Again that peculiar word, "unimpressive," the aggrieved tone, the ad hominem way of dismissing Snowden and a federal judge alike. So uncharacteristic of Phillips, yet strangely familiar.

Then I remembered why. Here was the same sharp, scornful focus on messenger over message that I'd so often heard retaliators use to undercut and discredit whistleblowers. Now I was hearing them from one of the world's chief architects of corporate whistleblowing.

I asked Phillips why he was so sure that Snowden didn't qualify as a whistleblower. How did he know that Snowden had harmed US interests? Phillips replied that since becoming ambassador, he had had access to a number of classified channels at the embassy, which had convinced him that Snowden had seriously harmed US intelligence capabilities.

"Can you give me one example?"

He shook his head. The information was classified, he said.

By now I too was irritated. This wasn't the first time that someone with access to secret intelligence had assured me they had seen proof of the immense damage

Snowden had done—proof they unfortunately couldn't share. "How on earth can we be expected to believe evidence that we can't see?" I asked. "Surely if any proof existed, it would have been splashed all over the front page of every newspaper?" (Or as Daniel Ellsberg later told me with characteristic verve, "If Defense officials could ever identify a single person physically harmed by the revelations of Manning and Assange, there would be a picture of that harm—ideally for them, a headless body—on the cover of *Time*.") I probably spoke more heatedly and sarcastically than I'd intended.

Phillips glared at me. "Don't you trust your government?" he barked angrily.

I was surprised by this uncharacteristic flare-up, but even more by the irony of the situation. Here was a lifelong critic and dissenter, someone who had made a highly successful career by *not* trusting the government and had fought countless battles against its agencies. Phillips himself had taught me why the qui tam provision was so essential to the success of the FCA: because it allowed private citizens to pursue corporate fraudsters when the government couldn't be relied on to do so. As Obama's own expert panel on NSA activities, which included a former counterterrorism chief and a former acting director of the CIA, warned, "Americans must never make the mistake of wholly 'trusting' our public officials."

We changed the subject, talked about the eternal contradictions and beguilements of Italy for a while, and enjoyed a good bottle of wine. But Phillips's question still hung in the air, ringing ever more rhetorical. Why on earth, after the events of the last quarter century, should we trust our government?

Consider, for example, a government report on two top-secret NSA surveillance programs titled "Requirements for the THINTHREAD and TRAILBLAZER Systems." It was issued on December 15, 2004, by the inspector general of the Department of Defense, and is marked "Top Secret/COMINT" on the header and footer of every page. Consequently, the version I'm reading—which Jesselyn Radack, then head of national security and human rights matters at GAP, obtained in June 2011 through a FOIA lawsuit—is so heavily redacted that a series of white strips and shapes swallow about 90 percent of the words. On many pages, only the header and footer remain. Trying to understand this report is a bit like reading a medieval codex riddled by a millennium of bookworms.

Yet here and there, enough words cling together to emit flashes of meaning. In the Executive Summary, for example, we read that the IG's office began this investigation in response to a whistleblower complaint lodged with the DOD hotline, "which alleged that NSA actions in the development of THINTHREAD and TRAIL-BLAZER resulted in fraud, waste, and abuse. The specific allegations were: (1) TRAILBLAZER development wasted XXXXXXXX dollars; (2) NSA disregarded solutions to urgent national security needs; (3) NSA modified or suppressed studies XXXXXXXXXXXXXXXX; and (4) NSA did not XXXXXXXXXX XXXXXX THINTHREAD." On page 24, the authors state that they interviewed a number of NSA personnel and contractors during the preparation of their report, then add: "Many people we interviewed asked not to be identified for fear of management reprisal." They repeat this statement on page 35, and on page 111 they state further, "Because of fear of reprisal, we agreed to keep the sources anonymous."

On page 29, we learn that in July 2001, the House Permanent Select Committee on Intelligence (HPSCI) had ordered two studies of the Trailblazer program. The first, completed in July 2001, found that the program "was poorly executed and had an overly expensive XXXXXXXXXXXXXXX." The study team made a series of recommendations, contained in a paragraph that has been redacted in full, though these apparently included concerns about conflicts of interest among the developers of Trailblazer. We learn that the second study on Trailblazer was completed in December 2001: "Despite noting some changes made in NSA management and the TRAILBLAZER Program acquisition strategy that promised to address the conflicts and issues noted in the first report, the study team found that: XXXXXXXXXXXXXXXXXXXXXX." This second team's findings, which presumably gave a fuller account of the problems with Trailblazer, are two paragraphs of wordless white. On page 38, we learn that the inspector general of the NSA issued a report of his own on Trailblazer that "discussed improperly based contract cost increases, non-conformance in the management of the Statement of Work, and excessive labor rates for contractor personnel."

Clearly, the authors of this report believed that the three previous inquests into

Trailblazer, and the questions these raised about conflicts of interest, inflated contractor costs and the program's failure to deliver its promised results were pertinent to the accusations they had heard, via the whistleblower hotline, of fraud, waste and abuse in the program. This was a time when the quality of American intelligence was under intense scrutiny. In the few months between the two congressional investigations of Trailblazer came the terror attacks of 9/11.

When the fragments of evidence contained in this heavily redacted 2004 report are pieced together, the basic outlines of the case become clear. One or more whistleblowers had submitted a formal complaint to the DOD IG, alleging that senior NSA officials had committed serious improprieties in the management of the intelligence program called Trailblazer, which the whistleblower or whistleblowers claimed had wasted large sums of money, to the detriment of what was evidently a competing project, ThinThread. Trailblazer had evidently drawn attention for potential misconduct already, both in Congress and at the NSA IG's office; we also infer that the alleged wrongdoing involved private contractors. And the report clearly states that the atmosphere at the NSA, where some employees believed that internal studies could be doctored or suppressed, and that personnel who disagreed with senior management would likely suffer retaliation, was a classic chilled work environment—the perfect ecosystem for fraud.

Further disturbing aspects of this document appear in its margins. Each paragraph has a set of initials that indicates its level of classification, which descend in their level of restriction from TS ("Top Secret") to S ("secret") to FOUO ("For official use only") and at last to U ("unclassified"). Every redaction has a dotted line from the blanked-out text to an abbreviation in the margin that cites the legal justification for withholding that specific information. Remarkably, some eighty of the one hundred redacted paragraphs are marked "unclassified"; the law cited to justify their omission is Section 6 of the NSA Act of 1959, which essentially allows the agency to withhold anything that concerns its operations or personnel. The removal of so much unclassified material suggests an abuse of the redaction system. A former CIA military imagery analyst who read the original, unredacted IG report told me the vast majority of these redactions had been made not to shield legitimate national security secrets, but to avoid embarrassing senior NSA management, and especially its director, Michael Hayden. "This is the most damning government document I've ever seen, in all of my time in Washington," the analyst said.

Despite—and because of—its yawning lacunae, the report tells a powerful story of whistleblowing, to which forces inside the NSA, the Pentagon and the DOJ reacted with customary savagery. It was written on the basis of revelations by four whistleblowers who had recently left the agency or Congress, together with a fifth who verified their statements while still working at NSA. The brutal treatment these five people received after they blew the whistle convinced Edward Snowden to make his own disclosures about national security wrongdoing not through official channels as they had done, but to the press. The IG report also suggests how the failure of the whistleblower protection system in US national security contributed to the success of the terror attacks on September 11, 2001.

On April 24, 2017, Bill Binney picked me up at the Baltimore-Washington International Airport in a gray Ford pickup that had been modified to allow him to drive without the use of substantial portions of both legs, which he had lost to successive amputations, after chronic MRSA and MSSA infections entered the bone. A few days earlier, he'd undergone surgery to remove yet another chunk of his right leg; at several points in our conversation, the electronic pumping device he was wearing to drain fluid from the wound sounded an alarm, and he tended to it. He told me that as he had seen himself whittled away, he'd begun to compose potential epitaphs for his tombstone. "Rest in Pieces," he said, was too obvious. At the moment he favored the more mysterious "I'm Not Altogether Here," or perhaps, "Leaving This Earth a Bit at a Time."

We drove into the industrial park that surrounded the airport, a maze of boxy, mirror-glass low-rises. "Here's where one trillion of your tax dollars have gone every year since 9/11," Binney said. This neighborhood, Linthicum, is home to a massive NSA complex known as the "Friendship Annex" and is also a hub for major defense and intelligence contractors. We passed signs for Lockheed and Northrop Grumman, Booz Allen, Science Applications International Corporation (SAIC), and Leidos, all of which have thrived during the War on Terror. After an extended tour of NSA and intelligence contractor real estate in the area, we parked at the Bob Evans restaurant in Linthicum Heights. Over fried eggs, bacon, flapjacks and a steady flow of drip coffee, Binney described how the United States lost control of its national security establishment.

William Edward Binney is one of the NSA's greatest living code-breaking mathematicians, and a world authority on mass surveillance. Since 1965, he has watched from the inside as the intelligence community has grown exponentially in size and intrusiveness. Despite his poor health, Binney's humor abides: philosophical, acerbic, ruthless, earthy. In the first hour of our conversation, he explained the precise difference between bullshit and horseshit (bullshit dries into flat cow chips that you can pitch like a Frisbee, as Binney did as a boy), and shared his decryptions of several popular acronyms—"District of Corruption" and "Department of Just Us." He has dark, eager eyes with bags beneath, a domed forehead that seems to signal the brainpower behind, and a rapid-fire Pennsylvania-inflected delivery that occasionally grows countrified—"idea" becomes "ideer," and "over there" sounds like "over dere." He grew up in Reynoldsville, Pennsylvania, two hours west of Allen Jones's hometown of Beaver Springs. "The sign in town said '3,200 People, Watch Us Grow,' but Reynoldsville is down to about 2,800 now," Binney said. "The anthracite coal mines gave out long ago, and apart from some strip mining, the only two going concerns in town are the welfare office and the casket factory."

His father, who fought in World War II, spoke rarely and reluctantly about his wartime experiences. "Most people who served back then felt they were just doing their duty, then came back home and got on with their lives." Soldiers referred to themselves simply as "grunts" and "jarheads," not the glorified "warriors" and "warfighters" of today's professional army. Like Allen Jones and many other rural Pennsylvanians, Binney was a good shot with a hunting rifle, but as the war in Vietnam escalated, he volunteered rather than waiting to be called up, so he could choose what he'd be doing in the military, and not be assigned to a rifle company like many draftees from his area. "I didn't want to shoot people," he says. His aptitude for mathematics and logic suited him for intelligence, and he served as a communications traffic analyst in the Army Security Agency; while his fellow Cold Warrior Daniel Ellsberg was walking point in the Vietnamese jungles as a State

Department adviser, Binney was monitoring encrypted Soviet military communications at a surveillance base in Turkey. In 1967 he was reassigned to NSA headquarters in Washington, DC, and in 1970 he joined the agency as a civilian, beginning a swift rise through the ranks that culminated in his appointment as technical director of the World Geopolitical and Military Analysis Reporting Group, where he oversaw the work of six thousand intelligence analysts worldwide. His distinguished thirty-four-year career ended in October 2001, one month after 9/11, when he resigned from the agency in disgust.

Binney has a gift for reducing complex problems to their logical essentials. In an undergraduate course on differential equations at Penn State, he watched his professor fill ten blackboards to solve a higher-order differential equation with the laborious integrating factor method, then devised a technique that did the job in only ten lines. Later, while monitoring Soviet military signals, he isolated a handful of key parameters that distinguished between routine military activity, such as troop movements or war games, and a real attack. "When one or more of those warning indicators were present, as they were during the invasions of Czechoslovakia and Hungary for example, it was an attack," he said. "These indicators allowed us to see through the patterns of human behavior to the underlying intentions of the people involved."

As computers became commonplace, Binney used them to solve problems more swiftly and efficiently than human analysts could. In 1983, faced with a highly classified military problem that he wasn't allowed to describe to me, he and programmer Bill Davis wrote a program in the C computer language that, running on one IBM PC with 64K of RAM and two floppy drives, outperformed a massive bank of mainframes that were doing the same work in the basement of the NSA. "That little program was a mix of a mathematical solution, a systems solution, probability, set theory, all mixed in with very compact logic," he remembers with obvious satisfaction. "And it handled every possible thing that could happen—there were no exceptions." Binney also strove to make every solution easily comprehensible to the people who would ultimately be putting it to use—not techies like himself, but operations people, politicians, and generals. "Everything I did had to end up with a visual answer, because we think visually. People needed to be able to look at something complex in an efficient, organized way, and quickly get the essence of it."

In the late 1990s, Binney brought this same simplifying, visual approach to bear on digital communications, which were becoming a monumental problem for the agency. The burgeoning volume of data traveling across the internet and cellular networks was rapidly outstripping the NSA's ability to process it with conventional methods, which consisted of capturing and storing the data, and assigning human analysts to sift through it using keyword searches. Binney was determined to automate the analysis of this growing stream of information. He and a team of other NSA veterans, including cryptologic computer scientist Ed Loomis and analyst Kirk Wiebe, developed ThinThread, a suite of programs that could scan tens of terabytes per minute of digital information—emails, social media, web searches, cell and landline calls, faxes, GPS coordinates, information on travel and bank transactions—and pinpoint criminal activity and events of intelligence interest that took place outside the United States. "ThinThread was a way of looking *into* the data without looking *at* the data, and pulling out what's relevant," Binney said.

The program avoided data overload in two ways. First, it automated the information-gathering process, discarding the bulk of the data it received and homing in on vital nuggets of information. "We took human analysis, always the slowest part of the process, out of the loop," Binney explained. Second, ThinThread concentrated not on the content of the communications it processed—the words people actually said during phone calls and wrote in emails, for example—but on the "metadata," the circumstantial information about each communication: who was communicating with whom, when, where in the world, on which devices, and so forth. ThinThread used metadata to map the social networks among all people on earth who communicated digitally, and focus on the why of these communications: the intentions and capabilities of criminal actors, including terrorists. Once the metadata had revealed the telltale patterns of wrongdoing involving US citizens, the NSA could demonstrate probable cause, and request judicial approval for a wiretap, in accordance with the 1978 Foreign Intelligence Surveillance Act (FISA), passed after Watergate to prevent the kinds of intelligence abuses against

US citizens that the CIA, the FBI and the Plumbers had committed under Nixon. ThinThread even automated the process of requesting FISA warrants.

Binney explained ThinThread's basic capabilities by asking me to imagine the operations of a hypothetical drug cartel. "First of all, they have to make an agreement: who's gonna buy the dope? So you get that purchase, and see the buyer/seller relationship, okay? Once they have some kind of agreement, it [i.e., their communication stream] goes to a transporter—oops, they're getting ready to move drugs! Then it goes to a supplier and then it goes out to the supply people: you see the money exchange, and you see the dope exchange. Those kinds of transactions are the key to looking for the intentions and capabilities of dope smugglers." Over time, ThinThread would recognize structures in their communications that became fingerprints for their crimes. Binney and his colleagues aimed to use the program to flag a wide range of dangerous activity, including narcotics trafficking, money laundering, enemy military actions, the spread of weapons of mass destruction, and terrorism. By automating the identification of intelligence targets in this way, ThinThread also enabled human analysts to concentrate on the most serious threats and not to be distracted—or overwhelmed—by extraneous information.

ThinThread also protected innocent US citizens, who by law could not be surveilled without a warrant, using filters and encryption algorithms to shield or exclude their communications. Binney said that while he was working on ThinThread, he never worried that the program might one day be used illegally against Americans. "For decades I had been at the NSA, and for decades we'd said, 'USSID 18, USSID 18, USSID 18!'" Binney intoned, referring to United States Signals Intelligence Directive 18, which had long provided the ground rules for what data about American citizens the NSA and other intelligence agencies were allowed to collect, retain and share. "We were told again and again to follow the law. We all took the oath to 'protect and defend the Constitution.' Everybody in government service does. And everybody in Congress does, too." Another reason he says he didn't worry about illegal domestic surveillance by the NSA was that historically, the agency had strictly limited its activities to targets outside the United States. Jesselyn Radack, a national security and human rights lawyer who has represented prominent intelligence figures including Binney, Edward Snowden and Tom Drake, a former

NSA senior official who worked as an NSA contractor near the end of Binney's tenure, agrees. "Bill, Tom, Kirk [Wiebe], Ed, all of them had the first commandment of the NSA drilled into their brain: "Thou shalt not spy on Americans."

Throughout his intelligence career, Binney championed open, interdisciplinary work environments against a steady trend toward secrecy and compartmentalization, which he felt impeded creativity. In the late 1960s, programmers and engineers were separated from operations staff, raising pointless bureaucratic barriers. "Before, when the tech people were mixed right in with operations, if there was a problem, people could all see it and work on it together. After, when you take them out of there, you create a bureaucratic gap. Operations people now have to write a requirement and throw it over the wall, where it gets translated into all kinds of shit, and you get shit right back." Another source of compartmentalization was the increasingly specialized nature of intelligence work, and the proliferation of security clearances, both of which hindered interdisciplinary communication. Binney himself pointedly avoided obtaining security clearances. "Once you were cleared for one compartment, you couldn't talk about it outside of that compartment, which meant that nobody else will have the opportunity to think out of the box. I was never satisfied with that. So how does this box relate with that box? The answer is, all the boxes together." To foster an open intellectual environment, Binney and John Taggart, a leading NSA researcher, founded the Signals Intelligence Automation Research Center (SARC), an interdisciplinary group within Signals Intelligence (SIGINT), where techies and operations people continued to solve major cryptologic problems side by side.

The most serious bar to creativity and efficient problem solving in US intelligence, according to Binney, was the growing influence of corporate contractors, who performed an increasing percentage of the NSA's work. He saw existing contracts gain their own inertia, and managers strive to keep even useless projects alive because of the money they brought in. Binney first experienced this directly in 1985, while creating a new automation program, when he was required to continue to fund its preexisting, manually operated components even as his work was making them obsolete. "I had to support the contractors, give money to them, to keep their damned program going, which was a mess," he remembered. The NSA's growing dependence on contractors, Binney said, accentuated the agency's existing tendencies toward compartmentalization and incremental thinking, and further degraded its ability to meet big-picture intelligence challenges. Contractors and their NSA minders focused more on milestone payments and performance goals than on finding solutions: "This problem is too complicated to solve all at once—maybe a little bit will do," he said the NSA mentality became. "Solve one increment, and now we need more money for the next increment."

As at Hanford, project milestones focused the contractors' attention not on completing projects systematically and efficiently, but on gobbling up cash. "Each milestone becomes the basis for asking, 'Did we spend all of our money so we can actually gain more money?'" says Tom Drake. "Which means you don't really want to deliver. You incrementalize, leave out, cut off, claim that the project is so complicated, but you don't really want to solve it. Because if you solve it, you're not going to get your money. Do you see the perverse incentive?"

Bill Binney summed up the mentality succinctly: "Keep the problem going, to keep the money flowing." I'd first heard the phrase from Walt Tamosaitis, who had used it to describe the behavior he observed among Hanford contractors. Tamosaitis had learned it from a lawyer at GAP, Jesselyn Radack, who in turn had heard it from one of her whistleblower clients: Bill Binney. "You're incentivized to build an empire, and the fastest way to do this is to hire contractors," says Tom Drake. "You're incentivized to spend a lot of money, and to make sure to spend it all within the current financial year. If you actually came in under budget, or didn't spend all your money, you'd have that amount taken away from you in the following year. Late in the fiscal year there would be this mad rush to park the money somewhere, because you didn't want to lose it. This creates the perverse incentive to spend more money. Why spend it wisely or efficiently? Ultimately, it doesn't really matter what you develop, as long as you have your money. The money itself was reward enough, and the more you got, the higher your 'ranking,' as it were." Like Ernie Fitzgerald four decades earlier, Drake found that the quality of work in a project often declined as the amount of money spent on it increased.

Contractors also insisted on a free hand with how they used their money. Binney conceived a system in 1991 that would monitor all activity on the NSA network and identify any unauthorized access. Though it seems natural to keep close track of sensitive agency data—Binney believes that his system would have revealed Edward Snowden's illicit downloading of information—his idea met with fierce resistance at the agency, particularly by managers in charge of major government contracts. "You mean to tell me that you'll be able to see which programs are successes and which are failing, the money that's being spent on all the contracts, and how I move money around between programs?" Binney remembers one manager asking him. Yes, Binney replied. "And you also say that Congress could come out here and look at all that stuff?" Precisely, Binney said. "You are never doing this," the manager told him. Other managers agreed, and the program was scrapped. " 'You give me all this money and I get to play with it—it's my money once you give it to me, not yours anymore,' " Binney says the contractors believed. "I think it's universal throughout all government agencies and in industry. And that's why they can't even tell what [files] Edward Snowden took."

In 1999, as Binney and his colleagues neared the completion of ThinThread, the process of corporatization and compartmentalization of the NSA accelerated with the arrival of a new director, Michael Hayden, who later became Janine Wedel's colleague at George Mason University. Hayden, a former Air Force general who has subsequently woven his work in public service, private corporations, academia, think tanks and the media into a flourishing flexian career, was a military managerialist in the Robert McNamara mold. He commissioned a series of strategic studies of the agency by contractors and other industry-centric bodies—including a research group led by his friend and mentor James Clapper—which, unsurprisingly, urged the reshaping of the agency to make it operate like a corporation, and the wholesale outsourcing to private contractors of critical NSA work. "Less Making, More Buying" became the official policy of the agency.

Hayden implemented this new vision for the agency with gusto. He styled himself the CEO as well as the director of the NSA, and created new management posts, including chief information officer, chief financial manager and senior acquisition executive, which he filled with revolving-door recruits from intelligence contractors. He also created the office of the chief operating officer, the agency's second-in-command, where he installed William Black, a senior manager at SAIC and a serial revolver between the NSA and private intelligence firms. Hayden's communications both within the agency and to the outside world are so studded with management jargon—leadership schemata, strategic visions, missions, goals, tiger teams, and relentless refocusing on core activities—that they often read more like parodies of business-speak than guidance for one of the nation's most vital spy organizations. He also introduced a market-based compensation system, aiming, as he put it, "to use money as a management tool."

Many of Hayden's new activities, in fact, revolved around money: procuring more government funding for NSA, and using it to purchase the services of more contractors. In his revealing memoir, titled *NSA's Transformation*, Ed Loomis, a leading member of Binney's SARC team and one of the four intelligence veterans who blew the whistle on Trailblazer in 2002, explains that Hayden's "transformation initiative was very much dependent on increased funding. Without more funds flowing into the Fort [i.e., Fort Meade, the historic headquarters of the NSA], private sector talent could not be purchased to deliver an industrial-strength solution and bring NSA swiftly into the 21st century of the global network. If funds didn't materialize, NSA would then continue relying on its 'non-critical tradecraft' of computer scientists and engineers, thus putting a damper on the director's transformation of NSA's culture." In reality, Loomis writes, the outsourcing push was "a tactic to fleece an increase in funds from the U.S. Treasury, and an opportunity to engage friends and former associates in the private sector in the common goal of securing our country."

Hayden reorganized the NSA to fit his new contractor-centric strategy. He even outsourced the reorganization process to contractors, through a $2.4 billion program called Groundbreaker, which aimed, according to an internal memo, "to refocus agency assets on core functions that directly support its national security missions," and was run by Eagle Alliance, a consortium of intelligence and defense giants that included Northrop Grumman, General Dynamics, and Computer Sciences Corporation. The NSA announced that it would begin reducing its in-house team of computer scientists; at the same time, Eagle Alliance began offering hiring bonuses of up to $100,000, to entice these scientists to leave the agency and join the contractor consortium.

But the signature program at Hayden's new NSA was Trailblazer, which he described in internal memoranda as "the prototype of our future," and "the core of our strategy to exploit the global digital net and to transform how we satisfy our customers' information needs." From the outset, Trailblazer was to be developed primarily by external contractors, not NSA employees. To ensure this, in May 2001 William Black installed his friend and former colleague at SAIC, Sam Visner, as chief of the SIGINT programs office—the broad division under which Binney and Loomis's SARC unit worked. Here Visner was also responsible for several other programs, including ThinThread, which Binney's team was completing. ThinThread soon came to be viewed by NSA leadership as a competitor for government resources with Trailblazer, their flagship, much as the MRAP was perceived as a threat to funding for other armored vehicles. The battle between Trailblazer and ThinThread, Binney says, not only led to the predictable triumph of the big-money contract over the frugal in-house program, but actually helped ensure the success of the 9/11 attacks.

In early 2001, Trailblazer was a sprawling, amorphous undertaking that in concrete terms was little more than PowerPoint presentations and big ideas, but it promised to engage large teams of contractor personnel and attract billions of dollars in funding. (Hayden, in his memoir, *Playing to the Edge*, called Trailblazer "more a venture capital fund than a single program.") ThinThread, by contrast, had been built by a handful of NSA employees for a total cost of $3.2 million; in early 2001 it was largely complete, and had already been implemented in intelligence sites abroad. ThinThread was doomed by its own thrift, Binney says. "Six employees and $3.2 million? You can't build an empire with that. How many contracts can you list? That's why they had to kill us." At first, he says, NSA management tried to convince him to merge ThinThread and Trailblazer, a tactic he'd already encountered at the NSA for keeping useless contracts alive (and funded). As the redacted IG report suggests, Congress expressed repeated and serious concern about the poor management of the Trailblazer program. A Senate report criticized the NSA's management of Trailblazer, and congressional overseers soon decreed that if the program's management was not corrected by 2002, Congress would remove it from NSA control and reassign it to an acquisition office in the Department of

Defense—a radical indictment of NSA management, which had controlled its own acquisition programs since World War II. (In May 2003, Congress did just that, stripping the NSA of "milestone decision authority" over Trailblazer until at least October 1, 2006.)

By contrast, Congress had enough confidence in ThinThread to direct the NSA to deploy it in eighteen test sites, and to allocate about $9.5 million for this purpose. A classified Pentagon report praised ThinThread's data analysis capabilities, and directed that the program be implemented and enhanced. But launching Thin-Thread would show that the intelligence problem for which Trailblazer was being created had already been solved, Binney says, so the NSA slow-rolled ThinThread while proceeding with Trailblazer, for which he says Hayden had initially requested $3.8 billion and would eventually ask for even more.

NSA managers began to criticize ThinThread. Though Binney had built in pro-tections for the data and identity of US citizens, agency lawyers objected that the program would violate FISA and the Fourth Amendment. A consultant called in to evaluate ThinThread stated, without producing evidence, that the program "would not scale"—that ThinThread couldn't be expanded to analyze global internet and cell traffic. Meanwhile, Trailblazer contractors lobbied the intelligence committees on Capitol Hill to kill ThinThread as a distraction from a superior national security tool: their own program.

ThinThread nevertheless seemed to be gaining momentum. By November 2000 it was already operating in three research sites and producing usable intelligence for NSA analysts. News of the program began to circulate outside the agency. Charles Allen, a senior Homeland Security official and veteran of the CIA, requested a demonstration; Ed Loomis later wrote that when Allen arrived at the NSA for the briefing, he announced, "I hear you've got a cheap Trailblazer, and I'm here to see it!" Loomis reports that the senior NSA manager at the meeting, Maureen Bagin-ski, head of the Signals Intelligence Directorate of which SARC was a part, replied, "Charlie, we still need the money." Sam Visner warned Bill Binney not to brief any more outsiders on ThinThread.

But the meeting that sealed ThinThread's fate took place in April 2000, when a group of congressional staffers led by Diane Roark requested a briefing on it. Roark, a seventeen-year Republican staffer on HPSCI who had substantial responsibility for overseeing the NSA's budget, as well as the effectiveness and legality of its programs, had been monitoring the progress of both programs, and was as enthusiastic about ThinThread as she was skeptical about Trailblazer. In a 2015 interview, Roark described being surprised that numerous Trailblazer staff members were present at the ThinThread briefing, and being impressed by ThinThread's capabilities as Binney and Loomis described them. She turned to a member of the Trailblazer team and asked whether they were going to incorporate ThinThread into their program. "Wouldn't this help you?" she remembers saying. After the meeting, an NSA employee approached Roark and told her, "This is the real Trailblazer."

Word of this conversation soon reached the director's office. Hayden, Binney says, was furious about these exchanges with congressional staff. He promptly summoned to his office Binney and other members of SARC who had attended the briefing, and reprimanded them for insubordination. He also issued a message to the NSA workforce demanding obedience, loyalty and group cohesion from all employees, and implying that Congress was a potential antagonist rather than the legitimate supervisor of the agency's intelligence work. "Some individuals, in a session with our congressional overseers, took a position in direct opposition to one that we had corporately decided to follow," he wrote. "This misleads the Congress regarding our agency's direction and resolve. The corporate decision was made after much data gathering, analysis, debate, and thought. Actions contrary to our decisions will have a serious adverse effect on our efforts to transform the NSA, and I cannot tolerate them. I have dealt with the people involved." (Hayden was evidently referring to the dressing-down he had given Binney and the others.) He continued: "Once a corporate decision has been reached, I expect everyone to execute the decision to the best of their ability. I do not expect sheepish acquiescence, but I do expect that problems necessitating course corrections will be handled within these walls. I must insist on all of us having the personal discipline to adhere to our corporate decisions, including those with which we disagree."

Hayden's message reminded Binney of another historic call for loyalty and obedience to group mission, which he quoted to me from memory. "The principle of democratic centralism and autonomy of institutions means specifically freedom of criticism, complete and everywhere, as long as this does not disrupt the unity of action already decided upon—and the intolerability of any criticism undermining or obstructing the unity of action decided on by the party." Lenin pronounced these words in 1906.

In August 2001, senior NSA management terminated the ThinThread project. Having disposed of the competition, the agency pressed ahead with Trailblazer, awarding the prime contract for its development to SAIC, the company where William Black and Sam Visner had both worked only months before. Trailblazer limped on for five more years. In 2003, having secured the valuable Trailblazer contract for his former employer, Sam Visner rotated back to SAIC, with a promotion to senior vice president of the company's Intelligence, Security and Technology Group. By 2005, Michael Hayden admitted in congressional testimony that Trailblazer was badly over budget and behind schedule. In 2006, his signature program for the modernization of the National Security Agency was terminated, without ever having produced one piece of usable intelligence, at a loss to taxpayers that my sources have put at between $1.2 billion and $8 billion, though the total figure has never been made public.

But Trailblazer cost America more than money. "Trailblazer was the largest intelligence failure in the history of the NSA," Binney told me. "By killing Thin-Thread and going ahead with Trailblazer, the Agency traded the security of the nation in exchange for money."

This assessment isn't merely the sour grapes of a manager whose program lost out to a competitor in an office turf war. Tom Drake, who remained at the agency after Binney and the others retired, describes how, shortly after 9/11, he used Thin-Thread as a testbed to analyze information in the NSA databases from the weeks preceding the attacks. The program, he says, swiftly pinpointed each of the terrorists involved, their communications and movements before the hijackings and their dispersion patterns afterward.

"The promise of creating the national security state was that America would never again be surprised," Drake told me. "Instead, three thousand people were murdered. Instead of providing for the common defense, as per the Constitution, Trailblazer was used as an excuse to get more money."

After 9/11, top NSA management, far from being chastened by their failure to avert the worst foreign attack on the nation since Pearl Harbor, were emboldened to demand more funding. Binney remembers Sam Visner predicting that 9/11 would prove a boon to the agency: "We could milk this cow for fifteen years." Tom Drake recalls Maureen Baginski telling a group of NSA employees that "9/11 is a gift to NSA. We're going to get all the money we want and then some." At an event marking the fiftieth anniversary of the NSA in the fall of 2002, Drake watched a congressional staffer hand a large pasteboard check to Hayden, symbolizing the massive new funding that Congress was bestowing upon the agency. "It was like a Publishers Clearing House check," Drake remembers. "He was looking down at [CIA director George] Tenant and then pointing to the check that he's holding, and I could see him mouthing the words, kinda in slow motion, 'I got my money!' He was just gloating over the fact that he got his money. He really cared that he got his money, as if money was now the answer."

In the weeks following 9/11, one of ThinThread's core elements, Mainway, was swiftly stripped of its filtering and encryption and used to create StellarWind, a sweeping new program that the agency used to wiretap Americans without warrants. Trailblazer advocates in the NSA had claimed that ThinThread couldn't scale, yet the effectiveness of StellarWind proved they were wrong, or lying. Nor did their objections that ThinThread might violate the legal and constitutional rights of US citizens appear to concern NSA leaders any longer.

In October 2001, distraught about the sinister metamorphosis of their computer code and of their agency itself, which was now breaking its most time-honored pledges, Binney, Loomis and Wiebe resigned from the NSA. "I couldn't continue to be a party to what they were doing," Binney said. "I couldn't continue to violate the Constitution." But the three did continue trying to halt the serious crimes and constitutional violations they saw being committed by their former employer. With the help of their congressional ally Diane Roark, who remained on HPSCI until April 2002, they met with a number of senators and representatives involved in intelligence oversight. Binney particularly remembers a meeting that Roark arranged with Representative Richard Burr at HPSCI, which was held in the committee's Sensitive Compartmented Information Facility. Binney told Burr about the shocking new initiatives of the NSA, of which he assumed Burr was unaware: multiple violations of the Constitution and of a series of laws protecting US privacy rights, the illicit collection of data on US citizens, corruption in the Trailblazer program and the NSA's various other failures. "His quote at the end was, 'Well, we all know that NSA is really messed up, but now's not the time to fix it,'" Binney says. "And I knew right away that it was hopeless. What I didn't know at the time was that Nancy Pelosi and Porter Goss, the chair and the ranking member of HPSCI, and [Lindsey] Graham and [Richard] Shelby on the Senate intel subcommittee, those four people, the Gang of Four, had already agreed to all these programs at NSA. They had already given their imprimatur to violating the Constitution and any number of laws." In fact, as a document released by Edward Snowden later revealed, these four senior members of intelligence oversight had already been briefed by Michael Hayden on the NSA's mass surveillance activities on October 25, 2001.

Not suspecting this either, Diane Roark attempted to raise the alarm in Congress on what she considered a covert, illicit program being run by the NSA. Veteran national security reporter James Risen details the series of meetings and contacts that Roark had with senior congressional and intelligence officials, including Hayden himself, during which she sensed surprisingly little outrage on the part of her interlocutors. Gradually she began to realize that far more people knew about this program than she had initially imagined. Despairing of help from the executive and legislative branches, she tried the judiciary, delivering a back-channel letter to Supreme Court chief justice William Rehnquist and leaving an urgent voicemail for Colleen Kollar-Kotelly, a US district court judge and chief justice of the secret FISA court. Rehnquist did not respond, and Kollar-Kotelly, according to Risen's account, not only refused to meet Roark but reported her to the DOJ for asking questions about the StellarWind program. (Risen writes that Kollar-Kotelly had been persuaded by the Bush White House not only to accept the warrantless wiretapping program, but to keep it secret from her fellow FISA justices.)

Finally, in September 2002, Binney, Wiebe, Loomis and Roark made one last bid to halt what they saw as extreme corruption and illegality at the NSA. "Part of the oath you take at NSA, along with protecting and defending the Constitution, is that if you witness fraud, waste, abuse or corruption, you are required to report it," Binney told me. "Every government employee does, and everybody in Congress does too. Well, that's what we did. We fulfilled the requirements of employment with the US government." The four had already voiced their concerns about Trailblazer and about the NSA's other illicit activities to the appropriate intelligence committees in Congress, to no effect. Now, following agency protocol once more, they filed a whistleblower hotline complaint with the Department of Defense's Inspector General's Office. They offered the investigators their full cooperation, and requested anonymity because they feared retaliation for voicing their concerns even through official channels. They also mentioned the existence of a senior executive still working at the NSA who would substantiate their accusations with documents and testimony to which they no longer had access, on the condition of strict anonymity. This was Tom Drake.

After retirement, still convinced of ThinThread's remarkable potential for recognizing patterns of illegal behavior in massive data sets, Binney and his colleagues formed a private company, Entity Mapping LLC, and began pursuing a wide range of applications for their program, including the detection of healthcare fraud, drug trafficking, money laundering, insider trading, the spread of infectious diseases, the distribution of components used to make IEDs in Iraq, and the proliferation of weapons of mass destruction. They approached numerous government agencies, including the National Reconnaissance Office, the US Army's Intelligence and Security Command, the Department of Defense, the Defense Advanced Research Projects Agency and the CIA, as well as major corporations such as Boeing and Computer Sciences Corporation. In these contacts, time and again, after strong initial interest, the potential partner would abruptly terminate their dialogue. The company developed an application with Boeing that swiftly and accurately analyzed large encrypted data sets, only to see its client shut down the project and destroy both the software and the data it had produced. Binney and his colleagues came to believe that their attempts to launch the business were being blocked to avoid embarrassing top brass at the NSA.

Their already tense relations with their former employer took a darker turn on December 16, 2005, when an explosive article by James Risen and Eric Lichtblau appeared in the *New York Times* that revealed the existence of StellarWind, the NSA's ongoing domestic spying program. A furious George W. Bush ordered the DOJ to identify the source of Risen and Lichtblau's revelations. Bush's anger intensified on January 29, 2006, when *Baltimore Sun* reporter Siobhan Gorman published the first of a series of articles in which, citing unnamed sources at the NSA, she described mismanagement and potential corruption in the Trailblazer program. The article was headlined "Spy Data System a 'Boondoggle': After 6 Years and $1.2 Billion, NSA Still Hasn't Set Up Trailblazer."

A year and a half later, on the morning of July 26, 2007, Bill Binney stepped naked from the shower into the line of fire of an FBI special agent pointing a Glock semi-automatic at Binney's face. Other agents trained their weapons on his wife and son. The FBI detained the three of them in their living room for several hours, while agents ransacked the house and removed personal property, including Binney's computer, which was never returned. That same day, the FBI raided the homes of Loomis, Wiebe and Roark, and also carried away extensive personal property. Four months later, on November 28, 2007, the FBI gave Tom Drake the same treatment. All five were stripped of their security clearances, which put an end to their work at Entity Mapping and in all other intelligence matters. After distinguished careers during which, collectively, they had safeguarded the security of the United States for almost 150 years, they were now being treated as traitors.

In reality, neither Binney nor Loomis, neither Wiebe nor Roark, had spoken to the press; they had made their revelations exclusively through official agency channels. (The sources of Risen and Lichtblau's article turned out to be Thomas Tamm, a DOJ lawyer, and Russell Tice, an NSA intelligence analyst.) Drake, together with other NSA employees whose identities have never been publicly revealed, had spoken with Siobhan Gorman at the *Baltimore Sun*, after he saw that previous reports to Congress and the Department of Defense's IG failed to fix the dysfunction inside the NSA, but he had only supplied unclassified information that he felt proved fraud, waste and abuse by the NSA—an action that is protected by the First Amendment. (Despite widespread claims to the contrary, employees in even the most sensitive national security occupations are legally entitled to speak with the press on matters of public concern, so long as the information they provide is not classified.) NSA administrative policy does prohibit unauthorized contact with the press, and Drake knew he might lose his job if his conversations with Gorman were discovered. Nevertheless, after years of fruitless internal whistleblowing about what he considered to be colossal wrongdoing at the NSA, which he believed made the United States more vulnerable to terror attacks, Drake decided to take the risk, exercising his First Amendment rights in the public interest by releasing unclassified information to the press.

All five NSA whistleblowers were subjected to several years of interrogations, judicial intimidation and vilification in the media. A prosecutor threatened three times to indict Binney, Loomis, Wiebe and Roark on criminal charges. After a long stretch in legal limbo, they received immunity letters, in most cases on the condition that they testify against Tom Drake—a condition they accepted, knowing they had nothing to say against him.

Drake himself suffered far worse treatment. Prosecutors claimed they had found classified documents in his basement and in his personal email account, as well as evidence that he was part of a spy ring. They assured him that he would spend thirty-five years in jail. In reality, the documents they had discovered were copies of those he had supplied to the DOD IG during its audit of Trailblazer and Thin-Thread, and provided to Congress during its investigation of the NSA's response to 9/11. Drake had retained the files from the DOD IG investigation at the specific direction of the IG staff. The prosecutors were unmoved.

In 2009, when Obama took office, Drake hoped for a more reasonable DOJ. He got the opposite. Though failing to pursue Wall Street executives who had triggered the financial crisis, Eric Holder's DOJ was relentless in its prosecution of national security whistleblowers. The Justice team on his case included Lanny Breuer, head of the department's Criminal Division. Breuer put senior litigation counsel William Welch in charge of the Drake prosecution. "Bill is absolutely tenacious," Breuer said of Welch in a 2011 interview. "He'll follow every fact and research every legal issue." Extreme tenaciousness can, however, warp truth. In 2008, Welch had led the prosecutorial team that withheld exculpatory evidence in the disastrously failed prosecution of Senator Ted Stevens; subsequently Welch and two colleagues were briefly held in contempt of court. After an FBI whistleblower revealed the prosecutors' actions, District Court Judge Emmet G. Sullivan, who presided over the case, told the court: "In nearly twenty-five years on the bench, I've never seen anything approaching the mishandling and misconduct that I've seen in this case."

Welch indicted Drake on ten criminal counts under laws including the Espionage Act, the 1917 law passed, as its name implies, to prosecute spies serving foreign powers. Using a tactic that has since become standard procedure, Welch argued that the government didn't have to prove that Drake "intended to harm the country" in order to convict him of espionage, and that any discussion of the legal conception of whistleblowing was irrelevant to the case. (Welch actually filed a motion to preclude the defense from using the word "whistleblowing.") Tom Drake became the Obama administration's signature Espionage Act prosecution.

The case against Drake gradually unraveled. The overblown and intimidatory nature of the government's charges is captured by the real nature of the five purportedly "highly classified" documents that the DOJ used to suggest that Drake had illegally retained classified material. One, titled "Regular Meetings," was explicitly marked "UNCLASSIFIED" and had been posted on the NSA intranet; prosecutors argued that Drake should have known that it was actually classified. Another, "What a Success," was declassified shortly after Drake's indictment; the fact that it had ever been classified in the first place struck J. William Leonard, a former director of the Information Security Oversight Office under George W. Bush, as so outrageous that he filed a formal complaint against the NSA for having done so. The final three documents at the heart of the DOJ's prosecution, titled "Collections Sites," "Trial and Testing," and "Volume Is Our Friend," were part of the materials that Drake had shared with the DOD IG and Congress. After they were seized from Drake's house, NSA officials subjected them to a highly unusual—and illegal—"forced classification review," and retroactively pronounced them classified.

On June 9, 2011, just four days before Drake's trial was scheduled to begin, the DOJ abruptly made a plea deal with Drake in which they agreed to drop all charges in return for a token admission from Drake. Judge Richard Bennett berated the prosecutors for holding Drake hostage for years under the threat of a long jail term, on charges ultimately so weak that the department would abandon every one. "I find that unconscionable," Bennett said at a July 15 hearing. "Unconscionable," the judge repeated. "It is at the very root of what this country was founded on against general warrants of the British. It was one of the most fundamental things in the Bill of Rights that this country was not to be exposed to people knocking on the door with government authority and coming into their homes." Bennett noted that Drake had already paid a high price for the government's actions, including the loss of his lucrative NSA job and generous pension. Still, to end his extended legal ordeal, which had made Drake permanently unemployable in his chosen field and had stretched his personal finances to the snapping point, he says he was forced to "throw the government a bone." He pleaded guilty to one misdemeanor charge of exceeding authorized use of a government computer, without any involvement of classified information, and received a sentence of a year's probation and 240 hours of community service. Drake served out his sentence by interviewing a series of American war veterans for the Library of Congress's Veterans History Project. Two of the former soldiers he interviewed were Bill Binney and Daniel Ellsberg.

This is what comes of reporting fraud, waste and abuse in national security through agency channels. But how did the DOJ and its FBI agents obtain the names of the NSA Five? All had contributed to the 2002 whistleblower complaint of wrongdoing in Trailblazer. When President Bush ordered a major investigation into the sources behind scathing press about the NSA, it appeared that someone at the DOD IG had handed their names to the prosecutors, despite all assurances of anonymity. The office that was created to serve as a haven for whistleblowers had become a whistleblower trap.

We have a good idea who at the IG revealed the names, thanks to three other national security whistleblowers.

More than once during her work as a whistleblower attorney, Jesselyn Radack has seen disclosures by one whistleblower prompt others to step forward, to denounce not only the original malfeasance but the wrongful retaliation they have witnessed against the first whistleblower. "These are like whistleblower chain reactions,"

Radack says, "when one outrage triggers another." The revelations of the NSA Five, and their subsequent treatment at the hands of federal authorities, set off this kind of chain reaction among a handful of people who not only believed their original accusations of fraud and abuse at the NSA, but knew from personal experience the Orwellian injustices that many whistleblowers suffer.

When Binney first came to Radack to ask for legal advice, after the FBI had raided his house, she remembers him warning her that if he turned up dead, it would not have been a suicide. Radack, a graduate of Yale Law School, did not dismiss his statement as grandstanding or paranoia, because she herself had experienced the acute stresses and potential dangers of blowing the whistle on high-level national security malfeasance. As an attorney in the DOJ's Professional Responsibility Advisory Office, which counsels its attorneys on professional ethics, Radack had revealed the department's violations against John Walker Lindh, the so-called American Taliban, whose illegal interrogation presaged the US government's later systematic torture of Iraqi and Afghan detainees. (Radack has described these violations and their subsequent cover-up in a wrenching memoir, *Traitor*.) Though she had explicitly informed a lawyer from the DOJ's Terrorism and Violent Crime Section, during an email exchange on December 7, 2001, that Lindh had retained legal counsel, and that the FBI should have Lindh's lawyer present whenever he was questioned, the FBI interrogated him without a lawyer anyway, and extracted a confession. When Radack learned this, she objected that such a confession might be invalid. Her concerns and advice about the interrogation were expressed in numerous emails; Radack herself wrote about a dozen messages. In them she made clear that the FBI's interviews might be inadmissible in court, and recommended against prosecuting Lindh criminally.

Nevertheless, when Attorney General John Ashcroft announced Lindh's criminal indictment on January 15, 2002, he said his department believed that Lindh had not retained legal counsel. Three weeks later, Ashcroft stated that the prisoner's rights had been "carefully, scrupulously honored." Radack knew that both of Ashcroft's statements were false. By now the infamous photo of Lindh, naked, blindfolded and duct-taped to a stretcher, had circulated in the press, our first glimpse of officially sanctioned torture. Soon lawyers at the White House and the DOJ's

Office of Legal Counsel, at the behest of George W. Bush and Dick Cheney, would write a series of memoranda that purported to exempt US officials from the Geneva Conventions in their dealings with war detainees in Afghanistan, and essentially immunized them for crimes they had committed in the detention or interrogation of prisoners.

Abruptly, Radack's boss, Claudia Flynn, handed her a scathing performance review, though Radack had recently received glowing evaluations and a merit raise. Radack needed to find another job, Flynn announced, or this evaluation would be included in her permanent personnel file.

What Radack didn't know at the time was that her emails with the FBI had suddenly become radioactive. The federal judge presiding over the Lindh case, T. S. Ellis, had ordered all internal DOJ correspondence concerning the conditions of Lindh's interrogation to be transmitted to him, for disclosure to Lindh's attorneys if he found them relevant to Lindh's defense. Without informing Radack, her superiors at the Professional Responsibility Advisory Office had sent Judge Ellis only three of her numerous emails on the case, none of which mentioned her official instructions as an ethics adviser, or her concerns about the validity of Lindh's subsequent confession. When Radack learned, in an email from the prosecutor, that the other emails had been omitted, she examined the department's official file on the Lindh case, which she knew was a stack of documents including hard copies of all the emails—she had stapled them into the file herself. To her shock, she saw that the file had been purged, and now consisted of a few inoffensive documents and fax cover sheets.

The electronic copies of her emails had also disappeared from the DOJ mail server, but with the help of a DOJ computer technician, Radack retrieved fourteen of the missing emails. She printed out new hard copies of these messages, handed them to Claudia Flynn, and asked whether Radack should send them to the prosecutor herself.

Flynn was visibly angry. "No, I'll handle it," Flynn replied.

Radack resigned from the DOJ, and joined the DC law firm of Hawkins Delafield & Wood. She continued to follow the Lindh case intently, however, and from press reports she concluded that her office never had turned over to the court her "missing" emails, which were so prejudicial to the prosecution's case. Meanwhile, political and popular pressure grew for a punitive sentence against Lindh, whom the press had branded as a terrorist sympathizer. Having failed to catch Osama bin Laden or any other senior al-Qaeda operative, the Bush administration appeared determined to make an example of their first high-profile detainee in the war in Afghanistan. Bush, Cheney, Ashcroft, Donald Rumsfeld, Colin Powell, Hillary Clinton and other leading figures made inflammatory claims that contradicted the known facts: Lindh, some declared, was an al-Qaeda operative; he had attended a terrorist training camp; and he had known in advance of plans for the September 11 attacks. "American leaders and the American people were still reeling from 9/11," Radack remembers, "and they were hungering for the legal lynching of John Walker Lindh." Because of this prejudgment, Radack saw that Lindh might become the victim of a colossal miscarriage of justice, which now threatened to land him in prison for three consecutive life sentences, largely on evidence wrung from him during illegitimate interrogations.

She also saw that her former office had become an accomplice. "I was working in the *Justice* Department, advising on *ethics* and *professional responsibility!*" she says, cadencing her words to emphasize the hypocrisy. "We were prosecuting Enron and Arthur Andersen for obstruction of justice and destruction of documents, yet here we were doing precisely the same things." She thought about the bat mitzvah she had celebrated when she was thirteen, during which she had spoken of the prophet Jeremiah, whose mouth God touched to encourage him to denounce the idolatry of the people and the greed of the priests. She remembered the Torah portion she had read during this ceremony, from Exodus: *Lo ti'eh aharay rabim* ("Thou shalt not follow a multitude to do evil"). "This verse warns not to follow the majority of the people blindly for evil purposes, especially to disrupt justice," she had told the congregation that day. "I hope that I will always be able to make the right decisions about my actions." Seventeen years later, she decided to live by these words. "Jewish teachings were always there in the deep recesses of my mind," she says today. "I'm not sure how much they guided my choices, and how much they simply affirmed what I had already decided to do."

Airing her concerns through official channels was not an option. Radack had already left the DOJ; what's more, when she'd reported these events to her superiors while still at the department, they'd reprimanded her and forced her out. She couldn't communicate with the court, because she lacked legal standing in the case. Nor could she contact Congress, because she lived in the District of Columbia, which had no voting representative. Her one remaining avenue for disclosure, she felt, was the press. In June 2002, she released the missing emails to Michael Isikoff, a reporter at *Newsweek*, who published a story about them on June 23. "I don't use the term 'leaker' for what I did, because I was exercising my legal rights to share my own emails with the press—emails that would have been destroyed if I hadn't rescued them. I was a whistleblower, not a leaker. Sometimes semantics matter."

Her whistleblowing worked. On July 15, the DOJ announced that it was dropping eight of the ten charges it had brought against Lindh, in return for his guilty plea on the last two, aiding the Taliban and carrying weapons during the commission of crimes of violence. The plea deal was widely interpreted as arising from the DOJ's realization, once the information in Radack's missing emails became public, that the court would not admit Lindh's confession as evidence.

No DOJ officials were reprimanded for their handling of the case. But when *Newsweek* inadvertently revealed that Radack had been the source of the emails, her former colleagues began a retaliation campaign, with familiar Kafkaesque contours. The department opened a federal criminal investigation against her, for charges they would not disclose in detail, and informed her law firm that she was the subject of that investigation (the firm promptly placed her on unpaid administrative leave). The department referred her for disciplinary action to the bars in states where she was licensed to practice law, on the basis of a secret report that she was not permitted to read. Various government officials, without supplying evidence and often speaking anonymously, called Radack a "criminal," a "terrorist sympathizer," a "turncoat" and a "traitor." She was placed on the federal No Fly List maintained by the Terrorist Screening Center.

All charges against Radack were eventually dropped and all allegations were proven false, but her career, at least in the Washington legal establishment, was over. "Having been a whistleblower myself, I decided to devote the rest of my life to defending them," she says. Radack joined GAP to head its national security practice, and subsequently went to work for ExposeFacts.org, an organization that encourages whistleblowers to release information on national security and human rights violations and corporate criminality that will help citizens to make informed decisions about their democratic process.

As a former whistleblower, Radack was able to see the world through her clients' eyes. "The experience is so surreal, the retaliation is so over-the-top, so strangely creative and aberrant, that when you're describing it to someone, it does seem impossible, almost crazy." Bill Binney's concern about a staged suicide did not strike her as overwrought. The day she met Tom Drake, sensing that he needed the moral and intellectual support of fellow whistleblowers, she called Daniel Ellsberg and handed Drake the phone; she also connected him with John Kiriakou and Jeff Sterling, two other national security whistleblowers who had been indicted on espionage charges. She knew how to create an informal support network that helped each whistleblower to cope with what Radack calls "the politics of personal destruction." "When you blow the whistle on the national security establishment, you're going up against a massive force, with endless resources and the biggest megaphone, which is set on squishing you. They're powerful, but they're also scared of what you know, so they try to isolate and delegitimize you to destroy your credibility. They intentionally demonize you, make you radioactive, so even allies and friends won't touch you." In the Tom Drake case, even the normally fearless ACLU balked when they learned that Drake had been charged with spying, and refused to join his defense team. "Oh, espionage. . . . We don't want to get involved in that," was the reaction she heard.

In Radack's own case, the demonization probed deep into her private life. Some news outlets reported that her husband had left her, which her enemies evidently believed made her appear unstable. A whispering campaign emerged at the school of her son Jake, then four years old, who one day was told that his mother was in the newspaper because she'd done something wrong.

"What did you do, Mommy?" Jake asked her.

Radack, unsure how to respond, asked Jake what *he* believed she'd done. "I think you were a big tattletale, and got a real long time-out," he said.

"Yes, maybe," Radack replied, "but sometimes it's good to be a tattletale."

She describes the retaliation process in the national security community as particularly destabilizing, because it creates disturbingly inverted images of whistleblowers and wrongdoers. "You will never recognize yourself from the portrait they paint of you. They say you can't be trusted, but in reality it's they who can't be trusted. They insist that you should follow the law and go through channels, but when you do, like Bill Binney and Tom Drake did, these channels turn out to be traps, because the people in them break the law. They charge you with espionage and call you a traitor against your country, when they are the ones who are violating the Constitution." Radack considers the popular image of national security whistleblowers as wild-eyed civil libertarians and hacktivists to be another such inversion, part of the government's attempt to make whistleblowers seem unpatriotic and untrustworthy. "Most of my clients are middle-aged, white, card-carrying Republican military guys. They're ultra-conformists, very patriotic and flag-waving. Bill Binney volunteered for the Army and had a distinguished thirty-four-year career at NSA. Tom Drake served in the Navy, worked in the CIA in Eastern Germany before the Wall fell—he's not some ACLU hippie dude. Ed Snowden was younger, but he was a true believer. He was already working for the CIA at a very young age; he volunteered for the military to go fight in Iraq. Hardly a crunchy-granola kind of guy."

Radack and her GAP colleagues filed a FOIA lawsuit to obtain documents concerning Tom Drake's testimony about Trailblazer, which would demonstrate that Drake had kept these documents not on his own initiative, but at the direction of the DOD IG and Congress. In particular, she stressed the importance to Drake's defense of obtaining a copy of the 2004 audit report on Trailblazer and Thin-Thread, which, as she wrote to the DOD IG, "is described by people briefed on its contents as highly critical of the agency's management." Her FOIA suit eventually resulted in the release of the heavily redacted version of the 2004 audit report we have today. However, the IG claimed that it could not hand over most of the other documents she had requested, because they had been destroyed. In a letter of February 15, 2011, prosecutor William Welch, evidently relying on information supplied by the DOD IG, informed the presiding judge in the case, Richard Bennett, that these records had been purged in accord with the IG's "standard document destruction policy."

When they read this statement, a number of people inside the DOD IG knew, just as Jesselyn Radack herself knew, that it was a lie. The IG had no standard document destruction policy. On the contrary, it had a "Records Management Program," which explicitly required the retention of such documents. Eventually, several senior executives at the DOD IG did what Radack had done a decade earlier within the DOJ. Convinced that their office was mishandling the Drake case and several other whistleblower matters, thereby shielding the DOD while obstructing justice and threatening upstanding employees with extended prison sentences, they blew the whistle on their own office's whistleblower practices. The chain reaction triggered by the NSA Five continued to escalate.

Assistant Inspector General John Crane was one of this new wave of national security whistleblowers who spoke out. He had watched from inside the DOD IG's office as the ThinThread-Trailblazer investigation unfolded, and witnessed the legal assault against the five people who had come to his office as confidential whistleblowers and witnesses. He knew better than most that one of the main responsibilities of every inspector general was to receive and investigate the reports of whistleblowers, while shielding their identity and guarding them from reprisal.

He had worked at the DOD IG since 1988, and had been part of the generation of federal employees who had founded the inspector general system after the Inspector General Act was passed in 1978. Earlier still, he'd worked on the staff of Congressman Bill Dickinson, ranking member of the House Armed Services Committee, who had advocated the creation of the first IG office in the Defense Department; Crane regularly consulted the authors of the IG Act about their original intent when they wrote it. He recalls the excitement in the air when he joined the fledgling DOD IG in 1988, at a time when the reforming zeal of the post-Watergate era was still strong. "The IG concept was an experiment, an evolving experiment, and we were the paradigm," Crane remembers. "We were building a new organization—it was like a Silicon Valley startup. I was part of that startup generation, I had that vision. At the DOD IG, we knew how important our job was. We were the oversight over the largest corporation in the history of the world, employing half the federal workforce, whose mission was world domination."

To this day, Crane carries a small blue booklet in his left inside jacket pocket that contains the text of the 1978 act and later amendments, together with the Bill of Rights and the Constitution. Now and then he produces it and reads out a passage from the law, often to underscore how it echoes the political philosophy of the Founders. In 2003, when the old rules of the pre-9/11 world had changed under Secretary of Defense Donald Rumsfeld, he gave a copy of the act to every employee in the office. "I thought it was really important for the IG workforce to understand the act. That's your raison d'être, your mission. But when you execute that mission, it needs to be within the larger context set by the Constitution and the Bill of Rights."

Crane also had a long-term commitment to fostering the practice of whistleblowing within the IG system. He'd written articles on whistleblowing while studying at Georgetown, and had worked with HPSCI to draft the Intelligence Community Whistleblower Protection Act of 1998, which created an important new avenue for intelligence and military officials to disclose classified information to Congress. Six years later, he helped to found an office to protect civilian members of the DOD from retaliation, headed by the wily investigator and staunch whistleblower advocate Dan Meyer. In 2010, Crane established the first Office of Whistleblowing and Transparency at the IG, which he led when Jesselyn Radack contacted the DOD IG with a whistleblower reprisal complaint on behalf of her client Tom Drake. Crane was responsible for ensuring that his office scrupulously followed the rules of engagement with whistleblowers defined by the Inspector General Act: whistleblowers must remain anonymous except under extraordinary circumstances, and must never be punished for coming forward. He was also the FOIA appellate authority at the DOD IG, which meant he would be in charge of gathering and transmitting documents, redacted as necessary by the NSA, to Radack.

One of the founding principles of the IG Act, and one of Crane's biggest challenges in implementing it, was that individual IG offices had to retain their independence from, and their ability to criticize and correct, the departments and organizations they were charged with overseeing. Things had begun well for Crane when he joined the DOD IG, then led by Deputy Inspector General Derek Vander Schaaf, an aggressive investigator who had served in Robert McNamara's Defense Department as a budget specialist, and who, like Ernie Fitzgerald, knew all the tricks of the military contractor trade. Vander Schaaf, John Crane and their office investigated and punished wrongdoing wherever they found it, including fraud by major military contractors and sexual misconduct by senior generals and admirals. "We were doing a very big number of audit reports and investigations," Crane remembers, "including Category One audits, on the biggest-ticket projects like aircraft carriers and fighter planes. Our work led to about twenty congressional hearings each year." Over time, however, the IG's independence and investigative zeal faded, as the office became less a critic of the Pentagon than its defender. "When I left in 2013, we were down to one or two investigations a year," he says, nearly all of which concerned lower-level cases. "They didn't want to do complex investigations and audits because they could cause controversy, newspaper articles, congressional hearings. The new attitude was, 'Don't make waves.'"

This shift is a natural consequence of the IG management structure. Every inspector general reports to the head of his agency, who writes his performance reviews and determines his bonuses. He also serves at the pleasure of the president, who can fire him at will. "It's hardly surprising that many IG offices are highly political in their selection and investigation of cases," Jesselyn Radack says. "All too frequently, their only real investigations center not on wrongdoing, but on the person who surfaced it—the whistleblower." (The DOJ's own investigation of Radack was led, in fact, by the DOJ IG.)

"Today, IG DOD is probably the most dysfunctional whistleblower program in the federal government," Crane says. Indeed, numerous investigations of the office between 2012 and 2019 by the GAO, POGO and Congress have revealed serious misconduct, needless delays and an absurdly high 84.6 percent dismissal rate of whistleblower cases by the department (other military IGs, on average, dismissed only 40 percent of whistleblower cases). One report found that "the culture of the OIG DoD has been, and continues to be, hostile to internal whistleblowers," and noted that a substantial number of employees "did not feel they could disclose a suspected violation of any law, rule or regulation without fear of reprisal." During Senate floor speeches in 2016 and 2017, Chuck Grassley condemned DOD IG leadership for allegedly "tampering with investigative reports and then retaliating against supervisory investigators who call them to account," which he said suggested that "a culture of corruption is thriving in the Inspector General's office." Among numerous examples of this disturbing pattern at the IG's office, Grassley reviewed one in detail, the case of Admiral Brian Losey, whom Grassley called a "serial retaliator" against whistleblowers; during the investigation of Losey's case, Grassley said, senior managers at the DOD IG allegedly ordered investigators to change facts and omit evidence of suspected retaliation from their reports, and even sent a letter clearing the admiral before investigators had finished reviewing the evidence. "Was this a cover-up to facilitate the admiral's pending promotion?" Grassley asked rhetorically.

The Tom Drake case, and several concurrent investigations that John Crane witnessed at the IG, reflected this politicization and partiality. When he read his own office's report on Trailblazer, Crane was amazed by the repeated mentions of widespread reprisal against employees. "I was floored by that language," he told me. "You almost never find an IG document that mentions reprisal, because the Inspector General Act of 1978 itself and the Whistleblower Protection Act both specifically prohibit reprisal. This was something we are obliged to investigate!" But, Crane says, when he asked Henry Shelley, the IG's associate general counsel, to refer the matter for investigation, Shelley refused. In a sworn affidavit of February 9, 2015, Crane described what happened next: "Over the next several years, Mr. Shelley engaged in a relentless campaign to curtail and undermine whistleblower reprisal investigations. . . . The mishandling of Mr. Drake's case is an example of this pattern."

Crane says that Shelley, though part of an IG office charged by Congress to serve as an independent watchdog over the DOD, seemed more intent on defending the military than on holding it accountable. "He was very explicit that he considered himself to be the defense attorney of the DOD," Crane remembers. "He said that his first priority was the Navy, then the secretary [of defense], and then the IG, in that order. And I would tell him, 'No, no, no! You're the attorney for the IG, and your responsibility is to defend this office's interests." Several times Crane made his point by pulling out his little blue book and reading relevant parts of the IG Act aloud, but Shelley seemed unmoved. "Our office made very few findings against senior naval officers," Crane says. "That was his mind-set. And even when we found against them, Shelley would send the Navy our IG report in advance, so they could attack the report."

Crane's disillusionment with his office grew after the publication of the *New York Times* article on NSA domestic surveillance by Risen and Lichtblau and the subsequent fallout. Shortly after the *Times* story appeared, Crane met with Shelley and then IG Thomas Gimble. The three men speculated whether the DOJ would contact their office. Shelley, Crane says, suggested that they should, of their own accord, alert the DOJ to the existence of the NSA whistleblowers who had filed the hotline complaint. After the first *Baltimore Sun* article claimed there had been mal-feasance in the Trailblazer program, the three again discussed the matter, and the possibility that one whistleblower had supplied the information for both the *Times* and the *Sun* articles; Shelley and Gimble hypothesized that the DOJ might now be able to concentrate its attention on the whistleblowers who had filed the hotline complaint about Trailblazer, including the anonymous "senior executive" who had helped to substantiate their charges. (Gimble had been involved in preparing the IG report on Trailblazer, and knew that this executive was Tom Drake.) According to Crane, Shelley again suggested that their office reach out to the DOJ. Crane objected that such an action would deviate from normal procedure for contact with DOJ, and that the IG Act specifically prohibited disclosing the identities of whistle-blowers without their prior consent.

After the FBI raided Binney, Loomis, Roark and Wiebe, and then Drake a short time later, Crane repeatedly asked Shelley who had provided the names of the NSA whistleblowers to the DOJ, whether they had consented to this disclosure, and what guarantees the whistleblowers had received that their identities would remain confidential. Crane also pointed out that, in his experience, no DOD IG material witness had ever become the target of an investigation for having cooperated with the DOD IG. Shelley, he says, admitted that the situation was "dicey," but refused to describe his communications with the DOJ.

On April 14, 2010, came the Drake indictment. "I saw that our witness was now being prosecuted as a spy," Crane told me. "Drake faced thirty-five years in federal prison—the rest of his natural life." He paused, then added vehemently, "This is a human being's life!"

In mid-June, Jesselyn Radack and GAP took the offensive on Tom Drake's behalf, with their expansive demand for documents under FOIA. Crane, as FOIA officer, was responsible for preparing this material and transmitting it to GAP. In her FOIA request, Radack wrote, presciently, "If any of the material covered by this request has been destroyed or removed, please provide all surrounding documentation including, but not limited to, a description of the action taken regarding the material and justification for those actions." Six months later, GAP brought a whistleblower reprisal lawsuit against the NSA, charging that Drake was being retaliated against for having served as an unnamed source in the Trailblazer investigation.

Crane felt a growing sense of disbelief. Several of the charges on which the DOJ was prosecuting Tom Drake appeared to have been derived directly from the confidential testimony that Drake had given to IG investigators during the Trailblazer audit. In other words, someone at the IG had not only fingered Drake, an anonymous source, to the DOJ, but had supplied the prosecutors with a copy of his testimony. "I now realized that we were deep in what might become the most explosive case of my career at the DOD IG," Crane remembers, "and the most contentious espionage trial since Daniel Ellsberg was prosecuted for releasing the Pentagon Papers." (An April 2018 report by the DOJ inspector general found no evidence for Crane's claim that DOD IG employees had "proactively" revealed the names of the NSA Five to law enforcers; yet the report also conceded that the DOD IG's confirmation of the identities of the NSA witnesses to the FBI could be considered "tantamount to disclosure of their identities." An intelligence expert with intimate knowledge of the affair dismissed the DOD IG's statements as hair-splitting. "Whether or not DOD OIG 'proactively' reached out, DOD OIG helped the FBI focus its criminal investigation on whistleblowers who reported malfeasance through channels. Regardless of which agency picked up the phone first, DOD OIG not only failed to protect, but actively compromised, its key witness.")

Gimble had left the IG's office, and had been replaced by an acting IG, Lynne Halbrooks. Crane told Halbrooks and Shelley of his grave concerns about their office's involvement in a high-stakes criminal trial in which one of their own deponents had become the defendant. He stated that, given the urgency of the matter, he needed to quickly locate all documents related to GAP's FOIA request. He also said that he had to know whether Drake had been misinformed about his confidential status, and if so, who had revealed the identities of Drake and the other NSA whistleblowers.

Their reactions, Crane says, were not reassuring: after consulting with the managers who had conducted the 2004 Trailblazer audit, Shelley said that some of them had "fucked up," because they had "'overpromised' to Drake in terms of confidentiality," and had destroyed extensive documentation. Without Crane's input, members of the DOD IG informed William Welch about the purged documents; Welch, in turn, wrote Richard Bennett, the presiding judge in the Drake case, that these records had been purged "pursuant to a standard document destruction policy."

Again Crane was astonished. The procedures in place for handling documents, particularly highly classified information, were so strict that he felt Welch's claim couldn't stand. "I knew what the rules were, and I knew these documents couldn't have been destroyed, period. And if we had in fact destroyed or couldn't find classified documents, the DOD and DOJ needed to be notified immediately." He saw that supplying these documents to Drake's lawyers was vital to their ability to defend him in court. When the DOD IG receives documents from a source during an investigation, it usually instructs the source to keep a copy of those documents. "You tell them to keep an alternative set of records, not at work, typically at home. I wanted to see whether Drake had followed a DOD IG request to keep records at his home, and whether the IG was aware of it. This could be important exculpatory information."

According to Crane, shortly before Drake's trial date of June 13, as Crane worked feverishly to prepare the documents that Radack and GAP had requested, both Shelley and Halbrooks instructed him not to release the 2004 audit report until after the trial had ended, even if it was ready before. Shelley stated that he did not want information released that could be used by the media in a public defense of Drake. Crane objected again, reminding his superiors that such stalling tactics violated the FOIA process, which mandates the immediate release of information as it becomes available. (A week later, the NSA sent Crane the massively redacted copy of the 2004 audit report, which he forwarded to Radack.)

By now Crane and his superiors were on a collision course. He continued to demand information on the purged documents, which he said seemed highly suspicious, and could lead to obstruction of justice charges against their office. Shelley repeatedly refused to tell him more about the circumstances in which the documents had been destroyed, and stopped sharing information with him about the Drake case, citing attorney-client privilege concerns in an active judicial proceeding. On numerous occasions, Crane nevertheless urged a vigorous investigation into their office's handling of the case, and the potential destruction of case files. Halbrooks and Shelley refused, and threatened to deprive him of his twenty-member staff if he began a probe himself. "Halbrooks told me that such an investigation could embarrass her and Henry Shelley, and that by pushing for one, I wasn't being a 'team player,'" Crane told me. In a later conversation, as Crane stated in a sworn affidavit, Halbrooks insisted that she wouldn't allow the Drake case to undermine her goal of becoming the next IG, and began retaliatory actions against him. (The 2018 DOJ IG report stated that Shelley did not remember Crane expressing concern about these issues, or requesting an investigation, and that Halbrooks had declined the IG's request for an interview.)

Crane was put on administrative leave in January 2013, and resigned the next month, but he has continued ever since to publicly denounce the wrongdoing he witnessed. In April 2017, when I met Crane in Washington, the Office of Special Counsel had recently issued a "finding of substantial likelihood" that his claim that the DOD IG had retaliated against Tom Drake was founded, and deserved a full investigation. A year later, the DOJ IG announced that key documents in the Drake case had not been destroyed after all. "By concealing those documents, the DOD IG committed a fraud on the court," John Crane says today, "just as it failed to protect Drake and the other whistleblowers."

Three months after Crane left the DOD IG, Patrick Eddington, a former military imagery analyst at the CIA, became the third former national security whistleblower to take up the cause of the NSA Five. At that time he was working on national security matters as senior policy adviser to Representative Rush Holt, a New Jersey Democrat who served on HPSCI from 2003 to 2011. Eddington spoke at length with Binney, Drake and the others. He was moved by what they said, but also by their human plight, because he himself had been a whistleblower while working at the CIA. When he discovered evidence that US soldiers had been exposed to unidentified toxins during and after the 1991 war with Saddam Hussein, possibly including Iraqi sarin nerve gas, and that the military and the CIA were covering up the exposures and the possible medical harm they caused, he and his wife, Robin, who also worked at the agency, blew the whistle, first internally, then to Congress, and finally to the *New York Times*. The medical disorders they pointed to became known as Gulf War syndrome; while the precise causes of this disorder remain mysterious to this day, a 2010 study by the National Academy of Sciences estimated that up to 250,000 of the troops who served in Kuwait and Iraq had been harmed.

Eddington left the agency in 1996, and in 2004 went to work in Congress. "I always said if I got the chance to get back into government again, especially on the Hill, I was going to do everything I could to be helpful to other whistleblowers. I knew how vital their disclosures could be. I also knew what it felt like to become an enemy of your own agency just to get the truth out. It takes an enormous toll. It hounds your every step."

He was also fascinated, and appalled, by what the NSA Five had revealed about the general condition of US intelligence just before 9/11. Since he was a teenager, Eddington had been intrigued by historic military disasters caused by intelligence failures, such as Pearl Harbor, the Chinese intervention in the Korean War, and the Tet Offensive in Vietnam. "The people in the field at Pearl Harbor had the information that would have alerted them to the attack—that the Japanese consulate in Hawaii was keeping very precise track of where ships were in the harbor, down to the location of individual ships. But they were told by the intel bureaucrats back in Washington not to go after Japanese diplomatic traffic. This was the kind of catastrophic intel failure that had made me join the CIA, to see if, maybe, I could do better." In the Trailblazer and ThinThread debacle, he felt he recognized another military disaster born of bad intel. "Once I'd heard their story, I was not going to let this go. To me it was too important, because it was all about Pearl Harbor again."

While serving on Holt's staff, Eddington held the necessary security clearances to view documents classified as top-secret and sensitive compartmented information. He eventually obtained the original, unredacted 2004 IG audit report—Eddington was the former CIA analyst who told me this document was the most damning he'd seen in his entire Washington career. "When I read it, I felt sick," he says. He believes that the vast majority of the redactions to the report were made not to shield legitimate national security secrets, but to avoid embarrassment to senior NSA management, especially its director, Michael Hayden. "The full, classified version of the DOD IG report issued in December 2004 essentially validates every allegation that they [the NSA Five] made."

After he joined the Cato Institute as a policy analyst in homeland security and civil liberties in 2014, Eddington filed a FOIA lawsuit against the NSA to obtain extensive documentation concerning the investigation into Trailblazer and Thin-Thread, most of which remains classified. "I'm going to get not just that IG report," he says today, "but every email, every memo, every single piece of paper that was ever generated relating to ThinThread and Trailblazer and submitted to the IG by the whistleblowers. Because this episode is a poster child of malfeasance—this is Government Corruption 101. There's no question in my mind that there was contract steering going on here."

As an expert in intelligence, Eddington, like Bill Binney and Tom Drake, believes that had ThinThread been implemented as directed by Congress, it would have averted the tragedy of 9/11. "This tiny handful of government employees came up with a system for $3.2 million, that if it had been in place even just six months before 9/11 would have stopped the attacks. They would have been able to identify every hijacker and where they were." Eddington notes that the Trailblazer fiasco was part of a larger failure of several intelligence agencies to process and share information, which was identified by the congressional Joint Inquiry and the 9/11 Commission, but never fully corrected. "Both the CIA and the NSA, just on the basis of the information that they had from other sources—forget about Thin-Thread for a minute—if they had shared what they had on al-Hazmi and al-Mihdhar [the two Saudi terrorists who traveled from Bangkok to Los Angeles before taking part in the hijackings] when they had it, and if that data had been passed to the FBI in a timely fashion, they would have *got* those guys." Eddington smacks the table with the flat of his hand to emphasize the word "got," and punctuates each successive statement with another flat-hand blow: "They would have *tailed* them, they would have *got* FISA taps, they would have *caught* them in communication with the safe house over in Afghanistan and elsewhere, they would have *figured out* the rest of the network, just from those two guys alone. They should have done that even without ThinThread. And if ThinThread had been operational, and if NSA and CIA had shared that information, they would have got them all—they would have got every last one of them. 9/11 would never have happened. And instead of being the greatest American intelligence failure in history, 9/11 would have been the greatest American intelligence success, ever. We would have put al-Qaeda out of business almost without firing a shot. That's what a lack of integrity among NSA's senior leadership made possible."

The redacted version of the 2004 audit report, Eddington says, proves that the NSA is effectively beyond oversight or control, since by invoking Section 6 of the NSA Act of 1959, the agency is able to withhold anything having to do with agency personnel or operations. "That report shows how the NSA, a government agency which is supposed to be subject to independent audit by the DOD IG, can basically thwart transparency efforts to expose waste, fraud abuse and criminal conduct, by maliciously invoking an over-broad statute. Is that something which the federal courts are willing to allow? Are they willing to allow NSA to have that level of a Mafia-style legal protection racket, to keep their dirty laundry hidden from the public? If you asked people in Congress who passed that law back in 1959, 'So, just to be clear, you want to give them the ability to hide rapes, murders, torture, assassinations, spying on Americans—you want to give them the ability to hide all that?' my sense is that most of the folks who signed that law would say, 'Well, wait a minute. . . .'" What's more, he says, if the agency succeeds in suppressing this vital IG report, they will have a precedent to suppress similarly compromising documents in the future.

Secrecy, Eddington says, is the main problem with US intelligence today. "Secrecy gives you the ability to effectively conceal waste, fraud, abuse and criminal conduct of every description—and for me, secrecy more often than not is in fact used for precisely that purpose. It is used to try to conceal conduct that people at senior levels of government don't want you to know about." He explains that the abuse of secrecy in the NSA Five case, as with the concealment of the torture of prisoners, extraordinary rendition, drone killings, and other illegal or unconstitutional activities, stems from a historic case of 1953, *United States v. Reynolds*, in which the widows of three civilian observers killed in the 1948 crash of a B-29 bomber filed a wrongful death suit against the government. The Air Force denied their request to be allowed to see the accident report and the statements of surviving crew members, claiming that the report described secret electronic equipment being tested during the flight, and that revealing it would harm national security. In a 6–3 decision, the Supreme Court accepted the military's argument and created an official "state secrets privilege," which gave the military and the executive branch the right not to disclose information they deemed might harm national security if released. When the accident report was published in 2004, however, it showed that the crash was due to engine failure, and made no mention of secret equipment.

"Government lawyers, Air Force lawyers, went in and lied to the Supreme Court about what had really happened in that aircraft crash," Eddington says. "There wasn't any sensitive national security–related technology involved. It was lousy maintenance that caused that aircraft to go down and those folks to die. Yet the court basically created the state secrets privilege, which the government has used for over fifty years to conceal from the surviving family members and the descendants of those guys that were killed on that plane what had really happened. Just as they've used it to conceal wrongdoing ever since. When the Supreme Court of the United States allows itself to be lied to by the executive branch through the use of secrecy, then there is no way for you to have a functioning democracy, in my judgment."

He notes that the judiciary's helping the executive branch to keep its illegitimate secrets is part of an ongoing pattern. He points to James Risen's reporting that Colleen Kollar-Kotelly, the former presiding judge of the FISA court, not only complied with the Bush administration's request to conceal StellarWind from her fellow FISA judges, but relayed Diane Roark's name to the DOJ. "Behavior like this destroys, literally vitiates, the entire purpose of the FISA court. I don't understand why she's still on the federal bench. I don't understand why an impeachment resolution was not offered against her after this whole episode had taken place, because she had no business giving the executive branch that kind of carte blanche. So the level of corruption and dishonesty, and lack of fidelity to duty here, particularly to the Bill of Rights, is what is so incredibly violative, and so incredibly destructive. Because it sets a precedent, right? These things then become normalized."

Ultimately, Eddington blames Congress for accepting secrecy and lack of accountability among the intelligence agencies as well as the military, both because they have been cowed by the executive branch, and for fear of being branded "soft on terror" by voters. He is particularly critical of the House and Senate intelligence committees, which in his view have become far more lapdogs than watchdogs. "The intel committees in Congress have become apologists and enforcers for the intelligence agencies that, by law, they're required to regulate," Eddington says. "There's a huge contrast with the natural investigative bent of something like the House Committee on Oversight and Reform, where one of the first things you see on the website is 'Blow the whistle.' Whereas in the House and Senate intel committees, they do everything in their power to keep things in-house, to prevent them from getting out." He points out that the two intel committees routinely refuse to provide information to other members of Congress about intelligence programs. "If you're a member of Congress, and these programs are affecting your constituents—and they are, they're affecting everybody's constituents—and the intelligence committees can deny you the ability to get legitimate information that you need for oversight purposes, then the system is truly broken, the system is corrupt." People are typically appointed to the committees because they won't rock the boat, and some have extreme conflicts of interest, like Dutch Ruppersberger, the former ranking Democrat on HPSCI, whose Maryland district contained the NSA, and Porter Goss, former chair of the committee, a lifelong member of the intelligence establishment. "This kind of behavior completely undermines the ability of Congress as an institution to engage in the oversight necessary to prevent major abuses from taking place."

Steven Aftergood, an expert on government secrecy, agrees. "The [Senate and House] intel committees mostly operate in a classified bubble and so they fail to accurately represent the public and even the Congress as a whole." He says this became obvious in the wake of the Snowden disclosures: the committees were aware of the programs that Snowden revealed, and in fact had signed off on them, but when they were disclosed and public opinion was inflamed, Congress enacted some legislative changes. "If the intel committees had been functioning properly," Aftergood says, "there should have been no reason to change course following the disclosure."

Eddington, who is currently completing a history of the national security state from McKinley to Trump, believes that early in Obama's first term, Congress, through timidity and cultural capture, missed a critical opportunity to demand accountability for, and therefore to end, the extreme abuses instituted by the Bush administration, like torture and domestic spying. "The Constitution gave Congress a powerful mechanism to remove folks in the executive branch: impeachment. And it's not just for the president or the cabinet: Congress can impeach any civil servant in the US government. It should have used impeachment aggressively to go after people in intelligence and folks elsewhere who were responsible for these really abhorrent programs. Instead, Congress appears to accept the intelligence community's right to absolute secrecy, almost as an article of faith. Until you find ways of stripping that away, the intelligence community feels, quite rightly, that they can get away with murder."

Eddington seems optimistic that his FOIA lawsuit not only will reveal serious wrongdoing by the NSA in the Trailblazer contract and the cancellation of ThinThread, but will prove why protecting national security whistleblowers from retaliation is vital to our national security, and thereby prompt better legislation and administrative rules to protect whistleblowers. However, we would be excused for remaining cautious. Eddington's FOIA case was initially assigned to Judge Gladys Kessler, which seemed propitious, given the healthy skepticism of government secrecy that Kessler had expressed in some of her earlier judgments. But two weeks later, the case was reassigned to a new judge: Colleen Kollar-Kotelly, whose support of the Bush administration's StellarWind program Eddington considers grounds for impeachment. Meanwhile, under Trump's former secretary of defense James Mattis, national security officials previously condemned for serious retaliation against whistleblowers quietly returned to their jobs, or were promoted. Despite Chuck Grassley's sharp condemnations of Admiral Brian Losey, regardless of a DOD IG report confirming that Losey had indeed been guilty of whistleblower retaliation, and notwithstanding requests from leaders of the Senate Armed Services Committee that the Navy block Losey's pending promotion, in early 2017 the Navy secretly promoted Losey, granting him back pay and an increased pension. Similarly, in May 2016, NSA inspector general George Ellard was found by an external review panel of the heads of other IG offices to have illegally retaliated against an unnamed whistleblower, whereupon then NSA director Michael Rogers recommended that Ellard be fired. Ellard appealed the decision, and the case went silent for a time. Soon after Trump's election, Eddington learned that Ellard was still working at the NSA.

"Cases like these send two messages, loud and clear, to the national security community," Eddington says. "First, if you're a senior official or officer and you retaliate against a whistleblower, you may well get away with it, and keep your job, too. Second, if you witness fraud or wrongdoing and are thinking about blowing the whistle, think again." The laws, regulations and whistleblower offices within the DOD are similar to the elaborate compliance departments and hotlines in major recidivist fraud corporations: not whistleblower havens, but whistleblower traps.

Nowhere is the human harm of white-collar crime greater than in what we call "national security," which has become a misnomer. Since 9/11, millions of Americans have been spied on, and the nation's fundamental civil liberties have been blighted. After 9/11, on the basis of invented weapons of mass destruction, the US government embarked on a series of immoral and unwinnable wars that have bled the country dry, morally as well as financially, and further destabilized the Middle East. In our name, the United States government instituted a program of systematic torture of detainees—torture that was then and remains now illegal, and which has widely been agreed to have produced little or no useful information. In our name, it participated in the kidnapping, extradition and killing of purported terrorists, some of whom later proved innocent. It created its own version of extraordinary rendition in Guantánamo Bay, where time-honored legal guarantees like habeas corpus and right to a fair trial have been denied to prisoners for over sixteen years. In our name, it instituted and continues a vast program of extrajudicial killings by unmanned drones.

In our name, yet without our consent, in strictest secrecy, justified by secret legal opinions and blessed by secret courts—a secrecy that in most instances has no operational justification, and merely serves to conceal abuses that would cause public outcry if widely known. Even more than in other fields, whistleblowers are essential in national defense, because the factors that facilitate fraud—secrecy, the sense of mission and mystique, the culture of impunity, and the flow of Other People's Money—are more extreme. As the executive branch urges the "national security" agenda, Congress and the courts have become impotent or complicit, subverting the main checks to militarism. Here is the mortal threat to democracy that is eternal war, which the Founders saw during the Revolution, and Eisenhower warned against during the Cold War. Their message has been taken up by a handful of whistleblowers within the hermetically sealed realm of the national security apparatus, who have the nerve to announce to us, aloud, what our government is actually doing, to others and to us.

The experiences of the NSA Five demonstrate how profoundly hostile to whistleblowing is the culture of secretive organizations, and how easily structures meant to encourage principled dissent can be warped into snares that silence the message and destroy the messenger. Not only do such organizations resist any oversight of their activities and budgets; they also insist on carveouts for national security that allow them to curtail the rights of whistleblowers. The landmark Civil Service Reform Act of 1978 had exceptions for the NSA, CIA, FBI and the other members of the intelligence community, and the Whistleblower Protection Act of 1989 likewise failed to cover employees of those organizations. The so-called Intelligence

Community Whistleblower Protection Act of 1998 does not afford any meaningful protection to national security whistleblowers, particularly against retaliation. The original text of the Whistleblower Protection Enhancement Act (WPEA), which Obama signed into law in 2012, would have extended coverage to members of the national security community and prohibited the suspension of security clearances, a common form of reprisal. But HPSCI blocked these important amendments, claiming they would endanger national security.

Despite its generally supportive attitude toward antifraud whistleblowers in the corporate sphere, Obama's DOJ prosecuted nine defense and intelligence whistle-blowers under the Espionage Act—more such prosecutions than had occurred under all previous presidents combined. Starting with the show-trial prosecution of Tom Drake, the administration's lawyers developed a new, restrictive interpretation of the act that allowed them to exclude any public interest defense for intelligence whistleblowers, and that willfully mischaracterized them as enemies of the people. Veteran journalist Leonard Downie Jr. called the Obama administration's efforts to clamp down on leaks and control information "the most aggressive I've seen since the Nixon administration," an opinion shared by many experts. "I'd hoped Tom Drake's indictment under the Espionage Act would be an exception, but instead unfortunately it turned into a pattern," says Jesselyn Radack. "The Bush adminis-tration was brutal and dogged in its attacks on dissenters of all kinds, including whistleblowers, but the Obama administration assault on national security whistle-blowers was downright pathological. These are the aggressive posture and the legal weapons he has bequeathed to his successor, Donald Trump. National security whistleblowers once had to choose between their conscience and their career, when they decided whether to inform the American public what its own government is doing, to them at home, and in their name abroad. Now people are forced to choose between their conscience and spending the rest of their lives in prison or in exile."

On October 10, 2012, Obama signed Presidential Policy Directive 19 (PPD 19), which provided limited new protections for national security whistleblowers, in-cluding the first presidential prohibition in the history of security clearance retalia-tions. Eight months later, after the first of Snowden's revelations were published, Obama condemned Snowden for failing to make his disclosures through the procedures sanctioned by PPD 19. "I signed an executive order well before Mr. Snowden leaked this information that provided whistleblower protection to the intelligence community—for the first time," Obama said during an August 2013 press conference. "So there were other avenues available for somebody whose conscience was stirred and thought that they needed to question government actions." But as Obama should have known, PPD 19 did not explicitly apply to the vast pool of intelligence contract workers like Snowden, nor did it protect national security employees from criminal prosecution. The avenue Obama claimed to have opened was a blind alley—or another trap.

A year earlier, Obama had already set in train a further anti-whistleblower development, his Insider Threat Program, in response to Chelsea Manning's release of extensive secret military and diplomatic materials. The program, implemented by a task force headed by the director of National Intelligence (DNI) and the attorney general, ordered millions of federal employees to be vigilant for "high-risk persons or behaviors," and noted that criminal charges could be brought against those who failed to report them. Yet the definition of "insider threat" is so vague that it allows people and acts to be targeted that have nothing to do with classified information. A DOD strategy paper for the program exhorted managers to hammer home the idea that "leaking is tantamount to aiding the enemies of the United States." A DNI official, Patricia Larsen, stated in a November 2015 briefing that leaks that harmed the reputation of a government organization were to be considered insider threats, as they "would be in the business world." Larsen included Tom Drake's face in a rogue's gallery of proven "Insider Threats" together with convicted Soviet spy Aldrich Ames, Navy Yard shooter Aaron Alexis, and Fort Hood killer Nidal Hasan. Predictably, the intelligence community, with DNI in the lead, has implemented this program with zest.

Most whistleblower allies see the program as an institutional crackdown on whistleblowing. Jesselyn Radack observed that equating disclosing classified information with espionage and "violent acts against the government" is both wrong and dangerous. "'Insider threat' programs will more likely be used as a pretext for targeting whistleblowers . . . than they will be used to stop actual threats to national security," she wrote, shortly after the program was announced. Chuck Grassley

publicly worried that the program would sweep up legitimate communications between government employees and Congress: "The Insider Threat Program has the
potential for taking the legs out from underneath all of the whistleblower protections we have."

"All presidents are exasperated by leaks," wrote Arthur Schlesinger shortly after
Nixon's downfall.

> They are really not, however, against leaks in principle. The selective leak is a
> familiar tool of government. What enrages Presidents are the leaks they do not
> ordain themselves—leaks that embarrass, expose or undermine their policies,
> which is to say leaks that stimulate and fortify national debate. Presidents like to
> claim that such leaks do ineffable harm to national security. What they mostly
> mean is that leaks do harm to the political interests of the administration. The
> harm to national security through leaks is always exaggerated. We have had leaks
> from the start of the republic. . . . No one has ever demonstrated that these leaks,
> or the publication of the Pentagon Papers either, harmed national security. No
> one can doubt that the disclosures benefited the democratic process.

Prosecutor William Welch argued in a 2010 hearing that Tom Drake's disclosures had potentially harmed soldiers on the battlefield—a claim that a close reading of the five documents at the heart of the government's indictment reveals to be
absurd. Nor has any substantiation been offered for assertions about the harm done
to American intelligence capabilities by the disclosures of Chelsea Manning and
Edward Snowden.

In contrast, the DOJ has been lenient to several intelligence leakers whose revelations were potentially far more harmful to the nation. While serving as director
of the CIA, David Petraeus handed eight highly classified binders to his mistress,
Paula Broadwell, from which to glean spicy details for the biography of Petraeus
that she was writing. Those binders, known in the trade as "Black Books," contained top-secret/SCI material, the identities of covert officers, code words for secret intelligence programs, and information about war strategy and intelligence
capabilities. Petraeus later lied to FBI agents, another federal crime, when he told

them he had never provided classified information to Broadwell. Petraeus settled his judicial troubles in a deal brokered by Eric Holder, under which he pleaded guilty to a single misdemeanor charge of mishandling classified material, received a sentence of probation and a fine, and continued his illustrious flexian career.

John Crane witnessed this stark double standard in cases handled by his own office. While authentic whistleblowers like Bill Binney and Tom Drake were being betrayed and prosecuted for following official procedures, other cases were being sandbagged by the DOD IG because they seemed likely to embarrass the intelligence community and presidents past or present. In 2006, the DOD IG investigated allegations by Anthony Shaffer, a former lieutenant colonel in the US Army Reserve who deployed twice to Afghanistan as a staff officer shortly after 9/11. In October 2003, Shaffer had informed the 9/11 Commission and Congress that elements of US intelligence had ignored the results of a top-secret data-mining program, Able Danger, which in 2000 had successfully identified two of the three terror cells that later carried out the 9/11 attacks. He also alleged that the DOD had failed to share critical information with the FBI, and had destroyed data produced by Able Danger to conceal their failures. Although Shaffer's disclosures were protected under whistleblower law, the DOD nevertheless revoked his security clearance and fired him. Senior politicians including Chuck Grassley and John McCain called on the DOD IG, John Crane's office, to investigate.

Crane remembers Henry Shelley announcing, before the investigation even began, "We will not find for Tony Shaffer." DOD leadership, Crane says, "didn't want anyone to say that they had missed an opportunity to avoid 9/11—that they had readily available to them intelligence developed by DOD that could have prevented the attacks." After Shelley expressed irritation that witnesses had supported Shaffer's statements, Crane recalls, an investigator offered to fix the problem: "Tell me what you want the witness[es] to say," he told Shelley at a staff meeting, "and I will make them say it." In September 2006, the DOD IG issued a report that comprehensively rejected Shaffer's allegations.

In another investigation by Crane's office, conversely, senior officials who had leaked sensitive information with no pretense of public interest were shielded. Reports alleged that Secretary of Defense Leon Panetta had revealed highly classified information to Mark Boal, screenwriter and co-producer of the 2012 film *Zero Dark Thirty*, about the hunt for Osama bin Laden, and allowed Boal to attend a June 24, 2011, ceremony at CIA headquarters honoring (and clearly identifying) the members of SEAL Team Six, the unit that had tracked down bin Laden. A DOD IG report condemning this flagrant breach was essentially complete by December 2011 but was not released. Members of Congress expressed their frustration at the delay, Crane says, especially since Michael Vickers, Panetta's senior intelligence adviser, was a leading candidate to replace the disgraced David Petraeus as CIA director. "The Senate Arms Services Committee was about to hold nomination hearings, and they needed to know what, if anything, our report said about Michael Vickers," Crane remembers.

At its direction, Crane's colleague Dan Meyer gave the committee a copy of the report. When the IG continued to delay its publication, someone on the committee leaked it to a reporter, who passed it to POGO, which promptly published it, together with a searching analysis. (Acting DOD IG Lynne Halbrooks quickly relabeled the leaked document "a pre-decisional working-draft.") The report confirmed that Panetta's public remarks at the ceremony contained secret and top-secret information; that he had identified the commander of the unit by name—a disclosure that violated federal law—and that senior members of the military were "universally surprised and shocked" that a Hollywood executive would be present at the ceremony, as such a breach in secrecy could lead to members of the team being targeted by terrorists.

The report also described the pressure the Obama administration had exerted to ensure official cooperation with Mark Boal and Kathryn Bigelow, the filmmakers of *Zero Dark Thirty*, which celebrated one of Obama's most striking foreign policy triumphs and was originally scheduled for release in October 2012, a month before the presidential election. (It was eventually released in December 2012.) The IG report quoted emails from Michael Vickers telling senior DOD officials that "Secretary Panetta wants the Department to cooperate fully with the makers of the UBL [Usama bin Laden] film," and from George Little, a DOD spokesman, to a senior Pentagon official suggesting Panetta's fascination with the project. "I hope they get Pacino to play [Secretary Panetta]. That's what he wants, no joke!" (Memos and emails later obtained from the CIA and DOD through FOIA by Judicial

Watch, a conservative government oversight group, reveal the extensive support that Vickers and Panetta gave the filmmakers, including classified information about officers directly involved in the bin Laden raid.)

The POGO article that accompanied the leaked report included an email exchange from December 2012 between an unnamed member of the DOD IG's office and a congressional staffer, in which the staffer asks for information on the report, saying he'd heard that the IG was "sitting on it until Secretary Panetta retires." The IG employee replies that the report has been ready for a long time, adding, "I have grave concerns that the message and findings are now controlled and subject to undue influence across the board at DoD IG." The employee also states that he is writing to Congress as a whistleblower—and implies that there is plenty to blow the whistle on within his office.

As in the Tom Drake matter, the *Zero Dark Thirty* investigation led to repeated clashes among John Crane, Lynne Halbrooks and Henry Shelley. In one exchange, Crane remembers, investigators asked Halbrooks when they would be interviewing Panetta, an obligatory step, as he was the target of the investigation. Halbrooks, Crane says, replied, "Never." Later Halbrooks met with Panetta, against Crane's advice that she should not be in contact with the subject of her office's Title 18 investigation, and informed him that their office would never release the report. After POGO published both the report and the email chain between the unnamed DOD IG whistleblower and Congress, Halbrooks angrily demanded that Crane tell her the identity of the whistleblower—had it been Crane himself? Crane refused to say, whereupon Halbrooks made the timeworn accusation that he wasn't a "team player." (The unnamed whistleblower, we now know, was Bill Rainey, former deputy for intelligence at the DOD IG, and his congressional correspondent was Charles Murphy, a veteran member of Chuck Grassley's staff.)

A month later, a security guard appeared at Crane's desk and escorted him from the DOD IG facility. He later lodged a complaint with the Office of Special Counsel, alleging serious wrongdoing by senior members of his office in this and other investigations. On October 11, 2017, the OSC wrote him to confirm that his allegations in the *Zero Dark Thirty* affair largely matched those made by Chuck Grassley in 2014; that the OSC had found a substantial likelihood of serious fraud, waste, abuse or criminal behavior; and that it had called for a full investigation by the appropriate oversight body, in this case the Integrity Committee of the Council of the Inspectors General on Integrity and Efficiency. However, the letter concluded, the Integrity Committee, after consulting Henry Shelley, had declined to investigate the matter, against the clear will of Congress. "This is how the Inspector General community shuts down allegations by whistleblowers despite the clear intent of the law," Crane told me not long after he'd received the letter. "With conduct like this by the IGs, why would anyone become a whistleblower?"

When even whistleblower-protectors like John Crane get the whistleblower treatment, as they routinely do in the national security arena, we know that the entire system for safeguarding legitimate disclosures is profoundly broken—or rather, has been optimized to draw in would-be whistleblowers with false assurances of confidentiality and intent to investigate, and then to silence them. National security insiders know they must report their concerns outside established channels, via the press, a government watchdog NGO, or WikiLeaks. "Too often, you have to have a death wish to go through 'established channels' in national security," says Tom Devine.

It is in the national security arena, too, that a crucial part of the whistleblower protection system, the Department of Justice, shows its true colors as an enforcer for national security rather than a protector of individual whistleblowers—or of American citizens. This mirrors the department's two-faced stance on FCA and other whistleblowers against corporate fraud. Perhaps this hostility toward whistleblowers of all stripes makes a twisted kind of sense. Despite its official role as attorneys for the American people, the department belongs to and serves the executive branch, and is led by an AG whom the president chooses, among other qualities, for loyalty. "After quite a bit of experience with the federal courts," Ernie Fitzgerald wrote in 1989, "I learned that the American people have no legal advocate to represent them at the federal level. . . . The United States attorney general is the top lawyer—not for the people but for the president who appoints him. And he has a large and powerful department prepared to battle any opponents the administration might have."

The DOJ has consistently fought enhanced legal status for whistleblowers as an encroachment on the authority of the department and the executive branch. In the courts and lobbying behind the scenes, it resisted the passage of the 1986 amendments to the False Claims Act, and subsequently challenged its constitutionality before the Supreme Court. Senior members of the department have portrayed qui tam whistleblowers as marginal to their investigations, untrustworthy, and in the words of the current attorney general, William Barr, as an "abomination." DOJ leaders likewise argued in public and lobbied in private against government whistleblowers, convincing Reagan to veto the Whistleblower Protection Act in 1989, and convincing Senator Jon Kyl to place a secret hold on the Whistleblower Protection Enhancement Act in 2012. The DOJ's position on certain government whistleblowers softened under Obama; for the first time the department supported the WPEA and even recommended jury trials for whistleblowers. Yet by and large, the DOJ's anti-whistleblower bias remains strong.

The department's record in adjudicating retaliation complaints brought by FBI whistleblowers is indicative. A 2015 GAO report found that the DOJ sided with whistleblowers in only three of the seventy-two cases reviewed, and that whistleblowers suffered savage retaliation that sometimes lasted over a decade. The "judges" at hearings for FBI whistleblowers are lawyers from the DOJ's Office of Attorney Recruitment and Management, who rarely find against their own department. In an interview with *60 Minutes*, Chuck Grassley once likened the bureau's ethos to the omertà of organized crime families. "The Mafia used to talk about being family. The FBI's not Mafia, at least they're not supposed to be. But you get the impression that that sort of peer pressure is what you have to [have], and you don't mess with the family."

But it's in the realm of national security that Department of Justice prosecutors, together with their counterintelligence and criminal-investigative counterparts at the FBI, seem most clearly to reveal their true priorities, organizational ethos and distorted perception of justice. The DOJ's calculated, dishonest use of the Espionage Act seems designed to punish current and intimidate future whistleblowers and silence debate on vital legal and constitutional questions, while depriving the accused of an opportunity to explain their motives to a jury, or to make clear to the general public the benefits of their disclosures. New precedents created during these prosecutions have further enhanced the retaliatory power of the act. Amazingly, in May 2016, shortly after leaving the DOJ, Eric Holder admitted that Edward Snowden had "performed a public service by raising the debate [about domestic surveillance] that we engaged in and by the changes that we made." Nevertheless, he added, Snowden deserved to go to prison. In contrast to his previous stance on international fugitive Marc Rich, Holder stated that Snowden needed "to get lawyers, come on back [from Russia] and decide—see what he wants to do, go to trial, try to cut a deal." Holder's contradictory, Orwellian positions highlight the vital need for a public interest defense against criminal prosecution of whistleblowers.

The DOJ has waged its war on national security whistleblowers against the press as well, by targeting as accomplices in espionage conspiracies journalists who have published classified disclosures. In a series of virtually unprecedented moves against First Amendment rights, Holder's DOJ secretly subpoenaed the phone records of the Associated Press; issued a search warrant to investigate Fox News reporter James Rosen as an "aider and abettor and/or co-conspirator" in a federal leak investigation; and litigated for seven years to force *New York Times* reporter James Risen to reveal his sources in a story on the CIA, chalking up in the process a federal appeals court ruling that abolished the "reporter's privilege," the widely respected right of a journalist to refuse to testify about confidential sources in a criminal case, and a judgment by the Supreme Court that essentially agreed with the DOJ that Risen could be obligated to provide evidence in a national security prosecution. Even before Risen's ordeal, in July 2013, James C. Goodale, the former *New York Times* general counsel who represented the newspaper before the Supreme Court in the Pentagon Papers case, wrote that "Obama will surely pass President Richard Nixon as the worst president ever on issues of national security and press freedom." "Until President Obama came into office, no one thought talking or emailing was not protected by the First Amendment," Goodale continued. "President Obama wants to criminalize the reporting of national security information. This will stop reporters from asking for information that might be classified. Leaks will stop and so will the free flow of information to the public. . . . Obama's view is that national security interests nearly always trump the First Amendment. No president has had this view before, except Richard Nixon."

Donald Trump may be such a president. He has employed the legal instruments crafted by Obama to continue the assault on leakers. His DOJ has charged employees at Treasury, IRS and the security establishment with leaking information to the press, in some cases to reveal suspicious financial activity by members of Trump's inner circle. Trump has also escalated the war on the free press that mirrors his aggressive dislike of what he has termed, apparently without a nod to Ibsen, the "enemy of the people." In a federal investigation into leaks of classified information, his prosecutors seized years of email and phone records from Ali Watkins, a *New York Times* reporter. And with its plan to extradite and prosecute WikiLeaks founder Julian Assange, a meta-whistleblower and publisher, Trump's administration has crossed the Rubicon, extending its prosecutions from leakers themselves to those who publish their leaks. The May 23, 2019, indictment condemns Assange's attempts "to receive and obtain documents, writings, and notes connected with the national defense . . . for the purpose of obtaining information respecting the national defense"—precisely what serious national security reporters do for a living, and what every major publication that drew data from WikiLeaks did as well.

Ultimately, the reasons why the DOJ so often targets whistleblowers are diverse. Some, as we've seen, may have to do with the instinctive aversion that people who choose to work for large, strongly hierarchical and authority-conscious organizations have for people who question authority and are willing to break the chain of command. The fact that many government prosecutors move on to jobs defending companies as white-collar defense lawyers, where whistleblowers are a critical enemy, likely adds to their aversion. And despite its mythology of impartiality, the department is highly politicized, with many attorney generals and senior staff directly appointed by the president manifestly serving the executive branch's political agendas. John Mitchell served as Nixon's co-conspirator and henchman during Watergate; John Ashcroft and Alberto Gonzales railroaded Bush's torture and domestic surveillance programs past Congress; Eric Holder orchestrated Obama's Wall Street whitewash as well as his jihad against national security whistleblowers. William Barr, a staunch advocate of the unitary executive, has denounced the investigation by special counsel Robert Mueller as an illegitimate encroachment on Trump's executive power, and carries on his aggressive prosecution of whistleblowers, leakers and the press.

A highly politicized tone at the top can affect behavior at every level of the DOJ, and, as Jesselyn Radack discovered, cause Justice to lash out at whistleblowers. But throughout history, under both parties, many Department attorneys have been inimical to whistleblowers in more basic terms: because they are not players. Whistleblowers are the antithesis of celebrity revolvers like Eric Holder, Michael Chertoff and Mary Jo White. As insiders with an outsider's conscience, whistleblowers are perhaps the most serious threat to the flexians' preferred mode of transacting business, by which senior officials cut deals among themselves, without interference from underlings or from irksome laws and ethics guidelines. For such people, whistleblowers seem threatening because they are not predictable, malleable or corruptible.

In his slim, brilliant book *On Tyranny*, historian Tim Snyder observes that the Nazis rose to power by "manufacturing a general conviction that the present moment is exceptional, and then transforming that state of exception into a permanent emergency. Citizens then trade real freedom for fake safety." The Reichstag fire gave Hitler the exception he needed, what James Madison had called "some favorable emergency," to suspend the basic legal rights of all Germans, including habeas corpus, search warrants, freedom of expression and of the press, freedom of assembly, and privacy of the post and telecommunications. "When politicians today invoke *terrorism* they are speaking, of course, of an actual danger," Snyder writes. "But when they try to train us to surrender freedom in the name of safety, we should be on our guard. . . . People who assure you that you can *only* gain security at the price of liberty usually want to deny you both. You can certainly concede freedom without becoming more secure."

We have watched the Reichstag burn twice in the last two decades. If 2008 was a quiet coup in finance, during which Wall Street, in the name of exceptional and emergency circumstances, appropriated vast wealth from ordinary citizens in ways those citizens never fully understood, and therefore couldn't effectively resist, so

9/11 began a takeover of the commonwealth by intelligence and military leaders, a putsch, unvoted and undiscussed, from which our constitutional rights and our democracy have yet to recover. In the aftermath of both crises, Barack Obama, though elected on a promise of change and transparency, explicitly chose to look forward rather than back. Instead of Pecora hearings or the systematic prosecutions that followed the savings and loan crisis, we had squabbling, partisan commissions and dead silence from the DOJ, regulators and the Treasury. Instead of the Church Committee, the Watergate Hearings, the Pike Committee and other penetrating investigations of intelligence abuses under Nixon, the Obama administration fought tirelessly, in the courts and the press, to conceal Bush's torture, rendition, domestic surveillance and targeted drone killing from public view (not least because Obama himself continued the surveillance and targeted killing).

The resulting popular incomprehension and apathy about post-9/11 and post-2008 abuses emboldened leaders in the financial world and national security to consolidate and further extend their powers, in a dysfunctional feedback loop that, by now, has effectively disabled many crucial checks and balances of our republic. The aftermath of 9/11 proved Eisenhower's military-industrial prophecy, as zealots welding fear and secrecy empowered America's dark side, a shift cemented by later apologists more intent on executive power than on justice. When, on the fifteenth anniversary of 9/11, Bush and Obama appeared on screens at NFL games across the nation to rehearse their joint national mythology of terror, redemption and business as usual, they were two facets on the same monolith of state control, two exponents of an enduring imperial presidency.

The key dramatis personae persist, ensuring continuity of abuse. Just as Robert Rubin, Lawrence Summers and others who helped create the 2008 financial crisis were summoned to the Obama White House to fix it, and continue to this day to share their economic wisdom at prestigious universities and think tanks and on the pages of leading newspapers, so the Mnuchins and Rosses of Trump's cabinet who enriched themselves in 2008 now help determine the nation's economic trajectory. The mandarins of intelligence and the military continue, despite their failures and betrayals, to dictate the nation's intelligence and military policies: Chertoff, Clapper, John Brennan, McConnell, Alexander, Ridge, Petraeus, Mattis, the perennial national security leaders, these high priests of warfare. They speak tirelessly in the media and on Capitol Hill, as masters of matters far too complex, we are assured, for ordinary citizens to grasp. Somehow they have eluded a few commonsense questions, like: How many wars have we won in the Middle East lately? How well did our intelligence establishment protect us from 9/11? How successfully have the trillions we've poured into intelligence since then been at preventing subsequent terror attacks in San Bernardino, Orlando, and Fort Hood; the shoe bomber, the underwear bomber, and the Boston Marathon bombers; not to mention Paris, Nice, Berlin, Barcelona? The national security sages foster a deep sense of dependence, a conviction that we need them for their vast expertise, though the conflicting public and private interests this expertise entails help explain why we're in so much trouble to begin with.

Michael Hayden is the living demonstration of Janine Wedel's "fail up" model of the flexian career trajectory (which Jesselyn Radack describes more piquantly as "fuck up, cover up, move up"). Hayden led the NSA from 1999 to 2005. Despite the abject failure of his signature Trailblazer program, and despite heading a leading intelligence agency in the run-up to the 9/11 attacks, among the worst intelligence failures in US history, he was next tapped to serve as deputy director of the new Directorate of National Intelligence, and then to lead the CIA. One of the documents leaked by Edward Snowden, a draft report by the NSA IG from 2009, revealed how Hayden chose in March 2004 to continue the bulk collection of internet metadata, even after the attorney general had withdrawn support for the program. In 2008, Obama's new attorney general, Eric Holder, stated that Bush's authorization of the NSA domestic surveillance program had broken federal law, namely FISA, and three federal judges later agreed. So quite apart from the Trailblazer–ThinThread fiasco brought to light by the NSA Five, one would expect that the people most directly responsible for this program, which clearly includes Michael Hayden, would be prosecuted for felony crimes.

Since then, the NSA and other intelligence agencies have not covered themselves in glory. Aside from failing to protect our elections from the Russian hackers and our sensitive military technology (including plans for Lockheed's trillion-dollar F-35 fighter) from the Chinese, they have at times actively aided our enemies. In the summer of 2016, for example, a mysterious group of hackers known as the "Shadow Brokers" announced they had stolen an arsenal of cyberweapons built by the NSA—malicious code to penetrate firewalls, bypass antivirus software, target weaknesses in Microsoft products, and wreak other digital havoc. Shadow Brokers made some of these tools available on the web; cybercriminals have since used them in attacks in over 150 countries. Victims include Federal Express and Nissan, the Spanish telecommunications giant Telefónica, Russia's Interior Ministry, Chinese universities, and a number of hospitals; in facilities of the British National Health Service, patient records were made unusable and operations had to be postponed. "Americans didn't know how dysfunctional our intelligence agencies had become before September 11, 2001," says Michael German, an intelligence expert and former FBI whistleblower. "But the repeated failures since amply demonstrate that simply expanding their power and inflating their budgets hasn't made them more effective."

Michael Hayden nevertheless continues failing up. He has appeared countless times as an expert television commentator, to assure us how vital the NSA and its various programs have been to our safety. Hayden writes op-eds in major papers, like the one the *New York Times* ran in February 2016 under the snappy headline "To Keep America Safe, Embrace Drone Warfare"; Hayden's bio at the foot of the article identifies him as a former general and CIA director, and an author, but fails to mention that he also serves on the boards of Motorola Solutions and Michael Baker International, which make or use drones; is a principal at the Chertoff Group, a security and private equity consultancy that helps clients land big government contracts to fight terror and cyber threats; and works for a number of other defense-related companies, consultancies and think tanks. The article also fails to note what Micah Zenko, a senior fellow at the Council on Foreign Relations, estimated in a 2013 report: that as CIA director, Hayden personally authorized forty-eight drone strikes that killed 532 people, 144 of whom—nearly a third—were civilians. The article omits what experts on drones often state: that drone killings radicalize target communities, increasing support for terror organizations and making us *less* safe. Hayden is much caressed in academia: Oxford made him its inaugural Humanitas Visiting Professor in Intelligence Studies, and he is a distinguished visiting professor at George Mason University, down the hall from Janine Wedel. In October 2017, George Mason founded the Michael V. Hayden Center for Intelligence, Policy, and International Security.

Throughout this book, we've seen how institutional hypocrisy in corporations—the radical disjunction between an organization's public mission and values on the one hand, and its real, often secret agendas on the other—often triggers whistle-blowing. The post-9/11 national security takeover of America and our descent into torture, extraordinary rendition, domestic spying, targeted drone killing and endless war has created intense institutional hypocrisy on a national scale that draws all of us into its sticky web, forces us all to live in the lie. The country in which we find ourselves pays little heed to the Declaration of Independence, the Constitution, and the other founding documents of our nation. We are compelled to forswear the self-evident truths we swear by: that we all are created equal, are entitled to enjoy liberty and pursue happiness, to be secure against warrantless searches and seizures, and other injuries and usurpations of the tyrant. And that it is to secure these rights, not to strip them away, that governments are instituted among us, deriving their just powers from the consent of the governed. When we celebrate people who illegally spied on us, while prosecuting as spies those who revealed that spying, the load of absurdity becomes intolerable for many citizens. When we claim to be the fountainhead of freedom and self-determination in the world, yet allow our government to lord it over us, the cognitive dissonance is crushing. We praise sunlight, yet our vital national decisions are made in darkness; we preach justice in the world, yet promote our worst perpetrators. Orwell is a bestseller in America again for good reason.

Whistleblowers remind us of all this. They cry out when doublespeak and doublethink have become second nature to many. They confront us with the lie that our national life has become, when the formal statements and aspirations of our republic clash with our daily actions. We must learn to hear their voices, to escape as they have the spell of secrecy and authoritarianism, if we hope to awake from this deadly daze.

The Banana Republic
Wasn't Built in a Day

Let not any one pacify his conscience by the delusion that he can do no harm if
he takes no part, and forms no opinion. Bad men need nothing more to compass their ends, than that good men should look on and do nothing. He is not
a good man who, without a protest, allows wrong to be committed in his name,
and with the means which he helps to supply, because he will not trouble himself to use his mind on the subject. It depends on the habit of attending to and
looking into public transactions, and on the degree of information and solid
judgment respecting them that exists in the community, whether the conduct
of the nation as a nation, both within itself and towards others, shall be selfish,
corrupt and tyrannical, or rational and enlightened, just and noble.

> John Stuart Mill, inaugural address delivered
> at the University of St. Andrews, 1867

The point of modern propaganda isn't only to misinform or push an agenda. It
is to exhaust your critical thinking, to annihilate truth.

> Garry Kasparov, Twitter, December 13, 2016

This book took shape long before Donald Trump entered politics. I conducted
the first interviews in 2012, shortly before Barack Obama's reelection, and its
themes emerged—and its scope widened—gradually over subsequent years, as I
spoke with more than two hundred whistleblowers, scores of attorneys, advocates,
politicians, historians, government watchdogs, intelligence analysts, cognitive scientists and other experts. Time and again, whistleblowers and their allies mentioned a handful of traits in their workplaces, private or public, that had pushed
them past obedience, fear or self-interest, and compelled them to speak out. They

mentioned conflicts of interest, revolving doors, and the resulting betrayal of the organization or the public good for the profit of the few. They described how corporate contractors, lamprey-like, drained the life out of government institutions they worked for, sapping the sense of public service. They denounced the normalization, even the celebration, of financial crime in corporate America; the spread of hypocrisy; and the idolization of money as an end in itself, which increasingly transcends law, morality and professional responsibility.

As these root causes of whistleblowing surfaced in my reporting, Donald Trump was becoming a political force, by speaking, in a sense, the language of whistleblowing, publicly denouncing the crimes that harm us all. He said that as a businessman, he was disgusted with the corruption and cronyism of Washington politics, promising to "drain the swamp" of DC lobbyists and to "make our government honest once again." He condemned pharmaceutical companies for "getting away with murder" with their price gouging and theft from Medicare; he lambasted hedge funds and Wall Street banks (Goldman Sachs in particular) as enemies of Main Street Americans. He condemned the "catastrophic" US intelligence blunders that had invented weapons of mass destruction in Iraq and missed the all too real attacks of 9/11, and he rejected the ensuing wars in the Middle East as colossal wastes of American blood and money, whose perpetrators, including George W. Bush, should be tried as war criminals. "I love WikiLeaks," he told a crowd in October 2016, after the organization had published damaging information on Hillary Clinton's actions when she was secretary of state, one of five times he publicly praised Julian Assange's activities on the campaign trail. On Inauguration Day, he announced that he was transferring power in government from Beltway elites to the American people. Whatever one may have thought of Donald Trump as a man, his broadsides hit home.

Having sealed the biggest deal of his life and become the United States' forty-fifth president, however, Trump proceeded as anyone with even a passing knowledge of his past should have expected. He put Big Pharma in charge of healthcare and the FDA, and Goldman Sachs and other banks in all important financial roles, and handed the Pentagon even more money to continue the killing in the Middle East. Corporate lobbyists and CEOs run many departments, where deregulation, de-penalization and de-supervision are their creed. Trump transacts much of his presidential business at Mar-a-Lago, his golf resort in Florida, and at other Trump-branded properties. His daughter and son-in-law have assumed outsize roles in running the country, while retaining their interest in the Trump Organization—an almost unimaginable conflict of interest.

When Americans encounter such behavior in foreign lands, most call it corruption. When they see fabulously wealthy foreigners assuming state powers to enrich themselves and their inner circle, placing their offspring in positions of unwarranted authority, they brand these people oligarchs or dictators, and their children princelings. Yet in Trump's America—in *our* America over the last quarter century—this same behavior has routinely been justified with pragmatic talk of free markets, deregulation, costs and benefits, and of running government like a business. We've dubbed our homegrown oligarchs billionaires, and now name buildings and libraries after them, let them secrete their wealth in offshore tax havens, allow them to pay politicians unlimited funds to buy access and push through the fiscal "reforms" and government downsizing they cherish, to buy sports teams for which they build new stadiums with taxpayer money, complete with sky boxes from which they can look down upon the taxpaying multitudes. And many of us revere these homegrown oligarchs as paragons of the American Dream.

The historical arc of this book, and the voices of its whistleblowers, suggest some of the shifts that made a person of Donald Trump's qualities eligible for the American presidency. Under Kennedy, LBJ, and Nixon, the doctrine of massive military overspending commandeered the US economy, as the Cold War fear entrenched a priestly caste of military leaders and fed an epidemic of secrecy in our national security apparatus. Reagan's poisonous yet seductively lucrative dogma held that greater military spending paid for by ballooning national debt made the United States safer; that government was a problem, to be solved by the aggressive privatization of public assets; and that deregulated free enterprise was the engine of national prosperity. Above all, Reagan championed the idea, succinctly expressed by his friend Margaret Thatcher, that society itself is a myth: that the essence of life is self-interested individuals locked in an endless struggle for economic dominance.

Bill Clinton, the beneficiary of a booming economy, traded the historic

Democratic voter base, the working middle classes, for the Wall Street financial class. George W. Bush seized on the nation's disorientation and moral numbness after 9/11 to bypass the traditional channels and conventions of government, embracing illegal wars, torture, assassination, kidnapping and domestic spying as tools of state, and allowing contractors to construct a parasitic shadow government whose unprecedented war profiteering and gross corruption it became unpatriotic, even treasonous, to challenge.

After years of endless war and institutionalized financial fraud had destabilized America, Barack Obama took office promising change, yet proceeded, through both acquiescence and action, to normalize the abuses Bush had introduced as wartime exigencies, and add a few of his own. He confirmed the de facto role of Wall Street as the ruler of the US economy, and war as America's default condition. He staunchly defended Bush's torturers, kidnappers and other war criminals from prosecution, or even from opprobrium. He endorsed extralegal drone assassinations as an appropriate policy of a nation of laws, and mass surveillance of innocent US citizens as the right and the duty of the US government. And throughout, he attacked, relentlessly and vindictively, the few national security insiders (and several journalists) who questioned his betrayals of the Constitution and the people.

Donald J. Trump's victory has revealed how hollow the edifice of American democracy has become, how insubstantial its checks and balances, after decades of self-interested chiseling, reaming, drilling and blasting by various experts and insiders—the lawyers, soldiers, scholars, financiers, think tankers and policy makers who have probed deep into every crevice of the body politic from which tax dollars could be extracted. Many Americans standing at the gates for the last two decades and looking in at this merry banquet, with its swirl of public and private players, its bewildering disappearing and reappearing acts, the vast sums of money carried in and consumed, believed that government in the United States—that democracy itself—was broken. Some chose Trump to fix it. After decades of self-dealing, financial pillage, legal chicanery and illegitimate wars, perhaps they felt, What do we have to lose?

Others stood aghast at his election, which seemed to them the hijacking of a nation. American exceptionalism had become so deeply ingrained, on the left and on the right, that most of us had missed what whistleblowers and a few other clear-eyed Cassandras were saying all along: that the banana republic we have long scorned in poor, distant lands has grown up around us, as big and brash as a Trump casino. That, believing ourselves immune to tyranny, we have surrendered, one by one, the laws, norms, customs and habits of mind that shielded us from the tyrant. As Bill Binney says, "We've stopped acting like Americans."

Donald Trump is the incarnation of the same corruptions that have inaugurated the age of whistleblowing. His presidency and business empire are shrouded in secrecy, and in corresponding doubts about their legitimacy and legality. His tax records, his over five hundred limited liability shell companies that release no audited financial statements, the repeated reports of organized crime figures and Russian oligarchs laundering money through Trump properties, his bizarre loans of over $2 billion from Deutsche Bank made when no other firm would loan him money, while the bank itself was laundering billions in Russian cash . . . all this remains opaque. Trump extracts NDAs from his White House employees and his corporate employees alike, and issues gag orders in executive branch agencies; when he can't buy silence in advance, he writes a check after the fact to porn stars and *Playboy* playmates with whom he is said to have had sex, or has accommodating tabloids catch and kill their stories. Secrecy shrouds his involvement with Russian election tampering, money laundering and obstruction of justice even after the completion of the report by Special Prosecutor Robert Mueller. Is democracy possible in a country where so little is publicly known about the constitutional leader?

Donald Trump personifies a morbid fusion of public and private. He and his immediate family proudly profit from the White House "brand," thumbing their noses at the Constitution's emoluments clause. Unsurprisingly, Trump's picks to run his government are cut from the same cloth. An October 2017 analysis found that of the 341 people he nominated to Senate-confirmed posts, 105 had previously worked in the industries that they were now charged with regulating, while another 63 had lobbied or lawyered there. Trump's cabinet and senior advisers have such glaring conflicts of interest that conflicts appear to have been an important job qualification. Some have devoted their previous professional lives to bending or breaking the very rules that, as agency heads, they now profess to defend, and they stand to benefit richly from the further deregulation they have conducted. People like charter school advocate and entrepreneur Betsy DeVos at the Department of Education, Big Pharma executives Alex Azar at HHS and Scott Gottlieb at FDA, banker Steve Mnuchin at the Treasury, Wall Street lawyer Jay Clayton at SEC, finance moguls Carl Icahn and Stephen Schwarzman as White House economic advisers, union buster and distressed-debt guru Wilbur Ross at Commerce, mining and energy booster Ryan Zinke and his successor, David Bernhardt, at the Interior, and Big Ag farmer Sonny Perdue at Agriculture have all openly pursued their personal careers and industry agendas from positions of government authority. Other Trump nominees, like Scott Pruitt and his replacement, Andrew Wheeler, at the EPA, Rick Perry at Energy, Exxon CEO Rex Tillerson at State, and Mick Mulvaney at the Consumer Financial Protection Bureau, were evidently tasked with demolishing their government offices, and proceeded with gusto, scorning the laws they swore to uphold.

These people embody the sweeping redefinition of fraud as clever business that has occurred in our society. Mnuchin and Ross both made fortunes with banks that specialized in high-speed foreclosures after the 2008 crisis and were found in court to have systematically employed illegal methods. DeVos began her new job by disbanding a team of investigators looking into predatory for-profit colleges, some of which had already paid hundred-million-dollar settlements for fraud; for good measure, she placed deans and lawyers from those colleges in leading positions in Education. At the Consumer Financial Protection Bureau, Mulvaney quashed investigations and lawsuits into payday lenders and recidivist fraudster banks including Wells Fargo. Trump's DOJ gutted its Health Care Corporate Fraud Strike Force and reassigned most of its prosecutors; the number of white-collar crime cases they are pursuing has fallen to a twenty-year low. Meanwhile, Special Counsel Robert Mueller and New York prosecutors caught a series of key Trump operatives in an astonishing list of felony offenses, including bank fraud and tax evasion, conspiring to launder money, obstruction of justice, and lying to Congress and to the FBI.

Trump, of course, has set the tone at the top. Like most corporations and wealthy individuals, he has resolved decades of legal actions against him—antitrust violations, tenant intimidation, beauty pageant scandals, failing to pay hundreds of workers and contractors, the boiler room fraud vehicle known as "Trump University," and much else—by signing settlements, sealing the underlying facts, admitting no guilt and forging ahead. Trump behaves as if he were above the law—and, at least as laws against financial crimes are currently interpreted and enforced in the United States, he is. He often speaks like a gangland figure. "I need loyalty, I expect loyalty," he told FBI director James Comey. When Comey demurred, Trump fired him.

Trump is the supreme money dancer, whose career embodies the primacy of cash over ethics, the law, personal honor and public service: of life as a game scored in dollars, where the player with the biggest money roll wins, and only the winning matters. His entanglements with a cast of rich, slippery Russians and his fascination with Putin make perfect sense. When the oligarchic class arose from the Wild West of Soviet dissolution in the early 1990s, with a helping hand from the United States, these instant billionaires began secreting their money abroad—and where better to do so than in a Trump-branded condo in Manhattan or Miami? Other neo-billionaires in the United States, Africa, Asia, Europe and elsewhere, unwilling to risk losing their riches to taxes or unsympathetic governments, did the same. Trump, with his maze of shell companies, is just such a plutocrat, as are many of his circle. The Paradise Papers provide glimpses of the secret financial dealings of a dozen Trump advisers, donors and cabinet secretaries, cheek by jowl with a score of Russian oligarchs. Sometimes they do business together: Secretary of Commerce Wilbur Ross, we learn, was vice chairman of the Bank of Cyprus, a favorite financial haven for Russian oligarchs, as well as a partner in a shipping company tied to US-sanctioned oligarch Gennady Timchenko—a fact Ross forgot to mention during his January 2017 confirmation hearings. (Steven Mnuchin, with a similar lapse of memory, neglected to report in his Senate financial disclosures various shell companies, funds, and almost $100 million in real estate in the Cayman Islands and Anguilla.)

For such leaders, the notion of national allegiance, of "America First," is deeply foreign: their overriding loyalty is to their clans and their assets. Trump openly espouses oligarchy. At a June 2017 rally, he explained that he'd chosen the ultrarich for the key posts in his government "because that's the kind of thinking we want," adding, "I love all people, rich or poor, but in those particular positions, I just don't want a poor person." Living large, making a killing by abrogating laws, economic rules and social responsibilities and then flaunting that killing, isn't merely tolerated under Trump—it's applauded. Whatever help the Russians gave Trump in the 2016 elections, and whatever blackmail leverage Putin may have on Trump after decades of shadowy business deals in Russia, the two men have gravitated together because they share a worldview: the attitude of a czar over his serfs, not an elected ruler among his fellow citizens.

Unsurprisingly, the excesses of the Trump administration have triggered an unprecedented level of whistleblowing and leaking. According to data released by the DOJ in March 2019, the number of leaks of classified information reported by federal agencies reached record levels during the first two years of the Trump administration—an average of 104 leak referrals per year in 2017 and 2018, as compared with 39 leaks per year under Barack Obama. Officials in the EPA and the Department of the Interior, the FBI and Homeland Security have publicly denounced what they see as abrogations of their organization's central responsibilities. Members of the IRS and the Treasury have revealed evidence of wrongdoing by two disgraced members of Trump's circle, Michael Cohen and Paul Manafort—and been swiftly prosecuted for doing so. Within the White House, whistleblowers both named and anonymous have disclosed scores of irregularities, including Trump's approval of dozens of security clearances despite the concerns of career security advisers that the recipients of the clearances might be subject to foreign influence or blackmail.

DOJ officials have also denounced what they saw as wrongdoing within their department. In January 2017, Acting Attorney General Sally Yates ordered DOJ lawyers not to defend Trump's executive order on travel and immigration because it might be illegal, and also warned Trump that his national security adviser Michael Flynn had lied about his contacts with Russia. (Trump fired Yates for insubordination; two weeks later Flynn was forced to resign.) Hui Chen, a compliance adviser in the DOJ's fraud section, resigned because, she said, the cognitive dissonance in her work had become unsustainable: while questioning companies about their commitment to ethics and compliance, Chen saw her own executive branch become embroiled in conflicts, potential violations of the Constitution and possible treason. "Those are conducts I would not tolerate seeing in a company, yet I worked under an administration that engaged in exactly those conduct[s]. I wanted no more part in it."

An even higher-profile DOJ whistleblower was James Comey, who as FBI director in the early weeks of Trump's presidency released a memorandum to the press in which he described Trump appearing to ask Comey to end his investigation into Flynn. This seems surprising behavior from an FBI director who was such a fervent adversary of Edward Snowden and other national security whistleblowers, and before that, as Lockheed Martin's top lawyer, was in charge of combating whistleblower complaints. Comey told Congress he leaked the memo because he felt he "needed to get that [information] out into the public square"—a motivation he'd often heard from national security whistleblowers whom he'd pursued. (With delicious irony, Vladimir Putin offered Comey political asylum in Russia, as he had to Snowden, and Snowden himself denounced Comey's firing on Twitter: "This FBI Director has sought for years to jail me on account of my political activities. If I can oppose his firing, so can you.") Comey said he considered this memo and others he'd prepared after meetings with Trump to be unclassified, though a subsequent review by the bureau concluded that at least four of them contained classified information; Comey may also have violated the confidentiality agreement that he signed when he joined the FBI. So, like many whistleblowers he had targeted, Comey may have broken certain oaths and agreements in order to obey a higher allegiance.

In response to the unprecedented surge in unauthorized disclosures that began with his election, Trump has imposed gag orders and anti-leak training on government departments, and has forced senior White House staff to sign lifetime nondisclosure agreements—moves that violate whistleblower law. At Trump's urging, the DOJ has stepped up its pursuit of leakers and whistleblowers, and has continued the Obama administration's pursuit not just of government leakers but also of the reporters they communicate with. On May 23, 2019, underscoring how much Trump "loved" both WikiLeaks and journalistic freedom, his Justice Department indicted Julian Assange on seventeen counts of violating the Espionage Act, for helping Chelsea Manning to obtain and publish a trove of classified documents about the wars in Iraq and Afghanistan. (The British authorities had arrested

Assange on April 11, after Ecuadorian officials withdrew his citizenship.) Such novel charges could criminalize the acquisition and publishing of classified documents. Daniel Ellsberg says: "The arrest of Julian Assange and the two unprecedented indictments against him constitute the most significant and ominous attack on the First Amendment and freedom of the press since the Nixon administration's attempt to enjoin the *New York Times* from publishing the Pentagon Papers in 1971 and my subsequent prosecution (as a source) for copying them. This is the first use of the Espionage Act against a journalist, and I'm sure it won't be the last, especially if Assange is extradited to the US and stands trial." Yet for all his wrath at truth tellers within his government, Donald Trump himself, knowingly or not, sometimes acts like a leaker: during a May 10, 2017, meeting in the White House, for example, he revealed highly classified information about a possible ISIS terror tactic to senior Russian officials, data that an intelligence source told the *Washington Post* was so sensitive that the United States had not even shared it with American allies. Technically, US presidents can't be leakers or whistleblowers, because they instantaneously declassify virtually any information by the act of expressing it. But how do we know about Trump's revelation to the Russians in the first place, which took place behind closed doors in the Oval Office? How do we know that during the same meeting, Trump bragged to the Russians of having fired FBI director James Comey the previous day because of his Russia investigation, and called Comey "a real nut job"?

These revelations, and many others that have emerged from the heart of Trump's cabinet, can only have come from high-level sources in his administration and in US security agencies. But were these revelations made by a low-level staffer based on a more senior person's notes about an event, or directly by the senior official, who could put the event in a larger context? Were they motivated by love of country or a desire to discredit Trump—or both? If some of the legion of Trump leakers were to reveal their identities and become public whistleblowers, this might help us to assess the nature and value of their information. (Of course, as under past administrations, they would promptly be prosecuted, and would cease to provide information from inside the White House.) Trump himself has repeatedly attacked these anonymous leakers as "un-American," "criminal," and "a grave threat to our national security." If they were public whistleblowers, perhaps we'd know whether he's right.

On September 5, 2018, the *New York Times* took the rare step of publishing an anonymous op-ed by what the paper called "a senior official in the Trump administration." Though celebrating the deregulation, tax cuts and military buildup achieved under Trump, the author lamented the president's lack of commitment to "free minds, free markets and free people," his amorality, and the mental instability that could, he implied, make Trump unfit to discharge the duties of the presidency according to the Twenty-Fifth Amendment. The author announced that he and a cabal of senior Trump officials, whom he referred to as the "adults in the room," moved by their sense of duty to the country and its democratic institutions, had vowed to "steer the administration in the right direction," to "frustrate" and to "thwart" Trump's "more misguided impulses."

This isn't whistleblowing, an act intended to call out but also to halt wrongdoing. It is the self-serving announcement of an unelected shadow government, an authentic deep state that wishes to distance itself from the aberrant acts of the constitutionally elected leader while employing the power he lends them to advance agendas of their own. In this situation, a true whistleblower would have stepped into the spotlight, bolstering his assertions with professional gravitas and personal conviction, and launched a movement to remove Trump on constitutional grounds. Instead, this anonymous writer claims to defend US democracy while tearing up the Constitution. For once, I'm with Trump: this is treason.

The authentic whistleblowers we need now are not figures like these, who leak anonymously while continuing to wield (illegitimate) power. Nor are they likely to be the James Comeys or Robert Muellers, who are simply moving from one node to the next in their flexian networks. Comey's earlier stint in government during the Clinton and then the Bush administration—where, as deputy attorney general, he endorsed the use of waterboarding, wall slamming and other brutal interrogation methods—was followed by his time as general counsel at Lockheed Martin and on the senior management committee of Ray Dalio's hedge fund Bridgewater, from which he received a $3 million payout upon returning to government as director of the FBI. Special Counsel Robert Mueller served stints of his own at white-collar defense law firms and lobby shops, and, as FBI director for twelve years beginning just before 9/11, presided over an era of government-sanctioned torture, kidnapping, illicit interrogation and erosion of constitutional rights; Mueller defended warrantless surveillance and admitted using data from illegal NSA intercepts in his investigations, through a legally dubious practice known as "parallel construction." Robert Khuzami followed his term at the SEC with a stint at Kirkland & Ellis, then revolved back into government service in the Southern District of New York after Trump's election, perhaps to mitigate any awkward questions that might arise about Trump's odd, ruble-tinged debts to Deutsche Bank. Here Khuzami led the investigation of Trump's former attorney Michael Cohen—but, given Khuzami's history, we may be skeptical of his pronouncement, on the day of Cohen's guilty plea, that the case's outcome proved that "we are a nation of laws, with one set of rules that applies equally to everyone."

Real whistleblowers enjoy far less illustrious careers—and after their revelations, typically have no careers at all. Some may see sharper lines between right and wrong than more "successful" people. By temperament, they may be more straightforward and down-to-earth, more egalitarian, less respectful or fearful of authority. They may perceive the harm they witness as having specific victims. Most of us experience tragedies in our lives, but as Margaret Heffernan suggests in *Wilful Blindness*, certain people learn through such hardships to see not "through the eyes of power, but through the eyes of the vulnerable." A parent's early death or a struggle with illness or disability, a family's sudden descent into poverty, sometimes heightens a whistleblower's sensitivity to the human suffering of others. On a family car trip, Daniel Ellsberg's father fell asleep at the wheel, and his mother and sister died in the ensuing crash. Ellsberg said in a 2009 interview, "I think it did probably leave the impression on me that someone . . . you loved, like my father, or respected, an authority, could fall asleep at the wheel, and had to be watched."

A poor, rural upbringing gives certain whistleblowers the ability to shake off fear of retaliation. "How are you going to scare me by taking away my stuff, when I grew up without any stuff?" asks Rick Parks, who also cites his childhood in a small town, where everyone knew everyone else, as having made him less willing to ignore what might happen if he failed to call out the threat of nuclear disaster at

Three Mile Island. A humble background also appears to lend some whistleblowers a sense of resilience, an awareness of alternative ways of being that can break the spell of the team. "It was hard to give it all up, to stop being the Golden Boy," one anonymous whistleblower, born and raised in blue-collar Birmingham, told me of his decision to blow the whistle on his posh bank in the City of London. "But I'd never really felt part of the club to begin with." It may be for this reason that Justice Louis Brandeis, like Thomas Jefferson before him, praised small communities, where an engaged citizenry could learn to serve and preserve the common good, as the best incubators of democracy; and why Brandeis conversely warned of the "curse of bigness"—unhealthy concentrations of power and capital that lead to inequality, inefficiency, and competition-killing oligarchy.

Often, though, it seems mere chance, a lucky trick of timing, that makes whistleblowers see the world differently. Noreen Harrington, a corporate finance executive whose bank was using little-known practices to skim about $4 billion a year off mutual funds, mostly from smaller investors, found the courage—or the clarity—to blow the whistle after she happened to review her own sister's 401(k) savings account, and saw how such financial tactics were bleeding her sister's retirement fund dry. "Up until then, I hadn't really thought about the human toll," Harrington said in a 2004 interview. "After I looked at it from the bottom up, then I couldn't sleep at night. I knew I had to call somebody." She called Eliot Spitzer, then attorney general of New York, who successfully prosecuted her bank and other offenders.

The truth is, there is no whistleblower "type," no one personality with unique potential to call out wrongdoing. "People are constantly asking what kind of person would blow the whistle," says Kathleen McClellan of ExposeFacts. "For me, it's a bad question. Everyone, in the right circumstances, could do it—or could fail to."

Which means we all have the capacity to speak truth to power. The scores of whistleblowers in this book, the hundreds I've spoken with and the thousands I've never heard of, embody an independence of spirit, a fearlessness, we desperately need. They take responsibility for seeing with their own eyes and following their individual conscience, cutting through cant and rationalization to comprehend things as they really are. They show us why we cannot always accept the technical artifacts of "experts"—their algorithms and spreadsheets—as anything more than the objective-looking concretizations of their own subjectivity and self-interest, or confuse their expertise with probity. Whistleblowers understand that people in groups do things that group members individually would never dream or dare. They know to be leery of the motives of large organizations—that David is typically a more trustworthy and committed ally of the common good than Goliath. They remind that nearly all of us are the children of Stanley Milgram; that we must constantly question authority in all of its forms, and resist the false solace of submission. Whistleblowers strip away absurd euphemisms, revealing bedrock meanings: that corporations are not people, any more than dollars are speech; that "campaign contribution" has become shorthand for "bribe," and "legal settlement" for hush money; and that "deregulation," like "privatization," usually translates into generous gains for the few at great cost to the many. At the same time, whistleblowers reveal the dark side of loyalty, patriotism, and devotion to the team, and show that other words, however debased by cynicism, still have a substance that we long for: honor, duty, justice, virtue, truth.

Many of us, at some level, understand all this, but often, in a frenetic, attention-deficit world, we forget. Whistleblowers remind us to slow down, teach us to remember. They show through their actions that life, after all, is not a game, that all acts have consequences, and that we may choose not to dance to even the most seductive music. They tell us to listen instead for the quiet but insistent drumbeat of our conscience. Whistleblowers prove the remarkable power of one righteous voice, and the possibility of setting aside cynicism and pragmatism to live a life guided by ideals, with all the risks and sacrifices this implies. This affirmation of idealism, and its attendant hope, may be the whistleblower's most precious gift.

Their self-possession may even lend us the courage we will need to reclaim entire realms of civic life—politics, justice, teaching, lawmaking, warfighting—that have steadily been removed from our sight and control. They remind that to witness wrongdoing and fail to intervene is to become an accomplice. As Hannah Arendt said after the Reichstag fire, "I was no longer of the opinion that one can simply be a bystander." Or as another refugee from Nazi-dominated Europe, Lotte Scharfman, reportedly observed: "Democracy is not a spectator sport." Whistleblowers demonstrate how citizenship in dangerous times must be dynamic—how it demands not just pure thoughts and good words but strong, sometimes dangerous deeds, which in turn become narratives that spur others to act. In a very real way, whistleblowing *is* citizenship.

For we cannot rely on a handful of whistleblowers alone to save our democracy. As Edward Snowden said in a 2015 interview, "If we as a society are reliant on asking volunteers to stand up and self-immolate to report a wrongdoing, we will very quickly find ourselves out of volunteers." In a sense, the concept of blowing the whistle needs to disappear—it must become a routine act, just as many whistleblowers consider it: simply a part of working, and living, right. The changes our society needs run deeper than better laws, regulations, compliance programs and hotlines. We need to affirm the essential patriotism of dissent, to celebrate sharp tongues and sovereign minds as our purest duties.

Can this really be so hard, in a nation that professes to revere its Founders, those bold, rebellious, tirelessly provocative truth tellers?

Notes

CHAPTER 1. BECOMING A WHISTLEBLOWER

These annotations aim to help readers explore the legal underpinnings of my narrative—the complaints, indictments, amicus curiae briefs, depositions, trial transcripts, judicial opinions and other court documents that provide a rich yet often undervalued record of vital events. They suggest a few pathways into the broad landscapes of learning that relate to whistleblowing as a social, legal, economic, psychological, biological, philosophical and historical phenomenon. I hope their breadth, if not their comprehensiveness, conveys the importance of whistleblowing as a symptom and a potential cure to many ills of our age. Much of the information in this book derives from interviews with whistleblowers and their attorneys, as well as prosecutors, defense lawyers, government and private investigators, congressional staffers, scholars, consultants, bankers, soldiers, intelligence officials, federal judges and other experts. I would have liked in these annotations to acknowledge, by name, the hundreds of people who aided and guided my work, but many agreed to speak with me only anonymously. So to all of my sources, named and nameless, and particularly to the whistleblowers: thanks for your generosity, acumen and courage, which have made this book possible.

Chapter 1 is based in part on personal communication with Natalie Arbaugh, Howard Berman, Jim Breen, Patrick Burns, Tom Devine, Linda Douglass, Clark Kent Ervin, Peggy Finerty, Neil Getnick, Chuck Grassley, Eric Havian, Jim Helmer, Mary Inman, Allen Jones, Craig Karch, Steve Kohn, Greg Krakauer, Colette Matzzie, Vince McKnight, Tom Melsheimer, Marcia Miceli, Margaret Moore, Rick Morgan, Mickey Nardo, Janet Near, Cynthia O'Keeffe, John Phillips, Marc Raspanti, Shelley Slade, Tom Smith, Patrick Sweeten, Claire Sylvia, Jennifer Verkamp and Jason Zuckerman.

Details of the investigation of pharmaceutical companies that Allen Jones performed while working at the Pennsylvania OIG, his civil rights and whistleblower lawsuits against members of the Pennsylvania OIG, and his qui tam lawsuit under the Texas Medicaid Fraud Prevention Act against Janssen, Johnson & Johnson and other organizations, are available in the extensive court filings from these cases: Dwight L. McKee and Allen L. Jones v. Henry Hart et al., US District Court for the Middle District of Pennsylvania, case no. 4:CV-02-1910; Allen L. Jones v. Jeffrey Goble et al., US District Court for the Middle District of Pennsylvania, case no. 3:04-CV-1914; Allen L. Jones v. Jeffrey Goble et al., US District Court for the Middle District of Pennsylvania, case no. 3:04-CV-1914-ARC; and State of Texas ex rel. Allen Jones v. Janssen LP et al., 250th District Court of Texas, case no. D-1-GV-04-001288. (Full video of the trial is available at the Courtroom View Network.)

Quotes from Jones's colleagues at the OIG, and accounts of the workplace retaliation and eventual termination he underwent, are available in depositions taken during the above-cited litigation in Pennsylvania. The design and evolution of TMAP, PennMAP and similar schemes in other states are detailed in the extensive court documents from *State of Texas ex rel. Allen Jones*. Of particular importance in these documents are testimony and written reports prepared by distinguished expert witnesses retained by Allen Jones's legal team, who analyzed voluminous internal documentation supplied by the defendants during legal discovery and pieced together the details of the alleged wrongdoing. For the purposes of this book, the most significant expert witness reports are by Joseph Glenmullen, MD; David J. Rothman, PhD; Robert Rosenheck, MD; and Arnold I. Friede, Esq. For further insights on the Texas trial, see a series of perceptive, scientifically rigorous blog posts written by Dr. Mickey Nardo, a veteran psychiatrist and professor of residency training at Emory University in Atlanta, who attended the trial and got to know Allen Jones (his blog is *1 Boring Old Man*).

Also helpful in delineating the role of Alex Gorsky, current CEO of Johnson & Johnson and former senior executive at Janssen, in the development of the Risperdal marketing plan, are these two documents, both filed with the Court of Common Pleas, First Judicial District of the Pennsylvania Civil Trial Division in the case of AB, a minor, et al. v. Janssen Pharmaceuticals, et al., in re: Risperdal Litigation, March Term 2010, No. 296: a memorandum filed on September 9, 2012, by Brian J. McCormick, Esq., of the Sheller Law Offices, in re: Risperdal Litigation, March Term 2010, No. 296; and the deposition of Alex Gorsky taken on May 18, 2012, at the law offices of Drinker, Biddle & Reath, LLP, in Princeton, New Jersey. The "drug usage evaluation" that Allen Jones reviewed is a memorandum prepared by the Pennsylvania Office of Mental Health & Substance Abuse Services and other entities, dated January 2002, available in the filings to *State of Texas ex rel. Allen Jones*.

On Tom Ridge, see Clark Kent Ervin, *Open Target* (New York, 2006). Ervin was the inspector general of Homeland Security under Ridge, and became a whistleblower-like figure at the Department for pointing out security vulnerabilities there, for which Ridge viewed him "as a traitor and a turncoat." In Ervin's account, Ridge told him angrily: "Look, Clark. Are you *my* Inspector General? When I was Governor of Pennsylvania, I had an Inspector General, but he wasn't out there like you constantly criticizing and embarrassing us." Clark replied: "Well, sir, you've put your finger on the problem we're having here. The fact is I'm not *your* Inspector General; I'm the American people's Inspector General."

Important analyses of Johnson & Johnson's marketing of Risperdal, the TMAP program, and the involvement in TMAP of distinguished psychiatrists like Allen Frances, David Kahn and John Docherty include Paula Caplan, "Diagnosisgate: Conflict of Interest at the Top of the Psychiatric Apparatus," *Aporia* (January 1, 2015); and Steven Brill's fifteen-part "America's Most Admired Lawbreaker," *Huffington Post Highline* (published online starting September 15, 2015), which considers a civil suit against Johnson & Johnson by parents of children harmed by Risperdal. See also Brill's book, *Tailspin* (New York, 2018), which contains priceless insights into the DOJ's prosecution of Johnson & Johnson—and failure to prosecute Alex Gorsky. About corruption and conflict of interest in psychiatry more generally, see Robert Whitaker and Lisa Cosgrove, *Psychiatry Under the Influence* (New York, 2015); Lisa Cosgrove and Sheldon Krimsky, "A Comparison of *DSM*-IV and *DSM*-5 Panel Members' Financial Associations with Industry: A Pernicious Problem Persists," *PLoS Medicine* (March 2012); Michael Makhinson, "Biases in Medication Prescribing: The Case of Second-Generation Antipsychotics," *Journal of Psychiatric Practice* (January 2010); David Healy, "Manufacturing Consensus," *Hastings Center Reports* (July–August 2004); and Mark Olfson, Carlos Blanco et al., "National Trends in the Outpatient Treatment of Children and Adolescents with Antipsychotic Drugs," *Archives of General Psychiatry* (June 2006). Allen Frances, one of the psychiatrists who helped shape and disseminate TMAP, has subsequently taken a very different position on overmedication and financial conflicts of interest in psychiatry; see, for example, his book *Saving Normal: An Insider's Revolt Against Out-of-Control Psychiatric Diagnosis, DSM-5, Big Pharma, and the Medicalization of Ordinary Life* (New York, 2013). Regarding the activities of Dr. Joseph Biederman, see the legal motion filed on September 9, 2012, by Brian J. McCormick, Esq., in re: Risperdal Litigation, March Term 2010, No. 296, and the May 18, 2012, deposition of Alex Gorsky, Court of Common Pleas, Pennsylvania. See also the annual report from 2002 of the Johnson & Johnson Center for Pediatric Psychopathology at the Massachusetts General Hospital. More generally, see Gardiner Harris, "Research Center Tied to Drug Company," *New York Times* (November 24, 2008); and Marcia Angell, "Drug Companies & Doctors: A Story of Corruption," *New York Review of Books* (January 15, 2009). (More on conflict of interest in various professions below, in notes to Chapters 3 and 4.)

For the general historical background on qui tam laws and the False Claims Act, see the exhaustive treatment by James Helmer, *False Claims Act: Whistleblower Litigation* (7th ed., New York, 2017); and a clear encapsulation by J. Randy Beck, "The False Claims Act and the English Eradication of Qui Tam Legislation," *North Carolina Law Review* (April 1, 2000). See also Charles Doyle, "Qui Tam: The False Claims Act and Related Federal Statutes," Congressional Research Service (rev. version, February 25, 2013); the Supreme Court briefs and amicus curiae briefs to the important case of Vermont Agency of Natural Resources v. United States ex rel. Stevens 529 US 765 (2000), decided May 22, 2000; and T. J. Halstead, "Constitutional Aspects of Qui Tam Actions: Background and Analysis of Issues in Vermont Agency of Natural Resources v. United States ex rel. Stevens," Congressional Research Service (March 8, 2000). On the evolution of whistleblowing more broadly, see Robert G. Vaughn's seminal *The Successes and Failures of Whistleblower Law* (Cheltenham, 2012), with its invaluable range of insights into the rise of whistleblowing written by a former Nader's Raider and protagonist in that rise. See also Steve (Stephen Martin) Kohn, *The Whistleblower's Handbook* (3rd ed., Guilford, CT, 2017); Tom Devine and Tarek F. Maassarani, *The Corporate Whistleblower's Survival Guide* (Washington, DC, 2011); "Caught Between Conscience and Career," a whistleblowing guide published online by POGO (March 20, 2019); GAO report *Whistleblowers: Key Practices for Congress to Consider When Receiving and Referring Information*, May 7, 2019; and *International Handbook on Whistleblowing Research* (Cheltenham, UK, 2014), edited by A. J. Brown, author of important analyses of the nature of the whistleblowing act.

Regarding whistleblowing in the Revolutionary period, see *Journals of the Continental Congress*, vol. 7 (January 1–May 21, 1777), at Tuesday, March 25, p. 202; vol. 11 (May 2–September 1, 1778), at Thursday, July 30, p. 732; and vol. 14 (April 23–September 1, 1779) at Saturday, May 22, pp. 627–28. An overview and contextualization of these incidents is provided in *The Whistleblower's Handbook*. (For an account that defends Esek Hopkins's position in the affair, see Edward Field, *Esek Hopkins, Commander-in-Chief* . . . [Providence, RI, 1898].) Texts that examine the intellectual background of the Founders include Daniel Robinson and Richard Williams, eds., *The American Founding* (New York, 2012); Bernard Bailyn, *To Begin the World Anew* (New York, 2003); Richard B. Bernstein, *The Founding Fathers Reconsidered* (New York, 2009); Saul K. Padover, ed., *World of the Founding Fathers* (South Brunswick, NJ, 1977); Carl J. Richard, *The Founders and the Classics* (Cambridge, MA, 1994); and David Colclough, *Freedom of Speech in Early Stuart England* (Cambridge, UK, 2005).

On the Civil War–era enactment of the False Claims Act, in addition to Helmer, Beck, Halstead and Doyle cited above, see also the discussion of the FCA in the Cong. Globe, 37th Cong., 3rd Sess. (February 14, 1863), pp. 952–58; and *A Century of Lawmaking for a New Nation: U.S. Congressional Documents and Debates, 1774–1875*, Bills and Resolutions, Senate, 37th Cong., 3rd Sess., S. 506 introduced on February 6, 1863. See the excellent discussion in Shelley Slade and Brian Leneis, "Congressman Charles H. Van Wyck: Anti-Fraud Warrior of the 37th Congress," published by Vogel, Slade & Goldstein, LLP, a Washington, DC, law firm that represents FCA whistleblowers; the report of the House Committee on the Judiciary on the False Claims Act Correction Act of 2009, May 5, 2009; and Ron Soodalter, "The Union's 'Shoddy' Aristocracy," *New York Times* (May 9, 2011).

The World War II–era defanging of the law is thoroughly reviewed in Helmer, *False Claims Act*, and Beck, "The False Claims Act and the English Eradication," as well as in the amicus curiae brief by Chuck Grassley in the Supreme Court case of Rockwell International Corp. and Boeing North American, Inc. v. United States of America and United States ex rel. James S. Stone, 549 US 457 (2007), decided March 27, 2007. See also Senate report 1708 published during the 77th Cong., 2d Sess. (1942).

Regarding the 1986 amendments and the strengthening of the FCA, see the transcripts of the hearing before the Subcommittee on Administrative Practice and Procedure of the Senate Committee on the Judiciary, September 17, 1985. An excellent review of the Gravitt case, the 1986 amendments and John Phillips's work with Chuck Grassley and Howard Berman appears in Henry Scammell, *Giantkillers*

(New York, 2004). See also the hearings before the Subcommittee on Administrative Law and Governmental Relations of the House Committee on the Judiciary, February 5–6, 1986; and Senate report 99-345 from the Committee on the Judiciary on the False Claims Reform Act of 1985, July 28, 1986. For the widespread nature of defense contractor fraud at the time, see in particular the three-part GAO report from 1981, *Fraud in Government Programs: How Extensive Is It? How Can It Be Controlled?* For the DOJ's hostility to the FCA and in particular to its qui tam provision, see William P. Barr, Assistant Attorney General, opinion of the Office of Legal Counsel, "Constitutionality of the Qui Tam Provisions of the False Claims Act," July 18, 1989. (Barr was confirmed as US attorney general on February 14, 2019.) See also Jack Meyer, "The Importance of Whistleblowers to Reducing Fraud Against the Federal Government and Recovering Funds for Taxpayers," report for Taxpayers Against Fraud (2012).

More general considerations of the whistleblowing phenomenon include: Marcia Miceli, Janet Near et al., *Whistle-Blowing in Organizations* (New York, 2008); Paul Rosenzweig, Timothy McNulty et al., eds., *Whistleblowers, Leaks and the Media* (Chicago, 2014); Myron Glazer and Penina Glazer, *The Whistle-Blowers* (New York, 1989); Charles Peters and Taylor Branch, *Blowing the Whistle: Dissent in the Public Interest* (New York, 1972); C. Fred Alford, *Whistleblowers: Broken Lives and Organizational Power* (Ithaca, NY, 2001); Terance Miethe, *Whistleblowing at Work* (Boulder, CO, 1999); Alan Westin, ed., *Whistle-Blowing! Loyalty and Dissent in the Corporation* (New York, 1981); Gerald Vinten, ed., *Whistleblowing: Subversion or Corporate Citizenship?* (London, 1994); Roberta Johnson, *Whistleblowing: When It Works—and Why* (Boulder, CO, 2003); Rania Milleron and Nicholas Sakellariou, eds., *Ethics, Politics, and Whistleblowing in Engineering* (Boca Raton, FL, 2018); and Albert Hirschman's philosophically important *Exit, Voice, and Loyalty* (Cambridge, MA, 1970). On the FCA's evolution since 1986, and on the development of a wide range of other whistleblowing laws and provisions, see works by Kohn, *The Whistleblower's Handbook*; Scammell, *Giantkillers*; and Devine and Maassarani, *The Corporate Whistleblower's Survival Guide*.

CHAPTER 2. QUESTION AUTHORITY

This chapter is based in part on personal communication with Scott Amey, Elliot Aronson, Andrea Ashworth, Bill Astore, Howard Berman, Danielle Brian, Tom Carpenter, Ed Davis, Shanna Devine, Tom Devine, Daniel Ellsberg, Randy Fertel, Nancy Fitzgerald-Greene, Conchita Gayl, Franz Gayl, Chuck Grassley, Dan Grazier, Mark Greenberg, Liz Hempowicz, James Ledbetter, Tim Macht, Ralph Nader, Rick Parks, Jane Pejsa, John Phillips, Dina Rasor, Nick Schwellenbach, Michael Smallberg, Mandy Smithberger, Chuck Spinney, Andy Thomson, Robert Vaughn, Dave Wilton and Kit Wood.

For a thorough review of evidence and sources of Franz Gayl's whistleblowing activities and the MRAP incident, see Gayl's testimony before the House Committee on Oversight and Reform on HR 1507, the Whistleblower Protection Enhancement Act of 2009, May 14, 2009; statement by Christopher Lamb at a hearing before the House Armed Services Committee, *Impediments to Acquisition Excellence Illustrated by the MRAP Case*, June 24, 2014; Christopher Lamb, Matthew Schmidt et al., "MRAPs, Irregular Warfare, and Pentagon Reform," paper of the National Defense University's Institute for National Strategic Studies (June 2009); *Marine Corps Implementation of the Urgent Universal Needs Process for Mine Resistant Ambush Protected Vehicles*, report no. D-2009-030 by the DOD Office of Inspector General, December 8, 2008; *Procurement Policy for Armored Vehicles*, report no. D-2007-107 by the DOD Office of Inspector General, June 27, 2007; Andrew Feickert, *Mine-Resistant, Ambush-Protected (MRAP) Vehicles: Background and Issues for Congress*, Congressional Research Service report (order code RS22707), updated January 24, 2008; GAO report, *Rapid Acquisition of Mine Resistant Ambush Protected Vehicles*, July 15, 2008; GAO report, *Improvements to DOD's Urgent Needs Processes Would Enhance Oversight and Expedite Efforts to Meet Critical Warfighter Needs*, April 30, 2010; and Naval Audit Service, audit report N2007-0060, *Marine Corps Urgent Universal Need Statement Process*, September 28, 2007.

See also the fine profile of Franz Gayl and his ordeal by James Verini, "The Unquiet Life of Franz Gayl," *Washington Monthly* (July/August 2011); the series of incisive articles on the subject by Tom Vanden Brook in *USA Today*; Richard Lardner, "Marines Fail to Get Gear to Troops," Associated Press (May 25, 2007); and John McClean, "One Single Nail," *Marine Corps Gazette* (February 2008). The Urgent Universal Need Statement by Roy McGriff, signed by General D. J. Heljik, is unclassified, and dated February 17, 2005. See in addition the letters from Senator Joseph Biden, Senate Committee on Foreign Relations, to President George W. Bush, May 23, 2007; and from Biden and Senator Christopher Bond to Secretary of Defense Robert Gates, June 28, 2007. On General Richard Zilmer's achievements in Iraq, and specifically in Anbar Province, see especially Timothy McWilliams and Kurtis Wheeler, eds., "Al-Anbar Awakening," *American Perspectives, US Marines and Counter-Insurgency in Iraq*, vol. 1 (Quantico, VA, 2009).

Ernie Fitzgerald "committed truth" about the Lockheed C5-A in *The Economics of Military Procurement*, hearings before the congressional Joint Economic Committee, Subcommittee on Economy in Government, November 11–13, 1968, and January 16, 1969. See also *The Dismissal of A. Ernest Fitzgerald by the Department of Defense*, hearings before the same committee, November 17–19, 1969. On Ernie Fitzgerald's career, the essential sources are his two books, *The High Priests of Waste* (New York, 1972) and *The Pentagonists* (New York, 1989), as well as his numerous articles and reports. Good background is from Dina Rasor, Fitzgerald's longtime collaborator, in *The Pentagon Underground* (Washington, DC, 1985) and in the volume that Rasor edited, *More Bucks, Less Bang* (Washington, DC, 1983). On how the Pentagon mentality in Fitzgerald's time has given rise to today's drone warfare, see *Kill Chain* (New York, 2015) by veteran military-industrial-complex critic Andrew Cockburn, who knew Fitzgerald, Spinney, John Boyd and other Pentagon insiders. See also the interview with Fitzgerald by Alison Ross Wimsatt, "The Struggles of Being Ernest," *Industrial Management* (January/February 1999). Details of investigations into Fitzgerald's personal life, and the various lawsuits he brought against government officials, are in *High Priests*. (His Supreme Court case is Nixon v. Fitzgerald, 457 U.S. 731 [1982], decided June 24, 1982.) Fitzgerald died on January 31, 2019, at the age of ninety-two; reviews of his career include a moving Senate floor speech by Chuck Grassley, "A Tribute to Ernie Fitzgerald" (February 6, 2019); extensive obituaries in the *Washington Post* (February 7, 2019) and the *New York Times* (February 14, 2019); and an article by his friend and fellow whistleblower Chuck Spinney, "The Man Who 'Committed Truth': Remembering Ernie Fitzgerald," *Counterpunch* (February 7, 2019). On Fitzgerald's relationship with Chuck Grassley, see Eric Woolson, *Grassley* (Parkersburg, IA, 1995).

On Robert McNamara, the Whiz Kids and managerialism, see Deborah Shapley, *Promise and Power* (New York, 1993); the fascinating documentary film by Errol Morris, *The Fog of War* (2003); Richard Barnet, *Roots of War* (New York, 1972); Paul Hendrickson, *The Living and the Dead* (New York, 1996); and John Byrne, *The Whiz Kids* (New York, 1993). On systems analysis and its use in the military, see Ben Connable, *Embracing the Fog of War*, a RAND monograph (Santa Monica, CA, 2012); and Philip Caputo, *A Rumor of War* (New York, 1977). McNamara praised the art of management during his convocation address at Millsaps College on February 24, 1967. See also Phil Rosenzweig, "Robert S. McNamara and the Evolution of Modern Management," *Harvard Business Review* (December 2010); Leo McCann, "Killing Is Our Business and Business Is Good," *Organization* (2017); and further references on managerialism in notes to Chapter 3.

On the C5-A case, see Berkeley Rice, *The C-5A Scandal* (New York, 1971). For a look at Lockheed's current military-industrial clout, see William Hartung, *The Prophets of War* (New York, 2010). On waste and fraud in Afghanistan and Iraq, see the report "Transforming Wartime Contracting, Commission on Wartime Contracting" (August 2011; the commission was shuttered on September 30, 2011), and numerous, hard-hitting reports by the Special Inspector General for Afghanistan Reconstruction (SIGAR), including *Corruption in Conflict* (September 14, 2016). The DOD IG's report that revealed the "grand plug" was *Army General Fund Adjustments Not Adequately Documented or Supported*, July 26, 2016. In-depth analysis of $21 trillion in unauthorized spending by the DOD and other government bodies by Michigan State University economist Mark Skidmore, at the website The Missing Money. See also Robert Pollin and Heidi Garrett-Peltier, *The U.S. Employment Effects of Military and Domestic Spending Priorities*, report for the Political Economy Research Institute (Amherst, 2011). On Lockheed's disastrously over-budget and behind-schedule F-35 Joint Strike Fighter, see excellent coverage over the last decade by POGO and multiple reports by the GAO, e.g., Dan Grazier, "F-35 Far from Ready to Face Current or Future Threats" (March 19, 2019). See also "Achieving Full Combat Capability with the Joint Strike Fighter (JSF) Is at Substantial Risk," a memorandum prepared by the DOD Operational Test and Evaluation Office for the Under Secretary of Defense for Acquisition, Technology and Logistics, dated August 9, 2016.

On the military-industrial complex and defense contractor fraud more generally, see James Ledbetter's superb *Unwarranted Influence* (New Haven, CT, 2011); Andrew Cockburn, "The Military-Industrial Virus," *Harper's* (June 2019); Tom Englehardt's indispensable blog *Tom Dispatch*; Bill Astore's penetrating analysis and publications at his blog *Bracing Views*; two reports by the World Security Institute's Center for Defense Information, "America's Defense Meltdown" (Washington, DC, 2008) and "The Pentagon Labyrinth" (Washington, DC, 2011); Pierre Sprey, *Nothing's Too Good for Our Boys!*, report for the Straus Military Reform Project of the Center for Defense Information (2007); and Chuck Spinney, "Why Is Boeing Imploding? Part III," in his blog *The Blaster* (April 25, 2019), with references to a prescient analysis by Pierre Sprey eleven years earlier. On how the military pervades civilian life, see Nick Turse, *The Complex* (New York, 2008). See also Robert Coram, *Boyd: The Fighter Pilot Who Changed the Art of War* (New York, 2002). On the revolving-door phenomenon in the military, see Mandy Smithberger, "Brass Parachutes: The Problem of the Pentagon Revolving Door," report for POGO (November 5, 2018); Bryan Bender, "From the Pentagon to the Private Sector," *Boston Globe* (December 26, 2010); Katherine Silz Carson, "Tarnished Brass?" on the blog of the Edmond J. Safra Center at Harvard (March 3, 2014); and "Strategic Maneuvers," report by Citizens for Responsibility and Ethics in Washington (November 19, 2012).

On Ron Ridenhour and the My Lai massacre, see Ridenhour's 1969 letter, and several of his articles, which are available at the website of the Ridenhour Prize, an annual award given to whistleblowers and other truth tellers. Ridenhour, Hugh Thompson, Seymour Hersh and others discussed the My Lai massacre at a three-day conference held at Tulane University, proceedings of which were published as David Anderson, ed., *Facing My Lai* (Lawrence, KS, 2000). Government reports on My Lai include Lieutenant General William Peers, *Report of the Department of the Army Review of the Preliminary Investigations into the My Lai Incident*, vol. 1 (1970); *Investigation of the My Lai Incident*, hearings before the Armed Services Investigating Subcommittee of the House Committee on Armed Services (April 15–June 22, 1970); the final report of the same subcommittee (July 15, 1970); and *Records of the William L. Calley General Court-Martial, 1969–1981* (substantial excerpts available at Famous Trials, a website maintained by Professor Douglas Linder of the University of Missouri–Kansas City School of Law). Key works on My Lai include two groundbreaking books by Seymour Hersh, *My Lai 4* (New York, 1970) and *Cover-up* (New York, 1972); Michael Bilton and Kevin Sim, *Four Hours in My Lai* (New York, 1993); and Kendrick Oliver, *The My Lai Massacre in American History and Memory* (Manchester, UK, 2006). On Hugh Thompson, see Trent Angers, *The Forgotten Hero of My Lai* (Lafayette, LA, 2014), which contains H. R. Haldeman's cryptic memo. On reports and cases of extensive torture and summary executions of prisoners by US military in Vietnam, see Nick Turse, *Kill Anything That Moves* (New York, 2013); and Seymour Hersh, "My Lai, and Its Omens," *New York Times*, March 16, 1998. John Kerry's Senate testimony during *Legislative Proposals Relating to the War in Southeast Asia*, hearings before the Committee on Foreign Relations, April 23, 1971. Herbert Kelman and V. Lee Hamilton, *Crimes of Obedience* (New Haven, CT, 1990), provides a valuable analysis of group psychology and attitudes toward obedience in the Calley trial, among soldiers and the US public alike.

On Ralph Nader, see Nader, *Unsafe at Any Speed* (New York, 1965); Robert Vaughn, *The Successes and Failures of Whistleblower Law* (Cheltenham, UK, 2012); and Vaughn, "Public Employees and the Right to Disobey," *Hastings Law Journal* (November 1977). See also *Federal Role in Traffic Safety*, hearings before the Subcommittee on Executive Reorganization of the Senate Committee on Government Operations (March 22, 1965–March 22, 1966). On the Pinto cost-benefit analysis, see Gail Baura, "1978: Ford Pinto Recall," Chapter 3 of *Engineering Ethics* (Cambridge, MA, 2006); Mark Dowie, "Pinto Madness," *Mother Jones*, September/October 1977. Excerpts and analysis of Nader's January 1971 "Conference on Professional Responsibility" published as *Whistle Blowing*, ed. Ralph Nader, Peter Petkas et al., (New York, 1972). On the etymology of the term "whistleblower," see the Wordorigins.org website; *Oxford English Dictionary*; *Oxford Dictionary of American Political Slang*; Ben Zimmer, "A Whistlestop Tour of 'Whistleblowers,'" *Visual Thesaurus* (July 19, 2013); and William Safire, "Blowing My Whistle," *New York Times* (February 6, 1983). Text of the Powell Memorandum with useful context online at Moyers & Company, "The Powell Memo: A Call-to-Arms for Corporations" (September 14, 2012).

On Daniel Ellsberg's career and whistleblowing, see Daniel Ellsberg's books *Papers on the War* (New York, 1972), *Secrets* (New York, 2002), and *The Doomsday Machine* (New York, 2017). See also the absorbing documentary film by Judith Ehrlich and Rick Goldsmith, *The Most Dangerous Man in America* (2009); and Timothy Naftali, interview of Daniel Ellsberg for the Richard Nixon Oral History Program (May 20, 2008). The unredacted text of the Pentagon Papers is available online at the National Archives. For the history of RAND, game theory and its broader implications, see William Poundstone, *Prisoner's Dilemma* (New York, 1992); S. M. Amadae, *Prisoners of Reason* (New York, 2015); and Fred Kaplan, *The Wizards of Armageddon* (Stanford, CA, 1991). Books by RAND stalwarts that brought game theory, bargaining theory and decision theory to bear on warfare include: Herman Kahn and Irwin Mann, *Game Theory* (Santa Monica, CA, 1957); Thomas Schelling (2005 Nobel laureate in economics for "having enhanced our understanding of conflict and cooperation through game-theory analysis"), *Strategy of Conflict* (Cambridge, MA, 1960) and *Arms and Influence* (New Haven, CT, 1966); and Melvin Drescher, *Games of Strategy* (Englewood Cliffs, NJ, 1961). More generally on the Vietnam War and Ellsberg's national security milieu, see David Halberstam, *The Best and the Brightest* (New York, 1972); Neil Sheehan, *A Bright Shining Lie* (New York, 1988); and Max Hastings, *Vietnam: An Epic Tragedy, 1945–1975* (New York, 2018). The Supreme Court case is New York Times Company v. United States 403 U.S. 713 (1971), decided June 30, 1971; and United States v. Daniel Ellsberg and Anthony Russo before the US District Court, Central District of California no. A-150 (reviewed and analyzed at the Famous Trials website). Erwin Griswold's contradictory statements appear in his Supreme Court oral arguments, June 26, 1971, and in Griswold, "Secrets Not Worth Keeping," *Washington Post*, February 15, 1989.

Complete text of the Watergate tapes is in Douglas Brinkley and Luke Nichter, *The Nixon Tapes* (New York, 2015), and online at Nixontapes.org. See also Stanley Kutler, *The Wars of Watergate* (rev. ed., New York, 1992); and J. Anthony Lukas, *Nightmare* (New York, 1976). The Butterfield memo is described in *Nixon v. Fitzgerald*. This case is discussed in Richard Ellis, *Judging Executive Power* (Lanham, MD, 2009); and A. Robert Smith, "The Butterfield Exchange," *New York Times*, July 20, 1975. Nader's suit against Bork is Nader v. Bork, U.S. District Court for the District of Columbia, DDC 1973, decided November 14, 1973. For the text of the Malek Manual, see "Federal Political Personnel Manual, The 'Malek Manual,'" *The Bureaucrat* (January 1976). The influence of Watergate and other political scandals of the 1960s and 1970s on whistleblower legislation is examined by Vaughn, *The Successes and Failures of Whistleblower Law*.

See introductions to the history and to key aspects of social psychology in Elliot Aronson and Joshua Aronson, *The Social Animal* (12th ed., New York, 2018); Carol Tavris and Elliot Aronson, *Mistakes Were Made (but Not by Me)* (New York, 2007); Lee Ross, Mark Lepper et al., "History of Social Psychology," in *Handbook of Social Psychology* (5th ed., Hoboken, NJ, 2010); and Daniel Kahneman, *Thinking Fast and Slow* (New York, 2011). On the Milgram experiments, see Stanley Milgram, *Obedience to Authority* (New York, 1974); Thomas Blass, *The Man Who Shocked the World* (New York, 2004); Blass, "The Roots of Stanley Milgram's Obedience Experiments and Their Relevance to the Holocaust," *Analyse & Kritik*

(1998); and Arthur Miller, *The Obedience Experiments* (New York, 1986). For a replication of the Milgram experiments fifty years later, with very similar behavior among subjects to that which Milgram originally observed, see Dariusz Doliński, Tomasz Grzyb et al., "Would You Deliver an Electric Shock in 2015?" *Social Psychological and Personality Science* (March 14, 2017). Transcripts of the Eichmann trial are available online at the Nizkor Project, and extensive video is online at Yad Vashem, the World Holocaust Remembrance Center. See also Gabriel Bach, "Eichmann Trial," in *Encyclopedia of the Holocaust* (New York, 1990); Deborah Lipstadt, *The Eichmann Trial* (New York, 2011); and the classic, though controversial, account by Hannah Arendt, *Eichmann in Jerusalem* (New York, 1963).

CHAPTER 3. THE MONEY DANCE

This chapter is based in part on personal communication with Steven Aftergood, Elliot Aronson, Elin Baklid-Kunz, Alison Bass, Max Bazerman, Sara Miron Bloom, Donna Boehm, Lori Brown, Diane Burton, Richard Condit, Daniel Fessler, Skip Freedman, Adrian Furnham, Susan Gouinlock, Mark Greenberg, Eric Havian, Jim Helmer, Marianne Jennings, Erika Kelton, Don Kettl, Brian Knutson, Steve Kohn, Sheldon Krimsky, Jeanne Lenzer, Harry Lewis, Harry Litman, Iain McGilchrist, Cheryl Eckard Mead, Tom Melsheimer, Russell Mokhiber, Mickey Nardo, Cliff Palefsky, Roy Poses, Robert Prentice, Jim Ratley, Lesley Ann Skillen, Lynn Stout, Skyler Swisher, Paul Thacker, Janine Wedel, Marlan Wilbanks, Scott Withrow and Lin Wood.

On the case of Elin Baklid-Kunz and Halifax Health, see extensive court records for United States of America ex rel. Baklid-Kunz v. Halifax Hospital Medical Center d/b/a Halifax Health a/k/a Halifax Community Health System, a/k/a Halifax Medical Center and Halifax Staffing, Inc., case no. 6:09-CV-1002-ORL-31 DAB, US District Court for the Middle District of Florida, Orlando Division. See in particular:

- Second amended complaint, filed by Baklid-Kunz February 18, 2011, with Exhibits 1-7
- DOJ's complaint in intervention, filed November 4, 2011 (United States of America ex rel. Baklid-Kunz v. Halifax Hospital Medical Center et al.)
- Depositions by Elin Baklid-Kunz, William Kuhn, Arvin Lewis, Eric Peburn, Audrey Ann Pike, George Rousis, Federico Carlos Vinas
- Notice of Deposition of Arvin Lewis, August 22, 2012
- Transcript of Motions Hearing, May 7, 2013
- Declaration of Mary Ann Norvik, filed on September 10, 2012
- Expert Report of Kathy McNamara, filed on December 21, 2012
- Email from Stephanie Herder, MD, of Allmed to Elin Baklid-Kunz, March 23, 2010, filed on January 24, 2014, as Exhibit 7 to Motion in limine No. 2
- Memorandum from Dave Davidson to Alberto Tineo, June 3, 2010, which contains a heavily redacted version of the Allmed report (filed on January 24, 2014, as Exhibit 9 to Motion in limine No. 2)
- Order of Judge Presnell, July 1, 2014
- Report and Recommendation of United States Magistrate Thomas B. Smith on May 8, 2014
- See also the Corporate Integrity Agreement between the Office of Inspector General of the Department of Health and Human Services and Halifax Hospital Medical Center, signed March 10, 2014; "Whistleblower: Halifax Health Sent Patients to Unnecessary Surgeries Like 'Sending Lambs,'" WFTV (ABC) News Channel 9, October 28, 2013; Peter Whoriskey and Dan Keating, "Spinal Fusions Serve as Case Study for Debate over When Certain Surgeries Are Necessary," *Washington Post*, October 27, 2013; and John Perry, "Lessons Learned from Halifax," *Hospitals & Health Systems Rx* (May 2014).

On criminal and civil wrongdoing at Columbia/HCA, see DOJ press release, "Columbia/HCA, the Hospital Chain That Pled Guilty to Substantial Criminal Conduct and Paid a Then-Record $1.7

Billion Settlement," June 26, 2003. Peburn and Feasel awards were from *Becker's Hospital Review* in 2015: "150 Hospital and Health System CFOs to Know" and "130 Nonprofit Hospital & Health System CEOs to Know 2015." Rick Scott and Feasel received the Mary McLeod Bethune Legacy Awards Gala, "for their dedication and continuous contribution to education and the community." For local news of the trial and the hospital's public statements about it, see especially coverage by Skyler Swisher in the *Daytona Beach News-Journal* (e.g., in 2014: August 18, August 20, September 26); and by Lori Brown of WFTV, Channel 9 in Orlando, Florida (e.g., in 2014: May 28, August 6, March 3). See more local coverage at the Wilbanks & Gouinlock website under Case Histories: Halifax Medical Center.

Court filings, press releases and media for other cases brought by Wilbanks and Gouinlock are available at the Wilbanks & Gouinlock website, under Results, Case Histories and In Litigation. Specific cases mentioned are: United States of America ex rel. Vainer and Barbir v. DaVita Inc. and Gambro Healthcare Inc. et al.; United States of America, Florida et al. ex rel. Payne, Church and Pryor v. Adventist Health System—Sunbelt, Inc. et al.; United States of America and Georgia ex rel. Williams v. Tenet Healthcare, Health Management Associates et al.; and United States of America ex rel. Bibby and Donnelly v. Wells Fargo Bank et al.

On the psychology of money in a social and historical context, see Michael Sandel, *What Money Can't Buy* (New York, 2012); Karl Polanyi, *The Great Transformation* (2nd ed., Boston, 2001); Margaret Heffernan, *Willful Blindness* (London, 2011); Max Weber, *The Protestant Ethic and the Spirit of Capitalism*, trans. Talcott Parson, esp. Chapter 2, "The Spirit of Capitalism" (London, 1992); Iain McGilchrist's magisterial *The Master and His Emissary* (New Haven, CT, 2009); Richard Seaford, *Money and the Early Greek Mind* (Cambridge, UK, 2004); Adrian Furnham, *The New Psychology of Money* (Hove, East Sussex, 2014); Charlie Munger, "The Psychology of Human Misjudgment," a speech delivered at Harvard University in 1995; and James Buchan, *Frozen Desire* (London, 1997). For the text of Mark Twain's "corn pone opinions," see his *"What Is Man?" and Other Philosophical Writings*, ed. Paul Baender (Berkeley, CA, 1973). Socrates's comment is in Plato, *The Republic*, 551a.

For perspectives on the neuroscience and evolutionary psychology of money, see Hans Breiter, Itzhak Aharon et al., "Functional Imaging of Neural Responses to Expectancy and Experience of Monetary Gains and Losses," *Neuron* (May 2001); Brian Knutson, "FMRI Visualization of Brain Activity During a Monetary Incentive Delay Task," *NeuroImage* (July 2000); Knutson, G. E. Wimmera et al., "Nucleus Accumbens Activation Mediates the Influence of Reward Cues on Financial Risk Taking," *NeuroReport* (March 26, 2008); Knutson and Jaak Panksepp, "The Role of Brain Emotional Systems in Addictions: A Neuro-evolutionary Perspective and New 'Self-Report' Animal Model," *Addiction* (April 2002); Kathleen Vohs, Nicole Mead et al., "The Psychological Consequences of Money," *Science* (November 17, 2006); Long Wang, Deepak Malhotra et al., "Economics Education and Greed," *Academy of Management Learning and Education* (December 2011); Paul Piff, Daniel Stancato et al., "Higher Social Class Predicts Increased Unethical Behavior," *Proceedings of the National Academy of Sciences* (March 13, 2012); Maryam Kouchaki, Kristin Smith-Crowe et al., "Seeing Green," *Organizational Behavior and Human Decision Processes* (May 2013); Cassie Mogilner, "The Pursuit of Happiness," *Psychological Science* (August 23, 2010); Geoffrey Miller, "Sexual Selection for Moral Virtues," *Quarterly Review of Biology* (June 2007); Miller, "Sex, Mutations and Marketing," *European Molecular Biology Organization Reports* (October 2012); Miller, "Sexual Selection for Cultural Displays," in Robin Dunbar, Chris Knight et al., eds., *The Evolution of Culture* (Edinburgh, 1999); and Andrew Lo, *Hedge Funds, Systemic Risk, and the Financial Crisis of 2007–2008*, testimony before the House Committee on Oversight and Government Reform, *Hearing on Hedge Funds*, November 13, 2008.

For Richard Posner's positions on organs, babies and the free market, see Posner, "Sale of Body Parts—Posner," *The Becker-Posner Blog*, October 21, 2012; and Posner, "The Regulation of the Market in Adoptions," *Boston University Law Review* (1987). On cost-benefit analyses, the shareholder value argument, the Chicago School and homo economicus, see notes to Chapter 4 below.

Regarding the history and psychological contradictions of the compliance industry, see the compelling analysis by Max Bazerman and Ann Tenbrunsel, *Blind Spots* (Princeton, NJ, 2012); as well as John MacKessy, "Knowledge of Good and Evil," *Finance Professionals' Post* (May 26, 2010); and "Defense Industry Initiative on Business Ethics and Conduct," *Annual Report to the Public and the Defense Industry* (1996). See also Uri Gneezy and Aldo Rustichini, "A Fine Is a Price," *Journal of Legal Studies* (January 2000); Donna Boehme, "From Enron to Madoff: Why Most Corporate Compliance and Ethics Programs Are Positioned for Failure," presented on March 5, 2009, at a RAND conference titled "Perspectives of Chief Ethics and Compliance Officers on the Detection and Prevention of Corporate Misdeeds"; Lisa Ordóñez, Maurice Schweitzer et al., "Goals Gone Wild" (working paper, Harvard Business School, January 2009); and George Loewenstein, Cass Sunstein et al., "Disclosure," *Annual Review of Economics* (August 2014).

On the spread of financial conflicts of interest in US healthcare, see Roy Poses's blog *Health Care Renewal* (tags: conflict of interest, financialization, corporatism), and Poses, "A Cautionary Tale," *European Journal of Internal Medicine* (May 2003). See also Maggie Mahar, *Money-Driven Medicine* (New York, 2006); Paul Starr's essential *The Social Transformation of American Medicine* (2nd ed., New York, 2017); Sheldon Krimsky, *Conflicts of Interest in Science* (New York, 2019); Krimsky, "Funding Effect in Science," Chapter 5 of *Corrupted Science*, an online resource that grew out of Krimsky's book *Science in the Private Interest* (Lanham, MD, 2003); Arnold Eiser, *The Ethos of Medicine in Postmodern America* (Lanham, MD, 2014); Justin Bekelmanet, Y. Li et al., "Scope and Impact of Financial Conflicts of Interest in Biomedical Research," *Journal of the American Medical Association* (January 2003); Aaron Kesselheim, Michelle Mello et al., "Strategies and Practices in Off-Label Marketing of Pharmaceuticals: A Retrospective Analysis of Whistleblower Complaints," *PLOS Medicine* (April 5, 2011); and David Lewis, *Science for Sale* (New York, 2014).

For more on the related problems of managerialism and financialization in medicine, see Paul Komesaroff, Ian Kerridge et al., "The Scourge of Managerialism and the Royal Australasian College of Physicians," *Medical Journal of Australia* (June 2015); and Arnold Relman, "Medical Professionalism in a Commercialized Health Care Market," *Journal of the American Medical Association* (December 12, 2007). More broadly, see William Lazonick, "The Financialization of the U.S. Corporation," *Seattle University Law Review* (2013); Lazonick, "Profits Without Prosperity," *Harvard Business Review* (September 2014); Robert Kuttner, *Everything for Sale* (New York, 1997); Kuttner, *The Squandering of America* (New York, 2007); and H. Thomas Johnson and Anders Broms, *Profit Beyond Measure* (New York, 2000). On Enthoven and RAND in healthcare: Howard Waitzkin, "The Strange Career of Managed Competition," *American Journal of Public Health* (March 1994); and P. M. Ellwood and A. C. Enthoven, "'Responsible Choices': The Jackson Hole Group Plan for Health Reform," *Health Affairs* (Summer 1995). (See also notes to Chapter 6 below.)

Regarding corporate influence on research and universities, see Derek Bok, *Universities in the Marketplace* (Princeton, NJ, 2003); and Bok, *Higher Education in America* (rev. ed., Princeton, NJ, 2013); *Recommended Principles to Guide Academy-Industry Relationships*, American Association of University Professors (Washington, DC, 2014); a special issue of *Nature Outlook* devoted to research commercialization (May 5, 2016); Joshua Hunt, *University of Nike* (Brooklyn, NY, 2018); Harry Lewis, *Excellence Without a Soul* (New York, 2006); Henry Heller, *The Capitalist University* (London, 2016); and Benjamin Ginsberg, *The Fall of the Faculty* (Oxford, UK, 2011). See also Paul Starr, "Law and the Fog of Healthcare," *St. Louis University Journal of Health Law & Policy* (June 2013); and Frank Grad, "The Antitrust Laws and Professional Discipline in Medicine," *Duke Law Journal* (May 1978).

For the increasing influence of billionaire oligarchs over the educational agendas of US universities, and how self-interested philanthropy serves their public policy goals, see Jane Mayer, *Dark Money* (New York, 2016); Nancy MacLean, *Democracy in Chains* (New York, 2017); and "Why the Koch Brothers Find Higher Education Worth Their Money," online at *Public Integrity* (June 5, 2018). The

1975 Supreme Court ruling that undercut the existing ethical codes of doctors and other professional societies was Goldfarb v. Virginia State Bar 421 US 773.

On conflicts of interest in medicine, in addition to references in Chapter 1 above and Chapter 4 below, see the full May 2, 2017, issue of the *Journal of the American Medical Association* devoted to medical conflicts; Don Moore, Daylian Cain et al., *Conflicts of Interest* (Cambridge, UK, 2005); Marc Rodwin, *Conflicts of Interest and the Future of Medicine* (Oxford, UK, 2011); Bernard Lo and Marilyn Field, eds., *Conflict of Interest in Medical Research, Education, and Practice*, Committee on Conflict of Interest in Medical Research, Education, and Practice, National Academy of Sciences (Washington, DC, 2009); Michael Davis and Andrew Stark, eds., *Conflict of Interest in the Professions* (Oxford, UK, 2001); and Ray Moynihan, "Who Pays for the Pizza? Redefining the Relationships Between Doctors and Drug Companies," *British Medical Journal* (May 31, 2003). See also Marcia Angell, *The Truth About the Drug Companies* (New York, 2004); Angell, "Drug Companies & Doctors: A Story of Corruption," *New York Review of Books* (January 15, 2009); Angell, "Transparency Hasn't Stopped Drug Companies from Corrupting Medical Research," *New York Times* (September 14, 2018); David Healy, *Pharmageddon* (Oakland, CA, 2012); Carl Elliott, *White Coat, Black Hat* (Boston, 2010); and Troyen Brennan, David Rothman et al., "Health Industry Practices That Create Conflicts of Interest," *Journal of the American Medical Association* (January 25, 2006). See also extensive publications on medical and other professional conflicts by scholars at Harvard's Edmond J. Safra Center for Ethics, including the 2011 symposium titled "The Scientific Basis of Conflicts of Interest"; as well as resources about conflicts at the Ethical Systems website. Brown University's conflict of interest policy, dated May 22, 2009, is titled "Conflict of Interest Policy for Officers of Instruction and Research."

On the case of David Kern and flock worker's lung, Kern, rather than sit for an interview, supplied an extensive file of published and unpublished materials, on which, together with independent sources, I based this account. See David Kern, Robert Crausman et al., "Flock Worker's Lung," *Annals of Internal Medicine* (August 15, 1998); Kern, "The Unexpected Result of an Investigation of an Outbreak of Occupational Lung Disease," *International Journal of Occupational Environmental Health* (January–March 1998), with extensive discussion in the same issue titled "Right, Wrong, and Occupational Health"; Kern, "Confidentiality Agreements and Scientific Independence," *Medical Decision Making* (January 1998); Kern, "A Recent Case Study," a talk delivered on March 29, 1999, as part of a conference at MIT titled "Secrecy in Science: Exploring University, Industry and Government Relationships"; Kern, letter to Frank Davidoff, editor of the *Annals of Internal Medicine*, dated October 1, 1998; Kern, Charles Kuhn et al., "Flock Worker's Lung," *Chest* (January 2000); and Kern, Eli Kern et al., "A Retrospective Cohort Study of Lung Cancer Incidence in Nylon Flock Workers, 1998–2008," *International Journal of Occupational Environmental Health* (October–December 2011). See also extensive coverage of the Kern case by Aubrey Blumsohn at his *Scientific Misconduct Blog*, by Roy Poses at the *Health Care Renewal* blog, and in Jennifer Washburn's valuable *University, Inc.* (New York, 2008). For Kern's views on whistle-blowing and free speech, see Owen Fiss, *The Irony of Free Speech* (Cambridge, MA, 1996).

Study 329 was published as Martin Keller, Neal Ryan et al., "Efficacy of Paroxetine in the Treatment of Adolescent Major Depression," *Journal of the American Academy of Child and Adolescent Psychiatry* (July 2001), where it remains online to this day, with no indication that its scientific validity has been refuted. See Alison Bass, *Side Effects* (Chapel Hill, NC, 2008), and Bass's series of articles in the *Boston Globe* that chronicled the affair, as well as further publications at her blog, *Alison Bass*. The two most important recent articles on Study 329 were both published in the *British Medical Journal* on September 19, 2015: Joanna Le Noury, John "Mickey" Nardo, David Healy et al., "Restoring Study 329" (which is a reanalysis of the full clinical trial data underlying Study 329); and Peter Doshi, "No Correction, No Retraction, No Apology, No Comment" (a trenchant review of the wider implications of the study, and the reactions by academic officials and editors). Original documents from Study 329 and other pharmaceutical causes célèbres are online at the Industry Documents Library of the University of California, San Francisco. See also extensive coverage by Mickey Nardo at his *1 Boring Old Man* blog, Roy Poses at *Health Care Renewal*, and Aubrey Blumsohn at *Scientific Misconduct Blog*.

On financial conflicts of interest among other prominent medical researchers, see Paul Thacker, the investigator for Chuck Grassley and for POGO, who reviewed the evidence in a series of data-dense publications in the *POGO Blog*: Thacker and Danielle Brian, "POGO Letter to NIH on Ghostwriting Academics," addressed to Francis S. Collins, Director, National Institutes of Health (rev. version, December 22, 2010); Thacker, "Author of Ghostwritten Study Runs for Parliament in Canada" (May 12, 2011); and Thacker, "The Ugly Underbelly of Medical Research" (January 13, 2011). See also Thacker, "How an Ethically Challenged Researcher Found a Home at the University of Miami," *Forbes* (September 13, 2011).

The suit brought by Eliot Spitzer against GSK is The People of the State of New York, by Eliot Spitzer, Attorney General of the State of New York vs. GlaxoSmithKline plc, SmithKline Beecham Corporation, filed with the Supreme Court of the State of New York on June 2, 2004. See also Cheryl J. Cunningham et al. v. SmithKline Beecham d/b/a GlaxoSmithKline, heard before the US District Courts of the Northern District of Indiana and the Eastern District of Pennsylvania, case no. 2:07-CV-174; and the remarkable March 15, 2007, deposition of Sally Laden in this suit, which details the practice of ghostwriting employed by GSK and other major pharmaceutical companies. For GSK's $3 billion criminal and civil settlement with the DOJ, see US ex rel. Greg Thorpe et al. v. GlaxoSmithKline plc et al., case no. 11-10398-RWZ (complaint, exhibits and other documents are available at the DOJ website, including a detailed press release titled "GlaxoSmithKline to Plead Guilty and Pay $3 Billion to Resolve Fraud Allegations and Failure to Report Safety Data"). See also US ex rel. Thomas Gerahty and Matthew Burke v. GlaxoSmithKline plc et al., case no. 1:03-cv-10641, before the US District Court for the District of Massachusetts.

For perceptions of increasing incidence of fraud and corruption in many parts of US society, see Harry Lewis, *Excellence without a Soul*, and Bazerman and Tenbrunsel, *Blind Spots*, as well as Lawrence Lessig, *America, Compromised* (Chicago, 2018); Lessig, *Republic, Lost* (2nd ed., October 20, 2015); and the extensive work of Lessig and colleagues on institutional corruption published by Harvard's Edmond J. Safra Center for Ethics (e.g., Lisa Cosgrove and Robert Whitaker, "Finding Solutions to Institutional Corruption" [working paper, Edmond J. Safra, May 9, 2013]). See also Zephyr Teachout, *Corruption in America* (Cambridge, MA, 2014); and Teachout, "The Anti-Corruption Principle," *Cornell Law Review* (January 2009); Marianne Jennings, *The Seven Signs of Ethical Collapse* (New York, 2006); Lynn Stout, *Cultivating Conscience* (Princeton, NJ, 2010); Ann Tenbrunsel and David Messick, "Ethical Fading," *Social Justice Research* (June 2004); David Callahan, *The Cheating Culture* (New York, 2004); Dan Ariely, *The Honest Truth About Dishonesty* (New York, 2012); Linda Treviño, "The Ethics of Managers and Employees," in *The Routledge Companion to Business Ethics*, ed. Eugene Heath, Byron Kaldis et al. (Abingdon, UK, 2018); and Treviño, *Managing Business Ethics* (7th ed., Hoboken, NJ, 2017). See also William Lazonick, "How American Corporations Transformed from Producers to Predators," AlterNet (April 2, 2012); and Lazonick's extensive, insightful publications online at the Institute for New Economic Thinking.

On sports misconduct, see Lisa Kihl, ed., *Corruption in Sport* (Abingdon, UK, 2017); *Mapping of Corruption of Sport in the EU*, report to the European Commission (December 2018); Transparency International, *Global Corruption Report: Sport* (February 23, 2016); and Graham Brooks, Azeem Aleem et al., *Fraud, Corruption and Sport* (London, 2013). Regarding academic fraud, see above references to ghostwriting and conflicts of interest; as well as Nachman Ben-Yehuda and Amalya Oliver-Lumerman, *Fraud and Misconduct in Research* (Ann Arbor, MI, 2017); R. Grant Steen, "Retractions in the Scientific Literature: Do Authors Deliberately Commit Research Fraud?" *Journal of Medical Ethics* (February 2011); John P. A. Ioannidis, "Why Most Published Research Findings Are False," *PLoS Medicine* (August 2005); and latest news on academic misconduct by Adam Marcus and Ivan Oransky on their

Retraction Watch website. See also Ferric Fang, R. Grant Steen et al., "Misconduct Accounts for the Majority of Retracted Scientific Publications," *Proceedings of the National Academy of Sciences* (October 16, 2012). On tax evasion, see the IRS report *Federal Tax Compliance Research*, Publication 1415 (May 2016), and more broadly, Gabriel Zucman, *The Hidden Wealth of Nations* (Chicago, 2015); Oliver Bullough, *Moneyland* (London, 2018); Nicholas Shaxson, *Treasure Islands* (New York, 2011); James Henry, *The Price of Offshore Revisited*, report prepared for the Tax Justice Network (July 2012); and James Henry, "Taxing Tax Havens," *Foreign Affairs* (April 12, 2016). On healthcare fraud, aside from extensive references above, see exhaustive coverage by Roy Poses, *Health Care Renewal* blog, under the tag health care corruption. See also Transparency International, "Corruption in the Pharmaceutical Sector" (June 2016); Karen Hussmann, "Addressing Corruption in the Health Sector," report for the U4 Anti-Corruption Resource Centre (January 2011); and Jim Gee and Mark Button, "The Financial Cost of Healthcare Fraud 2015," report prepared by PKF Littlejohn LLP and the University of Portsmouth. On misconduct in the defense industry, in addition to notes to Chapter 2 above, see the GAO's March 2019 report, *High-Risk Series—Substantial Efforts Needed to Achieve Greater Progress on High-Risk Areas*, as well as the online version of the GAO High Risk List for fraud, waste, abuse and mismanagement in government programs and operations. See also POGO's online Federal Contractor Misconduct Database.

On outsourcing and the revolving door, see Reed Karaim, "Privatizing Government Services," report for *CQ Researcher* (December 8, 2017); Thomas Frank, *The Wrecking Crew* (New York, 2008); Frank, *Listen, Liberal* (New York, 2016); John DiIulio, *Bring Back the Bureaucrats* (West Conshohocken, PA, 2014); Paul Verkuil, *Outsourcing Sovereignty* (Cambridge, UK, 2007); Donald Kettl, *Escaping Jurassic Government* (Washington, DC, 2016); and Paul Chassy and Scott Amey, "Bad Business," report by POGO (September 13, 2011). Recent litigation against pharmaceutical companies is neatly tallied in Sammy Almashat, Sidney Wolfe et al., "Twenty-Five Years of Pharmaceutical Industry Criminal and Civil Penalties," report for Public Citizen (March 31, 2016). For wrongdoing by banks, see the Corporate Research Project's online Corporate Rap Sheets, and the Good Jobs First online Violation Tracker, as well as the websites of two Wall Street veterans, Dennis Kelleher at *Better Markets*, and Pam Martin's probing and provocative *Wall Street on Parade* blog (search for terms like "rap sheet" and "recidivist"). Director of National Intelligence James Clapper lied to Congress under oath while being questioned by Senator Ron Wyden during a March 12, 2013, hearing before the Senate Select Committee on Intelligence. On the decline in prosecutions and the concurrent rise of settlements, deferred prosecution agreements and non-prosecution agreements, see Brandon Garrett, *Too Big to Jail* (Cambridge, MA, 2014), and Jesse Eisinger, *The Chickenshit Club* (New York, 2017). The Supreme Court decided the case of *McDonnell v. United States*, docket no. 15-474, on June 27, 2016.

Regarding secrecy and overclassification, see Steven Aftergood, "An Inquiry into the Dynamics of Government Secrecy," *Harvard Civil Rights–Civil Liberties Law Review* (Spring 2013); Aftergood's statement was made before the Subcommittee on the Constitution of the Senate Judiciary Committee, *Hearing on Secret Law and the Threat to Democratic and Accountable Government* (April 30, 2008); Mary-Rose Papandrea, "Lapdogs, Watchdogs, and Scapegoats," *Boston College Law School Faculty Papers* (February 27, 2008); testimony of David Cuillier at a hearing before the Senate Judiciary Committee, *Open Government and Freedom of Information: Reinvigorating the Freedom of Information Act for the Digital Age* (March 11, 2014); the op-ed by Elizabeth Goitein and J. William Leonard, "America's Unnecessary Secrets," *New York Times* (November 7, 2011); and Michael Barclay, "Democracy Behind Closed Doors," report for the Freedom Forum Institute (March 9, 2015).

On secrecy in business, nondisclosure agreements, and mandatory arbitration, see Orly Lobel, "NDAs Are Out of Control," *Harvard Business Review* (January 30, 2018); Katherine Stone and Alexander Colvin, "The Arbitration Epidemic," briefing paper for the Economic Policy Institute (December 7, 2015); testimony of Cliff Palefsky, House Judiciary Committee, Subcommittee on Commercial and

Administrative Law, at the hearing *Mandatory Binding Arbitration: Is It Fair and Voluntary?* (September 15, 2009); and Michael Barr, "Mandatory Arbitration in Consumer Finance and Investor Contracts," *New York University Journal of Law & Business* (special issue, 2015). See also Jed Rakoff, "Why You Won't Get Your Day in Court," *New York Review of Books* (November 24, 2016); and Erwin Chemerinski, *Closing the Courthouse Door* (New Haven, CT, 2017). On secret tax havens and the use of shell companies, see Casey Michel, "The United States of Anonymity," a briefing paper for the Hudson Institute's Kleptocracy Initiative (November 2017); and "Just for Show? Reviewing G20 Promises on Beneficial Ownership," a Transparency International report (November 12, 2015). For in-depth looks at the Panama Papers, Paradise Papers and other tax evasion and financial secrecy scandals, see investigations by the International Consortium of Investigative Journalists on their website. The Tax Justice Network's Financial Secrecy Index ranks nations' jurisdictions according to their secrecy and the scale of their offshore financial activities. See also David Resnik, "Openness Versus Secrecy in Scientific Research," *Episteme* (February 2006).

Sociologist Claude Fischer's analysis of the individualism and the obedience and conformism of Americans appears in "Sweet Land of . . . Conformity?" *Boston Globe*, June 6, 2010; and in a related post on his *Made in America* blog, "American Individualism—Really?" (April 19, 2010). See also his fascinating book *Made in America* (Chicago, 2010).

CHAPTER 4. BLOOD IVORY TOWERS

This chapter is based in part on personal communication with Gary Aguirre, Max Bazerman, Bill Black, Sara Miron Bloom, Charles Davidson, Daniel Fessler, Jon Haidt, Kiley Hamlin, Marianne Jennings, Rob Kurzban, Harry Lewis, David McClintick, Karen Stenner, Lynn Stout, Steven Teles, Andy Thompson, David Warsh, Janine Wedel and Ilya Zaslavskiy.

On Lynn Stout's objections to the Lowell Milken gift, UCLA's reaction, and the question of dubious philanthropy, see "UCLA School of Law Receives Transformative $10 Million Gift from Alumnus Lowell Milken," UCLA Law website (August 5, 2011); UCLA chancellor Gene Block's letter to the editor about the Lowell Milken gift, *Los Angeles Times* (September 2, 2011); Larry Gordon, "UCLA Law Professor Opposes Naming Institute After Lowell Milken," *Los Angeles Times* (August 24, 2011); Julie Creswell and Peter Lattman, "Milken's Gift Stirs Dispute at UCLA Law School," *New York Times DealBook* (August 22, 2011); Stephen Bainbridge (a professor of law at UCLA), "LA Times Has More Details on Milken to UCLAW Gift Controversy," on his blog, *ProfessorBainbridge.com* (August 23, 2011); and Nick Baumann, "Apparently We've Forgotten Who the Milkens Are," *Mother Jones* (August 18, 2011).

The criminal case in which Michael Milken pleaded guilty to felony charges and received a ten-year prison sentence is United States of America v. Michael R. Milken, Lowell J. Milken et al., case no. SS 89 Cr. 41 (KMW), in the US District Court for the Southern District of New York; see findings of presiding judge Kimba Wood, December 13, 1990. Among the many suits filed against Milken, Drexel and others in the Southern District of New York and in the Northern and Central Districts of California, see especially Federal Deposit Insurance Corporation, et al. v. Michael R. Milken, et al., Southern District of New York no. 91 Civ. 0433 (MP), opinion and order of December 19, 1991; and Securities and Exchange Commission v. Drexel Burnham Lambert Inc., et al., Southern District of New York no. 88 Civ. 6209 (MP) (1988)—see the SEC's 184-page complaint documenting Mike Milken's alleged conspiracies and insider trading, litigation release no. 11,859, 41 SEC Docket 1047 (September 7, 1988); and settlement details in litigation release no. 12061 (April 13, 1989).

The definitive book on the Milkens, Ivan Boesky and Drexel Burnham Lambert is *Den of Thieves* (New York, 1991), by James Stewart, who won a Pulitzer Prize for his *Wall Street Journal* reporting that formed the basis of the book. *Den of Thieves* underwent extensive pre-publication fact-checking by the publisher, Simon & Schuster, to avert libel suits from people mentioned in the book. Stewart nevertheless faced such a lawsuit, surreptitiously funded by Lowell Milken, though he prevailed after seven years of litigation (see Roger Parloff, "Milken's Revenge?" *Legal Affairs* [July–August 2002]). Also essential is the sixty-page article by George Akerlof and Paul Romer, both subsequent recipients of the Nobel Prize in economics, titled "Looting: The Economic Underworld of Bankruptcy for Profit," *Brookings Papers on Economic Activity*, no. 2 (1993), which details what Akerlof and Romer describe as systematic market manipulation by Michael Milken. See also Connie Bruck, *The Predators' Ball* (New York, 1988); William Cohen, "The Michael Milken Project," *Institutional Investor* (May 1, 2017); and Edward Cohn, "The Resurrection of Michael Milken," *American Prospect* (November 14, 2001).

For a radically different interpretation of the Milkens' banking careers, see Daniel Fischel, *Payback: The Conspiracy to Destroy Michael Milken and His Financial Revolution* (New York, 1995); Fenton Bailey, *Fall from Grace* (New York, 1992); and "The Mythology of Michael Milken" on Milken's website, mikemilken.com. Revisionist publications on junk bonds and the S&L scandal published by the Milken Institute include Glenn Yago and Susanne Trimbath, *Beyond Junk Bonds* (New York, 2003); and Glenn Yago and James Barth, *The Savings and Loan Crisis: Lessons from a Regulatory Failure* (Santa Monica, CA, 2004). In addition to the Lowell Milken Institute for Business Law and Policy at UCLA, Milken centers, institutes, foundations and archives include the Lowell Milken Center for Unsung Heroes, Lowell Milken's and Michael Milken's personal websites, the Milken Family Foundation, the Milken Institute, and the Milken Archive of Jewish Music.

On Milton Friedman's ideas and their impact on economic and public policy, see Friedman's influential *Capitalism and Freedom* (40th anniversary ed., Chicago, 2002); Friedman, "The Social Responsibility of Business Is to Increase Its Profits," *New York Times Magazine* (September 13, 1970); obituary of Friedman by Lawrence Summers in the *New York Times*, "The Great Liberator" (November 19, 2006); and Andrei Shleifer, "The Age of Milton Friedman," *Journal of Economic Literature* (March 2009). The definitive edition of Friedrich von Hayek's *The Road to Serfdom*, originally published in 1944, is volume 2 of *The Collected Works of F. A. Hayek* (Chicago, 2009). Representative texts by other leading University of Chicago economists and legal scholars include: James Buchanan, *The Limits of Liberty*, published as volume 7 of *Collected Works of James M. Buchanan* (Carmel, IN, 1975); Henry Manne, *Insider Trading and the Stock Market* (New York, 1966); Ronald Coase, *The Firm, the Market, and the Law* (Chicago, 1990); Coase, "The Problem of Social Cost," *Journal of Law & Economics* (October 1960); Gary Becker, "Crime and Punishment," *Journal of Political Economy* (March–April 1968); Becker, "Nobel Lecture: The Economic Way of Looking at Behavior," *Journal of Political Economy* (June 1993); Becker and Julio Jorge Elías, "Introducing Incentives in the Market for Live and Cadaveric Organ Donations," *Journal of Economic Perspectives* (Summer 2007); Richard Posner, "The Problematics of Moral and Legal Theory," *Harvard Law Review* (May 1998); Posner, "An Economic Theory of the Criminal Law," *Columbia Law Review* (October 1985); and Posner, *Frontiers of Legal Theory* (Cambridge, MA, 2001). See also Frank Easterbrook and Daniel Fischel, "Antitrust Suits by Targets of Tender Offers," *Michigan Law Review* (May 1982); Easterbrook and Fischel, *The Economic Structure of Corporate Law* (Cambridge, MA, 1991); Fischel, "The Corporate Governance Movement," *Vanderbilt Law Review* (November 1982); Andrei Shleifer and Robert Vishny, "Corruption," *Quarterly Journal of Economics* (August 1993); Oliver Williamson, *The Mechanisms of Governance* (Oxford, UK, 1996); and Gregory Mankiw, *Principles of Economics* (8th ed., Boston, 2017); the passage that contrasts economics with physics and Japanese appears in the preface to the first edition of *Principles* (2000).

On the law and economics movement, free-market fundamentalism, homo economicus and ethics (or lack thereof) in finance, see particularly Lynn Stout, *Cultivating Conscience* (Princeton, NJ, 2010); Steven Teles, *The Rise of the Conservative Legal Movement* (Princeton, NJ, 2008); Teles, "Transformative Bureaucracy," *Studies in American Political Development* (April 2009); Bill Black, *The Best Way to Rob a Bank Is to Own One* (Austin, TX, 2005); and Black's extensive writings posted at the New Economic Perspectives website, including: "Mankiw Mendacity and Morality and His League of Failed

Economists" (April 24, 2015), in which he describes Mankiw's response to Akerlof and Romer's "Looting" paper during a discussion at the Brookings Institution (the transcript of the discussion appears in Akerlof and Romer, "Looting"); and "Mankiw Morality in a Mash Up with Mankiw Myths" (May 9, 2016). Lynn Stout's casebook on law and economics is David W. Barnes and Lynn A. Stout, *Cases and Materials on Law and Economics* (Eagan, MN, 2006). On shareholder value and the nature of the corporation, see Roger Martin's brilliant *Fixing the Game* (Boston, 2011); Michael Jensen and William Meckling, "Theory of the Firm," *Journal of Financial Economics* (October 1976); and Paul Hirsch, "From Ambushes to Golden Parachutes," *American Journal of Sociology* (January 1986). On the widespread use and abuse of cost-benefit analysis, see Edward Fuchs and James Anderson, "The Institutionalization of Cost-Benefit Analysis," *Public Productivity Review* (Summer 1987); *Setting the Record Straight on Cost-Benefit Analysis and Financial Reform at the SEC*, report by Better Markets (Washington, DC, July 30, 2012); and a positive view of the practice in Eric Posner and E. Glen Weyl, "Cost-Benefit Analysis of Financial Regulations: A Response to Criticisms," *Yale Law Journal* Forum (January 22, 2015).

See also Martin Gelter and Kristoffel Grechenig, "History of Law and Economics," *Max Planck Institute for Research on Collective Goods Preprint* (April 1, 2014); Lanny Ebenstein, *Chicagonomics* (New York, 2015); Richard Posner, "Gary Becker's Contributions to Law and Economics," *Journal of Legal Studies* (June 1993); Paul Zak, ed., *Moral Markets* (Princeton, NJ, 2008); David Wilson and William Dixon, *A History of Homo Economicus* (Abingdon, UK, 2012); Daniel Cohen, *Homo Economicus* (Paris, 2013); and Steven Levitt and John List, "Homo Economicus Evolves," *Science* (February 15, 2008). See also David Harvey, *A Brief History of Neoliberalism* (Oxford, UK, 2005); Richard Sennett, *The Culture of the New Capitalism* (New Haven, CT, 2006); Sennett, *The Fall of Public Man* (40th anniversary ed., New York, 2017); Sennett, *The Corrosion of Character* (New York, 1998); Fred Block and Margaret Somers, *The Power of Market Fundamentalism* (Cambridge, MA, 2014); James Galbraith, *The Predator State* (New York, 2008); Bernard Harcourt, *The Illusion of Free Markets* (Cambridge, MA, 2011); Steve Keen, *Debunking Economics* (rev. ed., London, 2011); and Justin Fox, *The Myth of the Rational Market* (New York, 2009). Oliver Wendell Holmes expounded his "bad man" theory in "The Path of the Law," *Harvard Law Review* (March 25, 1897). (Further references to the free-market mantra and homo economicus appear in notes to Chapter 6 below.)

For details on the founding of Compass Lexecon and on economists serving as highly paid expert witnesses, see Jesse Eisinger and Justin Elliott, "These Professors Make More Than a Thousand Bucks an Hour Peddling Mega-Mergers," online at *ProPublica* (November 16, 2016). See also Charles Ferguson's 2010 documentary film *Inside Job*, and his book by the same title (London, 2014). Michael Milken's 1986 remark on junk bonds reported in David Vise "Market Dynamo Defends Use of Junk Bonds for Takeover Bids," *Washington Post* (December 7, 1986). For Milken's later travails with the SEC, see Securities and Exchange Commission v. Michael R. Milken and MC Group, case no. 98 Civ. 1398 in the Southern District of New York, filed February 26, 1998; SEC Administrative Proceeding in the Matter of Guggenheim Partners Investment Management, LLC, filed August 10, 2015 (File no. 3-16735); and Matt Levine, "Guggenheim, the SEC and Milken's Shadow," *Bloomberg Opinion* (August 10, 2015).

On aspects of evolutionary psychology relevant to whistleblowing, see David Buss, *Evolutionary Psychology* (6th ed., Abingdon, UK, 2019); Buss, ed., *Handbook of Evolutionary Psychology* (2nd ed., Hoboken, NJ, 2015); and work by pioneering scholars Leda Cosmides and John Tooby, including "Evolutionary Psychology," *Annual Review of Psychology* (January 2013); Cosmides, Michael Price et al., "Punitive Sentiment as an Anti-Free Rider Psychological Device," *Evolution and Human Behavior* 23 (2002); and "Evolutionary Psychology," Cosmides and Tooby's excellent online synopsis posted at the Center for Evolutionary Psychology of the University of California–Santa Barbara (January 13, 1997). See also Andy (J. Anderson) Thomson and Clare Aukofer, *Why We Believe in God(s)* (Durham, NC, 2011); and Daniel Fessler, Jason Clark et al., "Evolutionary Psychology and Evolutionary Anthropology," in Buss, *Handbook of Evolutionary Psychology*.

Other pertinent research in evolutionary psychology includes Robert Trivers, "Deceit and Self-Deception," in Peter Kappeler and Joan Silk, eds., *Mind the Gap* (Berlin, 2010); Trivers and William von Hippel, "The Evolution and Psychology of Self-Deception," *Behavioral and Brain Sciences* (February 2011); Robin Dunbar, *How Many Friends Does One Person Need?* (London, 2010); Dunbar, Clive Gamble et al., *Thinking Big* (London, 2014); Denise Cummins, "Dominance, Status, and Social Hierarchies," in Buss, *Handbook of Evolutionary Psychology*; Cummins, "Emergence of Deontic Reasoning," in T. K. Shackelford and V. A. Weekes-Shackelford, eds., *Encyclopedia of Evolutionary Psychological Science* (Basel, Switz., 2016); Francisco Gil-White, "Are Ethnic Groups Biological 'Species' to the Human Brain?" *Current Anthropology* (August–October 2001); Michael Bang Petersen, "Healthy Out-Group Members Are Represented Psychologically as Infected In-Group Members," *Psychological Science* (October 19, 2017); Peter Singer, "Ethics and Intuitions," *Journal of Ethics* (2005); Richard Joyce, "Ethics and Evolution," in Hugh LaFollette and Ingmar Persson, eds., *The Blackwell Guide to Ethical Theory* (2nd ed., Hoboken, NJ, 2013); Robert Kurzban and Daniel Houser, "Experiments Investigating Cooperative Types in Humans," *Proceedings of the National Academy of Sciences* (February 1, 2005); Kurzban and Steven Neuberg, "Managing Ingroup and Outgroup Relationships," in Buss, *Handbook of Evolutionary Psychology*; Kurzban and Peter DeScioli, "A Solution to the Mysteries of Morality," *Psychological Bulletin* (March 2013).

Regarding morality in infancy and early childhood, see J. Kiley Hamlin, "Moral Judgment and Action in Preverbal Infants and Toddlers," *Current Directions in Psychological Science* (June 2013); Hamlin, "Context-Dependent Social Evaluation in 4.5-Month-Olds," *Frontiers in Psychology* (June 2014); Hamlin, Karen Wynn et al., "Social Evaluation by Preverbal Infants," *Nature* (November 22, 2007); Hamlin, Neha Mahajan et al., "Not Like Me = Bad," *Psychological Science* 24, no. 4 (2013); Marco Schmidt and Michael Tomasello, "Young Children Enforce Social Norms," *Current Directions in Psychological Science* (July 2012); Schmidt, Susanne Göckeritz et al., "Young Children's Creation and Transmission of Social Norms," *Cognitive Development* 30, no. 1 (2014); Schmidt and Jessica Sommerville, "The Development of Fairness Expectations and Prosocial Behavior in the Second Year of Life," *Infancy* 18, no. 1 (2013); and Yarrow Dunham and Andrew Baron, "Consequences of 'Minimal' Group Affiliations in Children," *Child Development* (May–June 2011). On justice in animals, see Jessica Pierce and Marc Bekoff, "Wild Justice Redux," *Social Justice Research* (June 2012); and Martin Nowak, Corina Tarnita and E. O. Wilson, "The Evolution of Eusociality," *Nature* (August 2010).

On authoritarianism, see Karen Stenner, *The Authoritarian Dynamic* (New York, 2005); Cass Sunstein, *Can It Happen Here?* (New York, 2018); Sunstein, *Why Societies Need Dissent* (Cambridge, MA, 2003); Marc Hetherington and Jonathan Weiler, *Authoritarianism and Polarization in American Politics* (Cambridge, UK, 2009); Robert Altemeyer, *The Authoritarians* (self-published, 2007); and the classic text by Theodor Adorno, Else Frenkel-Brunswik et al., *The Authoritarian Personality* (New York, 1950). Works on Holocaust rescuers include Patrick Henry, *We Only Know Men* (Washington, DC, 2007); Samuel Oliner and Pearl Oliner, *The Altruistic Personality* (New York, 1988); Eva Fogelman, *Conscience and Courage* (New York, 1994); Fogelman, "The Rescuer Self," in Michael Berenbaum and Abraham Peck, eds., *The Holocaust and History* (Bloomington, IN, 1998); and Nechama Tec, *When Light Pierced the Darkness* (Oxford, UK, 1987).

The Scalia–Cheney case before the Supreme Court was captioned Richard B. Cheney, Vice President of the United States, et al. v. United States District Court for the District of Columbia et al., case no. 541 US 913, decided on June 24, 2004. See Scalia's memorandum of March 18, 2004, and the motion to recuse by Alan Morrison, counsel for the Public Citizen Litigation Group, February 23, 2004, as well as the two underlying suits brought by Judicial Watch Inc. against the National Energy Policy Development Group before the US District Court for the District of Columbia, civil case numbers 01-1530 (EGS) and 02-631 (EGS); and the July 11, 2002, opinion in the latter suit by Justice Emmet Sullivan. Good analysis of Scalia's position by Edward Lazarus, "Scalia's Refusal to Recuse," online at FindLaw, US Supreme Court Center, Legal Commentary (April 1, 2004). See the relevant law at 28

US Code § 455, "Disqualification of Justice, Judge, or Magistrate Judge." Scalia wrote his 1974 memo to Kenneth Lazarus, associate counsel to LBJ, dated December 18.

On the unconscious nature of decision making, see Jonathan Haidt, "The New Synthesis in Moral Psychology," *Science* (May 18, 2007); Haidt, "Moral Psychology and the Law: How Intuitions Drive Reasoning, Judgment, and the Search for Evidence," *Alabama Law Review* 64, no. 4 (2013); Haidt, Silvia Helena Koller et al., "Affect, Culture, and Morality, or Is It Wrong to Eat Your Dog?" *Journal of Personality and Social Psychology* (October 1993); Haidt, Simone Schnall et al., "Disgust as Embodied Moral Judgment," *Personality and Social Psychology Bulletin* (August 2008); Haidt, *The Righteous Mind* (New York, 2012); Daniel Kahneman, *Thinking Fast and Slow* (New York, 2011); Joshua Greene, *Moral Tribes* (London, 2014); Greene, "The Cognitive Neuroscience of Moral Judgment and Decision Making," in Michael Gazzaniga and George Mangun, eds., *The Cognitive Neurosciences* (Cambridge, MA, 2014); Greene, R. Brian Sommerville et al., "An fMRI Investigation of Emotional Engagement in Moral Judgment," *Science* (September 14, 2001); Greene, "The Secret Joke of Kant's Soul," in W. Sinnott-Armstrong, ed., *Moral Psychology*, vol. 3 (Cambridge, MA, 2008); Greene, "The Rise of Moral Cognition," *Cognition* (February 2015); and Judith Jarvis Thomson, "The Trolley Problem," *Yale Law Journal* (May 1985).

On reciprocity and conflicts of interest, see Robert Cialdini, *Influence* (rev. ed., New York, 2006); Lawrence Lessig, *Republic, Lost* (2nd ed., October 20, 2015); Anthony Pratkanis, "Social Influence Analysis," in Pratkanis, ed., *The Science of Social Influence* (New York, 2007); and Pratkanis and Doug Shadel, *Weapons of Fraud* (Seattle, 2005). See also Dolly Chugh, Max Bazerman et al., "Bounded Ethicality as a Psychological Barrier to Recognizing Conflicts of Interest," in Don Moore, Daylian Cain et al., *Conflicts of Interest* (Cambridge, UK, 2005); Chugh and Mary Kern, "A Dynamic and Cyclical Model of Bounded Ethicality," *Research in Organizational Behavior* (2016); Bazerman and Don Moore, "Is It Time for Auditor Independence Yet?" *Accounting, Organizations and Society* (May–July 2011); Bazerman, George Loewenstein et al., "Why Good Accountants Do Bad Audits," *Harvard Business Review* (November 2002); Carol Tavris and Elliot Aronson, *Mistakes Were Made (but Not by Me)* (New York, 2007); and Don Moore and Philip Tetlock, "Conflicts of Interest and the Case of Auditor Independence," *Academy of Management Review* (January 2006). Marcel Mauss's classic work is *The Gift*, trans. W. D. Halls (London, 1990).

On Arthur Andersen, Enron and conflicts of interest in accounting, in addition to references regarding conflict of interest in the notes to Chapters 1 and 3 above, see Malcolm Salter, *Innovation Corrupted* (Cambridge, MA, 2008); and *Financial Oversight of Enron*, report by the staff of the Senate Committee on Governmental Affairs (October 7, 2002). Interview with Peter Thiel by Maureen Dowd, "Peter Thiel, Trump's Tech Pal, Explains Himself," *New York Times* (January 11, 2017).

The case against Blankenship is United States of America v. Donald L. Blankenship, US District Court for the Southern District of West Virginia, case no. 5:14-cr-00244; see the grand jury indictment of November 12, 2014, and the sentencing memorandum of March 28, 2016. Full details of the disaster are available in a preliminary report from the West Virginia Governor's Independent Investigation Panel, led by J. Davitt McAteer, titled *Upper Big Branch, the April 5, 2010, Explosion* (May 2011). The original 1998 fraud lawsuit against Blankenship's company is Caperton et al. v. A. T. Massey Coal Co. et al., in the Circuit Court of Boone County, West Virginia, case no. 98-C-192. See the November 12, 2009, decision by the Supreme Court of Appeals of West Virginia, no. 33350; and the Supreme Court decision (556 US 868) of June 8, 2009, which contains full details of Blankenship's and the West Virginia Supreme Court's machinations, and Scalia's dissent. (Justices Roberts, Thomas and Alito likewise dissented, for similar reasons.) See also Laurence Leamer, *The Price of Justice* (New York, 2013); Jeff Goodell, "The Dark Lord of Coal Country," *Rolling Stone* (November 29, 2010); and Russell Mokhiber, "Bruce Stanley on Corporate Crime in West Virginia," *Corporate Crime Reporter* (December 15, 2014).

Regarding Janine Wedel, the Harvard Project, and the evolution of Russian kleptocracy, the first definitive telling of the scandal was David McClintick, "How Harvard Lost Russia," *Institutional Investor* (February 2006). See also David Warsh's recent, in-depth book *Because They Could* (CreateSpace Publishing, 2018); Warsh covered the case for the *Boston Globe* as it unfolded, and also wrote about it on his website, Economic Principals. More good coverage in the *Harvard Crimson,* including Nicholas Ciarelli and Anton Troianovski, "'Tawdry Shleifer Affair' Stokes Faculty Anger Toward Summers" (February 10, 2006). See also Harry Lewis, *Excellence Without a Soul* (New York, 2006).

The DOJ lawsuit against Harvard and members of the Harvard Project is United States of America v. President and Fellows of Harvard College, Andrei Shleifer and Jonathan Hay, civil action before the US District Court, District of Massachusetts, case no. 00-11977-DPW; see especially the government's complaint filed on September 26, 2000; Judge Douglas Woodlock's memorandum and order of June 28, 2004; the civil jury's conclusion regarding Shleifer's directorship of the project, December 9, 2004; and depositions of Lawrence Summers (March 13, 2002) and Andrei Shleifer (October 16, 2001). See also Forum Financial Group LLC and Johnny Y. Keffer v. President and Fellows of Harvard College, Jonathan R. Hay and Andrei N. Shleifer, civil action before the US District Court, District of Maine, case no. 00-306-PH (complaint filed October 24, 2000).

For the anthropological analysis of flex networks, Western aid, the "corruption industry" and the rise of the oligarchs, see Janine Wedel's books *Collision and Collusion* (updated ed., New York, 2001); *Shadow Elite* (New York, 2009); and *Unaccountable* (updated ed., New York, 2016); as well as Wedel, "Clique-Run Organizations and US Economic Aid," *Demokratizatsiya* (Fall 1996); Wedel's testimony before the House Committee on International Relations, for a hearing titled *US Aid to Russia: Where It All Went Wrong* (September 17, 1998); Wedel, "Tainted Transactions," *National Interest* (Spring 2000); Wedel, "Rethinking Corruption in an Age of Ambiguity," *Annual Review of Law and Social Science* (December 2012); and Wedel, "Mafia Without Malfeasance, Clans Without Crime," in *Crime's Power,* ed. Philip Parnell and Stephanie Kane (New York, 2003). See also Adam Podgórecki, "Polish Society: A Sociological Analysis," *Praxis International* (April 1987); Antoni Kaminski and Joanna Kurczewska, "Main Actors of Transformation," in Eric Allardt and Wlodzimierz Wesolowski, eds., *The General Outlines of Transformation* (Warsaw, 1994); Leonid Kosals, "The Clan Capitalism and Its Long Run Future in Russia," in Robert Trappl, ed., *Cybernetics and Systems 2008* (Vienna, 2008); Wojciech Pawlik, "Intimate Commerce," in Janine Wedel, ed., *The Unplanned Society* (New York, 1992); James Millar, "From Utopian Socialism to Utopian Capitalism," *George Washington University 175th Anniversary Papers* (1996); and Rubén Berríos, *Contracting for Development* (Santa Barbara, CA, 2000). See also Anne Williamson, testimony at hearings before the House Committee on Banking and Financial Services titled *Russian Money Laundering* (September 21, 1999); comments on Wedel's article "Tainted Transactions" by Jeffrey Sachs, Wayne Merry, Michael Hudson et al. in *National Interest* (Summer 2000); Jeffrey Sachs, "What I Did in Russia," posted on his blog, *Jeffsachs.org,* on March 14, 2012; Maxim Boycko, Andrei Shleifer et al., "Privatizing Russia," *Brookings Papers on Economic Activity,* no. 2 (1993); Shleifer and Robert Vishny, "Corruption," *Quarterly Journal of Economics* (August 1993); Shleifer and Vishny, *The Grabbing Hand: Government Pathologies and Their Cures* (Cambridge, MA, 1999); and useful interviews with Wedel, Merry et al. in the PBS *Frontline* episode titled "Return of the Czar," which aired May 9, 2000.

Regarding the Chubais clan and the rise of Russian oligarchs, see Karen Dawisha, *Putin's Kleptocracy* (New York, 2014); Ilya Zaslavskiy, "How Non-State Actors Export Kleptocratic Norms to the West," briefing paper for the Hudson Institute's Kleptocracy Initiative (September 2017); and Zaslavskiy's valuable website www.underminers.info. See also Zaslavskiy and Scott Stedman, "How to Select Russian Oligarchs for New Sanctions?" report prepared for Underminers.info (June 2018); Zaslavskiy, "Making Life Hard for Russia's Robber Barons," *Foreign Policy* (May 18, 2016). On Leonard Blavatnik's philanthropy, see Zaslavskiy, "Why Comrade Sir Leonid (Len) Blavatnik Is a Putin Oligarch . . . ," posted at Underminers.info on February 13, 2019; Ann Marlowe, "Is Harvard Whitewashing a

Russian Oligarch's Fortune?" *New York Times* (December 5, 2018); Harry Lewis, "Some Russian Money Flows Back to Harvard," posted at his blog *Bits and Pieces* on January 19, 2014; and Max de Haldevang, "Major GOP Donor Len Blavatnik Had Business Ties to a Russian Official," *Quartz* (online, January 22, 2019). See also McClintick, "How Harvard Lost Russia."

The *Time* magazine cover with Greenspan, Rubin and Summers is dated February 15, 1999. See Sheila Bair, *Bull by the Horns* (New York, 2012); testimony by Brooksley Born at the hearing *Over-the-Counter Derivatives Market*, before the House Committee on Banking and Financial Services (July 24, 1998); and the *Frontline* episode "The Warning" (segment aired October 20, 2009; with transcripts of additional interviews online), about Born's efforts to regulate over-the-counter derivatives, a root cause of the 2008 financial crisis, and the concerted, and ultimately successful, campaign by Alan Greenspan, Robert Rubin and Lawrence Summers to thwart her.

CHAPTER 5. REAPING THE NUCLEAR HARVEST

This chapter is based in part on personal communication with David Anderson, Dave Berick, Bill Black, Donna Busche, Tom Carpenter, John Carreyrou, Mary Louise Cohen, Richard Condit, Sally Denton, Tom Devine, Dana Gold, Gary Gwilliam, Eric Havian, Marco Kaltofen, Erika Kelton, Laton McCartney, Russell Mokhiber, Rick Parks, James Ratley, Gary Rogers, John Swain, Sandy Tamosaitis, Walt Tamosaitis and Eileen Welsome.

On the history of Hanford and its surrounding community, its nuclear weapons program and its myriad environmental hazards, see Harry Thayer, *Management of the Hanford Engineering Works in World War II* (New York, 1996); Bruce Hevly and John Findlay, eds., *The Atomic West* (Seattle, 1998); S. L. Sanger, *Working on the Bomb: An Oral History of World War II* (Portland, OR, 1995); Pap Ndiaye, *Nylon and Bombs*, trans. Elborg Forster (Baltimore, 2007); David Harvey, *History of the Hanford Site: 1943–1990*, report by the Pacific Northwest National Laboratory (Richland, WA, 2001); Robert Bauman and Robert Franklin, eds., *Nowhere to Remember: Hanford, White Bluffs, and Richland to 1943* (Pullman, WA, 2018); and Melvin Adams, *Atomic Geography* (Pullman, WA, 2016). For recent news, scientific analysis and historical information, see the Hanford Challenge website, as well as the extensive resources available online at the Hanford History Project and the DOE's Hanford website. Sharp reporting on Hanford whistleblowers, tank leaks and other contamination events is on *KING 5 News*, which airs on an NBC-affiliated station based in Seattle (www.king5.com). Good daily coverage of the site and surrounding communities is in the *Tri-City Herald*, a local daily newspaper.

On Hanford's place in the US nuclear weapons program and the Manhattan Project, see Kate Brown, *Plutopia* (New York, 2013); Max Power, *America's Nuclear Wastelands* (Pullman, WA, 2012); Fred Pearce, *Fallout* (Boston, 2018); Michael D'Antonio, *Atomic Harvest* (New York, 1993); Lesley Groves, *Now It Can Be Told* (New York, 1983); Richard Rhodes, *The Making of the Atomic Bomb* (New York, 1986); Gregg Herken, *Brotherhood of the Bomb* (New York, 2002); Andrew Blowers, *The Legacy of Nuclear Power* (Abingdon, UK, 2016); and Dan Zak, *Almighty* (New York, 2016). See also Ellsberg, *The Doomsday Machine* (New York, 2017). For an understanding of the current worldwide nuclear weapons complex and ongoing arms race, see also the website of Nuclear Watch.

On the fraught environmental cleanup effort at Hanford, see Roy Gephart, *Hanford: A Conversation About Nuclear Waste and Cleanup* (Columbus, OH, 2003); Steven Blush and Thomas Heitman, *Train Wreck on a River of Money*, report prepared for the US Senate Committee on Energy and Natural Resources (March 1995); Robert Alvarez, "Reducing the Risks of High-Level Radioactive Wastes at Hanford," *Science and Global Security* 13, nos. 1–2 (2005); Alvarez, "Plutonium Wastes from the US Nuclear Weapons Complex," *Science & Global Security* 19 (2011); *Hanford Cleanup: The First 25 Years*, report by the Oregon Department of Energy (September 2014); the DNFSB's Annual Reports to Congress (see esp. reports no. 23–28 for the years 2013–2018); and *Competing Visions for the Future of Hanford*, report by the nonprofit group Columbia Riverkeeper (July 17, 2018).

For Hanford's natural landscape and the threat that radiation poses to it, see J. L. Downs, W. H. Rickard et al., *Habitat Types on the Hanford Site*, report by the Pacific Northwest Laboratory (December 1993); Blaine Harden, *A River Lost* (New York, 1996); "Geology and Ground-Water Characteristics of the Hanford Reservation," Geological Survey Professional Paper 717 (Washington, DC, 1972); Andrew Barto, Y. James Chang et al., "Consequence Study of a Beyond-Design-Basis Earthquake Affecting the Spent Fuel Pool for a US Mark I Boiling Water Reactor," report for the USNRC's Office of Nuclear Regulatory Research (September 2014); Brett Tiller and Ted Poston, "Mule Deer Antlers as Biomonitors of Strontium-90 on the Hanford Site," *Journal of Environmental Radioactivity* (2000); and "Hanford and the River," report by Columbia Riverkeeper (2013).

Specifically regarding the Hanford tank farms and their danger to workers, see the excellent overview in court filings for the lawsuit captioned Hanford Challenge, United Association of Plumbers and Steamfitters Local Union 598, and the State of Washington v. Ernest Moniz, in his official capacity as Secretary, United States Department of Energy, and Washington River Protections Solutions, LLC, before the US District Court, Eastern District of Washington, case no. 4:15-cv-05086-TOR. See esp. Washington state's motion for preliminary injunction (July 21, 2016); the citizen plaintiffs' reply in support of this motion (October 5, 2016); and the presiding justice Thomas Rice's order denying motion for judgment on the pleadings (November 3, 2016).

For a review of the research on vapor and worker exposure in the Hanford tank farms, see Robert Alvarez, "Chronology Regarding Hanford High-Level Radioactive Waste Tank Vapor Exposures," report prepared for Hanford Challenge (December 29, 2015). Key reports on tank farm vapors include W. R. Wilmarth et al., "Hanford Tank Vapor Assessment Report" (the "TVAT report"), prepared for Savannah River National Laboratory (October 30, 2014); "Hanford Site-Wide Risk Review Project," by the Consortium for Risk Evaluation with Stakeholder Participation (CRESP) led by Vanderbilt University (August 31, 2015); and A. D. Maughan, J. G. Droppo et al., "Health Risk Assessment for Short- and Long-term Worker Inhalation Exposure . . . ," report prepared by Pacific Northwest National Laboratory (March 1997). Important GAO reports include *Hanford Cleanup: Condition of Tanks May Further Limit DOE's Ability to Respond to Leaks and Intrusions* (November 2014); and *Nuclear Waste: DOE Lacks Critical Information Needed to Assess Its Tank Management Strategy at Hanford* (June 2008).

For insights into the serious dangers and compromised safety culture in the tank farm, see DNFSB letter of April 1, 2013, to Senator Ron Wyden; letter of July 24, 2003, from Nancy Beaudet, industrial hygienist at the Occupational and Environmental Medicine Program, Harborview Medical Center, Seattle, to Kathy Lombardo, a vice president at CH2M Hill; "Follow-up Assessment of Progress on Actions Taken to Address Tank Vapor Concerns at the Hanford Site," a study by the DOE's Office of Worker Safety and Health Assessments (January 2017); "Knowing Endangerment: Worker Exposure to Toxic Vapors at the Hanford Tank Farms," report by GAP (September 2003); and D. J. Washenfelder, "Forensic Investigation of Hanford Double-Shell Tank AY-102 Radioactive Waste Leak—14178," a presentation at the Waste Management Conference (March 2–6, 2014).

On downwinders, the "Green Run" and experiments on humans, see Eileen Welsome's engrossing *The Plutonium Files* (New York, 1999); Michelle Gerber, *On the Home Front: The Cold War Legacy of the Hanford Nuclear Site* (3rd ed., Lincoln, NE, 2007); Lisa Martino-Taylor, *Behind the Fog* (Abingdon, UK, 2017); *The Human Radiation Experiments: Final Report of the Advisory Committee on Human Radiation Experiments* (New York, 1996); and *Lessons Learned from the Fukushima Nuclear Accident for Improving Safety and Security of US Nuclear Plants: Phase 2*, report by the National Academies of Sciences, Engineering, and Medicine (Washington, DC, 2016). See also *Radiation Exposure Compensation Act Trust Fund: FY 2013 President's Budget*, report by the DOJ Civil Division (February 2013); the online DOE Openness Project: Human Radiation Experiments; "A Listing of Radionuclides Released from Hanford," online at Hanford Health Information Network, Washington Department of Health; M. A. Robkin, "Experimental Release of 131I: The Green Run," *Health Physics* (June 1992); and "The Green Run," Technical Steering Panel of the Hanford Environmental Dose Reconstruction Project,

Fact Sheet 12 (March 1992). The Hanford Project and Hanford Challenge offer further information online.

Regarding Walt Tamosaitis's experiences at Hanford and the WTP, see court documents in Tamosaitis's various lawsuits, which include his federal suit captioned Walter L. Tamosaitis, PhD, and his marital community v. URS Energy & Construction, Inc., an Ohio Corporation and wholly owned subsidiary of Aecom, before the US District Court, Eastern District of Washington, case no. 2:11-cv-05157-LRS; see especially the second amended complaint (filed on July 8, 2015); the deposition of Frank Russo (July 14, 2011); and emails among Bechtel, URS and DOE employees revealed in discovery. See also the contract concluded between DOE and Bechtel titled "Performance Evaluation and Measurement Plan . . . Design, Construction, and Commissioning of the Hanford Tank Waste Treatment & Immobilization Plant," which details the financial incentives and awards to be triggered by closure of the M3 mixing issue; and the opinion by Circuit Judge Marsha Berzon, US Court of Appeals for the Ninth Circuit, filed November 7, 2014.

Tamosaitis filed his first whistleblower suit with the US Department of Labor (OSHA), alleging violations of the whistleblower provisions of the Energy Reorganization Act relating to his removal from the WTP: see the first amended complaint, filed December 15, 2010. The complaint for his second OSHA whistleblower suit, asserting claims and requesting damages resulting from his termination by URS in 2013, was filed March 27, 2014. Tamosaitis's suit against Bechtel, URS et al., alleging civil conspiracy, was heard by the Benton County Superior Court, case no. 10-2-02357-4, complaint filed September 13, 2010. See also the settlement agreement between Tamosaitis and URS, filed August 12, 2015; and Tamosaitis's two statements at hearings before the Subcommittee on Financial and Contracting Oversight of the Senate Committee on Homeland Security and Governmental Affairs, *Whistleblower Protections for Government Contractors* (December 6, 2011); and *Whistleblower Retaliation at the Hanford Nuclear Site* (March 11, 2014). Tom Carpenter's 163-page statement with attachments at the latter hearing is a definitive review of systemic dysfunction at the WTP, the DOE and Hanford contractors.

Numerous official reports and testimony catalog problems at the WTP of the kind that both Walt Tamosaitis and Donna Busche encountered. See Gary Brunson's two essential memoranda: "Summary of Actions and Design Outcomes That Erode Confidence in the Ability of Bechtel National Inc. to Complete Their Assigned Role as Design Authority for the WTP," memorandum 12-WTP-0274 to Scott Samuelson, Office of River Protection, et al. (August 23, 2012); and "Stop Work Recommendation and Basis," memorandum 12-WTP-0399 to Steven Chu, Secretary of Energy, et al. (December 19, 2012). See also "Safety Culture at the Waste Treatment and Immobilization Plant," Recommendation 2011-1 of the DNFSB (June 9, 2011). Key GAO reports critical of the WTP include *Hanford Waste Treatment: DOE Needs to Evaluate Alternatives to Recently Proposed Projects and Address Technical and Management Challenges* (May 2015); *Hanford Waste Treatment Plant: DOE Needs to Take Action to Resolve Technical and Management Challenges* (December 2012). Two audit reports by the DOE IG are likewise critical of the facility and its management: "Department of Energy Quality Assurance: Design Control for the Waste Treatment and Immobilization Plant at the Hanford Site" (September 2013); and "Quality Assurance Standards for the Integrated Control Network at the Hanford Site's Waste Treatment Plant" (May 2007). See also *Assessments of Safety Culture at the Hanford Site Waste Treatment and Immobilization Plant*, prepared by the DOE's Office of Worker Safety and Health Assessments, dated June 2014 and June 2015; and *Independent Oversight Assessment of Nuclear Safety Culture and Management of Nuclear Safety Concerns at the Hanford Site Waste Treatment and Immobilization Plant*, prepared by the DOE's Office of Health, Safety and Security (January 2012). Problems at the facility were highlighted years earlier in the *Hearing on Oversight of the Department of Energy's Waste Treatment Plant at Hanford*, House Committee on Appropriations, Subcommittee on Energy and Water Development, and Related Agencies (April 6, 2006), with associated GAO testimony, "Contractor and DOE Management Problems Have Led to Higher Costs, Construction Delays, and Safety Concerns" (April 6, 2006).

See Donna Busche's whistleblower lawsuit with OSHA, Donna Busche v. URS Energy and Construction, Inc. and Bechtel National, Inc., case no. 10-1960-14-002, third amended complaint filed June 16, 2014, which reviews the previous lawsuits brought by Busche. See also the undated memorandum produced in discovery in which consultant John Parker Stewart details his findings from his interviews of Busche and coworkers conducted in July 2011 (WTP-URS-00015); Busche's October 3, 2013, letter to Patricia Zarate at the DOE Employee Concerns Program succinctly describing her position and concerns in the case; and the DOE IG "Special Review: Issues Pertaining to the Termination of Ms. Donna Busche, a Contractor Employee at the Waste Treatment Plant Project" (October 2014), which explains how Bechtel and URS refused IG Gregory Friedman's demand for documents related to Busche's case.

For an excellent overview of the problem-plagued history of the WTP project, see the FCA lawsuit that Busche filed jointly with Tamosaitis and Brunson against Bechtel and URS, captioned United States of America ex rel. Gary Brunson, Donna Busche, and Walter Tamosaitis, Ph.D., v. Bechtel National Inc., Bechtel Corporation, URS Corporation et al., before the US District Court, Eastern District of Washington, case no. CV-13-5013-EFS, complaint filed August 23, 2013. See also Busche's statement at the March 11, 2014, hearing titled *Whistleblower Retaliation at the Hanford Nuclear Site*, as well as transcripts of the three DNFSB public hearings held in Kennewick, Washington (October 7–8, 2010; March 22 and May 22, 2012).

On regulatory capture and the revolving door at DOE, the department's contracting policies, and its attitude to whistleblowing, see Jonathan Brock, "Filling In the Holes in Whistleblower Protection Systems: Lessons from the Hanford Council Experience," *Seattle Journal for Social Justice* 11, no. 2 (2013); Tom Carpenter, "Whistleblowers in the Nuclear Age," a presentation at the Public Interest Environmental Law Conference (March 2, 2013); and Irwin Stelzer and Robert Patton, "The Department of Energy: An Agency That Cannot Be Reinvented," publication of the American Enterprise Institute (Washington, DC, 1996). Key GAO reports criticizing DOE contracting, conflicts and whistleblower protection include *Department of Energy—Contracting Actions Needed to Strengthen Subcontract Oversight Report to Congressional Requestors* (March 2019); *Department of Energy—Performance Evaluations Could Better Assess Management and Operating Contractor Costs* (February 2019); *Department of Energy—Whistleblower Protections Need Strengthening* (July 2016); *Nuclear Waste—Absence of Key Management Reforms on Hanford's Cleanup Project Adds to Challenges of Achieving Cost and Schedule Goals* (June 2004); and *Department of Energy—Contract Reform Is Progressing, but Full Implementation Will Take Years* (December 1996). A GAO report from 2019 points out that the NNSA and the DOE have been on the GAO High Risk List for project mismanagement for twenty-seven consecutive years: *High-Risk Series—Substantial Efforts Needed to Achieve Greater Progress on High-Risk Areas* (March 2019).

A recent lawsuit concerning whistleblowing and retaliation at Hanford is Julie M. Atwood v. Mission Support Alliance, LLC, Steve Young, et al., in the Superior Court of Washington for Benton County, case no. 15-2-01914-4, complaint filed August 20, 2015. See also letter of July 22, 2014, by Steve Grossman, Assistant Regional Administrator, OSHA, to Sandra Kent, General Counsel of Washington River Protection Solutions, Re: Washington River Protection Solutions, Inc./Doss/0-1960-12-002. Part of Ed Bricker's saga is described in Edwin L. Bricker, Cynthia Bricker v. Rockwell International Corporation et al., 10 F.3d 598, US Court of Appeals for the Ninth Circuit, decision of October 25, 1993. The FCA fraud suit against Lockheed Martin, Mission Support Alliance and others is United States of America v. Mission Support Alliance, LLC, Lockheed Martin Services, Inc., et al., US District Court for the Eastern District of Washington, case no. 4:19-cv-05021-RMP; see complaint filed February 8, 2019, and DOJ press release on the same day titled "United States Files False Claims Act Suit Against Mission Support Alliance LLC. . . ."

On the privatization of America's nuclear weapons research and production complex, and the cartel that now controls it, see Robert Alvarez, "Under Siege: Safety in the Nuclear Weapons Complex,"

Bulletin of the Atomic Scientists (August 30, 2018), and Alvarez's extensive further publications on the *Bulletin's* website; William Hartung and Christine Anderson, "Bombs Versus Budgets: Inside the Nuclear Weapons Lobby," a publication of the Center for International Policy (June 2012); the hearing before the Subcommittee on Strategic Forces of the House Committee on Armed Services titled *Governance, Oversight, and Management of the Nuclear Security Enterprise to Ensure High Quality Science, Engineering, and Mission Effectiveness in an Age of Austerity* (February 16, 2012) (see esp. the letter from Jeff Colvin and Roger Logan on Behalf of the University Professional and Technical Employees Union); and *Managing for High-Quality Science and Engineering at the NNSA National Security Laboratories*, report by the Committee to Review the Quality of the Management and of the Science and Engineering Research at the Department of Energy's National Security Laboratories, National Academy of Sciences (Washington, DC, 2011).

On major delays, cost overruns and bad management at nuclear facilities like the MOX project at Savannah River and the UPF at Oak Ridge, see the excellent GAO report *Project Management: DOE and NNSA Should Improve Their Lessons-Learned Process for Capital Asset Projects* (December 2018); Robert Alvarez, "Y-12: Poster Child for a Dysfunctional Nuclear Weapons Complex," *Bulletin of the Atomic Scientists* (August 4, 2014); and two reports by DOE inspector general, *Management Alert: Remediation of Selected Transuranic Waste Drums at Los Alamos National Laboratory* (September 2014); and *Special Report: Management Challenges at the Department of Energy—Fiscal Year 2015*, DOE inspector general, Office of Audits and Inspections (October 2014). See also Michael Lucibella and Alaina Levine, "It's a Bumpy Ride to Private Management for Los Alamos, Livermore," *American Physical Society* (June 2010); Greg Mello, "Declining Federal Oversight at Los Alamos, Increasing Production Incentives: A Dangerous Divergence," presentation to the DNFSB (March 22, 2006); the DOE IG's "Special Inquiry: Alleged Attempts by Sandia National Laboratories to Influence Congress and Federal Officials on a Contract Extension" (November 2014); Patrick Malone, Peter Cary et al., *Nuclear Negligence*, an excellent six-part online report by the Center for Public Integrity (June–August 2017); and extensive resources at the Los Alamos Study Group website.

For the point of view of nuclear-industrial complex insiders, see *Interim Report of the Congressional Advisory Panel on the Governance of the Nuclear Security Enterprise* (April 2014); and George Shultz, Sidney Drell, Henry Kissinger and Sam Nunn, *Nuclear Security: The Problems and the Road Ahead* (Stanford, CA, 2014). Ongoing attempts to weaken or abolish the DNFSB were discussed at a public hearing held by DNFSB in Albuquerque, New Mexico (February 21, 2019), and the Los Alamos Study Group's page on the DNFSB. See also Greg Mello and Robert Alvarez, briefing to the DNFSB on the history and importance of the board (October 27, 2017); and "The U.S. Nuclear Weapons Complex: Major Facilities," online at the Union of Concerned Scientists. Barack Obama's 180-degree shift from nuclear disarmament to nuclear modernization is succinctly described in Chuck Spinney and Pierre Sprey, "Sleepwalking into a Nuclear Arms Race with Russia," *The Blaster* (February 24, 2017); and William Broad and David Sanger, "US Ramping Up Major Renewal in Nuclear Arms," *New York Times* (September 21, 2014). For revolving-door behavior among nuclear industry insiders, see extensive research at the POGO website, including "Nuclear Official Allowed to Oversee Former Client" (February 4, 2015) and "Ashton Carter Takes Revolving Door to Higher Level" (January 6, 2015).

On the history of Bechtel, the firm's activities at Hanford and Three Mile Island, and Rick Parks's career as a nuclear whistleblower, see Sally Denton, *The Profiteers* (New York, 2016); Laton McCartney, *Friends in High Places* (updated ed., New York, 1989); Jackall, *Moral Mazes*; Stephen Unger, *Controlling Technology* (3rd ed., New York, 2017); "Bechtel: Profiting from Destruction," report jointly written by the nonprofit watchdog groups CorpWatch, Global Exchange and Public Citizen (June 2003); and Bechtel's own account of its history, *Bechtel: Building a Century, 1898–1998* (Kansas City, MO, 1997). See also the exhaustive online resources and bibliography at "Three Mile Island: The Inside Story," Smithsonian National Museum of American History; and the Three Mile Island website.

On the theory and practice of white-collar crime, see the historic speech of December 27, 1939, by Edwin Sutherland, published as "White-Collar Criminality," *American Sociological Review* (February 1940). An essential resource, in print and online, is the weekly publication *Corporate Crime Reporter*. See also David Anderson, "The Cost of Crime," *Foundations and Trends in Microeconomics* 7, no. 3 (2011); Anderson, "The Aggregate Burden of Crime," *Journal of Law & Economics* (October 1999); and *The Cost of Crime: Understanding the Financial and Human Impact of Criminal Activity*, hearing before the Senate Judiciary Committee on September 19, 2006. For an early formulation of the concept of "tone at the top," see the findings of the so-called Treadway Commission: *Report of the National Commission on Fraudulent Financial Reporting* (October 1987). Recent rulings that narrow the interpretation of fraud laws include the Supreme Court's McDonnell v. United States, 136 S. Ct. 2355 (2016); Skilling v. United States, 561 U.S. 358 (2010); Nike, Inc. v. Kasky, 539 U.S. 654 (2003); and the Second Circuit Court of Appeals' United States v. Caronia, case no. 09-5006-cr, decided December 3, 2012. For general discussion of judicial narrowing of corruption laws, see Zephyr Teachout, *Corruption in America* (Cambridge, MA, 2014), and Lynn Stout, *Cultivating Conscience* (Princeton, NJ, 2010).

Noam Chomsky was interviewed in the 2003 film *The Corporation*, written by Joel Bakan after his book by the same title, directed by Mark Achbar and Jennifer Abbott. A few highlights in the lengthy bibliography on corporate influence in society include: Sheldon Whitehouse, *Captured: The Corporate Infiltration of American Democracy* (New York, 2017); Samuel Buell, *Capital Offenses* (New York, 2016); Gordon Lafer, *The One Percent Solution* (Ithaca, NY, 2017); Adam Winkler, *We the Corporations* (New York, 2018); Gregg Barak, *Unchecked Corporate Power* (Abingdon, UK, 2017); Alfred Chandler and Bruce Mazlish, eds., *Leviathans* (Cambridge, UK, 2005); Kent Greenfield, *The Failure of Corporate Law* (Chicago, 2007); William Laufer, *Corporate Bodies and Guilty Minds* (Chicago, 2006); Steve Tombs and David Whyte, *The Corporate Criminal* (Abingdon, UK, 2015); and Jeffrey Clements, *Corporations Are Not People* (2nd ed., San Francisco, 2014).

On the ethics and psychology of corporate bureaucracy, see David Ewing, *Freedom Inside the Organization* (New York, 1977); Jackall, *Moral Mazes*; Sissela Bok, *Secrets: On the Ethics of Concealment and Revelation* (New York, 1983), and Bok, *Lying: Moral Choice in Public and Private Life* (updated ed., New York, 1999). Franklin Raines is quoted on incentives in "Getting Money to Where It Hasn't Gone," *BusinessWeek* (May 19, 2003). Bill Black tells the story of Raines and Sampath Rajappa in "Adam Smith Was Right About Corporate CEOs' Incentives Absent Effective Regulation," on the Cato Unbound website (December 4, 2008). William Douglas's comment on the corporation is from his speech at the Annual Dinner of the Fordham University Alumni Association, February 9, 1939. General Robert Wood is quoted in W. Grant Ireson and Eugene Grant, eds., *Handbook of Industrial Engineering and Management* (Englewood Cliffs, NJ, 1971).

On the still-unfolding saga of Theranos and Elizabeth Holmes, see Carreyrou's book *Bad Blood* (New York, 2018), as well as his extensive coverage of the story in the *Wall Street Journal*. See SEC press release, "Theranos, CEO Holmes, and Former President Balwani Charged with Massive Fraud" (March 14, 2018); and SEC's complaint filed on March 14, 2018, with the US District Court, Northern District of California, San Jose Division, case no. 18-cv-01602. See also the DOJ press release, "Theranos Founder and Former Chief Operating Officer Charged in Alleged Wire Fraud Schemes" (June 15, 2018), and the grand jury indictment filed with the US District Court, Northern District of California, San Jose Division, case no. 18-cr-00258. See also the 2019 documentary film *The Inventor*, written and directed by Alex Gibney.

Emails between Elizabeth Holmes and James Mattis were published by the *Washington Post* in two articles by Carolyn Johnson: "E-Mails Reveal Concerns About Theranos's FDA Compliance Date Back Years" (December 2, 2015) and "Trump's Pick for Defense Secretary Went to the Mat for the Troubled Blood-Testing Company Theranos" (December 1, 2016).

CHAPTER 6. MONEY MAKES THE WORLD GO ROUND

This chapter is based in part on personal communication with Gary Aguirre, Chris Arnade, Bradley Birkenfeld, Bill Black, Richard Bowen, Patrick Burns, Louie Clark, Bill Cohan, Richard Condit, Raimund Herden, Erika Kelton, Steve Kohn, David Lane, Harry Markopolos, Russell Mokhiber, Cliff Palefsky, Wally Turbeville, Michael Winston and Martin Woods.

A number of blogs, including *Naked Capitalism, Wall Street on Parade, Jesse's Café Américain, Zero Hedge* and *Michael Hudson*, provided essential insights often absent from mainstream media. Matt Taibbi's profiles of whistleblowers in *Rolling Stone* are invaluable (as is much else he writes about the financial system). See, for example, "Gangster Bankers" (February 14, 2013); "The $9 Billion Witness" (November 6, 2014); "A Whistleblower's Horror Story" (February 18, 2015); and "Julian Assange Must Never Be Extradited" (May 30, 2019).

For Bowen's experiences in banking during the savings and loan crisis, and the failure of Penn Square and First National Bank of Oklahoma City, see the extensive report published by the FDIC: *History of the Eighties*, vol. 1, *An Examination of the Banking Crises of the 1980s and Early 1990s* (Washington, DC, 1997); and *Managing the Crisis: The FDIC and RTC Experience*, vol. 1 (Washington, DC, 1998). See also Phillip Zweig, *Belly Up: The Collapse of the Penn Square Bank* (New York, 1985); Mark Singer, *Funny Money* (New York, 1985); and further references below concerning the savings and loan crisis.

For Bowen's experiences at Citigroup, see Richard Bowen's April 7, 2010, testimony before the FCIC (read the full text that he submitted, without the redactions required by the FCIC, which became public on March 11, 2016); the transcript of his interview by FCIC staff (February 27, 2010); and the letter of December 17, 2010, from Richard Bowen's attorney, Steven Kardell, to Gary Cohen, general counsel of the Financial Crisis Inquiry Commission, "Re: Richard Bowen quotes." See also extensive discussion of Citi's business in the FCIC Report and other expert testimony; and the consolidated class action complaint In Re Citigroup Inc. Securities Litigation, US District Court, Southern District of New York, Master File No. 07-civ-990 1 (SHS), filed December 1, 2008, with rich detail on the bank's multifarious alleged frauds involving residential mortgage-backed securities and CDOs built on subprime mortgages. See also Citigroup's settlement agreement, statement of facts and other documents from its $7 billion settlement of July 11, 2014, with the US government and five states, available online from the corporate monitor's website Citi Monitorship. For a broader examination of the illegal merger that created Citigroup in 1998, the bank's collapse in 2008 and subsequent bailout, see the cogent discussion by Arthur Wilmarth, "Citigroup: A Case Study in Managerial and Regulatory Failures," *Indiana Law Review* 47 (2013); Andrew Cockburn, "Saving the Whale, Again," *Harper's* (April 2015); and Pam Martens, "The Rise and Fall of Citigroup," on her blog *Wall Street on Parade*, which contains many other posts about Citi's wrongdoing. See also James Freeman and Vern McKinley, *Borrowed Time: Two Centuries of Booms, Busts, and Bailouts at Citi* (New York, 2018); and the Supervisory Letter 2008-05 sent by the National Bank Examiners, Comptroller of the Currency, to Vikram Pandit, CEO of Citigroup (February 14, 2008). Interesting historical context in *Citibank*, a report by Nader's Raiders, David Leinsdorf and Donald Etra (New York, 1973).

On the nature and causes of the 2008 financial crisis, the essential starting point is *The Financial Crisis Inquiry Report*, the final report of the FCIC published in January 2011, which reads like a murder mystery, and is filled with insights from financiers, regulators, auditors, economists and other experts in American finance. The commission also published voluminous testimony by these and other insiders, together with valuable regional studies of the genesis and the impact of the crisis on communities throughout the United States. Equally vital and engrossing is the staff report of the Senate Permanent Subcommittee on Investigations, which, unlike the FCIC, was a strongly bipartisan effort, led by Senators Carl Levin and Tom Coburn, titled *Wall Street and the Financial Crisis: Anatomy of a Financial Collapse* (April 13, 2011); together with transcripts of the four hearings held by the subcommittee on April 13, 16, 23 and 27, 2010, during which they confronted key bankers and regulators behind the 2008 crisis.

Other helpful analyses from the vast bibliography on the 2008 financial crisis include: Martin Wolf, *The Shifts and the Shocks* (New York, 2014); Frank Partnoy, "Financial Systems, Crises, and Regulation," *Legal Studies Research Paper Series* of the University of San Diego School of Law (May 2014); Arthur Wilmarth, "The Dark Side of Universal Banking: Financial Conglomerates and the Origins of the Subprime Financial Crisis," *Connecticut Law Review* (May 2009); Alan Blinder, *After the Music Stopped* (New York, 2013); Blinder, Andrew Lo et al., eds., *Rethinking the Financial Crisis* (New York, 2012); Joseph Stiglitz, *Freefall* (New York, 2010); Adair Turner, *Between Debt and the Devil* (Princeton, NJ, 2015); Atif Mian and Amir Sufi, *House of Debt* (Chicago, 2014); Yves Smith, *Econned* (New York, 2010); and Adam Tooze, *Crashed* (New York, 2018). Also interesting are Andrew Sorkin, *Too Big to Fail* (New York, 2009); Tim Geithner, *Stress Test: Reflections on Financial Crises* (New York, 2014); and Ben Bernanke, Tim Geithner and Henry Paulson, *Firefighting: The Financial Crisis and Its Lessons* (New York, 2019). The two dissenting statements by Republican FCIC commissioners are "Dissenting Statement of Keith Hennessey, Douglas Holtz-Eakin, and Bill Thomas, Causes of the Financial and Economic Crisis" (January 26, 2011); and Peter Wallison, "Dissent from the Majority Report of the Financial Crisis Inquiry Commission" (January 14, 2011).

Useful discussions of specific root causes of the 2008 financial crisis (without any attempt at comprehensiveness) include: (re: ethics and morality) Gregg Fields, "Reflections on a Global Crisis: How Ethical Failures and Institutional Corruption Produced the Great Recession," compendium of blog posts from the Edmond J. Safra Center for Ethics at Harvard; Geoffrey Miller and Gerald Rosenfeld, "Intellectual Hazard: How Conceptual Biases in Complex Organizations Contributed to the Crisis of 2008," *Harvard Journal of Law & Public Policy* (Spring 2010); Arnold Kling, "The Financial Crisis: Moral Failure or Cognitive Failure?" *Harvard Journal of Law & Public Policy* (Spring 2010); David Tuckett, "Addressing the Psychology of Financial Markets," *Economics: The Open-Access, Open-Assessment E-Journal* (November 2009); (re: deregulation) David Moss, "Reversing the Null: Regulation, Deregulation, and the Power of Ideas" (working paper, Harvard Business School, October 28, 2010); (re: economists and the Fed) Adair Turner, *Economics After the Crisis* (Boston, 2012); Neil Fligstein, Jonah Brundage et al., "Seeing Like the Fed," *American Sociological Review* (September 2017); Alan Blinder, "Federal Reserve Policy Before, During and After the Fall," in Martin Baily and John Taylor, eds., *Across the Great Divide: New Perspectives on the Financial Crisis* (Stanford, CA, 2014); (re: toxic mortgages) Edward Kane, Gerard Caprio et al., "The 2007 Meltdown in Structured Securitization: Searching for Lessons Not Scapegoats," *World Bank Research Observer* (February 2010); Neil Fligstein and Alex Roehrkasse, "The Causes of Fraud in Financial Crises," *American Sociological Review* (June 2016); Tomasz Piskorski, Amit Seru et al., "Asset Quality Misrepresentation by Financial Intermediaries: Evidence from RMBS Market," *Journal of Finance* (December 2015); (re: derivatives) Gillian Tett, *Fool's Gold* (New York, 2009); Wally Turbeville, testimony at the hearing on *Examining Legislative Improvements to Title VII of the Dodd-Frank Act*, before the House Committee on Agriculture (March 14, 2013); Jesse Eisinger, "The $58 Trillion Elephant in the Room," *Portfolio* (November 2008); René Stulz, "Credit Default Swaps and the Credit Crisis," *Journal of Economic Perspectives* (Winter 2010); (re: AIG bailout) Better Markets, amicus curiae brief in Starr International Company, Inc. v. United States of America and American International Group, Inc., before the US Court of Appeals Federal Circuit, filed December 15, 2015; Malcolm Salter, "Annals of Crony Capitalism: Revisiting the AIG Bailout" (working paper, Edmond J. Safra Center, December 5, 2013); (re: Lehman Brothers) report of Anton R. Valukas, Examiner, in the Chapter 11 bankruptcy proceedings of Lehman Before the US Bankruptcy Court for the Southern District of New York (March 11, 2010); Rosalind Wiggins, Thomas Piontek et al., *The Lehman Brothers Bankruptcy*, an eight-part case study by the Yale Program on Financial Stability (rev. version, 2015); and the letter by Lehman whistleblower Matthew Lee to Martin Kelly, controller, and other senior executives at the bank (May 16, 2008); (re: Bear Stearns) William Cohan, *House of Cards* (New York, 2009); (re: the repeal of Glass-Steagall) *Repealing Glass-Steagall Contributed to the 2008 Financial Crash*, report by Better Markets (Washington, DC, May 1, 2017); (re: Moody's) written statement of Richard Michalek, former VP/senior credit officer, Moody's Investors Service, submitted to the Senate Permanent Subcommittee on Investigations Committee on Governmental Affairs (April 23, 2010); (re: Fannie and Freddie) Bethany McLean, "The Fall of Fannie Mae," *Fortune* (January 24, 2005); and Bill Black, "How Liar's Loans and Accounting Control Fraud Destroyed Fannie and Freddie," published on Bank Whistleblowers United website (March 8, 2016).

On the failure of the US government and its citizens to reregulate and otherwise bring major banks under control after 2008, thus increasing the likelihood of another financial crisis, see Susan Strange's prescient works *Casino Capitalism* (Oxford, UK, 1986) and *Mad Money: When Markets Outgrow Governments* (Ann Arbor, MI, 1998); Anat Admati, "Rethinking Financial Regulation," in Olivier Blanchard, Raghuram Rajan et al., eds., *Progress and Confusion: The State of Macroeconomic Policy* (Boston, 2016); Sheila Bair and Ricardo Delfin, "How Efforts to Avoid Past Mistakes Created New Ones," in Martin Baily and John Taylor, eds., *Across the Great Divide: New Perspectives on the Financial Crisis* (Stanford, CA, 2014); Arthur Wilmarth, "Turning a Blind Eye: Why Washington Keeps Giving In to Wall Street," *University of Cincinnati Law Review* 81 (2013); Simon Johnson, "The Making of Lehman Brothers II," published online by the Peterson Institute for International Economics (February 26, 2018); Johnson and Antonio Weiss, "Financial Regulation Calls for 20/20 Vision," *Bloomberg Opinion* (June 1, 2017); Joseph Stiglitz, "10 Years After the Financial Crisis" (working paper, Roosevelt Institute, September 2018); Edward Kane, "Ethical Failures in Regulating and Supervising the Pursuit of Safety-Net Subsidies," *European Business Organization Law Review* (June 2009); Elizabeth Warren, "The Unfinished Business of Financial Reform," speech at the Levy Institute's 24th Annual Hyman P. Minsky Conference (April 15, 2015); and Nouriel Roubini and Stephen Mihm, *Crisis Economics* (New York, 2010).

On the cost of the 2008 financial crisis, and the ongoing social harm it has caused, see *The Cost of the Crisis*, report by Better Markets (July 2015); *FCIC Field Hearings on the Impact of the Financial Crisis*, in Miami, Bakersfield, Sacramento and the State of Nevada; *Financial Regulatory Reform*, report by the GAO (January 2013); Scott Keeter, Carroll Doherty et al., "The Politics of Financial Insecurity," report for the Pew Research Center (January 8, 2015); İnci Ötker-Robe and Anca Maria Podpiera, "The Social Impact of Financial Crises" (working paper, Policy Research of the World Bank, November 2013); David Luttrell and Tyler Atkinson, *Assessing the Costs and Consequences of the 2007–09 Financial Crisis and Its Aftermath*, report by the Dallas Federal Reserve (September 2013); Barb Rosewicz, Ruth Mantell et al., "States' Personal Income Shows Uneven Economic Recovery," online article at Pew Charitable Trusts (November 1, 2016); Neil Fligstein and Zawadi Rucks-Ahidiana, "The Rich Got Richer: The Effects of the Financial Crisis on Household Well-Being, 2007–2009" (working paper, Institute for Research on Labor and Employment, Berkeley, CA, 2015); *Occupational Fraud: A Study of the Impact of an Economic Recession*, report by the Association of Certified Fraud Examiners (2009); Michael Hurd and Susann Rohwedder, "Effects of the Financial Crisis and Great Recession on American Households" (working paper, National Bureau of Economic Research, September 2010).

For aspects of deteriorating social conditions in the United States since the 2008 crash, see Philip Alston, *Report of the Special Rapporteur on Extreme Poverty and Human Rights on His Mission to the United States of America*, UN Human Rights Council (May 4, 2018); Angus Deaton, "The Financial Crisis and the Well-being of Americans," *Oxford Economic Papers* (January 2012); Deaton and Anne Case, "Mortality and Morbidity in the 21st Century," *Brookings Papers on Economic Activity* (Spring 2017); Deaton, *The Great Escape* (Princeton, NJ, 2015); Matthew Desmond, *Evicted* (New York, 2016); and Wally Turbeville, *The Detroit Bankruptcy*, report for Demos (November 2013).

On the Citi collapse and repeated bailouts, see the report by the redoubtable Neil Barofsky, special inspector general for the Troubled Asset Relief Program, "Extraordinary Financial Assistance Provided to Citigroup, Inc." (January 13, 2011); and Pam Martens, "The Untold Story of the Bailout of Citigroup," *Wall Street on Parade* (August 8, 2012). For events behind the scenes during Richard Bowen's FCIC testimony, see William Cohan, "Was This Whistleblower Muzzled?" *New York Times* (September 21,

2013). On Bradley Karp, see *Wall Street on Parade*, and Karp's biography at the website of his law firm, Paul, Weiss, which lists fourteen "significant representations" involving Citigroup, including its Enron- and Lehman-related litigation, and its Second Circuit victory "allowing corporations to enter into federal regulatory consent judgments without admitting wrongdoing." For Sherry Hunt's qui tam case, see United States of America ex rel. Sherry A. Hunt v. Citigroup, Inc., Citibank NA, Inc. et al., US District Court for the Southern District of New York, case no. 11-civ-05473 (VM): the DOJ's complaint in intervention was filed February 14, 2012; the settlement agreement was filed February 15, 2012; and the DOJ issued its press release on the same day, "Manhattan US Attorney Files and Simultaneously Settles Fraud Lawsuit Against CitiMortgage, Inc. for Reckless Mortgage Lending Practices."

On widespread recidivist fraud by Citigroup and the other five largest US banks, see two invaluable reports by Better Markets, "Wall Street's Six Biggest Bailed-Out Banks: Their RAP Sheets & Their Ongoing Crime Spree," and "RAP Sheet Rundown," both published on April 9, 2019. See also Ryan Chittum, "200 Years of Citi," *Columbia Journalism Review* (March 9, 2012). For JPMorgan's rap sheet, see the JPMadoff website and the book by the same title (North Charleston, SC, 2016), both authored by Helen Chaitman and Lance Gotthoffer. Regarding the FCIC referring Robert Rubin to the DOJ for investigation, see Richard Bowen, "Now We Know—The DOJ Ignored Two FCIC Citi Criminal Referrals!" on his blog, *Richard Bowen* (March 24, 2016).

The SEC "sweetheart" settlement rejected by Judge Rakoff is captioned US Securities and Exchange Commission v. Citigroup Global Markets Inc., US District Court for the Southern District of New York, case no. 11-cv-7387, complaint filed October 19, 2011; and SEC press release "Citigroup to Pay $285 Million to Settle SEC Charges for Misleading Investors About CDO Tied to Housing Market" (October 19, 2011). Judge Rakoff delivered his opinion on this case on November 28, 2011; the Second Circuit reversed his ruling in United States Securities & Exchange Commission v. Citigroup Global Markets, Inc., docket nos. 11-5227-cv (L), 11-5375-cv (con), 11-5242-cv (xap), United States Court of Appeals for the Second Circuit, decided June 4, 2014. Rakoff rejected the SEC settlement with Bank of America in Securities and Exchange Commission v. Bank of America Corporation, US District Court for the Southern District of New York, case no. 09-civ-6829 (JSR), order filed September 14, 2009. Eric Holder's admission that some banks are too big to jail came in an exchange with Chuck Grassley during testimony before the Senate Judiciary Committee on March 6, 2013; see transcript in "Attorney General Eric Holder on 'Too Big to Jail,'" *American Banker* (March 6, 2013).

The platform of Bank Whistleblowers United is discussed in their First Annual Bank Whistleblowers Press Conference in Washington, DC (February 25, 2016). Aspects of Bill Black's fraud-fighting and professional ethics are profiled in James Bowman, Jonathan West et al., *The Professional Edge* (Armonk, NY, 2004); Norma Riccucci, *Unsung Heroes* (Washington, DC, 1995); Tim Schultz, "These Rogues of the Dismal Science Have Been Vindicated by the Economic Crash," *Playboy* (June 2012); and Thomas Frank, "Finally, Wall Street Gets Put on Trial," *Salon* (September 7, 2014).

For details of the defamation case of Lexecon against Milberg Weiss, see Lexecon, Inc. and Daniel R. Fischel v. Milberg Weiss Bershad Hynes & Lerach, et al., no. 96-1482, decided March 3, 1998; and Melody Petersen, "Law Firm to Pay Longtime Foe $50 Million," *New York Times* (April 14, 1999).

Regarding Bradley Birkenfeld and UBS, see grand jury indictment United States of America v. Marco Parenti Adami, Emanuel Agustoni et al., US District Court for the Eastern District of Virginia, case no. 1:11-cr-95, filed February 23, 2011; Birkenfeld's book *Lucifer's Banker* (Austin, TX, 2016); and the extensive legal documentation available at Birkenfeld's website, *Lucifer's Banker*. On Mr. ABC, see "Testimony of Mr. ABC—a Confidential Witness," before the Senate Finance Committee (July 21, 2004). Regarding Harry Markopolos's revelations about Bernard Madoff, see his book *No One Would Listen* (Hoboken, NJ, 2010); and a different viewpoint in Diana Henriques, *The Wizard of Lies* (New York, 2011). On the recent money-laundering revelations known as the Panama Papers, Paradise

Papers, etc., see detailed reports of each leak on the website of the International Consortium of Investigative Journalists (ICIJ), whose reporters, together with *Süddeutsche Zeitung* reporters, developed and broke the stories. On the controversial figure of Hervé Falciani, see Patrick Radden Keefe, "The Bank Robber," *New Yorker* (May 23, 2016); and Martha Hamilton, "Whistleblower? Thief? Hero? Introducing the Source of the Data That Shook HSBC," ICIJ online (February 8, 2015). ICIJ also considers the revelations by Antoine Deltour and Raphaël Halet of Luxembourg tax avoidance schemes, in its coverage of "Luxembourg Leaks." The investigation of the failure of Eric Holder's DOJ to prosecute HSBC, run by partisan Republican Jeb Hensarling, chair of the House Committee on Financial Services, produced a final report titled *Too Big to Jail: Inside the Obama Justice Department's Decision Not to Hold Wall Street Accountable* (July 11, 2016), which is ironic given that Hensarling is a staunch Wall Street promoter. Regarding Danske Bank whistleblower Howard Wilkinson and his EU testimony in favor of financial whistleblowers, see the data sheet titled "Meet the Whistleblower" at the website of Wilkinson's attorney, Steve Kohn; and the CBS *60 Minutes* episode "How the Danske Bank Money-Laundering Scheme Involving $230 Billion Unraveled," which aired on May 19, 2019.

For bank commodity manipulation/monopoly, see *Wall Street Bank Involvement with Physical Commodities*, an investigation of the Senate Permanent Subcommittee on Investigations, Committee on Homeland Security and Governmental Affairs, released with the hearings of November 20–21, 2014. On dark pools and algorithmic trading, see Walter Mattli, *Darkness by Design* (Princeton, NJ, 2019). On the 1MDB scandal, see Tim Leissner's guilty plea in United States of America v. John Doe, US District Court for the Eastern District of New York, case no. 18-cr-439 (MKB), hearing of August 28, 2018, redacted transcript filed November 9, 2018.

Documents outlining the recidivism of specific banks include: Kara Stein's remarks on Deutsche Bank in "Dissenting Statement in the Matter of Deutsche Bank AG, Regarding WKSI," SEC Public Statement (May 4, 2015); Edward Wyatt, "Promises Made, and Remade, by Firms in S.E.C. Fraud Cases," *New York Times* (November 7, 2011); and Assistant Attorney General Leslie Caldwell's remarks about UBS at DOJ press conference on Foreign Exchange Spot Market Manipulation in Washington, DC (May 20, 2015).

For a look at some of HSBC's money laundering, see *US Vulnerabilities to Money Laundering, Drugs and Terrorist Financing: HSBC Case History*, the report of the hearing before the Permanent Subcommittee on Investigations of the Senate Committee on Homeland Security and Governmental Affairs, July 17, 2012; and the DOJ statement of facts in its lawsuit against the bank, United States of America v. HSBC Bank USA, NA and HSBC Holdings PLC, US District Court for the Eastern District of New York, case no. 1:12-cr-00763-ILG, filed November 12, 2012.

Lanny Breuer's and Eric Holder's remarks on reluctance to criminally prosecute major banks reported in "Lanny Breuer on UBS: Our Goal Here Is Not to Destroy a Major Financial Institution," *Corporate Crime Reporter* (December 20, 2012).

Regarding the savings and loan crisis, see two definitive studies published by the FDIC: *History of the Eighties*, vol. 1, *An Examination of the Banking Crises of the 1980s and Early 1990s* (Washington, DC, 1997); and *Managing the Crisis: The FDIC and RTC Experience*, vol. 1 (Washington, DC, 1998); along with the valuable chronology and resources at a page at the FDIC website "FDIC: The S&L Crisis: A Chrono-Bibliography"; and Robert Rubinovitz, "Moral Hazard in the Thrift Industry," DOJ Antitrust Division, Economic Analysis Group Discussion Paper (1990). Important analyses, in addition to Bill Black's *The Best Way to Rob a Bank Is to Own One*, include: *The US Government's War Against Fraud, Abuse, and Misconduct in Financial Institutions: Winning Some Battles but Losing the War*, report of the House Committee on Government Operations (Washington, DC, 1990); Bruce Green, "Financial Institutions and Regulations, the S&L Crisis: Death and Transfiguration," *Fordham Law Review* (January 1991); Kathleen Day, *S&L Hell* (New York, 1993); Michael Lowy, *High Rollers* (New York, 1991);

Martin Mayer, *The Greatest Ever Bank Robbery* (New York, 1992); and Lawrence White, *The S&L Debacle* (New York, 1991). For a very different account of the crisis, which it ultimately blames on "regulatory chokeholds and policy missteps," see James Barth, S. Trimbath et al., eds., *The Savings and Loan Crisis: Lessons from a Regulatory Failure,* from the Milken Institute Series on Financial Innovation and Economic Growth (Dordrecht, Netherlands, 2004).

On Keating, Lincoln Savings and Loan, and the link with Milken's junk bonds, see Michael Binstein and Charles Bowden, *Trust Me: Charles Keating and the Missing Billions* (New York, 1993); Kitty Calavita, Henry Pontell et al., *Big Money Crime* (Berkeley, CA, 1997); George Akerlof and Paul Romer, "Looting: The Economic Underworld of Bankruptcy for Profit," *Brookings Papers on Economic Activity*, no. 2 (1993); James Stewart, *Den of Thieves* (New York, 1992); Stephen Pizzo, Mary Fricker and Paul Muolo, *Inside Job: The Looting of America's Savings and Loans* (New York, 1989); and James Adams, *The Big Fix* (New York, 1990). See also hearings before the Senate Select Committee on Ethics, *Preliminary Inquiry into Allegations Regarding Senators Cranston, DeConcini, Glenn, McCain, and Riegle and Lincoln Savings and Loan*, published in five parts between November 15, 1990, and January 16, 1991. News stories published during the crisis include: Rick Atkinson and David Maraniss, "Gray the 'Re-Regulator' and Wright Lock Horns," *Washington Post* (June 16, 1989); Richard Berke, "Officials Say House Speaker Intervened in Texan's Case," *New York Times* (June 22, 1987); James Granelli, "Angry Bondholder Grabs Keating," *New York Times* (August 3, 1991); and Douglas Frantz, "Inquiry Looks at Links to Milken in S&L Scandal," *Los Angeles Times* (December 6, 1989). Keating received the ten-year sentence from Judge Lance Ito in The People, Plaintiff and Appellant, v. Charles H. Keating, Jr., et al., Defendants and Respondents, Superior Court of Los Angeles County, case no. BA 025236, sentencing on April 10, 1992. The sentence was overturned in April 3, 1996, by the US District Court for the Central District of California, Keating v. Hood, 922 F. Supp. 1482 (C.D. Cal. 1996).

George Akerlof describes Gresham's Dynamic in "The Market for 'Lemons': Quality Uncertainty and the Market Mechanism," *Quarterly Journal of Economics* (August 1970).

On the history of Goldman Sachs, see William Cohen, *Money and Power* (New York, 2011); Charles Ellis, *The Partnership* (New York, 2008); and Lisa Endlich, *Goldman Sachs* (New York, 1999). On the psychology of traders, see Mark Fenton-O'Creevy, Nigel Nicholson et al., *Traders* (Oxford, UK, 2004); Donald Langevoort, "Chasing the Greased Pig Down Wall Street: A Gatekeeper's Guide to the Psychology, Culture, and Ethics of Financial Risk Taking," *Cornell Law Review* (July 2011); Robert Frank, Thomas Gilovich et al., "Does Studying Economics Inhibit Cooperation?" *Journal of Economic Perspectives* (Spring 1993); and Thomas Noll, Jérôme Endrass et al., "A Comparison of Professional Traders and Psychopaths in a Simulated Non-Zero Sum Game," *Catalyst* (2012). On Henry Paulson's conflicts of interest, see the cogent analysis by Greg Gordon, "How Hank Paulson's Inaction Helped Goldman Sachs," *McClatchy Newspapers* (October 10, 2010).

On how financial hypertrophy harms a nation's economy, see Thomas Philippon, "Finance vs. Wal-Mart: Why Are Financial Services So Expensive?" in Blinder and Lo et al., *Rethinking the Financial Crisis*; Gerald Epstein and Juan Antonio Montecino, *Overcharged: The High Cost of High Finance*, report for the Roosevelt Institute (July 2016); Epstein, "How the FED's QE Contributed to Inequality," interview available online at the Institute for New Economic Thinking (August 3, 2016); and Epstein and Montecino, "Have Large Scale Asset Purchases Increased Bank Profits?" More broadly, see Michael Hudson, *Killing the Host* (Islet Publisher, 2015); Hudson, *J Is for Junk Economics* (Islet Publisher, 2017); Robert Kuttner, *Can Democracy Survive Global Capitalism?* (New York, 2018); John Kay, *Other People's Money: The Real Business of Finance* (New York, 2015); Joseph Stiglitz, *People, Power, and Profits* (New York, 2019); James Kwak, *Economism* (New York, 2017); Nomi Prins, *Other People's Money* (New York, 2004); and Daniel Cohen, *The Infinite Desire for Growth*, trans. Jane Marie Todd (Princeton, NJ, 2018). On how the long-term health of corporations is degraded by stock buybacks and financialization, see William Lazonick, "Stock Buybacks," Brookings Institution (April 2015); Lazonick,

"The Financialization of the US Corporation," *Seattle University Law Review* 36, no. 2 (2013); SEC Commissioner Robert Jackson, "Stock Buybacks and Corporate Cashouts," a speech in Washington, DC (June 11, 2018); Lucian Bebchuk, Jesse Fried et al., "Managerial Power and Rent Extraction in the Design of Executive Compensation," *University of Chicago Law Review* 69, no. 3 (2002); Lawrence Mishel and Jessica Schieder, "CEO Compensation Surged in 2017," report for the Economic Policy Institute (August 16, 2018); and Lazonick, "Taking Stock: Why Executive Pay Results in an Unstable and Inequitable Economy," a white paper for the Roosevelt Institute (June 5, 2014). On the social and economic harm caused by private equity, see the lucid study by Eileen Appelbaum and Rosemary Batt, *Private Equity at Work* (New York, 2014); and Danielle Ivory, Ben Protess et al., "When You Dial 911 and Wall Street Answers," *New York Times* (June 25, 2016).

Evidence for ethical decline in the finance industry is in Ann Tenbrunsel and Jordan Thomas, "The Street, The Bull and The Crisis," a study published jointly by Notre Dame and the whistleblower law firm of Labaton Sucharow (May 2015); Thomas, "Wall Street, Fleet Street, Main Street," published by Labaton Sucharow (July 30, 2012); Alain Cohen and Ernst Fehr, "Business Culture and Dishonesty in the Banking Industry," *Nature* (December 4, 2014); Luigi Zingales, "Does Finance Benefit Society?" a working paper of the National Bureau of Economic Research (January 2015); and John Bogle, "Financial Reform: Investment Standards and Ethical Values," the Community Forum Distinguished Lecture Series of the Bryn Mawr Presbyterian Church (April 28, 2014). See also Mark Egan, Gregor Matvos et al., "The Market for Financial Adviser Misconduct," *Journal of Political Economy* (February 2019).

Regarding Ferdinand Pecora's investigations into Wall Street wrongdoing that caused the 1929 crash, see Pecora's memoir *Wall Street Under Oath* (New York, 1939); the recent biography of Pecora by Michael Perino, *The Hellhound of Wall Street* (New York, 2010); and Susie Pak, *Gentlemen Bankers* (Cambridge, MA, 2013). The hearings that prompted the passage of Glass-Steagall, the Securities Act of 1933 and the Securities Exchange Act of 1934 (together with the founding of the SEC), held from April 11, 1932, to May 4, 1934, by the Senate Committee on Banking and Currency, were titled *Stock Exchange Practices*, and are available online at the St. Louis Federal Reserve; see, for example, the testimony of J. P. Morgan (May 26–June 9, 1933) and "Sunshine" Charley Mitchell, head of National City Bank, the predecessor of Citigroup (April 23–June 3, 1933).

On the causes of the 1929 crash, see the final report from the 1933–1934 hearings, *Stock Exchange Practices* (June 6, 1934), with an exhaustive catalog of financial frauds, many of which strongly resemble modern-day wrongdoing. Further analysis includes: John Kenneth Galbraith, *The Great Crash 1929* (New York, 1938); Galbraith, *A Short History of Financial Euphoria* (New York, 1990); Louis Brandeis, *Other People's Money and How the Bankers Use It* (New York, 1913); Arthur Wilmarth, "Prelude to Glass-Steagall: Abusive Securities Practices by National City Bank and Chase National Bank in the Roaring Twenties," *Tulane Law Review* (June 2016); Peter Temin, *Lessons from the Great Depression* (Boston, 1990); Jon Wisman, "The Financial Crisis of 1929 Reexamined: The Role of Soaring Inequality," *Review of Political Economy* 26, no. 3 (2014); and Liaquat Ahamed, *Lords of Finance* (New York, 2009). On the Supreme Court's blunting of 1930s securities laws, see E. Thomas Sullivan and Robert Thompson, "The Supreme Court and Private Law: The Vanishing Importance for Securities and Antitrust," *Emory Law Journal* (2004).

On Gary Aguirre's whistleblowing against the SEC, see *The Firing of an SEC Attorney and the Investigation of Pequot Capital Management*, the comprehensive report of the investigation conducted by the Senate Committees on Finance and Judiciary (August 2007); as well as the hearings titled *Examining Enforcement of Criminal Insider Trading and Hedge Fund Activity*, held before the Senate Committee on the Judiciary (June 28, September 26 and December 5), with extensive testimony by Aguirre (June 28 and December 5) and his accusers, and keen questioning by Senators Specter and Grassley. Aguirre lays out his case in two letters to SEC chair Christopher Cox (September 2, 2005, and January 2, 2009). See also the remarkable memorandum opinion and order by District Judge Ellen Huvelle of

April 28, 2008, in the case Gary Aguirre v. Securities and Exchange Commission, US District Court for the District of Columbia, case no. 06-cv-1260 (ESH); and two reports by SEC IG H. David Kotz titled *Re-Investigation of Claims by Gary Aguirre of Improper Preferential Treatment and Retaliatory Termination* (September 30, 2008); and *Allegation of Perjury and Obstruction of Justice by Former SEC Enforcement Attorney* (March 17, 2009).

For low morale and revolving-door attitudes at the SEC, see the GAO reports *Securities and Exchange Commission: Improving Personnel Management Is Critical for Agency's Effectiveness* (July 2013); and *Securities and Exchange Commission: Actions Needed to Address Limited Progress in Resolving Long-Standing Personnel Management Challenges* (December 2016). On David Zilkha's interactions with Art Samberg and Pequot, see the SEC administrative proceeding in the matter of David E. Zilkha, proceeding no. 3-13913, hearing held on November 1, 2010; and Securities and Exchange Commission v. Pequot Capital Management, Inc. and Arthur J. Samberg, US District Court for the District of Connecticut, case no. 3:10-cv-00831, complaint filed May 27, 2010.

On Aguirre's attempts to warn of misconduct by banks and other financial institutions that soon caused the 2008 crash, see his letter to Senators Christopher Dodd and Richard Selby on the eve of Bear Stearns's collapse (February 13, 2008); and his analysis of the failure of the SEC and other offices of the US government to pursue and punish the financial criminals, in "A Tale of Two Frauds," a two-part article in *Wall Street Lawyer* (August and October 2013). See also his letter to Mary Schapiro, chair of the SEC, re: threats to the SEC whistleblower program (December 17, 2010); and his letter to Preet Bharara regarding the SEC's apparent gaming of its own whistleblower system, Re: US v. David Zilkha and Arthur Samberg (November 30, 2010).

Robert Khuzami's response to Chuck Grassley's questions about coordination between DOJ and SEC whistleblowers is in a letter of February 18, 2011. The SEC IG's investigation of Khuzami's alleged secret conversation with his friend and Citigroup defense attorney (Brad Karp?) is titled "Investigation into Allegations of Improper Preferential Treatment and Special Access in Connection with the Division of Enforcement's Investigation of Citigroup, Inc." (September 27, 2011). On the figure of John "Mack the Knife" Mack, see the priceless account by Frank Partnoy in *F.I.A.S.C.O.* (New York, 1997). (Partnoy, a fixed income derivatives salesman under Mack at Morgan Stanley, became a finance and legal scholar, a sharp critic of Wall Street and an authority on market regulation.)

James Kidney gave his retirement speech in March 2014. Kidney's story and his views of the ABACUS transaction are told in detail in Jesse Eisinger, *The Chickenshit Club* (New York, 2017). Full details of the ABACUS 2007-AC1 deal appear in the 2011 report of the Senate Permanent Subcommittee on Investigations, *Wall Street and the Financial Crisis: Anatomy of a Financial Collapse*. See also Securities and Exchange Commission v. Goldman Sachs & Co. and Fabrice Tourre, US District Court for the Southern District of New York, case no. 10-cv-3229, complaint filed April 16, 2010; SEC IG's report *Allegations of Improper Coordination Between the SEC and Other Governmental Entities Concerning the SEC's Enforcement Action Against Goldman Sachs & Co.* (September 30, 2010); and further analysis in McLean and Nocera, *All the Devils Are Here.* For an admiring look at John Paulson's speculation against the subprime mortgage market in ABACUS, see Gregory Zuckerman, *The Greatest Trade Ever* (New York, 2009).

On the pardon of Marc Rich, see *Justice Undone: Clemency Decisions in the Clinton White House*, Chapter 1, "Take Jack's Word"; *The Pardons of International Fugitives Marc Rich and Pincus Green*, Second Report by the Committee on Government Reform (May 14, 2002); and *The Controversial Pardon of International Fugitive Marc Rich*, Hearings Before the House Committee on Government Reform, held February 8 and March 1, 2001.

For Michael Winston's litigation against Countrywide and Bank of America, see Michael Winston v. Countrywide Financial Corporation, Bank of America et al., in the Superior Court for the County of

Los Angeles, Van Nuys Courthouse East, case no. LC085895, second amended complaint filed January 6, 2010; the Moody's report on Countrywide and related correspondence, Exhibit 544 in this case; and the transcript of the hearing on Bank of America's motion for judgment notwithstanding verdict (April 6, 2011). The appeals court reversal is captioned Winston v. Countrywide Financial Corporation, case no. B232823, Court of Appeals of California, Second District, Division Seven, filed February 19, 2013. See also Ted Mathews's letter to LA district attorney Steve Cooley regarding perjury (November 3, 2011); GAP's May 14, 2013, amicus brief to the California Supreme Court in re: Winston v. Countrywide Financial Corp. et al., case no. S209196; and the useful case study "Michael Winston and Countrywide Financial Corporation," prepared by GAP in 2014.

Other major lawsuits against Countrywide include: Securities and Exchange Commission v. Angelo Mozilo, David Sambol et al., US District Court for the Central District of California, case no. 09-cv-03994, complaint filed June 4, 2009 (details the SEC's charges against Angelo Mozilo, David Sambol et al. of securities fraud and insider trading, which Mozilo eventually settled for $67.5 million and Sambol for $5.5 million); Federal Trade Commission v. Countrywide Home Loans, Inc. and BAC Home Loans Servicing, LP, before the US District Court, Central District of California, Los Angeles, case no. 10-cv-04193-JFW-SS, complaint filed (June 7, 2010) and consent judgment filed (June 15, 2010); and the consolidated class action suit In Re Countrywide Financial Corporation Securities Litigation, before the US District Court for the Central District of California, Western Division, lead case no. 07-cv-05295-MRP-MAN, Second Consolidated Amended Class Action Complaint filed January 6, 2009.

Gretchen Morgenson covered the Winston trial in the *New York Times* in "How a Whistle-Blower Conquered Countrywide" (February 19, 2011) and "He Felled a Giant, but He Can't Collect" (June 30, 2012). See also her book on Countrywide, its role in the 2008 crisis, and the subsequent (and ongoing) illegal foreclosure scandal: Morgenson and Joshua Rosner, *Reckless Endangerment* (New York, 2011); McLean and Nocera, *All the Devils Are Here*; and David Dayen, *Chain of Title* (New York, 2016).

The false claims lawsuit against Bank of America and Countrywide was brought by qui tam whistle-blower Edward O'Donnell, a former head underwriter at Countrywide; see United States of America ex rel. Edward O'Donnell v. Bank of America Corporation, successor to Countrywide Financial Corporation, et al., before the US District Court for the Southern District of New York, case no. 12-cv-1422-JSR, complaint in intervention by DOJ filed October 24, 2012; Judge Jed Rakoff's opinion delivered on July 30, 2014; and the reversal on appeal, captioned United States ex rel. O'Donnell v. Countrywide Home Loans, Inc., before the United States Court of Appeals for the Second Circuit, case nos. 15-cv-496 (L) and 15-cv-499 (Con), decided May 23, 2016.

Jed Rakoff discussed the eclipse of the jury trial in two important articles for the *New York Review of Books*: "Why You Won't Get Your Day in Court" (November 24, 2016) and "Don't Count on the Courts" (April 5, 2018). Research suggesting appeals court bias includes: Adam Bonica and Maya Sen, "The Politics of Selecting the Bench from the Bar," *Journal of Law & Economics* (November 2017); Kevin Clermont and Stewart Schwab, "Employment Discrimination Plaintiffs in Federal Court: From Bad to Worse?" *Harvard Law & Policy Review* 3 (2009); Kevin Clermont and Theodore Eisenberg, "Appeal from Jury or Judge Trial: Defendants' Advantage," *American Law and Economics Review* (Spring 2001); and Michael Heise and Martin Wells, "Revisiting Eisenberg and Plaintiff Success," *Journal of Empirical Legal Studies* (September 2016). See also Billy Corriher, *Big Business Taking Over State Supreme Courts*, report for the Center for American Progress (August 2012); and Stratos Pahis, "Corruption in Our Courts: What It Looks Like and Where It Is Hidden," *Yale Law Journal* (June 2009).

Tom Devine made his remarks on judicial bias during his testimony during a June 11, 2009, *Hearing on the Whistleblower Protection Enhancement Act of 2009*, before the Subcommittee on Oversight of

Government Management, the Federal Workforce, and the District of Columbia, Senate Committee on Homeland Security and Governmental Affairs.

CHAPTER 7. MINISTRIES OF TRUTH

This chapter is based in part on personal communication with Bill Binney, Louie Clark, John Crane, Ed Davis, Tom Devine, Tom Drake, Pat Eddington, Ed Loomis, Kathleen McClellan, John Phillips and Jesselyn Radack.

Key rulings and opinions on the legality or constitutionality of NSA domestic surveillance program include Larry E. Klayman, Charles Strange et al. v. Obama et al., US District Court for the District of Columbia, case no. 13-civ-0851 (RJL), opinion of Judge Richard Leon filed December 16, 2013; American Civil Liberties Union et al. v. James R. Clapper et al., US District Court Southern District of New York, case no. 13-civ-3994 (WHP), memorandum and order of Judge William Pauley filed December 27, 2013; American Civil Liberties Union, American Civil Liberties Union Foundation et al. v. James R. Clapper, Michael S. Rogers et al., US Court of Appeals for the Second Circuit, docket no. 14-42-cv, decided May 7, 2015; and Richard Clarke, Michael Morell et al., *Liberty and Security in a Changing World*, report and recommendations of the President's Review Group on Intelligence and Communications Technologies (December 12, 2013). See also "The President's Surveillance Program," report prepared by the inspectors general of the DOD, DOJ, CIA, NSA and Office of the Director of National Intelligence (July 10, 2009); and Declaration of Thomas Andrews Drake filed on May 26, 2017, in the case of Mary Josephine (Josie) Valdez, Howard Stephenson, et al. v. National Security Agency, George W. Bush et al. before the US District Court District of Utah, Central Division, case no. 15-cv-00584-RJS.

On national security whistleblowers under the law, and particularly on the application of the Espionage Act since 9/11, see the good introduction to the main issues in Louis Fisher, "National Security Whistleblowers," report for the Congressional Research Service (December 30, 2005); Jess Radack and Kathleen McClellan, "The Criminalization of Whistleblowing," *The Labor & Employment Law Forum* 2, no. 1 (2011); Yochai Benkler, "A Public Accountability Defense for National Security Leakers and Whistleblowers," *Harvard Law & Policy Review* (Summer 2014); Richard Moberly, "Whistleblowers and the Obama Presidency: The National Security Dilemma," University of Nebraska College of Law, Faculty Publications (2012); Pamela Takefman, "Curbing Overzealous Prosecution of the Espionage Act: Thomas Andrews Drake and the Case for Judicial Intervention at Sentencing," *Cardozo Law Review* (December 2013); Stephen Vladeck, "The Espionage Act and National Security Whistleblowing After Garcetti," *American University Law Review* (June 2008); and Daniel D'Isidoro, "Protecting Whistleblowers and Secrets in the Intelligence Community," *Harvard Law School National Security Journal* (September 29, 2014).

See also James Bruce and W. George Jameson, *Assessing the Department of Defense's Approach to Preventing and Deterring Unauthorized Disclosures*, report prepared for the Office of the Secretary of Defense by the RAND National Defense Research Institute (Santa Monica, CA, 2013); Blake Norvell, "The Constitution and the NSA Warrantless Wiretapping Program: A Fourth Amendment Violation?" *Yale Journal of Law & Technology* (2009); Harold Edgar and Benno Schmidt, "The Espionage Statutes and Publication of Defense Information," *Columbia Law Review* (May 1973); as well as two congressional hearings: *National Security Whistleblowers in the Post–September 11th Era: Lost in a Labyrinth and Facing Subtle Retaliation*, before the House Subcommittee on National Security, Emerging Threats, and International Relations of the Committee on Government Reform (February 14, 2006); and *Examining the Administration's Treatment of Whistleblowers*, before the House Subcommittee on Federal Workforce, US Postal Service and the Census, Committee on Oversight and Government Reform (September 9, 2014). Barack Obama issued Presidential Policy Directive 19, "Protecting Whistleblowers with Access to Classified Information," on October 10, 2012.

On leak prosecutions, press freedom and the First Amendment, see Yochai Benkler, "A Free Irrespon-sible Press: Wikileaks and the Battle over the Soul of the Networked Fourth Estate," *Harvard Civil Rights-Civil Liberties Law Review* (Summer 2011); Heidi Kitrosser, *Reclaiming Accountability* (Chicago, 2015); Kitrosser, "Leak Prosecutions and the First Amendment," *William & Mary Law Review* (March 2015); Mary-Rose Papandrea, "Lapdogs, Watchdogs, and Scapegoats: The Press and National Security Information," *Indiana Law Journal* (2008); Papandrea, "Leaker Traitor Whistleblower Spy: National Security Leaks and the First Amendment," *Boston University Law Review* (March 2014); and Stephen Vladeck, "Inchoate Liability and the Espionage Act: The Statutory Framework and the Freedom of the Press," *Harvard Law & Policy Review* (Winter 2007).

For the Obama administration's aggressive stance against reporters who publish national security leaks, see Leonard Downie, *The Obama Administration and the Press: Leak Investigations and Surveil-lance in Post-9/11 America*, report for the Committee to Protect Journalists (October 10, 2013); Steven Aftergood, "Reporter Deemed 'Co-Conspirator' in Leak Case," *Secrecy News* blog of the Federation of American Scientists (May 20, 2013); the FBI application for a search warrant in the investigation into a suspected leak of classified information by Stephen Jin-Woo Kim, a State Department contractor, dated May 28, 2010; and James Goodale, "Only Nixon Harmed a Free Press More," *New York Times* (July 31, 2013).

For Edward Snowden as a Russian agent, see Edward Epstein, *How America Lost Its Secrets* (New York, 2017), and the comprehensive rebuttal by Michael German, "The NSA Won't Shut Up About Snowden, But What About the Spy Who Stole More?" online at the Brennan Center for Justice (March 11, 2014). German writes: "Real spies don't blow whistles or publish the materials they steal. This makes their actions more damaging, since it's more difficult for victim intelligence agencies to discover the breach, assess the resulting damage, and correct it. Were Snowden really a spy, his Russian handlers would have been as angry about the documents' publication as Clapper is, as it diminished their intelligence value."

For discussions of excessive government secrecy, the overclassification of data, and the relation of these to leaks, see references on government secrecy in notes to Chapter 3 above, as well as: Steven After-good, "National Security Secrecy: How the Limits Change," *Social Research* (Fall 2010); Aftergood, "What Should Be Classified? Some Guiding Principles," report prepared for the Open Society Justice Initiative (May 2011); Aftergood, "An Inquiry into the Dynamics of Government Secrecy," *Harvard Civil Rights-Civil Liberties Law Review* (Spring 2013); and Aftergood, "Reducing Government Se-crecy," *Yale Law & Policy Review* (Spring 2009). See also Rahul Sagar, *Secrets and Leaks: The Dilemma of State Secrecy* (Princeton, NJ, 2013); Timothy Edgar, *Beyond Snowden: Privacy, Mass Surveillance, and the Struggle to Reform the NSA* (Washington, DC, 2017); Jason Ross Arnold, *Secrecy in the Sunshine Era: The Promise and Failures of US Open Government Laws* (Lawrence, KS, 2014); Lloyd Gardner, *The War on Leakers: National Security and American Democracy, from Eugene V. Debs to Edward Snowden* (New York, 2016); and David Pozen, "The Leaky Leviathan: Why the Government Condemns and Condones Unlawful Disclosures of Information," *Harvard Law Review* (December 2013).

On the current feeble state of oversight on the intelligence community, see Michael German, ed., "Strengthening Intelligence Oversight," report for the Brennan Center for Justice (January 27, 2015); "Strengthening Intelligence Oversight," proceedings of a conference held at the Brennan Center (May 27–28, 2015); Daniel Byman and Benjamin Wittes, "Reforming the NSA: How to Spy After Snowden," *Foreign Affairs* (May–June 2014); Karen Greenberg, *Rogue Justice: The Making of the Security State* (New York, 2016); Mark Ambinder and D. B. Grady, *Deep State: Inside the Government Secrecy Indus-try* (Hoboken, NJ, 2013); Dana Priest and William Arkin, *Top Secret America: The Rise of the New American Security State* (New York, 2011); Tim Shorrock, *Spies for Hire: The Secret World of Intelligence Outsourcing* (New York, 2008); and Linda Weiss, *America Inc.?: Innovation and Enterprise in the Na-tional Security State* (Ithaca, NY, 2014).

Concerning US intelligence and national security overspending, dysfunction, and failures in the ongoing cyberwar with various adversaries, see "America's $1 Trillion National Security Budget," report by the POGO Defense Monitor (January–March 2014); Michael German, "The Spies Who Bilked Us: Lavishing Intelligence Agencies with Money and Power Has Only Magnified Their Failures," *American Conservative* (June 25, 2014); German, "The US Intelligence Community Is Bigger Than Ever, but Is It Worth the Cost?" online at *Defense One* (February 6, 2015); and David Cay Johnston, "The True Cost of National Security," *Columbia Journalism Review* (January 31, 2013). See also Benjamin Friedman, Tim Harper et al., eds., *Terrorizing Ourselves: Why U.S. Counterterrorism Policy Is Failing and How to Fix It* (Washington, DC, 2010); and two interviews conducted at the Brennan Center by Michael German: with Benjamin Friedman, "Rethinking Intelligence" (January 27, 2015); and with Babak Pasdar, "Why Doesn't the Intelligence Community Care Whether Its Security Programs Work?" (August 19, 2014). Further important reading includes Glenn Greenwald, *With Liberty and Justice for Some* (New York, 2011); Paul Pillar, *Intelligence and US Foreign Policy* (New York, 2014); David Sanger, *The Perfect Weapon* (New York, 2018); and Fred Kaplan, *Dark Territory* (New York, 2016). For a very different perspective, see Michael Hayden, *Playing to the Edge: American Intelligence in the Age of Terror* (New York, 2016; note his terminology, which characterizes American intelligence as a game and himself as a player); Hayden, *The Assault on Intelligence: American National Security in an Age of Lies* (New York, 2018); and James Clapper, *Facts and Fears: Hard Truths from a Life in Intelligence* (New York, 2018). On America's eternal wars and their broader effects on society, see notes to Chapter 2 above, and Tom Engelhardt, *A Nation Unmade by War* (Chicago, 2018); Andrew Bacevich, *America's War for the Greater Middle East* (New York, 2016); Bacevich, *The New American Militarism* (Oxford, 2013); Michael Mandelbaum, *Mission Failure* (Oxford, 2016); and Rosa Brooks, *How Everything Became War and the Military Became Everything* (New York, 2016).

Regarding the perils and inadequacies of drone warfare, see Micah Zenko, "Evaluating Michael Hayden's Defense of CIA Drone Strikes," posted on the Council on Foreign Relations blog (February 20, 2016); Zenko, "Reforming US Drone Strike Policies," report for the Council on Foreign Relations (January 2013); Andrew Cockburn, *Kill Chain* (New York, 2015); David Cortright, Rachel Fairhurst et al., eds., *Drones and the Future of Armed Conflict* (Chicago, 2015); and Hugh Gusterson, *Drone* (Boston, 2016). See also John Horgan, "Are Drone Strikes Really Making Us Safer?" published online at *Scientific American* (March 15, 2016); "Living Under Drones: Death, Injury, and Trauma to Civilians from US Drone Practices in Pakistan," report prepared jointly by the Stanford Law School's International Human Rights and Conflict Resolution Clinic and the NYU School of Law's Global Justice Clinic (September 2012); and "Drones and State Terrorism," a special edition of *Critical Studies on Terrorism* 11, no. 2 (2018).

On the dangers to US democracy posed by outsize executive branch power and growing authoritarianism, see Timothy Snyder, *On Tyranny* (New York, 2017); Snyder, *The Road to Unfreedom* (New York, 2018); Bruce Ackerman, *The Decline and Fall of the American Republic* (Cambridge, MA, 2010); Frederick A. O. Schwarz and Aziz Huq, *Unchecked and Unbalanced: Presidential Power in a Time of Terror* (New York, 2007); Charlie Savage, *Takeover: The Return of the Imperial Presidency and the Subversion of American Democracy* (New York, 2007); and the classic work by Arthur Schlesinger, *The Imperial Presidency* (New York, 1973).

The audit report of the DOD IG that details the disclosures of the "NSA Five," titled *Requirements for the TRAILBLAZER and THINTHREAD Systems*, was released on December 15, 2004. It is available online, in heavily redacted form, at the Federation of American Scientists website. A less redacted version of the report was obtained by Patrick Eddington through FOIA; see this document, and Eddington's lucid analysis, in "Hayden, NSA, and the Road to 9/11," posted on *Just Security* (December 7, 2017).

Jane Mayer did a superb investigation of the Tom Drake case in "The Secret Sharer," *The New Yorker* (May 23, 2011). The articles that triggered the reprisal against the NSA Five were: James Risen and Eric Lichtblau, "Bush Lets U.S. Spy on Callers Without Courts," *New York Times* (December 16, 2005); and Siobhan Gorman, "System Error," *Baltimore Sun* (January 29, 2006), the first of a series of articles by Gorman. The DOJ's suit against Drake is United States of America v. Thomas Andrews Drake, before the US District Court for the District of Maryland, case no. 10-cr-00181-RDB; see in particular the Defendant's Response to Government's Motion in Limine to Preclude Evidence of Necessity, Justification, or Alleged "Whistle-blowing," filed March 15, 2011.

A complete record of the varied legal actions against Chelsea (originally Bradley) Manning, including charges and pleas, verdict and sentencing, and unofficial transcripts at the court martial, is available at the website of Alexa O'Brien, an independent researcher in national security and law enforcement matters. The Freedom of the Press Foundation has also published extensive materials, including a leaked recording of Bradley Manning's statement before the military court in Fort Meade explaining his motivations for leaking voluminous government documents including the infamous Apache helicopter video and the Afghanistan and Iraq Wars Logs to WikiLeaks (full recording released March 12, 2013): Manning wanted to "spark a domestic debate on the role of the military and our foreign policy in general as it related to Iraq and Afghanistan"; "hoped that the public would be as alarmed as me about the conduct of the aerial weapons team crew members"; and "wanted the American public to know that not everyone in Iraq and Afghanistan are targets that needed to be neutralized, but rather people who were struggling to live in the pressure cooker environment of what we call asymmetric warfare."

Essential sources for the case of Bill Binney and the NSA Five include Ed Loomis's detailed and perceptive insider's memoir, *NSA's Transformation* (Kindle, 2014); James Risen, *Pay Any Price* (New York, 2014); and *A Good American*, a searching 2017 documentary film directed by Friedrich Moser, with extensive interviews with and input from members of the NSA Five. See also James Bamford, *The Shadow Factory* (New York, 2008); and interviews with Bill Binney, Ed Loomis, Diane Roark, Tom Drake and others in "United States of Secrets," *Frontline* (December 13, 2013). Michael Hayden's message to the NSA workforce (DIRgram) regarding failure of certain employees to adhere to the Agency's "corporate decisions" is DIRgram-87: "Personal Obligations" (April 14, 2000). See also his DIRgram-00: "100 Days of Change" (November 10, 1999); DIRgram-37: "Transformation Begins with TRAILBLAZER" (January 14, 2000); DIRgram-183: "GROUNDBREAKER Employment Opportunities for the NSA Work Force" (June 14, 2001); and DIRgram-196: "GROUNDBREAKER Award Contract" (July 31, 2001). For Hayden's decision to continue bulk domestic surveillance after the attorney general stopped endorsing the program in March 2004, see "ST-09-0002 Working Draft: Review of the President's Surveillance Program" (March 24, 2009), available at the Snowden Surveillance Archive, an online database of all documents released by Edward Snowden that have been published by the media.

Jess Radack's meticulous and moving account of her DOJ whistleblowing experience is in *Traitor: The Whistleblower and the "American Taliban"* (Washington, DC, 2012). See also Laurie Abraham, "Anatomy of a Whistleblower," *Mother Jones* (January/February 2004). The suit against John Walker Lindh is United States of America v. John Phillip Walker Lindh, in the US District Court for the Eastern District of Virginia, Alexandria Division, case no. crim. 02-37-A; see memorandum opinion of Judge Ellis delivered on July 11, 2002. For contrasting views of John Walker Lindh, see Frank Lindh (John's father), "America's 'Detainee 001'—The Persecution of John Walker Lindh," *The Guardian* (July 10, 2011); and Dan De Luce, Robbie Gramer et al., "John Walker Lindh, Detainee #001 in the Global War on Terror, Will Go Free in Two Years. What Then?" *Foreign Policy* (June 23, 2017).

John Crane details the events he witnessed in the DOD IG in his sworn affidavits of January 23 and February 9, 2015, and September 14, 2017. See also Jess Radack's letter to Richard Bennett, judge in the Tom Drake case, Re: United States v. Thomas Andrews Drake, case no. 10 CR 00181 RDB (April

17, 2015); as well as two letters to Crane from Karen Gorman, chief of the OSC Retaliation and Disclosure Unit, re OSC File No. DI-15-2333 (March 18, 2016; October 11, 2017); and a letter from Danielle Brian and Mandy Smithberger at POGO to Glenn Fine, DOD Acting Inspector General (March 8, 2016), rehearsing numerous instances of serious misconduct and anti-whistleblower culture in the DOD IG (March 8, 2016). See also Mark Hertsgaard, *Bravehearts: Whistle-Blowing in the Age of Snowden* (New York, 2016). Chuck Grassley sharply criticized the DOD IG for corrupt behavior and serial retaliation against whistleblowers, in two Senate floor speeches: "Admiral Losey Whistleblower Investigation" (April 6, 2016) and "Defense Department Inspector General Hotline Backlog" (April 27, 2017). Numerous recent GAO reports highly critical of national security whistleblower procedures and protections include: *Whistleblower Protection: Additional Actions Needed to Improve DOJ's Handling of FBI Retaliation Complaints* (February 2015); *Whistleblower Protection: Analysis of DOD's Actions to Improve Case Timeliness and Safeguard Confidentiality* (March 2019); and *Whistleblower Protection: DOD Needs to Enhance Oversight of Military Whistleblower Reprisal Investigations* (May 2015). See also testimony of Michael German at the hearing *Whistleblower Retaliation at the FBI: Improving Protections and Oversight*, before the United States Senate Committee on the Judiciary (March 4, 2015). On dysfunction in the OSC and MSPB, two administrative bodies that are vital to whistleblower protection, see two further GAO reports: *Office of Special Counsel: Actions Needed to Improve Processing of Prohibited Personnel Practice and Whistleblower Disclosure Cases* (June 2018); and *Whistleblower Protection: Additional Actions Would Improve Recording and Reporting of Appeals Data* (November 2016). On the conduct of FISA, see Andrew Nolan, Richard Thompson et al., *Reform of the Foreign Intelligence Surveillance Courts*, report for the Congressional Research Service (March 21, 2014); and Emily Berman, "The Two Faces of the Foreign Intelligence Surveillance Court," *Indiana Law Journal* (Summer 2016).

Patrick Eddington and his wife, Robin, blew the whistle on the concealment of the Gulf War Syndrome in Philip Shenon, "Ex-CIA Analysts Assert Cover-Up," *New York Times* (October 30, 1996). Eddington tells his CIA whistleblowing story in his memoir, *Long Strange Journey* (Shelbyville, KY, 2011). His forthcoming book on the history of domestic surveillance and political repression from McKinley to Trump is titled *The Triumph of Fear*. For the history of intelligence failures producing military fiascos, see Sam Adams, *War of Numbers: An Intelligence Memoir of the Vietnam War's Uncounted Enemy* (Hanover, NH, 1995); Edwin Layton, *And I Was There: Pearl Harbor and Midway—Breaking the Secrets* (New York, 1985); and Erik Dahl, *Intelligence and Surprise Attack: Failure and Success from Pearl Harbor to 9/11 and Beyond* (Washington, DC, 2013).

The 1953 case that established the state secrets privilege was United States v. Reynolds, 345 U.S. 1 (1953), decided March 9, 1953. See also Barry Siegel, *Claim of Privilege: A Mysterious Plane Crash, a Landmark Supreme Court Case, and the Rise of State Secrets* (New York, 2008), and Hampton Stephens, "Supreme Court Filing Claims Air Force, Government Fraud in 1953 Case," posted on *Inside the Air Force* (March 14, 2003). On February 7, 2003, after a federal judge threatened to block a false claims suit against Boeing and TRW for falsifying data behind the Star Wars antimissile program, citing the state secrets privilege, Chuck Grassley and Howard Berman, the original architects of the FCA, wrote a letter to Attorney General John Ashcroft warning against this misuse of the privilege.

DNI official Patricia Larsen's November 2015 briefing on insider threats is available via a link in Kenneth Lipp, "Government Compares NSA Whistleblower to Ft. Hood Shooter, Soviet Spies," *Daily Beast* (November 18, 2015). David Petraeus's plea deal resulted from the case United States of America v. David Howell Petraeus, before the US District Court for the Western District of North Carolina, Charlotte Division, case no. 3:15-cr-00047-RJC-DCK; see the DOJ's factual basis document and plea agreement, both filed on March 3, 2015. The leaked DOD IG report on the *Zero Dark Thirty* affair is the DOD IG draft report "Release of Department of Defense Information to the Media" (undated). See also Adam Zagorin and David Hilzenrath, "Unreleased: Probe Finds CIA Honcho Disclosed Top Secret Info to

Hollywood," POGO website (June 4, 2013); "Judicial Watch Obtains Stack of 'Overlooked' CIA Records Detailing Meetings with bin Laden Filmmakers," posted on the *Judicial Watch* website (August 28, 2012); and Jason Leopold and Ky Henderson, "Tequila, Painted Pearls, and Prada—How the CIA Helped Produce 'Zero Dark Thirty,'" *Vice* (September 9, 2015), which is based on extensive CIA internal documents obtained through FOIA.

Chuck Grassley's interview with *60 Minutes* appeared in the episode "FBI Whistleblower Harassed?" (November 25, 2002). Eric Holder's reference to Edward Snowden's "public service" appears in his interview with David Axelrod, *The Axe Files* (May 24, 2016, transcript released May 30, 2016).

EPILOGUE. THE BANANA REPUBLIC WASN'T BUILT IN A DAY

This epilogue is based in part on personal communication with Bill Binney, Tom Drake, Pat Eddington, Daniel Ellsberg, Kathleen McClellan, Marcia Miceli, Janet Near, Jesselyn Radack and Jeff Rosen.

The key source on some of Donald Trump's most significant wrongdoing is the so-called Mueller Report, by special counsel Robert S. Mueller III, which was released, with heavy redactions by Trump attorney general William Barr, on April 18, 2019. At this writing it has not been released in unredacted form. Helpful data on Donald Trump's financial methods, secrecy and past lawsuits is supplied by Jean Eaglesham, Mark Maremont et al., "How Donald Trump's Web of LLCs Obscures His Business Interests," *Wall Street Journal* (December 8, 2016); David Cay Johnston, *The Making of Donald Trump* (updated ed., London, 2017); Craig Unger, *House of Trump, House of Putin* (New York, 2018); Luke Harding, *Collusion* (Vintage, 2017); and Timothy O'Brien, *TrumpNation* (New York, 2005).

For case studies of Trump's business dealings with Russian oligarchs and Deutsche Bank, his association with money laundering, and his dealings with figures such as convicted felon Felix Sater, see Nathan Layne, Ned Parker et al., "Russian Elite Invested Nearly $100 Million in Trump Buildings," Reuters (March 17, 2017); Michael Hirsh, "How Russian Money Helped Save Trump's Business," *Foreign Policy* online (December 21, 2018); Timothy O'Brien, "Deutsche Bank's Troubles Are Donald Trump's Troubles," *Bloomberg Opinion* (November 29, 2018); Luke Harding, "Is Donald Trump's Dark Russian Secret Hiding in Deutsche Bank's Vaults?" *Newsweek* (December 21, 2017); "Bailed Out by Russia," posted online at The Moscow Project; Alex Ward, "Felix Sater, the Spy, Criminal, and Mafia-Linked Executive Tied to Trump Tower Moscow, Explained," *Vox* (updated January 18, 2019); David Cay Johnston, "Just What Were Donald Trump's Ties to the Mob?" *Politico* (May 22, 2016); and Craig Unger, "Trump's Russian Laundromat," *The New Republic* (July 13, 2017).

Investigations of Trump's finances, with particular reference to Deutsche Bank, are ongoing at the Southern District of New York, the House Financial Services Committee and elsewhere, and are producing useful materials. See, for example, "Status of the Russia Investigation," a summary of ongoing investigations issued by the HPSCI Minority (March 13, 2018). See also Garrett Graff, "A Complete Guide to All 17 (Known) Trump and Russia Investigations," *Salon* (December 17, 2018); and The Online Trump-Russia Timeline, published online at Just Security. For a reckoning of Trump's lawsuits and settlements before his election to the presidency, see David A. Graham, "The Many Scandals of Donald Trump," *The Atlantic* (January 23, 2017).

Regarding Trump University, a paradigm higher education fraud scheme, a number of complaints provide rich details of the case, which was settled by Trump for $25 million in November 2016; see, for example, The People of the State of New York by Eric T. Schneiderman, Attorney General of the State of New York v. The Trump Entrepreneur Initiative LLC, formerly known as Trump University LLC, et al., complaint filed with the Supreme Court of the State of New York on August 24, 2013. See also Ulrich Boser, Danny Schwaber et al., "Trump University: A Look at an Enduring Education Scandal," Center for American Progress (March 30, 2017).

On Trump's revolving-door nominees to major government posts: Sam Stein and Lachlan Markay, "Swamp Things: More Than 50% of President Trump's Nominees Have Ties to the Industries They're Supposed to Regulate," *Daily Beast* (October 29, 2017). On accusations of past financial illegalities by Treasury Secretary Steve Mnuchin and Commerce Secretary Wilbur Ross, particularly with illegal mortgage foreclosures after the 2008 crisis, see David Dayen, *Chain of Title* (New York, 2016); Dayen, "Treasury Nominee Steve Mnuchin's Bank Accused of 'Widespread Misconduct' in Leaked Memo," *The Intercept* (January 3, 2017); Senator Ron Wyden's statement for the confirmation hearings of Steve Mnuchin, "Wyden Statement on Senate Floor on Steven Mnuchin to be Treasury Secretary" (February 10, 2017, delivered as a Senate floor speech on February 13); transcript of Mnuchin's Senate confirmation hearing to become Treasury secretary (January 19, 2017); and Dan Alexander, "New Details About Wilbur Ross' Business Point to Pattern of Grifting," *Forbes* (August 7, 2018). On Ross's financial dealings as revealed by the Panama Papers, see the fascinating article by lead Panama Papers journalists Frederik Obermaier and Nicolas Richter, "The Secretary's Ties to Russia," *Süddeutsche Zeitung* (November 5, 2017); and extensive coverage of Ross at the International Consortium of Investigative Journalists website.

On Betsy DeVos's assault on public education, see Erica Green, "Betsy DeVos Reinstated College Accreditor over Staff Objections," *New York Times* (June 11, 2018); Bill Black, "Trump Admin Halts Investigation of For-Profit Colleges," *The Real News Network* (May 19, 2018); and David Whitman and Arne Duncan, "Betsy DeVos and Her Cone of Silence on For-Profit Colleges," Brookings Institution (October 17, 2018). On Mick Mulvaney's actions as "unit killer" at the CFPB, see Nicholas Confessore, "Mick Mulvaney's Master Class in Destroying a Bureaucracy from Within," *New York Times Magazine* (April 16, 2019).

On the decline in white-collar prosecutions under Trump, and his administration's weakening or elimination of anti-fraud units, see "White Collar Prosecutions Hit All-Time Low in January 2019," Transactional Records Access Clearinghouse (TRAC), Syracuse University (March 13, 2018); Brandon Garrett, "Declining Corporate Prosecutions," *American Criminal Law Review* (March 26, 2019); and Roy Poses, "Gutting the Health Care Corporate Strike Force," *Health Care Renewal* blog (July 13, 2017).

On the increase in leaks and leak investigations under Trump, see Steven Aftergood, "Leaks of Classified Info Surge Under Trump," based on information Aftergood obtained via FOIA, published in *Secrecy News*, a blog of the Federation of American Scientists (April 8, 2019); former Attorney General Jeff Sessions's testimony during an oversight hearing of the House Committee on the Judiciary (November 14, 2017); and Betsy Woodruff, "Leak Investigations Rise 800% Under Jeff Sessions," *Daily Beast* (November 14, 2017). On Trump's efforts to curb leaks throughout the government, see Valerie Volcovici and P. J. Huffstutter, "Trump Administration Seeks to Muzzle US Agency Employees," Reuters (January 24, 2017); Michael Biesecker, "Federal Employees Ordered to Attend Anti-Leaking Classes," Associated Press (September 21, 2017); and Esha Bhandari, "No, the President Can't Legally Gag White House Staffers," Speech, Privacy, and Technology Project of the ACLU (March 20, 2018). For a snapshot of the rapidly evolving status of Julian Assange, see Matt Taibbi, "Why the Assange Arrest Should Scare Reporters," *Rolling Stone* (April 11, 2019).

On EPA whistleblowers helping to force the dismissal of its widely reviled former head Scott Pruitt, see April Glaser, "The Ousting of Scott Pruitt Is a Victory for Whistleblowers," *Slate* (July 6, 2018). A prominent Department of Interior whistleblower is Joel Clement, a climate scientist and policy expert; see Nicky Sundt, "Interior Department Whistleblower Joel Clement Receives Award for Civic Courage," published online at the GAP website (September 21, 2017). Medical doctors Scott Allen and

Pamela McPherson were contractors with the Department of Homeland Security who turned whistle-blowers; see their letter to Chuck Grassley and Ron Wyden, chair and vice chair of the Senate Whistle-blowing Caucus (July 17, 2018). For details on recent IRS, Treasury and FBI whistleblowers, see three articles in the excellent online US Press Freedom Tracker: "IRS Employee Charged with Leaking Suspicious Financial Transactions to Prominent Lawyer and the Media" (February 27, 2019); "Treasury Employee Charged with Leaking Details of Manafort's Suspicious Bank Transactions to BuzzFeed News" (October 18, 2018); and "Former FBI Agent Terry Albury Accused of Leaking Documents to The Intercept" (April 6, 2018). A veteran White House security adviser who blew the whistle on ir-regular security clearances is Tricia Newbold; see analysis and excerpts from her testimony before the House Oversight and Reform Committee in "Re: Summary of Interview with White House Whistle-blower on Security Clearances," a memorandum released by the staff of the House Committee on Oversight and Reform on April 1, 2019.

On former Acting Attorney General Sally Yates's public rejection of certain Trump policies, see her letter stating that Trump's executive order on immigration might be unlawful (January 27, 2017), and her testimony before the Senate Judiciary Committee describing how she warned the White House about the vulnerability of former national security adviser Michael Flynn (May 9, 2017). Hui Chen explained her motives for resigning from the DOJ in a telling post on LinkedIn titled "Mission Mat-ters" (June 25, 2017); see also Russell Mokhiber, "Hui Chen on Corporate Crime in the Age of Trump," *Corporate Crime Reporter* (July 19, 2017).

On James Comey's leak of FBI memoranda, see the memoranda themselves in redacted form (released April 19, 2018); Comey's testimony before the Senate Intelligence Committee on June 7, 2017; and Comey's book *A Higher Loyalty* (New York, 2018). For an example of his own retaliatory dealings with whistleblowers, see the account of Coast Guard whistleblower Michael DeKort, "Lockheed Whistle-blower—When I Faced James Comey," *Medium* (November 20, 2017); and Rick Perlstein, "Will a Botched Coast Guard Contract Come Back to Bite James Comey?" (July 29, 2013). Comey's endorse-ment of waterboarding and other torture, while serving as deputy assistant attorney general under George W. Bush, is concisely described in Alex Emmons, "FBI Director James Comey, Who Signed Off on Waterboarding, Is Now Losing Sleep over an iPhone," *The Intercept* (February 25 2016). Em-mons also supplies links to compromising original DOJ memoranda from 2002 and 2004. On Mueller and parallel construction, see Bill Binney and Ray McGovern (twenty-seven-year former CIA analyst), "Robert Mueller: Gone Fishing," online at *Consortium News* (May 1, 2018); and "Dark Side: Secret Origins of Evidence in US Criminal Cases," a report by Human Rights Watch (January 9, 2018). For astute accounts of the flexian careers of Comey and Mueller, see Mattathias Schwartz and Ryan Devereaux, "James Comey, a Washington Operator, Knows How to Play the Game," *The Intercept* (June 8, 2017); and Coleen Rowley (an FBI whistleblower), "Russia-gate's Mythical 'Heroes,'" online at *Consortium News* (June 6, 2017).

On the arc of American history that has led to Donald Trump, see Daniel Rodgers, *Age of Fracture* (Cambridge, MA, 2011); Haynes Johnson, *Sleepwalking Through History* (New York, 1991); Benjamin Page and Martin Gilens, *Democracy in America?* (Chicago, 2017); Joseph Stiglitz, *The Price of Inequal-ity* (New York, 2012); Reed Hundt, *A Crisis Wasted* (New York, 2019); and in particular Francis Fuku-yama's ambitious and endlessly stimulating two-volume *The Origins of Political Order* (New York, 2011) and *Political Order and Political Decay* (New York, 2014). Fukuyama enjoys the dubious distinc-tion of having predicted the ascent of post-democratic leaders like Donald Trump, in his earlier work *The End of History and the Last Man* (New York, 1992), where he actually identifies Trump by name, and points to Trump's excesses, ostentation and yearning for domination as cardinal symptoms of the fall of liberal democracy in America.

On Louis Brandeis, democracy, small communities and the "curse of bigness," see Jeffrey Rosen, *Louis D. Brandeis* (New Haven, 2016). On Thomas Jefferson's views about these themes, see Francis

Cogliano, ed., *A Companion to Thomas Jefferson* (Hoboken, NJ, 2011), and Cogliano, *Thomas Jefferson* (Edinburgh, 2006). On Noreen Harrington's serial whistleblowing, first on mutual funds and then on Madoff, see Abigail Hofman, "Wall Street's Whistle-blower," *Daily Telegraph* (January 2004); "Meet a Major-League Whistleblower," *60 Minutes* (February 17, 2004); and Richard Sandomir, "A Court Filing Says a Mets Owner Knew of Madoff Concerns," *New York Times* (February 10, 2012). Edward Snowden's observation is from an interview with Mike German on October 12, 2015, during that year's Computers, Freedom, and Privacy Conference.

Index